FRANÇOIS-XAVIER MARTIN.

THE
HISTORY OF LOUISIANA,

FROM THE EARLIEST PERIOD,

BY

FRANÇOIS-XAVIER MARTIN.

" Hæc igitur formam crescendo mutat et olim,
Immensi caput orbis erit sic dicere vates."
—OVID METAM. XV., 434 and 435.

WITH A

MEMOIR OF THE AUTHOR,

By JUDGE W. W. HOWE,

(NEW ORLEANS BAR.)

———

TO WHICH IS APPENDED

ANNALS OF LOUISIANA,

FROM THE CLOSE OF MARTIN'S HISTORY, 1815; TO THE COMMENCEMENT
OF THE CIVIL WAR, 1861,

By JOHN F. CONDON.

———

A
FIREBIRD
PRESS
BOOK

Gretna 2000

Entered according to the Act of Congress in the year 1882, *by*
JAMES A. GRESHAM,
In the office of the Librarian of Congress, at Washington.

Manufactured in the United States of America

Published by Pelican Publishing Company, Inc.
1000 Burmaster Street, Gretna, Louisiana 70053

ISBN 1-56554-536-2

PUBLISHER'S NOTICE.

In issuing this New Edition of MARTIN'S HISTORY OF LOUISIANA, the publisher feels assured that he is supplying a general want, and preventing the almost total disappearance of a rare and valuable record of our State. In addition to the original work, which has been faithfully reproduced, will be found much new and important matter, consisting of a Memoir and Portrait of the distinguished author; the Act of Purchase of Louisiana from the French; Brief Annals of the leading events in the History of the State, from 1815 to the beginning of our Civil War, with other information that cannot but interest the general reader.

The mechanical portion of the work, which has been entirely executed in this city, will compare favorably with that of similar publications issued elsewhere.

The Publisher offers thanks to his numerous subscribers, whose generous encouragement has done much to promote the success of this enterprise.

James A. Gresham, Publisher

PUBLISHER'S NOTE FOR THE THIRD EDITION

Martin's History of Louisiana has long been out of print. The first edition, which came out nearly 150 years ago, is rare. Even the reprint which James A. Gresham issued in 1882 is now becoming scarce.

Gresham's reprint, the publisher asserted, is a careful copy of Martin's original work. However, in checking a copy against the 1827 edition, slight changes were found in punctuation; in modernizing the spelling (show for shew); in capitalization (spelling Jesuits with a capital "J"); in hyphenating words, and other unessential alterations. The paragraphs are the same.

Gresham's reprint includes a biography of Francois Xavier Martin, the Act of Purchase of Louisiana from France, the history of the State from 1815 to 1861, and information about Secession.

The present, or third edition of Martin's History, is an exact reproduction of Gresham's edition, and, in addition, contains an introduction by Dr. Robert C. Reinders, Assistant Professor of History at Tulane University. It also contains an Index which is missing from the other editions, thus making it more useful to scholars and those interested in research.

PELICAN PUBLISHING COMPANY

New Orleans, U.S.A.

CONTENTS.

CHAPTER III.

CHAPTER IV.

CHAPTER V.

CHAPTER VI.

CHAPTER VII.

CHAPTER IX.

CHAPTER X.

CHAPTER XI.

CHAPTER XII.

CHAPTER XIII.

CHAPTER XIV.

CHAPTER XV.

CHAPTER XX.

CHAPTER XXI.

CHAPTER XXII.

CHAPTER XXIII.

PAGE

CHAPTER XXVII.

CHAPTER XXVIII.

CHAPTER XXIX.

CHAPTER XXX.

CHAPTER XXXI.

CHAPTER XXXII.

CHAPTER XXXIII.

A CRITICAL STUDY OF FRANÇOIS XAVIER MARTIN'S "HISTORY OF LOUISIANA"

by

Robert C. Reinders, Ph.D.

(Assistant Professor of History at Tulane University)

The first concern of any historian is with his sources. An historian uses his sources as building blocks in constructing his literary edifice; he fits the proper pieces together to form a coherent pattern and, to stretch the metaphor further, cements or nails his structure together with the aid of his reason, judgment, and interpretation. In dealing with F. X. Martin's *History of Louisiana,* the critic has the difficult task of discovering exact sources without the aid of the author since Martin did not employ a system of footnoting or include a bibliography. He merely listed at the end of each chapter (in the 1827-1829 edition) the last names of the authors—or the type of materials as "Gazettes," "Archives," "Records"—whose books he utilized in preparing the particular chapter.

The first major source[1] utilized in the *History of Louisiana* is Garcilaso de la Vega, *La Florida del Ynca.*[2] Martin used Garcilaso to chronicle the explorations of Hernando de Soto. Though Martin does not hesitate to offer value judgments throughout his work, this is the only source he treats critically. He notes that Garcilaso referred to lions in Florida and to large Indian armies and concludes that the Spaniards who provided him with

---

[1] In Martin's first chapter, on the geography of Louisiana, he uses a report of an exploration of the Red and Washita rivers by John Sibley, William Dunbar, and a Dr. Hunter. *Message from the President of the United States Communicating Discoveries Made in Exploring the Missouri, Red River, and Washita by Captains Lewis and Clark, Doctor Sibley, and Mr. Dunbar. . . .* (New York, 1806). Several pages of chapter one are copied almost *verbatim ac litteratim* from Sibley's account. Martin also employs a report on the Red river sent to the Secretary of War in 1826; Antonio de Ulloa, *Mémoires Philosophiques, Historiques, Physiques, Concernant de la Découverte de l'Amerique . . .* (2 vols.; Paris, 1787); and Jabez Wiggins Heustis, *Physical Observations, and Medical Tracts and Researches on the Topography and Diseases of Louisiana* (New York, 1817).

[2] The full title is: *La Florida del Ynca. Historia del Adelantado Hernando de Soto, Governador y capitan general del Reyno de la Florida, y de otros hericos cavalleros Españoles e Indios* (Lisbon, 1605). The most recent English translation was published by the University of Texas Press in 1951.

information "were less fond of truth than of the marvellous." (p. 35).[3] After concluding his account of de Soto's tragic wanderings, Martin commented again on his source:

> Garcilasso de la Vega. . . . entitles his work the history of the *conquest* of Florida. With as much propriety, an English writer might entitle his memoirs of of Sir Edward Packenham's expeditions in 1814, the history of the *conquest* of Louisiana. Perhaps Garcilasso wrote more as a lawyer than a soldier, and imagining that this perambulation of the country had acquired a title to the Crown of Spain, considered Florida as thereby *acquired*. . . . (p. 38).

Unfortunately Martin's point is somewhat vitiated by the fact that Garcilaso's account was not entitled the conquest of Florida; this was the title given to an abbreviated French translation which Martin employed.[4]

Martin's major source for the French in North America from the first voyages until early in the eighteenth century was the work of a Jesuit priest, Pierre François Xavier de Charlevoix.[5] Indeed Martin borrowed so extensively that entire sections of his *History of Louisiana* are hardly more than loose translations from Charlevoix. Examples of Martin's borrowings would fill pages, but the following three examples will suffice to illustrate the judge's technique.

> Charlevoix: "Here [Sable Island] Mr. de la Roche landed forty wretched men, whom he had drawn from the prisons in France. . . ." (I, p. 243).

---

[3]All page references to Martin's *History of Louisiana* are from the 1882 edition.

[4]Pierre Richelet, *Histoire de la conquete de la Floride: ou Relation de ce que s'est passé dans la découverte de ce pais par Ferdinand de Soto; composée en espagnol par l'Inca Garcilasso de la Vega.* (The Hague, 1735). Note that Martin follows Richelet's incorrect spelling of Garcilaso.

[5]*Histoire et description génerale de la Nouvelle Français, avec le Journal historique d'un voyage fait par ordre du roi dans l'Amerique Septenrionalle* (6 vols.; Paris, 1744). There is an English edition translated and edited by John Gilmary Shea, *History and General Description of New France* (6 vols.; New York, 1900). All references to Charlevoix will be from the English translation.

Martin: "He [de la Roche] left on it [Sable Island] forty wretches, whom he had taken out of the prisons of Paris." (p. 43).

Charlevoix: In the year 1609, Champlain, who had wintered in Quebec, having been joined then by Pontgrave, when a party composed of Huons, Algonquins, and Montagnez was preparing to march against this common enemy [Iroquois], allowed himself to be persuaded to accompany them." (II, p. 89).

Martin: Champlain was joined here [Quebec] in the spring by Pontgrave. Parties of the Hurons, Algonquins, and Montagnes, were preparing for an expedition against the Iroquois, and he was induced to accompany them." (p. 49).

Charlevoix: Cartier "crossed the gulf [of St. Lawrence], approached the continent, and entered a very deep bay, where he suffered greatly from the heat, whence he called it Chaleurs Bay." (I, pp. 112-113).

Martin: Cartier "crossed the gulf and entered a bay, which from the heat at the time, he called Chaleur bay. . . ." (p. 33).

Martin is never critical of Charlevoix as a source but he is critical of him as a person. On page 62, Martin refers to the superstition of the Canadians and Indians and on the following pages implies that the "reverend writer," Charlevoix, was in the same category. In fact, Father Charlevoix was also critical of the excessive fears of the natives and while he was more willing to accept some of the stories than the skeptical Martin, he does not deserve the Judge's facetious appellation. On page 147, Martin states that Charlevoix in 1721 "gave out that he had the king's order to seek a northwest passage to China, and to inquire into the state of the southern province [Louisiana]; but as he produced no official letter, not much credit was given to his assertion." Martin, who was following an account by Bernard de la Harpe for this period, evidently ignores de la Harpe's statement that Charlevoix did have an order from the King. Since de la Harpe disliked Charlevoix it seems obvious he would have mentioned any false credentials the priest carried.[6]

For events in the English colonies from the sixteenth through the eighteenth century, Martin largely utilizes John Marshall's *Life of George Washington* (1803). Evidently feeling that writings of a fellow judge were in the common market, Martin liberally and literally copied from Chief Justice Marshall's work. For example, Marshall states that John Cabot sailed from Bristol "on board a ship furnished by the king, which was accompanied by four barks fitted out by merchants of that city." (I, p. 4). Martin states that "this navigator [Cabot] sailed in a ship furnished by the crown, and four barques, supplied by the merchants of Bristol." (p. 31). And another example:

> Marshall: "The first vessel fitted out by the company in 1606, was captured and confiscated by the Spaniards, who at that time asserted a right to exclude the ships of all other nations, from navigating the American seas." (I, p. 85).
>
> Martin: "the northern company fitted out a vessel the same year [1606]; but she was taken by the Spaniards, who claimed the exclusive right of navigating the American seas." (p. 48).

Another English source found in Martin for the colonial period is Daniel Coxe, *A Description of the English Province of Carolana [,] by the Spanish called Florida, and by the French, La Louisiane* (London, 1722). Martin appears to accept Coxe's contention that New Englanders were in Louisiana and New Mexico as early as 1678, even to copying directly from Coxe, though these facts were patently wrong. Martin as a judge should have recognized special pleading, for Coxe had purchased Sir Robert Heath's claim to the Carolinas and with it a claim to Louisiana; he needed to prove that Englishmen had been in Louisiana before the French.

The only section on France in the New World during the seventeenth century Martin did not adapt from Charlevoix con-

---

[6]The title of Charlevoix's work specifically mentions the King's order; furthermore the book was published in Paris and would probably have been suppressed if Charlevoix's credentials were not correct. Perhaps Martin was piqued by Charlevoix's suggestion that lawyers as a rule lacked curiosity.

cerned the details of Robert LaSalle's discoveries.[7]   On La Salle's efforts in Canada and his voyage down the Mississippi, Martin follows Henri de Tonty's *Dernieres Découvertes dans l'Amerique Septentrionale de M. de La Sale* published in 1697.   Martin was evidently unaware of the fact that de Tonty several times denied authorship, though Charlevoix clearly calls it a "romance." (III, p. 207).   To compound his error further Martin also relies, to a lesser extent, on Father Louis Hennepin's *Description de la Louisiane,* a work of questionable veracity.[8]   For LaSalle's ill-fated attempt to discover the mouth of the Mississippi river by sea, Martin seems to follow Joutel[9] and de Tonty, the latter in turn a close paraphrase of an account by Chrestien le Clerq.[10] He relies on Joutel for the earliest part of LaSalle's ventures to America and into Texas; he then shifts to LeClerq-Tonty apparently without noticing Joutel's criticism of LeClerq's account.   Joutel's relation is a first hand one and all modern historians insist that it is the most accurate.   As in the case of Charlevoix and Marshall cited above, Martin paraphrases closely and copies.

Martin relies very heavily on Bernard de la Harpe for his account of the French in Louisiana from the time of Iberville to about 1723.[11]   He also continues to use Charlevoix—the romantic

---

[7]LaSalle had an implacable hatred of the Society of Jesus; Charlevoix reciprocated by passing over LaSalle's endeavors in a few paragraphs.

[8]Perhaps Martin used Jean Frédéric Bernard, ed., *Recueil de Voyage au Nord Contenant Divers Memoirs Trés-utiles au Commerce a la Navigation,* (10 vols.; 3rd edition; Amsterdam, 1734).   Volume five of this set contains the de Tonty and Hennepin narrations.

[9]The English version is: Henri Joutel, *A Journal of the Last Voyage Perform'd by Monsr. de la Sale, to the Gulph of Mexico to find out the Mouth of the Mississippi River. . . .* (London, 1714).   Martin lists his sources as Charlevoix, Hennepin and de Tonty, but none of the authors follow as closely to Joutel as Martin.

[10]Chrestien le Clerq, *Premier Etablissement de la Foy dans la Nouvelle France. . . .* (2 vols.; Paris, 1691).   There is an English translation by John Gilmary Shea published in New York in 1881.

For example, LeClerq states: "The Sieur de la Salle put all his force under arms to enter the village. . . ." (II, p. 235); Martin writes: "LaSalle ordered his men under arms as they entered the village." (p. 85).

[11]*Journal Historique concernant l'établissement des Français a la Louisiane. . . .* (New Orleans, 1831).   There is an English translation in B. F. French, *Historical Collections of Louisiana. . . . Part III* (New York, 1851). Martin may have been using de la Harpe's manuscript account.

account of St. Denis' trip to Mexico is paraphrased from Charlevoix
—and for the events of the Natchez massacre of 1729 and a few
smaller points he makes use of two contemporary narratives by
the French officer, Jean Bernard Bossu.[12] A description of the
severe hurricane of 1772 Martin takes from an account of Bernard
Romans. Other details on eighteenth century Louisiana he took
from the studies of Vergennes, Hutchins, Le Page du Pratz, Stoddard, and St. Méry.[13]

For the period after 1723 he made use of the Superior
Council proceedings, a wide variety of judicial records, and the
dispatches of the French and Spanish governors. These manuscript sources were available in the Cabildo where Martin held
court. The Judge employed federal records including a report to
the United States State Department in 1803 on the condition of
the new territory.[14] One of Martin's most interesting sources, at
least to the modern historian, is the *Moniteur de la Louisiane*, the
first newspaper in New Orleans.[15] It should probably be men-

---

[12]Jean-Bernard Bossu, *Nouveaux Voyages aux Indes Occidentales.* . . .
(Paris, 1768). An English translation by John Reinhold Forster was pub-
lished in London in 1771 under the title, *Travels Through that Part of North
America Formerly Called Louisiana.* Martin also used Bossu, *Nouveaux
Voyages dans l'Amerique Septentionale.* . . . (Amsterdam, 1778).

[13]Bernard Romans, *A Concise Natural History of East and West Florida.*
. . . (New Orleans, 1961); Charles Gravier Vergennes, *Memoire Historique
et Politique sur la Louisiane* (Paris, 1802); Le Page du Pratz, *Histoire de la
Louisiane* (Paris, 1758); Thomas Hutchins, *An Historical Narrative and
Topographical Description of Louisiana and West Florida.* . . . (Philadelphia,
1784); Amos Stoddard, *Sketches, Historical and Descriptive of Louisiana*
(Philadelphia, 1812); Moreau de St. Méry, *a Topographical and Political
Description of the Spanish Part of Saint Domingo.* . . . (Philadelphia, 1798).

[14]*American State Papers* (Walter Lowrie and Walter S. Franklin, eds.;
38 vols.; Washington, 1832-1861), Miscellaneous Papers, Vol. I, pp. 344-356,
381-383.

[15]The use of newspapers as sources was almost unknown in Martin's
time; it is not until the first volume of John Bach McMaster's *History of the
People of the United States from the Revolution to the Civil War* in 1883 that
newspapers are used with any regularity.

In addition to the sources cited above, Martin also relies on the following:
in chapter 2, Joannes de Laet,*L'histoire du Nouveau Monde ou Description
des Indes Occidentales.* . . . (Leyden, 1640) and Samuel Purchas, *Purchas
His Pilgrimage. Or, Relations of the World and the Religions Observed in all
Ages and Places Discoured from the Creation Unto the Present* (London,
1613); in chapter 3, William Robertson, *The History of America* (2 vols.;

tioned that where Martin had to rely on manuscripts, documents, and newspaper accounts his history improves in interest and accuracy.

Martin unfortunately did not evaluate his sources in the manner expected of a judge or an historian. He relied on single sources for extended chronological periods and did not seek to discover other sources which might have been more accurate or offer alternative interpretations. This led him to repeat the errors of his sources[16] and it led him into false statements or conclusions which could easily have been avoided.[17]

2nd American edition; Philadelphia, 1822); in chapters 29-32, Arsène Lacarrière Latour, *Historical Memoir of the War in West Florida and Louisiana in 1814-15* (Philadelphia, 1816) and John Henry Eaton, *The Life of Andrew Jackson. . . .* (Philadelphia, 1817); in chapters 19-25, Daniel Clark, *Proofs of the Corruption of Gen. James Wilkinson, and of his connexion with Aaron Burr. . . .* Phildelphia, 1809); in chapters 22-24 and 27-30, James Wilkinson, *Memoirs of My Own Times* (3 vols.; Philadelphia, 1816).

[16]Following are a few examples. Martin repeats Charlevoix's statement that the word Canada came from a misinterpretation of *aca nada*, "nothing there" repeated by two Spaniards shipwrecked off the coast of Newfoundland. This is not true and if Martin had read Charlevoix's footnote he would have seen that the Jesuit declared that the account was only a tradition and an Indian word was a more likely source. Martin, following Charlevoix, places the arrival of the first horse in Canada as June, 1665; contemporary sources mark the date as June 20, 1647. Martin repeats Charlevoix's incorrect and skimpy data concerning Father Marquette after the latter's exploration of the Mississippi. LeClerq's description of a formidable French fort in Texas housing twelve cannon is accepted by Martin; Joutel insists it had only eight cannon and was in a pitiful condition. All modern historians think Joutel was correct. The DeGourges expedition to revenge the massacre of the Huguenots in South Carolina was taken by Martin from Charlevoix. Historians have discounted the event completely. Martin refers to Sauvolle as the brother of Bienville and Iberville using de la Harpe as evidence. Even though later historians such as Gayarré accept this view, recent scholarship denies the relationship. The spurious de Tonty book leads Martin into several errors of which the preposterous account of a Mascoutin Indian, Mausolia, who attempted to create dissension between the French and the Illinois Indians, is probably the most blatant.

[17]For example: Martin on page 190 states that Diaz Anna, a ship captain from Jamaica, was arrested in New Orleans in 1759 and because he was a Jew his ship was seized. Kerlerec, the French Governor, had Diaz Anna released, and arrested seven French officials responsible for the affair including Bossu. By checking Bossu, a contemporary, Martin would have discovered that the ship was confiscated because it was English, and England and France were at war. Nor was Bossu arrested; he was in a fort on the

Over and beyond the errors of his sources which, given Martin's method's, could not be avoided, there are a plethora of mistakes that Martin seems to have compounded himself—often in the face of his sources.[18] Only a few examples can be offered in the limited space of this essay. Martin is "evidently erroneous" when he contends that de Soto traveled as far north as Kentucky; the Spaniards were moving west not north.[19] De la Harpe very clearly states that a group of Tonica Indians visited Bienville on December 21, 1704, but Martin, who is following de la Harpe's account, writes the date as November; in another case Martin speaks of a French officer stationed on the Wabash sending hides to Mobile—de la Harpe's narrative indicates he was already dead.[20] Charlevoix and the Abbé Pénicaut (used by Charlevoix) state that St. Denis

---

Tombigbee at the time. In relating the fate of the remnants of LaSalle's colony, Martin insists that the Spaniards found no one remaining in Texas. Yet Charlevoix, using Spanish and French documents, clearly indicates the survival of the LaSalle colony and its eventual disposition. Furthermore Bossu writes of meeting a half breed son of a survivor of the expedition.

[18]There are some examples which indicate that Martin simply mistranslated. Charlevoix in describing an ambush of the French by the Seneca Indians states that the Indian allies of the French being "better trained to bush-fighting than the French [Canadian militia and regular army], held firm, and gave the army time to collect itself. Then the enemy was repulsed on all sides. . . ." (III, p. 287). Martin ignores the Indians and states that the "regulars, to whom this kind of warfare was quite novel, were not so useful as the [Canadian] militia. The army, now collected, dispersed the Indians." (p. 8). In other cases Martin mis-copied. On page 55 he refers to "father Philibert, Noult and Anne de Noue and a brother spiritual." Charlevoix lists them as Father Philibert Noyrot, Anne de Noue, and a brother." (II, p. 37). Sibley mentions a lake near Natchitoches "sixty miles in circumference;" Martin writes six.

[19]Theodore Irving, The Conquest of Florida (New York, 1869), p. 239. Typical of Martin's errors in dealing with de la Vega are the following: Garcilaso has 1,000 men and 350 horses began the expedition; Martin gives the figure as 900 foot soldiers and 350 horsemen. Martin has de Soto halt at a village called Herriga; Garcilaso refers only to a "cacique" (chief) named Herrihigua.

[20]Martin had special difficulties with de la Harpe. He refers to a fifty gun ship, de la Harpe has it 40 guns; he speaks of nine Frenchmen being robbed, de la Harpe says six; he has 200 passengers arriving on a ship, de la Harpe has 190. The dramatic account of the surrender of Pensacola in 1719 in Martin is from de la Harpe, but Martin presents the facts in a wholly inaccurate manner. There is a conflict between the accounts of the surrender in Charlevoix and de la Harpe which Martin evidently did not observe.

had twenty-four horsemen on his Mexican trip; Martin lists twenty. The Judge concludes that LaSalle established a second fort on the Cow River in Texas in April, 1685; Joutel, the only source, states it was in June. LaSalle shortly before his death did not observe a "number of buzzards" as Martin states; Joutel and LeClerq-Tonty clearly refer to them as eagles. Sir Walter Raleigh did not grant his letters to John Smith, but to a Thomas Smith; and if Martin considered this to be the John Smith of Virginia fame, he would be more inaccurate since Smith was at the time serving as a soldier of fortune in Europe. The colony of Maryland was not founded by "all Roman Catholics, and chiefly from Ireland;" only a small minority of the settlers on the *Ark* and *Dove* were Catholics.[21] Marquette belonged to the Society of Jesus; he was not a Recollect father. The Abbé de Fénélon imprisoned by Frontenac was not the famous Archbishop of Cambrai and author of *Telemachus*. The two Fénèlons were step brothers and the more famous was only seventeen years old when the events are described by Martin. O'Reilly before his appearance in New Orleans was received by Lafrénière, Marquis, and Milhet, not by Lafrénière, Grandmaison, and Mazent; Boisblanc, one of the conspirators against Spanish rule, was sentenced to six years, not life. O'Reilly was not refused an audience with Charles III after his return from Louisiana; on the contrary the monarch in a personal interview highly commended the Spanish governor. Martin was unaware of the difference between the Pilgrims and the Puritans; in any case the Pilgrims did not found Salem or Boston.

Dates are frequently wrong in Martin's history. The remainder of LaSalle's company reached Fort St. Louis on September 14, 1687 not, as Martin states, on September 4. Even more confusing Martin has the same travellers reach Quebec on October 9, 1687; all sources conclude that they arrived on August 27, 1688— on October 9, 1688 they arrived at La Rochelle in France. The French fleet carrying LaSalle to the Gulf of Mexico left on July 24, 1684 not on July 4. Baron d'Avaugou replaced Viscount d'Argenson in 1661 not 1662. George Washington was made commander-in-chief of the Continental army on June 15, 1775 not on June 1. Burgoyne surrendered on October 17, 1777 not on the 20th. The first Acadians did not arrive in Louisiana until 1764, not, as Martin writes, in 1755.

---

[21] John Marshall, whom Martin follows, uses the phrase "chiefly roman catholics" which is at least less in error than Martin.

There are also errors of omission in Martin which, even within the frame of his available sources, are serious defects. Two examples will illustrate this point. Martin's anti-clericalism blinded him to the role of the French clergy in the explorations of Canada and the Mississippi valley. There is no indication in Martin that the better known explorers used missionary posts as way-stations on their trips or that geographical reports were largely the work of Jesuit or Recollect fathers. For the same reasons Martin fails to properly assess the religious impulse in the French and Spanish conquests. Martin's pro-American feeling led him to contend that the American colonists welcomed with open doors the Acadians after their expulsion by the British. As Francis Parkman has observed, the opposite was true; colony after colony refused to accept these French Canadians. There is no evidence, other than Martin's wishful thinking, upon which he could have based his viewpoint.

There are a few serious errors in Martin which perhaps he could not avoid due to a lack of available sources. He was unaware that the Pinckney Treaty was signed because the Spanish feared John Jay, our representative in London, might make a treaty with England to despoil the Spanish dominions in North America. Martin's contention that W. C. C. Claiborne followed a policy of not offering government positions to Creoles was not true. Claiborne's letters, published many years later, reveal that he was willing to grant favors to native-born Louisianians. It was the Creole reticence to accept that prevented more of them from serving under the new American government.

A work of history, like any other form of writing, allows the author a chance to sermonize. The modern historian "preaches" by such indirect techniques as the juxtaposition of data, the interpretation he gives to certain information, and by the selected use of adjectives and chosen phrases. Martin seldom employs these techniques (an exception is his critical treatment of Governor Alejandro O'Reilly); his history is almost pedantically objective, often reading like a brief in a civil court case. When Martin wishes to offer advice or commentary he does so openly, almost in the form of an "aside". These "asides" or annotations mostly center around two themes and reveal a strong bias in the mind of Judge Martin.

First, he calls the reader's attention to the superiority of republican institutions and specifically to American political institutions.

> Judge [John] Marshall has shown in his history of the colonies [*Life of George Washington*] planted by the English in North America, how immense and rapid are the advances of a community, allowed to manage their own concerns, unaided, and even checked at times, by a distant administration. Mine shall be the humble task to show how small and tardy are those advances in a colony, absolutely guided by the mother country notwithstanding the great assistance the latter may afford to the former. (p. 95).

This theme Martin labors throughout his book. The English colonies were more prosperous and grew faster because they were democratic and developed representative institutions. The French and the Spanish were never able to command a sizable population as they were limited by the character of a monarchical system. In the struggle between monarchy and democracy, the latter would prevail: "Providence had not destined the shores of the mighty stream [Mississippi] for the abode of the vassals of any European prince." (p. 67). A corrupt Europe, saddled by nobles and "popery" could never produce a George Washington, "a man whose name will long attract the admiration of the world and forever that of his country." (p. 184).

The French also failed, Martin argues, because they were so engrossed in the search for riches and the glory of exploration that they did not turn to the cultivation of the land. "Government, instead of concentrating the population, seemed more intent on making new discoveries where other settlements might be made, and to seek in the bowels of the earth for metals and ochres." (p. 103). Wealth rested in the "dull and steady process of tillage," but the French forsook the "immediate, real and secure advantages . . . for distant, dubious and often visionary ones." (p. 114).

It is interesting to note that Martin's thesis precedes by two decades a similar one propounded by the celebrated American historian, Francis Parkman, except that Parkman felt that religious differences between the French and English were also a factor in the English success. Martin asserts that a French "spirit of intolerance" prevented a large Huguenot population from settling in the new world, but he never suggests any superiority of Protestantism over Catholicism. Modern historians would not reject the limitation placed on French colonization by an authoritarian government nor the advantages accruing to the English colonies operating under a policy of "salutary neglect". But the recent tendency is to attribute more influence to geographical factors which limited the English colonies to a narrow tidewater area and easily opened to the French via the St. Lawrence-Great Lakes and Mississippi drainage systems over one-half of the North American continent. Religion is a factor only in the sense that the English came to settle an area where they could practice their faith, thus leading to a concentration of population; the French came to convert the Indians who were widely dispersed. The most significant reasons for the failure of the French and Spanish are not suggested by either Martin or Parkman. The industrial revolution, a large navy, and a foreign policy directed toward the formation of an Empire allowed England to defeat France and weaken Spain in the New World while these countries were involved in continental engagements. It was, in the last analysis, the English naval and military forces that defeated the French, not the American colonials. The Spanish were, in spite of at times brilliant delaying actions, ultimately removed by the inexorable press of American population westward.

A second theme stressed by Martin centers around the money question. In several places Martin discusses the issuance of paper money in Canada, Louisiana, and in the English colonies. Usually his account is out of context, occasionally irrelevant, and it always interrupts his narrative as if to call the reader's attention to the practice. Martin, very obviously, was a conservative, hard-money man who viewed inflationary currency as a cancer on the body politic, and did not hesitate to employ his history as a vehicle to expound his opinions.

> Indolence, improvidence and extravagance, at times, occasion private distress, and this the public. Industry, economy and order alone can relieve the first; and if the latter be curable by the same means only, it is vain to resort to alterations in the value of money, a paper currency, or tender laws—indeed to any such

> artificial remedies. . . . They may for a moment,
> mitigate the effect of the disease; but they foment the
> cause, which should be removed, if a radical cure be
> intended. (p. 154).

In view of the above it is hardly likely that Martin disapproved of Hamiltonian banking plans or Jackson's Specie Circular.

The purpose of this essay has been to appraise critically Martin's *History of Louisiana,* but it would be less than just not to point out its commendable aspects.

The book has an historical value as the "first history of Louisiana which merits this name."[22] As a work of history it is not notably inferior to most of the histories of the day and is better than many. The age of Ticknor, Prescott, Bancroft, and Parkman was only beginning and it would be remiss to judge a busy New Orleans professional man by the works of these men. Martin's history was certainly thought worthy of the interest of Charles Gayarré, Louisiana's outstanding nineteenth century historian, who in 1830 published his *Essai Historique sur la Louisiane,* which is hardly more than a French translation of Martin.

For the present-day student interested in Louisiana history the most valuable section covers the events from 1803 to 1815. Indeed no researcher studying this period could afford to ignore Martin's history. Martin played a significant role in Louisiana during most of these years and much of his account is based on his own experience and knowledge. Only Claiborne's letters offer a fuller contemporary view of the territorial and early statehood era. Even here Martin, by his sympathy with the Creole population along with his fervent commitment to the American government, is probably able to present the more balanced picture of the times. The good Judge was, and remains to this day, the prime example of the bridge between the two major ethnic groups whose interrelations color and make unique the history of Louisiana.

---

[22]Marc de Villiere du Terrage, *Les Dernières Annèes de la Louisiane Française* (Paris, 1903), p. vi. Another scholar has stated that "notwithstanding its dryness, [it] was the best which had been written until then." Edward Laroque Tinker, *Les Écrits de Langue Française en Louisiane aux XIXe Siècle* (Paris, 1932), p. 222.

MEMOIR OF

FRANÇOIS-XAVIER MARTIN.

I.

THE history of Louisiana will always be an interesting chapter in the history of the world. It does not concern merely the area which is now included within the boundaries of the present State; it embraces of necessity the story of the repeated and persistent attempts of France to found an empire in the new world, which should extend from the mouth of the St. Lawrence across the great Lakes to the mouth of the Mississippi. The Louisiana of the seventeenth century extended from the Alleghanies to the Rocky Mountains, and from the Rio Grande and the Gulf to the dim regions which now constitute British America; while Canada or New France stretched from the upper Mississippi to the Atlantic Ocean. There have been few plans of colonization more vast, and whatever may be the judgment of the historian upon the policy or the work of France in this bold scheme, there can be little difference of opinion as to the qualities displayed by the Frenchmen who were leaders in the movement. They were certainly cast in the heroic mould. Their voyages and their marches, their gay contempt of danger, their patience under suffering, their cheerful adaptation of means to end, place them easily in the front rank of pioneers. Such men as De Gourges, Champlain, Marquette, Frontenac and Lasalle, do honor to their race. Nor should Iberville and Bienville be omitted from the list, for though born in Canada, they may be credited to France, and it was for her good and glory they lived their laborious days in Louisiana.

Indeed, it seems well for those of us who have been nurtured on the English literature of the last three centuries to make now and then some careful study of the lives of the French explorers during the same period, if only to keep our perceptions achromatic respecting the French character. Of course, we do not really think that the French have at all times been given over now to frivolity and now to ferocity. We are not quite sure that their character is chiefly compounded of ape and tiger. Such an opinion would have to be relegated, now-a-days, to the limbo of superstitions. Yet, without doubt, there are many good people of Anglo-Saxon descent who have a vague feeling that a Frenchman has always

been, comparatively, a poor creature, a fop, a fribble, destitute of true
earnestness of character, and quite beyond the reach of saving grace,
whether of the political or the theological sort.   For such an inadequate
estimate of a great nation there can be no better corrective than a study
of the story of Louisiana.   When this story is diligently considered, it
will be seen that beneath the superficial errors and follies of France are
found and found abundantly those elemental virtues of courage, tenacity,
self-denial, and keen intelligence, which have made her great in the past,
and will make her great in the future.

Ten years ago it was said by many that France was ruined; and for
some, there seemed to be a kind of satisfaction in the thought.   Yet, in
July of the present year, the editor of the Fortnightly Review says of her,
in view of the adjournment of her legislature :

"The expiring parliament has remitted taxes amounting to over eleven
millions sterling, redeemed a milliard of debt, devoted £60,000,000 to
public works—spending over the latter £1,600,000 more per annum than
the Empire—and closes its accounts with a surplus of two millions
sterling.   France has regained her place among the nations.   Even the
deplorable Tunis expedition proved that she dare transgress with a high
hand.   While absorbing Tunis, she has annexed Tahiti, and is extending
her influence in Eastern and Western Africa and the Further East.   The
war against Clericalism, marked as it has been by many unfortunate
features, seems to have provoked no perceptible reaction, while it gratified
the *odium anti-theologicum* of the most energetic Republicans.   Education
has been made free, compulsory, and secular.   Steps have been taken to
shorten the period of military service.   Order has been maintained
without the sacrifice of liberty, and the peasants have learned to identify
the Republic with prosperity and peace."

Such results seem surprising.   They need surprise no one who is
familiar with the story of the French in America during the sixteenth,
seventeenth and eighteenth centuries.

II.

Judge Martin's History of Louisiana was originally published in the
year 1827.   It has long been out of print, and for some time it has been
difficult to obtain even a single copy.   In republishing the work, it has
been thought proper to preface it with some details of the life of its
author.

François-Xavier Martin was born in Marseilles, in France, on the 17th
of March, 1762, and his boyhood was passed in that busy and cosmopolitan
seaport.   His family seem to have been plain and quiet people, from
whom he derived, as his sole inheritance, a rugged physique, a keen
intelligence, and a robust will.   So far as we may judge, he seems to have

been in many respects such a solid and serious youth as was Jules Grevy, now President of the French Republic. He must have received some early education; but it was too brief for much exactitude or finish; for at the age of eighteen years, he left Marseilles for the island of Martinique, and never afterwards returned to the place of his birth, except for a brief visit near the close of his life. At this time Martinique was a French colony, famous, then as now, for producing considerable quantities of sugar, coffee and logwood, and an inordinate amount of rum. Young Martin appears to have gone thither to engage in some kind of mercantile business, and was not very successful; for in the last years of the American Revolution he had come to this country, landing at Newbern, North Carolina.

It is said that he volunteered in the Continental Army, but his military career was short. Tradition relates that being on outpost duty, one day, he came rushing in with the report that the enemy was at hand. His regiment turned out to meet the foe and found instead of the fiery coats of the British, a row of red flannel shirts hung out to dry. The fact was that the young scout was painfully near-sighted, and his vision was so defective that he was entirely unfit for military service. He must have returned at once to Newbern, for at the close of the Revolution we find him there, endeavoring to keep soul and body together by teaching French.

Such limited employment could not long satisfy his active and ambitious disposition. He proposed to himself to be a printer; and thereafter to be whatever a printer might become. He boldly applied for employment as a practical printer. "Can you set type?" was of course the first question addressed to the applicant, who had never set a type in his life. "Without doubt, I can," replied Martin, believing, we must presume, that a man of sense and determination need not be daunted by merely mechanical difficulties, but ought to be guided by the rule that "what man has done, man may do." He was immediately employed, and such were his ingenuity and keenness of observation, that the foreman of the establishment, though he may have scolded him now and then, for an error, never discovered but that his journeyman had previously learned the trade. In after life, the Chief Justice used to tell this story with the same gusto as that which is sometimes displayed by a bishop in relating his college pranks.

He soon after established a newspaper of his own, which he was not ashamed to peddle, newsboy fashion, not only in Newbern, but in the adjoining counties; and at the same time he published almanacs, spelling-books, and translations from the French. But he could not rest content with work like this. He studied law, at leisure moments, and in the year 1789, being then twenty-seven years of age, he was admitted to the bar of North Carolina. He soon took position—not as a brilliant advocate—for he had neither the taste nor the qualities which make the brilliant advocate; but as a student of laws and of jurisprudence who was destined to become a jurist.

On the occasion of a visit of President Washington to North Carolina, about this time, Mr. Martin was one of a committee appointed to receive that distinguished man. Mr. Gayarré says that this was one of the events of Martin's life of which he always loved to talk.

"When Washington, whom he had never seen before, showed himself to his admiring eyes, in a coach and four, with that majestic bearing which is attributed to kings, and which made that illustrious individual look like the very incarnation of intensified aristocracy, the young Frenchman, who had been dreaming of Cincinnatus with spade and plough, and dirt-stained, hard-fisted hands, was rather disconcerted. The committee conducted this Louis Fourteenth of republicanism to his apartments; but, before entering them, Washington said with a smile to those who reverently surrounded him: 'Gentlemen, I am in the habit of attending to the comfort of my horses before thinking of my own : please, therefore, be so kind as to lead me to the stables.' And to the stables the founder of an empire went with a measured and august step, not assumed, but prescribed to him by nature. With placid dignity he patted his horses, and gave the minutest directions to his groom, much to the edification of the astonished committee." *

Martin was a man whose industry could not be appeased by any single employment. Moreover, he was fond of money as well as of fame, as we shall have occasion to notice more especially hereafter. While practicing law he continued to carry on business as a printer, and began to busy himself with the composition and publication of books. Among these may be mentioned a collection of the Statutes of the Parliament of England in force in the State of North Carolina, published according to a resolve of the General Assembly, at Newbern, from the Editor's Press, 1792; a Treatise on the Powers and Duties of a Sheriff, according to the laws of North Carolina; and a Treatise on Executors.

In 1802, he published a translation of Pothier on Obligations, a book for which he had a profound respect; and at this time so complete was his skill as translator and type setter, that in executing the work he used no manuscript, but rendered the French directly into English type in the composing stick.

In 1804, he published a revision of the Statutes of North Carolina, and some three years after issued a second edition. The copy to be found in the Law Library of New Orleans is a stout quarto, two volumes in one, with an appendix, which brings the work down to 1807. It is printed by the firm of Martin & Ogden, Newbern. Between the revision proper and the

---

* Fernando de Lemos : p. 245.

appendix is a page, which shows that the senior partner of the house while on jurisprudence bent, yet had a frugal mind. This page is not wasted by being left blank, but is discreetly filled with a list of " Books printed and for Sale at this Office," and in which we find not only Martin's Sheriff, and Martin on Executors, but a list of novels which, it is to be hoped, amused and instructed the literary people of North Carolina in that day, such as " Lord Rivers, " "The Female Foundling, " " Delaval," and so on. There is even announced, " The Rural Philosopher, a Poem." Who the poet was is a mystery which remains unrevealed. It is quite certain that it was not Martin himself.

Those who visit the Land of the Sky, and breathe the pleasant air of Buncombe County, might be interested to know, that as appears by this volume, the county was established in 1791, and included the larger part of western North Carolina, extending from the head of "Swannanoe Creek" to the Tennessee line on the west, and to South Carolina on the south. It was a magnificent domain, for scenery at least, and the member who insisted at every turn on saying something "for Buncombe," had a large and interesting subject.

In 1806, Mr. Martin was elected and served for one term as a member of the Legislature.

His researches into the statutes of North Carolina suggested to him a collection of materials for a history of that State, which he published some years later, chiefly in the form of annals.

In this busy and useful method, he passed, in North Carolina, some twenty-eight years of his life. The youth who had come to Newbern, a forlorn and friendless foreigner, had grown to be a man of mature years and assured position. He had wasted no time. He had become a proficient in the common law and in the laws of the United States, and had not neglected the jurisprudence of Rome and of his native country. He had learned to express himself with force, if not with perfect purity of idiom. He had acquired a wide knowledge of history. He had attained the age of about forty-seven years, and had, with an economy like that of a French peasant, laid up a modest competence. To some men it might have seemed that the work of life was about completed, and that it was nearly time for rest. For Martin, life had just begun. His work thus far had been provisional and preparatory. He was to live and labor for nearly forty years longer, and was to use his acquirements and talent in a very different field. He had exhausted the possibilities of the little town of Newbern, and the same spirit of intelligent enterprise which led him from Marseilles to Martinique, and from Martinique to North Carolina, prompted him to leave North Carolina for newer fields.

III.

JAMES MADISON had just been inaugurated President of the United States, a judge was needed in the territory of Mississippi, and the new President offered the place to Mr. Martin. He accepted the position and filled it about one year, when he was transferred, on the 21st of March, 1810, to the bench of the Superior Court of the territory of Orleans, and this brought him to the city of New Orleans. He found himself once more in a strange city, a place most singular in its peculiarities of situation and of history, but one for whose advantage he was peculiarly fitted to work.

The territory of Orleans then embraced the present limits of the State of Louisiana. * Its previous history had been such as to produce a remarkable complexity in its population, its society and its laws. States, like individuals, are largely a result of race tendencies and of the modifying power of events and circumstances. In these respects few modern States have been subjected to such peculiar and varied influences as Louisiana; and this fact should be borne in mind, even in any estimate of its present condition, and any comparison with the other parts of our Union. Its principal river was opened to the world in a peculiar way. For more than a century the Spanish navigated the waters of the Gulf without seeming aware that the largest river in the world was pouring into it. For nearly two centuries after the discovery of America, the great stream was not entered from its mouth for commercial purposes, and it was not until that heroic pioneer, Lasalle, in the year 1682, picked out his perilous path from Canada, by the way of Lake Michigan and the Illinois river, and descended the Mississippi to the Gulf of Mexico, that the world began to dimly conjecture the capacity of this vast natural highway, and the possibilities of the valley through which it flows.

Lasalle was exploring under the patronage of Louis Fourteenth and the Prince of Conti. He gave the name of Louisiana to the region he passed through, while in after years the name of his other patron was given to one of the streets of New Orleans.

The first important settlement resulting from these discoveries was made at Biloxi, on the northern shore of the Gulf, and now in the State of Mississippi. It was founded by Iberville in 1699, and was the chief town until 1702, when Bienville moved the headquarters to the west bank of the Mobile River. The soil of Biloxi is exceptionally sterile, and the settlers seem to have depended mainly on supplies from France or St. Domingo. The French government, so distant and necessarily so ignorant of the true interests of the colony seemed intent on the search

* This is understood to be the legal effect of the Act of Congress of March 26, 1804; and it is not deemed necessary to discuss here the question of the "Florida Parishes."

for gold and pearls. " The wool of buffaloes," says Martin, "was pointed out to the colonial officers as the future staple commodity of the country, and they were directed to have a number of these animals penned and tamed." To those who know Biloxi, there is something delicious in tl.e idea of building up a colony there on pearls and "buffalo wool."

On the 26th September, 1712, the entire commerce of Louisiana, with a considerable control in its government, was granted by charter to Anthony Crozat, an eminent French merchant. The territory is described in this charter as that "possessed by the crown, between Old and New Mexico and Carolina and all the settlements, port, roads and rivers therein— principally the port and road of Dauphine Island, formerly called Massacre Island, the river St. Louis, previously called the Mississippi, from the sea to the Illinois, the river St. Philip, before called Missouri, the river St. Jerome, before called the Wabash, with all the lands, lakes and rivers mediately or immediately flowing into any part of the river St. Louis or Mississippi."

The territory thus described " is to be and remain included under the style of the government of Louisiana, and to be a dependence of the government of New France, to which it is to be subordinate." *

By another provision of this charter " the laws, edicts and ordinances of the realm and the custom of Paris were extended to Louisiana." †

The grant to Crozat, so magnificent on paper, proved of little use or value to him, and of little benefit to the colony, and in 1718 he surrendered the privilege.

In the same year, on the 6th September, the charter of the Western or Mississippi Company was registered in the Parliament of Paris. The history of this enormous scheme, with which John Law was so closely connected, is well known. The exclusive commerce of Louisiana was granted to it for twenty-five years, and a monopoly of the beaver trade of Canada, together with other extraordinary privileges, and it entered at once on its new domains. Bienville was re-appointed governor a second time. He had become satisfied that the chief city of the colony should

---

* A young French engineer, Franquelin, hydrographer to the king at Quebec, made, in 1684, an interesting map, which is still preserved in Paris in the Dépôt des cartes of the Marine. " It exhibits the political divisions of the continent, as the French then understood them; that is to say, all the regions drained by streams flowing into the St. Lawrence and the Mississippi are claimed as belonging to France, and this vast domain is separated into two grand divisions, La Nouvelle France and La Louisiane. The boundary line of the former, New France, is drawn from the Penobscot to the southern extremity of Lake Champlain, and thence to the Mohawk, which it crosses a little above Schenectady in order to make French subjects of the Mohawk Indians. Thence it passes by the sources of the Susquehanna and the Alleghany along the southern shore of Lake Erie, across southern Michigan, whence it sweeps northwestward to the sources of the Mississippi. Louisiana includes the entire valley of the Mississippi and the Ohio, besides the whole of Texas. The Spanish province of Florida comprises the peninsula and the country east of Mobile drained by streams flowing into the Gulf; while Carolina, Virginia and the other English provinces form a narrow strip between the Alleghanies and the Atlantic."—Parkman: Discovery of the Great West, p. 411.

† Martin : Vol. I., Chap. viii.

be established on the Mississippi, and so, in 1718, New Orleans was founded. Its location was plainly determined by the fact that it lies between the river and Lake Pontchartrain, with the Bayou St. John forming a natural connection which extends a large portion of the way from the lake to the Mississippi. And even at this early day there was a plan of constructing jetties at the mouth of the great river, and so making New Orleans the deep water port of the Gulf. It was about this time that the engineer, Pauger, reported a plan for removing the bar at the mouth of one of the Passes, by a system substantially the same as that so successfully executed recently, under the Act of Congress, by Captain James B. Eads.* It was a mooted question for some time, however, whether New Orleans, Manchac, or Natchez should be the colonial capital; but in 1722 Bienville had his way, and removed the seat of government to New Orleans.

In the same year, the place was visited by the Jesuit traveller, Charlevoix, who speaks of it as " this famous town which has been named New Orleans," having been so called in compliment to the Regent Duke who was at the head of the French government during the minority of Louis Fifteenth. It was famous, probably, at that time only, because the speculators of the Western Company had puffed it into a premature reputation. Charlevoix himself was grievously disappointed with the town, and says in a melancholy way:

" It consists really of one hundred cabins disposed with little regularity, a large wooden warehouse, two or three dwellings that would be no ornament to a French village, and the half of a sorry warehouse which they were pleased to lend to the Lord,"—for a church—" but of which he had scarcely taken possession, when it was proposed to turn him out to lodge under a tent."

He goes on, nevertheless, to make the prediction, that " this wild and dreary place, still almost covered with woods and reeds, will one day be an opulent city and the metropolis of a great and rich colony."

The Western Company possessed and controlled Louisiana some fourteen years, when, finding the principality of little value, it surrendered it in January, 1732. The system which thus came to an end was essentially vicious, yet the supply of means to the colony was advantageous, and " it cannot be denied," says Martin, " that while Louisiana was part of the dominion of France, it never prospered but during the fourteen years of the company's privilege." †

In 1732, Le Page Du Pratz describes New Orleans in these words:

" In the middle of the city is the Place d' Armes,"—now Jackson

---

*Martin: Vol. I., Chap. ix.

† Martin : Vol. I., Chap. ix.

Square. "Midway of the rear of the square is the parish church dedicated to Saint Louis, where the reverend fathers, the Capuchins, officiate. Their residence is on the left of the church, on the right are the prison and guard house. The two sides of the square are occupied by two sets of barracks. It is entirely open on the side next the river. All the streets are regularly laid out in length and width, cross each other at right angles, and divide the city into sixty-six squares, eleven in length along the river, and six in depth."

In 1763, occurred an event which left a deep impression on the history of Louisiana. On the third of November of that year, a secret treaty was signed at Paris, by which France ceded to Spain all that portion of Louisiana which lay west of the Mississippi, together with the city of New Orleans, "and the island on which it stands." The war between England, France and Spain was terminated by the treaty of Paris, in February, 1764. By the terms of this treaty, the boundary between the French and British possessions in North America was fixed by a line drawn along the middle of the river Mississippi, from its source to the river Iberville, and from thence by a line in the middle of that stream and lakes Maurepas and Pontchartrain to the sea. France ceded to Great Britain the river and port of Mobile and everything she had possessed on the left bank of the Mississippi, except the town of New Orleans and the island on which it stood. As all that part of Louisiana not thus ceded to Great Britain had been already transferred to Spain, it followed that France had now parted with the last inch of soil she held on the continent of North America.

The French inhabitants of the colony were astonished and shocked when they found themselves transferred to Spanish domination. Some of them were even so rash as to organize in resistance to the cession; and finally, in 1766, even went so far as to order away the Spanish Governor, Antonio de Ulloa. But the power of Spain, though moving with proverbial slowness, was roused at last, and in 1769, Alexander O'Reilly, the commandant of a large Spanish force, arrived and reduced the province to actual possession. The leaders in the movement against Ulloa, to the number of five, were tried, convicted and shot. Another was killed in a struggle with his guards. Six others were sentenced to imprisonment, and from that time "order reigned."

The colony grew slowly from this time until the administration of Baron de Carondelet, but under his wise management, from 1792 to 1797, marked improvements were made. The streets began to be lighted; fire companies were organized; the Canal Carondelet, connecting the rear of the city with the Bayou St. John and so with the Lake, was constructed; the defenses of the city were strengthened and a militia organized. In 1794, the first newspaper, the *Moniteur*, was established.

2*

On the 1st October, 1800, a treaty was concluded between France and
Spain by which the latter promised to restore to France the province of
Louisiana.   France, however, did not receive formal possession until the
30th of November, 1803, when in the presence of the French and Spanish
officers, the Spanish flag was lowered, the tri-color hoisted, and a formal
delivery made to the French Commissioners.

But France did not remain long in possession.   The cession to her had
been procured by Napoleon, and he did not deem it politic to retain such
a province.   While, therefore, it was being thus formally transferred, it
had already, in April, 1803, been ceded to the United States, and on the
20th December, 1803, the United States took possession.

In 1804, the territory of Orleans was established by act of Congress.
The rest of the immense purchase was at first erected into the district of
Louisiana; then, in 1805, into the territory of Louisiana, and then in
1812, into the territory of Missouri.   So Missouri and Louisiana parted
company in the juridical way, the former to receive eventually the
common law as fundamental, the latter to continue its adherence to the
civil law in many important matters.

At the time of the transfer to the United States, the population of New
Orleans was about eight thousand.   At the time of Judge Martin's
arrival it was over seventeen thousand.

IV.

IT requires but a glance at the foregoing facts to reveal the singular
situation of this new American territory.   It was not American in history
or even in name.   It had been governed, both by French and Spanish,
with ideas and by methods which were in many respects medieval.   In
1754, a soldier who had been guilty of mutiny at Cat Island was "sawed
in two parts.   He was placed alive in a kind of coffin, to the middle of
which two sergeants applied a whip saw." *   In 1778, a royal schedule
was published in New Orleans, forbidding the reading of Robertson's
History of America, and ordering all copies which might be found to be
destroyed. †   In 1785, an attempt was made to introduce the Inquisition
into the province, and "a clergyman of New Orleans received a commission
of commissary of the Holy Office in Louisiana."   Governor Miro did not
approve of the Inquisition, and so one night while the commissary " was
peacefully slumbering, he was disturbed by an officer heading eighteen
grenadiers, who lodged him on board of a vessel, which at break of day

* Martin : Vol. I., Chap. xiii.
† Ib. Vol. I., Chap. iii.

sailed with him for Spain." * In 1786, Miro issued a set of police regulations in the form of a proclamation, giving minute directions as to demeanor in church, dress, passports, late hours and similar subjects. †

Naturally, with such a state of affairs, came corruption of all kinds. In a dispatch of May 24, 1803, Laussat, the French Colonial Prefect, declares that justice was then administered "worse than in Turkey." In the same year, Daniel Clark, then the Consul of the United States at New Orleans, and whose name has since become so famous in the Gaines cases, wrote to the Department of State at Washington, with bitter complaints of the delays of justice and the venality of all officials. ‡

With the American domination came new ideas, new complications, new elements, good and bad. The matter of law and the administration of justice demanded immediate attention in what was to be one of the United States. The early colonists had brought with them the Jurisprudence of France. The charter of Crozat, had, as we have seen, specially extended to Louisiana the laws, edicts and ordinances of the realm and the Custom of Paris. When the Spanish took possession, O'Reilly caused a code of instructions to be published, in reference to practice, according to the laws of Castile and the Indies, to which was annexed an abridgment of the criminal laws, and some directions in regard to wills. "From that period," says Judge Martin, "it is believed that the laws of Spain became the sole guide of the tribunals in their decisions. As these laws and those of France proceed from the same origin as the Roman code, and there is great similarity in their dispositions in regard to matrimonial rights, testaments and successions, the transition was not perceived before it became complete, and very little inconvenience resulted from it." §

The acts of Congress in regard to the territory of Orleans provided for trial by jury, for habeas corpus, and for the prohibition of cruel and unusual punishments, thus pointing to the Common Law as the proper basis of jurisprudence in criminal matters in every American State: and the territorial legislature laid down this basis in a statute which is still in force. ‖

In 1808, a civil code of law was for the first time adopted by a legislature in Louisiana. It was based to a large extent on a draft of the Code Napoleon; was prepared by Messrs. Brown and Moreau Lislet; and was entitled, "A digest of the civil laws now in force in the territory of Orleans, with alterations and amendments adapted to the present form of government." It did not repeal anterior laws, except so far as they

---

* Martin : Vol. II., Chap. v.
† Ibid.
‡ Gayarre's Hist. of La.: Vol. I., p. 584.
§ Martin : Vol. II., Chap. i.
‖ Revised Statutes of Louisiana, 1870, § 976.

were in conflict with its provisions. In practice, then, it was used "as an incomplete digest of existing statutes which still retained their empire, and their exceptions and modifications were held to affect several clauses by which former principles were absolutely stated. Thus the people found a decoy, in what was held out as a beacon. The Fuero Viejo, Fuero Juezgo, Partidas, Recopilationes, Leyes de las Indias, Autos Accordados and Royal Schedules remained parts of the written law of the territory, when not repealed expressly or by necessary implication. Of these musty laws copies were extremely rare; a complete collection was in the hands of no one; and of very many of them not a single copy existed in the province. To explain them, Spanish commentators were consulted, and the corpus juris civilis and its own commentators were resorted to; and to eke out any deficiency, the lawyers who came from France or Hispaniola, read Pothier, d'Aguesseau, Dumoulin, etc.

"Courts of justice were furnished with interpreters of the French, Spanish and English languages. These translated the evidence and the charge of the court when necessary, but not the arguments of the counsel. The case was often opened in the English language, and then the jurymen who did not understand the counsel, were indulged with leave to withdraw from the box into the gallery. The defense, being in French, they were recalled, and the indulgence shown to them was enjoyed by their companions who were strangers to that language. All went together into the jury room, each contending the argument he had listened to was conclusive; and they finally agreed on a verdict in the best manner they could."*

It is easy to perceive that Judge Martin coming in 1810 to be a member of the Superior Court of the territory, had before him a formidable task. There were conflicts of decision to be reconciled, anomalies to be reduced to order, a jurisprudence, in fact, to be created. How well he performed his part of the task, with what patience, clear sightedness and vigor, is matter of history. He has been called the Mansfield of the southwest. Such comparisons are little worth. They are always defective, and sometimes very deceptive. In many respects, Mansfield and Martin were entirely unlike. Yet, in some respects, their work was similar. In the department of what may be called constructive jurisprudence, in the skilful blending of the best principles of the English and the Roman law, in the apt illustration of one by the other, a resemblance may be traced.

Martin's companions on the territorial bench, at the time he was appointed, were George Matthews, the presiding judge, and John Lewis.

---

*Martin: Vol. II., Chap. xiv.

V.

BY act of Congress of 1811, the inhabitants of the territory were authorized to form a constitution, with a view to the establishment of a State government. The debates in the national House of Representatives on this bill were long and entertaining. Josiah Quincy, of Massachusetts, opposed the measure with something like ferocity; denied the right to admit the proposed new State, and declared that "if this bill passes, the bonds of the Union are virtually dissolved; that the States which compose it are free from their moral obligations, and that, as it will be the right of all, so it will be the duty of some, definitely to prepare for a separation, amicably if they can, violently if they must." Mr. Quincy was here interrupted and called to order by Mr. Poindexter, the delegate from Mississippi; but repeated his remarks, committed them to writing, and handed the paper to the clerk of the House. *

That a Quincy, of Massachusetts, should maintain the right of secession on the floor of Congress, and should be called to order by a Poindexter of Mississippi, is certainly a fact which may be classed among the curiosities of history and politics.

The bill having been passed, however, the Constitution of 1812 was framed and adopted, and in April of that year, the Congress passed an act for admission of the State to the Union, by the name of Louisiana. The territorial courts ceased to exist, and Martin was no longer a judge. He was, however, appointed Attorney-General of the new State, and so acted during the exciting events of the war with England, and until February, 1815, when he was appointed a judge of the Supreme Court of the State. At this time he was fifty-three years of age. He seemed to take a new lease of life, for he sat upon that bench until 1846, a period of thirty-one years. During this lengthy term, he was not content with a formal discharge of his official duties. He did not permit himself to shrink and wither away into a clever clerk, attending to what was barely necessary and nothing more. On the contrary, while his duties as judge were performed with entire strictness, his labors in adjacent fields of intellectual work were immense.

He prepared and published reports of the Supreme Court of the territory of Orleans from 1809 to 1812, in two volumes. He began this work while he was still on the bench of that Court. The title page contains a characteristic quotation, which indicated his own views as to the necessity of reports in a community where none had ever existed. It is an extract from instructions given by the Empress of Russia to a Commission created for the purpose of framing a code of law, and is as follows:

* Gayarré: Vol. III., p. 250.

" Ces tribunaux donnent des décisions ; elles doivent être conservées, elles doivent être apprises, pour que l'on juge aujourd'hui comme on y a jugé hier, et que la propriété et la vie des citoyens y soient assurées et fixés comme la constitution mêmes de l'état."

The preface to the first volume is dated at New Orleans, October 30th, 1811, and expresses the views of the reporter with regard to the Court of which he was a member, the duties of a judge, and the unusual condition of jurisprudence in the territory. He says :

" No one could more earnestly deplore, for no one more distressingly felt, the inconveniences of our present judicial system. From the smallness of the number of the judges of the Superior Court, the remoteness of the places where it sits and the multiplicity of business, it has become indispensable to allow a quorum to consist of a single judge who often finds himself compelled, alone and unaided, to determine the most intricate and important questions, both of law and fact, in cases of greater magnitude as to the object in dispute than are generally known in the State courts —while from the jurisprudence of this newly acquired territory, possessed at different periods by different nations, a number of foreign laws are to be examined and compared, and their compatibility with the general constitution and laws ascertained—an arduous task anywhere, but rendered extremely so here, from the scarcity of works of foreign jurists. Add to this, that the distress naturally attending his delicate condition is not a little increased by the dreadful reflection that if it should be his misfortune to form an incorrect conclusion, there is no earthly tribunal in which the consequences of his error may be redressed or lessened."

The case of Detournion *vs.* Dormenon, reported in this volume, is rather a curious one. The Parish Judge of Louisiana has always been a subject of more or less derision. Thus, a well known advocate in New Orleans once said to the Supreme Court, " May it please your honors, it is a settled rule that every man is presumed to know the law, except, perhaps, a Parish Judge." The defendant Dormenon was Judge of the Parish of Point Coupee. He seems to have been a peppery person, for in 1809, Governor Claiborne was obliged to make a journey to that Parish to allay a feud between Dormenon and the Abbé Lespinasse, the Parish priest, which had set the whole community by the ears. * However this may be, it appears that, according to the practice which then prevailed, Dormenon was acting as an *ex-officio* Sheriff, and while he was engaged in selling, at auction, property which he had seized upon an execution issued by himself, conceived that Detournion had insulted him. He, thereupon, issued an attachment and fined and imprisoned Detournion. The latter paid the fine and costs, and brought this action to recover the money thus paid and damages for the imprisonment. The court held that the alleged insult offered to the defendant while acting as a Sheriff could not be considered as a contempt of his authority as a judge, and therefore gave judgment for the plaintiff.

As a study in the genesis of anecdotes, it may be noted that in the New Orleans Monthly Review for February, 1875, the facts of the foregoing case appear in the following form, as handed down doubtless by tradition, and slightly embellished by some one who had a talent for epigram:

Under the old system the Parish Judge also acted as auctioneer, in selling the property of successions. It fell out once, in a well known sugar parish, that while the judge was knocking down some goods and chattels of a deceased person, a neighbor in the crowd behaved with some levity. The magisterial heart was fired.

"See, here, Sam Cooley, if you don't behave yourself, I will commit you for contempt of court."

"But, Judge, you are not in court now. There is no such offense as contempt of auction or an auctioneer."

"What, sir—what, sir? Why, I'll have you know, sir, that I'm an object of contempt at all times and in all places!"*

The territorial court having come to an end, Judge Martin continued his work as reporter, by publishing the decisions of the Supreme Court of the State, which make eighteen volumes, from the third of Martin, old series, to the eighth of Martin, new series, inclusive, the last of these volumes being issued in the year 1830.

In 1817, his fame had so far reached his native place, that he was elected a member of the Academy of Marseilles. In 1841, he was made Doctor of Laws, by Harvard College.

In 1827, he published the History of Louisiana, which is now reprinted. †

So, in addition to the usual work of a lawyer and judge, we find that he prepared and published some thirty volumes of law and history.

---

* It is said that, some years before the late war, the Probate Judge in New Orleans committed a citizen for contempt under circumstances which displayed equally curious ideas of law and personal rights. The officer in question was walking down Chartres street clothed in white linen, and happened to step on a loose brick in the pavement under which the water had settled—a thing sometimes called a "dandy trap." The water squirted up and bespattered his honor from head to foot. Rushing on to his court room, he took his seat, sent for the shop keeper in front of whose house the accident had occurred, and punished him for contempt of court. All parties were of Latin descent, and this extraordinary exercise of arbitrary power does not seem to have had any sequel.

† It should be noted that the references in this sketch to Martin's History are necessarily to the old edition, which appeared in two volumes. In the present republication the two volumes are published in one.

VI.

THE Code of 1808 was revised in 1825. In the same year a Code of Practice was promulgated, which is a model of brevity and simplicity. There is a theory afloat that the American system of code practice was invented in New York, about the year 1848, but an examination of the Louisiana Code of Practice, will satisfy the reader that the greater share of credit, in this matter, belongs to its compilers, who were Edward Livingston, Pierre Derbigny and Moreau Lislet.

By an act of 1828, all the civil laws in force before the promulgation of the Codes with a single exception, were declared abrogated. It was decided, however, that the Roman, Spanish and French civil law, which the legislature thus repealed, were the positive written or statute laws of those nations and of Louisiana, and only such as were introductory of a new rule, and not those which were merely declaratory ; and that the legislature did not intend to abrogate those principles of law which had been established or settled by the decisions of courts of justice. *

The result is that the Codes of Louisiana—which have been again amended in 1870 for the purpose chiefly of omitting matters rendered obsolete by the late war—are interpreted, when necessary, firstly, by the decisions of her courts, and secondly, in the absence of such, by the principles of the civil law, so far as they can be applied to the subject matter and to modern life.

No code of commerce or of evidence has ever been adopted in Louisiana, and it has been settled that in commercial matters we will follow the law merchant of England, and of the other States of the Union ; † and that in matters of evidence, we will be governed by English and American decisions, so far as not modified by statute or code. ‡

When it is remembered that in the federal courts we have the admiralty and chancery in full operation, it will be seen that the strata are numerous, which have been from time to time deposited in the legal alluvion which lies about the mouth of the Mississippi, and that a New Orleans lawyer may be expected to profess an acquaintance with a good many different things.

It will be noticed also, that during the lengthy period in which Martin sat on the bench, the questions which came up for decision were, for these reasons, of unusual difficulty and importance. For not only were the complications of colonial jurisprudence to be untangled, but in addition to these came the problems of the territorial government, of the Code of 1808, of the relations between the civil law and the American

---

* Reynolds vs. Swain: 13 Louisiana, 193.
† McDonogh vs. Millaudon : 5 Louisiana, 403.
‡ Drauguet vs. Prudhomme : 3 Louisiana, 86.

system, of the relations between the federal and State power, of the Constitution of 1812, and of the Code of 1825.

The Supreme Court of Louisiana, from 1821 to 1833, was certainly one of the ablest courts of last resort in the United States, and its decisions have been cited with respect in other countries. During the period here referred to, it was composed of George Matthews, François-Xavier Martin, and Alexander Porter.

Judge Matthews was born near Staunton, Virginia, in the year 1774, while his father was absent on an expedition against the Indians, which terminated in the battle of the Great Kanawaha. His father afterwards served with credit in the war of the Revolution, and attained the rank of Colonel. In 1785, Colonel Matthews removed with his family to Georgia, and afterwards became Governor of that State. George was sent back to Virginia to be educated, and after completing his academical course, returned to Georgia, and studied law. In 1805, he was appointed by President Jefferson a judge of the territory of Mississippi. In 1806, he was appointed to a similar position in the territory of Orleans. On the formation of the State of Louisiana, he was appointed by Governor Claiborne, a judge of the Supreme Court, and in July, 1813, he became presiding judge and so continued until his death, in 1836. He was a man of excellent sense, of sweet temper, and of that broad physique which is such an important foundation for a judicial temperament. Judge Watts, in a note to his memorial discourse on Matthews, printed in the tenth of the Louisiana Reports, says:

"In his personal appearance, Judge Matthews was of the middle stature and constitutionally disposed to corpulence, which even much exercise could not repress. His countenance was always placid, with a lurking expression of humor, indicating playfulness of mind and a disposition to repartee, and many excellent ones are told of him."

It is a matter of regret that Watts should not have reported some of these excellent jokes, for this allusion, standing alone, is rather tantalizing. But one story of the kind, so far as can now be ascertained, still survives, which Mr. Christian Roselius used to tell with his well known hearty laugh. It seems that Matthews was not only like Wolsey, a man of an "unbounded stomach," but he was, what some stout men are not, a great eater. A friend said to him one day:

"I am told, Judge, that you are the man who first complained that a turkey was an inconvenient bird for human food, being too much for one and not enough for two."

"Impossible," replied Matthews, "I could not have said that, for I never thought a turkey too much for one."

Alexander Porter was born near Omagh, County Tyrone, Ireland, in the year 1786. In 1801, he emigrated to the United States and settled in

3*

Nashville, Tennessee, where he was admitted to the bar, in 1807. In 1810, he removed to Louisiana, and settled on the Teche, where it appears that he was not received with entire hospitality. The story goes, at least, that at one plantation, where he stopped as a wayfarer, asking for a glass of water, the proprietor set dogs on him and drove him off the place. Porter had a fine, poetic revenge, however. In a short time, it was discovered that he was the best lawyer in that region. In 1812, the reports show that he was engaged as counsel in every important case in the district. And, not long after, the same planter who had behaved towards him in such a ruffianly style, was obliged to come to him with questions that involved an estate. Porter caused him to make an abject apology, and then, it is said, by way of further expiation, to pay a royal fee.

It is related that on another occasion, when Porter represented a plaintiff on the trial of a hotly contested suit, he felt it his duty, in summing up the cause, to make a terrible onslaught on the defendant. After the trial was over, the defendant, who was a rustic giant, met him in the courthouse square and threatened to break his head. Porter looked up at the angry person with the utmost serenity, and said:

"Did you ever see a man throw a stone at a dog?"

"Yes."

"And did you ever see the dog bite at the stone?"

"Yes."

"And don't you think it would be better, in such a case, for the dog to bite at the man that threw the stone?"

"Yes."

"Well, sir, you are the dog, and I am the stone. If you wish to bite any one, go find the man that threw the stone."

And, thereupon, the puzzled party defendant turned away and was seen no more.

Judge Porter, was not only scholar and lawyer, but also an enthusiastic planter and lover of fine stock. He imported several thoroughbred horses, one of whom, Hark Forward, was a brother of Harkaway, a famous winner of cups and plates.

Porter was appointed a member of the Supreme Court in 1821, and resigned in 1833, having been elected to the Senate of the United States. He died in 1844. During the time he sat upon the bench, the court was thus composed of elements most curiously, and, it would seem, most fortunately combined. The presiding judge was a Virginia gentleman, well-bred, amiable, full of that common sense, which is, unhappily, not so common on the bench as its name might indicate. Next came Martin, the Frenchman, with his immense industry, his unusual experience, his varied knowledge of history and law. And to these, Porter added still another element, the presence of an Irish scholar, learned, eloquent, full of insight, gifts and graces.

From the death of Matthews, Martin was presiding judge. Judge Bullard, who was one of his associates, says, that in this position, " in his deportment towards the bar, he rarely, if ever, evinced anything like petulance or censoriousness, while at the same time, on every proper occasion, he uttered rather the censure of the law than of the Court upon such persons, whether parties or advocates, as merited reproof." *

This is a high compliment. It too often happens that a judge, in a spirit of impatience or vanity, treats with arrogance or even insolence the counsel or the parties who appear before him. It is said that Thurlow ruined the business and broke the heart of a deserving solicitor by an unjust attack upon him from the bench. Such conduct is most reprehensible, not only because it may inflict a wanton injury, but because the lawyer when thus attacked, is attacked with his hands tied, and cannot well respond in kind. A judge might, at least, if he happen to feel dyspeptic or truculent, remember the school boy rule to " take one of your size," and not assail those whom the law, for reasons of public policy merely, has placed, for the time being, in a defenseless position. We may be sure that Martin never violated the rules of an intelligent generosity in this regard.

Yet there are limits to human endurance, and on one occasion, as tradition relates, the massive patience of Martin gave way. He was growing old, and was in the habit sometimes of thinking aloud. A young lawyer, fresh from the Emerald Isle, was making his maiden speech before the court. It was a vile mass of rubbish and bombast. One of the associates whispered to his chief:

" I don't know what this young man means by all this ranting?"

" He don't know himself," shouted Martin, "let him sit down—let the other lawyer speak."

And so the ambitious youth sat down.

VII.

WHEN Martin published his History of Louisiana, in 1827, he seems to have considered himself an old man, because he was sixty-five. He says of himself, in the preface, what he probably would not have wished any one else to say:

"Age has crept on him, and the decay of his constitution has given more than one warning that if the sheets now committed to the

* 1 Ann. viii.

press were longer withholden, the work would probably be a posthumous one."

Yet he was destined to labor for nineteen years longer. His imperfections of vision increased under his incessant and protracted work, and in 1838, he became quite blind. For all practical purposes, this blindness was total during the last eight years of his judicial life. Yet he continued to sit on the bench and to discharge the duties of his office with a regularity that was surprising. His last reported opinion was delivered in February, 1846, in which it was held that an inspector of elections, who has illegally and maliciously prevented one from voting, will be responsible to such person in damages.*

In the year 1844, Judge Martin made a brief visit to France, in the hope of obtaining some relief for his eyes—a hope which was entirely fruitless. Before his departure, he was entertained with a dinner, given to him by the New Orleans bar, at the City Hotel, at which a brief speech composed by him, was read by Judge Morphy.

In March, 1846, in consequence of the adoption of a new State Constitution, the Court of which he was a member, ceased to exist, and he was thus retired from the bench. By reason of strength, his days had become four score and four, and there was little left for him to do in this world. For him, the pathetic question of the poet, "What can an old man do, but die?" was but a natural one. On the 10th of December, 1846, the end came. On the 12th, the usual proceedings were had in the Supreme Court. The deceased was buried in the St. Louis Cemetery, and a shaft of granite marks the grave. Its inscriptions were placed upon it by some of his friends of French descent, and briefly sum up the chronology of his life, as follows:

FRANÇOIS–XAVIER MARTIN: né à Marseille, 17 Mars, 1762, mort à la Nouvelle Orleans le 10 Decembre 1846. Membre de la chambre de l'état de la Caroline du Nord 1806. Juge de la Cour du Territoire du Mississippi 1809. Juge de la Cour Superieure du Territoire d'Orleans 1810. Juge de la Cour Supreme de l'état de la Louisiane pendant 31 ans, du 1 Fevrier 1815 au 18 Mars 1846. Membre associé étranger de l'Academie de Marseille 1817. Docteur de l'Academie de Harvard 1841.

VIII.

IN personal appearance, Martin was rather below the medium height, with a large head, a Roman nose, and a thick neck. The portrait which accompanies this history, was taken when he was about sixty years old.

---

* Bridge vs. Oakey : 12 Rob. 638.

As he further advanced in years and began to lose his eyesight, he became a somewhat uncouth, and to those who knew him, a pathetic figure. Mr. Gayarré, writing from personal recollection, says of his appearance at this time:

" He walked along the streets of New Orleans with his eyes closed, and with tottering and hesitating steps, feeling his way like a blind man, absorbed in thought, probably lost in utter darkness, or at best, guiding himself only by the twilight of his imperfect vision, running one of his hands abstractedly over the side walls of the houses, mechanically and unconsciously twirling round with his index the iron catches intended to hold fast the outside shutters of windows and doors, muttering to himself half-formed sentences, and frequently ejaculating in a dolorous undertone, ' poor me ! poor me ! ' He was always shabbily, and sometimes even dirtily dressed, for he could not see, with his own eyes, what was the condition of his clothes, which, after all, he had a profound aversion to renew, being of an extremely penurious disposition. He had to trust to his black housekeeper for information as to the necessities of his wardrobe, and any one who knows the carelessness of that incorrigibly shiftless race, can be at no loss to form for himself an idea of the peculiar physiognomy of the Judge's apparel. His uncouth and odd figure used to attract the attention of the juvenile blackguards of the city, who loved to serve him with tricks, which the old gentleman bore with philosophic serenity, for he never permitted his displeasure to go beyond a slight expression of disgust, manifested by something which partook of the snort and the grunt. He never recognized any of his acquaintances or friends, who passed by him in the streets in perfect incognito. Frequently, on addressing him, they had to name themselves, when he did not know them by the sound of their voice. Everywhere, and invariably, Judge Martin kept his eyes closed, and very few, I believe, ever caught a glimpse of their color.

" His conversation was argumentative, and he was fond, after the Socratic method, of proceeding by questions, which he accompanied with a grunt. Question after question, logically linked together, each one more shrewd and insidious than the other, and leading to some conclusion, to which he vigorously drove the person interrogated, whilst he emitted grunt after grunt, was the sum total of his colloquial powers. He was not destitute of humor, and relished a joke. * * * On such occasions, when pleased, he showed his satisfaction by laughing after a manner peculiar to himself. He threw his heavy and massive head back, opened his mouth wide, without uttering a sound, and drew up to his bushy eyebrows the deep wrinkles of his face. There was something striking in that silent laugh. When he met with a knotty point of law which perplexed him, his habit was to drop in, as it were, in a friendly

way, at the offices of those lawyers for whom he had the most consideration, and who were not interested in the case he had under advisement.
After a few minutes of desultory conversation, he would slyly approach
the subject which he had in mind. 'Well, counsellor,' he would say,
'suppose such a point, what would be your views on it?' Whatever
opinion the counsellor might express, the judge would take the other
side, raise objection after objection, insinuate plausible doubts, puzzle the
counsellor, and after having pumped his antagonist dry, would leave his
office with his usual grunts and with ejaculations of 'poor me, poor me,'
as soon as he was again on the street and thought himself alone. Thus he
went round repeating the same scene, until he was satisfied with the result
of his investigations. When, after having duly weighed a case, he found
that the arguments for and against were equally balanced, it is said that
he wrote two judgments adverse to each other, which he would read to
his associates, and between which he desired them to decide, as he was
ready to adopt either of them as correct. It is related that, one day, he
had thus prepared two judgments, one for the plaintiff and the other for
the defendant. The decision for the defendant was adopted by the Court.
As chance would have it, the two judgments got mixed up, and Judge
Martin, to the dismay of the Court, delivered from the bench, the one
which was in favor of the plaintiff, and which had been rejected. The
defendant, either from his own impulse, or from a hint which he received,
made an application for a rehearing, which was granted, and the error
was rectified." *

Martin never married. Some said he could not afford such an extravagance as a wife. Absorbed in the study of law and the practice of
parsimony, it does not appear that the thought of domestic happiness
ever entered his imagination, and much less his heart.

Lord Campbell relates the story of an English barrister, who, having
been married one morning, and finding the day to hang heavily on his
hands, went to his office and began to study an intricate case. He became
so interested in his investigations that he studied all night, and not until
the next morning did he remember that he had a bride at home. It is
likely that Martin would have made a husband as little flattering and
attentive as the hero of this anecdote. He was an inveterate recluse, and
the presence of a wife would only have been annoying to him, and his
habits would surely have annoyed her.

It is matter of regret that his private life seems so cheerless, when
compared with that of other men who have been great in his profession.
It might be pleasant to record that, like Coke, he married in due time,
and reared up ten children in the ways of wisdom; though, perhaps, the

---

* Fernando de Lemos : p. 247.

reader might also recall the additional fact that Coke tried matrimony a second time and had a termagant for his second spouse, who led him a dreadful life. But yet, it would be agreeable if one could detail some romance of his early life, like that of John Scott, afterwards Lord Eldon, who, at the age of twenty, before he had begun to study law, and while romance was possible, fell in love with the beautiful Bessy Surtees, eloped with her by the help of a real rope ladder, married her in Scotland, and strange to say never repented of the rash act, but loved her as well when she was sixty-three, and Countess of Eldon, as when she was Bessy, the belle of Newcastle,

We do not find in his life any such incident as that which occurred to Mansfield, when he cast the longing eye of youth upon a young lady, whose father was not fond of young lawyers, but proceeded to marry her off to a booby squire with broad acres and broad face.

Nothing of the sort glistens in Martin's life. He seems to have needed no companion or consort. The truth is that he had the temperament and the habits of a miser. His frugality was innate, and this instinctive trait, developed by the struggles of his early poverty assumed proportions which might have furnished a subject for the pen of Moliere, or a supplemental scene for Les Cloches de Corneville. His painful economy in North Carolina enabled him to bring to New Orleans a considerable sum. From that time, he received an average salary of about five thousand dollars a year, besides the proceeds of his reports and other books. He lived, so to speak, on nothing, and heaped up his savings with compound interest. For a long time his household in New Orleans consisted of an old slave and his wife, and a body servant and factotum, named Tom. "The judge had said to the cook and her husband : 'I intend to be a generous master; I will permit you a room, but you must feed yourselves and supply my table with decent fare, besides cleaning the house in which we all reside, and which is yours as well as mine. This is all I require of you. The rest of the time is yours, and whatever money you may make and save after having nourished me and kept my clothes in a good state of repair, is your absolute property.' Such was the peculiar idiosyncrasy of the judge, that I am convinced he thought himself very generous on that occasion. It may be easily imagined what fare he had and what an infinite variety of stains and patches adorned his garments, which really were a nondescript curiosity. Fortunately he had the digestive powers of an ostrich. * * When he dined out, he swallowed with indiscriminate voracity all that was piled upon his plate. His apartment was never swept, his scanty furniture never dusted, and the spider festooned his ceilings with its airy drapery, serenely conscious, I presume, of reaching old age in undisturbed repose. From this den the miser would come out, year after year, to ascend the bench in the hall of justice, where he was transformed into an impartial, high-minded and inflexible judge, shedding on the subject before him the rays of his luminous, but cold intellect, and pouring the treasures of his vast erudition with a profusion and appropriateness which won the confidence and excited the admiration of an appreciative bar. It was no longer Shylock but Daniel come to judgment.

"Tom, the body servant of Martin, was as much of a character in his way, as the personage he waited upon, and was well known throughout the State, for he never failed to accompany the judge on his annual circuit. The slave looked upon his master as a sort of helpless grown-up baby of whom he had to take care, and for whose safety and welfare he was accountable to the State, of which that master, as he proudly knew, was one of the highest dignitaries. Tom very naturally came to the conclusion that, notwithstanding the color of his skin, he was a man of much importance, and even assumed authority over the great personage whom he considered as his ward. For instance, when at home, where Tom had full sway, the judge rose from his seat, Tom would sometimes say : 'Where are you going, sir ?'

" ' I am going to take a walk.'

" ' What ! without consulting me? Don't you know it's raining?'—or— 'Don't you know you've walked enough to day ? sit down, sir, sit down.'

" And taking his master by the shoulder, Tom would gently force him back to his seat.

" The judge was overheard once saying to his faithful companion in a hotel where he had stopped :

" 'Tom, have I dined to-day ?"'

"'What ?' replied Tom in a scolding tone. 'What a question, sir. Are you getting clear out of your mind ? Don't you recollect you ate a whole duck ?'

" ' Oh, very well then, all right.'

" One day, Tom said to him, ' I want a whip for our buggy?'

" ' Well, Tom, if you want a whip, buy a whip, of course. I do not see any objection to it.'

" After awhile, Tom came to him, whip in hand.

" 'Master,' he said, ' I want a dollar?'

" ' A dollar from me. Monstrous. What for? On what tenable ground do you establish your petition?'

" ' To pay for the whip.'

"' Why, Tom, I thought you were a man of sense. Did you not buy the whip for your own accommodation?'

" ' I bought it for your buggy, sir.'

"'My buggy! Our buggy, you mean. You called it our buggy,

yourself. Don't you ride in it? Tush! Don't trouble me any more about it.'

"Tom might have replied: Master, if we are in partnership, you ought at least to pay for one-half of the whip. He might have had other points to urge, but did not think of them, and failed to argue his master into recognizing the justice of his claim. Besides, opinionated and conceited as he was, there was one subject on which he never hazarded a conflict, which was—anything bordering on the law—anything concerning legal rights or claims. 'I can rule the old man as my master,' Tom would say, 'but as judge, it is no go. He's too mighty awful on the law. He can't be beaten there by anybody.'

"This eccentric black man possessed a good deal of sense and a good deal of humor. Judge Martin, being once on a judicial tour through the State, was occupying the same room with one of his associates on the bench, who was an Irishman by birth, and a gentleman of fine abilities, a scholar and a wit. * Tom, who was in attendance on them, now and then had a word to put in with all the freedom of speech of a privileged servant.

"'Tom, Tom,' said the judge, 'where did you get the expression you have just used? Have you not been with me long enough to learn pure English? Do you intend to disgrace me?'

"'I beg pardon, master,' replied Tom. 'Have the goodness to excuse me. If I talk broken English, it is due to my having lately kept bad company,' and he glanced with a mischievous smile on his thick lips at the Irish gentleman, who relished the joke and gave it circulation by repeating it.

"Tom thought himself very learned in the law, although, as I have said, it was the only subject on which he never ventured to enter into a conflict with his master; and was frequently heard expounding it with the most comical gravity to his ebony friends, for whom his word had indisputable authority. Poor Tom! He died in a distant part of the State where he had followed his master, who left him there when taken sick, as he could not spare time to wait for his recovery. The tavern-keeper, at whose house he had departed from this world, knowing the peculiar relations which existed between Tom and the judge, had him decently buried, and sent to the latter a bill for twenty dollars for the cost of the funeral. The judge broke out into the fiercest grunts he had ever been heard to emit, and refused to pay the bill, because the expenses had been unauthorized and excessive; and one dollar, which he tendered, was, he said, all that could be required for the burying of a negro. The landlord sued the judge in the parish were Tom had died; but the judge excepted to the

4*

* Porter.

jurisdiction of the court on the ground of his being domiciliated in the parish of Orleans.   The plea was sustained, and the plaintiff was thrown out of court with costs.   Pitiful human nature!   What shades and lights there are in the character of a man!   And must they not be faithfully though regretfully reproduced, to give a correct knowledge of the individual to be portrayed, and to adorn a tale, or point a moral?"*

It appears that in a solitary moment of weakness, Martin once loaned a brother jurist the sum of one thousand dollars.   It was not repaid when promised, and the lender was in a dreadful state of anxiety about the matter.   Finally, a bright idea struck him.   He would marry his debtor to a lady of fortune.   In due time, he found a person answering to that description, in a way.   She was a widow up on Red river.   He reported his " find " to his impecunious friend, as follows :

" My dear C ——, I have found you a wife.   She is healthy and sober, and she owns three thousand turkeys !"

Strange to relate, the borrower was not fascinated by the widow and her numerous fowls, and the match never came off.   Whether Martin ever recovered his money does not appear.   Probably not.

Some years before his death, the judge sent for a brother, who came over from France and took up his abode in New Orleans.   This brother, Paul Barthelemy Martin, was somewhat younger, though between sixty and seventy years of age.   But he was a younger brother still to the imagination of the judge, who always called him by the affectionate diminutive of Mimi.   Mimi was not so excessively frugal, and tried to introduce a little comfort into the home of the chief justice, and even went so far as to insist upon having some decent table claret to enliven the dinner.   It goes without saying that the judge groaned in spirit at such wild extravagance as wine at twenty-five dollars the cask, but Mimi carried his point.

IX.

JUDGE Martin's will was written in 1844, in the olographic form, on a sheet of coarse foolscap, in English, and with a certain common law flavor, as if in his extreme old age, he was mentally recurring to the studies of his earlier life.   A fac-simile is to be annexed to this sketch, but it may be a convenience to the reader to have it presented in ordinary type.   It is as follows :

" I institute my brother, Paul Barthelemy Martin, heir to my whole estate, real and personal, and my testamentary executor and detainor of my estate.   In case of his death, absence or disability, I name my friend and

---

* Fernando de Lemos : p. 249.

colleague, Edward Simon, my testamentary executor and detainor of my estate. New Orleans, this twenty-first day of May, eighteen hundred and forty-four.   F.-X. Martin."

It would seem that a man who had been profoundly versed in law for some sixty years, might make a will which no one would dispute; and that after having himself been advocate or judge in so many lawsuits, his bones might rest undisturbed by any din of forensic warfare over his grave.

If he had died in poverty, as many good lawyers and judges have done, the result might have been different from what it proved to be; but he died rich. His estate was inventoried at $396,841.17, and it is likely that its full value was about a half million.

The will above copied was proved and ordered to be executed, and Paul B. Martin entered into possession of the estate. A few weeks after, the State of Louisiana commenced its suit against him, alleging that he had caused himself to be recognized as executor under a pretended olographic will of François-Xavier Martin, dated 21st May, 1844, and had taken possession of his estate. That the said pretended olographic will was void and of no effect, for this, that when it was made, François-Xavier Martin was physically incapable, on account of blindness, of making an olographic will. That the estate of the deceased (who on this theory died intestate) fell to heirs domiciliated out of the United States, viz: in France, and was, therefore, subject to a tax of ten per cent. by the Statute of 1842; and the State, therefore, demanded that the executor, P. B. Martin, be adjudged to pay up this tax amounting to the sum of $39,684.11. The State by a supplemental petition further alleged, that for the illegal purpose of depriving the State of this ten per cent., the deceased had bequeathed all his property to his brother, P. B. Martin, a resident of New Orleans, with a secret understanding and agreement that he, Paul, was to hold it as a resident, and so evade the State tax on estates going to non-residents, and yet, that eventually the property should go to these non-resident relatives in France; that this agreement, and the will made in view of it, were illegal and contrary to public policy and order, and therefore void.

In short, the State claimed two things:

1. That the will was void as a legal and physical impossibility.

2. If it was not void for these reasons, it was void as an attempted fraud on the fiscal rights of the State.

The suit was defended and the court below gave judgment in favor of the State, but the defendant appealed, and the questions, both of fact and law, came up before the Supreme Court at the June term, 1847, in the tribunal where Judge Martin had presided so long.

A great deal of testimony had been taken; and among other witnesses, Judge Bullard, who had been long associate on the bench with the deceased, had been called. He stated that Judge Martin wrote an opinion in 1834, at Baton Rouge, at which time his sight was quite dim, and he wrote further than the paper and on the table, so that when the clerk came to examine the opinion, a part was on paper and a part written on the table. That since 1836, he had never seen him write more than to sign his name. That it was necessary in all cases where he had to sign his name, to place a pen in his hand and direct him where to sign. It was not necessary to hold his hand. He sometimes signed his name well. He could not tell if he had ink in his pen or not. He could not read what he had written, nor had he read anything since 1836, or at latest, since 1838. Being shown the will of Judge Martin, witness said the testator could not have read it; he was totally blind in 1844, when he went to France on a visit; *but it is written in his handwriting:* believes the testator could have written the will by means of bars to confine the edges of the paper, or other mechanical means, or by feeling the edges, but thinks he required assistance to take his pen, and get the ink. Witness was present when the will was opened. It was folded in the form of a letter. Thinks that the testator could have folded the will by feeling, but does not know about the sealing. The testator told witness on one or two occasions, when they had cases before them growing out of this ten per cent. tax, that it might be easily evaded. Has no recollection of Judge Martin's ever having revealed to him the manner in which it might be evaded, nor does he believe Judge Martin had the intention of evading it himself.

The defendant, Paul Martin, was interrogated in regard to the alleged fraudulent agreement, as to the eventual disposition of the property, and in rather acidulated French, denied it flatly. Being asked if his intention was not to give the property to the other heirs of Judge Martin, he replied :

"Je n'ai la dessus d'autre intention que celle de disposer de ma fortune selon ma volonté. La dessus je dis que je ne me crois pas obligé de faire dans ce moment un testament public. Je ferai mon testament comme je l'entendrai."

The case was elaborately argued by Mr. Attorney General Elmore, assisted by Mr. Musson and Mr. Pèpin, for the State, and by Mr. Grima, Mr. Mazureau, and Mr. Legardeur, for the defendant.

The use of French in court was common, even at that late day, and Mr. Mazureau's brief, published in the report of the case, is written entirely in this language. Its introduction is worth translating, though, of course, a translation cannot present the vivacity of the original. He says :

"He who amasses a great fortune sows the seeds of a great lawsuit, which germinate after his death. This apothegm of an Indian Philosopher, if I am not deceived, has never prevented some men, in every country of the civilized world, from piling up during all the days of their life, riches, which they knew how to enjoy but in one way, in looking at them. But experience has often proved that the saying is correct, and the present action is an example of its truth."

"François-Xavier Martin, the architect of his own fortune, arriving in his youth in the United States, was one of those men not often met with now-a-days, to whom study, obstinate toil, and the constant exercise of the thinking faculty were prime necessities of life. Two passions appeared to rule him : that of fame as a savant and jurist, and that of riches. His external life was in some sort that of a philosopher dwelling apart from all mundane vanities. And, in his interior life, almost always alone with himself, he developed with peculiar wisdom the resources which his own talent created for him, whether to enlarge his reputation as a lawyer and a magistrate, or to augment the cash which he had laid up by his toil and his economy. * * For thirty years his ear was carressed by the most flattering testimonials of a high consideration, both as a savant, and as a judge of integrity and purity. He has descended to the tomb, escorted by a numerous procession composed of all that our city contains of respectability. But in giving up his mortal part to the earth, our. common mother, he has left a will, by which he, disposes, in favor of his brother, of a fortune of nearly $400,000. And this judge, this president of our Supreme Court, celebrated for his intellectual capacities, and his distinguished judicial mind, who has been able for thirty years, during nine or ten of which he had lost his sight, to write out and to pronounce decisions which many considered as oracles, has not been able to escape the severity of the sentence of the Hindoo philosopher. His death has given life to a lawsuit; and in this suit, brought in the name of the State, he is represented as incapable of making an olographic testament, and its annulment is demanded ! A supplemental petition is presented, in which we recognize manifestly that this alleged incapacity springs only from an imagination burning to obtain at least some scrap of this opulent succession; and, in which, wishing to arrive more surely at this goal, they accuse him of having made by his will a trust prohibited by our Code."

Mr. Mazureau proceeds at great length to argue the questions presented, and the counsel on both sides ransacked the history of the legal world, from the time of the Ten Tables down. There was some plausibility, at first sight, in the theory that a blind man could not make an olographic will. To be such a will, it must be dated, written, and signed, entirely by the testator ; it was not necessary that it should be witnessed, and it was not ; and could it be said that a blind man, who could not read what he had written, who could not tell whether he had ink in his pen or not, who

could not be supposed to know, of himself, whether his intentions had
been correctly expressed, be able to write a will of this sort, which would,
by itself, satisfy the requirements of a will; that is, make proof that the
dispositions it contained, emanated from the testator, and embodied all
his intentions?

But the Supreme Court decided, firstly, that the will was valid, it being
clearly proved that it was dated, written and signed by the testator, that
if he made use of mechanical contrivances, to assist him, they could only
be considered as "helps to write," in the nature, for example, of spectacles ;
that such helps would not deceive him as an amanuensis might deceive a
blind man, and that the document must be presumed, in the absence of
clear proof to the contrary, to express the intentions of the testator.

Upon the second point, the Court found, as matter of fact, that the
venerable man had not been guilty of violating the laws he had so long
labored to expound and to perfect. They found that the relatives, in
whose favor he was accused of having made secret dispositions, were
persons with whom he was really unacquainted, and they enquired,
through their organ, Judge Rost, who delivered the opinion :

"Upon what principle of human action can it be explained that a man
of great intellect, occupying the highest judicial position of the State,
known to us all from our youth as having been a law unto himself and
who, whatever may have been his oddities and faults, justly prided
himself on the purity of his life, should have died perpetrating a vile
fraud for the benefit of relatives unknown to him?"

"There is another view," continues Judge Rost, "far more consistent
with his character. The love of independence was a passion with him,
and the things of this earth, by which independence is secured, had a
large share in his affections. His desire that his worldly goods should
be kept together after his death, exhibited by the pain he felt at the mere
suspicion that his brother would sell them and leave the country, far out-
weighed in his mind his attachment for those persons. We believe in
the sincerity of his anguish. The last looks of the man of wealth, dying
without posterity, are cast upon the property he has amassed; his last
hope on earth is, that his estate may live and continue to represent him.
The defendant in this case, (the brother), was the instrument selected
to give life to that cherished fiction. We have no doubt of his being
really universal legatee, nor that the intentions of the testator were, as he
expressed them, that his brother should continue to be, in all respects, *un
autre lui-même.*

"The representative of the State has faithfully discharged, what, under
the information he had received, he conceived to be an official duty. On
us devolves the more grateful task, to determine that he was misled by

that information, and that the name of François-Xavier Martin stands unsullied by fraud.

" It is ordered, that the judgment rendered in this case, in favor of the State, be reversed, and that there be judgment for the defendant."

And so terminated this singular suit.

It may be added, as a pleasant fact, that after the death of Paul Barthelemy Martin, the bulk of the estate went to a niece, who is still, it is believed, living in southern France, and by reason of her character, is known as the Providence of the community where she resides. Such a result may, perhaps, justify the painful economies of the venerable judge.

X.

LOOKING back at the life of Martin, it appears, that aside from the eccentricities, which, in a certain sense made him all the more picturesque, he was a man of exceptional robustness, who, in a profession which may be easily perverted, found opportunity to do something of permanent value to his adopted country and his race.

A distinguished orator of New England said of one of her most eminent advocates, as the net result of his career, that " he was one who made it safe to murder, and of whose health thieves enquired before they began to steal." This epigram, like most epigrams of the kind, was unjust in its special application, yet it contained a kernel of abstract truth.

No matter how successful a mere advocate may be, his reputation after all is little better than that of the actor who struts and frets his little hour upon the stage, and then is heard no more; or of the sweet singer, like Malibran, whose voice could not be described even by those who had heard it, and whose fame for those who never heard it rests in a tradition vague as moonlight. And after the death of the great lawyer, when he comes to be tried in the Egyptian fashion, to find what manner of man he was, the question will be, not how many verdicts did he gain by appeals to the passions of a jury; not, how many times did he success-fully wrench and twist the rules of law in such a way as suited his client's case; but, what was his influence in developing in fair and fruitful forms the jurisprudence of his country; what old abuse did he destroy, what new and needed reform did he construct; did he, like Tribonian, convert the laws of an empire which had been a wilderness into a garden; did he, like Domat, trace the civil law in its natural order as it flows from those two great commands of love to God and love to man; did he, like Lord Hardwicke, become the father of equity; did he, like Stowell, well nigh create for modern commercial nations the rules

of belligerent rights; did he, like John Marshall, expound the constitution of a great and new country; did he put the results of his
experience in a good book, for the benefit of his successors in the
profession?

If any of these questions can be answered in favor of the lawyer, fame
and honest fame, shall be decreed him.

But if he has lived merely for himself, a sharp attorney, an agile
advocate, he might almost as well have been an opera dancer, and over
his grave we could only think with Hamlet:

" Where be his quiddets now, his quillets, his cases, his tenures and his
tricks ? Why does he suffer this rude knave to knock him about the
sconce with a dirty shovel and will not tell him of his action of battery ?
Humph ! This fellow might be in's time a great buyer of land with his
statutes, his recognisances, his fines, his double vouchers, his recoveries.
Is this the fine of his fines and the recovery of his recoveries, to have his
fine pate full of fine dirt ? Will his vouchers vouch him no more of his purchases * * than the length and breadth of a pair of indentures ? The very
conveyances of his lands will hardly lie in this box, and must the inheritor
himself have no more ? "

We may be sure that over the tomb of Martin the grim jests of the
melancholy Dane could find no proper place.

A marble bust, which adorns the rooms of the Supreme Court of
Louisiana, represents the features of the venerable man, but it recalls no
such sarcasm. They are the features of one who was truly honest, who
was soundly learned, and who, above all, made his laborious life of lasting
value to the world.

WILLIAM WIRT HOWE.

NEW ORLEANS, December, 1881.

HISTORY

OF

LOUISIANA.

PRELIMINARY CHAPTER.

Topographical View of the State of Louisiana.

LOUISIANA, admitted into the Confederacy of the United States of America, on the thirtieth of April, 1812, is the southwesternmost state.

It lies from about the twenty-ninth to the thirty-fourth degree of north latitude and between the eighty-ninth and ninety-fifth degree and thirty minutes west longitude from Greenwich.

Its limits are fixed in the preamble of its constitution, and an act of its legislature of the twelfth of August, 1812.

The southern limit is the gulf of Mexico, from Pearl to Sabine river.

The western separates the state, and the United States, from the Spanish province of Texas. It begins on the gulf, at the mouth of the Sabine, and follows a line drawn along the middle of that stream, so as to include all islands to the thirty-second degree of north latitude and thence due north to the thirty-third degree.

The northern separates the state, on the western bank of the Mississippi from the territory of Arkansas, and on the eastern from the state of Mississippi. The line begins on the point at which the western limit terminates, and runs along the northern part of the thirty-third degree, to a point in that parallel, in the middle of the Mississippi river; on the western side, it begins at a point in the middle part of the river in the northern part of the thirty-first degree, and runs on that parallel to the eastern branch of Pearl river.

The eastern separates, in its whole length, the states of Louisiana and Mississippi. It is a line drawn in the middle of the Mississippi river between the two points, already mentioned, and another drawn from the eastern termination of the north boundary on Pearl river, running along the middle of that stream to its mouth in the estuary, which connects lake Pontchartrain with the gulf.

The area, within these limits, is a superfice of about forty-eight thousand square miles: Louisiana being, in extent, equal to North Carolina, and superior to every other state in the union, except Virginia, Missouri, Georgia and Illinois.

The population to the square mile is three persons; equal to that of Alabama and Indiana, and inferior to that of every other state, except Illinois and Missouri.

The aggregate population is of one hundred and forty-six thousand persons; inferior to those of every state, except Alabama, Rhode Island, Delaware, Mississippi, Missouri and Illinois; considerably below the one-half of the averaged population of the states, which is about four hundred thousand.

The free population is of eighty thousand one hundred and eighty-three persons; of which seventy thousand four hundred and seventy-three are white, and nine thousand seven hundred and ten colored.

Agriculture employs fifty thousand one hundred and sixty-eight, and manufactures five thousand seven hundred and ninety-seven. The number of foreigners not naturalized is three thousand and sixty-two.

Although Louisiana lies between the twenty-eighth and thirty-fourth degrees of north latitude, its temperature widely differs from that of the countries lying between the same parallels in the old world: the Cape de Verd islands and the southern parts of Algiers, Tripoli, Tunis, Morocco, Egypt, Arabia Felix, Persia, China and Japan.

We must ascend the Mediterranean, to reach a country in which the degree of cold, which is felt in Louisiana, is experienced, and descend about ten degrees towards the equator to find a country in which the heat felt in Louisiana prevails.

Cold is seldom so intense in the city of Nice, or Savoy, nor heat greater in Havana, than in New Orleans, which lies within the thirtieth degree of northern latitude, and is consequently never approached by the sun, in his zenith, nearer than six degrees and a half; for the variety of temperature, observable as the result of other circumstances than the relative propinquity to the equinoctial line, is nowhere more obvious than in Louisiana. In New Orleans, during the months of June, July and August, the thermometer rises to the ninety-eighth and even the hundredth degree of Farenheit's scale; which is the greatest degree heat of the human body when in health. In winter it sometimes falls to seventeen; and Ulloa relates that he has seen the Mississippi frozen, before New Orleans, for several yards from the shore. The variations in the thermometer are frequent and sudden: it falls and rises, within a few hours, from ten to twenty-four degrees.

Summer is the longest season; it continues for five months, besides many hot days in March and April, October and November. In June and July heat is diminished by eastern breezes and abundant rains; the hottest days are in August. In this month, and the first part of September, heat is less supportable than in the West Indies, from the absence of the eastern breeze.

The principal causes of heat, in New Orleans and its vicinity, are the equality of the soil, the great timber with which the neighboring country is covered, and the feebleness of the wind, which does not allow it to penetrate the inhabited parts of the country: add to this, the distance from the sea, which prevents the wind, that reigns there, from reaching the city, in which the air is commonly still during the hot months. If the wind comes from the north, it reaches New Orleans, after passing over a vast extent of plains and woods, loading itself with their hot vapor.

Heat, intense as it is, does not seem as in other countries, to concentrate itself in the earth and warm it to a certain depth; on the contrary, the water of the Mississippi, taken from the surface is warm, and from below, cold. This demonstrates that the heat, which prevails in the country, does not penetrate below, and is accidental, generated by the absence of wind, or the action of the sun on woods, marshes and swamps.

The effect of great heats is felt in a manner not common elsewhere. In walking, after the setting of the sun, one passes suddenly into a much hotter atmosphere than that which preceded, and after twenty or thirty steps, the cooler air is felt: as if the country was divided into bands or zones of different temperatures. In the space of an hour, three or four of these sudden transitions are perceptible.

This is not easily accounted for. It results probably from the burning of the woods, which takes place after gathering the crop, and is one of the ordinary causes of heat in the air, in the direction of the fire. The land being equal in quality and form, it cannot be imagined that the rays of the sun are more fixed in one spot than another. It is likely that some of the columns of air, considered horizontally, remain unmoved since the setting of the sun, and thus preserve the heat it communicated; while others, set in motion by a light or variable wind, lose theirs. These mutations are perceived when there is no wind.

In the fall, which is the most pleasant season in Louisiana, and often prolongs itself during the first winter months, the sky is remarkably serene; especially, when the wind is northerly. In October, the thermometer frequently rises to the seventy-eighth degree, which is the greatest heat in Spain.

In a country, in which the heat of summer is so great and so long, it might not be presumed that the cold of winter should be, at times, so severe as experience shows. Sharp frosts have occurred as early as November, but their duration, at this period, is extremely short. In the latter part of December, in January and the first part of February, the mercury has been known to fall many degrees below the freezing point. But cold days are rare in Louisiana, even in winter. In this season, heat succeeds to cold with such rapidity, that after three days of hard frost, as many generally follow, in which the average heat of summer prevails.

Spring is an extremely short season. A Louisianian is hardly sensible of its presence, when the suffocating air of summer is felt, for a while, and then winter days return.

The winds are generally erratic and changeable, blowing within a short space of time, from every point of the compass without regularity, and seldom two successive days from any one.

In July, August and September, there are frequent squalls, with much rain, thunder and lightning, and sometimes gales of wind from the south and southwest.

From the middle of October to April, the northern wind prevails and sometimes blows very hard : when it changes to the eastward or southward, it is commonly attended with close hazy or foggy weather.

In April, May and the first part of June, sea and land breezes prevail and refresh the air.

The south and southwest winds bring rain in winter; when they cease, the northwest wind prevails, and cold weather begins. When it continues, and its strength increases, it infallibly freezes. When the wind passes from east to west, without stopping, cold is neither great nor lasting; for the wind passes promptly to the east and from thence to south and south-west, and the rain begins.

The north and northwest winds are those which bring cold and hard frost in winter, and a suffocating heat in summer.

The cause of the cold they bring is the same in Louisiana, as in all the eastern parts of North America. The immense extent of country, covered with snow over which they pass, probably from the pole; while, on the opposite side of the Atlantic, the continents of Europe and Asia end in the seventy-fifth degree of latitude, and are separated from the pole, by a vast expanse of sea. But there cannot be any other cause of the heat they bring than the large plains, thick woods and wide pieces of water, which they cross; the humidity of which, acted upon by the intense heat of the sun, gives rise to ardent vapors, the heat of which being communi-cated to the air, instead of cooling, renders it more suffocating than in calm weather.

Ulloa noticed in Louisiana a particularity, which he says is not observed elsewhere. At certain times, when rains are abundant, a yellow, thick coat, resembling brimstone appears floating on puddles and the big vats or butts, in which rain water is collected and preserved: it is gathered in abundance along the brims of these receptacles. The atmosphere, he observes, is loaded with sulphureous particles, as is evinced by frequent tempests; it being rare that rain should not be accompanied by violent thunder. This, he concludes, experience demonstrates to proceed from thick woods, filled with resinous trees, the subtle parts of which are exhaled, and mixing with the sulphureous parts of the atmosphere, unite with them, and are together precipitated with the clouds that bring down the tempest. This sulphureous substance is so abundant and ordinary, and at times so much more perceptible than at others, that this circum-stance has given rise to the popular error that a rain of sulphur falls.

Before we proceed to take a view of the face of the country, the gulf on which the state is situated, and the mighty stream which traverses it, attract our attention.

The gulf of Mexico may be considered as a great whirlpool. The general course of the waters, in the Atlantic ocean, as well as the current of the air, within and near the middle zone, being from east to west, the force of the sea comes upon the West India islands and their lengths are in that direction. When the waters get into the great gulf, they are obstructed everywhere, and as it were turned round by the land. The great velocity of this body of water is towards the equator, and it must get out, where it meets with the least resistance, that is on the side towards the pole, where it forms the strong current, or passage, called the gulf stream.

The natural course of the waters therefore, on the northern part of the gulf should be from west to east: but it is partially changed, by frequent currents which are very unequal, depending certainly on the winds, but seldom on that which blows on the spot.

By the general law of the tides, there should be flood for six hours and ebb during the six following. But here, an ebb will continue for eighteen or twenty hours, and a flood during six or four only, and *vice versa.*

A southern wind always raises and keeps the waters up in the bays, and a northern almost entirely empties them. Yet, it must be allowed that these ebbs and flows are not equable in their continuance. Upon an accurate observation of them, we discover a tendency to two ebbs and flows in twenty-four hours, though they be overpowered by the winds and currents.

The entrance of the bays and rivers on the gulf is defended generally by a shallow sand bank, forming a bar farther out towards the sea than is usual elsewhere. The depth on the bar is not at all proportioned to that within. The mouths of the rivers are frequently divided into different channels, by swamps covered with reeds, owing probably to the conflict between the currents and the rise of the river, in certain seasons of the year.

The water of the gulf is not much heavier than the common. An aerometer, immersible in common water with a weight of two ounces and twenty-two grains was found so in that of the gulf, with one or two ounces and fifty-three grains, according to an experience of Father Laval, at the distance of ninety leagues from the coast. Fifty leagues inside of the Mediterranean, on the coast of Spain, near Almeria, the same instrument floated on sea water with a weight, less than two ounces and sixty-six grains. The reason of this difference, he concluded was, that larger rivers flow into the gulf, especially the Mississippi, bringing into it a greater quantity of fresh water than those which flow into the Mediterranean.

The Mississippi is remarkable by its great length, uncommon depth, and the muddiness and salubrity of its waters, after its junction with the Missouri.

The source of this mighty river is supposed to be about three thousand miles from the gulf.

From the falls of St. Anthony, it glides with a pleasant and clear stream, and becomes comparatively narrow before it reaches the Missouri, the muddy waters of which discolor those of the Mississippi to the sea.

Its rapidity, breadth and other peculiarities, now give it the majestic appearance of the Missouri, which affords a more extensive navigation, and is a longer, broader and deeper river, which has been ascended near three thousand miles, and preserves its width and depth to that distance.

From their junction to nearly opposite the Ohio, the western bank of the Mississippi (with the exception of a few places) is the highest, thence to bayou Manshac, it is the lowest, and has not the least discernible rise or eminence for seven hundred and fifty miles. Thence to the sea, there is not any eminence on either bank, but the eastern appears a little the highest, as far as the English turn, from whence both gradually decline to the gulf, where they are not more than two or three feet higher than the common surface of the water.

The direction of the channel is so crooked, from the mouth of the Ohio to New Orleans, that the distance is eight hundred and fifty-six miles by water, and four hundred and fifty only by land.

The water of the Mississippi appears foul, turbid and unwholesome, but in reality it is not so. It is so loaded with mud, that being put in a vase, it yields a sediment; and the sight of a quantity of earthy particles is offensive. In the highest floods, it unroots and carries with it large trunks of trees to a great distance: some covered with verdure, others dry and rotten. This abundance of sound and decayed timber cannot fail to impart some of their substance to the element on which it floats. Yet the mixture is not perceptible, and experience has shown that the water is wholesome.

The river, receives a number of other streams, the waters of some of which are saltish and impregnated with metallic particles : but the water of the main river predominates so much over those of the tributary branches, that it preserves its salubrity.

During the summer, while the Mississippi is low, the water is clear, but not so good as at its flood. That of the sea then ascends to a great distance and affects that of the river, without rendering it unwholesome. The latter is then warm on the surface, but preserves its coolness below.

Although it is so loaded with dirt, yet it does not generate the stone. It being supposed that, however clarified it may be, it still continues to contains some earthy particles. In many families, a number of jars are used, in order to give time to the water to yield its deposit, and the oldest is used. After having thus remained for a long time, even for a year, if a portion of the water be taken in a glass, not the least extraneous particle can be discovered, but it appears as diaphanous as crystal; yet if it remain one or two days, there will be seen at the bottom a subtle earth resembling soap. A coat of this is seen floating in the large jars, in which the water is put to settle. Common people, especially those who navigate the Mississippi, use its water in the most turbid state : and although they do so, while they are weary and sweating, there is no example of its having proved hurtful.

The coolness of the water may be attributed to the northern clime, in which the river has its source, and the great quantity of snow which it receives, or in which it is said to originate, and the ice it brings down from the vast plains west to north, as far as the forty-fifth degree. In this long course, it carries away a prodigious quantity of earthy particles, which, being kept constantly in motion, are so subtilized, that viewed in a glass, they appear like a smoke, filling its capacity. This great subtility is doubtless what communicates to the water, that wholesome quality, which facilitates digestion, excites appetite and maintains health, without producing any of the inconveniences, which other waters occasion.

The Mississippi rises at its flood higher than the neighboring land, and inundates it, where it is not protected by an artificial bank or levee. Although the river be deep and wide, its ravages, before it was confined by such banks, on the contiguous fields was not very great, owing to the profundity of its bed, which occasions the great strength of its current to be below, where the rapidity and weight of the water unite.

The water that escapes over the levees, or oozes through them, joined to that which flows in places that are unprotected, as well as the rain water, never returns into the river, but fills the vast cypress swamps beyond the tillable land, and finally find their way into these lakes, on both sides of the stream, in the vicinity of the sea. The declivity of the land on the eastern side towards lakes Maurepas and Pontchartrain, shows that the earth which the water of the Mississippi deposited, formed, in course of time, the island on which the city of New Orleans stands.

It is clear that the bed of the river rises in the same proportion as its banks. This is manifested by the constant necessity there is of raising, the levees.

At the mouth of the river, there is also some evidence that its bed rises. About the year 1722, there were twenty-five feet of water on the bar : Ulloa found twenty in 1767, at the highest flood, and now in 1826 there are sixeeen; while the depth within has ever remained the same. It is possible that the bar, at the different mouths of the river, may have risen, while the bottom of the bed within may have remained unaltered. But the mass of water, which passes through these mouths, being the same as formerly, it follows that its force against the waves of the sea is not altered, and no good reason can appear why the sea should retain the sand to a higher level than before on the bank. It is much more natural to conclude that the bed of the river has risen, whereby its mouths are widened and it meets the waves of the sea with less force, than when it came through deeper and narrower channels.

The strength and rapidity of the current are such in high water, that before steam was used in propelling boats, it could not be stemmed without much labor and waste of time; although the sturdy navigators were greatly aided by eddies or countercurrents, which everywhere run in the bends, close to the shore. The current in high water descends at the rate of five and even six miles an hour, and in low water at the rate of two only. It is much more rapid in those places, where shoals, battures or clusters of islands narrow the bed of the river: the circumference of these shoals or battures is in some places of several miles: and they render the voyage longer and more dangerous, at low water.

The many beaches and breakers which have risen out of the channel, are convincing proofs that the land on both sides forming the high ground near Baton Rouge is alluvial. The bars that cross most of the channels, opened by the current, have been multiplied by the means of trees brought down by the stream. One of them, stopped by its roots or branches, in a shallow place, is sufficient to obstruct the passage of a thousand, and to fix them near it. Such collections of trees are daily seen between the Balize and Mississippi, which simply would supply a city with fuel for several years. No human force being adequate to their removal, the mud brought down by the water cements and binds them together, they are gradually covered, and every inundation not only extends their lengths and widths, but adds another layer to their heights. In less than ten years, canes and shrubs grow on them and form points and islands, which forcibly shift the bed of the river.

The Mississippi discharges itself into the gulf by several mouths or passes of different lengths. The east pass, which is that principally used, is the shortest, being twenty miles in length; the south pass is twenty-two, and the southwest twenty-five.

The bars that obstruct these passes are subject to change; but, immediately on entering the river there are from three to seven, eight and ten fathoms, as far as the southwest pass, and thence twelve, fifteen, twenty and thirty fathoms, which is the general depth to the mouth of the Missouri. The depth of water over the bar of the first pass is sixteen feet; over those of the other two there are from eight to nine or ten feet.

The shoals about the mouth of the Mississippi, like those in its bed, have been formed by the trees, mud leaves and other matters continually brought down, which being forced onwards by the current, till repelled by the tide, they subside and form what is called a bar. Their distance from the entrance of the river, which is generally about two miles, depends much on the winds being occasionally with or against the tides. When these bars accumulate sufficiently to resist the tide and the current of the river, they form numerous small islands, which constantly increasing, join each other, and at last reach the continent.

All the maritime coast of Louisiana is low and marshy: that from the mouth of Pearl river, where the southern boundary of the state begins, is like that from the Perdido to Pearl river, faced by low and sandy islands; the principal of which are those of Chandeleur and a considerable number of islets. Near the mouth of the Mississippi is Round bay, in which vessels often fall, and where they wait, not without danger, and often for a long time for a fair wind, to reach one of the passes of the Mississippi, which it would be difficult to find, were it not for the houses at the old and new Balizes, and the flag staff at the former, which are visible from some distance at sea. The white clayey color of the water, remaining unmixed on the surface of the salt, is also an indication that the mighty stream is not far. It has the appearance of a shoal and alarms strangers : but the soundings are much deeper off the Mississippi, than anywhere else on the coast.

It is an observation founded on experience, that when the water of the river incorporates itself with that of the sea, and is apparently lost in the gulf, the current divides itself, and generally sets northeasterly and south-westerly; but, off soundings, the currents are, in a great measure, governed by the winds, and, if not attended to, will drive vessels south-westward, beyond the Balize, into the bay of St. Bernard, which is full of shoals, and consequently of a difficult, nay dangerous navigation.

The old Balize, a post erected by the French towards the year 1724, at the mouth of the River, is now two miles above it. There was not then the smallest appearance of the island, on which, forty-two years after, Don Antonio de Ulloa caused barracks to be erected for the accommodation of the pilots, which is now known as the new Balize.

The French had a considerable fort and garrison at the old Balize : but the magazine and several other buildings, and a part of the fortifications, gradually sunk into the soft ground. The Spaniards had a battery with three or four guns, and a subaltern's command on each island. Such is the situation of these islands, that they neither defend the entrance of the Mississippi, nor the deepest channels. The small establishments on them appear to have been made for the purpose of affording assistance to vessels coming into the river, and forwarding intelligence and dispatches to New Orleans.

In ascending the stream, there are natural prairies and a prospect of the sea on both sides, for most of the distance to the bend of Plaquemines, where a fort on each bank defends the passage, and is sufficient to stop the progress of any vessel. The British in 1815 warmly bombarded, during several days, the fort on the eastern bank. The distance from the Balize to it is thirty-two miles. From thence to the beginning of the settlements there are about twenty miles. The intermediate space is a continued tract of low and marshy ground, generally overflowed. It is covered with thick wood and palmetto bushes, which seem to render it impervious to man or beast. The banks of the river above this are thickly settled on each side for the space of thirty-five miles to the English turn, where the circular direction of the river is so considerable, that vessels cannot proceed with the wind that brought them up, and must either wait for a more favorable one, or make fast to the bank and haul close, there being a sufficient depth of water for any vessel entering the river.

At the bottom of the bend of the English turn, on the east side, is a creek running in that direction into Lake Borgne, on the elevated banks of which a number of Spanish families, brought by government from the

Canary islands in 1783, found an asylum. They were aided by the public treasury, and procured a scanty subsistence in raising vegetables for the market of New Orleans. They were in time joined by several Acadian families. A church was built for them at the king's expense: it was dedicated to St. Bernard, in compliment to Don Bernardo de Galvez, the governor of the province, under whom the migration was made. In course of time, several colonists removed thither, and it was then that the sugar cane began to be cultivated, after the abortive efforts to naturalize it to the climate of Louisiana, under the French government. This part of the country was called Terre-aux-Bœufs, from its having been the last refuge of the buffaloes or wild oxen.

By a singularity, of which Louisiana offers perhaps the only instance, the more elevated ground in it is found on the banks of its rivers, bayous and lakes. This elevation of a soil generally good, rarely too strong, often too weak, owing to a mixture of sand, varies considerably in its depth, and reaches, in very few places indeed, the elevated land of another stream or lake. Hence, the original grants of land were made of a certain number of arpents (French acres) fronting the stream, *face au fleuve*, with the eventual depth, which was afterwards fixed at forty arpents, and ordinarily carries the grant to a considerable distance into the cypress swamp.

These back swamps draining the arable ground, receive, during the high water, that which comes from the clouds, and that which filters through, or overflows the levee—that which finds its way through the breaches of these levees or crevasses, occasioned at times by the negligence of some planter, and that which others draw from the river to irrigate their fields or turn their mills. It may therefore be correctly said, in Louisiana, that water does not run to the river. But, unfortunately the mass of stagnant water, during several months of the year, to the north of the Mississippi, between its left bank and the right of the Iberville, the lakes Maurepas, Pontchartrain and Borgne and those of Round bay, and to the south from the Atchafalaya, between its left bank and the right one of the bayous and lakes, which discharge themselves in the wide estuary near the sea, finds but a partial and insufficient issue at high water, and produces, especially in uncovered spots, the deadly evaporation of the fœtid miasmata of the marshes and swamps it covers. Fortunately, on either side of the Mississippi, is found the greatest depth of arable and open ground, varying from the fraction of an arpent to thirty generally, rarely to sixty, and in very few places indeed to one hundred. The banks of the lakes, generally narrower, are much nearer to the swamps, which empty their contents through a number of bayous; they are interspersed with prairies and spots of high land, covered with oak and cypress.

This gives to this part of the state a disagreeable aspect, obstructs communications and insulates planters. It gives it a dismal and dangerous appearance, which must be well known before it may be trodden with safety. Nature seems not to have intended it for the habitation of man; but rather to have prepared it for the retreat of alligators, snakes, toads and frogs, who at dusk, by their united, though discordant vociferations, upbraid man as an intruder, assert their exclusive right, and lay their continual claim to the domain they inhabit.

It might be concluded from this picture, that Louisiana is an unhealthy country; but this would be to judge of the whole by the part. The city of New Orleans has been visited (principally since the beginning of the current century) with disastrous and almost annual epidemics, which, at a first view, justify the conclusion, if they are not the effect of local circumstances. But, it is universally admitted, that planters on the Mississippi, whom an imperious necessity compels to range themselves on the banks of the stream, especially above the city, suffer nothing from the influence of the climate or their position.

Agriculture, on both sides of the river, from the sea to the vicinity of Baton Rouge, demands the protection against its inundations, of artificial banks or levees. Public and private interest have made them the object of the solicitude and attention of the legislature. Yet, as interest excites not the vigilance of those to whom the execution of laws, in this respect, is committed, the negligence of a planter occasions, at times, a breach or crevasse on his levee, in some part of the river. If it be not immediately discovered or prompt attention given, the impetuous waves force their passage and widen the breach; the crop of the heedless planter is soon destroyed; the rails of his fences float and his house is borne away. But the alarming flood increases in extent, strength and rapidity; the angry stream seems to have found a new channel; the back swamps are filled to a considerable extent; the water rises in them and overflowing for numbers of miles, above and below the breach, inundates the cultivated fields, reaches the levee and despoils a whole neighborhood of the fruit of the sweat and labor of its inhabitants. The mischief does not end here. The Mississippi does not, like the Nile, deposit a fattening slime on the land it overflows. On the contrary, it leaves on it a large quantity of sand, destructive of its fertility, or scatters the seeds of noxious weeds. Immediately around New Orleans, the culture of sugar and even gardens hath been abandoned, on account of the prodigious growth of nut grass, the seeds of which have been spread by the water of the Mississippi.

From the English turn to the city, the Mississippi is bordered on each side by plantations, and the houses are as close to each other as in many parts of the United States that are dignified by the appellation of town. The planters are all wealthy, and almost exclusively engaged in the culture of the cane. There are a few who cultivate cotton. The distance is eighteen miles.

The city of New Orleans rises on the bank of the Mississippi, in the middle of a large bend. The circular direction of the stream here is so great, that although the city stands on the eastern side the sun rises on the opposite bank. The city proper is an oblong square of about twenty-eight arpents in front, on the Mississippi, and fourteen in depth, which under the French and Spanish governments, was surrounded and defended by a line of fortifications and a ditch. It has in its middle, on the river, a large square, or *place d'armes*, surrounded by an iron pallisado, and is adorned by three elegant public edifices, the cathedral, city hall, and a building in which the courts of the state are accommodated with halls and offices. These occupy one side of the square; that towards the river is open; each of the two others is covered by a block of uniform houses, with upper galleries. The city is intersected by seven streets parallel, and twelve perpendicular, to the river. The direction of the latter is northwest and southeast. With its suburbs, New Orleans extends along the river about three miles, and in its utmost depth on the outer line of the uppermost suburb, about one. We speak of the parts covered by contiguous buildings: that within the chartered limits is much greater.

The middle steeple of the cathedral is in 29° 57' north latitude, and 92° 29' of west longitude from Greenwich.

The three first streets parallel to the river and most of the perpendicular ones, as far as they are intersected by the former, have a considerable number of elegant brick buildings, three stories high; but the rest of the city has nothing but small wooden houses, one story high; some very mean. The proportion of the latter is much greater than in any other city of the United States.

Besides the public buildings on the square, there are the old and new nunneries, a presbyterian and an episcopal church, the jail, customhouse, courthouse of the United States, three theatres, an university, hospital and market house.

The city has three banks, besides the office of discount and deposit of that of the United States.

Two public institutions offer an asylum to the orphan youth of both sexes.

In the rear, towards the middle of the city, is a basin for small vessels, which approach New Orleans through lake Borgne; a canal about two miles in length, leads from it to bayou St. John, a small stream which empties in lake Pontchartrain; another canal, in suburb Marigny, affords also a communication with the lakes; it begins within a few yards of the Mississippi and falls into bayou St. John, at a short distance from the place, where it receives the waters of the other canal.

In population, New Orleans is superior to every city in the union, except New York, Philadelphia, Baltimore and Boston. It appears from official documents, that it contained in 1769 three thousand one hundred and ninety persons of all colors, sexes and ages: in 1788, five thousand three hundred and thirty-one: in 1797, eight thousand and fifty-six: in 1810, seventeen thousand, two hundred and forty-two, and according to the last census, in 1820, twenty-seven thousand, one hundred and fifty-six.

The city is protected from the inundation of the river, by a levee or bank, twenty feet in width, which affords a convenient walk.

Both sides of the Mississippi, from the city of New Orleans to the town of Donaldsonville, a space of seventy-five miles, are occupied by the wealthiest planters in the state, principally engaged in the culture of the sugar cane. This part of the country has been denominated the German and Acadian coasts, from its original settlers; and the wealth of the present has procured to it the appellation of the golden coast. There are five parochial churches and a convent of nuns, between New Orleans and Donaldsonville. No water course runs into, or flows from, the Mississippi in this distance, if we except a small canal, on the western side, near the city, which affords a communication with lake Barataria and others.

Donaldsonville stands on the western side of the river, at the angle it forms with bayou Lafourche, or the fork of the Chetimachas.

This town, though destined to be the seat of government, by an act of the legislature, is but a small place. It has an elegant brick church, and contains the court house and jail of the parish. The bank of Louisiana has here an office of discount and deposit, and there is a printing office, from which an hebdomadary sheet is issued. A large edifice is now rearing for the accommodation of the legislature.

The bayou Lafourche is an outlet of the Mississippi river, which has probably been the first channel through which it discharged its water into the gulf of Mexico, by the way of Big and Little caillou, the Terrebonne, Bayou du large, Bayou du cadre and Bayou black, besides several others.

For the soil, on the banks of all those streams, although of alluvial origin, like the Mississippi bottoms, which they resemble in every respect, appear of older formation; at least it is more impregnated with oxide of iron, its vegetable fossils more decayed, and the canes and timber which it produces, are generally larger than those on the banks of the Mississippi. Every one of these water courses is from one to four hundred feet in width, and has an extensive body of sugar land, capable of making fine settlements and producing the best sugar, as well as the olive tree, like in Berwick's bay to the N. W. of this. The land would produce from two to two thousand five hundred pounds of sugar to the acre.

The climate is mild and frost is seldom seen in this region, before the last of December: the land is easily cleared for cultivation, which consists simply in cutting the sticks, canes, and a few large magnolia, or sweet gum, perhaps three or four per acre, to let the canes dry and set them on fire. Nothing then remains except the bodies of the trees and stumps: the fertility of the soil is inferior to none; it produces everything susceptible of growing in the climate.

The banks of most of these rivers, several feet above the high water mark, require no levee, like those of the Mississippi: the land wants little or no ditching, as it drains naturally: the water has traced with the hand of time its own gullies. The whole country affords great facility to new settlers, for providing fish, oysters, and game, all at hand; even large droves of buffaloes are often met with in the great cane brakes of that fine country, which has remained so long unsettled, only on account of the difficulty of penetrating through them.

However, it is probable a communication will soon be established: a great portion of that country has been viewed within the last five years, by the board of internal improvements; roads have been laid out, and a canal route traced all the way to New Orleans, fit for steamboat navigation, and having not more than ten miles to cut; six miles of which pass through firm and floating prairies. The fact is that thirty-seven arpents of canal in the firm prairie would join the waters of the Mississippi with those of the Lafourche, which already communicates to bayou Terrebonne by fields, lake and a canal of twelve feet in width, cut with saws through about two miles of floating prairies, by a few inhabitants of that bayou; but this passage is only fit for small paddling boats, as there are twelve arpents of cypress swamp joining the Terrebonne, where the boats have to paddle through the cypress knees, logs and brush.

The water of the lakes, which are very numerous between the Lafourche and the Terrebonne, are five feet and a half above the level of the waters of Terrebonne, which already communicates with Black river, on bayou Cleannoir by the way of bayou Cane; but a canal of twenty arpents would join those two bayous six miles above that, and at the same time join the Grand caillou by means of five locks; the level of Black river is six feet below the latter water, and Grand caillou six feet and a half, so that this canal can be dug at little expense, above the actual level of the water, before letting in that of the lakes.

The benefits resulting from these improvements are incalculable: the immense forest of oak wood on the bayou Lafourche could be brought to New Orleans in a very few hours. The quantity of clam shells on the big Catahoula and neighborhood, might be transported to New Orleans, at a moderate expense and make a fine pavement for the streets of that city. At no great cost, the fish market would offer a new branch of trade.

Oysters could be brought to market for half the actual price.

The magnificent live oak of Grande isle and Cheniere Caminada, would not only afford fine timber for building durable ships and steamboats, but yet offer an hospitable shade, under their ever green foliage to the inhabitants of New Orleans, who would resort to those places, in preference to any other, if they could get to them without difficulty.

Yet, those are comparatively matters of little consideration, when we reflect that this canal passes through the greatest body of land, fit for the culture of the sugar cane, and in fact the only one in the U. S. fully adapted to that culture, which affords the prosperous staple of this state; and that this canal will cause the whole of that country to settle, which, in a few years, will double the quantity of sugar now made in the whole state, notwithstanding the increase of trade, which must naturally take place by the facility afforded by such canal, for the intercourse between New Orleans and the western coast of the gulf of Mexico.

About thirty miles higher up, the Mississippi has another outlet, through bayou Plaquemines, the waters of which, united to those of Grand river, flow into several lakes and lagoons on the sea coast. Bayou Plaquemines is a rapid stream; but is dry at the upper end, during winter. Its northern bank is not inhabited, being a great part of the year under water; and the agricultural establishments, on the southern bank, protected by a small levee, are scarce and insignificant.

Between these two outlets, the banks of the Mississippi are thickly settled; but the sugar plantations are few, and the planters not so wealthy as below Donaldsonville. Under the Spanish government, it was believed the sugar cane could not well succeed so high up, and there were but two plantations on which it was cultivated; they were close to Donaldsonville. But, since the cession, the industry of the purchasers of Louisiana has proved that the cane succeeds well as high up as Pointe Coupee.

The orange tree does not thrive well above bayou Plaquemines: the sweet is no longer seen, though the sour is found as far as the northern limit of the state, on the west of the Mississippi.

The only outlet, which the Mississippi has through its eastern bank, is a few miles above bayou Plaquemines—it is called bayou Manshac. At about ten miles from the Mississippi, it receives the river Amite from its right side, and takes the name of Iberville river.

From the Mississippi to the mouth of Iberville on lake Maurepas, the distance along the stream is sixty miles; the first ten of which do not admit of navigation during more than four months of the year. There are, at all times, from two to six feet of water for three miles farther, and the depth, in the remaining part of the way to the lake, is from two to four fathoms.

The river Amite falls into bayou Manshac on the north side, twenty miles from the Mississippi: the water of the Amite is clear, running on a gravelly bottom. It may be ascended by vessels, drawing from five to six feet of water, about twelve, and with batteaux one hundred, miles farther.

It forks about seventeen miles above its mouth : the eastern fork is the Comite; the western, which preserves its name, is the most considerable and rises near Pearl river. Both run through a fertile, rolling country, which as well as the low land, is covered with cane, oak, ash, mulberry, hickory, poplar, cedar and cypress.

The united waters of bayou Manshac and the Amite form the Iberville, the length of which is thirty-nine miles. The land and timber on its banks are similar to those on the Amite, with the difference that the banks of the Iberville are in general lower, and the country less hilly, with a greater proportion of rice land, and cypress and live oak of an excellent quality for ship building.

Lake Maurepas is about ten miles long and seven wide, and from ten to twelve feet deep. The country around it is low and covered with cypress, live oak and myrtle.

The Tickfoa is the only river that falls into lake Maurepas. It rises in the state of Mississippi and runs a middle course between Amite and Pearl rivers, it has a sufficient depth for steam boat navigation to the mouth of bayou Chapeaupilier, a distance of about fifty miles.

The pass of Manshac connects lake Maurepas and lake Pontchartrain. It is seven miles in length, and about three hundred yards wide; divided by an island, which runs from the former to within a mile from the latter; the south channel is the deepest and shortest.

The greatest length of lake Pontchartrain is about forty miles, and its width about twenty-four, and the average depth ten fathoms.

It receives on the north side the rivers Tangipao, Tchefuncta and Bonfouca, with the bayous Castin and Lacemel, and on the side of the city, bayou St. John, and higher up bayou Tigouyou.

Tangipao has at its mouth a depth of water of four feet, Tchefuncta seven, and Bonfouca, six.

Two passes connect lake Pontchartrain with an estuary called lake Borgne, the Rigolets and the pass of Chef Menteur, both of which are defended by a fort, surrounded by deep morasses.

The passes are about ten miles long, and from three to four hundred yards wide.

By bayous that fall into lake Borgne, a number of fishermen, who dwell on its banks, find their way to the market of New Orleans, which they supply. Through one of these, bayou Bienvenu, the British army under general Packenham, proceeded, with all its artillery to within a very few miles of the city.

There are from sixteen to eighteen feet of water on the sides of lake Borgne; in the middle from ten to twelve fathoms; but in its upper part, from eleven to twelve feet.

Opposite to the entrance into lake Borgne, and at the end of the Rigolets, on the north side near the gulf, is the mouth of Pearl river.

This stream rises in the northern part of the state of Mississippi, and after traversing it centrally, sends its waters into the gulf by two main branches. The eastern which, we have seen, divides the states of Louisiana and Mississippi, falls into lake Borgne. The western, which leaves the main branch in the latitude of thirty degrees, runs entirely through the former state and falls into the Rigolets.

Above the fork, the navigation is good for steam boats, during six months of the year; some have already ascended to Monticello.

It is evident from an inspection of this river, that at no very distant period, its eastern branch was its only channel, meandering through an extent of above one hundred miles to lake Borgne. During some inundation, the western branch broke from the main channel, through the swamps, and found a nearer course, of sixty miles only, to the Rigolets.

Above Manshac, the land gradually rises on the eastern side of the river, to Baton Rouge, a small town distant about one hundred and twenty miles from New Orleans. The plantations are not all, as below, ranged side by side on the immediate banks of the river; but, many are scattered in the intermediate space, between the Mississippi, the rivers Amite, Comite and others flowing into the lakes Maurepas and Pontchartrain. On one of these the Spaniards made an abortive effort to establish a town, called Galveztown.

Sugar plantations are now much fewer; but those on which cotton is cultivated are more numerous and extensive. The part of the state to the east of the Mississippi and the lakes, having been occupied by the British for nearly twenty years, the descendants of its original French inhabitants are in very small number, indeed; and a great many of the people who have come to Louisiana from other states, since the cession, have settled there: during the possession of the British, several colonists from the Atlantic provinces, principally Virginia, the Carolinas and Georgia, flocked thither. There was a considerable migration in 1764 and 1765 from the banks of the Roanoke, in North Carolina; so that the population differs very little from that of the Atlantic states. The mixture of French and Spaniards being small indeed, except in the town of Baton Rouge.

This town is built on a high bluff, on the eastern side of the river. The United States have extensive barracks near it. It contains the public buildings of the parish, and has two weekly gazettes and a branch of the bank of Louisiana.

On the opposite side of the river from bayou Plaquemines, the arable land is only a narrow slip between the bank and the cypress swamps, that empty themselves in the Atchafalya.

At a distance of about thirty miles from Baton Rouge and on the same side, on an elevated ridge parallel to and near the river, is the town of St. Francisville. The land around, as far north as the boundary line, which is only fifteen miles distant, and far to the east, is rolling, and tolerably well adapted to the culture of the cotton, which engages the attention of the settlers. St. Francisville has a house of worship, a weekly paper and a branch of the bank of Louisiana, and the public buildings of its parish.

Opposite to it, is the settlement of Pointe Coupee, the principal part of which is a peninsula, formed by the old bed of the Mississippi, called False river, the upper part of which is stopped up at present. The French had a fort there, the vestiges of which are discernible. This parish is populous and wealthy: cotton is its principal staple, but it has few sugar plantations. It has no town; but the plantations throughout, principally on both banks of False river, are much closer to each other than in any other parish in the state. It is at high water insulated, by the Atchafalaya and the Mississippi on the northeast and west, and by a dismal swamp which separates it from the parish of West Baton Rouge, and which is then inundated.

To the west, and at the distance of forty miles from St. Francisville, is the small town of Jackson, and about sixty miles to the south of the latter, that of Springfield, near the mouth of the Tangipao river, which falls into lake Maurepas.

On the eastern side of lake Pontchartrain, near the mouth of the Tchefuncta is the town of Madisonville, and seven miles higher up, that of Covington. The land in this neighborhood along the water courses is a rich alluvial bottom, and terminates in pine barrens.

The country near Springfield, Covington and Madisonville, especially the two last, is sandy and sterile in general, and covered with pine trees; although there are, along most of the water courses, several spots well adapted to the culture of cotton. The inhabitants apply their industry to making tar and pitch, gathering turpentine, cutting timber, burning bricks and lime; the immense ridges of shell, on the margin of the gulf facilitating greatly, the last operation.

A little above the northern extremity of the settlement of Pointe Coupee, Red river pours its waters into the Mississippi. This stream has its source in the vicinity of Santa Fe. The Mississippi, a little below, sends part of its accumulated flood to the sea through a western branch, its first outlet from its source called the Atchafalaya; a word, which in the Indian language means a long river. The form of the country and this name, not at all applicable to the stream at present, have given rise to the opinion, that, in former time, the northern extremity of the settlement of Pointe Coupee prolonged itself to, and joined the bank of the Mississippi, above the mouth of Red river, leaving a piece of ground between the two streams; so that the Red river did not pay the tribute of its waters to the Mississippi, but carried them, and the name of Atchafalaya, which it then bore, and was particularly applicable to it, to the sea; the present stream, which has retained its name, being only a continuation of it, and that in course of time the waves of the long and great rivers destroyed the ground that separated them, and divided the former into two; the upper one of which has received the name of Red river from the Europeans, on account of the color of its water, which is occasioned by the copper mines near it, the impregnations of which prevent them from being potable.

The confluence of Red river and the Mississippi is remarkable as the spot, on which the army of Charles I. of Spain, under De Soto, towards the middle of the sixteenth century, committed the body of their chief to the deep, in order to prevent its falling into the hands of the Indians.

On entering Red river, the water appears turbid, brackish and of a red color. For the first sixty or seventy miles, its bed is so crooked, that the distance through its meanderings is two-thirds greater than in a straight line. The general course is nearly east to west; the land for upwards of thirty miles from its mouth is overflowed at high water, from ten to fifteen feet. Below Black river, the northern bank is the highest. The growth in the lower or southern part is willow and cotton wood; in the higher, oak, hickory and ash.

Six miles from the mouth of the river, on the south side, is bayou Natchitoches, which communicates with lake Long, from whence another bayou affords a passage to the river. At high water, boats pass through these bayous and lake, and go to the river after a route of fifteen miles, while the distance from one bayou to the other is forty-five.

Black river comes up from the north, about twenty-four miles from bayou Natchitoches; its water is clear and limpid, when contrasted with that of Red river, and appears black.

Above the junction, Red river makes a regular turn to the south, for about eighteen miles, forming a segment of about three-fourths of a circle. Twenty miles above, the bayou from lake Long comes in, and thirty-three miles still farther is the first landing of the Avoyelles : the river all the while being so crooked that, at this place, the guns of Fort Adams are distinctly heard ; although the distance by the river is upwards of one hundred and fifty miles. The sound appears a little south from east.

At this landing is the first arable soil immediately on the banks of the river, which, in the whole space, are higher than the land behind. At a short distance from this landing, to the south is the prairie des Avoyelles, of an oval form and about forty miles in circumference. It is very level, covered with high grass and has but very few clumps of trees ; its soil is not very fertile ; that of the timber land around it, when cleared, is far preferable. The lower end of the prairie has the richest land. The timber around it is chiefly oak, which produces good mast. The inhabitants raise cotton ; but the settlement is better for cattle and hogs ; in high water it is insulated, and at others communicates with those of Rapides, Opelousas and Pointe Coupee.

The upper landing is fifteen miles higher, and sixteen miles above, a few years ago, was laid the foundation of the town of Cassandra, on the north side, opposite to bayou L'amoureux, which connects Red river and bayou Bœuf. The intermediate land on the northern bank is tolerably good, moderately hilly, covered chiefly with oak, hickory and short leaved pine. But at the distance of a few miles from the water, begins a pine barren tract, that extends for upwards of thirty miles to the settlements of Catahoula. On the south side, is a large body of rich low ground, extending to the borders of the settlements of Opelousas, watered and drained by bayou Robert and bayou Bœuf, two handsome streams of clear water that rise in the high land between Red river and the Sabine.

Bayou Bœuf falls into bayou Crocodile, which empties itself into the Atchafalaya to the south of the settlement of Avoyelles, at a short distance from the large raft in the latter stream. In point of fertile soil, growth of timber, and goodness of water, there is not perhaps an equal quantity of good land, in the state, than on the banks of bayou Bœuf.

The town of Alexandria stands on the south side of Red river, fifteen miles above that of Cassandra, and immediately below the rapids or falls, which are occasioned by a sudden rise of the bed of the river, which is here a soft rock, extending quite across. From July to November, there is a sufficiency of water, over the falls, for the passage of boats. The rock is extremly soft and does not extend up and down the river more than a few yards, and a passage could easily be cut across.

The town is regularly built. It has an elegant court house and college, built of bricks, a strong jail and a neat market house. The bank of Louisiana has here an office of discount, and there is a printing office, from which a weekley paper is issued.

The settlement of Rapides is a valley of rich alluvial soil, surrounded by pine hills, extending to the east towards the Washita, and in the opposite direction to the Sabine. The pine hills come to the river, opposite to the town.

Immediately above the town, the river receives from the same side bayou Rapides, a semi-circular stream, about thirty miles in length, the upper part of which receives a portion of the water of Red river.

Bayou Robert, which is now almost stagnant, formerly ran out of bayou Rapides, about a mile above its mouth and winding through a rich valley united with bayou Bœuf. But, a dyke has been thrown up, at its former mouth and the current confined to bayou Rapides.

Both these bayous pass through bodies of extremely fine land, of great depth.

Twenty miles above Alexandria are two deserted villages of the Biloxi Indians.

Near these, bayou Jean de Dieu or Coteille, falls into Red river, from the right side. The stream of bayou Rapides, of which the channel is continuous, was formerly a navigable branch of Red river, which returned to the parent stream, below and at the foot of the rapids but the gradual deepening of the bed and the widening of the stream have left it a small bayou, which is fed by springs and branches from the pine hills; one-half emptying at the former outlet above; the other at the foot of the rapids, below. The lower half is called bayou Rapides. The whole length is about thirty miles. The land throughout is of the finest quality and great depth, and now in the highest state of culture. These bayous are not used for the purpose of navigation, but are capable of forming with little expense, a fine natural canal.

Thirteen miles above bayou Jean de Dieu, is an island of seventy miles in length and three in width, the northern channel of which is called the Rigolet du bon Dieu and the other the river aux Cannes.

There is not much good land on the west side of the river; the high lands generally confine it on one side and the island thus formed is, on the side of it bordering on the rigolet, subject to inundation.

On the east side of the river the valley is narrow but of inexhaustible fertility; the rest of the land between the river and the Washita, is oak and pine land, of little value, except in spots on the water courses.

The principal settlements of Natchitoches are on the immediate banks of the river, on each side. The land is red alluvion, of singular fertility, but not cultivable to a great extent from the rivers. The swamps commencing within a very few acres.

The town of Natchitoches is at the distance of one hundred and nine miles from Alexandria and on the same side of Red river. It is the westernmost town of the state, being two hundred and sixty-six miles from the Mississippi, about four hundred from New Orleans and five hundred from the gulf by water.

The old town stood on a hill, about half a mile behind the present, which is immediately on the bank of the river. On the second street, is a hill the area of which covers about two hundred acres of ground; on it a fort and barracks have been built, the site of which is thirty feet above the bank of the river. The old town is an extensive common of several hundred acres entirely tufted with clover and covered with sheep and cattle. Nothing of it is discoverable except the forms of the gardens and some ornamental trees. It began to be abandoned soon after the cession of the province to Spain. Before, most of the settlers dwelt in town; the hill is of stiff clay and the streets were miry; the people found the place inconvenient, on account of their stock and farms, and filed off one after the other, and settled on the river. The merchants found its banks convenient for lading and unlading: the mechanics followed and the church and jail were removed. The soil on the river, though much richer, is of a loose sandy texture and the streets are not miry, nor much dusty. The town is nearly twice as large as Alexandria. The well water is hardly potable, that of the river brackish, and the inhabitants, as in Alexandria, have large cisterns for collecting rain water. The public buildings of the parish are in this town and a weekly gazette is published.

There are two lakes near, within one and six miles. The larger has a circumference of six miles, the other of thirty. They rise and fall with the river: the stream that connects them with it, during high water, runs into them with great velocity, and in like manner to the river, during the rest of the year. The quantity of fish and fowls which are obtained on these lakes appears incredible. It is not uncommon, in winter, for a man to kill from two to four hundred fowls in an evening. They fly between sun down and dusk: the air is filled with them. A man loads and fires, as quickly as he can, without taking aim, and continues on the same spot, till he thinks he has killed enough. Ducks and geese, brant and swan are thus killed. In summer, fish abound equally. An Indian with a bow and arrow, kills more than two horses can carry away, while he is thus engaged. Some of the fish weigh from thirty to forty pounds. The lakes afford also a plenty of shell for lime. At low water, their bottoms are most luxuriant meadows, where the inhabitants fatten their horses.

Stone coal is found in abundance, in the neighborhood, with a quarry of good building stone.

Similar lakes are found all along Red river for five or six hundred miles. They are natural reservoirs, for the surplus quantity of water, beyond what the banks of the river may contain; otherwise, no part of the ground could be inhabited, the low land, from hill to hill, would be inundated.

Twelve miles north of Natchitoches, on the opposite side of the river is lake Noir, a large one; the bayou of which comes into the Rigolet du bon Dieu, opposite to the town; near it are salt works, from which the town is supplied.

Three miles up the stream, is the upper mouth of the Rigolet du bon Dieu, where the settlement of the grand ecor, or great bluff begins. This eminence stands on the south side, and is about one hundred feet high. Towards the river, it is almost perpendicular, and of a soft white rock: the top is a gravel loam of considerable extent, on which grow large oaks, hickory, black cherry and grape vines There is a small bluff near, at the foot of which is a large quantity of stone coal, and several springs of the best water in this part of the country. Near them is a lake of clear water, with a gravelly margin.

The river makes a large bend above the bluffs, to the north, and a long reach, nearly due east by it. About a mile above, from the south shore, a large bayou comes in from the Spanish lake, which is about fifty miles in circumference, and rises and falls with the river, from which the largest boats may ascend to the lake, and through it up several bayous, particularly bayou Dupin, up which, boats may go within one mile and a half from the old French fort, at the Adayes.

Two miles above this place, the river forks; the southwestern branch running westerly for sixty miles, then forming and meeting the other.

The country, bounded to the east and north by this branch of the river, is called the bayou Pierre settlement, from a stream that traverses it.

Part of the land was granted by the French government. The inhabitants raised large herds of cattle and made some cheese. The settlement is interspersed with prairies, and the land is equally rich, as the river bottoms. The hills are of a good grey soil. The creek, called by the new settlers, Stony creek, affords several good mill seats. Its bed and banks furnish a good kind of building stone. The upland is high, gently rolling, and produces good corn, cotton and tobacco. A few miles to the west is an abundant saline.

Higher up on the river, on a hill, to the northeast is the Campti settlement. The river land is here much broken by bayous and lagoons.

Between lake Bistineau and tributary streams of the Washita is a new and extensive settlement, which has grown up within a few years, called Allen's settlement. The land is second rate upland, finely watered and well adapted to raising stock.

The country to the west of Red river, extending to the Sabine, furnishes but a small proportion of even second rate land. It is generally covered with oak and pine. There are some choice spots of land; but of small extent.

Cantonment Jessup is situated half way between Red river and the Sabine and on the highest ridge, which separates the streams flowing into these rivers.

The land on the Sabine is unfit for cultivation to any extent. The part of it, which is not subject to sudden overflow, is high land of no value but for raising stock.

Above is the obstruction, commonly called the great raft, choking up the channel for upwards of one hundred miles, by the course of the river. It was examined, during the winter of 1826, by capt. Birch and lieutenant Lee, with a detachment from cantonment Jessup, by order of the secretary of war of the United States, with the view of ascertaining the practicability of opening a passage for steam boats.

They found, within one hundred miles of the bed of the river, above one hundred and eighty rafts or jams of timber, from a few to four hundred yards in length. They thought that to break through, or remove them, so as to admit the passage of a steam boat, would be a work of immense labor and expense, and that, if done, the loose timber would probably form other rafts below.

The bank of the river appeared to them very rich; but so covered with canes, briars and vines, as to render it impossible to advance, without cutting a passage all the way, and they judged a man could cut but a few yards in a day.

They crossed over an island hauling a light skiff to bayou Pierre, from which a canal of less than half a mile, through an alluvial soil, would open a communication with lake Scioto. This lake is about one hundred miles long and five or six wide; a channel ten feet deep runs through it. The high water mark is at least fifteen feet above the surface of the lake in winter. The lake has an indented shore, parallel to the river, and a communication with it about twenty-five miles above the raft, and another might be easily opened many miles higher up.

In ascending bayou Pierre, which falls into the river six miles above the town of Natchitoches, the principal obstruction consists of a number of cypress stumps, that might be easily removed at low water. This once effected and a canal cut into lake Scioto, there would be nothing, at high water, to prevent steam boats ascending Red river one thousand miles above the town of Natchitoches, even into New Mexico, through a fertile and salubrious country. It is believed, that the passage through bayou Pierre is one hundred miles shorter than through the main branch of the river.

Cotton is exclusively cultivated for sale in the settlement of Rapides, and almost so in that of Natchitoches, in which tobacco is also raised; it is of a superior quality; the planters do not put it up as elsewhere in hogsheads, but bring it to market in carrots.

Black river, at its mouth, is about one hundred yards in width, and is twenty feet deep. Its banks are covered with pea vine, and several kinds of grasses, bearing a seed which geese and ducks eat greedily. Willows are generally seen on one side or the other, with a small growth of black oak, pecan, hickory, elm, etc. It takes its name at the distance of sixty-six miles from Red river, where it branches out into the Catahoula, Washita and Tensa. Its width here does not exceed eighty yards. The soil is a black mould mixed with a moderate proportion of sand, resembling much the soil of the Mississippi. Yet the forest trees are not like those on that stream, but resemble those on Red river. The cane grows on several parts of its right bank, and a few small willows are seen on either. In advancing up the river, the timber becomes large, rising in some places to the height of forty feet. The land is at times inundated, not by the waters of the river, but from the intrusion of its powerful neighbor, the Mississippi. The land declines rapidly from the banks, as in all alluvial countries, to the cypress swamps, where more or less water stagnates, during the whole year. Towards the upper end of Black river, the shore abounds with muscles and perrywincles, the first of the kind called pearl muscles.

The land, at the mouth of the Catahoula is evidently alluvial. In process of time, the river, shutting up its ancient passage, and elevating the banks over which its waters pass no longer, communicates with the same facility as formerly. The consequence is, that many large tracts, before subject to inundation, are now exempt from that inconvenience.

There is an embankment running from the Catahoula to Black river (enclosing about two hundred acres of rich land) at present about ten feet high, and ten feet broad. This surrounds four large mounds of earth at the distance of a bow shot from each other; each of which may be twenty feet high, one hundred feet broad, and three hundred feet long at the top, besides a stupendous turret, situated on the back part of the whole, or farthest from the water; the base covers about an acre of ground, rising by two steps or stories, tapering in the ascent; the whole surmounted by a great cone with its top cut off. This tower of earth, on admeasurement, was found to be eighty feet perpendicular.

The Tensa is a creek thirty-six miles long, the issue of a lake of the same name, twenty-four miles in length and six in breadth, which lies west from the mouth of the Catahoula, and communicates with Red river, during the great annual inundations.

To the west and northwest angle of this lake, a stream called Little river enters, and preserves its channel of running water during all the year: meandering along the bed of the lake, the superfices of which, in all other parts, during the dry season from July to November, and frequently later, is completely drained, covered with the most luxuriant herbage, and becomes the retreat of immense herds of deer, of turkeys, geese and crane.

The Tensa serves only to drain off a part of the waters of the inundation from the low land of the Mississippi, which communicates with Black river during the season of high water.

Three miles up the Washita and on the right side comes a stream called the Haha, one of the many passages through which the waters of the great inundation penetrate and pervade all the low land; annihilating, for a time, the current of lesser streams in the neighborhood of the Mississippi.

Five miles above is the *prairie Villemont*, thus named from its having been included in a grant from the French government to an officer of that name.

In the beginning of the last century, the French projected, and began here extensive settlements, but the massacre in 1730, and the subsequent destruction of the Natchez Indians, broke up all their undertakings, and they were not renewed by the French.

The timber, on both sides of the Washita to this prairie, is chiefly the red, white and black oak, interspersed with a variety of other trees.

The plains of the Washita lie on its east side, and sloping from the bank, are inundated in the rear by the Mississippi. In certain great floods, the water has advanced so far, as to be ready to pour into the Washita over its margin.

On approaching towards bayou Lowes, which the Washita receives from the right, a little below its first rapid there is a great deal of high land on both sides of the river, producing the long leaved pine.

At the foot of the rapids, the navigation is obstructed, by beds of gravelly sand; above the first rapid is a high ridge of primitive earth, studded with abundance of fragments of rocks or stone, which appear to have been thrown up to the surface in a very irregular manner. The stone is of a very friable nature, some of it having the appearance of indurated clay; the rest is blackish, from exposure to the air; within, it is of a greyish white. It is said that the strata in the hill are regular and might afford good grindstones.

The other rapid is formed by a ledge of rocks crossing the entire bed of the river: above it, the water appears as in a mill pond and is about one hundred yards wide.

Twelve miles higher, a little above a rocky hill, comes in the bayou Aux Bœufs. The river is here, at low water, about two fathoms and a half deep, on a bottom of mud and sand. The banks of the river appear to retain very little alluvial soil: the high land earth which is a sandy loam of a grey color, has streaks of red sand and clay. The soil is not rich; it bears pines, interspersed with red oak, hickory and dogwood.

A third rapid created by a transverse ledge of rock, narrows the river to about thirty yards.

Similar rapids occur as far as the settlement. It is a plain or prairie, which appears alluvial from the regular slope of the land from the bank of the river, the bed of which is now sufficiently deep to preserve it from inundation. Yet, in the rear, the waters of the Mississippi approach, and sometimes leave dry but a narrow strip of land along the bank of the Washita. The soil is here very good, but not equal to the Mississippi bottoms; it may be estimated second rate. At a small distance to the east, are extensive cypress swamps, over which the waters of the inundation always stand, to the depth of from fifteen to twenty-five feet. On the west, after passing once the valley of the river, the breadth of which is from one-quarter to two miles, the land assumes an elevation from one hundred to three hundred feet, and extends to the settlements of Red river. It is there poor and what is called pine barrens.

On this part of the river, lies a considerable tract of land, granted in 1795 by the Baron de Carondelet to the Marquis of Maison Rouge, a French emigrant, who proposed to bring into Louisiana, thirty families from his country, who were to descend the Ohio for the purpose of forming an establishment, on the banks of the Washita, designed principally for the culture of wheat, and the manufacture of flour. This tract was two leagues in width, and twelve in length, traversed by the river.

The town of Monroe stands on the side of the Washita, and at high water is approached by large steamboats; but the navigation is interrupted during a great part of the year by many shoals and rapids. The general width of the river to the town is from eighty to one hundred yards. Its banks present very little appearance of alluvial soil, but furnish an infinite number of beautiful landscapes.

A substance is found along the river side, nearly resembling mineral coal; its appearance is that of the carbonated wood, described by Kirwan. It does not easily burn, but being applied to the flame of a candle, it sensibly increases it, and yields a faint smell, resembling that of gum lac, or common sealing wax.

Soft friable stone is common, and great quantities of gravel and sand are upon the beach; on several parts of the shore a reddish clay appears in the strata of the banks, much indurated and blackened by exposure to light and air.

The land above the town is not very inviting, the soil being poor and covered with pine wood.

About thirty-six miles higher up is bayou Barthelemy, on the right. Here begins Baron de Bastrop's grant of land, by the Baron de Carondelet in 1795, obtained nearly on the same terms as that of the Marquis de Maison Rouge. It is a square of four leagues on each side, containing about one million of acres.

The bank of the river continues about thirty feet in height, of which eighteen from the water are clayey loam of a pale color, on which the water has deposited twelve feet of light sandy soil, apparently fertile, and of a dark brown color. This description of land is of a small breadth, not exceeding one-half of a mile on each side of the river; and may be called the valley of the Washita, between which there is high land covered with pine.

The soil continues with a growth of small timber to the bayou des butes, which has its name from a number of Indian mounds along its course.

The margin of the river begins now to be covered with such timber as grows on inundated land, particularly a species of white oak, vulgarly called the overcup oak, the wood of which is remarkably hard, solid, ponderous and durable. It produces a large acorn, in great abundance, on which bears feed, and which is very fattening for hogs.

A few miles higher up is a long and narrow island. Here the face of the country begins to change. The banks of the river are low and steep, its bed deeper and more contracted, being from twenty-five to thirty feet in depth. The soil, near the water, is a very sandy loam, covered with such vegetation, as is found on the inundated land of the Mississippi. The tract presents the appearance of a new soil, very different from what is below.   This alluvial spot may be supposed the old site of a great lake, drained by a natural channel, by the abrasion of the water—since which period, the annual inundations have deposited the superior soil.   Eighteen or twenty feet are wanting to render it habitable for man.   It appears now well stocked with the beasts of the forest.

Mallet's island is above.   Its upper point has been ascertained to be within 32½ seconds to the northern line of the state.   The bed of the river along this alluvial soil is generally covered with water, and its navigation, uninterrupted.   Near it is *marais des Sabines*, on the right.   A stratum of dirty white clay, under the alluvial tract, shows the end of the sunken and the approach of the high land.   The salt lake marsh does not derive its name from any brackishness in its water; but from its contiguity to some of the lakes, generally found, on a clayey soil, compact enough for potters' ware.

Opposite to this place is a point of land, forming a promontory, advancing within a mile of the river, and to which the boats resort, when the low lands are covered with water.

Great salt lick creek, a stream of considerable length, and navigable for small boats, comes in above.   The hunters ascend it three hundred miles, and affirm that none of the springs that feed it are salt.   It has obtained its name from the many buffalo salt licks discovered in its vicinity.

Although many of these licks, by digging, furnish water, holding marine salt in solution, there exists no reason for believing that any of them would produce nitre.

Notwithstanding this low, alluvial tract appears in all respects well adapted to the growth of the long moss, or Spanish beard, (tilansia) none is obtained in the thirty-third degree of latitude.

The long leaf pine, frequently the growth of rich and even inundated land, is here in great abundance.   The short leaf pitch pine, on the contrary, is generally found upon arid land and frequently in sandy and lofty situations.

Some sand beaches and rapids are higher up; there are cane brakes on both sides of the river.   The canes are small, but demonstrate that the water does not surmount the bank more than a few feet.

The river here begins to widen.   Its banks show the high land soil, with a stratum of three or four feet of alluvion deposited by the river upon it.   Their superstratum is greyish and very sandy, with a small admixture of loam, indicative of the poverty of the upland and mountains in which the river rises.

At the distance of a few miles is the confluence of the little Atipouse, on the left hand.   The navigation of the Washita is much impeded by numerous rapids and shoals.

Coal mines are to be found on the northwest side of the river, at the distance of one mile and a half from its banks, and a saline was discovered by Dr. Hunter, in 1804.

It is situated at the bottom of the bed of a deep gully.   The surrounding land is rich and well timbered, but subject to inundation; except an Indian mound, having a base of eighteen or one hundred feet in diameter and twenty feet high.   After digging about three feet through the clay, he came to quicksand, from which the water flowed in abundance.   Its taste was salt and bitter, resembling that of sea water.   In a second hole, it required him to dig six feet before he reached the quicksand: in doing which he struck several pieces of Indian pottery. The brine yielded a solid mass, by evaporation, of ten quarts or half a pound in weight, when dry. It is, therefore, of the same strength as the water of the ocean on our coast, and twice that of the famous lick in Kentucky, called Bullet's lick, and Mank's lick, from which so much salt is made.

The part of the state lying north of Red river is interspersed with numerous lakes and water courses, and presents every variety of the soil, from the low inundated land to the highest hills in Louisiana. As in the lower region of the Mississippi, the margin of the rivers is (with the exception of a few tracts of high cane brake land) higher than that in the rear, taking a southern direction with that noble stream. The shores of lake Providence, the first high land that presents itself, are about three miles west from the river. That lake is evidently an ancient bed of the Mississippi; about thirty-six miles due south, lake St. Joseph presents the same appearance. On Bruine's bayou, twelve miles south, part of the banks are sufficiently high for cultivation. Lake St. John is not far from Concordia. The shores of both these lakes are partly cultivated; their features indicate also that they formerly were beds of the Mississippi. From Concordia to the mouth of Red river, the land descends suddenly from the banks into what makes a part of the Mississippi swamp. The first water course of any importance running west of and in a nearly parallel course with the Mississippi is the river Tensa, which uniting with the bayou Mason runs into the Washita. The Tensa and Mason might easily be made navigable far steamboats, which have already ascended the Tensa upwards of thirty miles. In the upper part of those rivers, the land is high in many places, chiefly on the Mason; the land is rolling, far above high water mark, but not sufficiently elevated to merit the appellation of hills. Beautiful specimens of calcareous spath have been brought from that part of the country, found in ploughing. In the lower part of those streams the land is low and unfit for cultivation. Between the Mississippi and the Tensa, bayous intersect the swamp, always running west or southwestwardly; lakes, joined the one to the other by those bayous, are scattered over it. The greatest part of those lakes becomes dry at low water, and in a dry autumn, except those which were formerly beds of the Mississippi. These retain invariably a considerable quantity of water. The same observation applies to the country between the Mississippi and Black river, which empties into Red river thirty miles above its mouth. When the Mississippi rolls on its full tide, those bayous, receiving an immense addition from its waters, run with the rapidity of torrents; chiefly at their issue from the Mississippi into the Tensa and river Aux Bœufs, mixing their waters with the Washita and Black river, and carrying back into its bosom by Red river, what it had yielded to them above.

The head waters of the Tensa are at or near lake Providence; the Mason heads higher up and westerly.

The next river west of these is the Aux Bœufs, thus called by the first hunters (French) on account of the innumerable herds of buffaloes which then roamed in the large prairies bordering its banks. That river has its rise not far north of the thirty-third degree of latitude, in the territory of Arkansas. The middle part of its course presents high rich land; it gets lower towards its mouth, near which it is overflowed to the Washita river.

Between river Aux Bœufs and the Mason the land is low, with here and there a tract of high rich soil.

West of river Aux Bœufs, Barthelemy river, (often called bayou) is a considerable stream; it heads in the territory of Arkansas, and empties into the Washita, thirty miles by water above the town of Monroe, the only re-union of houses or hamlets in the parish of Washita. The land on that bayou is high on both sides; its water pure, and its current brisk, even at the lowest stage of water. It is navigable for barges or batteaux, and could be rendered fit for steam boat navigation at a small expense. Among the numerous water courses, which either are or could easily be made a *medium* of water communication, from the Mississippi to the northwestern part of the state, it will ultimately be this river, which will be found to afford the best, the easiest and the most important.

Among the numerous creeks and bayous which carry their tribute to the Washita river, bayou Louis ought not to be forgotten; it is not on account of the extent of its course, but on account of the land on its borders or adjacent thereto. It comes out of a lake of the same name, the western and northwestern banks of which are inhabited, being high and fertile. That lake and bayou, the Washita, river Aux Bœufs and Turkey creek surround the high land, called Sicily Island. In it are found high hills, generally much broken, containing sand stones and some silex in pebbles; that spot is the most remarkable for being the only one covered with slight hills between the Mississippi and Washita, and also, because it appears to have been among the first inhabited by the French, who settled in Louisiana, who probably abandoned it at the epoch of the massacre by the Natchez Indians. It is about thirty miles from Concordia, in a west by north direction. French axes have been found there, canon balls, even mill stones and iron tools much disfigured by rust, but evidently of French manufacture.

The next stream, to which all those mentioned above are tributary, is the Washita; that river has its source in the territory of Arkansas, in the Rocky mountains. In the vicinity of its head waters are found the celebrated warm springs. It runs almost parallel with the Mississippi. At the mouth of the Tensa, Little river or Catahoula river, arrives from the west. The Washita, running between the two, takes their additional supply at the same place, in its course, but there loses its name: from this place to its junction with Red river, during a meandering course of about sixty miles, it assumes the name of Black river, an appellation probably derived from the color of the soil through which it runs; the fertility of which often induced emigrants to settle on its banks; but they are too low; very few years elapse without seeing them inundated; they are now deserted. Many bayous empty their waters into Black river, all rising in the Mississippi swamp, and at high water communicating with that noble stream. The largest is bayou Crocodile, which comes out of lake Concordia; when its current is considerable, the largest kind of canoes have navigated it to Black river.

The Washita is navigable for steam boats of any burthen during six or eight months in the year, as far as the town of Monroe, a distance of about two hundred and forty miles from its mouth, or as it is there called the mouth of Black river. Steam boats of upwards of one hundred and fifty tons have ascended it more than two hundred miles above Monroe. From its mouth to the Mississippi, the banks of Red river are low, and during high water offer nothing to the eye but an immense sea covered with forests.

The features of the country, west of Washita river, are very different from those of the eastern side: between Washita and Red river, extensive pine hills, some of which are several hundred feet high, cover the surface of the earth, nearly as far south as the mouth of Little river, with the exception of the bottoms of creeks; some of which are fertile and above inundations—others, chiefly near their mouth, covered with water at every great swelling of the stream. On that side, the Mississippi has no effect; no power, there ceases its dominion, except occasionally when at the highest stage, it recedes on Red river, and Black river, and consequently such of their tributary streams, the entrance of which are situated low enough to be affected by this retrograde motion. Such is Little river, which runs through a lake called Catahoula, almost dry at low water, and which could be navigated by crafts of heavy burthen, when the adjacent low land is inundated. That river has its head waters about thirty miles south of the 33d degree of N. latitude; its northernmost branch originates at 32 degrees and 35 seconds; it then takes the name of Dogdemene and forms the boundary between Washita and Natchitoches parishes. It retains that name to its junction with the bayou or rather creek Castor, thence it is called Little river. In the same manner as the Tensa, Washita and Little river, uniting at one point, form Black river.

The country, through which Little river (sometimes called Catahoula river) runs, wears not a uniform aspect, sometimes reaching between hills, bluffs and banks, then strongly dragging its waters through lands inundated from one and a half to three miles on each side; in some instances, it flows through rich bottoms, not subject to inundation. Its navigation could be easily improved, and no doubt will be so, when its banks are more thickly settled.

Several large creeks flow between Washita and Little river, formed by innumerable branches, a great proportion of which are never failing springs; they only swell by rains; the water running with rapidity from the hills, subsides a few hours after the rain ceases. But few countries can boast of being better supplied with good water than the tract bounded north by the 33d degree of latitude, west by the Dogdemene, south by Catahoula lake and Little river, and east by the Washita river. That country is covered with hills, some of which are very good land, especially about the head waters of bayou D'Arbonne a large creek, which empties into the Washita about seven miles above Monroe. Between its mouth and that place, the bayou Siard, has its entrance into the river. It may not be amiss to observe here in order to find the true meaning of the words bayous and creeks, in the state of Louisiana; the early French settlers in Louisiana called bayous, small bays; any water course, which at its mouth and even higher up did appear like stagnating water, was called bayou, a diminutive of bay. The appellation would be correctly given to all water courses, having hardly any current, or the current of which would run some times to, and some times from, the river; as it is the case with a great many in this section of the state. When the river is lower than the low lands, those bayous run into the river; when those lands are dry and the river rising, they run from it with equal velocity. Those low lands are like reservoirs; did they not exist, lower Louisiana could not be inhabited; it would yet be part of the dominion of the sea; they retain an immense quantity of water, which could be calculated, had we an accurate map of the state, showing minutely all the land overflowed and to what depth. The name of creek could be given (although its true signification is nearly the same as the one expressed by bayou before) to all water courses running with some velocity and always in the same direction. Thus with any further explanation and by the bare inspection of a map, it would be understood, what sort of stream is delineated and even the elevation of the land it runs through. Thus we would say bayou Siard, Barthelemy creek or river, creek D'Arbonne until it meets the overflow, thence bayou D'Arbonne, etc.

The bayou Siard has two entrances, one into Barthelemy, about six miles east from its mouth, the other into Washita river, mentioned before. It runs to and from that river, according to the stage of waters in either stream; it is navigable for barges some distance from the river and could be easily made so for steam boats; on the hills between Washita and Dogdemene, are occasionally very sandy stones, strongly inpregnated with oxide of iron, siliceous probably. Plaster of Paris is found at a distance of about ninety miles below Monroe, and near the Washita, a few lime stones are scattered on the hills adjacent to those containing plaster of Paris. In the same vicinity and in the deep curbs formed by the swift running branches, have been found petrified shells of several kinds of bivalves, also of belemita and cornua ammonis.

The land between Catahoula lake, Little river, Black river and the lower part of Red river is almost an uninterrupted overflow, not quite as low as the Mississippi swamps, which is in many instances more than twenty feet below high water mark; some lakes or ponds are scattered over that country. Those ponds are nothing more than overflowed land, without any timber. Several inundated (at high water) prairies more elevated than these ponds, are met with in this section of the state, always near the rivers, and often on their banks, particularly in the lower parts of Washita and Bœuf rivers. Prairies never covered with water and bordering the banks of Washita higher up, existed formerly, such as prairie de Lait, (yet considerable) prairie du Manoir, de Brin d'amour, des Chicots, des Canots, where Monroe is built (names all nearly forgotten) prairie Chatellerault, prairie Bonde, on Barthelemy river. These are now cultivated, or covered with timber; a circumstance which never fails taking place as soon as the borders of the prairies are settled. Those named Merrouge, Galleer, Jefferson, alias 4th Prairie, are situated far from the river, about east north east, thirty miles from Monroe. Higher up, on the bayou Barthelemy, are several prairies of high but not first rate land; they are not yet inhabited. In the parish of Catahoula, the prairie of that name about fifteen miles south west from Catahoula courthouse, called also Harrisonburg, is some time inundated. It seems to have been formerly part of the lake of the same name. Prairie des Bois, south south east from Monroe, nine miles distant, is also subject to inundation. Another kind of prairie not so necessary, are those found on the summit of the hills—prairie des Cotes is one of that description. It lies almost due south, rather westerly, from Monroe, distant thirty-six miles in a straight course; the land there is poor, but, like these mentioned above afford very good pasturage for cattle. The direction of the hills between Washita and Dogdemene is rather from north to south, as far as bayou Castor; they afterwards generally run from east to west. The valleys, which separate them, are evidently the work of the water courses, the directions of which are always from about north to south, the hills appearing to follow that course, are at the lowest end but very short, and at a bird's eye view, have the appearance of having been thrown together in that manner by the waves of the sea, which probably, at some remote period, rolled over this whole tract of country.

The settlements of Opelousas are separated from those of Red river, by a ridge of piny and sterile hills. These are succeeded by extensive prairies, which continue without any important interruption, as far as the sea. They are almost entirely destitute of trees, except along the water courses : so much so, that when a cluster of trees is accidentally met with, it is called an island. The facility these prairies offer in raising cattle, had induced the original settlers of Opelousas and Attakapas to prefer the pastoral to the agricultural life. Those who followed them, were invited by rich spots of land on the water courses, to the cultivation of indigo and afterwards cotton, besides corn, rice and other provisions.

The town, near the parochial church of Opelousas, dedicated to St. Landry, has not the advantage of standing upon navigable water ; and this circumstance has contributed to check its growth. It has a branch of the Louisiana bank.

At a few miles below it, is a convent of nuns, the inmates of which devote themselves to the education of young persons of their sex. This establishment is a new one, and entirely due to the piety of a lady of the neighborhood.

The upper part of the settlements of Attakapas, which lie between Opelousas and the sea, differ very little from the former. Emigrants from the other states, having settled on the land near the sea, have given themselves to the culture of the sugar cane, and meet with great success.

There are two towns in the Attakapas—St. Martinsville and Franklin, on the river Teche, which rises in the Opelousas. The first, though not considerable, has a weekly gazette, and a branch of the state bank, a church and the other public buildings of the parish. The other is as yet an embryo.

The Spaniards made an abortive attempt to establish a town, called New Iberia, about sixteen miles below St. Martinsville.

The prairies in this part of the state are not natural ones : they owe their origin to the Indian practice of setting fire to dry grass during the fall and winter, in order that the tender herbage, in the spring, may attract game ; this destroys young trees, and the prairie annually gains on the woodland, as long as the practice prevails. When it ceases, the woodland gains on the prairie.

To the west is a collection of houses on Vermilion river, near the public buildings of the parish of Lafayette.

Towards the sea, near the base of the delta formed by bayou Lafourche and the Mississippi, are a number of lakes, the principal of which are Barataria and Salvador. Of the streams that fall into the gulf, west of the mouth of the Mississippi, the most important are Lafourche, Atchafalaya, Teche, Mentao, Calcasu and Sabine.

All the space between these streams, near the gulf, is interspersed with trembling prairies, lagoons and numerous bayous. There are, however, many spots of high ground; but the difficulty of access and distance from inhabited tracts have prevented migration to them.

The Teche has its source in the prairies, in the upper part of the settlements of Opelousas, and during the season of high water, flows partially into the Courtableau. As it enters the settlements of Attakapas, it receives from the right side bayou Fusilier, which bayou Bourbeux connects with Vermilion river. A little more than twenty miles farther, it passes before the town of St. Martinsville and reaches, fifteen miles after, the spot on which the Spaniards, soon after the cession, made a vain attempt to establish a city, to which the name of New Iberia was destined; twenty miles, from the mouth of the Teche, is the town of Franklin.

Above St. Martinsville, cotton is universally cultivated on the banks of the Teche: below it, are a number of sugar plantations. which succeed remarkably well. The low price of cotton has of late induced many of the planters to attempt the culture of the cane, above St. Martinsville, even as high as bayou Bœuf.

On the east of the Teche, and between that stream and the Atchafalaya, is Prairie Grand Chevreuil, occupying the ground beyond the reach of inundation. On the opposite side, and to the east of Vermilion river is the Attakapas prairie; the land of which, especially on the banks of the latter stream, is of good quality and well adapted to the culture of sugar, cotton, indigo, tobacco and corn.

The Vermilion river has its source in the upper part of the Opelousas settlements: between it and the Mentao is the Opelousas prairie, which is more extensive than the two just mentioned; being about seventy-five miles in length and twenty-five in breadth. Its direction is S. W. to N. E. It affords an extensive range for cattle.

The Mentao and Calcasu rise near the sandy ridge separating the settlements of Red river from those of Opelousas. These streams are nearly parallel to the Vermilion and Sabine. The land on their banks is of less fertility than near the Mississippi. Agricultural establishments are rare, and the few settlers confine their attention to raising cattle.

At the mouth of Sabine river, where the western boundary of the state begins, the country exhibits a wild state of desolation. A line of shell banks extends along the shores of the lake, into which the river expands, at the distance of twenty miles from its mouth; they are covered with trees of a stunted growth. The country around is a morass to the distance of twenty miles above the lake.

The whole coast from the Mississippi to the Sabine, as from the former stream to Pearl river, is low and swampy, and except in a very few places indeed, can only be approached through the water courses.

CHAPTER I.

CHARLES the eighth, the seventh monarch of the house of Valois, wielded the sceptre of France, and Henry the seventh that of England, in 1492, when Columbus, under the auspices of Ferdinand of Aragon and Isabella of Castile, discovered the western hemisphere.

Charles, during a reign of nineteen years, sought military glory, and an extension of territory, in the invasion of Italy. Success, for a while attended his arms, and with the aid of the Pope, he caused himself to be crowned Emperor of Constantinople and King of Naples; but, he was soon driven back, and died in 1496, the fiftieth year of his age, without having ever sought to avail himself of the advantages the discovery of the new world offered. Less ambitious of warlike fame, Henry made an early effort to share them. He fitted out a small fleet, the command of which he gave to Cabot, a Venetian adventurer, settled in Bristol, whom he sent on a voyage of discovery. No historical record informs us of the success of this expedition; but in 1496, this navigator sailed in a ship furnished by the crown, and four barques, supplied by the merchants of Bristol. He discovered a large island, to which he gave the name of *Prima vista*, now known by that of Newfoundland, and soon after the continent. He sailed southwardly along the coast, as far as the bay of Chesapeake. It is not known that he effected or even attempted a landing, and the ocular possession he took of the country is the origin and basis of the claim of the English nation to all the land in North America, from the Atlantic to the Pacific Ocean.

Charles the eighth, having left no issue, was succeeded by Louis the twelfth, a distant kinsman; their common ancestor being Charles the seventh, the grandfather of the deceased monarch. Louis continued the war in Italy with the same spirit, and with as little success as his predecessor; and viewed the progress of the Spaniards in America with equal unconcern. His subjects, however, extended their industry and their commerce to the new world. In 1504, the Biscayans, the Bretons and the Normans, visited Newfoundland, in quest of fish. Two years after, Denys entered, and made a map of the Gulf of St. Lawrence; and in 1508, Aubert carried over the first American Indians who trod the soil of France. The crown of England in the following year, passed, on the death of Henry the seventh, in his fifty-second, to his son Henry the eighth.

The southernmost part of the continent of North America, was first discovered by a Spanish adventurer in 1513. Not impelled by avarice or ambition, but led by credulity and chance, Ponce de Leon, believing that the island Binimi, in the archipelago of Bahama, possessed a fountain, the waters of which had the virtue of repairing the ravages of time on the human frame, sailed from the island of Porto Rico, in search of this renovating stream. A violent storm disappointed his hopes, and threw him on the cape, opposite to the northern side of the island of Cuba. He called the country thus discovered Florida, either from its flowery appearance, or from the circumstance of his having discovered it on Palm Sunday, *Pasqua de Flores*. Erecting a large cross on the beach, he took formal possession in the name of his sovereign, Charles the first of Spain,

the grandson of Isabella, the late Queen of Castile.   He returned in the
following year and landed on the same spot, with a number of his countrymen; but the natives fell on the intruders and killed them all but six, who
were grievously wounded.   The chief was among the latter.   He sailed
for the island of Cuba, where he and his five surviving companions died
of their wouuds.

Louis the twelfth died on the first of January, 1515, the fifty third year
of his age, without issue.   His successor was Francis the first; their
common ancestor was the Duke of Orleans, a brother of Charles the sixth.

The first attempt of the French to plant a colony in America, was made
in the second year of Francis' reign.   A few adventurers of that nation,
were led by the Baron de Levy to the small island, in the forty-fourth
degree of northern latitude, now known as Sable Island, part of the
province of Nova Scotia.   The spot was most unfavorable; at a great
distance from the continent, or any other island; the soil is rocky and
sterile.   These men were unable to derive their subsistence from it.   They
suffered much from the cold; many sickened and died.   The Baron carried
back the survivors to France, leaving some cattle and hogs on the island.

In 1520, Vasquez de Aillon sailed from Hispaniola for the northern
continent, with views not quite so unexceptionable as those of Ponce de
Leon.   His object was to seize some of the Indians, transport them to
Hispaniola and sell them to his countrymen, who could not obtain from
Africa a sufficient number of negroes to work the mines.   He made land
on the coast of the present state of South Carolina, near the mouth of a
river to which he gave the name of Jourdain, after a man on board of one
of his ships, who first descried it; it now bears that of Santee.   He was
received with hospitality: after staying awhile, and supplying himself
with provisions, he invited a number of the natives to a banquet on board
of his ship, made them dance at the sound of his trumpets, plying them
with abundant doses of ardent spirits.   When exercise and ebriety had
lulled their senses, he hoisted his sails and brought off his unwary guests.
Heaven did not allow him to reap the fruits of his treachery.   One of the
ships perished in a storm.   The sturdy captives in the other, for a long
while, refused to take any food; the voyage was long, and disease made a
great havoc among the Spaniards and the Indians.

Velasquez made another voyage to Florida in 1552, with two ships; he
was quite unsuccessful.   He lost one of the ships, and the Indians killed
a great part of his people.

Veranzany, a Florentine, employed by Francis the first, appears to have
been the first navigator, who visited America at the expense of the crown
of France.   He reached it in the month of March, 1524, a little below Cape
Hatteras, near the spot on which sixty years after, the first attempt towards
English colonization in America was made, under the auspices and at the
cost of Sir Walter Raleigh.   He sailed up the coast, as far as the fiftieth
degree of northern latitude, entered a few of the rivers, had some little
intercourse with the aborigines, by whom he was every where friendly
received, and returned to France, without any attempt towards a settlement.

He made other voyages, in the two following years, and it is supposed
perished in the last.

The misfortunes of Francis, made a prisoner at Pavie, his long captivity
in Spain, and his distresses till the peace of Cambray, prevented the

execution of the plan he had formed of planting a French colony in the new world.

Pamphilo de Narvaez, having obtained from Charles the first of Spain, the government of all the countries he could discover from Rio de Palma, to the undefined limits of Florida, sailed from the island of Cuba, with four ships and a barque in March, 1528, with four hundred foot and eighty horse. He landed near the bay del Spiritu Santo, called, in modern times, the bay of Tampa. The Indians cheerfully supplied him with corn and other provisions. He landed a part of his force and took solemn possession of the country, in the name of his imperial master. Noticing, at this ceremony, a cymbal of gold, in the hands of an Indian, his hope of securing a large quantity of this metal was greatly excited. He was told that the Apalachians, a nation not far distant, had much of it. Under the influence of the excitement which the information created, he put the shipping under the orders of Cabeca de Vacca, with directions to sail along the coast; he landed the rest of his force, and marched up the country the last day of May. On the next, he crossed a river, on the banks of which was a town, where the Indians supplied him with provisions. He ranged the country for several days, without meeting a human being; at last he overtook a chief preceded by men blowing flutes, and followed by a large party. He gave them to understand, he was going towards the Apalachians; the chief told him these Indians were at war with his nation: Narvaez travelled with him to his village, in which he was hospitably entertained. Proceeding, he reached on the 25th the first village of the Apalachians, which consisted of about forty cabins. He took possession of it without opposition, and found corn, venison and skins; but no metal. He sojourned near this village for several days, making occasional excursions into the country; during which, he had frequent skirmishes with the natives, who darted their arrows at his people and hid themselves in the swamps. At last, destitute of provisions, seeing nothing but a sterile country and unpassable roads, he determined on marching towards the sea, and reached Aute, an Indian town, not far distant from the spot on which the Spaniards afterwards erected the fort of St. Mark of the Apalaches. The Indians followed on the flanks of their invaders, harrassing them at times by clouds of arrows. Their countrymen at Aute, strongly defended themselves and killed a number of Spaniards. Cabeca de Vacca approached the coast, and Narvaez and his men took shipping; but the greatest part perished through fatigue, hunger, disease and shipwreck. Those who escaped these complicated disasters, reached Rio de Palma. Narvaez was not among them; his vessel foundered in a storm and he never was heard of.

Francis, having married his rival's sister, and released his sons, detained as hostages in Spain, availed himself of the tranquillity that followed the peace of Cambray, to resume his plan of adding a part of America to his dominions.

For this purpose, he directed two barques of sixty tons, with one hundred and fifty men, to be fitted out at St. Maloes, and gave the command of them to Cartier, who sailed on the 30th of April, 1534. He reached Bonavista in the island of Newfoundland in twenty days, crossed the gulf and entered a bay, which from the extreme heat at the time, he called Chaleur bay; it is a little to the south of the mouth of the river St. Lawrence. Two sailors (the wretched remnant of the crew of a Spanish ship, which had been wrecked there) were wandering on the beach, when Cartier's boat approached.   The French inquired what country they were in; one of the Spaniards, who, being pressed by hunger, imagined he was asked whether there was any thing to eat, replied, *Aca nada;* "there is nothing here."   The French in the boat, on returning to Cartier, told him the Spaniard said the country was called *Canada.*   Cartier visited several parts of the gulf, and took possession of the country for the crown of France.

The king, on the return of Cartier, ordered a new expedition, consisting of three ships; the largest, commanded by Cartier, was of one hundred and twenty tons; they sailed on the 19th of May, 1535.   On reaching the continent, Cartier was obliged by stress of weather, to put into a port which he called St. Nicholas.   He gave the name of St. Lawrence to the gulf and the river; leaving the two small vessels at the mouth of the stream, he proceeded to an Indian town called Hochelaga, near the spot on which the city of Montreal now stands.   The friendly reception the Indians gave him, induced him to send for the vessels he had left, and to build a number of cabins, which he surrounded with a strong palisado, that might enable him to resist a sudden attack; and he made other preparations to winter there.   The season proved extremely severe, and the scurvy broke out among his men; he was himself attacked by it.   Twenty-five of his people had already perished, and two alone escaped the disease, when a specific remedy was pointed out by the Indians, in a decoction of the bark of the *Abies Canadensis,* (the Canadian fir.)   Eight days after it had been resorted to, Cartier found all his men perfectly recovered.   Some who had been afflicted with another disease, and had been but partially cured, were perfectly restored to health by the use of this specific.   In the spring, Cartier brought back such of his men as the fell disorder had spared; but nothing more was done in Francis' reign, towards the settlement of a French colony in America.

Two years after, Charles the first of Spain gave the government of St. Yago de Cuba to Hernandez de Soto, with permission to prosecute the discovery of, and subjugate, Florida; and on the twelfth of May of the following year, he sailed from the Havana with an army of nine hundred foot and three hundred and fifty horse.   The fleet was equipped, and the naval and land forces raised and supported at Soto's expense.   He had amassed considerable wealth in Peru, in the conquest of which he had accompanied Pizarro.   The fleet was delayed by contrary winds, and at last reached the bay in which Narvaez had landed eleven years before. Three hundred men, having landed and marched a short distance, were repelled with great loss.   Soto now disembarked his horse and foot, and sent back the large vessels.   He proceeded northerly, his march being retarded by frequent interruptions from the natives, who hung on his flanks; and he halted at Herriga, the first town he came to, at the distance of six miles from the shore.   He spent some days there, to give time to the baggage to come up and afford some rest to his men, and began his march for the country of the Apalachians, which was at the distance of about four hundred miles.   The country was divided into small districts, each governed by a cacique; the chief, the district and its principal town, generally bearing the same name.   The town was a collection of from fifty to two hundred houses; surrounded by a strong palisado.   Garcilasso de la Vega, in his history of this expedition, has recorded the names of the towns through which Soto passed, from the bay del Spiritu Santo to the Apalachians. They are many, but it is believed the name of none of them corresponds with that of any of the present divisions of the country. Two of the principal districts, or provinces, were governed by a female cacique. After advancing into the country, Soto's progress ceased to be obstructed, and at several towns he was hospitably received, and obtained abundant supplies of corn and venison. One of the female caciques added to this needed succor, presents of pearls. If we credit Garcilasso, these presents in the quantity and value of the pearls, were immense; they were often as large as hazel nuts and were dealt out by the bushel, except those of the smallest kind, called *seed of pearls*, which were weighed. But this writer speaks of lions in the forests of Florida, and of a number of caciques, who commanded several thousands of warriors. It is believed those who furnished this Indian author with the memoirs on which he wrote, were less fond of truth than of the marvellous.

Several caciques opposed the passage of the Spaniards through the country, but none could resist, with bows and arrows, an army with musketry and artillery. By courtesy, threats and violence, Soto made his way to the country of the Apalachians. There, after taking some rest, a part of his army was sent in strong detachments to reconnoitre the ground; while the rest proceeding southwesterly, reached *Aute*, a town near the sea shore, which Narvaez had visited. There, this party dividing itself in two detachments, one of them marched westerly to Anchusi, another large town, on the spot on which, about a century and a half after, was built the town of Pensacola; while the latter, proceeding at first easterly, then southerly, reached the bay in which the army had landed, from which one of the small vessels was sent to Cuba, with an account of Soto's progress, and to obtain supplies.

The two detachments uniting again at Aute, joined the main body at the Apalachians, where Soto had determined on wintering.

The army resumed its march early in the spring; its direction was at first northwesterly; passing through the back parts of the present state of Georgia, it marched for some time northerly, then northwesterly through the country of the Cherokees, then a large and warlike nation, crossing the present state of Tennessee and proceeding to that of Kentucky, as high up as the thirty-seventh degree of northern latitude. It marched thence southwesterly to the bay of Mobile. Of the Indians thus visited by Soto, the Tuscaloosas, Mobilians and Alabamans, are the only ones who, at this day retain their names. The Mobilians made a furious resistance, but were at last overpowered. Garcilasso reckons they lost in several skirmishes, a pitched battle and the defence of their principal town, upwards of eleven thousand men, and that more than one thousand women were burnt in a single house. Soto, having subdued the Mobilians, gave one month's rest to his army; then continued his march to the Chickasaws, among whom he wintered.

A party of these Indians attacked him at night, in the latter part of January following, by torch light. The torches were formed of a grass, which made into a rope, takes and retains fire like a match. The Chickasaws darted arrows, armed with this grass thus lighted, on the huts of their invaders, principally those used as stables, thus setting the provender on fire; several horses were burnt at their mangers, to which they were made fast with small chains. The Indians, hovering round their enemy, became visible only when they agitated their torches. The musketry, artillery and cavalry, however, soon compelled them to disperse; the Spaniards had forty men and fifty horses killed in this attack. Soto removed his camp to what he conceived a more defensible spot, about three miles to the west. But notwithstanding his utmost vigilance and the alertness of his men, the army, while it remained in the country of the Chickasaws was incessantly harrassed by hovering parties, and every individual who straggled to any distance from the camp, was almost instantly made a prisoner or killed.

Early in April, Soto marched northwesterly through the country of the Choctaws, and the western parts of the present states of Mississippi and Tennessee. He reached the mighty stream then called by the Indians, Cicuaga, and now Mississippi, a little below the lowest Chickasaw bluff. Having employed some time in building flats, he overcame without much difficulty the opposition made by the Indians to his crossing it. On the western bank, he proceeded as high up as White river, and then downwards in a circuitous route, to avoid the swampy shore, through the present territory of the Arkansas, to his winter quarters. On the left side of the Mississippi, the Spaniards met with the same reception from the Indians, as on the opposite. At times the natives were confident and friendly, at others reserved, often cruel and treacherous; rarely, though some times, approaching in hostile array.

In the spring, the army proceeded southerly by slow marches; but in the beginning of the summer, fatigue, dearth of provisions, the intense heat and the impure air of the swamps, greatly injured the health of the Spaniards; many sickened and died. At last, after long and frequent halts, the army reached the mouth of Red river. Here the chief was seized with a fever, the mortal character of which became manifest in a few days. It was not long before he became conscious of his situation, and he contemplated approaching dissolution with composure. He appointed Luis Muscoso de Alvarado his successor, calmly conversed with his officers on the most proper movements of the army, had almost all the individuals in it brought to his bedside, received their oaths of fidelity to the future chief, recommended to the men obedience to him, and affection to each other, discipline, unanimity and perseverance. Then, giving his remaining moments to the rites of the church of Rome, expired about the 30th of June.

He was in his forty-second year. Ambitious to have his name as conqueror of Florida, in the page of history, between those of Cortez and Pizarro, the conquerors of Mexico and Peru, he spent in this scheme an immense fortune, acquired in the conquest of the latter kingdom, and was the indiscreet cause of the death of the greatest portion of his followers, without any advantage to his country or himself. In republics, as wealth is seldom acquired with great rapidity and ease, and is more generally divided, it is seldom so profusely lavished, and it rarely enables the possessor to command the sacrifice of the lives of men to his ambitious views.

His remains were inclosed in a strong coffin, which was filled with bullets and sunk in the Mississippi, opposite to the mouth of Red river, to prevent them from falling into the hands of the Indians.

In the meanwhile, the plan of settling a colony in Canada, though abandoned by the monarch, had been resumed by individuals, in France.

Francis de la Roque, Lord of Robertval, a man of considerable influence in the province of Picardy, had solicited Francis the first to permit him to prosecute the discoveries of Cartier. He had been, by letters patent of the fifteenth of January, 1540, created "Lord of Norimbegue, Viceroy and Lieutenant-General of Canada, Hochelaga, Saguenay, Newfoundland, Belisle, Carpen, the great bay and Baccaloes."

The Viceroy, in the following year, sailed with five ships, having taken Cartier as his first pilot. The voyage was prosperous. He built a fort (some say on the river St. Lawrence, others on the island of St. John) of which he gave the command to Cartier. Leaving a good garrison in it, and a barque for the prosecution of Cartier's discoveries, he sailed for France, in search of farther aid for his colony.

Incessantly annoyed by the natives, assailed by disease, and unable to withstand the severity of the weather, the colonists prevailed on their chief, in the following year, to carry them back to France. Near the island of Newfoundland, they met Robertval, who, by solicitations and threats, induced them to return. Having restored order among them, he proceeded up the rivers St. Lawrence and Saguenay to explore their shores. He sent one of his pilots in quest of a northwest passage to China, and went back to France.

Muscoso, the successor of Soto in the command of the Spaniards on the Mississippi, conducted the remainder of the army up Red river, through that part of the country now called Natchitoches and Nagodoches, to a nation of Indians, whom from the number of wild cattle he found among them, he called *los vaqueros;* probably, in that part of the country now known as the province of Texas. Proceeding about one hundred miles further, the army reached the foot of a mountainous country. Muscoso had been induced to march this way in the hope of getting to Mexico by land. He now determined, on account of the distance which he received from the Indians, to retrograde, and float down the Mississippi to the sea. The army accordingly marched into winter quarters, at the mouth of Red river.

During the month of January, Muscoso employed his carpenters in the construction of vessels, to convey his men to Mexico. The neighboring caciques, apprehensive that his views, in going thither, were to apprise his countrymen of the fertility of the land on the Mississippi, and to solicit aid to return and subjugate the Indians, leagued themselves for the purpose of raising a sufficient force to destroy the Spaniards, or at least to set fire to the vessels they were building. Garcilasso relates the league was so general, that the caciques, who entered in it, agreed to raise forty thousand men. The plot, however, became known to some Indian women, who attended the Spanish officers, and was disclosed to Muscoso. The measures he took to defeat it, induced most of the caciques to withdraw from the league. Those who dwelt immediately on the river and their nearest neighbors, persevered in their intention, and collected a considerable number of canoes and pirogues and made rafts, with the view of pursuing the Spaniards down the stream.

On the twenty-fourth of June, the vessels were launched, and soon after the army went on board; hides having been placed around the bows, as a protection against the arrows of the Indians. Out of the twelve hundred and fifty men who were landed at the bay del Spiritu Santo, there remained now but three hundred and fifty, and the three hundred and fifty horses were reduced to thirty. On the second day after their departure, the Indian fleet hove in sight towards noon; Garcilasso says, it consisted of one thousand pirogues, canoes or rafts of various sizes; the largest containing eighty men and the least having four oars on each side. Each pirogue was neatly painted in and outside, with blue, red, yellow or white. The oars and feathers, bows and arrows of the warriors in each pirogue, was of the same color with it. The oars were plied in measure and cadence, the rowers singing to mark the time. The fleet advanced in five divisions, each pouring a volley of arrows, as it passed the Spaniards; the pursuit was continued during ten days, when it was given up. Almost every Spaniard was wounded, and of the thirty horses that were embarked, twenty-two were killed. The Spaniards had been unable to defend themselves, having no longer any powder.

Muscoso perceiving a village near the shore, and concluding he was approaching the sea, deemed it prudent to land one hundred of his men in quest of provisions. As they advanced toward the village, the Indians left it, flying in all directions. The Spaniards found in it abundance of corn, venison and dried fruit. But a part of the Indian fleet, having landed above, a junction was formed between it and the Indians of the village, and they marched down against the Spaniards, who were compelled to return in great haste to their shipping; leaving their horses behind, which the Indians destroyed with their arrows.

Four days after, the Spaniards reached the sea, and sailing slowly along the coast, arrived at Panuco, a port distant about sixty leagues from the city of Mexico.

Garcilasso de la Vega, who has written the best account that has reached us of this expedition, entitles his work the history of the *conquest* of Florida. With as much propriety, an English writer might entitle his memoirs of Sir Edward Packenham's expeditions in 1814, the history of the *conquest* of Louisiana. Perhaps Garcilasso wrote more as a lawyer than a soldier, and imagining that this burthensome perambulation of the country had acquired a title to the crown of Spain, considered Florida as thereby *acquired,* and called the act an acquisition or conquest. So might the sailing of Cabot in 1498, in a vessel fitted out by Henry the seventh of England, be called the acquisition or *conquest* of the northern continent of America. Although the name was not given, the effect was claimed; and General Hill, in 1711, demanded the surrender of the fortress of Quebec, on the incontestible title, acquired to the crown of England to all North America, by the discovery, or ocular occupation, of the country, by Cabot.

The sceptre of England, on the twenty-eighth day of January, 1547, passed from the hands of Henry the eighth, in the fifty-seventh year of his age, into those of his infant son, Edward the sixth; and that of France, on the thirty-first of March following, from those of Francis the first, in his fifty-third year, into those of his son, Henry the second. Francis had entirely lost sight of the new world, during the war with England, in the latter part of his reign.

History has not recorded any attempt of Henry the eighth, to extend his dominions to the western hemisphere. English vessels, however, were employed during his reign, in the fisheries of Newfoundland; and in the reign of his youthful successor, was passed the first English statute, which relates to America. Its object was to repress the extortions of the officers of the Admiralty, who demanded a duty, or part of the profits made on every voyage to Ireland, Iceland or Newfoundland.—2 Ed. vi. 6.

Edward died in 1553, at the age of sixteen, and was succeeded by Mary, his sister.

America does not appear to have attracted the attention of this princess, nor that of Henry the second of France, who prosecuted the war his father had begun with England. At the conclusion of it, he entered into a league with the elector of Saxony and the Margrave of Brandenburg, against Charles the first; but when his antagonist had reconciled himself to his German adversaries, Henry was left to maintain the war alone. Philip the second of Spain, on the abdication of his father in 1556, prosecuted it with great vigor, aided by the English, whose queen he had married.

Mary, who ended her life, on the seventh of November, 1558, at the age of forty-one, without issue, had for her successor Elizabeth, her sister; and on the 10th of July of the following year, Henry the second died, at the same age, in consequence of a wound he had accidentally received in a tournament. The wars that desolated France during almost the whole reign of this prince, were probably the cause that the French made no progress in the new world.

His son and successor, Francis the second, the husband of the unfortunate Mary Stuart of Scotland, reigned but seventeen months, and was succeeded by Charles the ninth, Henry's second son.

In the beginning of Charles's disturbed reign, Admiral Coligny sought in Florida, an asylum for his protestant adherents. He equipped two ships at Dieppe, under the direction of Jean Ribaud, whom he put at the head of a small military force, and a considerable number of colonists. Ribaud weighed anchor on the eighteenth of February, 1562, and made land in the thirtieth degree of northern latitude, near a cape, to which he gave the name of *Cap Francais*: it is one of the promontories of the estuary on which the town of St. Augustine now stands. He landed on the banks of the river St. Mary, which now separates Georgia from Florida. He called it the river of May, from the circumstance of his entering on the first day of that month. The Indians received him with much hospitality. He erected a column on the banks of the stream, and affixed to it an escutcheon of the armorial of France, in token of his having taken solemn possession of the country. After a short stay, he proceeded northerly to an island, at the mouth of Edisto river, in the present state of South Carolina. He called this stream the great river, a fort which he erected on the island Charles's Fort, or *Arx Carolina*, and the place, before which he anchored, Port Royal; an appellation, which it retains at this day. Having settled his colony around it, he placed Albert at the head of the colonists, and returned to France. Although he had been very friendly received by the natives, he in vain endeavored to prevail on some of them to accompany him.

Albert visited the Indian tribes near the fort, and found them all disposed to live on the most friendly terms with the whites. These were more anxious to ramble over the country, in search of mines of the precious metals, than to till the earth; and the stock of provisions left by Ribaud, although considerable, was at last exhausted. This chief, on his arrival in France, had found his countrymen distracted by a civil war, and his patron out of favor at court, so that he was unable to procure for the colony the needed supplies he had come after. For awhile, Albert procured relief from the natives; corn and peas were obtained in tolerable abundance: but fire consumed the building in which the succor had been stored. The Indians became unable or unwilling to minister to the increasing wants of the colonists. The distress, attending the penury that followed, heightened the discontents which the ill conduct or misguided severity of Albert had excited, and the colonists rose against and slew their chief.

Nicholas Baree was called by the insurgents to the supreme command. They had ascertained that there was no gold mine near them, and thought it preferable to return to the old world, than to seek a scanty and precarious subsistence by labor, in the new. Unanimity strengthened their efforts; a vessel was built and corked with Spanish beard; ropes were made of grass, and sails, with the tents, bags and linen cloth that remained; but as famine drove them from the land, the stock of provisions they carried to sea, was not abundant; calms retarded their progress; they were reduced to a scanty ration of eighteen grains of corn a day to each man; and the moment came when there was not a single grain to deal out. Lots were cast, and the wretch pointed out by chance, tamely submitted his neck to the butcher's knife, to appease the hunger of his companions. Soon after this, they were met by an English ship, which enabled them to reach France.

Coligny had been restored to favor, and he did not solicit in vain his sovereign's aid, for the prosecution of his plan to settle a colony in Florida. Three ships were fitted out at Havre de Grace; and Laudonniere, to whom the command of them was given, sailed on the twenty-second of April, 1564, and landed on the shores of the river St. Mary, near the monument erected two years before by Ribaud, as an evidence of his having taken possession of the country around it, in the name of Charles the ninth.

The Indians manifested great joy at the arrival of the French, and led Laudonniere to the column. He directed a fort to be built, on the southern bank of the stream, and called the country Caroline, in honor of his king. Parties of his men went in different directions, to explore the country. The Indians, discovering that the precious metals were the main object of the pursuit of the whites, played on their credulity, amused them with fanciful stories, and pointed to the westward as the part of their country in which mines of gold could be found. No success attended a search for metals; but a ship arrived from France, laden with provisions.

Laudonniere's administration did not please the colonists. A mutiny ensued, but its consequences were not so fatal to the chief, as the former had been to his predecessor. Some of the mutineers possessed themselves of two barques, which Laudonniere had caused to be constructed, and sailed on a piratical cruize down the canal of Bahama, towards the Havana.

On the third of August, in the following year, Sir John Hawkins, a renowned English navigator, visited Caroline, with four vessels. Laudonniere obtained one of them, and made preparations to sail in her for France. He was near his departure, when, on the twenty-fifth, a small fleet was descried approaching the coast. It consisted of seven sail, and was commanded by Ribaud. Complaints against Laudonniere had been made to the King; he was represented as oppressing the men under him, and it had been strenuously urged that unless he was recalled, there was much ground to apprehend that the garrison would redress their own wrongs, in the same manner as the former colonists had redressed theirs. Ribaud was accordingly appointed governor of Caroline, and instructed to send his predecessor home. Contrary winds compelled the fleet to seek shelter successively in the ports of Havre de Grace and Portsmouth; it had sailed from the latter towards the middle of June, and the passage had been tedious. Ribaud had hardly delivered the minister's dispatches to Laudonniere, when a Spanish fleet hove in sight.

Philip the second, apprised of the progress of the French in Caroline, had ordered a fleet to be equipped at Cadiz, under the orders of Don Pedro Menendez, for the purpose of destroying their colony. Don Pedro had sailed on the twenty-ninth of June. At the departure of Ribaud from France, notice of the preparations making at Cadiz had reached Paris, and although the object of them was not known, an attack on Caroline was suspected. He was, therefore, instructed, whilst he was charged to attempt nothing against the rights of the Spanish King, to resist any encroachment on those of his own sovereign.

Don Pedro landed near the mouth of a stream, which the French had called the river of the dolphins, to which he gave the name of St. Augustine, who, on the day of his arrival was honored in the Romish Church; it is now known by that of St. John. He took formal possession of the country in Philip's name, and gave orders for the immediate erection of a fort. Ribaud thought it best to set sail, and attack the Spanish fleet before the land forces could be put ashore, and invest the French fort. Leaving, therefore, a few men with Laudonniere, he took in all the rest, and hoisted sail. A violent storm overtook and dispersed his vessels, and drove several of them on shore. In the meanwhile, the Spanish chief had landed his troops and marched towards the fort. He reached it on the nineteenth of September, before sunrise. The weather was foggy, and the Spaniards were in the fort, while several of the French were still in bed. An immediate slaughter began. But Laudonniere, with a few of his men, effected his escape on board of a vessel, in which they sailed for France.

Don Pedro now went in quest of Ribaud; he found him at anchor; after a parley of twenty-four hours, the French chief surrendered his vessels and the men under his orders. Two hundred soldiers or sailors, having refused to yield themselves prisoners, escaped during the night, and marched through the woods southerly. Notwithstanding his pledged faith, Don Pedro caused all such of his prisoners as were protestants to be hung or slaughtered. The Catholics, who were in a small number indeed, were spared. The bodies of those who were hung were left on the trees along the shore; and an inscription was set up announcing they were hung " not as French, but as heretics."

Laudonniere's fort was repaired and garrisoned, and it, as well as the river on which it stood, was called San Matheo, after the saint, the festival of which was celebrated in Spain, on the day on which Don Pedro entered the stream.

A strong party was sent after the men who parted from Ribaud, the night preceding his surrender; they were overtaken at a place, afterwards called by the Spaniards, *Punta de Canaveral*, in the 28th degree of latitude, and made prisoners.

Six hundred French are reckoned to have fallen victims to the cruelty of the Spaniards, whose force, at the end of this tragedy, is said to have been reduced to four hundred, who were divided between the forts of San Matheo and St. Augustine.

This is the first act of hostility between European nations in the new world.

Charles the ninth, took no measure to avenge the murder of his protestant subjects. The apathy of the monarch, of the court and the nation, excited the valiant spirit of Dominique de Gourgues, of Pont Marsan, in the province of Gascony. Having sold his patrimony, aided by two of his friends, he equipped three vessels in the port of Bordeaux, engaged two hundred men to accompany him, and left the Garonne on the second of August, 1567. As he approached the river of San Matheo, the Spaniards mistaking his vessels for some of their nation, fired a salute. De Gourgues, unwilling to undeceive them, returned the compliment, and passed on. He landed at the mouth of the river then called the Seine, now Alatamaha. With the neighboring Indians, who ran to the shore on the approach of the vessels, came some of Laudonniere's men, who had found a refuge in their towns. By their assistance, De Gourgues was enabled to converse with the natives, who greatly dissatisfied with their new neighbors, offered to join him if he would dislodge the Spaniards. De Gourgues told them his voyage had not been undertaken with any hostile intention; but, if the Indians desired it, he was ready to assist them in getting rid of their unwelcome neighbors. He was informed that besides the fort at St. Matheo and St. Augustine, the Spaniards had a third, which they called St. Helen, at a small distance to the south of the second; and their effective force, in the three, was about four hundred men.

A number of warriors, from the more distant tribes, came and joined those from the sea shore who had put themselves under De Gourgues.

The combined army was soon in the neighborhood of the northernmost fort. De Gourgues sent some of his allies to form a cordon around it, into the woods; he went after them, accompanied by a considerable part of his men, whom he placed as near the edge of the woods as could be, without being seen by the enemy; while the rest of his force, in a small body, approached slowly in front, and halted out of the reach of the artillery of the fort. On their being perceived by the Spaniards, a strong detachment sallied out to attack them. De Gourgues then came forth, placing the detachment between him and the party they expected to attack. They were completely routed. He now turned against the fort, and the Indians contracting the circle they had formed around it, rushed forward, giving the war whoop. The garrison, intimidated by this unexpected manœuvre, became an easy prey. A great carnage ensued. A few Spaniards flew to the woods, where they were pursued and dispatched by the Indians. De Gourgues had the survivors hung on trees along the shore, with an inscription announcing they were thus treated "not as Spaniards, but as murderers."

De Gourges next marched against St Augustine, and the other fort; there were but fifty men in each; they surrendered, and were not ill treated. The buildings were burnt and the forts dismantled.

The French being too few in number to hold possession of the country, De Gourgues brought them back to France. He was obliged to conceal himself to avoid falling a victim to the resentment of Philip II., who offered a large price for his head, and whose Ambassador, at Paris, demanded that he should be punished, for having waged war against a prince in amity with his own sovereign. Thus are often the most heroic, useful and disinterested services that an individual renders to his country, not only unrewarded, but the source of chagrin, distress and misery. *Sic vos, non vobis.*

During the remainder of the reign of Charles the ninth, the kingdom was distracted by the struggles of the Condes, the Guises and the Colignys; so that the re-establishment of the French colony in Florida, was not attempted. Charles died on the thirtieth of May, 1574, at the age of twenty-four, and was succeeded by his brother, Henry the third.

Elizabeth of England, who, during her long reign, saw the crown of France on the heads of five kings, does not appear to have thought of the new world till 1578. On the eleventh of June of that year, she authorized Sir Humphry Gilbert, by letters patent, to discover and take possession of such remote, heathen and barbarous countries, as were not possessed by any christian prince or people.

Sir Humphry was not successful in his attempt. He made no settlement, and his country gained no advantage, but the formal possession which he took of the island of Newfoundland. In his pursuit of farther advantages, he lost his fortune and his life.

Henry the third does not appear to have turned his attention towards the western hemisphere till the ninth year of his reign; when he granted to the Marquis de la Roche, the powers which the Marquis de Robertval had enjoyed under Francis the first, and which Henry the second had granted to the former, who had been prevented by the distresses of the times to avail himself of them. The grant is of the twelfth of January, 1583. It states that the king, in compliance with the wishes of his predecessor, appoints the Marquis, his Lieutenant-General in Canada, Hochelaga, Newfoundland, Labrador, the river of the great bay, (St. Lawrence) Norembegue and the adjacent country.

The condition of the grant is, that the grantee shall have in particular view, the extension of the catholic faith. His authority is declared to extend over persons in the land and sea service. He is to appoint the captains and officers of the ships, and they are to obey him; he is authorized to press ships and to raise troops, declare war, erect fortifications and towns, baronies, earldoms and fiefs of less dignity, to enact laws and punish those who break them. The exclusive commerce of the country is granted him, and he is empowered, in case of death, or sickness, to appoint, by will or otherwise, one or more lieutenants, in his stead.

The success of the grantee did not correspond to the extent of his powers. Desirous of visiting the country, over which they were to be exercised, he fitted out a ship. The island of Sable, on which the Baron de Levy had stopped in 1508, was the first land he saw. He left on it forty wretches, whom he had taken out of the prisons of Paris. A Spanish ship had lately been cast on it; the timber, these men took from the wreck, enabled them to build huts. The cattle and sheep left by the baron had greatly multiplied, and afforded them meat. The Marquis from thence proceeded to the continent, and explored the shores of the country which was after called Acadie, and now Nova Scotia. He

returned to France and died, without having been able to advance his
interest or that of his country, by his grants.

Sir Humphry Gilbert had a half brother, who makes a most conspicuous
figure in the history of the new world, and of England—Sir Walter
Raleigh, who had taken an interest in the expedition that followed the
grant.   To him, the Queen granted a new one, on the twenty-sixth of
March, 1584.   Within a month from that day, the grantee equipped two
vessels, which reached the northern continent of America, on the coast of
the present state of North Carolina.   They entered Pamplico sound, by
Occacock inlet, and proceeded to Roanoke island.   A short time was
spent in exploring the country, and trafficking with the natives.

On the return of the adventurers, their report greatly excited the hopes
of their patron.   The new discovered country was called Virginia, in
honor of the maiden queen, and Sir Richard Grenville was dispatched to
convey thither a small colony, which Sir Walter abundantly supplied
with provisions, arms and ammunition.

Sir Richard landed one hundred and eight colonists, whom he left
under the orders of Ralph Lane, after having visited the barren shores of
Albemarle and Pamplico sounds.

The English, like the French in Caroline, instead of employing their
time in the tillage of the soil, wasted it in the search after ores.   The
stock of provisions brought over, not being renewed by agriculture, was
exhausted; and the colonists scattered themselves along the shore, in
small parties, with the hope of finding a precarious subsistence in fishing
and hunting.   Sir Francis Drake, returning in the following year from a
successful expedition against the Spaniards, (the first act of hostility of
England against Spain, in the new world) visited Virginia; and at first
determined on adding one hundred men to those under Ralph Lane, and
leaving one of his vessels with them; but, at last, at their request, he
took him and his men on board of his fleet and carried them back to
England.

Sir Richard arrived some time after, with three vessels.   Finding the
country deserted, and desirous of keeping possession of it, he left as many
of his men as he could spare, fifty in number, on Roanoke island.   Some
time after his departure, these men were massacred by the natives.

The ill success of Sir Walter Raleigh's attempt, did not discourage him.
He fitted out three ships, in which a number of colonists embarked; some
women accompanied them; an ample supply of provisions was provided,
and John White was placed at the head of the colony, with twelve assistants,
who were to act as his council.   On reaching the island of Roanoke, in
the latter part of July, 1587, they erected cabins for their accommodation
during the winter, and made preparations for a crop in the spring, and in
the following year, their chief crossed the Atlantic to solicit further aid
from the knight.

On his reaching England, he found the nation in great alarm, at the
formidable preparations of the King of Spain for the invasion of the country,
and Sir Walter Raleigh and Sir Richard Grenville, too much engaged, in
providing the means of defending their country, to attend to the affairs of
Virginia. Sir Walter, at last, assigned his patent to a company of merchants,
at the head of whom was John Smith.

On the first of August, 1589, Henry the third of France fell, in his
thirty-ninth year, under the knife of Jacques Clement, a fanatic priest.

Ninety-six years had rolled away since the discovery of America, at the death of Henry, the last Monarch of the house of Valois. The French, the Spaniards and the English had made a number of attempts at colonization, on the northern continent; yet, besides a few soldiers, whom the Spaniards had sent to garrison fort St. Augustine, the few colonists left by John White on Roanoke island, and the forty, by the Marquis de la Roche, on Sable island, there was not an European, living under his national flag in North America, the northern part of which was now known to Europe under the appellation of Canada, the middle by that of Virginia, and the southern by that of Florida.

CHAPTER II.

AT the death of Henry the third, the house of Valois became extinct. Its princes had occupied the French throne, for two hundred and sixty-one years; the first king of that branch, having been Philip VI., who succeeded to Charles V. Henry of Bourbon, was the nearest, though a very distant kinsman of the deceased monarch; their common ancestor being Louis IX., more commonly called St. Louis, who died in 1226.

The assignees of Sir Walter Raleigh's patent, in March, 1590, fitted out three ships, in which White embarked for Virginia. So much time was lost in a fruitless cruise against the Spaniards, that these vessels did not reach their destination till the month of August. The colonists, whom White had left on Roanoke island, three years before, were no longer there, and every effort to discover them was fruitless. No other attempt was made to find them, and the period and manner of their perishing was never known.

A French vessel came to Sable Island for the forty wretches, whom de la Roche had left there. Twenty-eight had perished; the survivors were taken back to France.

Henry the fourth, the first king of France of the house of Bourbon, did not obtain at once the peaceable possession of the throne. He had been bred a protestant, and the catholics suspected the sincerity of his attachment to their faith, which he had embraced. He confirmed his power by the victories of Arque and Ivry, and to silence all opposition, pronounced his abjuration, and his adherence to the catholic faith, in St. Denys, before his coronation, and in the following year, the fifth since his predecessor's demise, the city of Paris opened its gates to him.

On the thirteenth of September, 1593, the crown of Spain, by the death of Philip the second, in the seventh-second year of his age, passed to his son, Philip the third. The revolution, which severed the Spanish provinces in the low countries, from the dominions of Spain, began in the latter part of the reign of the deceased monarch; and the war, which ended in the beginning of the next, left the house of Nassau in possession of these provinces. The loss of territory, thus sustained, was followed in the latter part of the life of Philip III., by a considerable diminution of population, through the ill advised expulsion of the Moors.

The attention of Henry the fourth, nor that of his subjects, does not appear to have been drawn to America, till many years after his accession.

Pontgrave, an experienced navigator of St. Maloes, who had for several years traded to Tadoussac, on the northern shore of the river St. Lawrence, at a short distance below the spot on which the city of Quebec has since been built, and Chauvin, a captain of the king's ships, who had obtained a patent, nearly similar to that of the Marquis de la Roche, made a voyage to Canada, in 1602.   They proceeded up the river St. Lawrence, as far as the place, on which the city of Trois Rivieres now stands, where Pontgrave wished to begin a settlement; but Chauvin, more anxious of promoting his interest, by traffic with the Indians, than that of his country, by planting a colony, refused his consent.   A few men, however, were left at Tadoussac, who would have perished, if the Indians had not relieved them.

The English now kept pace with the French, in their endeavors to make a settlement in the new world.   Bartholomew Gosnold, a bold navigator, departed from Falmouth, with thirty-two men in a barque, and sailing as nearly west as possible, made the continent on the eleventh of May of the same year, towards the forty-third degree of northern latitude.   He gave the names, which they still bear, to Cape Cod, Martha's Vineyard and Elizabeth Island, in the present state of Massachusetts; but no account has reached us of his leaving any person behind.   Indeed, the small number of men he took out, precludes any idea of it.

On the third of May, 1603, Queen Elizabeth died in the seventieth year of her age, without issue, and was succeeded by James VI., of Scotland, the son of the unfortunate Mary Stuart.

At the accession of the House of Stuart to the throne of England, there was not a single individual of the English or French nation in North America, living under the protection of his national flag.

The Commander de la Chatte, who had acquired the rights of Chauvin, formed a company, chiefly composed of merchants of Rouen, to whom were joined several persons of distinction.   It prepared an expedition, the command of which was given to Pontgrave, to whom Henry the fourth had granted letters patent, authorising him to make discoveries and settlements on the shores of the river St. Lawrence.   Samuel de Champlain, an experienced seaman, who makes a conspicuous figure in the history of the new world, accompanied him.   They sailed in 1603.

After a short stay at Tadoussac, they left the shipping there; and proceeded, in a light boat, with five sailors to the rapids of St. Louis, or the Indian town of Hochelaga, which Cartier had visited sixty-eight years before.   They carried on some traffic with the natives, and joining the shipping, returned to France.

Their patron, the Commander de la Chatte, had died during their absence, and his powers had been vested by the king, in Pierre de Guard, Sieur du Monts, to whom had also been granted the exclusive trade, in furs and peltries, from the 40th to the 50th degree of north latitude, with the authority of granting land, as far as the 46th.   He was also created Vice Admiral, and Lieutenant-General over that extent of country.   He was allowed the free exercise of his religion (the Calvinist) in America, for himself and his people.   He covenanted to settle the country, and establish the Roman Catholic religion among the Indians.

The grantee fitted out four vessels, one of which was intended for the fur trade, at Tadoussac.   Pontgrave was directed to proceed with another to Canceaux, to sail through the canal between Royal Island and that of

St. John, and to drive interlopers away. Dumontz intended to go to Acadie with the other two.

The expedition left Havre de Grace, the seventh of May, 1604. In the following month, Dumontz entered a port of Acadie, in which he found a vessel trading, in violation of his exclusive privilege; he confiscated it, and gave the name of Rossignol (that of his master) to the port. He proceeded to another place, to which he gave the name of Port Mouton, from the circumstance of a sheep being drowned there. He landed his men here, and stayed one month, while Champlain was exploring the coast. They afterwards proceeded to an island, to which the name of St. Croix was given. They there committed some wheat to the ground, which succeeded amazingly.

During the winter the French suffered for want of water. The difficulty they found in procuring a supply from the continent, induced them to use melted snow. This brought on the scurvy, which made great havoc among them. As soon as the weather grew moderate, Dumontz went in search of a more favorable spot. He sailed along the coast, and up the rivers Penobscot and Pentagoct. Unable to find a suitable place, he returned to the island, where he was soon met by Pontgrave. Despairing of success there, he moved his men to Port Royal. Pontgrave was so delighted with the place, that he solicited and obtained from Dumontz a grant of it, which was afterwards confirmed by the king.

More attentive to acquire wealth by a trade in furs and peltries, than a subsistence by the culture of the soil, Pontgrave derived but little advantage from his grant.

In the autumn Dumontz returned to France. The complaints of the merchants of Dieppe and St. Maloes, who represented his privilege as destructive of the fisheries, from which these cities derived great advantages, induced the king to revoke it. Undismayed by this untoward event, he prevailed on Poutrincourt to fit out a ship for the relief of the colonists at Port Royal.

Acadie had, in the meanwhile, attracted the attention of the English. The earls of Southampton and Arundel fitted out a ship, the command of which they gave to Weymouth. He sailed from the Downs on the thirtieth of March, 1605, and after a passage of forty-four days, reached the continent between the forty-first and forty-second degrees of north latitude; coasting it northerly, he entered the river Penobscot, and ascended it upwards of sixty miles. The plans of his employers were not agricultural; the discovery of mines of the precious metals, and the purchase of furs and peltries, were the objects they had in view. After trafficking for awhile with the Indians, and setting up crosses (in token of his having taken possession of the country) in different parts of the banks of the river, he returned to England, carrying thither a Sagamore and five other chiefs.

The ship, which Dumontz had induced Poutrincourt to fit out for Acadie, left La Rochelle on the twelfth of May, 1606; her passage was tedious. Left so long without assistance, the colonists began to despair. Pontgrave had used in vain his best efforts to inspire them with confidence and patience. At last, unable to withstand their clamors any longer, he embarked with them for France; leaving behind two men only, who willingly remained in the fort, to preserve the property, which the smallness of the only vessel he could procure prevented him from

carrying away.   He had not left sight of French bay when he met a
barque, by which he was informed of the arrival of Poutrincourt at
Canceaux.   This induced him to retrograde, and on re-entering Port
Royal, he found there Poutrincourt, who had passed between the
continent and the island of Cape Breton.

Abundance being thus restored to the colony, the chiefs gave their
undivided attention to its security.   Fortifications were erected, and land
inclosed and cultivated.   Employment checked idleness and its consequence, disease; the friendship of the natives was secured, and the
colony began to thrive.   Dumontz' affairs in France had not been equally
prosperous.   He was unable to recover his privilege, and received a very
trifling indemnification.   He was at last permitted to exercise it during
one year; at the expiration of which, it was to be enjoyed by the Marchioness of Guercheville, a lady of great distinction at the court of France;
but this favor was burdened with the obligation of making a settlement
on the banks of the St. Lawrence.   His former friends had not abandoned
him; but their object was not colonization, but traffic with the Indians.
They fitted out two ships, which they placed under the orders of Champlain and Pontgrave, who were sent to trade at Tadoussac.

In the meanwhile, a plan had been adopted in England, under the
auspices of James the first, which was the origin of the extension of his
dominions to the western hemisphere.   Letters patent had been issued on
the tenth of May, 1606, granting to Sir Thomas Gates and his associates,
the territories in America, lying on the coast, between the thirty-fourth
and forty-fifth degrees, either belonging to the king, or not possessed by
any christian prince or people.   The grantees were divided into two
companies.

The southern was required to settle between the 34th and 41st, and the
northern between the 38th and 45th.   But neither was to settle within one
hundred miles from any establishment made by the other.

The northern company fitted out a vessel the same year; but she was
taken by the Spaniards, who claimed the exclusive right of navigating the
American seas.   During the next, they sent two vessels, in which were
embarked about two hundred colonists, who were landed near Sagadehoc,
in the fall.   They erected a small fortification, to which they gave the
name of Fort George.   The winter was extremely severe.   The leader, and
some of the principal colonists, fell victims to the diseases, which the great
cold produced.   The rest, hearing of the death of their most influential
patron, by the vessel that brought them provisions in the spring, returned
to England quite dispirited.

The southern company was more fortunate.   Its first expedition consisted
of a vessel of one hundred and twenty tons, and two barques, which
besides their crews, carried one hundred and fifty colonists.   The command
of it was given to Newport.   It sailed from the Thames, on the nineteenth
of December, 1606, and did not enter the bay of Chesapeake, till the
seventeenth of April following.   It proceeded up the river, then called
Powhatan, but to which Newport gave the name of James river, on the
shores of which was laid the foundation of the oldest town of English
origin, now existing in the new world; it was called James Town.   St.
Augustine in Florida, and Port Royal in Acadie, now Annapolis of Nova
Scotia, are the only towns on the northern continent, which, in point of
antiquity, rightly claim the precedence of it.

About fifteen months after, on the third of July, 1608, Champlain laid, on the northern shore of the St. Lawrence, the foundation of the city of Quebec, at the distance of three hundred and sixty miles from the sea.

The place was called by the Indians Quebecio, a word indicating a narrowed place; the width of the stream there diminishing from three to one mile, while about thirty miles below, it expands to twelve and fifteen.

Champlain was joined here, in the spring, by Pontgrave. Parties of the Hurons, Algonquins and Montagnes, were preparing for an expedition against the Iroquois, and he was induced to accompany them. He imagined, that aided by these three nations who were numerous, and had a strong interest to unite with him, he would be able successively to subdue all others; but he was ignorant that the Iroquois, who kept in awe every Indian within a circle of three hundred miles, were about to be supported by an European nation, jealous of the progress of his own in Canada.

This year Henry Hudson, an English seaman, in the service of the Dutch East India Company, sent to seek a northwest passage to China, discovered the river which still bears his name, though sometimes called the North river, and now separates the states of New York and New Jersey.

Champlain, ascending the St. Lawrence, entered the river to which the name of Sorel was afterwards given, in the company of his red allies. They went up this stream, as far as its rapids, near the place now called Chambly. Here, finding it impossible to proceed farther in their boats, they marched along the shore: the Indians bearing on their shoulders their bark canoes, which alone could now be of any use.

A few days after, towards sunset, they perceived the camp of the Iroquois. The allied army, having taken some slight precaution, went to rest. Before dawn, Champlain placed two Frenchmen in the woods, that they might, as soon as light beamed, fall on the flank of the enemy. The Algonquins and Hurons were divided into two bands. All were armed as the foe, with bows and arrows; but great reliance was placed in the fire-arms of the French, to whom it was recommended to take good aim at three Iroquois chiefs, whom high feathers, decorating their heads, rendered conspicuous.

The Algonquins and Hurons advanced side by side, till within one hundred and fifty yards from the Iroquois; they then opened, and the French, rushing betweeen, poured in their fire. Two of the obnoxious leaders of the enemy, who had been designated to the French, fell; the third was wounded. The Algonquins and Hurons yelled and discharged vollies of arrows, while the French gave a second fire. This put the enemy to flight; he was pursued; several of his men were killed, and a greater number made prisoners, The victors lost none of their men; about fifteen were wounded, but not one dangerously. A large supply of provisions was found in the enemy's camp, of which the pursuers were in much need.

Champlain returned, with his allies, to Quebec, where Pontgrave soon after arrived. They sailed together for France, leaving the command of the colony to Pierre Chauvin.

Henry the fourth was much pleased with the account Champlain gave him of the settlement on the St. Lawrence, and gave to his American dominions the name of New France. Dumontz was then at court, using his best efforts, especially with the Marchioness of Guercheville, to recover his privilege; but without success. His associates, the principal of whom were le Gendre and Collier, did not forsake him. They fitted out two ships, the command of which they gave to Champlain and Pontgrave. The views of these men were quite different. Champlain had most at heart the success of the colony; Pontgrave thought of nothing but the acquisition of wealth, by traffic with the Indians.

The first reached Tadoussac on the twenty-sixth of April, 1610, and proceeded to Quebec without delay. He found the colony in a prosperous condition. Wheat and rye had been sown the preceding year, and succeeded well; vines had been planted, but the event had disappointed the hope of the farmer. The people were healthy, and the Indians much pleased with their new neighbors, among whom they found a supply of provisions, when the precarious resource of the chase rendered it necessary; but they valued the whites most, on account of the protection they afforded against the irruptions of the Iroquois. The Hurons, the Algonquins and the Montagnes were the most immediate neighbors of the French. The first dwelt above Quebec, and the two other below, towards Tadoussac.

These Indians pressed Champlain to accompany them, on a second expedition against the Iroquois; their warriors being already assembled at the mouth of the river Sorel. On his arrival there, he found the number of these much smaller than it had been represented. A party, of about one hundred of the enemy, was hovering in the neighborhood; he was told he might surprise them if, leaving his boat, he went up in a light canoe of the Indians. He did so, with four of his countrymen, who had accompanied him, and he had hardly proceeded three miles up, when his Indians, without saying one word, jumped out of the canoe, and without leaving a guide with the whites, ran along the shore as fast as they could.

The country was swampy, and the musquitoes and other insects extremely troublesome. Champlain was advancing slowly, in uncertainty and doubt, when an Algonquin chief came to hurry him, saying the battle was begun. He hastened, and soon heard the yells of the combatants. The Iroquois had been found, and attacked in a small entrenchment, and had repelled the assailants. These, taking courage on the approach of their white allies, returned to the charge. The conflict was obstinate; Champlain was wounded in the neck, and one of his men in the arm. This did not prevent a galling fire from being at first poured in; but at last, the ammunition was exhausted; the enemy, greatly distressed by the musketry, was elated on its silence. The French, placing themselves at the head of their allies, marched to the attack and were repelled; but others, whom Champlain had left behind, coming up, the charge was renewed, and the Iroquois were mostly killed or wounded, and those who attempted to escape were drowned in the stream.

On the fourteenth of May, Henry the fourth fell under the dagger of Ravaillac, in the fifty-seventh year of his age, and was succeeded by his son, Louis the thirteenth.

The Marchioness of Guercheville was now in the enjoyment of the privilege, which had been granted to Dumontz; who, after its revocation, had been permitted to resume it for one year. Her avowed object was the conversion of the Indians, and the promotion of the Catholic religion in Acadie. For this purpose, she sent thither, in the following year, two

Jesuits, fathers Briart and Masse, as missionaries to Port Royal. This is the first spiritual succor sent to this part of the continent from France.

Champlain discovered the lake to which he gave, and which still bears, his name.

The Dutch began, in 1613, their first establishment on the northern continent, in the island of Manhattan. They called it Nova Belgica, and its principal town (now the city of New York) New Amsterdam.

The Marchioness of Guercheville fitted out two ships at Honfleur, for Acadie. She gave the command of them to De la Saussaie, whom she intended placing at the head of her affairs there. He sailed on the twelfth of March, 1613, and cast anchor in the port de la Haive, on the sixth of May. He erected there a pillar, with the armorial escutcheon of the Marchioness. From thence he went to Port Royal, where he found only an apothecary, who commanded, two Jesuits and three other persons —Becancourt, whom she had entrusted with her affairs there, being gone with the rest of the colonists, into the country in quest of provisions. Having taken the Jesuits on board, De la Saussaie proceeded to the river Penobscot, on the northern shore of which, he erected a small fort with the aid of his crew, and of twenty-five colonists, whom he had brought from France, and a few cabins for their accommodation. He called the place St. Sauveur.

He was hardly settled there, when Samuel Argal, an Englishman from Virginia, with eleven men of his nation, came into the neighborhood, and hearing of the French settlement, determined on destroying it; viewing it as an encroachment on the rights of the northern company, within whose grant he conceived it to be. The French, being unprovided with artillery (and the English having four pieces of cannon) made but a feeble resistance. They had several men killed. After their surrender, the settlement was abandoned to pillage and destruction; the vanquished were permitted to return to France; some of them, however, voluntarily followed Argal to Virginia. The escutcheon of the King of England was substituted for that of the Marchioness. Argal, before he sailed, sent some of his men to St. Croix and Port Royal, where, as at St. Sauveur, the houses of the French were consumed by fire.

The death of Henry the fourth had left Dumontz without support; Champlain had found a patron in the Earl of Soissons, whom the queen regent had placed at the head of the affairs of New France; but this nobleman died soon after, and was succeeded by the Prince of Conde. Under the auspices of the latter, Champlain sailed with Pontgrave, who had lately returned from Acadie. Landing at Quebec, on the seventh of May, 1613, and finding every thing in good order, he proceeded up the river, and laid the foundation of the city of Montreal. He visited the Ouatamais, and joining Pontgrave, whom he had left trading below, returned with him to St. Maloes. He formed there an association with merchants of that city, of Rouen and of la Rochelle, and by the aid of the Prince of Conde, obtained a charter for it.

The English northern company, deterred by the ill success of the colony they had sent to Sagadehoc five years before, had in the meanwhile limited their enterprise to a few voyages, undertaken for the sole purposes of fishing and trading for furs and peltries with the natives. In one of these, John Smith made in 1614, an accurate map from Cape Cod to Penobscot river. He laid it before the Prince of Wales, who gave the country the appellation of New England, under which the territory between the Dutch colony of Nova Belgica, and the French of Canada became known to Europe.

The company, lately formed by Champlain, at St. Maloes, fitted out their first expedition for New France, in the following year. He carried thither four recollet friars, whom he landed at Quebec, on the twenty-fifth of March, 1615. He next proceeded to Montreal, where he found a large party of the Hurons, who proposed a third expedition against the Iroquois.

He assented to it, provided they would wait till his return from Quebec, where his presence was absolutely necessary; this was agreed to, and he set off.

The Indians, however, grew soon tired of waiting for him, and proceeded with a few Frenchmen he had left in Montreal and father Joseph le Caron, one of the recollet friars lately arrived. Champlain reached Montreal, a few days after their departure, and was much vexed at their conduct. He would have desisted from following them, had he not feared the friar, who was with them, might be ill treated. He embarked with two Frenchmen and ten Indians, and joined the Hurons in the village. Placing himself at their head, he led them towards the Iroquois, who were found in an entrenchment, the approaches to which were in every direction, obstructed by trunks of large trees, still armed with all their branches. The assailants, repulsed on their first approach, attempted to set fire to the trees; but the besiegers had provided themselves, against this mode of offence, with a large supply of water. Champlain now erected a high scaffold, on which he placed his countrymen, whose galling fire greatly annoyed the enemy and would have insured victory, if the Hurons had not become untractable and unmindful of the orders of their leader. He was at last wounded in the leg, an accident, which drove his allies from presumption to despair; and he found himself compelled to order a retreat. It was made in a better order than he had expected; for, notwithstanding the pursuit, he did not lose one man.

Champlain wintered in the neighborhood, unable to procure a guide for his return to Quebec. He visited the villages near him, as far as Lake Nipissing. In the spring, he induced a few Indians, who had become attached to him, to pilot father Joseph and himself to Quebec, where they landed on the eleventh of July. He soon after went over to France.

During his absence, two Frenchmen, on a trading excursion, were killed by the Hurons. On his return, he was planning an expedition against his former allies, in order to avenge his countrymen's death; but the former, apprehensive of the conseqences, if they gave him time to make his preparations, determined on striking the first blow, and destroying every white man in Canada. With this object in view, they assembled about eight hundred warriors, near Trois Rivieres. Brother Pacific, a lay recollet friar, who had been stationed as a school master in the settlement, having received early information of their design, successfully exerted himself to dissuade them from it, holding out the hope that, if they abandoned it, and give up the assassins, Champlain would be prevailed on to forbear taking the just revenge he meditated. Accordingly, at their request, he went down to Quebec. Champlain demanded two Indians, who had been designated, as the perpetrators of the murder. One of them was sent and with him a large quantity of furs and peltries, in order, aocording to the

Indian custom, to cover the dead or atone for the crime. Prudential considerations induced Champlain to appear satisfied with this.

The troubles that distracted France during the minority of Louis the thirteenth, prevented the regency from attending to the possessions of the crown in America. Champlain continued to make frequent, but unsuccessful voyages to France, in search of aid; and his associates, satisfied with advancing their own interests by traffic, did not think of promoting the settlement or agriculture of the colony.

The prince of Conde sold, in 1620, his vice royalty to his brother-in-law, the Marshal of Montmorency. This nobleman, appointed Champlain his lieutenant, who, encouraged by the promises of his new patron, took his family over. On his landing at Tadoussac, he found three traders of la Rochelle, who, in contempt of the king's orders, and in violation of the company's rights, were trafficking with the Indians, and so far forgot themselves as to supply them with fire arms and ammunition; a measure which, until then, had been cautiously avoided.

On the twentieth of December, a ship from England landed one hundred and twenty men near Cape Cod, who laid the foundation of a colony, which, in course of time, became greatly conspicuous in the annals of the northern continent. They called their first town New Plymouth.

Philip the third, on the twenty-first of March of the following year, the forty-third of his age, transmitted the crown of Spain to his son, Philip the fourth.

This year, James the first of England, granted to Sir William Alexander, all the territory taken by Argal from the French in America, giving it the appellation of Nova Scotia, instead of that of Acadie, under which it was then known. The grantee divided it into two provinces: the first, which included the peninsula, retained the name in the royal grant; the second, including the rest of the territory, was called Nova Alexander. The king proposed to create fifty baronets, from among the associates of Sir William, who would contribute most liberally to the settlement of the territory granted.

The Iroquois, apprehending, that if the French were suffered to gain ground in Canada, the Hurons and Algonquins would acquire with their help, a preponderance over their nation, determined openly to attack the whites. Accordingly they fell on a small party of the latter, near the falls of St. Louis; but timely information of the approach of the Indians, enabled the French to repel them. On their return, they led away father William Poulain, a recollet monk; but the French had taken an Iroquois chief of considerable note, and the holy man, as they were tying him to the stake, received his freedom and his life, on the proposal of his countrymen to give the warrior in exchange for him.

Another party, in thirty canoes, came to Quebec and surrounded the convent of the recollets, on St. Charles river. The pious monks had fortified their, till then, peaceful monastery. The Iroquois hovered for several days around it, and retreated after having captured a small party of Hurons, who had come to the relief of their godly fathers. After destroying their huts and burning some of their prisoners, near the holy place, the Iroquois withdrew. Champlain found the force he could command too weak to venture on a pursuit. At the solicitation of the principal inhabitants, he sent father George le Baillif to France, to lay the distressed situation of the colony before the sovereign, and implore the needed relief.

Quebec in 1622, fourteen years after its settlement, had only fifty inhabitants, men, women and children. A brisk trade was carried on with the natives at Tadoussac below, and at Montreal and Trois Rivieres above the city.

The charter, which the Prince of Conde had procured to the company of merchants of St. Maloes, Rouen and la Rochelle, which Champlain had formed, was now revoked and its privilege granted to William de Caen and Edmund de Caen, his nephews.

The uncle came to Quebec, and although a protestant, was cordially received. He gave the direction of his affairs in Canada to Pontgrave, who was, by the ill state of his health, obliged to follow his principal to France, in the following year.

Champlain, having received intelligence that the Hurons, his former allies, meditated an union with the Iroquois against the French, sent among them three recollet monks—Fathers Joseph le Caron and Nicholas Viel and brother Nicholas Saghart. The timely exertion of the influence of these pious men, had the effect of averting the impending calamity He now laid the foundation of the fortress of Quebec, and went to France with his family.

Henry de Levy, Duke of Ventadour, had succeeded his uncle the Marshal of Montmorency, in the vice-royalty of New France. All the relief, which the solicitations of Champlain could obtain from the new viceroy, who had lately withdrawn from court, and received holy orders, was of the spiritual kind. Father Lallemand, who had accompanied de la Saussaie in Acadie, father Masse, of whom mention has already been made, and father Jean de Brebeuf, all three of the order of the Jesuits, were sent as missionaries to Canada, and were accompanied by two of their lay brethren, and father Daillon, a recollet. They all landed at Quebec, in 1625.

On the twenty-ninth of April of the same year, on the demise of James the first, in the fifty-ninth year of his age, his son, Charles the first, ascended the thrones of England and Scotland. This year is remarkable as the one in which the French and English made their first settlements in the West India islands. They both landed, on the same day, in different parts of the island of St. Christopher.

Charles the first, in some degree, pursued the intentions of his father, by granting patents of knight baronets to the promoters of the settlement of Nova Scotia. The original scheme was, however, defeated, and Sir William Alexander sold his property in that country to the French. He was Charles' secretary of state for Scotland, and was created Lord Stirling. The person who had inherited his title in 1776, took part with the Americans, and served the United States with distinction, as a general officer during the war which terminated by the recognition of their independence, by their former sovereign.

Fathers Daillon and Brebeuf, some time after their arrival at Quebec, set off for Trois Rivieres, where they met with a party of the Hurons, who offered to escort them. As their object was to go and preach the gospel to the Indians, they accepted the offer, and were about starting, when the news of the death of father Viel induced them to remain. This father, having spent some time with the Hurons, left them on a visit to Quebec in a canoe, with two of their young men. Instead of the usual pass, they took the branch of the river which runs between the islands of Montreal and Jesus, commonly called the river of the meadows, in which there is a fall, and neglecting to make a small portage, they attempted passing over the fall. In doing so, the canoe upset, and the father with an Indian boy who waited on him, were drowned. The fall was, from this circumstance, called *le sault du recollet*. The Indians made their escape. As they carried away the father's baggage, and did not appear well disposed before, they were strongly suspected of premeditated murder.

Three Jesuits, father Philibert, Nouet and Anne de Noue and a brother, came to Quebec in 1626, in a vessel chartered by their order. This spiritual was accompanied by worldly aid. A number of useful mechanics came also. They added much to the appearance of the place, which now began to take that of a town, having had before that of a plantation only. The Indians were often troublesome; at times, killing such of the whites as straggled to any distance. Animosities arose between the inhabitants and the agents of the de Caens, who were protestants. They paid but little attention to the culture of the ground, being solicitous only of collecting furs and peltries. Such was the situation of the colony when Champlain returned, in 1627.

Gustavus Adolphus, king of Sweden, having patronized the plan of Gulielm Usselin, for establishing a colony near that of the Dutch on Hudson river, a number of Swedes and Fins came over this year, and landed on Cape Henlopen, which they called Paradise point; they purchased from the natives all the land from the Cape to the falls of the Delaware, and began their settlement.

In the month of May, Louis the thirteenth, at his camp before la Rochelle, issued an edict by which a number of individuals, which was to be carried to one hundred, were incorporated under the style of "the company of New France." The privilege of the de Caens was expressly revoked. New France and Caroline or French Florida, were transferred to the company; the sovereign reserving only the faith and homage of its members and the inhabitants of the country, with a golden crown, on the accession of every king, the right of commissioning the officers of the highest tribunal of justice, presented to him, by the company, the power of casting cannons, erecting forts and doing whatever might be needed for the defence of the country. The company was invested with the power of granting land, erecting dukedoms, marquisates, earldoms, baronies, etc. An exclusive trade in furs and peltries was granted forever; and in everything else, during fifteen years. The right was, however, reserved to the king's subjects in the country, to purchase furs, peltries and hides from the Indians; under the obligation of selling beaver skins to the factors of the company at a fixed price.

The company covenanted to transport in the course of the first year, two or three hundred mechanics of different trades to Canada; to increase the number of its inhabitants, within fifteen years, to sixteen thousand; to lodge, feed and maintain the people they should send thither, during three years, and afterwards to grant them cleared land, sufficient for their support, and supply them with grain for seed. It was stipulated that all the colonists should be native French and Roman catholics, and no alien or heretic was to be received; it was provided that in every settlement there should be at least three priests supported by the company: cleared land was to be allotted for their support.

The company was composed of several noblemen, wealthy merchants and other influential characters, at whose head was the Cardinal of Richelieu. The Duke of Ventadour surrendered his office of viceroy to the king.

The first efforts of the company were unsuccessful. Its vessels were taken by the English, although there was no war between them and the French; but the cabinet of St. James had taken umbrage at the siege of la Rochelle.

David Kertz, a native of Dieppe, but a refugee in the service of Charles the first, instigated, as was supposed, by William de Caen, who was exasperated at the loss of his privilege, cast anchor with a small fleet before Tadoussac, early in the spring of the following year, and sent one of his ships to destroy the houses and seize the cattle at Cape Tousmente; and another to summon Champlain to surrender Quebec. The French chief was in the utmost distress for provisions and ammunition. He, however, returned a bold answer. Kertz having, in the meanwhile, received intelligence of the approach of a number of vessels, sent by the company to carry men and provisions to Canada, thought it more advisable to go and meet them than to attempt a siege.

Roquemont, who commanded the company's ships, cast anchor at Gaspe, from whence he dispatched a light vessel to Quebec, in order to apprise Champlain of his approach, and deliver him a commission, by which he was appointed governor and lieutenant general of New France. Miscalculating the relative forces of the French and English fleets, Roquemont went in search of Kertz, and fought him; but his ships, being overladen and encumbered, were all captured.

The joy, which Roquemont's messenger had excited in Quebec, was not of long duration. It was soon followed by the melancholy tidings of the capture of the vessels loaded with the needed supplies. This misfortune was attended by another. The crops failed throughout the country. The Indians for a while yielded some relief from the produce of their chase; but this precarious aid did not, nor could it, last long. The colonists had still some hope from another quarter. Father Nouet, superior of the Jesuits, and father Lallemand, were gone to solicit succor in France. They found, in the generosity of their friends, the means of chartering a vessel and loading her with provisions, and took passage in her with father Alexander Vieuxpont and a lay brother. A storm cast her ashore on the coast of Acadie. The superior and lay brother were drowned. Father Vieuxpont joined father Vimont in the island of Cape Breton. Father Lallemand sailed for France, but experienced a second shipwreck near San Sebastian, from which he however escaped.

Famine was not the only calamity that afflicted Canada. The Indians had grown turbulent and intractable, on the approach of the English. The ill will which a difference of religious opinions often creates, was greatly excited, and the Huguenots, whom the de Caens had introduced, refused obedience to the constituted authorities. Champlain had need of all his firmness and energy to suppress the disorder. Iu this state of affairs, he thought the best measure he could adopt was to march against the Iroquois, who of late had given him great cause of complaint, attack them and seek subsistence for his men in their country. But he was without ammunition and could not reasonably expect any for many months. Brule, his brother-in-law, whom he had sent to France to lay the distressed situation of the colony before the king, had sailed but a few weeks before.

Towards the middle of July, he was informed that a number of English vessels were behind Pointe Levy. This intelligence. which at any other time would have been very unpleasant, received a different character from circumstances. He viewed the English less as enemies than as liberators who came to put an end to the horrors of famine. A few hours after, a boat, with a white flag advanced and stopped in the middle of the port, as if waiting for leave to approach. A similar flag was hoisted in town, in order to intimate a wish that it might come to shore. An officer landed, and brought to Champlain a letter from Louis and Thomas Kertz, brothers to David, the Commodore. One of them was destined to the command of Quebec, the other had that of the fleet, which was at Tadoussac. The vessel that carried Brule, had fallen into their hands, and the distressed situation of the colony had become known to them, from the report of some of her sailors. Champlain was offered to dictate the terms of the capitulation; the place was yielded.

On the twentieth, the English cast anchor before it. They had but three ships; the largest was of one hundred tons, and had ten guns; the other two were of fifty tons, and had six guns each.

The conquest of Canada added but little to the wealth or power of England. Quebec, the only part of it which could be said to be settled, was a rock on which one hundred individuals were starving. It contained but a few miserable huts. All the wealth of the place consisted in a few hides and some peltries of inconsiderable value.

Thus, one hundred and twenty years after the French first visited the northern continent of America, notwithstanding a great waste of men and money, they were without one foot of territory on it.

The English colonies were in a more prosperous condition. The sturdy pilgrims who had landed but a few years before, in the north, had already wrested from the metropolis the government of their colony; and spreading their population along the sea shore, had laid the foundation of the towns of Plymouth, Salem and Boston.

The settlements in Virginia were extended to a considerable distance along the banks of James and York rivers to the Rapahanoc, and even the Potomac. They had subdued the neighboring tribes of Indians, who had attempted a general massacre of the whites. They enjoyed already the privilege of making their own laws. Regular courts of justice were established among them, and they had victoriously stood a contest, which terminated in the dissolution of the company, at whose cost the country had been settled; too spirited to submit to the arbitrary sway of Sir John Harvey, whom the king had sent to govern them, they had seized and shipped him to England.

On the thirtieth of October, Charles the first granted to Sir Robert Heath, his attorney-general, all the territory between the thirty-first and thirty-sixth degrees of northern latitude, not yet cultivated or planted, from the Atlantic to the Pacific ocean, with the islands of Viaries and Bahama. This immense tract, including all the country now covered by the states of North and South Carolina, Georgia, Tennessee and Mississippi with parts of that of Louisiana, the territory of Arkansas, with a considerable portion of New Mexico—was erected into an English province by the name of Carolana. This is the largest grant of a king of England to an individual. Sir Robert does not appear to have made an attempt to occupy any part of it. In 1637, he transferred his tittle to Lord Maltravers, who some time after on the death of his father, became Earl of Arundel and Surry, and Earl Marshal of England. This nobleman is said to have been at considerable expense in an attempt to transplant a colony there, but the civil war which began to rage soon after, prevented his success. The province afterwards became the property of Dr. Coxe of New Jersey, whose right, as late as the 21st of November, 1699, was recognized by the attorney-general of king William, and reported by the lords commissioners of trade and plantations as a valid one. The Virginia company loudly complained of the grant to Sir Robert as an encroachment on their charter.

While a new government was thus sought to be established in the south, by the king's authority, new establishments were formed by the northern company in the neighborhood of the French : Sir Ferdinando Gorges and John Mason, two members of that corporation, built a house at the mouth of Piscataqua river, and afterwards others erected cabins along the coast from Merrimack eastwardly to Sagadehoc, for the purpose of fishing. In 1631, Sir Ferdinando and Mason sent a party, under one Williams, who laid the foundation of the town of Portsmouth in the present state of New Hampshire.

By the treaty of St. Germain, which put an end to the war between France and England, on the twenty-ninth of March, 1632, the latter restored to the former, Canada and Acadie, without any description of limits ; Quebec, Port Royal and the island of Cape Breton were so by name.

CHAPTER III.

EMERY DE CAEN was dispatched with a copy of the treaty to Quebec. His principal object in bringing it was the recovery of the property he had left in Canada, for the restoration of which provision had been made by an article of the treaty. With the view of yielding to him some indemnification for the loss of his privilege, Louis the thirteenth had granted him the exclusive commerce of New France, in furs and peltries, for one year.

Kertz surrendered the country to de Caen.

Charles the first, on the twenty-eighth of June, granted to Cecilius, Lord Baltimore, a large tract of country, between the settlements of Virginia and the river and bay of Delaware. It was called Maryland, in honor of Henrietta Maria, sister to Louis the thirteenth of France. Lord Baltimore, soon after sent thither two hundred colonists. They were all Roman catholics, and chiefly from Ireland.

The company of New France resumed its rights in 1633, and Champlain, who, on its nomination, had been appointed governor of Canada, returned to Quebec, bringing with him a few Jesuits.

Acadie was granted to the commander of Razilly, one of the principal members of the company. He bound himself to settle it, and began a small establishment at la Haive. A party of his people attacked a trading house of the colony of New England on Penobscot river. In the following year, he erected a small military post there. It was attacked by an English ship and barque, under Captain Girling; but it successfully defended itself.

The Plymouth company, dividing its territory among its members, the land between Merrimack and Piscataqua rivers was granted to Mason. It now constitutes the state of New Hampshire. That to the northeast, as far as Kennebeck river, was allotted to Sir Ferdinando Gorges, another member. It is now the state of Maine.

Roger Williams, a popular preacher, and a Mrs Hutchinson, being banished from Massachusetts, purchased each a tract of land from the Naraganset Indians, on which they settled, with a few of their adherents, and laid the foundations of Providence and Rhode Island. Nearly about the same, time, Hooker, a favorite minister in Boston, with leave of the government, led a small colony farther southerly, and laid in the towns of Hartford, Windsor and Wetherfield, the foundation of the present state of Connecticut.

In December 1635, a college was established by royal authority at Quebec, and in the following year, Champlain died, and was succeeded by the Chevalier de Montmagny.

The piety of the Dutchess d'Aiguillon procured to the colony two useful establishments—that of the Sisters of the Congregation, who came from Dieppe in 1637; and that of the Ursuline Nuns from Tours, in 1638, to devote themselves to the relief of suffering humanity in the hospital, and the education of young persons of their sex.

With the view of checking the irruptions of the Iroquois, who greatly distressed the upper settlers, and came down the river that falls into the St. Lawrence on its right side, at a small distance from the town of Montreal, Montmagny had a fort erected on its banks; it was called Fort Richelieu, in honor of the Cardinal, then prime minister, and afterwards communicated its name to the stream.

Justice had hitherto been rendered to the colonists, by the governor and commandants; in 1640, provision was made for its more regular administration, by the appointment of judges at Quebec, Montreal and Trois Rivieres, and a grand seneschal of New France. The former had original, and the latter appellate jurisdiction.

Louis the thirteenth, on the fourteenth of May, 1643, the forty-second year of his age, transmitted his sceptre to his son, Louis the fourteenth.

The English settlements, near the French, suffering as much from the Indians as Canada, the colonies of New Hampshire, Massachusetts, Rhode Island and Connecticut, sought protection in the union of their efforts. They entered into a league of alliance, offensive and defensive, and gave to five commissioners, chosen by each colony, the power of regulating the affairs of the confederacy. Accordingly the governor of Massachusetts, in behalf of the united colonies, in the following year, concluded a treaty of peace and commerce, with Monsieur d'Antouy, governor of Acadie; it was laid before, and ratified by, the commissioners.

In 1646, d'Aillebout succeeded Montmagny in the government of New France.

The Indians continuing to distress the back settlers of New England, the commissioners of the united colonies sent a deputy to Quebec; who, in their behalf, proposed to d'Aillebout, that the French and New England colonies should enter into a perpetual alliance, independent from any rupture between the parent countries. D'Aillebout, approving the measure, sent father Dreuilletes, a Jesuit, to meet the commissioners in Boston. The envoy, it appears, was instructed not to agree to any treaty, unless the aid of New England was afforded to New France against the Iroquois. Time has destroyed every trace of the final result of this mission.

Democracy now prevailed in England, over the monarch and its nobles. The House of Lords was abolished, and Charles the first lost his head on the scaffold, on the 30th of January, 1648, in the forty-eighth year of his age. Oliver Cromwell, under the title of protector, assumed the reins of government. During the struggle that preceded the king's fall, the northern colonies spiritedly adhered to the popular party; Virginia remained attached to the royal cause, which did not cease to prevail there till the arrival of a fleet, with the protector's governor. Some resistance was even made to his landing.

The commissioners of New England resumed their negotiations to induce the governor of New France to enter into an alliance with them. The English and French colonies were now much distressed by irruptions of the Indians. The French had sent among the latter, a considerable number of missionaries, who proceeded, in their efforts to propagate the gospel, much in the same manner as methodists now do in new and thinly inhabited countries. Besides travelling missionaries, who performed regular tours of duty, among the more distant tribes, they had stationed ones in the nearer. The stationed missionary was generally attended by a lay brother, who instructed young Indians in their Catechism. The father had often around him a number of his countrymen, who came to sell goods and collect peltries. His dwelling was the ordinary resort of the white men whom necessity, cupidity or any other cause, led into the forests. A number of Indians gathered near the mission, to minister to the wants of the holy man, and his inmates or visitors. His functions gave him a great ascendency over his flock, amused and increased by the pageantry of the rites of his religion. His authority often extended over the whole tribe, and he commanded and directed the use of its forces. As he was supported by, and did support, the government of the colony, he soon became a powerful auxiliary in the hands of its military chief. The union which existed among the travelling and stationed missionaries, all appointed and sent or stationed, and directed by their superior in the convent of Quebec, had connected the tribes who had received a missionary, into a kind of alliance and confederacy, the forces of which government commanded, and at times exerted against the more distant tribes. In return, it afforded the confederates protection against their enemies. The Iroquois, Eries and other nations, not in this alliance, considered the members of it as their foes, made frequent irruptions in their villages, and at times captured or killed the missionary and the white men around him. The parties engaged in these expeditions did not always confine the violence they thus exercised to Indian villages; they often attacked the frontier settlements of the whites, and at times approached their towns. These circumstances rendered it desirable to New France, to secure the aid of New England against the Indians. Accordingly, in June, 1651, d'Aillebout, calling to his council the head of the clergy and some of the most notable planters, who recommended that Godefroy, one of the latter, and father Dreuillettes, should proceed to Boston, and conclude the alliance, which the commissioners of the New England colonies had proposed. Charlevoix has preserved the resolutions of the notables, the letter they wrote to the commissioners, and the passport or letter of credence which the governor gave to the envoys; but he was not able to transmit us the result of the mission.

New France received a new governor, in the person of Lauson, in 1652.

A large party of the Iroquois, advancing towards Montreal, Duplessis Brocard, who commanded there, putting himself at the head of the inhabitants, marched out. He lost his life in an encounter, and his followers were routed. This accident, although it inspired the Indians with much confidence, did not embolden them to attack the town.

On the failure of an expedition, which Cromwell had directed to be prepared in Boston, under the command of Sedwick, for the attack of the Dutch in Nova Belgica, this officer took upon himself to dislodge the French from Acadie.

The French and English were not the only European nations annoyed by the Indians. The Swedes, who, at this time, had several settlements over the territory, which is now covered by the states of New Jersey, Pennsylvania and Delaware, finding themselves in too small a number to stand their ground with the natives, abandoned New Sweden; and John Rising, their governor, in 1655 by order of his sovereign, transferred to Peter Stuyvesant, governor of Nova Belgica, all the rights of the Swedish crown in this quarter, for the use of the states-general.

In 1659, New France received new civil and ecclesiastical chiefs. The Viscount of Argenson succeeded Lauson, and Francis de Laval, Bishop of Petrea, appointed by the holy see, its apostolic vicar, arrived with a number of ecclesiastics. The island of Montreal was erected into a seignory, and the priests of St. Sulpice in Paris, were made lords of it. A seminary was established in the city of Montreal; it being the intention of government, to substitute a secular clergy to the Jesuits and recollets, who till now had ministered to the spiritual wants of the colonists. A similar establishment had been begun in Quebec. Regulations were made for the collection of tithes. Societies of religious ladies in France sent some of their members to Montreal, for the relief of the sick and the education of young persons of their sex.

While Canada was advancing in its internal improvements, the Virginians extended their discoveries over the mountains. Daniel Coxe, in his description of Carolana, published in 1722, relates that Col. Woods of Virginia, dwelling near the falls of James river, about one hundred miles from the bay of Chesapeake, between the years 1654 and 1664, discovered at different times, several branches of the Ohio and Mississippi. He adds, he had in his possession, the journal of a Capt. Needham, who was employed by the Colonel.

In 1660, the people of Virginia, at the death of Mathews, the protector's governor, called on Sir William Berkely, the former governor under the king, to resume the reins of government, and proclaimed Charles the second as their legitimate sovereign, before they had any intelligence of Cromwell's death. Charles' restoration was soon after effected in England, and his authority recognized in all his American colonies.

This year was a disastrous one in Canada: large parties of the Iroquois incessantly rambled over the country, in every direction, killing or making prisoners of the whites, who strayed to any distance from their plantations. The culture of the earth was much impeded by the terror they inspired. Even in Quebec, the people were alarmed. The Ursuline and hospital nuns were frequently compelled to seek shelter out of their monasteries, at night. In the following year, an epidemic disease made great havoc. It was a kind of whooping cough, terminating in pleurisy. Many of the whites, and the domesticated Indians fell victims to it. Its greatest ravages were among the children. It was imagined to be occasioned by enchantment, and many of the faculty, did, or affected to, believe it. Others were terrified into credulity, and the strangest reports were circulated and credited. Time and the progress of knowledge have dispelled the opinion (which at this period prevailed in Europe, and the colonists had brought over) that at times, malignant spirits enabled some individuals to exercise supernatural powers over the health and lives of others. It was said, a fiery crown had been observed in the air at Montreal; lamentable cries were heard at Trois Rivieres, in places in which there was not any person; that at Quebec, a canoe all in fire had been seen on the river, with a man armed cap-a-pie, surrounded by a circle of the same element; and in the island of Orleans, a woman had heard the cries of her fruit in her womb. A comet made its appearance; a phenomenon seldom looked upon as of no importance, especially in calamitous times.

The alarm at last subsided. The parties of Iroquois, who desolated the country, became less numerous and less frequent; these Indians finally sued for peace. The governor did not appear at first very anxious to listen to their proposals; but prudence commanded the acceptance of them.

The Baron d'Avaugour relieved the Viscount d'Argenson in 1662.

Serious discontents now arose between the civil and ecclesiatical chiefs. Much distress resulted from the inobservance of the regulations, made to prevent the sale of spirituous liquors to the Indians. A woman, who was found guilty of a breach of them was sent to prison, and at the solicitation of her friends, the superior of the Jesuits waited on the Baron to solicit her release. He received the holy man with rudeness; observing that, since the sale of spirituous liquors to the Indians was no offence in this woman, it should not, for the future, be one in anybody. Obstinacy induced him afterwards to regulate his conduct according to this rash declaration; the shopkeepers (thinking themselves safe) suffered cupidity to direct theirs, and the regulations were entirely disregarded. The clergy exerted all their influence to suppress the growing evil, and withheld absolution from those who refused to promise obedience to the regulations. The Bishop resorted to the use of the censures of the church against the obstinate; this created much ill will against him and his clergy, and he crossed the sea, to solicit the king's strict orders for the suppression of this disorder.

A dreadful earthquake was felt in Canada on the fifth of February, 1663. The first shock is said by Charlevoix, to have lasted half an hour; after the first quarter of an hour, its violence gradually abated. At eight o'clock in the evening, a like shock was felt; some of the inhabitants said they had counted as many as thirty-two shocks during the night. In the intervals between the shocks, the surface of the ground undulated as the sea, and the people felt in their houses. the sensations which are experienced in a vessel at anchor. On the sixth, at three o'clock in the morning, another most violent shock was felt. It is related that at Tadoussac, there was a rain of ashes for six hours. During this strange commotion of nature, the bells of the churches were kept constantly ringing by the motion of the steeples; the houses were so terribly shaken that the eaves on each side, alternately touched the ground. Several mountains altered their positions; others were precipitated into the river, and lakes were afterwards found in the places on which they stood before. The commotion was felt for nine hundred miles from east to west, and five hundred from north to south.

This extraordinary phenomenon was considered as the effect of the vengeance of God, irritated at the obstinacy of those, who, neglecting the admonitions of His ministers, and contemning the censures of His church, continued to sell brandy to the Indians. The reverend writer, who has been cited, relates it was said, ignited appearances had been observed in the air for several days before; globes of fire being seen over the cities of Quebec and Montreal, attended with a noise like that of the simultaneous discharge of several pieces of heavy artillery; that the superior of the nuns, informed her confessor some time before, that being at her devotions she believed "she saw the Lord, irritated against Canada, and she involuntarily demanded justice from him for all the crimes committed in the country; praying the souls might not perish with the bodies: a moment after she felt conscious the divine justice was going to strike; the contempt of the church exciting God's wrath. She perceived almost instantaneously four devils at the corners of Quebec, shaking the earth with extreme violence, and a person of majestic mien alternately slackening and drawing back a bridle, by which he held them." A female Indian, who had been baptised was said to have received intelligence of the impending chastisement of heaven. The reverend writer concludes his narration by exultingly observing, "none perished, all were converted."

The bishop was favorably heard at court, and returned with de Mesy, who, at his recommendation, was sent to relieve the Baron d'Avaugour.

The company of New France, drawing but little advantage from its charter, had surrendered it; and Gaudais, the king's commissioner to take possession of the country, arrived with the governor and bishop. One hundred families came over with him. A number of civil and military officers, and some troops were also sent.

After having executed the object of his mission, received the oaths of fidelity of the former and new colonists, and made several ordinances for the regulation of the police and administration of justice, the commissioner returned to France.

The governors had hitherto claimed cognizance of all suits which the plaintiff brought before them, and disposed of them, in a summary way, and without appeal. They, however, seldom proceeded to judgment without having previously tried in vain to induce the parties to submit their differences to the arbitration of their friends; and the final decisions of the governors, when the attempt failed, had generally given satisfaction. We have seen, however, that in 1640, a grand seneschal of New France and inferior judges at Quebec, Montreal and Trois Rivieres, had been appointed. By an edict of the king, of the month of March, 1664, a sovereign council was created in New France. It was composed of the governor, the apostolic vicar, the intendant, and four counsellors, (chosen among the most notable inhabitants, by, and removeable at the pleasure of these three officers) an attorney general and a clerk. This tribunal was directed to take the ordinances of the king, and the custom of Paris, as the rules of its decisions. The military and ecclesiastical chief had precedence over the intendant in council, though the latter exercised the functions of president. A majority of the judges was a quorum in civil, but the presence of five of them was required in criminal cases.

Inferior tribunals were established at Quebec, Montreal and Trois Rivieres.

The occupation, by the Dutch and Swedes, of the territory between New England and Maryland, had never been viewed in England as the exercise of a legitimate right, but rather as an encroachment on that of the crown, the country having been discovered by one of its subjects, Henry Hudson. The circumstance of his being, at the time, in the service of the states general, was not deemed to affect the claim of his natural sovereign. Charles the second, accordingly made a grant to his brother, the Duke of York, and Lord Berkeley, of all the territory between New England and the river Delaware, and a force was sent to take possession of it in 1664.

Governor Stuyvesant, who commanded at New Amsterdam, would have resisted the English forces, but the inhabitants were unwilling to support him. He was therefore compelled to yield. The town of New Amsterdam received the name of New York, which was also given to the province, and fort Orange that of Albany.

The territory between the Hudson and the Delaware, the North and South river, was erected into a distinct province, and called New Jersey. In New France, de Mesy did not live on better terms with the bishop and clergy, than his predecessor. Great discontents prevailed also between him and the members of the council. They rose to such a height that he ordered Villere, a notable inhabitant, who had been called to a seat in the council, and Bourdon, the attorney general, to be arrested, and, after a detention of a few days, he shipped them to France. The stern wisdom and unshaken integrity of the prisoners were universally acknowledged. Their complaints were favorably heard at court. The answer of the governor to the charges exhibited against him, appeared unsatisfactory, and de Courcelles was sent to relieve him.

Louis the fourteenth had, in the preceding year, appointed the Marquis de Tracy, his viceroy and lieutenant general in America. This officer was directed to visit the French islands in the West Indies, to proceed to Quebec and stay as long as might be necessary, to settle the disturbed government of the colony, and provide for its protection against the irruptions of the Iroquois.

In June, 1665, the viceroy landed at Quebec, with four companies of the regiment of Carignan Salieres. He dispatched a part of this small force, with some militia, under the orders of captain de Repentigny, who met several parties of the Iroquois, whom he reduced to order. The rest of the regiment arrived soon after, with de Salieres its colonel, and a considerable number of new settlers and tradesmen, and a stock of horses, oxen and sheep. The horses were the first seen in Canada. The addition to the population of the colony, which then arrived, much exceeded its former numbers.

The viceroy proceeded with a part of the troops to the river Richelieu, where he employed them in erecting three forts. The first, was on the spot on which had stood fort Richelieu, built by Montmagny in 1638, and which was gone to ruins. The new one was built by an officer of the name of Sorel, who was afterwards left in command there. It received his name, and communicated it to the river. The second fort was erected at the falls. It was at first called Fort Louis; but Chambly, the officer who built and commanded it, having acquired the land around, it took his name. The third was nine miles higher up, and was called St. Theresa, from the circumstance of its having been completed on the day on which the catholics worship that saint. These fortifications were intended as a protection against the Iroquois, who generally came down that river to invade the colony. They were greatly emboldened by the expectation of aid from the English, at Albany. The new forts effectually guarded against their approach by the stream; but the Indians soon found other parts of the country affording them as easy a passage. They became so troublesome, that the viceroy and governor were, for a considerable time, compelled to keep the field with the regular forces, and as many of the inhabitants as could be spared from the labors of agriculture. They had several encounters with large parties of Indians, whom they defeated. The latter found it of no avail to continue their irruptions, while the colony was thus on its guard.

The tranquillity, which the retreat of the foe and the vigilance of the chiefs gave to the colony, was, however, soon disturbed by events over which human foresight can have no control. Several shocks of an earthquake, attended with the appearance of the meteors that had accompanied that of 1663, now excited great alarm. A deadly epidemic disease added its horrors to those which the commotions of nature had produced.

Charles the second, unmindful of his father's charter to Sir Robert Heath, about a third of a century before, had in 1663 granted to Lord Clarendon and others, the territory from the river San Matheo, or St. John, in Florida, to the thirty-sixth degree of northern latitude. There was as yet but an insignificant settlement in this vast extent of country. It was on the north side of Albermarle Sound, and had been formed by stragglers from the colony of Virginia, who, traveling southerly, had stopped at a small distance beyond its southern limit, and had been joined by emigrants chiefly of the Quaker profession, driven by the intolerant spirit of the people of New England. The new proprietors having discovered valuable tracts of land, not included in their charter, obtained in June, 1665, a second and more extensive one. It covers all the territory from the twenty-ninth degree to Wynock, in 30 degrees, 30 minutes of northern latitude. They effected, shortly after, a small settlement on Cape Fear river, which was afterwards removed farther south, and became the *nucleus* of the state of South Carolina, as that on Albermarle Sound, extending southerly and westerly, became that of North Carolina.

On the seventeenth of September, 1665, Philip the fourth of Spain died in his sixtieth year, and was succeeded by his son, Charles the second.

The French king had, in 1662, transferred to the West India Company all the privileges which that of New France had enjoyed; the former, not being in a situation to avail itself immediately of the royal favor, requested that the colonial government might for a while be administered by the king's officer. In the spring of 1667, the Marquis de Tracy, according to the king's order, put the company in formal possession of the country, and soon after sailed for France. Neither the colony nor the company appear to have derived any great advantage from this arrangement; and in the following year, the freedom of commerce in New France was proclaimed.

By the treaty of Breda in 1667, Acadie was restored to the French.

The ecclesiastical government of New France had been hitherto confided to an apostolic vicar, a bishop *in partibus infidelium*, that of Petrea. The pope now erected the city of Quebec, into a bishop's see, and St. Vallier was appointed its first incumbent. This gentleman, however, did not receive the canonical institution till four years after.

The lords of manors in New France did not enjoy any ecclesiastical patronage; and the bishop who, receiving all the tithes collected in the diocese, was burdened with the support of the curates, had the uncontrolled appointment of them.

It does not appear that with the exception of the seminary of St. Sulpice, any lord in New France, ever claimed the administration of justice by his own judges. This corporation was in the exercise of this right as lords of the island of Montreal; but they surrendered it to the king in 1692.

The Chevalier de Grandfontaine and Sir John Temple, plenipotentiaries of the French and British crowns, signed in Boston, on the seventh of July, 1670, a declaration by which the right of France to all the country from the river of Pentagoet, to the island of Cape Breton (both inclusive) was recognized. The chevalier was appointed governor of Acadie.

Count de Frontenac succeeded Courcelles in the government of New France, in the following year. He found it desolated by repeated irruptions of the Iroquois, who came down along the eastern shore of lake Ontario and descended the St. Lawrence. With the view of checking their approach this way, he built a fort at Catarocoui on the lake, near the place where its waters form the river.

The western company by an edict of February, 1670, had been authorized to send to the islands, small coins expressly struck for circulation there to the amount of one hundred thousand livres, (about $20,000) and the edict especially provided they should not circulate elsewhere. In November, 1672, however, their circulation was authorized in the king's dominions in North America, and their value was increased one-third; pieces of fifteen sous being raised to twenty, and others in the same proportion. At the same time, the practice that had prevailed in the islands and in New France, of substituting the contract of exchange to that of sale was forbidden. The king ordered that in fnture, all accounts, notes, bills, purchases and payments should be made in money, and not by exchange or computation of sugar, or other produce, under pain of nullity. Former contracts, notes, bills, obligations, leases, etc., in which a quantity of sugar, or other produce, was stipulated to be delivered, were resolved by the royal power into obligations to pay money. This interference in the concerns of individuals created confusion, and the great demand it occasioned for coin, increased its value and occasioned a consequent decrease of land and other property, which had a most mischievous effect.

The Canadians had learnt from the Indians that there was a large stream to the west, the course of which was unknown; but they had ascertained it did not flow northerly nor easterly; and great hopes were entertained that it might afford a passage to China, or at least to the Gulf of Mexico. Talon, the first intendant of New France, was about returning home and determined on discovering before he sailed the course of this great river.

He engaged for this purpose father Marquette, a recollet monk, who had been for a long time employed in distant missions, and Joliet, a trader of Quebec, and a man of considerable information and experience in Indian affairs. The two adventurers proceeded to the bay of lake Michigan and entered a river, called by the Indians Outagamis, and by the French *des renards*. Ascending almost to its source, notwithstanding its falls, they made a small portage to the Ouisconsing. Descending this stream, which flows westerly, they got into that they were in quest of on the seventh of July, 1673. History has not recorded any account of its having been floated on by any white man since Muscoso, with the remainder of his army, descended it from Red river to its mouth, about one hundred and thirty years before.

Committing themselves to the current, the holy man and his companion soon reached a village of the Illinois, near the mouth of the Missouri. These Indians gladly received their visitors. Their nation was in alliance with the French, and traders from Canada came frequently among them; a circumstance which had rendered them obnoxious to the Iroquois, whom they found too numerous to be successfully resisted, without the aid of their white friends. The guests were hospitably entertained, and their influence, with the governor and ecclesiastical superior, was solicited, that some aid might be afforded them, and that a missionary might come and reside among them.

After a short stay, the current, which now began to be strong, brought the travellers in a few days to a village of the Arkansas. Believing now they had fully ascertained that the course of the river was towards the Gulf of Mexico, their stock of provisions being nearly exhausted, they deemed it useless and unsafe to proceed farther, among unknown tribes, on whose disposition prudence forbade to rely. They therefore hastened back to the river of the Illinois, ascended it and proceeded to Chicagou, on lake Michigan. Here they parted; the father returning to his mission, among the Indians on the northern shore of the lake, and the trader going down to Quebec, to impart to their employer the success of their labors. Count de Frontenac gave to the river they had explored the name of Colbert, in compliment to the then minister of the marine.

Joliet's services in this circumstance, were remunerated by a grant of the large island of Anticosti, near the mouth of the river St. Lawrence.

This important discovery filled all Canada with joy, and the inhabitants of the capital followed the constituted authorities of the colony to the cathedral church, where the bishop, surrounded by his clergy, sung a solemn *Te Deum*. Little did they suspect that the event, for which they were rendering thanks to heaven, was marked, in the book of fate, as a principal one among those, which were to lead to the expulsion of the French nation from North America, that Providence had not destined the shores of the mighty stream for the abode of the vassals of any European prince; but had decreed that it should be for a while the boundary, and for ever after roll its waves in the midst of those free and prosperous communities that now form the confederacy of the United States.

CHAPTER IV.

THE people of New England saw, with a jealous eye, the French in possession of Acadie. On the tenth of August, 1674, Chambly, who commanded there, was surprised in the fort of Pentagoet, by an English adventurer, who had lurked in his garrison for several days. This man had procured the aid of the crew of a Flemish privateer, about one hundred in number. The French being but thirty in the fort, were soon subdued. The victor marched afterwards with a part of his force to the fort on the river St. John. Manson, who commanded there, was found still less prepared for defence than his chief. By the capture of these two forts, the only ones which the French had in Acadie, the whole country fell into the power of the invaders. Charles the second disavowed this act of hostility, committed in a period of profound peace. It had been planned, and the means of its execution had been procured in Boston.

The absence of causes of external disturbance, gave rise to internal, in Canada. The colonists complained that, through the ill-timed exertion of the influence of Count de Frontenac, the seats in the superior council, which were destined for notable inhabitants, were exclusively filled by men entirely devoted to him—that more suits had been commenced in the last six months, than during the six preceding years. An act of arbitrary power had greatly excited the clergy against him. He had imprisoned the abbe de Fenelon, then a priest of the seminary of St. Sulpice at Montreal, who afterwards became Archbishop of Cambray, and acquired great reputation in the literary world, as the author of Telemachus, on the alleged charge of having preached against him, and of having been officiously industrious in procuring attestations from the inhabitants, in favor of Perrot, whom the count had put under arrest. They also complained that he had, of his own authority, exiled two members of the council, and openly quarrelled with the intendant.

Much ill will was created between him and the bishop, clergy and missionaries, by the sale of spirituous liquors to the Indians, which they had hitherto successfully opposed, and the count now countenanced. The priests complained it destroyed the whole fruits of their labor among the converted Indians, and the bishop had declared the breach of the law, in this respect, a sin, the absolution of which was reserved to him alone, in his diocese.

These dissensions were made known to the king, who, with the view of putting a stop to them, directed that an assembly of the most notable inhabitants of the colony, should be convened and express its opinion on the propriety of disallowing the traffic, and that their determination should be laid before the archbishop of Paris and father de la Chaise, an eminent Jesuit confessor of the king. It was urged in France that a discontinuance of the sale would deprive the colonial government of the attachment of the natives, who would be induced to carry their furs and peltries to Albany and New York. The two high dignitaries of the church, to whom the sovereign had committed the examination of this question, having conferred with St. Vallier, the Bishop of Quebec, (who had been induced by his zeal in the cause of humanity, to go over and solicit the King's interference) decided that the sale should not be allowed. This report became the basis of an ordinance, the strictest observance of which was enjoined on the count, and the prelate pledged himself to confine his interference to cases of the most flagrant violation of the ordinance.

Father Marquette had died; and the great joy which the discovery of the Mississippi had excited, had subsided. Joliet was, perhaps, too much engaged by his own private concerns to prosecute the plans of further discoveries, and the utmost apathy on this subject prevailed in the colonial government. To the enterprise of a then obscure individual, France owed her success in colonization on the Mississippi.

Robert Cavelier de Lasalle, a native of Rouen, who had spent several years in the order of the Jesuits, and whom this circumstance had prevented from receiving any part of the succession of his parents, who had ended their lives, while he was thus civilly dead, came to Canada, in search of some enterprise that might give him wealth or fame. Such appeared to have been the prosecution of Marquette and Joliet's discoveries. He did not doubt that the mighty stream poured its waters into the Gulf of Mexico; but he fostered the idea, that by ascending it, a way might be found to some other river running westerly and affording a passage to Japan and China.

He communicated his views to count de Frontenac, to whom he suggested the propriety of enlarging the fort at Catarocoui, increasing its force, and thus by holding out protection, induce settlers to improve the surrounding country, which would afford a strong barrier to the rest of the colony in case the Iroquois renewed their irruption. He presented, as a farther advantage, the facility, which this would give for the building of barques for the extension of trade, along the shores of the lakes, and of the limits of the colonies and the dominions of the king over distant tribes of Indians. The count entered into Lasalle's views; but, as the execution of the proposed plan required considerable disbursements, which he did not choose to order without the minister's directions, he ordered the projector to go over, to present and explain his plans.

Lasalle, on his arrival, was fortunate enough to procure an introduction to, and gain the notice of the Prince de Conti, whose patronage secured him the most ample success at court. The king granted him letters of nobility, and an extensive territory around the fort at Catarocoui, now called fort Frontenac, on condition of his rebuilding it with stone, and invested him with ample power for prosecuting the projected discoveries, and carrying on the trade with the natives. The prince desired Lasalle to take with him the chevalier de Tonti, an Italian officer, who had served in Sicily, where he had lost a hand. He had substituted to it, one made of copper, of which habit enabled him occasionally to make a powerful use. He was the son of the projector of a plan of placing money at interest (not unknown now in the United States) called a tontine; in which the principal, paid in by those who die, is lost to their estates, and enures to the benefit of the survivors.

Daniel Coxe mentions, in his description of the English province of Carolana, that this year, 1678, a considerable number of persons went from New England, on a journey of discovery, and proceeded as far as New Mexico, four hundred and fifty miles beyond the Mississippi, and on their return rendered an account of their discoveries to the government of Boston, as is attested among many others by Colonel Dudley, then one of the

magistrates, and afterwards Governor of New England, and since Deputy
Governor of the Isle of Wight, under Lord Cutts.

Lasalle, accompanied by the prince's protege and thirty colonists, among
whom were useful mechanics, landed at Quebec on the 15th of September,
1678, and proceeded without tarrying, to the entrance of lake Ontario, then
called Frontenac.   He immediately employed his men, in rebuilding the
fort, and put a barque of forty tons on the stocks.   The expedition with
which the fort and vessel were completed, gave to the colonial government
a high idea of his activity.   He was a man of genius, enterprise and
perserverance, firm and undaunted.   Power rendered him harsh, capricious
and haughty.   He was ambitious of fame; but this did not render him
inattentive to pecuniary advantages.

The barque being launched, Lasalle thought of nothing but trade and
discoveries, and left the fort on the 18th of November.   After a tedious
and dangerous passage, he reached a village called Onontarien, where he
purchased provisions, and proceeded to one of the Iroquois, near the falls
of Niagara.   He stayed but one night there : next morning he went nine
miles higher up, where selecting a convenient spot, he traced the lines of
a fort, and set his men to work : but observing this gave umbrage to the
Indians, he desisted; to preserve however what was already done, he
surrounded it with a palisade.

The season being now far advanced and the cold very severe, he deemed
it best to place his men in winter quarters, and sent a party to reconnoitre
the way to the Illinois; leaving the rest at Niagara, with the Chevalier de
Tonti, he returned to fort Frontenac.   In the spring he came back with a
considerable stock of merchandise, provisions and ammunition : but his
vessel was wrecked on approaching the shore; most of the lading was
however saved, and put on board of another barque, which his men had
constructed during the winter.

He now dispatched the chevalier with a few men to explore the shores
and country on the northeast side of lake Erie, then called Conti.   The
chevalier, after performing this service, passed to lake Huron, and landed
on the northern shore.   He there heard of the party who had gone
towards the Illinois; they had passed higher up.   After viewing the
country he returned to Niagara.   Lasalle had sold all his goods, and was
gone for a new supply; on his return he brought, besides merchandise, a
large stock of provisions and three recollet monks to minister to the
spiritual wants of his people.   The whole party now crossed 'lake Erie
without accident, but were detained for a long time by tempestuous
weather at Michillimackinac.   Lasalle took a view of the isthmus, traded
with the Indians, and laid the foundation of a fort.   The chevalier
proceeded northeasterly, in search of some men who had deserted, and to
obtain a better knowledge of the land in those parts.   He went ashore
near a strait called St. Mary, and following the coast, reached a river
which runs from the lake, and after a circuit of two hundred miles falls
into the St. Lawrence.   After a ramble of eight days he returned to his
boat, and reaching the point of the lake, took the southern pass, and
landed near a plantation of the Jesuits, where he found the men he was
in quest of, and prevailed on them to go back to the party.

In the meanwhile, Lasalle had in the latter part of September, crossed
the lakes Huron and Michigan, then called Tracy and Orleans, and landed
in the bay of the Puants on the 8th of October.   From thence he had

sent back the barque to Niagara loaded with furs and skins. Equally attentive to the improvement of his fortune by commerce, and the acquisition of fame by prosecuting his discoveries he proceeded in canoes with seventeen men to the Little Miami, which he reached on the first of November. He there carried on some trade with the natives whom he induced to put themselves under the protection of his sovereign, and with their consent took formal possession of their country for the crown of France—erecting a fort near the mouth of the stream.

The chevalier though impatient of joining his leader had been compelled by contrary weather and want of provisions to put ashore. His men were fatigued and refused to proceed till they had taken some rest. They gathered acorns and killed deer. The chevalier, taking the boat, committed himself to the waves, promising shortly to return for them; after being tossed during six days by a tempest, he reached the fort Lasalle was building on the Little Miami.

In expressing his pleasure at the return of the chevalier the chief observed it would have been much greater if he had seen also the men, who were left behind. This kind of reproof induced the former, as soon as he had rested a while, to return for these men. He had hardly left land when a storm arose and cast him ashore; dragging his boat along he reached the spot from whence he had started. Calm being restored on the lake, the whole party re-embarked and soon joined Lasalle who was much pleased at this addition to his force, viewing it as essential to the completion of his plan. Little did he think these men would prove a source of vexation and distress and a great obstruction to his views.

He had been successful in his trade, and the fort he had just completed enabled him to keep the Indians in awe, and command the entrance of the lake; he now determined on prosecuting his journey three hundred miles further into the country of the Illinois. Leaving ten men in the new fort he proceeded up the river with the rest, and after a passage of four days reached the stream that now bears the name of that tribe, and to which he gave that of Seignelay.

Lasalle had now forty men besides the three friars and the chevalier. Advancing by small journeys and making frequent excursions to view the country, he came about Christmas to a village of nearly five hundred cabins. It was entirely deserted : the cabins were open and at the mercy of the traveller. Each was divided into two apartments generally and coarsely built; the outside covered with mud and the inside with mats. Under each was a cellar full of corn; an article which the French greatly needed, and of which they did not neglect the opportunity of supplying themselves. Pursuing their way ninety miles further they came to a lake about twenty miles in circumference in which they found a great deal of fish. Crossing it they found themselves again in the current of the river and came to two Indian camps. On perceiving the party, the natives sent their women and children into the woods, and ranged themselves in battle array, on each side of the stream. Lasalle having put his men in a posture of defence, one of the Indian chiefs advanced, and asked who they were and what was their object in thus coming among them. Lasalle directed his interpreter to answer the party were French, their object was to make the God of heaven known to the natives, and offer them the protection of the king of France, and to trade with them. The Illinois tendered their pipes to their visitors and received them with great cordiality. The French gave them brandy and some tools of husbandry, in return for the provisions taken in their village. Pleased at this token of good faith, the Indians desired Lasalle to tarry and allow them to entertain him and his men. The women and children came forward, and venison and dried buffalo meat with roots and fruit were presented, and three days were spent in convivial mirth.

With the view of impressing his hosts with awe, Lasalle made his people fire two volleys of musketry. The wonder excited by this unexpected thunder had the desired effect. It was improved by the erection of a fort near the river. Uneasy at his being without intelligence of the barque he had sent to Niagara, richly laden with furs and peltries, and at an appearance of discontent which forebode mutiny among his men, he gave the fort the name of Creve Cœur, Heart Break.

Till now his journey had been fortunate : he had carried his discoveries to the distance of fifteen hundred miles. Forts had been erected at reasonable distances to mark and preserve the possession he had taken of the country. The Indian nations had all willingly or otherwise yielded to his views : the most refractory had suffered him to pass. But his men appeared now tired down, from the length of a journey, the issue of which appeared uncertain, and displeased to spend their time in deserts among wild men ; always without guides, often without food. They broke out in murmurs against the projector and leader of a fatiguing and perilous ramble. His quick penetration did not allow anything to escape him. He soon discovered their discontent and the mischievous designs of some of them, and exerted himself to avert the impending storm. Assurance of good treatment, the hope of glory, and the successful example of the Spaniards were laid before his men to calm their minds. Some of the discontented who had gained an ascendency over part of the rest, represented to them how idle it was to continue the slaves of the caprice and the dupes of the visions and imaginary hopes of a leader who considered the distresses they had borne, as binding them to bear others. They asked whether they could expect any other reward, for protracted slavery, than misery and indigence, and what could be expected at the end of a journey, almost to the confines of the earth, and inaccessible seas, but the necessity of returning poorer and more miserable than when they began it. They advised, in order to avert the impending calamity, to return while they had sufficient strength ; to part from a man who sought his own and their ruin ; and abandon him to his useless and painful discoveries. They adverted to the difficulty of a return while their leader by his intelligence and his intrigues, had insured, at the expense of their labors and fatigues, the means of overtaking and punishing them as deserters. They asked whither they could go, without provisions or resources of any kind. The idea was suggested of cutting the tree by the root, ending their misery by the death of the author of it, and thus availing themselves of the fruits of their labors and fatigues. The individuals who were ready to give their assent to this proposal, were not in sufficient number. It was, however, determined to endeavor to induce the Indians to rise against Lasalle, in the hope of reaping the advantage of the murder, without appearing to have participated in it.

The heads of the mutineers approached the natives with apparent concern and confidence, told them that, grateful for their hospitality, they were alarmed at the danger which threatened them ; that Lasalle had entered into strong engagements with the Iroquois, their greatest enemies; that he had advanced into their country to ascertain their strength, build a fort to keep them in subjection, and his meditated return to Fort Frontenac had no other object than to convey to the Iroquois the information he had gained, and invite them to an irruption, while his force among the Illinois was ready to co-operate with them.

Too ready an ear was given to these allegations; Lasalle discovered instantly a change in the conduct of the Indians, but not at first its cause. He was successful in his endeavors to obtain a disclosure of it. He communicated to the Indians the grounds he had of suspecting the perfidy of some of his men. He asked how impossible it was that he could connect himself with the Iroquois. He said he considered that nation as a perfidious one, and there could be neither credit nor safety in an alliance with these savages, thirsting for human blood, without faith, law or humanity, and instigated only by their brutality and interest. He added, he had declared himself the friend of the Illinois, and opened his views to them on his arrival among them.

The smallness of his force precluded the belief of an intention in him to subdue any Indian tribe, and the ingenuous calmness with which he spoke, gained him credit; so that the impression made by some of his men on the Indians, appeared totally effaced.

This success was, however, of small duration. An Indian of the Mascoutans, (a neighboring tribe) called Mansolia, an artful fellow, was engaged by the Iroquois, to induce the Illinois to cut off the French. He loitered till night came on, in the neighborhood of the camp; then entering it, stopping at different fires, and having made presents to, and collected the big men, he opened the subject of his mission. He began by observing that the common interest of all the Indian tribes, but the particular one of his and the Illinois, had induced his countrymen to depute him to the latter, to consult on the means of averting an impending calamity; that the French made rapid strides in their attempt to subjugate every nation from the lakes to the sea; employing not only their own men, but the Indians themselves; that their alliance with the Iroquois was well known, and the fort they had erected among the Illinois was only a prelude to further encroachments, as soon as they were joined by their confederates; and if they were suffered to remain unmolested, it would soon be too late to resist, and the evil prove without a remedy; but while they were so small in number and that of the Illinois was so superior, they might be easily destroyed and the blow they meditated warded off.

This fellow's suggestions, deriving strength from their coincidence with those of Lasalle's men, had the desired effect. The suspicions which Lasalle's address and candor had allayed, were awakened, and the head men spent the night in deliberation.

In the morning, all the desultory hopes he had built on the apparent return of confidence, vanished on his noticing the cold reserve of some of the chiefs, and the unconcealed distrust and indignation of others. He vainly sought to discover the immediate cause of the change. He knew not whether it would not be better to entrench himself in the fort. Alarmed and surprised, but unable to remain in suspense, he boldly advanced into the midst of the Indians, collected in small groups, and speaking their language sufficiently to be understood, he asked whether

11

he would ever have to begin and ever see diffidence and distrust on their brows. He observed he had parted with them the preceding eve in peace and friendship, and he now found them armed and some of them ready to fall on him: he was naked and unarmed in the midst of them, their ready and willing victim, if he could be convicted of any machination against them.

Moved at his open and undaunted demeanor, the Indians pointed to the deputy of the Mascoutans, sent to apprise them of his scheme and connection with their enemies. Rushing boldly towards him, Lasalle, in an imperious tone, demanded what token, what proof existed of this alleged connection. Mansolia, thus pressed, replied, that in circumstances, in which the safety of a nation was concerned, full evidence was not always required to convict suspicious characters; the smallest appearances often sufficed to justify precautions; and as the address of the turbulent and seditious consisted in the dissimulation of their schemes, that of the chiefs of a nation did in the prevention of their success; in the present circumstances, his past negotiations with the Iroquois, his intended return to Fort Frontenac, and the fort he had just built, were sufficient presumptions to induce the Illinois to apprehend danger, and take the steps necessary to prevent their fall into the snare he seemed to prepare.

Lasalle replied, it behooved the Illinois to prepare means of defence; but not against the French, who had come among them to protect and unite them in an alliance with the other tribes, under the patronage of the king of France; that the Iroquois had already subjugated the Miamis, Quichapoos and the Mascoutans, they now sought to add the Illinois to these nations; but they durst not make the attempt while they were connected with the French, and with the view of depriving them of the advantage, they derived from their union, they had made use of an individual of a conquered tribe as an emissary, greatly apprehending little credit would be given to one of their own; that all the intercourse he had with the Iroquois, was the purchase of a few skins; that he had built Fort Frontenac and another on the Miami to arrest their progress (a circumstance that excited their jealousy) and Fort Crevecœur was erected to protect the Illinois, and such of his men as remained with them.

His uniform candor, since he came among the Illinois, gained him credit with them; and Mansolia at last confessed the Iroquois had caused the rumor of his connection with them to be spread, in order to excite distrust against him among the Illinois.

A good understanding being now restored, Lasalle finding himself on a stream that led to the Mississippi, divided his men into two parties; one of which was to ascend the great river, reconnoitre the country near its shores, visit the tribes below, as far as the sea, and enter into alliances with them. The other party was to remain in the fort.

Some of his men, seeing him making preparations for his departure, and finding it impossible to counteract his views, determined on destroying him. Accordingly, on Christmas day, they threw poison into the kettle, in which his dinner was preparing, expecting, that if they could get rid of him and his principal officers, they could obtain all the goods and other property in the fort. The scheme was very near being successful. A few minutes after the officers rose from the table, they were attacked with convulsions and cold sweats. Suspecting what had happened, they took theriack instantly, and this attention prevented the consequences of the dire attempt. These wretches, perceiving their conduct could not pass unnoticed, fled into the woods, and escaped the pursuit of their commander.

Dacan was selected for the command of the party, which was intended for the expedition to the Mississippi. Father Louis Hennepin, attended it as chaplain; it left Fort Crevecœur on the twenty-eighth of February, 1680. Descending the river of the Illinois to the Mississippi, Dacan ascended the latter stream to the forty-sixth degree of northern latitude, where his progress was stopped by a fall, to which he gave the name of St. Anthony, which it still retains. There the party was attacked and defeated by a body of the Sioux, and led into captivity. They did not experience much ill treatment, and were at last enabled to effect their escape, by the aid of some French traders from Canada. On regaining their liberty, they floated down the river to the sea, according to some accounts, and according to others to the river of Arkansas, and returned to Fort Crevecœur.

The year 1680 is remarkable for the grant of Charles the second, to William Penn of the territory that now constitutes the states of Pennsylvania and Delaware. The grantee, who was one of the people called Quakers, imitating the example of Gulielm Usseling and Roger Williams, disowned a right to any part of the country included within his charter, till the natives voluntarily yielded it on receiving a fair consideration. There exists not any other example of so liberal a conduct towards the Indians of North America, on the erection of a new colony. The date of Penn's charter is the twentieth of February.

Lasalle had remained in Fort Crevecœur after the departure of his men under Dacan, until the fall, and having given the command of its small garrison to the Chevalier de Tonti, left it for Fort Frontenac early in November. On the third day of his march he reached the first village of the Illinois. Noticing a beautiful situation in the neighborhood of several tribes, the Miamis, Outagemis, the Kickapoos, the Ainous and Mascoutans, he determined on building a fort on an eminence which commanded the country, as a means of keeping the Indians in awe, and a stopping place or retreat for his countrymen. While he was there, two men whom he had sent in the fall to Michillimachinac, in order to procure intelligence of a barque which he had ordered to be built there, joined him. They reported that they had not been able to obtain any information. In fact, they had set fire to her, after having sold her lading to the Iroquois; a circumstance which Lasalle strongly suspected. He sent them to the chevalier with a plan of the intended fort, and directions to come and execute it. He now proceeded on his way towards Fort Frontenac.

The chevalier had hardly arrived and began the fort before the officer he had left at the head of the garrison of Fort Crevecœur, sent to apprise him that the two men, lately come from Michillimachinac, having found associates among the soldiers and pillaged the fort and fled into the woods; leaving only seven or eight men who had refused to join them, This induced the chevalier to return. He found Fort Crevecœur entirely destitute, and took measures to conceal this misfortune from the Indians and to make it known to Lasalle.

A large party of the Iroquois fell on the Illinois, a circumstance which induced some of the latter to apprehend that there might be some truth in the report of an alliance between their enemy and the French. The chevalier having no force to assist the Illinois, successfully afforded them his good offices as a mediator with the aids of fathers Gabriel and Zenobe, who had remained with him.   It was believed in Canada that the Iroquois had been excited by the English at Albany and the enemies of Lasalle.

Charles the second having disowned the invasion of Acadie in 1674, and it having been accordingly restored to the French with the Fort of Pentagoet, and that of the river St. John, a small settlement had been formed at Port Royal.   The English had built a fort between the rivers Kennebeck and Pentagoet, which they had called Penkuit.   The Abenaquis claimed the country on which it stood and complained of its erection.   The English induced the Iroquois to fall on these Indians, who being unable at once to withstand these white and red enemies reconciled themselves to the former.   The English being so far successful invaded Acadie and took the forts at Pentagoet and the river St. John.   Valliere, who commanded at Port Royal, could not prevent the inhabitants from surrendering that place.   Thus were the French once more driven from the country.

Lasalle, in the meanwhile, arrived at Fort Crevecœur and placed a garrison of fifteen men there, under a trusty officer, and proceeded up with workmen to finish the other which he called Fort St. Louis.   Leaving the workmen in it, he hastened to meet the chevalier at Michillimachinac, which he reached on the fifteenth of August.   After having refreshed himself and his men for a few days, he set off with the chevalier and father Zenobe for Fort Frontenac.   After a day's sail he reached a village of the Iroquois where he traded for peltries, and leaving his two companions there he proceeded to the fort from whence he sent a barque loaded with merchandise, provisions and ammunition and a number of recruits.   The chevalier and the father went in her to the neighborhood of the falls of Niagara, where taking her lading over land to lake Erie, after a short navigation they landed on the shores of the Miami.   Here the chevalier exchanged some goods for corn, and the party increased their provision of meat by the chase; and were joined by a few Frenchmen, and a number of Indians of the Abenaquis, Loop and Quickapoos.

They here tarried till the latter part of November, when Lassalle having joined them, they ascended the river to the mouth of the Chicagou, and went up to a portage of a mile that led them to the river of the Illinois.   They spent the night near a large fire, the cold being extremely intense.   In the morning, the water courses being all frozen, they proceeded to an Indian village in which they staid for several days.   After visiting Fort St. Louis and Fort Crevecœur, the weather softening, they floated down the river of the Illinois to the Mississippi, which they entered on the second of February.

The party stopped a while at the mouth of the Missouri, and on the following day reached a village of the Tamoas, the inhabitants of which had left their houses to spend the winter in the woods.   They made a short stay at the mouth of the Ohio, floating down to the Chickasaw bluffs, one of the party going into the woods, lost his way.   This obliged Lasalle to stop.   He visited the Indians in the neighborhood, and built a fort as a resting place for his countrymen navigating the river.   At the solicitation of the Chickasaw chiefs, he went to their principal village, attended by several of his men.   They were entertained with much cordiality, and the Indians approved of his leaving a garrison in the fort he was building. The Chickasaws were a numerous nation, able to bring two thousand men into the field. Presents were reciprocally made, and the French and Indians parted in great friendship. Lasalle, on reaching his fort, was much gratified to find the man who was missing. He left him to finish the fort, and to command its small garrison. His name was Prudhomme; it was given to the fort—and the bluff, on which the white banner was then raised, to this day is called by the French *ecor a Prudhomme*. This is the first act of formal possession taken by the French nation of any part of the shores of the Mississippi. The spot was, however, included within the limits of the territory granted by Charles the first to Sir Robert Heath, and by Charles the second to Lord Clarendon and his associates.

Lasalle continued his route in the latter part of February, and did not land during the three first days. On the fourth he reached a village of the Cappas. As he advanced towards the landing, he heard the beating of drums. This induced him to seek the opposite shore, and to throw up a small work of defence; soon after a few Indians came across; Lasalle sent one of his men to meet them with a calumet, which was readily accepted. They offered to conduct the party to their village, promising them safety and a good supply of provisions. The invitation was accepted, and two Indians went forward to announce the approach of the French. A number of the chiefs came to the shore to meet the guests, and lead them to the village; where they were lodged in a large cabin, and supplied with bear skins to lie on. The object of Lasalle's expedition being inquired into, he told his hosts he and his men were subjects of the king of France, who had sent them to reconnoitre the country, and offer to the Indians his friendship, alliance and protection. Corn and smoked buffalo meat were brought in, and the French made presents of suitable goods. When Lasalle took leave, two young men were given him as guides to the Arkansas.

This tribe dwelt about twenty-five miles lower. They had three villages; the second was at the distance of twenty-five miles from the first. They gave the French a friendly reception. In the last village many Indians being assembled, Lasalle, with their assent, took possession of the country for his sovereign, fixing the arms of France on a lofty tree, and causing them to be saluted by a discharge of musketry. The awe which this unexpected explosion excited, increased the respect of the natives for their visitors, whom they earnestly pressed to tarry.

On the day after their departure, the French saw, for the first time, alligators, some of which were of an enormous size.

The next nation towards the sea was the Taensas, who dwelt at the distance of about one hundred and eighty miles from the Arkansas. On approaching their first village, Lasalle dispatched the Chevalier de Tonti towards it. It stood on a lake, at some distance from the river. The chief received the chevalier kindly, and came with him to meet Lasalle. The healths of the king of France and of the chief of the Taensas were drank in this interview, under a volley of musketry. A supply of provisions was obtained; some presents were made to the natives, and the French departed and floated down the river.

On the second day, a pirogue approached from the shore, apparently to reconnoitre the party. The chevalier was sent to chase her, and as he came near, about one hundred Indians appeared on the shore with bent bows. Lasalle, on seeing them, recalled the chevalier; and the French went and camped on the opposite shore, presenting their muskets. The Indians now laid their bows on the ground, and the chevalier went over with a calumet. Lasalle seeing it accepted, came over, and was led by the Indians to their village. The chief expressed much joy at the sight of the French, and detained them a few days. At their departure, he made his people carry dried fruit, corn and venison to their boats. Lasalle gave him a sword, an axe, a kettle and a few knives. After firing a salute, the French proceeded to a village of the Coroas, twenty-five miles further.

On the twenty-seventh of March, they encamped at the mouth of Red River.

Further down, they fell in with a party of the Quinipissas who were fishing, and who on perceiving them went ashore, where a drum was beaten and a number of men made their appearance armed with bows. Lasalle directed some of his men to advance, but they were briskly repulsed. Four Indians, whom he had taken as guides at the last village, advanced with as little success, and no further attempt to land was made.

Two days after, the French came to a village of the Tangipaos. It was entirely deserted and despoiled of everything. Several dead bodies lay in heaps. The scene was too disgusting to allow the party to stop.

After descending the river several days, Lasalle took notice that the water of the Mississippi became brackish, and shortly after the sea was discovered. This was on the seventh of April.

Lasalle sailed along the coast for awhile, and returning to the mouth of the river, caused a *Te Deum* to be sung. The boats were hauled aground, recaulked, and a few temporary huts erected. A cross was placed on a high tree, with the escutcheon of France, in token of the solemn possession taken for the king. Lasalle called the river St. Louis and the country Louisiana.

Parties of the Tangipaos and Quinipissas came on the next day to hunt buffaloes, which were in abundance in the neighboring cane brakes. The Indians were successful in their chase, and presented the French with three of these animals.

After resting a few days, the party set off. It now consisted of sixty persons, white and red. They were soon tired of stemming the current which was now very strong, and proceeded along the shore to the Quinipissas. As these Indians had manifested no hospitable disposition, Lasalle deemed it prudent to take some precautions. Accordingly, four Indians were sent forward; they returned in the evening with as many Quinipissas women, who were sent back in the morning with presents, and desired to inform their countrymen, the French requested nothing but a supply of provisions and their friendship; and were willing liberally to pay for what they might obtain. A few hours after, four chiefs came with provisions, and requested Lasalle to stop with his men in their village. On their arrival there, water fowls and fruit were given them, and at might they encamped between the village and the river. In the morning, their treacherous hosts attacked them, but they did not find them asleep. Lasalle had constantly a sentry, and warmly repelled the assailants. Five of them were killed, and the rest fled. After this blow, Lasalle preceeded on without stopping, till he reached the Natchez, who were much pleased at seeing the scalps of the Quinipissas in the hands of the Indians accompanying him.

The French, being invited to an entertainment, noticed with surprise that not a woman of their hosts was among them. A moment after, a number of armed men appeared. Lasalle immediately arose and ordered his men to take their arms. The head man requested him not to be alarmed, and directed the armed ones of his nation to halt; informing his guests they were a party, who had been skirmishing with the Iroquois, and assured them that no individual of his nation harbored any other sentiment towards the French, but that of esteem and friendship. Notwithstanding this assurance, the French set off in the belief that Lasalle's quick motion had averted a blow.

The Taensas and Arkansas received the party, with as much cordiality as when they went down. The French left the latter tribe on the twelfth of May, and stopped at Fort Prudhomme. Lasalle found himself too unwell to proceed: he therefore sent the Chevalier de Tonti forward, with twenty men, French and Indians. His indisposition detained him among the Chickasaws for nearly two months, and he joined the chevalier at Michill-imachinac, in the latter part of September. They spent a few days together there, and the latter went to take the command of Fort St. Louis of the Illinois, and the former continued his route to Quebec.

The Count de Frontenac had sailed for France some time before Lasalle's arrival. The relation the latter gave of his expedition, excited great joy in Canada. He was impatient to announce his success to his sovereign, and took shipping for France in October.

CHAPTER V.

LE FEVRE DE LA BARRE, the successor of Count de Frontenac in the government of New France, and de Meules, the new intendant, landed at Quebec in the spring of 1683.

Lasalle was received at court with all the attention due to a man who had planned and carried into execution an enterprise so useful to the nation; and the Marquis de Seignelay, who had succeeded Colbert, his father, in the ministry of the Marine, gave directions some time after for the preparation of an expedition, at la Rochelle, in order to enable Lasalle to plant a French colony on the banks of the Mississippi.

The vessels destined for this service were the king's ship the Joli, the frigate the Aimable, the brig la Belle, and the ketch St. Francis. The command of them was given to Beaujeau,

Twelve young gentlemen accompanied Lasalle as volunteers; a company of fifty soldiers was given him, and the king granted a free passage, and made a liberal advance in money, provisions and implements of husbandry to twelve families who consented to emigrate. A number of useful mechanics were also embarked, with some other individuals. In order to provide for the spiritual wants of these people, five clergymen, one of whom was Lasalle's brother, were sent. Thus, besides the officers and crews, about two hundred and fifty persons accompanied Lasalle.

Beaujeau did not, however, weigh anchor till the fourth of July, 1684. He shaped his course for Hispaniola; but before he reached it, a storm scattered his small fleet. The Aimable and the Belle reached together Petit Goave, where the Joli had arrived before them. The St. Francis, being a dull sailer, was overtaken and captured by two Spanish privateers. A severe indisposition detained Lasalle on shore for several days; during which, many of the people, yielding to the incitement of a warm climate, favored by the want of occupation, became the victims of intemperance and consequent disease; and several died.

The fleet set sail on the twenty-fifth of November, and was for many days becalmed; on the ninth of December it was before the Cape *de los corrientes* in the island of Cuba, and on the twenty-seventh, their observation showed them to be in the twenty-eighth degree of northern latitude. Their reckoning announced the approach of land, and towards sun down they found bottom in thirty-two fathoms. Lasalle and Beaujeu determined on sailing W. N. W., till the water shoaled to six fathoms, and on the twenty-ninth they saw land at the apparent distance of six leagues.

There was no person in the fleet acquainted with the coast. Lasalle noticing a strong current easterly thought himself near the Apalaches. The vessels continued sailing in the same direction, and on new year's day the anchor was cast in six fathoms, the land appearing distant about four leagues. Two boats were ordered ashore. Lasalle went in one of them. He had hardly landed when the wind growing fresher and fresher he was compelled to return; the other boat was behind and followed him back. The land was flat and woody. He took an observation and found himself in twenty-nine, ten.

The weather was hazy, and the wind continued high. The coast appeared lined with battures and breakers. Sailing again W. N. W., as soon as the wind abated they vainly sought for several days the mouth of the Mississippi. On the thirteenth they sent ashore for water; a number of Indians came along the beach; the wind was from the sea. The fleet cast anchor within half a league from the shore. The natives seemed by gestures to seek to induce the French to land. They showed their bows, then laid them on the ground, and walked composedly along with arms akimbo. A white handkerchief was waved at the end of a musket, as an invitation to approach. Throwing a log into the water they swam aboard each keeping one arm on the log.

Lasalle attempted in vain to make himself understood. The natives pointed to hogs, fowls and the hide of a cow, apparently desirous to convey the idea of their having such animals. Small presents were made which seemed to gratify them much. When they went back, the shallowness of the water prevented the close approach of the boats, the Indians swam away. The French thought the natives gave them to understand there was a great river near, which occasioned the battures.

Lasalle now began seriously to apprehend he had passed the Mississippi, and proposed to Beaujeu to sail back. The naval commander was of a different opinion and nothing was determined on for several days. At last, Lasalle selecting half a dozen of men, undertook to seek the mighty stream by a march along the shore. The weather was extremely hazy, the land low, flat and sandy, destitute of grass, and fresh water was only to be found in stagnant pools. He noticed numerous tracks of deer, and saw a great number of water fowls; having wandered from daybreak till three o'clock, Lasalle began to despair, and brought his men back; he spent several days in vain attempts to induce Beaujeu to come to some determination.

He next landed one hundred and twenty men, with the view of sending them along the shore, while the Belle sailed in the same direction, till they reached the river he was in quest of. He gave the command of them to Joutel, who marched at their head on the fourth of February, and on the eighth came to a wide stream, on the banks of which he halted for the Belle. Tired of waiting, Joutel had ordered a raft to be built to cross the stream, when the Joli and the Belle hove in sight, and Lasalle came soon after with the Aimable. Beaujeu now ordered out the boats of the three vessels to sound on the bar and in the channel, which he directed to be staked. Finding there was a sufficiency of water, it was thought best to bring the shipping over the bar. The Joli and the Belle accordingly came in and anchored in safety, but the Aimable struck on the bar, and soon after went ashore. It was believed that design, not accident, had occasioned this misfortune; Aigran, who commanded her, having refused to receive on board a pilot of the Belle, sent by Lasalle, to follow the stakes or permit an anchor to be cast, when the vessel struck. During the night the wind rose and the waves became violent; she went to pieces with a boat of the Joli, which had been used in saving part of her lading, and had been left fastened to the wreck. Lasalle had to lament, with the loss of this vessel, that of a quantity of provisions, ammunition, and implements of husbandry. He saved a few barrels of flour, wine and brandy, and some powder.

A party of Indians came to the camp; he made them some trifling presents, with which they appeared much pleased. At their request, he visited their village, consisting of about fifty cabins, at a small distance from the shore. Other parties on the following day hovered around the camp, without venturing to attack it. They captured and carried off two white men who had straggled to a distance. A party went in pursuit of them, and compelled the surrender of the prisoners. The Indians returned a few nights afterwards in great numbers, and, just at the dawn of day, the camp was assailed by a volley of arrows, which killed two and wounded several men in the camp. An instant and rapid flight enabled the Indians to avoid pursuit.

On the sixth of February, 1685, on the demise of Charles the second of England, at the age of fifty-five, without issue, his brother, James the second, succeeded him.

With the view of increasing the commerce of New France, and affording to the nobility of Canada the means of extending their fortunes, Louis the fourteenth, by an edict of the month of March of the same year, permitted them to engage in trade, by land and sea, without thereby committing any act of derogation.

This wise measure at home was followed by one of a different character in the colony. Canada was greatly distressed by the scarcity of a circulating medium, universally felt in all new settlements, and Champigny de Norroy, who succeeded de Meules in the intendancy, sought relief in an emission of card money, which was put into circulation, under an ordinance of the governor and intendant.

Each card bore the stamp of the king's arms, and its value was signed by the colonial treasurer, and had the coats of arms of the governor and intendant impressed on wax.

Beaujeu sailed for France on the fifteenth of March, in the Joli, taking with him the captain and most of the crew of the Aimable. He refused to land a number of cannon balls, which he had brought for the colony, on the pretence that they were in the bottom of his ship, and he could not unload her without risk. He left twelve pieces of cannon, but not a single ball.

After his departure, Lasalle occupied himself in building a fort at the western extremity of the bay, which now bears the name of St. Bernard, and garrisoned it with one hundred men. Leaving Morangies, his nephew, in command there, he set off with a party of fifty men, accompanied by the abbe de Lasalle, his brother, and two recollet friars, father Zenobe, who had descended the Mississippi with him a few years before, and father Maxime. His object was to seek for the mouth of the Mississippi river, at the bottom of the bay. The captain of the Belle was directed to sound this estuary in his boats, and to bring the vessel as far as he could; he followed the coast to a point which was called Point Hurier, after an officer who was left there with a few men to throw up a small work. The party now proceeded to the eastern extremity of the bay, and to a considerable distance beyond, and returned without finding the Mississippi.

In the middle of April, Lasalle established a new post sixteen miles up a river, which from the number of cows he found on its bank he called Cow river; it is believed to be the one called by the Spaniards *Rio Colorado de Texas*. A party of Indians came to attack him; but they were repulsed.

Towards the latter part of the month, Lasalle returned to the fort in which he had left Morangies. On Easter Sunday, divine service was performed with great solemnity, every one receiving the sacrament.

This fort and the small work thrown up by Hurier were now abandoned and demolished; all the colonists removing to the new settlement, with all their effects. The ground was prepared for cultivation, and a number of houses were erected for common and private use. A fort was built, in which twelve pieces of cannon were mounted, and a large subterraneous magazine made. The fort was called Fort St. Louis.

In the meanwhile, the Chevalier de Tonti having received intelligence from Canada of the departure of a fleet from France, in which Lasalle was bringing colonists to the Mississippi, left the fort at the Illinois, in order to meet his former chief. The Indians everywhere greeted the chevalier, who reached the mouth of the river without being able to receive any information of his countrymen. He staid there several weeks, and the boats which he sent towards the east and west in search of Lasalle, returned without any account of him. Despairing of being more successful if he staid longer, he reluctantly reascended the stream. The tree, on which Lasalle had two years before placed the escutcheon of France, had been uprooted in a storm, and the chevalier raised another token of the possession taken for the king, on the banks of the river, about twenty miles from the sea. Mortified and chagrined, he progressed slowly, stopping in the villages on the way, endeavoring to obtain some account of the French colonists. All his attempts proved fruitless, and he reached his fort, among the Illinois, in the month of May.

During the fall, most of the colonists on *Rio Colorado* sickened and many died.

The Indians frequently came near the fort, and at times killed such of the French who strayed into the woods. Lasalle marched against them, with a party whom he had provided with a kind of wooden jackets, that protected them against arrows. He killed several Indians, and made some prisoners. A little girl about four years of age, who was then taken, was the first of the natives who received baptism in the colony.

Disease and the fatigues of this kind of warfare, interrupted so much the labors of agriculture, that but a scanty crop was made. The seed grain having been brought shelled was a circumstance that had its effect, in disappointing the hopes of the sower; wheat seldom coming well in virgin ground, when the seed has not been kept in the ear.

The captain of the Belle, having gone a hunting with half a dozen of his men, was surprised by a party of Indians, who slew them all. After paying the last duty to their bodies, Lasalle and his brother attended by twenty men, left the fort with the view of resuming the search of the Mississippi.

The bay he was on received a number of rivers, none of which was of such a depth or width, as allowed it to be considered as a branch of the mighty one. Lasalle visited them all. He was impeded in his progress by the difficulty of crossing them, by almost incessant rains, and the necessity, at every stage, to provide against a sudden attack. On the thirteenth of February, 1686, he came to so wide and deep a stream, that he suspected it to be that he was looking for. He threw up a light work on its banks, in which he placed nine men. Proceeding higher up, he came to a large village of Indians, where he was cordially received. From the information he received, he was convinced his conjecture was erroneous; after a further progress, he retrograded, took back his nine men, and returned to the settlement which he reached on the last day of May.

The Iroquois encouraged and aided by governor Dongan of New York, continued their irruptions on the frontier settlements of Canada, and Louis the fourteenth was induced, at the pressing solicitations of the colonists, to send a body of troops to their succor. Labarre being old and infirm, the Marquis de Denonville was sent to relieve him. In his first communication to the minister, which is of the eighth of May, 1686, this officer recommended the erection of a fort, with a garrison of four or five hundred men at Niagara, to shut out the English from the lakes; secure exclusively the fur trade to Canada, afford an asylum to the allied Indians, and deprive deserters from the king's troops of the facility of joining the English at Albany; who employed them as guides in military and commercial excursions among the tribes in alliance with the French.

The Marquis increased the garrison of Fort Frontenac, and furnished it abundantly with provisions and ammunition. This gave umbrage to governor Dongan, who wrote him the Iroquois considered this reinforcement as the prelude to the invasion of their country; that these Indians were the allies, nay the subjects of the English crown, and an act of hostility against them could only be viewed as an infraction of the peace which existed between France and England; that he was informed a fort was about to be erected at Niagara; a circumstance which surprised him the more, as the Marquis, though but lately arrived in America, could not well be supposed ignorant of that part of the country being within the province of New York.

The Marquis answered, that the consciousness of the Iroquois, that they deserved chastisement, could alone excite their apprehensions: however, the supplies sent to Fort Frontenac ought not to have alarmed these Indians, as there had always been a large garrison at that post, and the difficulty of supplying it rendered it necessary to improve every opportunity; that the governor was under an error as to the right of his sovereign to the country of the Iroquois; he ought to have known that the French had taken possession of it, long before any Englishman came to New York; that, however, as the kings of England and France were now at peace, it did not behoove their officers in America to enter into any altercation about their rights.

Louis the fourteenth having approved the emission of card money made in Canada during the preceding year, another emission was now prepared in Paris in which pasteboard was used instead of cards. An impression was made on each piece of the coin of the kingdom of the corresponding value.

Pasteboard proving inconvenient cards were again resorted to. Each had the flourish which the intendant usually added to his signature. He signed all those of the value of four livres and upwards, and those of six livres and above were also signed by the governor.

Once a year, at a fixed period, the cards were required to be brought to the colonial treasury, and exchanged for bills on the treasury-general of the marine, or his deputy at Rochefort. Those which appeared too ragged for circulation were burnt, and the rest again paid out of the treasury.

For awhile the cards were thus punctually exchanged once a year; but in course of time, bills ceased to be given for them. Their value which till then had been equal to gold, now began to diminish; the price of all commodities rose proportionally, and the colonial government was compelled, in order to meet the increased demands on its treasury, to resort to new and repeated emissions; and the people found a new source of distress in the means adopted for their relief.

The English colonies in America in the latter part of the seventeenth and the first of the eighteenth century, had also recourse to emissions of paper currency. They everywhere yielded at first a momentary relief. The currency borrowed its value from confidence; moderation might have preserved, but profusion almost universally destroyed it, and the depreciated paper proved a greater evil than that it was intended to remedy.

The earliest emissions in these colonies, date in those of New England of 1696, in New York of 1709, in New Jersey of 1720, in Pennsylvania of 1722, in Delaware of 1730, in North Carolina and Barbadoes of 1705, and in South Carolina of 1703. If the colonies of Maryland and Virginia, during the period of their dependence on the crown, had no paper currency (a circumstance which has not been ascertained) it was probably owing to their finding in tobacco, their staple commodity, the means of substituting the contract of exchange to that of sale. Merchants there kept their accounts in pounds of tobacco, and the fees of the colonial officers were by law fixed and made payable in that article.

A few days after the return of Lasalle to the fort, the Belle was cast ashore in a hurricane and bilged. The officer who commanded her, the chaplain and four of her crew, alone escaped. With her thirty-six barrels of flour, some wine and a quantity of merchandise were lost. She was the only vessel remaining in the colony, and would have been of vast service to Lasalle; he expected to have sailed in her to Hispaniola, in search of succor. On the loss of this last vessel he determined .to proceed to Fort St. Louis of the Illinois, in order to apprise government of his miscarriage and solicit farther aid.

Accompanied by his brother and nephew, by father Athanase, fifteen other Frenchmen and two trusty Indians, who had followed him from Canada, on the twenty-second of May, mass having been said to implore the benediction of heaven on his journey, he set off and travelled north-easterly, taking with him two canoes and two sleighs.

He crossed several streams, and saw large herds of buffaloes, among which were a few horses, so wild that they could not be caught without great address and much difficulty. Every night he took the precaution of surrounding his camp with poles, to guard against surprise. On the twenty-fifth, towards noon, he met with four Indians on horseback, of a tribe called the Quoaquis; their dress was chiefly of leather; they had boots, saddles and a kind of shield of the same material, and wooden stirrups; the bits of their bridles were of wolf or bear's teeth. They inquired who the party were, and being informed, invited them to their village.

Two days after, Lasalle crossed a river which he called Riber, from one of the party who was drowned in crossing it. Here he halted for six days; his men killed a buffalo, and salted and smoked the meat. Three days after he crossed another stream, which he called Hiens, after one of the party who sank into the mud and was drawn out with great difficulty.

Lasalle now altered his course, travelling due east. After a march of several days, he came to a tribe called the Biscatonges, where he obtained dressed buffalo skins, of which his men made moccasins, a kind of covering for the foot, much used by the Indians, and resembling a mitten or a glove without fingers. These Indians also supplied Lasalle with canoes; the two he had brought from the fort being already so crazy as to be of but little use.

On the following day, as the French approached a village, one of them shot a deer; this so terrified the Indians that they all fled. Lasalle ordered his men under arms as they entered the village. It consisted of about three hundred cabins; the wife of one of the chiefs was still in hers, being so old that she could not move. She was given to understand she had nothing to fear. Three of her sons, who had remained at a small distance, noticing the peaceable demeanor of the strangers, called back her countrymen, who immediately returned. They offered the calumet to, and entertained the French with much cordiality.

Unwilling to put too much confidence in these friendly appearances, Lasalle encamped at night, on the opposite side of a cane brake that encircled the village, and surrounded himself with poles as usual. These precautions proved timely; for during the night, a party of Indians, armed with arrows, approached. The rustling of the canes warning Lasalle, he gave them to understand, without quitting his entrenchment, that if they did not retire, he would order his men to fire. The night passed without any further disturbance, and in the morning the hosts and the guests parted with apparent marks of friendship.

Eight miles further, they came to a village of the Chinonoas. These Indians dwelt in the neighborhood of the Spaniards, who often came among and vexed them. They immediately recognized the French as being of another nation, by their language and mien; and their hate of the Spaniards, inspired them with the opposite sentiment for their present visitors, who were not long without letting their hosts know, they were at war with the Spaniards. The Indians pressed Lasalle to tarry, and accompany them on an expedition they were projecting against their troublesome neighbors. He excused himself on the smallness of his party, who were ill provided with arms. He was supplied with provisions, and took leave.

On the next day, Rica, the Indian servant of Lasalle, stopped suddenly, exclaiming he was a dead man; he immediately fell, and in a few minutes, swelled to an astonishing degree. He had been bitten by a rattlesnake. After the scarification of the wound, and the application of such herbs as his countrymen quickly pointed out, he was relieved. This accident detained the party during two days.

They next came to a wide river, which rendered it necessary to make a raft with canes and branches covered with hides. Lasalle, his nephew and two servants, ventured on it first. When they reached the middle of the stream, the violence of the current carried them out of sight of their companions. After floating thus for a couple of miles, the raft rested on a large tree which had fallen into the river, almost torn out by the roots. By pulling on its branches, they found the means of reaching the opposite shore. The rest of the party remained all the night and the following day in distressing uncertainty, They proceeded along the river, loudly calling their leader, and night came on without their being relieved; but in the morning, the calls being resumed, were soon answered by Lasalle from the opposite shore. A stronger raft was made, and the rest of the party crossed.

They now reached a village of the Cenis, having overtaken an Indian on horseback, who was returning to it. His wife sat behind him, and other horses followed, with the produce of his chase. He gave part of it to Lasalle, and preceded the party into the village, leaving them. Some of the chiefs came out to meet the French, who staid several days, and traded with their hosts for some horses. This was the largest settlement Lasalle had come to. It extended for upwards of twenty miles, interspersed with hamlets of ten or twelve cabins. These were large, often exceeding forty feet in length. Dollars were seen among the people, and many articles of furniture, as spoons, forks, plates, etc., which manifested they traded with the Spaniards. Horses were in great plenty, and the Indians very willing to part with a serviceable one, for an axe. Lasalle saw, in one of the cabins, a printed copy of one of the Pope's Bulls, exempting Mexicans from fast during the summer. The natives made a very good map of their country on pieces of bark, and showed they were within six days' march from the Spanish settlements.

After staying five or six days, Lasalle proceeded to the Nassonites, where he was received with much courtesy. It was perceivable that the Indians of this tribe, had much intercourse with the Spaniards; for when they saw father Athanase, they made the sign of the cross and kneeled, to give him to understand, they were acquainted with the ceremonies of the mass. Here, four men of the party deserted, attracted, as was believed, by the charms of some of the Cenis women.

Lasalle and his nephew fell dangerously ill. Two months elapsed before they felt themselves in a situation to travel. His ammunition now was exhausted, and he was at the distance of four hundred and fifty miles in a straight line from his fort. The party unanimously agreed to return. On their march back, one of them attempting to swim across a river was devoured by an alligator. They reached the fort on the seventeenth of October.

There was a considerable tract of land cleared, and under cultivation. Comfortable houses had been built, and gardens were to be seen near most of them; the settlement was in a flourishing condition, and the Indians in the immediate neighborhood were friendly.

After a stay of two months with the colonists, Lasalle determined on returning by the way of Canada to France, in order to solicit a reinforcement of husbandmen and mechanics. He set off in the beginning of the new year, accompanied by his brother and nephew, father Athanase and seventeen men. He took the same route as before. There were in the party, when they left the settlement, two brothers of the name of Lancelot. The younger, being weak and infirm, was unable to keep up, and was sent back on the second day; the elder was desirous to return also; but Lasalle, thinking the party too weak, refused his consent. The young man was met near the settlement by a party of Indians, who killed him. Intelligence of this misfortune reaching the party, the surviving brother, casting the blame on Lasalle, did not conceal his resentment; but vented it in threats. At length, it seemed to have subsided. After a march of about two months, provisions failing, this man with Liotot, the surgeon, Hiens and Duhault, were sent to kill buffaloes, and salt and smoke the meat. These persons, displeased with Lasalle and his nephew, who commanded this small detachment, plotted their destruction. In the evening of the seventeenth of March, Liotot dispatched Lasalle's nephew, his servant and an Indian, with an axe. His companions standing by, ready to defend him with their arms, had any resistance been made. Lasalle, missing his nephew, left the party with father Athanase, and retrograded. Meeting Lancelot, he inquired whither his nephew was; the wretch pointed to a spot over which a number of buzzards were hovering; as Lasalle advanced, he met with another of the accomplices, to whom he put the same question; but Duhault, who lay concealed in high grass, fired; the ball lodged in Lasalle's head; he fell and survived an hour only. This was on the nineteenth of March, 1687, near the western branch of Trinity river.

The murderers, joined by other malcontents, taking possession of the provisions, ammunition and everything that belonged to the deceased, compelled the rest of the party to continue with them. In a quarrel among themselves, two of them were killed, and the rest sought an asylum among the Indians.

Lasalle's brother, father Athanase and five others continued their route towards the Illinois. A few days after, de Monte, one of them, bathing in a river, was drowned. In the latter part of July, this small party reached the country of the Arkansas. They noticed a large cross fixed in the ground, near a house built like those of the French in Canada. Here they found two of their countrymen, Couture and Delaunay, natives of Rouen, who had come thither from the fort at the Illinois. Here the party learned that the Chevalier de Tonti, on his way to the mouth of the Mississippi, to meet Lasalle, had left six Frenchmen at the Arkansas; four of whom had returned to the Illinois. After staying some time with Couture and Delaunay, the travellers disposed of their horses and procured canoes, in which they ascended the Mississippi and the river of the Illinois to Fort St. Louis, which they reached on the fourth of

September. The Chevalier de Tonti was absent, and Bellefontaine, his lieutenant, commanded. The travellers thought it prudent to conceal the death of Lasalle; they staid but a few days in the fort, and proceeded, by the way of Michillimachinac. to Canada, and landed at Quebec on the ninth of October, and soon after took shipping for France.

CHAPTER VI.

DURING the fall of 1687, a party of the Iroquois fell on some of the Indians in alliance with the French, near Michillimachinac. Father Lamberville, the missionary at that post, was informed that this attack had been determined on at a meeting of deputies of several tribes, the chiefs of which had been lately convened at Albany, by the governor of New York, who had assured them the Marquis de Denonville meant to wage war against them: the governor advised them to begin it themselves by falling on the French or their allies, whenever they met them, as, not suspecting any attack, they would be found an easy prey. He promised that whatever might be the consequences, he never would forsake his red allies.

While the government of New York was provoking its Indians to hostilities against Canada, James the second was apparently pursuing quite a different line of conduct. The Marquis received a letter from the Minister, informing him that the cabinet of St. James had proposed to the Ambassador of France, a treaty of neutrality, between the subjects of the two crowns in North America; and its offers having been accepted, one had been concluded in the preceding fall. The Marquis was accordingly directed to have the treaty published throughout the colony and registered in the superior council, and to see it faithfully executed by the king's subjects in Canada.

By the fourteenth and fifteenth articles, it was agreed that the two sovereigns should send orders to their respective governors and other officers, to cause to be arrested and prosecuted as pirates, the captains and crews of all vessels, sailing without a commission, and any of the subjects of either king, sailing under one from a prince or state at war with him.

It does not appear that the English had any other view, than to lull the French into security; for they fell on Fort St. Anne, in Hudson's Bay; but Iberville, who commanded there, repelled the assailants, took one of their ships and burnt a house which they had erected on the sea-shore.

Louis the fourteenth, with the view of increasing the crews of his galleys, and avenging the ill treatment of his subjects who fell into the hands of the Iroquois, had directed the Marquis' predecessor to send over all those Indians taken in war, to be employed on board of the galleys at Marseilles. The Marquis, under this order, had the imprudence of decoying, through various pretences, a number of Iroquois chiefs, into Fort Frontenac, where he had them put in irons and afterwards sent over. This unfortunate step was disowned at court, but the Indians were not ordered back. The disavowal had the effect of emboldening the Iroquois who attributed this act of justice and humanity to the king's apprehension of exciting the resentment of their nation. It attached them the more to the English.

In the summer, these Indians becoming more and more troublesome, it was deemed necessary to march against them. The Chevalier de Vaudreuil, who had been sent to command the troops took the field. He encamped on the island of St. Helen, opposite that of Montreal, with eight hundred regulars and one thousand militia. Champigny de Norroy, the intendant, preceded the army to Fort Frontenac; the Marquis followed it. At the fort, he received a letter from the governor of New York, complaining bitterly of the French making war against the allies of his sovereign. At the same time a piece of information was received, showing that but little reliance was to be placed on the writer's apparently peaceable disposition. A party of sixty white men from Albany, attended by a number of Indians, and guided by a French deserter, were surprised carrying goods and ammunition to Michillimachinac. The officer commanding there, seized the goods and ammunition, made the English prisoners, and sent the deserter to the Marquis, who had him shot.

The army now moved to the river *des Sables*, and marched into the country of the enemy. After having safely passed through two defiles, it was attacked by a party of about eight hundred Iroquois, who, pouring a destructive fire on its van, ran to attack its rear, while another party repeated the charge in front. This threw the army in some confusion; but the allied Indians, better used to fight in the woods, stood together, till the French rallied to them. The regulars, to whom this kind of warfare was quite novel, were not so useful in this instance as the militia. The army, now collected, dispersed the Indians. The French had only six men killed: the Iroquois forty-five killed and sixty wounded. The Marquis now marched to and encamped in one of the largest villages of the enemy, which was found quite deserted, and every house in it was burnt. After rambling for ten days, and laying waste every settlement and destroying every plantation, the Marquis, finding his regulars and militia much weakened by fatigue and disease, and his Indians impatient of returning, gave up the pursuit and returned to Niagara, where he employed his men in building a fort.

In the fall an epidemic disease ravaged the colony. Fort Chambly and Fort Frontenac were attacked in November; although the Indians were repelled in both places, they committed great ravages on the plantations of the neighborhood, and burnt several houses.

They made proposals of peace, in 1688, the following year, on condition that their chiefs in Marseilles should be brought back. The Marquis willingly accepted these offers. The frontier settlers had been prevented, by the dread of new irruptions, from cultivating their fields. Dearth prevailed all over the colony, and the enemy was the more to be feared, that he had a powerful aid in the English at New York.

According to a census of this year, Canada had a population of eleven thousand two hundred and forty-nine persons.

James, attempting to establish popery, had become obnoxious to the people; he was cruel and oppressive, and his subjects, who, half a century before, had led his father to the scaffold, offered his crown to the prince of Orange, the husband of his eldest daughter.

William landed in England, on the fourth of November, 1688. James, terrified, abdicated his crown and fled to France. The Irish for awhile supported his cause; but William and Mary were soon after recognised as sovereigns of the three kingdoms.

13

The people left by Lasalle in Fort St. Louis, not receiving any succor from France, and their stock of ammunition being exhausted, were unable to defend themselves against the neighboring Indians. Disease made great havoc among them; in the meanwhile, the Viceroy of Mexico, in compliance with a standing article of his instructions, by Philip the second, enjoining the extermination of all foreigners who might penetrate into the Gulf of Mexico, directed an expedition to be formed at Cohaguilla, unders the orders of Don Alonzo de Leon, to scour the country and hunt out the French colonists, if any were still remaining. This officer, with a small force, arrived on the twenty-second of April, 1689, at Fort St. Louis, and on the twenty-fourth, at the entrance of the bay, where he found the hull of the French vessel that had been wrecked. He saw no white man at either place. Having heard, on his march, that some of Lasalle's companions were still wandering about the country, or had taken refuge among the Indians, he shaped his course towards the Assinais, but found no trace of those he was in quest of. It is said that Don Alonzo was courteously received by the Assinais, and gave these Indians the appellation of *Texas* or friends. A few years after, the Spaniards sent missionaries into this part of the country, and afterwards established military posts or *presidios* among these Indians. These missions or posts were the beginning of the Spanish settlements in the province of Texas.

The Count de Frontenac was now appointed governor general of New France. In his instructions, which bear date of the seventh of June, 1689, it is stated that the reciprocal and repeated attacks of the French and English in Acadie and Hudson's Bay, had induced the appointment of commissioners, on the part of the two crowns, to report on their respective pretensions; but, as the facts alleged by either party were not admitted by the other, the conferences had been suspended till they could be verified. In the meanwhile, the late revolution in England had put, at least for the present, an end to these negotiations. The count was, therefore, instructed to aid the company trading to these places, and drive the English from the ground they had usurped. He was informed that, with regard to Acadie, the English commissioners had recognized the rights of France on the territory, as far as Pentagoet; and the attack of the forts on that river by the people of Boston, had been disavowed; and he was instructed to take, in concert with Monneval, governor of Acadie, the measures necessary to prevent the repetition of a like outrage. It was announced that the king, informed that the English of New York continued their intrigues with the Iroquois, inducing them to wage war against his Canadian subjects and his Indian allies, whom they supplied with arms and ammunition, had determined on carrying into execution, a plan projected by Callieres, the governor of Montreal, for taking possession of the city and province of New York, and had directed La Caffiniere to proceed with a naval force to Acadie and follow the count's directions.

On his arrival in Acadie, with this naval commander, while the governor general was concerting with him the plans of simultaneous attacks by the navy on the city of New York, and the land forces on Albany, the intelligence he received from Canada was such as to induce him to forego every plan of offensive operation against the English.

Fifteen hundred Iroquois made an irruption in the island of Montreal, on the twenty-fifth of August. This overpowering force struck every one on the island with consternation; no resistance was made. The Indians laid the plantations waste, burnt the houses and massacred the male inhabitants that fell into their hands. The females were made prisoners; but even all their lives were not spared. The bellies of pregnant women were ripped open, and the fruit torn out of the womb. Small children were put on the spit, and the mother compelled to turn it. Two hundred persons were killed in the small settlement of La Chine, the first they attacked. As they advanced towards the town of Montreal, destruction, fire and smoke marked their way. They made themselves masters of the fort, notwithstanding the vigorous and resolute resistance of Robeyre, who commanded there. Thus they were in possession of the whole island; they kept it till October.

On the arrival of the Count de Frontenac at Quebec, the Iroquois retreated for awhile, in order to provide the means of returning soon, in a situation to pursue their irruptions as far as the capital, where they intended to co-operate with an English fleet, which they expected to meet before it. They boasted that before the spring, there should not be one Frenchman alive in Canada.

In the meanwhile, war had been declared in France against England, on the twenty-fifth of June. The winter was spent in Canada, in making arrangements for the campaign of the following year. The chiefs lost not in their attention to the measures which the defense of the colony demanded, the view of the offensive ones, recommended by the king against New York and Albany—considering the reduction of the English colony, as the only means of protecting that committed to their care: but the spring vessels brought the king's orders to abandon the projected attack on the city of New York by sea, the immense armaments, which circumstances required in Europe, disabling the minister of the navy from sparing any ships for that purpose.

Three large detachments of the army advanced in the spring on the northern frontier of New York, and had considerable success. They took Corlaer, Sermantel and Kaskebe.

Afterwards, a party of the Iroquois came to the mouth of the river Sorel, and carried off a number of lads who were pasturing cattle. The Iroquois were pursued and the lads brought back, except one, whom they had killed, because he could not keep up with them.

Another party, who came to the island of Orleans, was attacked by a farmer, of the name of Columbet, who collected twenty-five of his neighbors. He was killed with a few of his followers; but the Iroquois were repelled and left twenty-five of their men on the field of battle.

A third made about thirty prisoners, men, women and children: they were followed, but the pursuit proved a fatal one to them, as the Indians, unable to escape with their captives, massacred them all.

The French had no naval force in North America. The English colonies supplied the mother country with one; and Sir William Phipps, sailing from Boston with a small fleet, on the twenty-second of May, took Port Royal, in Acadie, and soon after the other ports of that colony. Thence he proceeded to the island of New Foundland, where he pillaged the port of Plaisance.

On the sixteenth of June, his fleet, now consisting of thirty-four sail, cast anchor below Quebec, and he summoned the Count de Frontenac to surrender. On receiving a resolute answer, Sir William approached the city, and the fort began a fierce cannonade : the flag-staff of his ship was broken by a shot, and a Canadian boldly committed himself to the waves to take it : he succeeded, notwithstanding the brisk fire of the musketry, and the flag was triumphantly carried to the cathedral, where it was deposited as a trophy. On the eighteenth, fifteen hundred men landed, and were repulsed with the loss of three hundred. On the next day, the shipping drew near and cannonaded the lower town ; but the fire from the castle soon compelled them to retire in some confusion. On the twentieth a larger body was landed than before, at some distance below the city ; they boldly advanced towards it ; but the count sallied forth, with all his force, and repulsed them. They retreated to the place of their landing, where the vicinity of the shipping prevented him from following them. During the night, five pieces of artillery were landed, and in the morning the enemy advanced with these ; but the count coming out, with a larger force than the preceding day, the English retreated at first in tolerably good order ; but the galling fire of the French on the rear, and of their Indians on the land side, soon threw them in great confusion : those who reached the boats, embarking and pushing off in much haste, left their companions and cannon behind ; many of those were killed and the rest taken.

The fleet now weighed anchor and drifted down. They stopped out of the reach of the guns of the French, till an exchange of prisoners was made—Sir William having several on board of his fleet, taken in Acadie, New Foundland, and along the St. Lawrence as he ascended it.

He had expected that while he was attacking Quebec, a number of Iroquois, swelled and directed by some of his countrymen from Albany, would enter the island of Montreal and fall on the town : thus creating a necessity for the division of the forces of the colony, which would ensure the fall of Quebec, and finally enable him to make himself master of the whole province. But the English did not find among the Iroquois all the warriors they expected to join. The garrison of the upper fort had been reinforced and well supplied with arms and ammunition, and an attack being expected above, rather than below, the militia were able to disperse the parties of the Iroquois who approached.

Louis the fourteenth caused a medal to be struck in commemoration of this negative victory ; which is believed to be the first event, in the history of America, of which there is a numismatic record. The inscription on the medal is, *Francia in novo orbe victrix.*

In the fall, the scarcity of provisions was extreme. The alarm, in which the country had been the spring and the beginning of the summer, had drawn most of the people from their farms during seed time ; and although a small fleet of merchant vessels, which entered the river while the English were attacking Quebec, found a shelter, till after their departure, up the Saguenay, the supply they brought in afforded but a temporary relief and was soon exhausted. The famine was most severely felt in the capital : the troops were sent in small detachments in every parish, and the men scattered among such farmers, as could best afford them subsistence. They were all very cheerfully received.

The Iroquois came down in great numbers the following spring. A body of upwards of one thousand encamped near the island of Montreal : a detachment of one hundred and twenty was sent northerly, and one of two hundred southerly. The first fell on the settlements of the *Pointe aux trembles,* where they burnt upwards of thirty houses and made several prisoners, whom they treated with extreme cruelty. The other, among whom were about twenty Englishmen, went towards Chambly, where they laid all the plantations waste, capturing men, women and children. Several other parties went in various directions: all carrying desolation before them. The colonists could not keep any large force together, owing to the improbability of finding subsistence. Small bodies, however, kept the field, and scoured the country with so much success, that the foe was compelled to retreat.

A victualling convoy, which arrived during the summer, enabled the Canadians to wait for the season of reaping.

The Chevalier de Villebon, appointed governor of Acadie, arrived at Port Royal in November: finding no English force there, he called the inhabitants together and hoisting the white flag, took quiet and formal possession of the country.

Canada was greatly disturbed in the following year by the Iroquois; the French had several skirmishes with large parties of these Indians; but no decisive action took place.

In the latter part, a French fleet under the orders of Du Palais, came on the Canadian sea. The English attacked Plaisance, in the island of New Foundland without success: and the government of Massachusetts was equally unfortunate in an attempt against Villebon in Acadie.

In 1693, king William determined to indulge the people of New England and New York, with a second effort to reduce Quebec—the frontier settlements of these provinces being incessantly harrassed by irruptions of the Indians allied with France, often directed by the white people; but an attack on Martinique was the previous object of the naval and land forces destined against Canada. A contagious fever broke out in the fleet, while it was in the West Indies, and by the time the ships reached North America, had swept away upwards of three thousand soldiers and sailors. This disaster prevented any hostility against Canada or Acadie. Fort St. Anne, in the bay of Hudson, was taken by the English.

Iberville was, in the following year, sent thither with two ships, and a small land force. The English had a garrison of fifty men only in Fort Nelson. There was no military officer commanding there; but, they were under the orders of a factor of the company; he made no resistance. On its being reduced, its name was changed to Fort Bourbon; Iberville wintered there. The scurvy made a great havoc among his people. In the summer he left the command to Lasaut, to whom he gave Marigny, as his lieutenant, with a garrison of sixty Canadians and some Indians. He brought away a very considerable quantity of furs and peltries, collected from the natives.

In Canada, the Count de Frontenac, contrary to the representations of the intendant, the advice of his military officers, and the directions of the Minister, took upon himself to rebuild the fort at Catarocoui. He went up with seven hundred men for this purpose. It was in vain objected to him, that this force, and the funds that were thus to be employed, might be more usefully used in an offensive expedition against the Iroquois, who continued to annoy the distant settlements. He left in it a garrison of fifty-eight men.

In the fall, the count and the intendant recommended to the minister to send ten or twelve ships of the line against an English fleet that was expected in the Canadian sea, and to attempt the reduction of Boston. They represented that town as carrying on a considerable trade, and assured him its falling into the hands of the French would insure the fisheries exclusively to them.   The king's council, however, determined on confining the operations of the next campaign in America, to driving the English from the places they occupied in New Foundland, and the fort of Penkuit, from which they continued to harrass the settlements in Acadie, and which, being in the immediate neighborhood of the Abenaquis, gave the people of New England, a great opportunity of subduing these Indians, or at least of seducing them from their alliance with and dependence on the French crown.

Accordingly, in the next summer, Iberville arrived with two ships on 'the coast of Acadie, and on the third of July, met with three ships of war of the enemy ; one of which, the Newport, of sixty guns, he captured : a heavy fog that rose during the engagement, favored the escape of the other two.   Having taken fifty Indians on board at Beaubassin, he proceeded to Pentagoet, where the Baron of St. Castin had marched with twenty-five soldiers and two hundred and fifty Indians.   On the fifteenth, the Baron, having raised two batteries, sent a summons to the Commandant, representing the land and naval forces ready to co-operate against him, as too large to admit of a successful resistance.   The Englishman replied, that if the sea was covered with French ships, and the country around with French soldiers, he would not think of surrendering the fort as long as he had a gun to fire.   On this, a cannonade began from the batteries and shipping.   Iberville landed during the night and erected a bomb battery.   On the next day, fire bombs, thrown into the fort, appeared to create confusion : the baron now sent word that if the besieged waited for the assault, they would have his Indians to deal with, whom it might possibly be out of his power to control.   This threat had its effect, and the fort capitulated.

Iberville, after this, sailed for New Foundland.   An English fleet still hovered on the coast of Acadie : its commander, having landed four or five hundred men at Beaubassin, was shown by the inhabitants an instrument of writing, left with them by Sir William Phipps, declaring that as they had submitted to the forces of William and Mary, he had taken them under his sovereign's protection.   They were answered they should in no manner be injured.   Orders were accordingly given to the soldiers, who were prohibited from taking anything, except such cattle as might be needed for the fleet ; for which, payment was promised.   The commodore walked with the inhabitants who had waited on him, to the house of one Bourgeois, where he and his officers were entertained, and where the most respectable inhabitants came to visit him.   The soldiers, however, went about pillaging, and treating the Acadians as a conquered people, and when complaints were made to the chief, he did not restrain them. Walking out accidentally towards the church, he noticed a paper stuck on the door, subscribed by Count de Frontenac.   It contained regulations respecting the traffic with the Indians.   Pretending to be much irritated at this discovery, he charged the inhabitants with a breach of their sworn neutrality, ordered the church to be set on fire, and authorized his soldiers to continue the pillage.   The plantations were laid waste, and most of the houses burnt. The forces being re-embarked, the fleet went to the river St. John, where an unsuccessful attack was made on the fort.

In the meanwhile, Iberville went to New Foundland, where he had considerable success, and took the Fort of St. John. He was preparing to drive the English from the two only places which they held in that island, when he received orders to sail for the bay of Hudson with four ships which arrived from France. The English had captured Fort Bourbon, in that bay. He lost one of his ships in the ice, and a storm separated two of the others from him. The ship he was in was drove ashore in another gale: but the two who had disappeared, joining the one he had left, he gave battle to some English ships which he found in the bay. He sunk one of them and took another; the third escaped—and towards the middle of September he recaptured Fort Bourbon.

The peace of Riswick, in the meanwhile, put an end to hostilities. On the twentieth of September, Louis the fourteenth acknowledged William the third, king of England, and the two monarchs agreed mutually to restore to each other all conquests made during the war, and to appoint commissioners to examine and determine the rights and pretensions of each to the places situated in Hudson's Bay.

In the following year, Count de Frontenac died, and was succeeded, in the government-general of New France, by the Chevalier de Callieres.

At this period, the population of New France did not exceed sixteen thousand; that of Canada being thirteen, and that of Acadie three thousand.

We have seen that, before the accession of the Bourbons and the Stuarts, in the early part of the seventeenth century, all the efforts of France and England, towards colonization in the western hemisphere had proved abortive. The progress of these nations, under the princes of those houses, were simultaneous, but unequal, both in the means employed and the result. Vast were those of France: exiguous those of England. Yet the population of the colonies of the latter was sixteen times that of those of the former: it exceeded two hundred and sixty thousand.

Judge Marshal has shown, in his history of the colonies planted by the English in North America, how immense and rapid are the advances of a community, allowed to manage its own concerns, unaided, and even checked at times, by a distant administration. *Sequar, sed haud passibus equis.* Mine shall be the humble task to show how small and tardy are those advances in a colony, absolutely guided by the mother country, notwithstanding the great assistance the latter may afford to the former.

About three-fourths of a century, after Henry the fourth laid the foundation of Quebec, William Penn, an individual of the English nation, cut down the first tree, on the spot which Philadelphia now covers, and in about twelve years after, the quaker, by his unaided exertions, had collected twenty thousand persons around his city; one-fourth more than the efforts of three successive monarchs of France, commanding the resources of that mighty kingdom, and employing several ships of the royal navy in the transportation of the soldiers and colonists, had been able to unite in New France.

CHAPTER VII.

Louis the fourteenth seemed to have lost sight of Louisiana, in the prosecution of the war which the treaty of Riswick terminated. We have seen that Lasalle had lost his life in the attempt to plant a French colony on the Mississippi.

Iberville, on his return from Hudson's Bay, flattering himself with the hope of better success, offered to prosecute Lasalle's plan, and was patronized by the Count de Pontchartrain, the Minister of the Marine, who ordered an expedition to be prepared at la Rochelle.

Two frigates of thirty guns each, and two smaller vessels were employed in this service. The command of one of the frigates and of the armament was given to Iberville, and that of the other to the Count de Sugeres. A company of marines and about two hundred settlers, including a few women and children, embarked, Most of the men were Canadians, who had enlisted in the troops sent over from France during the war, and were disbanded at the peace.

This small fleet sailed on the twenty-fourth of September, 1698, for cape Francois, in the island of St. Domingo, where it arrived after a passage of seventy-two days. Here it was joined by a fifty gun ship commanded by Chateaumorant. Leaving the cape on new year's day, the ships cast anchor on the twenty-fifth of January before the island which now bears the name of St. Rose.

Iberville sent a boat to the main, where Don Andres de la Riolle had a short time before led three hundred Spaniards, on the spot on which, in the time of Soto, lay the Indian town of Anchusi, and now stands the town of Pensacola. Two ships of his nation were at anchor under the protection of a battery that had just been erected.

Don Andres received the officer in the boat with civility; but as his naval force was much inferior to that of the French, declined permitting Iberville to bring in his ships. They proceeded northerly to another island, not very distant, to which, from a heap of human bones near the beach, the name of Massacre Island was given. It is now known as Dauphine Island.

Sailing afterwards farther on, they entered a pass between two islands, which received the names of Horn and Ship Islands; but being stopped by the shallowness of the water, they came out, and shaping their course southwesterly, reached two other islands, now known as those of the Chandeleur, either from the circumstance of their having been first approached on the second of February, Candlemas day, or from their being covered with the myrtle shrub, from the wax of the berries of which the first colonists made their candles. The anchor was cast here, and the pass between Ship Island, and another called Cat Island, (from a number of these animals found on it) was sounded, and the smaller vessels entered through it. The fifty gun ship now returned to St. Domingo; and the two frigates remained before one of the Chandeleur islands.

Iberville went with most of his people to Ship Island, where they began to erect huts. He sent two boats to the main. They entered the bay of Pascagoula, where they discovered a number of Indians who fled at their approach, and were pursued in vain. On the next day a boat was again sent on shore. On the landing of the French, the natives ran away as before; but a woman, lagging behind, was caught, and was so much pleased at the behavior of the strangers, that she went and induced her countrymen to meet them. Four of these Indians were persuaded to go on board; Bienville, a brother of Iberville, who commanded the boat, remaining, in the meanwhile, as an hostage with the rest. After spending some time in the vessel, they returned, much gratified with their courteous reception, and a few presents that were made them. For want of an interpreter no other information could be obtained from them, except that they were of the Biloxi tribe.

On the following day, another party of Indians passed by. The same circumstance prevented any knowledge being obtained from them, except that they were Bayagoulas, that their tribe dwelt on the bank of a very large river, a little to the west, and that they were out on a war expedition against the Mobilians, who dwelt on a smaller stream, not far to the east.

On the twenty-seventh of February, Iberville and Bienville, each in a barge well manned, went in quest of the Mississippi. They were attended by father Athanase, a recollet monk, who had accompanied the unfortunate Lasalle, both in his descent of that river, and on his last voyage from France. The third day they entered a wide stream, which, from the turbidness of its waters, the friar justly concluded was the mighty river.

Having ascended it, according to their reckoning about one hundred and twenty miles, on the fifth day after they entered it, they discovered a party of Indians, who, on perceiving the barges, sought their safety in flight. One of them, however, soon turned and fearlessly awaited the approach of the strangers. His good will having been secured by a present, he went and brought back his companions. It was understood from them, that they were of the Bayagoula tribe. One of them was easily prevailed upon to get into Iberville's barge and accompany the French.

A few days after, the French overtook at the fork of the Chetimachas, a party of the Washitas, and two days after reached a village of the Bayagoulas.

Here they were shown some capots, or great coats, made of blankets, left there by some of Lasalle's companions. They were treated with great hospitality. The Indians supplied their guests with a few fowls, giving them to understand they proceeded from others, which they had received from a tribe of Indians (the Attakapas) dwelling northerly, near the sea; a vessel having been cast ashore there, from which a few of these animals came out.

Iberville was still apprehensive that father Athanase was mistaken, and the river he was on was not the Mississippi, until the natives produced a prayer book, in which the name of one of Lasalle's men was written, and at last, a letter from the Chevalier de Tonti, bearing date from the village of the Quinipissas, the twentieth of April, 1685. The chevalier lamented his being obliged to return, without having met his chief, whose departure from France with the intention of settling a French colony on the banks of the Mississippi, he had learned from Canada. He observed he had descended the stream, as far as the sea, with twenty Canadians and thirty Indians. Iberville was also shown a coat of mail, with double meshes of wire. From the accounts the Indians gave of the length of

14

time this piece of armor had been among them, Iberville guessed it to have belonged to one of the Spaniards who accompanied Soto.

Having left another fork of the Mississippi, (now known as the bayou Plaquemines) on the left hand, they soon came to another outlet of the river, on its opposite side, which separated the land of the Bayagoulas, from that of the Oumas. It is now called bayou Manchac.

Several days afterwards, they came to a place where the river made a considerable bend. Iberville, perceiving a large outlet, caused a number of trees that obstructed it to be cut down, and the barges were drawn through. The Mississippi afterwards so widened the outlet, that in time, the former bed of the river being much obstructed by trees, the stream altered its course, and the outlet became its bed. The place was hence called Point Coupee.

They afterwards came to another considerable bend through which the natives made a portage and had cut a road—the isthmus was but a few yards in width; the French gave it the name of the Portage de la Croix, from the circumstance of their having erected there a cross in token of having proceeded so far up the river, and of having taken possession of it. It is believed that this is the great bend of the Mississippi opposite the mouth of Red river. The Oumas Indians had a considerable village near this spot. The French repaired to it and were hospitably received.

Iberville now retrograded, and the barges having floated back as far as bayou Manchac, Bienville proceeded down the river to the sea, and Iberville entered the small stream and proceeded through two lakes, to which he gave the names of Maurepas and Pontchartrain, to a bay which he called St. Louis, and reached his shipping. Bienville arrived shortly afterwards.

It was now determined to fix the principal establishment of the colony at the eastern extremity of a bay which, from the Indians dwelling near it, was called the bay of Biloxi; it lies between the bay of Pencagonda and that of St. Louis. A fort with four bastions was immediately begun, and completed on the first of May. Twelve pieces of cannon were placed in it, and the command given to Sauvolle, a brother of Iberville; and Bienville, their younger brother, was appointed his lieutenant. The colonists settled around it, and Iberville and the Count de Sugeres sailed for France in the frigates, on the ninth, leaving the two small vessels for the service of the colony.

In the meanwhile, the Scotch had made an unsuccessful attempt to plant a colony near the isthmus of Panama. King William had given his assent to an act of the parliament of Scotland, incorporating a company to carry on trade in Africa and the Indies; and the association equipped three ships and two tenders, on which were embarked one thousand colonists.

This fleet cast anchor near cape Tiberon, in latitude 8. 40. N. on the second of November of the preceding year; the Indians received the adventurers with cordiality, and led their ships to a bay within Golden Island, about five miles wide and very deep. The Scotch, having sounded along the shore, found a lagoon on the southeast side of the bay, running up within the land for about two miles and a half, and selected a spot, which nature had rendered easily defensible, for the chief place for the colony. They called it New Edinburgh, and the harbor before it Caledonia harbor. They erected a platform, on which they placed sixteen guns, and dignified it with the name of Fort St. Andrews.

The Indians continued friendly; the colony was visited by small vessels from Jamaica and St. Domingo. It was several times harrassed by irruptions of Spaniards from the neighboring colonies, whom they always successfully repelled. In the spring, however, the cabinet of Madrid made loud complaints of this invasion of the territory of Spain, and William, being averse to a rupture with that nation, immediately after the conclusion of the war, disowned the Scotch colony, and the governors of Jamaica, Barbadoes, New York and Massachusetts issued proclamations, commanding the king's subjects, in their respective governments, to forbear holding any correspondence with, or giving any aid to the Scotch colony. William was deaf to the representations of the company, and the colonists, unable to repel the Spaniards, and to sustain themselves without aid from home, dispersed soon after.

Sauvolle, after the departure of the two frigates, dispatched one of his two vessels to St. Domingo for provisions. Nothing now appeared to him of greater importance than to secure a good understanding with the Indian tribes near the fort. For this purpose, in the beginning of June, he sent his young brother with a few Canadians, and a Bayagoula chief as a guide, towards the Colapissas, who dwelt on the northern bank of lake Pontchartrain. This tribe had three hundred warriors. On seeing Bienville approach, the Colapissas ranged themselves in battle array. He stopped and sent his guide to inquire into the cause of this hostile appearance. The Colapissas replied, that three days before, two white men, whom they took to be English from Carolina, came at the head of two hundred Chickasaws, attacked their village and carried away some of their people into captivity, and they had at first considered Bienville and his white companions as Englishmen. The Bayagoula chief undeceived them, and told them, that those who came to visit them were French, and enemies of the English—that their object, in coming to the village, was to solicit the friendship and alliance of its inhabitants. The Colapissas laid down their arms and received and entertained the French with great cordiality. Bienville made them a few presents, and exchanged with them promises of reciprocal friendship, alliance and support.

On his return to the fort he spent there but a few days, and set off easterly on a like errand; he ascended the Pascagoula river, on the banks of which the nation who gave it its name, the Biloxis and the Moetobies had villages—and he proceeded as far as the Mobilians. Having been as successful with these tribes as with the Colapissas, and equally anxious to live on good terms with his white as his red neighbors, he paid a visit to Don Andres at Pensacola.

Ever since the discovery of the Mississippi by Lasalle, Canadian huntsmen, or *coureurs de bois*, strayed at times to the banks of that river, and missionaries from that colony had been led by their zeal to locate themselves among the Indians on the Wabash, the Illinois and other streams that pay the tribute of their waters to the Mississippi, and of late among several tribes on the very banks of that river; and on the first of July, Sauvolle had the pleasure, which he little expected, of receiving the visits of two of these missionaries, who resided with the Tensas and Yazou Indians.

The holy men, coming to preach among the Oumas, had heard of a

French settlement on the sea shore; they floated down the Mississippi to visit it, and reached the fort through the lakes. Their names were Monteguy and Davion; the latter resided on an eminence, on the east side of the Mississippi, between the present towns of St. Francisville and Natchez, which the French called after him *La Roche a Davion.* While the English held this part of the country, the spot was called Loftus' heights. From a fort, built under the presidency of John Adams, it bears now the name of Fort Adams. These clergymen spent a few days with their countrymen, and returned to their respective missions.

Parties from the Mobile and Thome Indians visited their French neighbors in the month of August, and the vessel dispatched to St. Domingo on the departure of Iberville, returned with an ample supply of provisions, which began to be much needed.

Iberville, on ascending the Mississippi, had noticed three outlets; one on the eastern side, and two on the western, now called the fork of the Chetimachas, and bayou Plaquemines. He had descended through the first, and had instructed Sauvolle to have the two others explored. Perfect tranquillity reigning in the settlement, Bienville was sent, with ten Canadians in two pirogues, on this service.

They crossed lakes Pontchartrain and Maurepas, and ascending through bayou Manchac, reached the Mississippi and floated down to the fork. Taking always the western prong, whenever the stream forked, Bienville fell into a bayou in which the water failed; visiting several villages of Indians on the way, he returned to the Mississippi, which he descended, and on the sixteenth of September, met an English ship of sixteen guns. Captain Bar, who commanded her, informed Bienville he had left below another ship of his nation of the same force; these ships were sent by Daniel Coxe of New Jersey, who then was the proprietor of the immense grant of land from Charles I. of England to Sir Robert Heath, in 1627. The object of captain Bar and his companion was to sound the passes of the Mississippi. They were afterwards to return and convoy four smaller vessels, bringing several families, intended as the beginning of an English colony, on the banks of the river. Capt. Bar was uncertain whether the stream he was exploring was the Mississippi or not.

Bienville told him it was further west, that the country they were in was a dependence of the French colony of Canada, and the French had a strong fort and some settlements higher up, which induced Bar to retrograde. The part of the river, in which Bienville met him, was the beginning of a large bend, where the ship was detained; the wind which brought her up ceasing, from the very great turn of the river, to be favorable. From this circumstance, the place was called the English Turn; an appellation which it still retains.

While Bienville was on board, a French engineer, named Secon, handed him a memorial to be forwarded to the court of France. It stated, that the memorialist, and four hundred protestant families who had emigrated from France to Carolina, in consequence of the revocation of the edict of Nantz, in 1684, were anxious to come and live under the French government in Louisiana, provided liberty of conscience was promised them. This paper was accordingly forwarded; but the Count de Pontchartrain answered, that his sovereign had not driven these protestants from his kingdom to make a republic of them in America. Religious intolerance had greatly thinned the population of France, and was now to check that of her colonies. Its dire evils were not confined to Catholic countries nor to the old world—they have been felt even in "the land of the free." About sixty years before, the general court of Massachusetts excluded from the enjoyment of political rights, those who had not been received into the church as members; and even at this day, the constitution of North Carolina withholds some of them from those who deny the truth of the protestant religion.

Bienville, after the departure of the English ships, descended the river to the sea, and sounded its western pass; he found eleven feet of water on its bar.

Returning, he reached the village of the Bayagoulas on the first of October. These Indians were in the greatest consternation; having been lately surprised by the Oumas, who made several of their people prisoners. The war that had broke out between these two tribes was occasioned by a dispute about their limits. Bienville, on leaving them, promised to the Bayagoulas, that he would soon return with some of his men, and compel the Oumas to make peace with them.

On his way down, he was guided to a portage or crossing place; his pirogues were carried over to bayou Tigouyou, through which he reached lake Pontchartrain, and in four days arrived at the fort of Biloxi.

Several guns fired at sea, attracted the attention of the colonists on the seventh of December. Sauvolle sent out a light boat, which soon came back with the pleasing intelligence of the approach of a French fleet.

It consisted of a fifty and a forty gun ship, commanded by Iberville and the Count de Sugeres; Sauvolle had been appointed governor, Bienville lieutenant-governor of Louisiana; and Boisbriant major of the fort. This officer, with two others, St. Denys and Maton, came in the ships with sixty Canadians; they were accompanied by Lesueur, a geologist, who was sent to examine a greenish earth or ochre, which some of the men, who had accompanied Dacan up the Mississippi, had noticed on its banks.

Iberville, finding from Bienville's report that the English meditated an establishment on the Mississippi, determined on effecting one immediately. He departed for that purpose in the smallest vessel, with fifty Canadians, on the seventeenth of January, having sent Bienville by the lakes to the Bayagoulas to procure guides to some spot in the lower part of the river, secure from the inundation. They led him to an elevated one, at the distance of fifty-four miles from the sea, where Iberville met them soon after, and the building of a fort was immediately begun.

Towards the middle of February, they were met by the Chevalier de Tonti from the Illinois with seven men; he had left others, who had accompanied him, at the Bayagoulas. The object of his journey was to ascertain the truth of a report which had reached him of the establishment of a French colony.

Three days after, Iberville and Bienville set off with the chevalier and a small party for the upper part of the Mississippi. They stopped at the Bayagoulas, with whom they remained till the first of March, and proceeded to the Oumas, with the view of inducing or compelling them to release the prisoners they had taken from the Bayagoulas. On approaching the village of the Oumas, Iberville went forward with a few Bayagoula chiefs; as he approached their village, the Oumas met and received him with much respect. He was successful in his endeavors; peace was made between the two tribes, and the Bayagoula prisoners were liberated.

From the Oumas, the French proceeded to the Natchez; this nation had been lately reduced by wars to twelve hundred warriors. A missionary named St. Come had arrived some time before from Canada, and fixed his residence among them. The king, or Great Sun of the nation, on hearing of the approach of the French, came forward on the shoulders of some of his people, attended by a large retinue, and welcomed Iberville; those Indians appeared much more civilized than the others. They preserved in a temple a perpetual fire, kept up by a priest, and offered to it the first fruits of the chase.

The Tensas, a neighboring nation, were in alliance with the Natchez, and much resembled them in their manners and religion.

While Iberville remained there, one of the temples was struck and set on fire by lightning. The keeper of the fane solicited the squaws to throw their little ones into the fire, to appease the divinity; four infants were thus sacrificed before the French could prevail on the women to desist.

On the twenty-second of March, Iberville returned to the fort near the mouth of the Mississippi, and from thence to that at the Biloxi. He was much pleased with the country of the Natchez, and considered it as the most suitable part of the province for its principal establishment; he selected a high spot which he laid out for a town, and called it Rosalie, in honor of the Countess of Pontchartrain, who had received that name at the baptismal fount.

On the day that Iberville left the Natchez, Bienville and St. Denys, attended by a few Canadians and a number of Indians, set off for the country of the Yatassees, in the western part of Louisiana.

Iberville, on his arrival at the fort of Biloxi, was informed that the governor of Pensacola had come to Ship Island with a thirty gun ship, and one hundred and forty men, with the view of driving the French away. He found there a superior force, and contented himself with a solemn protest against what he called the usurpation of a country which he considered as part of the government of Mexico. He furnished the Count de Sugeres with a copy of this instrument, which the latter, sailing for France a few days afterwards, carried thither.

Lesueur, with a detachment of twenty men, set off for the country of the Sioux, in the latter part of April.

In the meanwhile, Bienville and St. Denys returned to Biloxi; they had found the country through which they intended to pass, entirely covered with water, and had proceeded to the village of the Washitas, in which they found but five huts; the Indians having mostly removed to the Natchitoches. They crossed Red river, and met six of the latter Indians who were carrying salt to the Coroas, a tribe who dwelt in the vicinity of the Yazou river. On the seventh of April they reached the village of the Ouitchouis, in which were about fifty warriors; here they were supplied with provisions, and one of the Indians accompanied them as a guide to the Yatassees, whose village was very large, as they had two hundred warriors. The information the travellers obtained of the country to the west was imperfect. They did not hear of any Spanish settlement in the vicinity.

On their way down the Mississippi, they stopped at the Bayagoulas, whose village was almost entirely destroyed by the Mongoulachas, a tribe who dwelt near them.

Iberville returned to France towards the last of May. He left Bienville in command, in the fort on the Mississippi, and sent St. Denys, with twelve Canadians and a number of Indians, to prosecute the discoveries he had begun on Red river.

Although the French had now been upwards of two years in Louisiana, they do not appear to have resorted to the culture of the earth for subsistence; they depended entirely on supplies from France or St. Domingo. Fishing and hunting afforded the colony fresh meat, and the people carried on a small trade with the Indian tribes on the sea coast. Government, instead of concentrating the population, seemed more intent on making new discoveries where other settlements might be made, and to seek in the bowels of the earth for metals and ochres. The attention of the colonial officers had been directed to a search for pearls. The wool of buffaloes was pointed out to them as the future staple commodity of the country, and they were directed to have a number of these animals penned and tamed. Nay, thoughts were entertained of shipping some of the young to France, in order to propagate the species there.

Charles the second, the fifth and last monarch of Spain of the house of Austria, died on the tenth of November, 1700, in the thirty-ninth year of his age, and without issue. His will called to the throne he was leaving Philip, Duke of Anjou, a grandson of Louis the fourteenth. Although the new king was received with acclamations in Madrid, his elevation was powerfully opposed by the Archduke Charles, who was supported by his father, and by England, Holland, Savoy, Prussia and Portugal. Thus, the flames of war began to rage in Europe in that contest, which is called the war of the Spanish succession.

St. Denys returned in the fall, after a very tiresome journey of upwards of six months, without any material information respecting the Indians in the upper part of Red river.

Lesueur had ascended the Mississippi, as high as the falls, to which Dacan and Hennepin had given the name of St. Anthony, proceeded up St. Peters' river upwards of one hundred and twenty miles, and entered a stream, which he called Green river, from the hue imparted to its water, by a greenish ochre, which covered the land around a copper mine, and was intermixed with the ore on the surface. The ice prevented his advance more than three miles, although it was now the latter part of September. He employed his detachment in building a small fort, in which they wintered. It was called Fort Thuillier, in compliment to a farmer-general of that name, one of Lesueur's patrons. In the spring, the party proceeded to the mine, at the foot of a mountain, which the Indians said was thirty miles in length. It was very near the bank of the river : thirteen thousand weight of a mixture of ochre and ore were gathered, brought to Biloxi, and shipped to France. From the circumstance of the mine having been abandoned, it is concluded that no value was attached to the shipment. Lesueur had left the greatest part of his men in the fort, to keep possession of the country.

A frigate arrived from France on the thirtieth of May, under the orders of Delaronde. Government, always under the impression that wealth was to be sought in the bowels of the earth, in Louisiana, rather than gathered from its surface, by the dull and steady process of tillage, and listening with unabated credulity to the tales of every impostor, who came from America, a Canadian, of the name of Mathew Sagan, who had furnished

the Count de Pontchartrain with feigned memoirs, in which he pretended
to have ascended the Missouri and discovered mines of gold, arrived in
this vessel.   The minister, yielding to the illusion which Sagan's memoirs
produced, had ordered his services to be secured at a great expense, and
instructed Sauvolle to have twenty-four pirogues built and one hundred
Canadians placed with them, under the orders of his man, to enable him
to proceed to the Missouri and work the mines.   He was well known to
most of the Canadians in Louisiana, who were conscious he never had
been on the Missouri.   Sauvolle, informed of the character of the man,
did not hurry the intended expedition, although, in obedience to his
instructions, he gave orders for the building of the pirogues.   The frigate
staid but a few days in Louisiana.

Sauvolle dying, on the twenty-second of July, Bienville succeeded him,
in the chief command and removed from the Mississippi to Biloxi.   Parties
of the Choctaws and Mobile Indians came a few days after his arrival, to
visit him.   Their object was to solicit the aid of the French against the
Chickasaws, who harrassed them by frequent irruptions in their villages.
The French chief, considering that his colony was too weak to be embroiled
in the quarrels of the Indian tribes near it, declined giving his visitors
any offensive aid, but sent an officer, accompanied by a few Canadians, to
afford the Choctaws his good offices as mediator.

A party of the Alibamons visited the fort, about the same time.

The utter neglect of agriculture, and the failure of the supplies which
had been relied on from France, St. Domingo and Vera Cruz, reduced the
colony to great distress during the summer; the people having nothing
to subsist on, but a few baskets of corn, occasionally brought in by the
natives, and what could be obtained by the chase or drawn from the water,
by the net or line.   In the fall, disease added its horrors to those of famine.
Most of the colonists sickened and many died; their number was reduced
to one hundred and fifty.   They were not relieved till late in December.

Iberville now arrived with two ships of the line and a brig, bringing a
reinforcement of troops.

In pursuance of the king's instructions, Bienville left twenty men
under the orders of Boisbriant, at the fort of Biloxi, and moved his headquarters to the western bank of the river Mobile.

The officer who had accompanied the Choctaws and Mobilians now
returned.   He had been successful in his mediation, and a peace had been
concluded between these Indians and the Chickasaws.

A supply of provisions from Vera Cruz, where Bienville had sent a light
vessel, added to a large one by the fleet, restored abundance in the colony,
and enabled him to afford relief to the garrison of Pensacola, which was
reduced to great distress.

Besides the new settlement on Mobile river, another was now begun on
Massacre Island, the ominous name of which was changed to Dauphine
Island.   Its fine port affording a much more convenient place to land
goods than Ship Island, the coast of Biloxi or Mobile river.   Barracks and
stores were built, with a number of houses, and a fort was erected to
afford them protection.

Iberville returned to France in the fleet.

William the third of England died on the sixteenth of March, in
consequence of a fall from his horse, in the fifty-third year of his age.

Mary, his queen, had died in 1694. Neither left issue. Anne, her sister, succeeded him.

The new queen declared war against France and Spain on the second of May.

There were other causes of irritation between England and France than the late increase of power and influence France had acquired in consequence of the occupation of the throne of Spain by a grandson of Louis the fourteenth. The late treaty of peace in 1696 had left the boundary line between the dominions of France and England unascertained. The queen claimed the whole country to the west of the river of St. Croix, as part of the province of Massachusetts; while the king sought to exclude her subjects from the fisheries on the coast, and from all the country east of the Kennebec river. De Callieres, Governor of Canada, proposed to Governor Dudley, of Massachusetts, that the colonies should forbear taking part in the war between the mother countries; but the offer was not acceded to, and hostilities began immediately, by irruptions of the French of Canada and their Indian allies, on the frontier settlements of Massachusetts and New Hampshire. Governor Moore, of South Carolina, on the first rumor of the declaration of war, proposed to the Legislature to furnish him the means of making an excursion into Florida. A war with Spain was already a popular measure in all the English American provinces. The colonists considered it as the readiest means they had of acquiring specie, of which there was generally a great scarcity among them. The application of Moore was successful, and he soon proceeded to the attack of St. Augustine.

This alarmed the Spaniards at Pensacola, and they solicited Bienville's aid. At the same time, an officer from the garrison of St. Augustine reached Mobile on a like errand. The French chief afforded to the governor of Pensacola arms and ammunition, and sent one hundred men, Canadians, Europeans and Indians, to St. Augustine. At the same time he dispatched a light vessel to Vera Cruz, to convey information to the viceroy, of the danger of the possessions of his sovereign, in the neighborhood of Louisiana and Carolina.

In the meanwhile, the English of Carolina had induced the Chickasaws to send emissaries among the Indians, in the vicinity of the settlements of the French on the gulf, to induce them to take part in the war; and in the fall, father Davion and father Limoges, who dwelt among the Natchez, came to Mobile and informed Bienville, the Coroas had killed Foucault their colleague, and three other Frenchmen. The commandant of the fort at Albany had also prevailed on the Iroquois to attack the frontier settlers in Canada. The Indians fell also on detached plantations, which the French had, to the south of the lakes, as far as the Wabash. Juchereau, a relation of St. Denys, had led thither a number of Canadians, who successfully employed themselves in collecting furs and peltries. Driven from this place, he had led his party westerly; and a pirogue with some of his men reached Mobile on the third of February. Their object was to solicit the assistance of the government of Louisiana: Bienville had been instructed to afford it. But the relief he had lately yielded to the Spaniards, the length of time he had been without succor from France, and the wants of his colony, limited the aid he gave Juchereau, to one barrel of powder.

In the summer, information reached Mobile of the death of the Chevalier

15

de Callieres, governor-general of New France, of which government Louisiana made a part. He was succeeded by the Marquis de Vaudreuil.

The men sent by Bienville to the relief of St. Augustine, found, on their arrival there, a naval force from the island of Cuba, on the approach of which, the troops of Carolina and their red allies had retreated. Becancourt who had gone to Vera Cruz to give information of the danger to St. Augustine, returned with a letter from the Duke of Albuquerque, viceroy of Mexico, in which that nobleman communicated to Bienville, the orders he had from his sovereign, to admit vessels from Louisiana in the ports of his government, and to allow them to export provisions.

The men, whom Lesueur had left at Fort Thuillier among the Sioux, for awhile thought that the Mississippi was a sufficient barrier between them and the Indians, under the influence of the English; but they now found themselves so vigorously attacked, that they could no longer retain their position. They descended the Mississippi, and reached Mobile on the third of March, 1704.

The government of South Carolina, after the forced retreat of its troops, from St. Augustine, had employed a part of them against the Indians, in its neighborhood, under the protection of Spain. Large parties of the Cherokees, Cohuntas, Talapooses and Alibamons, swelled by a number of negroes and headed by Englishmen, invaded the country of the Apalaches. An officer of the garrison of St. Marks, came to Mobile to inform Bienville that the Apalache Indians had applied to the commandant of that fort, for a supply of arms and ammunition, which it had not been thought prudent to grant. In consequence of this, two thousand of these Indians had been compelled to remove towards Carolina. Two of their villages, the inhabitants of which were catholics, had remained faithful to the Spaniards; their warriors had fought bravely, and two hundred of them had been killed. The enemy had committed much waste in the neighborhood, principally in the removal or destruction of cattle. Bienville was solicited to send a few soldiers to St. Marks; but he thought his garrison too weak to be divided, and supplied the Spaniards with military stores only.

At the same time, a number of Englishmen came among the Alibamons with the view of inducing them to fall on the French. These Indians resisted their solicitations, and sent word to Bienville to be on his guard, offering to furnish him with corn, of which, they said, they had great abundance. The garrison being ill supplied with this article, Dubreuil was sent with a few soldiers to effect a purchase. One of these returned soon after, with a broken arm. He related that the party had been met by twelve of these Indians, at the distance of two days' journey from their village, with the calumet of peace; but, at night, the Indians treacherously rose on them, and murdered his companions. He succeeded in making his escape by throwing himself into the river, after having received the stroke of an axe on his arm. The Indians fired several times at him while he was swimming.

A small fleet, composed of a French frigate, under the orders of Lefevre de la Barre, a son of the late governor of New France, and four Spanish sloops, made this year an unsuccessful attack on Charleston, in South Carolina. Sir Nathaniel Johnson, governor of that province, having had timely information of the approach of the enemy, made a powerful and successful resistance.

Louisiana now suffered greatly from the scarcity of provisions. But the governor of Pensacola, returning from a visit to Mexico, brought a very ample supply for his garrison, and cheerfully relieved his neighbors. They had been obliged to separate in small parties, along the coast, in order to seek a precarious subsistence out of the water. Shortly afterwards, the return of Becancourt, who had been sent to Vera Cruz, restored abundance. Bienville received by him the thanks of the viceroy, for the aid afforded to the garrisons of St. Marks and Pensacola, with assurance of his readiness to supply the French at Louisiana with anything they might need.

The arrival, soon after, of a ship from France (under Chateaugue, a brother of Bienville) loaded with provisions and military stores, removed for awhile the apprehension of famine. Seventeen new colonists came in her, and brought implements of husbandry.

The satisfaction which the restoration of plenty created was marred by the arrival of a party of Chickasaws, who reported that five Frenchmen had been killed by the Tagouiaco Indians, who dwelt on one of the streams which flow into the Wabash. These Indians had been excited to this aggression by some English traders who had lately arrived among them from Virginia.

These repeated and unprovoked outrages from the Indians induced Bienville to march against the Alibamons, whose treacherous conduct towards the men he had sent, on their invitation, to purchase corn in their village, remained unpunished. He left the fort about Christmas, with forty chosen men, attended by a few Chickasaws. He did not meet any of the enemy until after a march of several days, towards night, and was advised by his officers to delay the attack till daylight. The Alibamons occupied an eminence of difficult access, which the French approached. The night was dark and the ground covered with rushes, and the noise, necessarily made by the French in their progress, enabled the foe to pour in a destructive fire. Two men were killed, and one was dangerously wounded. The Indians now dispersed, and Bienville was compelled to return without inflicting any other injury than the capture of five pirogues laden with provisions. The Chickasaws pursued the Alibamons, and afterwards returned to the fort with five scalps, for which they were liberally rewarded.

The garrison received during the summer an addition of seventy-five soldiers, who arrived in a fifty gun ship, commanded by Decoudray. Two Grey Sisters came in the same ship to attend the hospital, and also five priests of the foreign missions (sent by the bishop of Quebec, of whose diocese Louisiana made a part.) Besides the military and spiritual supplies, an ample stock of provisions was brought. Neither were other wants of the colonists forgotten: twenty-three poor girls now landed, and immediately found as many husbands.

A vessel, in which Becancourt had been sent to Vera Cruz to obtain provisions, returned early in the fall; but he had died on the return voyage.

Ample as the stock of provisions in the colony was now, compared with that of former years, an accident happened in Pensacola, which rendered an early attention to future supplies necessary. The fort was consumed by fire, and the garrison lost its winter stock of provisions. They did not seek relief among their neighbors in vain.

A party of Choctaws brought to Mobile the scalps of five Alibamons.

From them and a party of Chickasaws, Bienville learned that a number of Englishmen were busily employed in their villages, in their endeavors to estrange these Indians from their alliance with the French.

Disease made this year considerable havoc in the colony, and small as its population was, it counted thirty-five deaths in the fall.

Father Davion, one of the missionaries who had lately descended the Mississippi, was still in the fort, and it had been thought hazardous to permit him to return. His flock greatly lamented the protracted absence of their pastor. In November, two Tunica chiefs came to escort him back. Bienville told them he could not consent to the return of the priest among them till they had avenged the death of father Foucault, his colleague, murdered by the Coroas, at the instigation of the English, and he expected they would seize the traders of that nation among them, and bring them prisoners to Mobile, with their goods; he offered to supply them with ammunition; his proposition was accepted, and St. Denys proposed to go with them, accompanied by twelve Canadians. The party was to be supported by another Canadian of the name of Lambert, who was returning to the Wabash with forty of his neighbors. The Tunica chiefs set off, having promised to meet St. Denys at the Natchez. Bienville gave orders for building pirogues; but before they were finished, accounts reached Mobile of the total destruction of the French settlements on the Wabash, by the Indian allies of the British. Lambert gave up his intended journey, and it being thought dangerous for St. Denys and his party to proceed without the escort which had been anticipated, the project was abandoned. Juchereau sent down to Mobile fifteen thousand hides, which he and his companions had collected on the Wabash.

The Indians near the French were not always in peace among themselves. In the spring, the Chickasaws made an irruption into the country of the Choctaws, captured a number of their people, carried them to South Carolina, and sold them as slaves. There were about forty of the former, men, women and children, around the fort of Mobile. These people solicited an escort from Bienville, as they could not return home without crossing the country of the latter. He detached St. Denys with twenty Canadians on this service. As they approached the first Choctaw village, he went in alone to beseech the chiefs to allow the Indians he escorted to pass. In granting this request, the chiefs stipulated that their head man, should be allowed to reproach the Chickasaws, in the presence of the French, for the treachery of their people. They were brought into an open field for this purpose, with their guns cocked and their knives in their hands. The Choctaw chiefs were surrounded by three hundred warriors. Their head man, holding a calumet, began by upbraiding the Chickasaws, with the perfidy of their nation. He assured them that, if the French took any interest in their safety, it was from a want of knowledge of their baseness, and it was just that they should expiate by their deaths the crimes of their people. He lowered the plumage of the calumet, and at this preconcerted signal, the Choctaws taking a correct aim, fired. The Chickasaw women and children alone escaped. This was not, however, effected without the destruction of some of the Choctaws. St. Denys, attempting to interfere, was himself wounded. The Choctaw chiefs brought him back to the fort and a great number of their warriors followed in mournful procession.

During the next month, a number of Chickasaw chiefs went to the

Tunicas, and embarking, at their village, descended the Mississippi and bayou Manchac. They crossed the lakes and came to Mobile, to solicit Bienville's mediation, in effecting a reconciliation with the Choctaws. Six other chiefs came, in another direction, on the same errand. He sent an officer, attended by three Canadians and a number of Thome Indians, to request some of the Choctaw chiefs to pay him a visit. They came accordingly, and peace was concluded between the Choctaws and Chickasaws, and the Thome and Mobile tribes.

The Choctaw chiefs had scarcely returned home, when their country was invaded by two thousand Cherokees, commanded by an English officer from Carolina. Several of their villages were destroyed and three hundred of their women and children were led away into slavery.

At the time the intelligence of this irruption reached Mobile, father Gratiot, a Jesuit missionary at the Illinois, reached the fort and reported that a party of white men from Virginia had come among these Indians, and instigated them to rise against the French, a number of whom had been killed. The holy man had with much difficulty effected his escape, but not without receiving a wound, which was still deemed dangerous.

A party of Choctaws brought the scalps of nine Alibamons to Bienville. These indians were incessantly committing hostilities against the French and their allies. Boisbriant was sent with twelve Canadians and the Choctaws, to chastise them; but this expedition had but little success. Two scalps of the Alibamons were brought by the Choctaws.

The peace, which through the mediation of Bienville, the Choctaws and Chickasaws had concluded, in the fort of Mobile, was but of short duration. Towards the end of March, the latter made an unprovoked invasion of the of the country of the former, and brought away one hundred and fifty persons. The French chief could not forget that the Choctaws had yielded to his representations in burying the hatchet; and he thought it his duty to assist them against the violators of the treaty. He sent them a considerable supply of powder and lead.

Hostilities among the Indian nations were not confined to the neighborhood of Mobile and Carolina; but extended across the country to the banks of the Mississippi. The Tensas, compelled by the Yazous to abandon their villages near the Natchez, had come down to the Bayagoulas, who received them with great cordiality. The treacherous guests, regardless of the laws of hospitality, rose, in the night, on their unsuspecting hosts and slaughtered the greater part of them. Fearful afterwards that the Oumas and Colapissas, the allies of the Bayagoulas, might be induced, by those who escaped, to avenge the death of their countrymen, the Tunicas sent four warriors of the Chetimachas and Yachimichas, to join them. The houses and fields of the Bayagoulas were destroyed and ravaged. The Tensas now turned their arms against their allies, made several prisoners and carried them into slavery.

The misfortune of the Bayagoulas excited no sympathy among the French. It was considered as a just retaliation for their treachery in destroying their former friends and neighbors, the Mongoulachas.

In the fall, a party of the Hurons, from Detroit, came down against the Arkansas; who being accidentally apprised of their approach, went forward, met, and destroyed most of them. A few of the invaders were made prisoners and brought to the village of the victors, where they were put to death with excruciating tortures.

The colonists learned, with much regret, in the fall of the year, the death of Iberville. He had sailed from France, with a large fleet, for the attack of Jamaica: but, learning that the English, conscious of their danger, had made such preparations as would probably prevent his success, he proceeded to the islands of St. Kitts and Nevis, on which he raised large contributions. He then proceeded to St. Domingo, where he intended taking one thousand troops for an expedition against Charleston. The yellow fever made a great havoc in his fleet. He fell a victim to the dire disease; and the expedition was abandoned.

An Englishman, trading among the Tunicas, was despoiled of his goods: he returned to Carolina and prevailed on some of the Chickasaws, Alibamons and other tribes in alliance with his nation, to accompany and assist him in taking revenge. The Tunicas, finding themselves too weak to resist this invasion, sought refuge among the Oumas; and, like the Tensas, rewarded the hospitality they received, by rising in the unsuspecting hour of rest on this party, and murdering or making prisoners of most of them. Some of the Oumas, who escaped, removed to a stream, now known as the bayou St. John, not very distant from the spot on which the city of New Orleans was afterwards built.

On new year's day, Bourgoing, appointed by the bishop of Quebec his vicar-general in Louisiana, arrived at Mobile by the way of the Mississippi. He brought accounts of the death of St. Cosme, a missionary and three other Frenchmen, by the Chetimachas. Bienville sent presents to his allies on the Mississippi, to induce them to declare war against these Indians. He was not able to raise more than eighty warriors. St. Denys joined them with seven Canadians, and led this little band into the country of the Chetimachas, destroyed their villages, ravaged their fields and dispersed the inhabitants.

During the summer an unsuccessful attempt was made on Acadie, from New England.

Two hundred Indians, headed by a few Englishmen, came to Pensacola, set fire to the houses near the fort, killed ten Spaniards and a Frenchman, and made twelve Apalache or Choctaw Indians prisoners.

A party of Touachas came to Mobile with two scalps and a slave of the Abikas in the beginning of November; they reported the Alibamons were in daily expectation of English troops from Charleston, with whom they were preparing to march to a second attack on Pensacola. Accordingly, in the latter part of the month, Bienville was informed that the place was actually besieged. At the head of one hundred and twenty Canadians and as many Indians, he marched to its relief. He reached it on the eighth of December; the besiegers had withdrawn on hearing of the approach of the French. Their force consisted only of three hundred and fifty Indians, and thirteen white men, commanded by one Cheney, commissioned by Sir Nathaniel Johnson, governor of South Carolina. The French, after staying three days in Pensacola, were ordered, on account of the scarcity of provisions, to return.

A vessel from Havana, laden with provisions, brandy and tobacco, came early in January to trade with the colony. This was the first instance, ten years after the arrival of the French in Louisiana, of a vessel coming to trade with them.

The Marquis de Vaudreuil, governor of Canada, had planned a considerable expedition against New England. His allied Indians kept the frontier settlers of that country in constant alarm. He was, however, disappointed in his expectation of raising the force he had contemplated. A strong party of Canadians and Indians, nevertheless, entered the province of Massachusetts, and destroyed a part of the town of Haverhill, killed one hundred of its inhabitants, and carried off seventy prisoners. In the pursuit, however, a number of the prisoners were retaken, and a few of the French killed.

In the following year, the British cabinet determined on vigorous and simultaneous attacks on Montreal and Quebec.

The first was to be conducted by General Nicholson, successively lieutenant-governor of New York and Virginia; he was to proceed through the Champlain. He led his force to Wood creek, where he was to wait the arrival of a British fleet at Boston, at which place it was to receive the troops destined to act against Quebec. The New England provinces, and that of New York had very cheerfully raised the men required for this service. The expectations which this armament had excited in the British provinces were disappointed, in consequence of the fleet, which was to proceed to Boston, being ordered on another service in Portugal.

The success of the settlement attempted in Louisiana not having answered the hopes of the court of France, it was determined to make a considerable change in the government of the colony. With this view, de Muys, an officer who had served with distinction in Canada during the preceding and present war, was appointed governor-general of Louisiana: the great distance from that colony to Quebec, the seat of the governor-general of New France, of which it was a dependence, had induced the belief that the former ought to be independent of the latter. Diron d'Artaguette was sent as commissary ordonnateur, with instructions to inquire into the conduct of the former administrators of the colony, against whom complaints had been made, to which the ill success of the establishment seemed to give consequence. The frigate in which these gentlemen had embarked, arrived at Ship Island in the beginning of the new year. The governor-general had died during the passage.

D'Artaguette found Louisiana in comparative tranquillity. Vessels from St. Domingo, Martinique and la Rochelle now came to trade with the colonists.

Early in September, a privateer from Jamaica landed his men on Dauphine Island, where they committed considerable depredations. This is the first instance of hostility of white people against the colony.

On the twenty-fourth, General Nicholson, with a corps of marines, and four regiments of infantry, arrived from Boston, before Port Royal in Acadie. He immediately invested the town, which soon after surrendered. Its name, in compliment to the British queen, was changed to that of Annapolis. Colonel Vetche was left there in command.

The settlement near the fort at Mobile suffered much in the spring from the overflowing of the river; in consequence of which, at the recommendation of D'Artaguette, the spot was abandoned, and a new fort built higher up. It was the one which, till very lately, stood immediately below the present city of Mobile.

The government of South Carolina prevailed again on the Chickasaws to attack the Choctaws, who were always the steadfast allies of the French. When intelligence of this reached Mobile, there were about thirty Chickasaw chiefs around the fort. Bienville, at their request, sent

Chateaugue with thirty men to escort them home. This service was successfully performed, notwithstanding the Choctaws made great efforts to intercept these Indians.

The government of France from this period ceased furnishing supplies to Louisiana, and trusted to the industry of private adventurers, to whom, however, it afforded some aid. A frigate arrived in the month of September, laden with provisions by individuals; the king furnished the ship only. D'Artaguette returned in her, much regretted by the colonists; observations, during his stay in Louisiana, perfectly convinced him that its slow progress could not be accelerated by Bienville, with the feeble means of which he had the command.

In the summer, General Hill, at the head of six thousand five hundred European and Provincial troops, sailed from Boston for the attack of Quebec. On the twenty-third of August, a violent storm cast eight of his transports on shore near Egg Island. One thousand of his men perished, the ships were greatly injured, and this disaster induced him to return. In the meanwhile, General Nicholson had led four thousand men, destined to the siege of Montreal, to Albany. The return of the fleet having enabled the Marquis de Vaudreuil to support Montreal with all his force, Nicholson retrograded.

A ship of twenty-six guns, under the orders of Laville Voisin, came to Ship Island in the beginning of the next year. This gentleman had made a fruitless attempt to sell her cargo to the Spaniards at Touspe. He had brought to the viceroy letters, which he supposed would have insured his admission into the ports of Mexico; but through some mismanagement his scheme failed; not, however, without his selling his cargo to some Spanish merchants, who engaged to receive it at Ship Island. He grew impatient of waiting for them, and went on a short cruise towards St. Antonio. The merchants arrived with their cash, waited awhile, and went away without seeing him.

On the arrival of d'Artaguette in France, and the report he made of the state of the colony, the king's council despairing of realizing the advantages which had been anticipated from it, as long as it remained on its former footing, and determined to grant the exclusive commerce of Louisiana, with great privileges, to Antony Crozat, an eminent merchant.

The war was terminated by the treaty of Utrecht on the thirtieth of March, of the following year: by its twelfth article, France ceded to Great Britain, "Nova Scotia or Acadie, with its ancient boundaries, as also the city of Port Royal, now called Annapolis, and all other things, in the said parts, which depends on these lands."

There were at this period in Louisiana two companies of infantry of fifty men each, and seventy-five Canadian volunteers in the king's pay. The rest of the population consisted of twenty-eight families; one half of whom were engaged, not in agriculture, but in horticulture: the heads of the others were shop and tavern keepers, or employed in mechanical occupations. A number of individuals derived their support by ministering to the wants of the troops. There were but twenty negroes in the colony: adding to these the king's officers and clergy, the aggregate amount of the population was three hundred and eighty persons. A few female Indians and children were domesticated in the houses of the white people, and groups of the males were incessantly sauntering, or encamped around them.

The collection of all these individuals, on one compact spot, could have claimed no higher appellation than that of a hamlet; yet they were dispersed through a vast extent of country, the parts of which were separated by the sea, by lakes and wide rivers. Five forts, or large batteries, had been erected for their protection at Mobile, Biloxi, on the Mississippi, and at Ship and Dauphine Islands.

Lumber, hides and peltries, constituted the objects of exportation, which the colony presented to commerce. A number of woodsmen, or *coureurs de bois* from Canada, had followed the missionaries who had been sent among the nations of Indians, between that province and Louisiana. These men plied within a circle, of a radius of several hundred miles, of which the father's chapel was the centre, in search of furs, peltries and hides. When they deemed they had gathered a sufficient quantity of these articles, they floated down the Mississippi, and brought them to Mobile where they exchanged them for European goods, with which they returned. The natives nearer to the fort, carried on the same trade. Lumber was easily obtained around the settlement: of late, vessels from St. Domingo and Martinique brought sugar, molasses and rum to Louisiana, and took its peltries, hides and lumber in exchange. The colonists procured some specie from the garrison of Pensacola, whom they supplied with vegetables and fowls. Those who followed this sort of trade, by furnishing also the officers and troops, obtained flour and salt provisions from the king's stores, which were abundantly supplied from France and Vera Cruz. Trifling, but successful essays had shown, that indigo, tobacco and cotton could be cultivated to great advantage: but hands were wanting. Experience had shown, that the frequent and heavy mists and fogs were unfavorable to the culture of wheat, by causing it to rust.

The French had been unfortunate in the selection of the places they had occupied. The sandy coast of Biloxi is as sterile as the deserts of Arabia. The stunted shrubs of Ship and Dauphine Islands announce the poverty of the soil by which they are nurtured. In the contracted spot, on which Sauvolle had located his brother on the Mississippi, the few soldiers under him, insulated during part of the year, had the mighty stream to combat. The buz and sting of the musquitoes, the hissing of the snakes, the croakings of the frogs, and the cries of the alligators, incessantly asserted that the lease the God of nature had given these reptiles of this part of the country, had still a few centuries to run. In the barrens around the new fort of Mobile, the continual *sugh* of the needle-leaved tree seemed to warn d'Artaguette his people must recede farther from the sea, before they came to good land.

It is true, during the last ten years, war had in some degree checked the prosperity of the colony, although during the whole of its continuance, except the descent of the crew of a privateer from Jamaica, no act of hostility was committed by an enemy within the colony; but the incessant irruptions on the land of the Indians, under the protection of Louisiana, by those in alliance with Carolina, prevented the extension of the commerce and settlements of the French towards the north. Yet all these difficulties would have been promptly overcome, if agriculture had been attended to. The coast of the sea abounded with shell and other fish; the lagoons near Mobile river were covered with water fowls; the forests teemed with deer; the prairies with buffaloes, and the air with wild turkeys. By cutting down the lofty pine trees around the fort, the colonists would have uncovered a soil abundantly producing corn and peas. By abandoning the posts on the Mississippi, Ship and Dauphine Islands, and at the Biloxi, the necessary military duties would have left a considerable number of individuals to the labors of tillage; especially if prudence had spared frequent divisions of them to travel for thousands of miles in quest of ochres and minerals, or in the discovery of distant land, while that which was occupied, was suffered to remain unproductive. Thus, in the concerns of communities, as in those of individuals, immediate, real and secure advantages are foregone for distant, dubious and often visionary ones.

According to a return made by the Marquis de Vaudreuil to the minister, there were, at this period in New France, including Acadie, four thousand four hundred and eighty persons capable of bearing arms, which supposes a population of about twenty-five thousand.

CHAPTER VIII.

CROZAT's charter bears date the twenty-sixth of September, 1712.

Its preamble states, that the attention the king has always given to the interests and commerce of his subjects, induced him, notwithstanding the almost continual wars he was obliged to sustain, since the beginning of his reign, to seek every opportunity of increasing and extending the trade of his colonies in America; that accordingly, he had in 1683, given orders for exploring the territory on the northern continent, between New France and New Mexico; and Lasalle, who had been employed in this service, had succeeded so far, as to leave no doubt of the facility of opening a communication between Canada and the Gulf of Mexico, through the large rivers that flow in the intermediate space; which had induced the king, immediately after the peace of Riswick, to send thither a colony and maintain a garrison, to keep up the possession taken in 1683, of the territory on the gulf, between Carolina on the east, and old and new Mexico on the west. But, war having broke out soon after in Europe, he had not been able to draw from this colony the advantages he had anticipated, because the merchants of the kingdom engaged in maritime commerce, had relations and concerns in the other French colonies, which they could not relinquish.

The king declares that, on the report made to him of the situation of the territory, now known as the province of Louisiana, he has determined to establish there a commerce, which will be very beneficial to France; it being now necessary to seek in foreign countries many articles of commerce, which may be obtained there, for merchandise of the growth or manufacture of the kingdom.

He accordingly grants to Crozat the exclusive commerce of all the territory possessed by the crown, between old and new Mexico, and Carolina, and all the settlements, ports, roads and rivers therein—principally the port and road of Dauphine Island, before called Massacre Island, the river St. Louis, previously called the Mississippi, from the sea to the Illinois, the river St. Philip, before called Missouri, the river St. Jerome, before called the Wabash, with all the land, lakes and rivers mediately or immediately flowing into any part of the river St. Louis or Mississippi.

The territory, thus described, is to be and remain included, under the style of the government of Louisiana, and to be a dependence of the government of New France, to which it is to be subordinate. The king's territory, beyond the Illinois, is to be and continue part of the goverment of New France, to which it is annexed; and he reserves to himself the faculty of enlarging that of Louisiana.

The right is given to the grantee, to export from France into Louisiana all kinds of goods, wares and merchandise, during fifteen years, and to carry on there such a commerce as he may think fit. All persons, natural or corporate, are inhibited from trading there, under pain of the confiscation of their goods, wares, merchandise and vessels: and the officers of the king are commanded to assist the grantee, his agents and factors, in seizing them.

Permission is given to open and work mines, and to export the ore to France during fifteen years. The property of all the mines he may discover and work, is given him: yielding to the king the fourth part of the gold and silver, to be delivered in France, at the cost of the grantee, but at the risk of the king, and the tenth part of all other metals. He may search for precious stones and pearls, yielding to the king one-fifth of them, in the same manner as gold and silver. Provision is made for the re-union of the king's domain of such mines as may cease during three years to be worked.

Liberty is given to the grantee, to sell to the French and Indians of Louisiana, such goods, wares and merchandise as he may import, to the exclusion of all others, without his express and written order. He is allowed to purchase and export to France, hides, skins and peltries. But, to favor the trade of Canada, he is forbidden to purchase beaver skins, or to export them to France or elsewhere.

The absolute property, in fee simple, is vested in him of all the establishments and manufactures he may make in silk, indigo, wool and leather, and all the land he may cultivate, with all buildings, etc.; he taking from the governor and intendant grants, which are to become void, on the land ceasing to be improved.

The laws, edicts and ordinances of the realm, and the custom of Paris are extended to Louisiana.

The obligation is imposed on the grantee to send yearly two vessels from France to Louisiana, in each of which he is to transport two boys or girls, and the king may ship free from freight twenty-five tons of provisions, ammunition, etc., for the use of the colony, and more, paying freight; and passage is to be afforded to the king's officers and soldiers for a fixed compensation.

One hundred quintals of powder are to be furnished annually to the grantee, out of the king's stores, at cost.

An exemption from duties on the grantee's goods, wares and merchandise, imported to, or exported from Louisiana, is allowed.

The king promises to permit, if he thinks it proper, the importation of foreign goods to Louisiana, on the application of the grantee, and the production of his invoices, etc.

The use is given him of the boats, pirogues and canoes, belonging to the king, for loading and unloading: he keeping and returning them, in good order, at the expiration of his grant.

The faculty is allowed him to send annually a vessel to Guinea, for negroes, whom he may sell in Louisiana, to the exclusion of all others.

After the expiration of nine years, the grantee is to pay the field officers and garrison kept in Louisiana, and on the occurrence of vacancies, commissions are to be granted to officers presented by the grantee, if approved.

A fifty gun ship, commanded by the Marquis de la Jonquere, landed at Dauphine Island, on the seventeenth of May, 1713, the officers who were to administer the government of the colony under the new system.

The principal of these were, Lamotte Cadillac, an officer who had served with distinction in Canada, during the preceding war, who was appointed governor; Duclos, commissary ordonnateur; Lebas, comptroller; Dirigoin, the principal director of Crozat's concerns in Louisiana, and Laloire des Ursins, who was to attend to them on the Mississippi.

The ship brought a very large stock of provisions and goods.

The governor and commissary ordonnateur, by an edict of the eighteenth of December, of the preceding year, had been constituted a superior council, vested with the same powers as the councils of St. Domingo and Martinico; but the existence of this tribunal was limited to three years from the day of its meeting.

The expenses of the king for the salaries of his officers in Louisiana, were fixed at an annual sum of ten thousand dollars. It was to be paid to Crozat in France, and the drafts of the commissary ordonnateur, were to be paid in Crozat's stores, in cash, or in goods, with an advance of fifty per cent. Sales in all other cases were to be made, in these stores, at an advance of one hundred per cent.

Commerce was Crozat's principal object, and he contemplated carrying it on chiefly with the Spaniards. His plan was to have large warehouses on Dauphine Island, and to keep small vessels plying with goods to Pensacola, Tampico, Touspe, Campeachy and Vera Cruz. His designs were however frustrated; the Spaniards, after the peace, refusing admittance to French vessels in those ports, on the solicitation of the British, to whom the king had granted privilege by the treaty of the Assiento.

He had recommended to Lamotte Cadillac, to whom he had given an interest in his concerns in Louisiana, to send a strong detachment to the Illinois, and towards the Spanish settlements in the west, to be employed in the search of mines and the protection of his commerce.

The benefits, which the French government had anticipated from a change of administrators in Louisiana, were not realized. An unfortunate misunderstanding took place between the new governor and Bienville— the former being jealous of the affection which the soldiers and Indians manifested to the latter.

La Louisiane, a ship belonging to Crozat, arrived in the summer with a large supply of provisions and goods, and brought a considerable number of passengers.

In the course of the winter, deputations from most of the neighboring nations of Indians came to visit and solicit the protection of the new chief of the colony.

Canada was so overwhelmed by repeated emissions of card money, and the consequent ruin and distress was so great that the planters and merchants united in a petition to the king, for the redemption of the cards at one half of their nominal value, offering to lose the other.

The British of Carolina, after the peace of Utrecht, gave a great extension to their commerce with the Indians near the back settlements of the province. Their traders had erected storehouses among the tribes in alliance with the French, as far as the Natchez and the Yazous. The Choctaws were so attached to the French, that they had heretofore refused to allow the British to trade among them. In the spring, however, a party of the British, heading two thousand Indians of the Alibamons, Talapouches and Chickasaws, came among the Choctaws; they were received in thirty of the villages: two only refusing to admit them. Violence being threatened against the minority, the Choctaws of these two villages built a fort, in which they collected, bidding defiance to their countrymen, the British and their allies. They held out for a considerable time: at last, on the eve of being overwhelmed, they escaped during the night, and made their way to the French fort at Mobile, where they were cordially greeted.

While the bulk of the Choctaws were thus diverted to the British, the Alibamons testified their attachment to the French by aiding them to build a fortress on their river. It was called Fort Toulouse.

Lamotte Cadillac being disappointed in his hope of trading with the Spanish ports on the gulf, made in the summer an attempt to find a vent for Crozat's goods, in the interior parts of Mexico. His object also was to check the progress of the Spaniards, whom he understood, were preparing to advance their settlements in the province of Texas, to the neighborhood of Natchitoches. St. Denys was therefore sent with a large quantity of goods, attended by thirty Canadians and some Indians, on this service.

In the month of August, Queen Anne, of Great Britain, died at the age of fifty, without issue, although she had given birth to nineteen children. She was the sixth and last sovereign of the house of Stuart. The crown, according to a statute for the exclusion of the children of James the second, passed to George, elector of Hannover, a grandson of princess Sophia, granddaughter of James the first.

The discovery of mines of the precious metals was a darling object with Lamotte Cadillac, and in the latter part of the winter his credulity was powerfully acted upon. A man named Dutigne, came from Canada, bringing from the Illinois two pieces of ore, which he asserted had been dug up in the neighborhood of the Kaskaskias. The governor had them assayed, and they were found to contain a great proportion of silver. Elated at the discovery, and eager to secure what he considered as a rich mine, he set off for the Illinois without disclosing the cause of his sudden departure, and had the mortification to learn on his arrival, that the pieces of ore which Dutigne had brought down came from Mexico, and had been left as curiosities, by a Spaniard, with a gentleman at the Illinois, from whom Dutigne had received them. Disappointed in his hope of the silver mine, he visited mines of lead on the western side of the Mississippi, and returned to Mobile without boasting of the object of his errand.

The British in the meanwhile, were progressing fast in their plan of establishing truckhouses among the Choctaws, Natchez, Yazous and other nations on the Mississippi. Bienville had sent for the principal chiefs of the Choctaws; he upbraided them for their treachery; urging that the French were the only people, from whom they could conveniently get the goods they wanted, as the British were at a comparative great distance from their villages. He prevailed on them to draw off all communication with them and the Indians in their alliance. The Choctaws kept their word, and on their return drove off every British trader from their villages.

An officer of the name of Young, a native of South Carolina, who was then with the Choctaws, made his way to the Natchez, and descended the Mississippi with the view of inducing the Oumas, Pascagoulas, Chouachas and Colapissas, to enter into an alliance with his nation. Laloire des Ursins, Crozat's principal agent on the river, went up in a pirogue to meet the intruder. He found him near bayou Manchac, arrested and sent him a prisoner to Mobile. Bienville allowed him to proceed to Pensacola, whence he attempted to reach Carolina by land, but was killed by some of the Thome Indians.

While Bienville was thus successful in preserving the attachment of the Choctaws and the natives on the Mississippi, he had the pleasure of learning that the Indians bordering on Carolina, imitating the Choctaws, had turned against the British, and invaded the frontier settlements of that province. The Yamassees, the Creeks and Apalachians spread desolation and slaughter in the south; while the Cherokees, Congarees and Catawbas, ravaged the northern part. It was computed the enemy were between seven and eight thousand strong. Indeed, every tribe from Florida to Cape Fear, had engaged in the war. The security of Charleston was doubted. It had not more than twelve hundred men fit to bear arms; but there were several forts near it, which offered places of refuge. Governor Craven marched with his small force against the enemy, who had advanced as far as Stono, where they burnt the church, as they did every house on their way. The governor advanced slowly and with caution, and as he proceeded, the straggling parties fled before him, till he reached the Saltketchers, where the Indians had pitched their great camp. Here a sharp battle ensued. The Indians were repulsed and the governor pursued them over the Savannah river. It is said the province lost, in in this war, upwards of eight hundred men, women and children. The Yamassees were driven from the land they had heretofore occupied, behind Port Royal Island, on the northeast side of the Savannah river. They settled in the neighborhood of the Spaniards, by whom the British alleged they had been instigated.

An officer of the garrison of Mobile, called St. Helen, who happened to be in a village of the Chickasaws, in which were fifteen British traders, was protected by a Choctaw chief, while these men were killed, but, being mistaken for one of them, by a young Indian who entered the cabin he was in, while he stooped to light a cigar, he was slain.

Bienville forwarded presents to the Indians, who had seceded from the British alliance, and directed his messengers to induce them to send to Mobile some of their head men, with whom a treaty might be made.

The Indians of the two villages of the Choctaws, who had remained steadfast in their friendship for the French, were still in the very neighborhood of Mobile. Bienville sent word to the chiefs of the other villages, he would not confide in them as friends, but cease to have any communication with them, if they persisted in refusing to receive their countrymen. He required them to send him the head of Ousachouti (the brother of the principal chief) who had been most active in introducing the British traders, and fomenting the civil war. The Choctaws, after some debate, slew the obnoxious chief, and sent for their countrymen of the two villages.

In the summer, the garrison was reinforced by two companies of infantry, commanded by Marigny de Mandeville and Bagot. With them came Rouzeau, sent to succeed Dirigoin, as principal director of Crozat's concerns in Louisiana.

At the same time, Bienville received the commission of commander-general of all the establishments on the Mississippi, and the rivers flowing into it.

A ship from la Rochelle and another from Martinico, came to Dauphine Island to trade. They were not permitted to land any goods as this would have been a violation of Crozat's privilege.

Louis the fourteenth died on the first of September, in his seventy-seventh year, and was succeeded by his grandson, Louis the fifteenth. The new monarch being in his sixth year only, his uncle, the Duke of Orleans, governed the kingdom during the minority.

The Cherokees fell in the beginning of the next year on the French settlements on the Wabash, and killed two men, named Ramsay and Longeuil. The father of the latter who was the king's lieutenant at Montreal, induced the Iroquois to declare war against the Cherokees. It was prosecuted with much vigor for a considerable time, and ended in the rout of the latter.

In execution of the king's order, Bienville assumed the command of the establishments on the Mississippi. A few French stragglers had settled among the Tunicas, Natchez, Yazous and Bayagoulas, and we have seen that clergymen from Canada visited, at times, these tribes as missionaries, and some of them had located themselves among these Indians: but there was as yet but one small fort on the mighty stream, not far from the sea. He was instructed to erect two others—one among the Natchez and the other on the Wabash. The connection of Louisiana with Canada was a favorite object at court, and it had been very strongly recommended to both the colonial governments. There was already a considerable population on that river, with whom the Canadians kept a regular intercourse by their huntsmen or coureurs de bois; this rising settlement afforded also a commodious resting place to emigrants from Canada to Louisiana.

Laloire des Ursins, who lived in the fort on the Mississippi, as director of Crozat's concerns on the river, had built six large pirogues for the intended expedition, and Bienville having reached the fort with a detachment, ordered his men to proceed to the landing of the Tunicas. These Indians had lately removed to the banks of a lake, which empties in the Mississippi through a bayou to which they gave their name which it still retains.

Bienville spent a few days with Laloire des Ursins, in order to have a conference with the head men of the Chouachas, a tribe who lived a little below the spot on which the city of New Orleans is built; on reaching his detachment he was informed the Natchez had lately killed two Frenchmen, and stopped and robbed nine Canadians who were descending the river. They had sent a messenger to solicit their aid in resisting the French. He sent an interpreter to the Natchez, directing him to conceal from them Bienville's knowledge of the murder—and to request them to meet him on friendly terms at their landing. In the hope that a show of confidence might induce him to overlook what had happened when he was informed of it, nineteen of these Indians attended with the nine Canadians. Among the former were five suns and seven village chiefs.

Bienville had pitched his tent on the bank of the Mississippi, and the Indians, as they approached, were told they could not be received as friends till the death of his countrymen was expiated. The head of the deputation, turning towards the sun, addressed that luminary in an invocation which he seemed to think would appease Bienville, to whom he tendered the calumet of peace. He was told no reconciliation could be expected till the head of the chief, at whose instigation the French had been killed, was brought to the camp. He replied that chief was a great warrior and a sun. On this, Bienville had him and some of his companions arrested and put under guard and in irons.

On the next day, the captives sent a messenger to the village for the desired head. He returned with that of an Indian who had consented to die for his chief: but Bienville, having been apprised of the deception, refused the proffered head. With as little success, the same imposition was attempted the following day.

The Canadians having informed Bienville that six pirogues were on their way from the Illinois, and would probably be stopped by the Indians if timely precautions were not taken, a canoe was dispatched at night, and the people on the pirogues, being thus apprised of the impending danger, were enabled to avoid it.

A number of the Natchez came to Bienville's camp and surrendered themselves, desirous to lose their lives, that they might in the next world wait on their captive chiefs, if their lives were not spared. He told them he had no doubt that Longbeard, one of his prisoners, had been concerned in the murder, and was one of those who had favored the admission of the British traders among the Natchez; but, as he had come into the camp of the French as a messenger of peace, his life would not be taken till the determination of the nation to refuse the head that had been demanded, was known. The Indians in the camp, however, expressed their wish that as he was a turbulent fellow, and had often disturbed their tranquillity, he might be sacrificed. Bienville declined doing so until he had the consent of the nation. The Indian was however secretly dispatched by his countrymen without the participation of any of the white people.

After this, Bienville and the French accompanied the Indians to their village. The property of the Canadians was restored, and with the consent of the Natchez a fort was begun on the spot which Iberville had chosen for a town. It was called Fort Rosalie, and a small garrison was left in it, under the order of Pailloux, in the latter part of June.

One of Crozat's ships arrived at Mobile in the following month, with a large supply of goods and provisions; she landed twenty passengers.

After a journey of upwards of two years, St. Denys reached Mobile, in the month of August. We have seen that he was sent in 1714 into the internal provinces of Spain, for the double purpose of finding a vent for Crozat's goods, and checking the advances of the Spaniards, who were preparing to form settlements, in the neighborhood of Natchitoches. He had reached this place, with his Canadians and Indians, without accident. He employed them in erecting a few huts for some of the Canadians he was to leave there, and having engaged some individuals of the neighboring tribes to join the Natchitoches, he supplied them with a few implements of husbandry, and useful seeds. Then, taking twelve chosen Canadians and a small number of Indians, he left Red river and marched westerly. After journeying for twenty days he came to a village of the Assinais, not far from the spot where Lasalle was murdered, about thirty years before. There he obtained guides, who led him one hundred and fifty leagues farther, to the easternmost settlement of the Spaniards on *Rio Bravo;* it was called St. John the Baptist, or Presidio del Norte. Don Pedro de Villescas, who commanded there, received the French with much hospitality. St. Denys informed his host he was sent by Lamotte Cadillac, to make arrangements for a commerce that might be equally beneficial to the Spanish and French colonists. Don Pedro said he could not do anything, without consulting the governor of Caouis, under whose immediate orders he was. This officer resided at a distance of about one hundred and eighty miles, and on receiving a communication from Don Pedro, dispatched twenty-five horsemen to bring St. Denys to him. He detained him until the beginning of 1715, when he informed him that he considered it his duty to send him to the viceroy. St. Denys being about to depart, wrote to his companions, whom he had left at the Presidio del Norte, to return to Natchitoches.

Caouis is distant from Mexico about seven hundred and fifty miles, and St. Denys was conducted by an officer, attended by twenty horsemen. On his arrival in the capital, the viceroy sent him to prison. He was enlarged, after a confinement of three months, at the solicitation of several French officers in the service of Spain. The viceroy now treated him with kindness, and made every effort in his power to induce him to enter the service of the Catholic king. Finding his endeavors useless, he made a present to St. Denys of a fine horse from his stable, supplied him with money and sent him back to Caouis, from whence he proceeded to the Presidio del Norte. Don Pedro was much affected at the removal of the Indians of five neighboring villages, who fatigued at the vexations they experienced from the officers and soldiers of the garrison of the Presidio, had determined to seek an asylum among a distant tribe of Indians. St. Denys offered to Don Pedro to go and bring them back; he soon overtook them, as their children and baggage much retarded their march. Placing a white handkerchief on the muzzle of his musket, as soon as he perceived them, he waved it as a token of his friendly intentions; they waited his approach. He placed before them the danger they ran, in removing among Indians who were utter strangers to them, and told them he was charged by Don Pedro to assure them, that, if they would re-occupy their villages, neither officers or soldiers of the Presidio, would be suffered to enter any of them, without their consent. They agreed to return with him, and Don Pedro, who feared that the departure of these Indians from the neighborhood of the Presidio should be attributed to his ill conduct or neglect, was gratified by the service St. Denys had rendered him.

During the short interval he had passed before, under Don Pedro's roof, the charms of the Spaniard's daughter had made a lively impression on St. Denys, and she had appeared to reciprocate his affection. He now pressed his suit, and obtained her hand. He staid six months with her, after their nuptials, and left her pregnant, returning to Mobile, accompained by Don Juan de Tillescas, her uncle.

Lamotte Cadillac was now convinced that a commerce with the Spaniards

17

was as impossible by land as by water; and he apprised Crozat of the inutility of any further attempt either way.

The period, for which the Superior Council of Louisiana had been established, being about to expire, the king, in the month of September, re-established it by a perpetual and irrevocable edict. It was however, new modelled, and to be composed of the governor-general and intendant of New France, the governor of Louisiana, a senior councillor, the king's lieutenant, two puisne councillors and an attorney-general and clerk. The edict gives to the council all the powers, exercised by the superior councils of other colonies: principally that of determining all cases, civil and criminal, in the last resort, and without costs. Its sessions are directed to be monthly, and a quorum is to consist, in civil cases of three judges, and in criminal of five. When necessary, in the absence and lawful excuse of the members, notables may be called to vacant seats. The intendant of New France, and, in his absence, the senior councillor, is to act as president, even, in presence of the governor-general of New France, or the governor of Louisiana. In provisional matters, fixing of seals, making inventories, etc., the senior councillor is authorized to act as a judge of first instance.

This edict was followed on the sixteenth of November, by an ordinance relating to redemptioners and muskets; it was not confined to Louisiana. Vessels, leaving the kingdom for any of the king's American colonies, were directed to carry thither, if under sixty tons four, and if above, six redemptioners, whose period of service was fixed at three years. They were required to be able bodied, between the ages of seventeen and forty, and in size not under four feet. It was provided that the redemptioners, whom the captain might not sell, should be given by the governor to some of the planters who had not any, and who were to pay their passage.

Crozat having recommended that notwithstanding the ill success of St. Denys, in his attempt to open a trade with the Spanish provinces bordering on Louisiana, the project should not be abandoned; three Canadians, named Delery, Lafreniere and Beaulieu, were supplied with goods out of his stores, in the month of October, and proceeded by the way of Red river to the province of New Leon; and to prevent the Spaniards from occupying the country of the Natchitoches, among whom St. Denys had left a few of his countrymen, a detachment was placed under the orders of Dutisne, who was directed to build and garrison a fort, among these Indians.

Three of Crozat's ships arrived from France on the ninth of March. They brought l'Epinai, who had been appointed governor, and Hubert commissary ordonnateur. Duclos, whom he succeeded, went in that capacity to St. Domingo. Three companies of infantry, under the orders of De Rome and Gouis, and fifty new colonists, accompanied them, among whom were Trefontaine, Guenot, Dubreuil and Mossy.

L'Epinai brought the cross of St. Louis to Bienville.

The Peacock, one of these ships, went into the bay of Ship Island, on the entrance of which they found twenty-seven feet of water; and two days after, she was unable to come out, without being unladen—the pass being entirely stopped up. After being lightened, she came out through the channel of the Island of Grand Grozier; where she found ten feet of water. This was more surprising, as since the arrival of Iberville, nineteen years before, no alteration had been noticed.

Another of the ships was sent to Havana for cattle; she went in under the pretence of distress, and was allowed three days to refit and procure provisions. She took in sixty cows; this excited surprise, and it being found they were intended for Louisiana, the captain-general insisted on forty-five of them being re-landed.

Although the services of Bienville had been rewarded by knighthood, the arrival of l'Epinai, as governor, gave him great mortification. The officers of the garrison were attached to him, and observed their new chief with a jealous eye. This was the source of an unfortunate schism in the colony, which for a while checked its progress. Hubert, who was a man of business, sided with l'Epinai, and his animosity against Bienville went so far as to charge him with being a pensioner of Spain, bribed to check the progress of the settlement.

Crozat's agents, finding but little vent for his goods in the colony, put a considerable quantity of them on board of one of his ships, which they sent to Vera Cruz, under the impression that they might be permitted to land them: but the viceroy was found inflexible. Her cargo was worth two hundred thousand dollars, at the costs in France, and the goods had mostly been selected with the view of being sold to the Spaniards at Mexico, and Crozat had made the attempt, in the hope of providing by the sale of these goods the means of discharging large sums that were due to the troops and workmen. On the return of the ship, they were compelled to offer to these people, in discharge of their claims, articles of luxury better suited for a great city, than for a rising colony. This excited great murmurs; Crozat's exclusive privilege had grown very unpopular in Louisiana. The colonial officers, who, heretofore had carried on an interlope trade with Vera Cruz, Havana and Pensacola, viewed with jealousy his agents and the new administrators, whom he had strongly attached to his interest, by a share in the privilege.

In the month of August, Crozat disappointed in the expectations he had entertained, surrendered his grant to the king. He complained that the weakness of the colony rendered it contemptible to the Indians, whom it could not prevent from incessantly waging war among themselves, whereby no trade could safely be carried on with them; that, the British drew nigher and nigher, and confined the French to their small settlements at Mobile, Biloxi and Dauphine Island—that the land on the island, and near the other two settlements, was sandy and sertile, while the rich land on the Mississippi was open to the British, whom nothing prevented from occupying it. The surrender was accepted on the twenty-third—about five years from the date of the charter.

During this period, neither the commerce nor agriculture of the colony was increased. The troops sent by the king and the colonists who came from France, did not swell its population to more than seven hundred persons of all ages, sexes or color. Two new forts were erected and garrisoned; Fort Toulouse among the Alibamons, and Fort Rosalie among the Natchez.

Arrangements having been made with three individuals of the names of Aubert, Renet and Gayon, for the commerce of Canada, which were to expire with the current year, government determined on creating a company, capable of carrying on the commerce of Canada and Louisiana, and improving the advantages which the cultivation of the soil, in these colonies presented. This was effected a few days after the surrender of Crozat's privilege was accepted.

CHAPTER IX.

The charter of the new corporation was registered in the Parliament of Paris on the sixth of September, 1717.

It is to be distinguished by the style of the Western Company, and all the king's subjects, as well as corporate bodies and aliens, are allowed to take shares in it.

The exclusive commerce of Louisiana is granted to it for twenty-five years; with the right, also exclusive, of purchasing beaver skins from the inhabitants of Canada, from the first of January, 1718, until the last day of the year 1742; and, the monarch reserves to himself the faculty of settling on information to be obtained from Canada, the number of skins the company shall be bound annually to receive from the inhabitants, and the price to be paid therefor.

All the other subjects of the king are prohibited from trading to Louisiana, under the penalty of the confiscation of their merchandise and vessels: but this is not intended to prevent the inhabitants from trading among themselves or with the Indians. It is likewise prohibited to any but the company, to purchase during the same period, beaver skins in Canada for exportation under the penalty of the forfeiture of the skins, and the vessels in which they may be shipped: but, the trade in these skins in the interior is to continue as heretofore.

The land, coasts, harbors and islands in Louisiana are granted to the company, as they were to Crozat, it doing faith and homage to the king, and furnishing a crown of gold of the weight of thirty marks, at each mutation of the sovereignty.

It is authorized to make treaties with the Indians, and to declare and prosecute war against them in case of insult.

The property of all mines it may open and work, is granted to it, without the payment of any duty whatsoever.

The faculty is given it to grant land, even allodially, to erect forts, levy troops and recruits even in the kingdom, procuring the king's permission for this purpose.

It is authorized to nominate governors and the officers commanding the troops, who are to be presented by the directors and commissioned by the king and removable by the company. Provisional commissions may, in case of necessity be granted to be valid during six months, or until the royal commission arrive.

The directors and all officers are to take an oath of fidelity to the king.

Military officers in Louisiana are permitted to enter into the service of the company, and others to go there with the king's license to serve it. All while in its service are to preserve their respective ranks and grades in the royal land and naval forces; and the king promises to acknowledge as rendered to himself all services they may render to the company.

Power is given to fit out ships of war and cast cannon, and to appoint and remove judges and officers of justice; but the judges of the superior council are to be nominated and commissioned by the king.

All civil suits to which the company may be a party, are to be determined by the consular jurisdiction of the city of Paris, the sentences of which under a fixed sum are to be in the last resort: those above are to be provisorily executed notwithstanding, but without prejudice of the appeal, which is to be brought before the Parliament of Paris. Criminal jurisdiction is not to draw with it that of the civil matter.

The king promises not to grant any letter of dispensation or respite to any debtor of the company; and he assures it of the protection of his name, against any foreign nation, injuring the company.

French vessels and crews alone, are to be employed by it, and it is to bring the produce of Louisiana into the ports of the kingdom. All goods, in its vessels are to be presumed its property, unless it be shown they were shipped with its license.

The subjects of the king, removing to Louisiana, are to preserve their national character, and their children (and those of European parents, professing the Roman Catholic religion) born there, are to be considered as natural born subjects.

During the continuance of the charter, the inhabitants of Louisiana are exempted from any tax or imposition, and the company's goods from duty.

With the view of encouraging it to build vessels in Louisiana, a gratification is to be paid on the arrival of each of them in France.

Four hundred quintals of powder are to be delivered annually to the company, out of the royal magazines, at cost.

The stock is divided into shares of five hundred livres each, (about one hundred dollars.) Their number is not limited; but the company is authorized to close the subscription at discretion. The shares of aliens are exempted from the *droit d'aubaine* and confiscation in case of war.

Holders are to have a vote for every fifty shares. The affairs of the company are, during the two first years, to be managed by directors appointed by the king, and afterwards by others, appointed triennially by the stockholders.

The king gives to the company all the forts, magazines, guns, ammunitions, vessels, boats, provisions, etc., in Louisiana, with all the merchandise surrendered by Crozat.

It is to build churches and provide clergymen; Louisiana is to remain part of the diocese of Quebec, it engages to bring in during its privilege, six thousand white persons and three thousand negroes; but it is stipulated, it shall not bring any person from another colony without the license of the governor.

Although the king had consented to redeem the card money that inundated Canada according to the petition of the planters and merchants of that colony, in 1713, he was tardy in the performance of his engagement, and it was not till this year, that the circulation of it was stopped. At the same time the value of coin there was reduced to the standard of the realm; dearly bought experience having shown that the rise of its legal value had not a tendency to retain specie in the colony, and that the only mean of preventing the exportation of it, was the payment of whatever was imported, in the produce of the country.

On the ninth of February, 1718, three of the company's ships arrived, with as many companies of infantry and sixty-nine colonists. Boisbriant, who came in this fleet, and who was appointed king's lieutenant in the colony, was the bearer of Bienville's commission as governor of the province; l'Epinai being recalled. Hubert had been made director-general of the concerns of the company in Louisiana. The troops and the inhabitants generally saw with great pleasure the chief command restored to Bienville.

He had spent twenty years in the colony and was well acquainted with its wants and resources.

The three Canadians, who had gone on a trading expedition to the province of New Leon, in 1716, returned to Mobile. They had been joined by St. Denys, and having supplied themselves with horses and mules at Natchitoches, they journeyed to a small village of the Adayes, which had but thirty warriors. Fording the river here, they came soon after to a group of about ten cabins of the Adeyches; near which the Spaniards had a mission composed of two friars, three soldiers and a woman.

Their next stage was at Nagogdoches, where they found the same number of friars, a lay brother and a woman. The first village of the Assinais was thirty miles farther. Here they met two friars and a woman. St. Denys now parted from his companions and went ahead with part of the goods. His companions, after journeying for twenty-five miles, reached the first presidio, garrisoned by a captain, lieutenant and twenty-five soldiers; they journeyed along, crossing two streams, about thirty miles to the last village of the Assinais, near which was a mission composed of two friars and a few soldiers. They halted seventy miles farther on the bank of the river Trinity. At nearly the same distance they crossed a river near which were immense herds of buffaloes. It had two branches, on the farthest of which was an Indian village of fifty huts. The travellers found Rio Colorado at the distance of about fifty miles. This is the stream near the mouth of which Lasalle built Fort Louis, which the Spaniards destroyed in 1696. Soon after crossing it, the party was attacked by about sixty Spaniards, on horseback, covered with hides, who, intimidated by its spirited conduct, fled; but, shortly after, came upon the rear of the French, and carried away a mulatto woman and three mules, one of which was loaded with a quantity of goods. The French reached, on the next day, the camp of a wandering tribe of Indians, who had erected about thirty huts and who gave them a friendly reception. After a stay of two days to rest, the party crossed on the second day the river St. Mark, and on the evening of the following, that of Guadeloupe. Fording afterwards that of St. Anthony, they stopped at the presidio of St. John the Baptist, on the western side of Rio Bravo or Del Norte, at the distance of about six miles from the stream.

The garrison of this post consisted of a captain, lieutenant and thirty-six soldiers. The settlement was confined to a square, surrounded with mud houses. Within this command were the missions of St. Joseph and St. Bernard.

The French were informed here that the goods brought by St. Denys had been seized, and he was gone to Mexico to solicit their release. To avoid a similar misfortune, they placed theirs in the hands of the friars, and afterwards disposed of them to merchants from Bocca de Leon. They were tarrying to receive their payment when accounts reached the presidio that St. Denys had been imprisoned. This induced them to depart abruptly, and make the best of their way to Mobile.

On their return they found a new mission had been established at the Adayes, under the name of San Miguel de Linarez.

The report of these people convinced the colonial government that it would be in vain to make any further attempt towards establishing a trade with the neighboring provinces of Spain.

Bienville, according to the last instructions he had received, dispatched

Chateaugue, with fifty men, to take possession of the bay of St. Joseph, between Pensacola and St. Marks. Chateaugue marked out the lines of a fort, and left Gousy to build and command it.

In the meanwhile, Bienville visited the banks of the Mississippi, in order to select a spot for the principal settlement of the province. He chose that on which the city of New Orleans now stands, and left there fifty men to clear the ground and erect barracks.

The company had been taught by the failure of all the plans of Crozat, that nothing was to be expected from a trade with the Spaniards, or the search after mines of the precious metals, in Louisiana; and, that no considerable advantage could attend an exclusive trade with an extensive province, thinly peopled, unless agriculture enabled the planters to purchase, and furnish returns for, the merchandise that might be sent thither. It was imagined the culture of the soil would be best promoted by large grants (many of several miles front on the rivers) to powerful and wealthy individuals in the kingdom.

Accordingly, one was made on the Arkansas river, of twelve miles square to Law, a Scotchman, who had acquired great credit at court, by several plans of finance, which he had proposed. Others of inferior, though still very large, extent, were made—particularly one on the river of the Yazous, to a company composed of Leblanc, secretary of state, Count de Belleville, the Marquis of Assleck and Leblond, who afterwards came to Louisiana, as a general officer of the engineers: others at the Natchez, to Hubert, and a company of merchants of St. Maloes; at the Cadodaquious, above the Natchitoches, up Red river, to Benard de la Harpe; at the Tunicas, to St. Reine; at Point Coupee, to de Meuse; at the place on which now stands the town of Baton Rouge, to Diron d'Arta-guette; on the right side of the Mississippi, opposite to Bayou Manchac, to Paris Duvernay; at the Tchoupitoulas, to de Muys; at the Oumas, to the Marquis d'Ancouis; at the Cannes Brulees, to the Marquis d'Artagnac; opposite to these on the right side of the river, to de Guiche, de la Houssaie and de la Houpe; at the bay of St. Louis, to Madame de Mezieres; and at the Pascagoulas, to Madame de Chaumont.

It has been stipulated with Law, that he should bring fifteen hundred persons from Germany or Provence, to settle the land granted him, on the Arkansas, and he was to maintain a small body of horse and foot for their protection. Each of the other grantees was bound to transport a number of settlers, proportioned to the extent of his grant. The company expected by these means, to fulfil the obligation imposed by the charter, to introduce six thousand white persons into the colony. Experience, however, showed that although these large grants facilitated the transportation of settlers, little was obtained from the labors of men, brought over from a distant clime, to cultivate land, the proprietors of which staid behind.

The first accession of population, which Louisiana received in this manner, consisted of sixty men, led by Dubuisson, to occupy the land granted to Paris Duvernay. They arrived in the month of April.

In June, three of the company's ships arrived; Richbourg, a knight of St. Louis, and Grandval, lately appointed major of the fort at Mobile, with a number of subaltern officers, came in these vessels. They were accompanied by Legas, an under-director, who brought thirty young men, to be employed as clerks, in the offices of the company: seventy settlers of the grant of de la Houssaie, and sixty of that of de la Houpe, with twelve companies of fifteen settlers, each of lesser grants; a number of soldiers and convicts, came also at the same time. The addition to the population of the colony by these vessels amounted to upwards of eight hundred persons.

The Spaniards complained grievously of the occupation of the bay of St. Joseph, as a military post. They had induced one-half of the garrison to desert; Chateaugue was sent to bring back the remainder. The fort, being thus abandoned by the French, was immediately after occupied by the Spaniards.

The former spread themselves widely over Louisiana in the fall. Benard de la Harpe, with sixty settlers, went to take possession of his grant, at the Cadodaquious, up Red river. Bizart was sent with a small detachment to the river Yazous, where he built fort St. Peter, and Boisbriant went to take the command at the Illinois. Thus the settlements of the French in Louisiana, acquired the utmost extension from east to west, they ever had, i. e., from fort Toulouse on the Alibamons, to a point on Red river, beyond the present limits of the State. This circumstance weakened much the colony, and was certainly unpropitious to its progress in agriculture. Its commerce was supposed to be favored by pushing the settlements among distant tribes of Indians, and facilitating the collections of furs and peltries.

A number of soldiers of the garrison of Mobile deserted this winter, and found their way by land, to the settlements of the British in South Carolina.

A large party of Spaniards from the neighboring provinces came to the Missouri with the view of descending and attacking the French at the Illinois. They fell on two towns of the Missouri Indians and routed the inhabitants. But, those at the mouth of the river, having timely notice of the approach of the foe, collected in vast numbers, attacked and defeated it. They made a great slaughter and tortured to death all the prisoners they took, except two friars. One of these died soon after: the other remained awhile in captivity. He had a fine horse and was very skilful in the management of it: one day as he was amusing the Indians with feats of horsemanship, he applied his spurs to the sides of the animal and effected his escape.

In the spring, l'Archambault, lately appointed director-general of the company's concerns, arrived at Mobile with upwards of one hundred passengers.

St. Denys now returned from Mexico. He had left the presidio of St. John the Baptist, with the view of procuring the release of his goods. On his arrival, the Marquis de Valero, who had succeded the Duke of Linarez in the viceroyalty, had flattered him with hopes of success. But Don Martin de Alacorne, governor of the province of Texas, having heard of the passage of St. Denys through his government, without having seen him, had written to the Marquis, representing St. Denys as a suspicious character, who was claiming property that was not his own. Too ready an ear was given to the misrepresentation of Don Martin, and St. Denys was arrested and imprisoned. One month after he obtained from the royal audience a decree for the release of his person and the restitution of his goods. He disposed of them to much advantage; but the person whom he employed for the collection of the proceeds, wasted them.

Exasperated by his misfortune, he vented his rage in abuses of the Spaniards, and in vaunting his influence with the Indians. This indiscretion occasioned an order for his arrest; but some of his wife's relations gave him notice of it, and furnished means of escape.

The only advantage the company derived from his excursion, was the evidence of his fidelity, and some information relating to the Spanish settlements.

The province of New Leon was thinly peopled, but rich in the gifts of nature. It had large meadows covered with cattle and vast fields highly cultivated, abounding in all kinds of grain and fruit; Monterey was its capital. Caldereto, Labradores, St. Antonio de Llanos, Linarez and Tesalve, were small open towns. The province had no mine; but the industry of its inhabitants made them sharers in the profits of their neighbors.

The Spaniards were seeking to avail themselves of the facility, which the union of the monarchies of France and Spain under princes of the same family, offered of penetrating into the western part of Louisiana. They remembered the bay of St. Bernard and the fort built there by Lasalle: they erected another on its ruins, in which they displayed the flag of Spain. They had called near it some wandering tribes of Indians, who, soon after, attacked by others less pacific, removed their village seventy miles farther westerly.

The Spaniards next brought over from the Canary Islands, a number of families, who, finding the soil, immediately on the margin of the sea, quite sterile, ascended the river San Antonio, one of those that fall into the bay of St. Bernard, and which, by the help of dykes, is made to cover and fertilize its banks. At the distance of about two hundred miles from the sea, on the border and near the source of this stream, they established the town of San Fernandez.

Another body, amounting to five hundred of these Islanders, came soon after and proceeded to the northwest. They settled among the Assinais and Abenaquis; tribes remarkable for the friendly reception they had given to Lasalle. Two friars and a few soldiers had detached themselves from this little colony, to catechise the Adayes, within twenty miles from the Natchitoches, among whom several French were domiciliated.

The Spaniards called the country they thus usurped from their neighbors, New Phillipine, in honor to the monarch of Spain, and in hope, too, that a name, dear to the French, might lessen the irritation, which the encroachment was calculated to excite.

Two company ships arrived from France, on the twenty-ninth of April. Serigny and thirty other passengers came in them. This officer was charged with the survey of the coast of Louisiana. He brought the account of the declaration of war by France against Spain, on the ninth of January, in consequence of Philip's refusal to comply with some of the stipulations of the triple alliance.

In a council of war composed of Bienville, Hubert, L'Archambault, Legas and Serigny, the attack of Pensacola was determined on.

Bienville, with as many soldiers of the garrison as could be spared, a number of Canadians and four hundred Indians, gathered around the fort, marched by land, while Serigny, with the shipping approached the place by water. Mattamore, the Spanish governor, having but a few soldiers, surrendered it without resistance, asking as an only condition, an

18

exemption from pillage for the inhabitants, and a passage to the Havana. Two of the company's ships went to Cuba on this service, and Chateaugue, was left in command.

Experience had shown the great fertility of the land in Louisiana, especially on the banks of the Mississippi, and its aptitude to the culture of tobacco, indigo, cotton and rice; but the laborers were very few, and many of the new comers had fallen victims to the climate. The survivors found it impossible to work in the field during the great heats of summer, protracted through a part of the autumn. The necessity of obtaining cultivators from Africa, was apparent; the company yielding thereto, sent two of its ships to the coast of Africa, from whence they brought five hundred negroes, who were landed at Pensacola. They brought thirty recruits to the garrison.

A number of soldiers having deserted this year, and it being supposed they had gone to South Carolina, Vauchez de la Tondiere was sent to Charleston to claim them. Governor Johnstone, far from listening to the request of Bienville, sent his messenger to England; an injustice, which the indiscreet confidence of Bienville by no means justified.

In violation of the laws of war, the captain-general of the island of Cuba, seized the company's ships, which had entered the port of Havana to land the garrison of Pensacola, pursuant to one of the stipulations of the capitulation. Having manned them with sailors of his nation, and put a small land force on board, he sent them back to retake the place. They appeared before it on the fifth of August.

L'Archambault was still there; Chateaugue and he determined on a vigorous defense, in the hope of being soon succored by Bienville and Serigny: but the confusion, which the unexpected approach of the enemy created, and the mutiny of some soldiers, excited by a few Spanish subaltern officers, who had been incautiously suffered to remain, compelled Chateaugue to surrender the next day.

Serigny, having learnt the arrival of the Spaniards, was advancing, when he heard of their success. Aware that they would not long remain idle, he hastened to Dauphine Island, and had hardly anchored, when the enemy hove in sight. Don Antonio de la Mandella, the commodore, sent a boat to summon the officer commanding the ship, in which Serigny had advanced, to an immediate surrender; threatening in case of delay, or injury to the ship, to give no quarters, and even to extend his rigor to Chateaugue and the other French prisoners, taken at Pensacola. Diouis, who commanded the shipping, sent the messenger on shore to Serigny, who received him surrounded by two hundred soldiers, and a greater number of Indians; the latter manifested anxiety and impatience to be permitted to present Serigny with the Spaniard's scalp. He was directed to make known to Don Antonio, the determined resolution of the French to defend the shipping and island. Fifty men were sent on board of the shipping to enable them to resist the landing.

Towards the evening, one of the enemy's ships entered Mobile river, and took a boat with five men and a quantity of provisions; and on the next day, another boat laden also with provisions, going from Dauphine Island to the fort at Mobile, was captured.

In the meanwhile, Bienville reached Dauphine Island, with a large body of Indians, and the Spaniards were repulsed in their attempt to land. Nineteen of their men were killed or drowned. Eighteen French deserters were taken by the Indians : seventeen of them were shot at Mobile, and the other hung on the island.

It appearing impracticable to prevent the enemy from entering Mobile river, it was determined no longer to attempt sending provisions to the fort. Every effort was directed to the protection of the island. The Spaniards did not attempt anything till the eighteenth, when two ships were discovered coming from Pensacola. They hovered around the island the two following days, and Serigny employed this time in erecting batteries near the places in which a landing was most to be apprehended. On the twenty-first, the enemy approached the western end of the island, and exchanged a few shots with a French ship, supported by a battery. They next moved to Point Guidery, at the eastern end of the settlement. Serigny ordered Trudeau, a Canadian officer, to take as many Indians as he could, and oppose the landing. About one hundred Spaniards came on shore ; but Trudeau, approaching with twelve Indians only, they were so alarmed at the yells and shrieks of those allies of the French, that they retreated in much confusion. Ten of their men were killed or drowned.

On the next day, the enemy succeeded in effecting a second landing at the same place, but the only advantage it procured was a supply of water, obtained before the force sent by Serigny to drive them back arrived. On the same day the garrison was reinforced by sixty Indians from Mobile ; at night the barracks were consumed by an accidental fire.

Shots were again exchanged the next morning by a Spanish and a French ship under a battery. The former sailed off on the following day after firing a few broadsides at the houses. The rest of the fleet, departing one after the other, were all out of sight on the twenty-eighth.

Three ships of the line under the orders of the Count de Champmeslin, escorting two company ships, hove in sight on the first of September. The garrison were greatly alarmed, mistaking them for a fleet from Vera Cruz, which it had been reported, was coming to prosecute the success of the Spanish arms, and reduce the whole province of Louisiana.

Villardo, a new director, with two hundred passengers, arrived with Champmeslin.

A council of war was held on board of the Count's ship, in which it was determined to attack Pensacola. Two hundred soldiers were accordingly taken on board of the fleet, and the anchors were weighed on the fifteenth. Bienville set off at the same time from Mobile, by land, with the same number of soldiers and about one hundred Indians ; those on Dauphine Island having gone to the fleet. Having invested the fort, he hoisted a white flag, a signal preconcerted with Champmeslin, who immediately brought the naval force into the harbor. The main fort did not fire a single gun ; the small one was defended for a couple of hours. The shipping made a brisk but unsuccessful resistance. The Indians were allowed to pillage the main fort ; but were prevented from scalping any one.

When the Spanish commodore presented his sword to Champmeslin, the latter immediately girt it on him, saying he deserved to wear it. The commander of the land forces was treated in a different manner ; Champmeslin ordered a common sailor to receive his sword, and reprimanded the Spaniard for his want of courage ; saying he did not deserve to serve his king.

The Spaniards lost many men, the French six only. The number of prisoners made was eighteen hundred.

The hope had been entertained that a large supply of provisions and ammunition would have been found in the forts; but it turned out they had provisions for a fortnight only. The discovery induced Champmeslin to hasten the departure of his prisoners. The officer who carried them to Havana was directed to bring back all the French prisoners there, and in order to insure their return, the field officers lately taken were detained as hostages.

A brig laden with corn, flour and brandy, sent from Havana to supply the fleet, which was expected from Vera Cruz, entered the harbor of Pensacola on the twenty-eighth, having mistaken the shipping in it for that of her nation. Her captain reported that when he sailed, it was confidently believed in the island of Cuba, that the Spanish flag was flying in every fort of Louisiana.

Early in October, a brig from Vera Cruz arrived with six hundred sacks of flour, and afterwards a smaller vessel from the same port. They were both deceived by the Spanish flag, which was kept flying over the forts for this purpose.

The French fleet sailed on the twenty-third; Delisle, a lieutenant of the king's ships, was left in command at Pensacola. Of forty deserters who were found with the Spaniards, twelve were hung on board of the ships; the others were condemned to hard labor for the benefit of the company.

The directors in France having drawn the attention of the king, to the alterations which the new order of things required in the organization of the superior council of Louisiana, this tribunal had been new modelled; and by an edict of the month of September, it had been ordered that it should be composed of such directors of the company, as might be in the province, the commandant-general, a senior councillor, the king's two lieutenants, three other councillors, an attorney-general and a clerk.

The *quorum* was fixed at three members in civil, and five in criminal cases. Those present were authorized to call in some of the most notable inhabitants to form a *quorum*, in case of the absence or legitimate excuse of the others. Judgments, in original, as in appellate cases, were to be in the last resort and without costs. The sessions were to be monthly.

Hitherto the council had been the sole tribunal in the colony. The suitors had no other to which they could resort. The increasing extension of the population demanded that judges should be dispersed in the several parts of the province. The directors of the company or its agents in the distant parts, with two of the most notable inhabitants of the neighborhood, in civil, and four in criminal cases, were constituted inferior tribunals. Their judgments, though subject to an appeal to the superior council, were carried into immediate but provisional execution, notwithstanding, but without prejudice to the appeal.

The gentlemen who composed the first superior council under this edict, were Bienville, as commandant-general, Hubert, as senior councillor, Boisbriant and Chateaugue, as the king's lieutenants, L'Archambault, Villardo and Legas, as puisne councillors; Cartier de Baune was the attorney-general and Couture the clerk.

Although the commandant-general occupied the first seat in the council the senior councillor performed the functions of president of that tribunal. He collected the votes and pronounced the judgments; and in provisory instances, as the affixing of seals, inventories and the like, the duties of a judge of the first instance were discharged by him.

The hope of acquiring riches, by the discovery of mines, had not yielded to the experience of upwards of twenty years; and the people of the Illinois thought their country possessed valuable ores, and their time was more engrossed by search after them than the tillage of the earth. On their application, an engineer, who was supposed to be skilled in mineralogy, was sent late in the fall to that distant part of the colony.

The desire of Bienville to remove the seat of government, and the head quarters of the troops, to the spot he had selected on the Mississippi for a city, was opposed by the other military officers, by Hubert and the directors of the company's concerns. An extraordinary rise of the Mississippi this year seemed to present an insuperable obstacle to his project; as the colony did not possess the means of raising at once the dykes or levees necessary to protect the place from the inundation of the stream, the idea was for the present abandoned. Hubert thought the chief establishment of the province should be in the country of the Natchez; but, as he had obtained a large grant of land there, his predilection for this part of the country was attributed to private motives, and he found no adherent. L'Archambault, Villardo and Legas, whose views were more commercial than agricultural, joined in the opinion to remove the seat of government to a spot on the sea shore, on the east side of the bay of Biloxi. This opinion prevailed; and Valdelure led there a detachment to be employed in erecting houses and barracks. The place was afterwards known as the New Biloxi.

Dutisne, who had been sent to explore the country of the Missouris, Osages and Panoussas, now returned, and made a report to Bienville.

He had ascended the Mississippi as far as the *bayou des Salines*, which is six miles from the Kaskaskias, and ninety from the Missouri. He afterwards traveled through stony hills well timbered, crossing several streams which flow into the Missouri. He reckoned there were three hundred and fifty miles from the salines to the principal village of the Osages, which stood on a hill, at the distance of five miles from the river of this name. It contained about one hundred cabins, and nearly double that number of warriors. These Indians spent but a small part of the year in their villages, hunting to a great distance through the woods, during the other part. About one hundred and twenty miles from the Osages, in a prairie country, abounding with buffaloes, he found the first village of the Panionkes, which had one hundred and thirty cabins, and he estimated the number of their warriors at two hundred and fifty. They had another village, nearly of the same size, about four miles further. There were near these two villages above three hundred horses, which these Indians appeared to prize much. The Pawonees were at the distance of four hundred and fifty miles. There was a saline of rock salt at about fifty miles from the Panoussas.

He had noticed mines of lead and ores of other metals, near the villages of the Osages. The villages of the Missouris were at the distance of three hundred and fifty yards from the mouth of the river, which bears their name, and those of the Osages, about ninety miles farther.

He formally took possession of the countries of these Indians, in the name of the king, and erected posts with arms, in testimonial of it.

Delochon, a gentleman who had been recommended by the directors for his skill in mineralogy, had been sent to the Marameg, a river that falls into the Mississippi, a little above the Missouri, and on the same side.

He obtained some ore, at a place pointed out by the Indians, and asserted, that a pound of it had produced two pennyweights of silver.

On his return to Mobile, he had been sent back with a number of workmen; and the process being repeated on a very large scale, a few thousand pounds of very inferior lead were obtained. It was believed he had been guilty of a gross imposition.

Accounts were received from Europe that the western and the eastern companies had been united: the aggregate body preserving the name of the former. The new directors sent positive orders to Bienville to remove the headquarters of the colony to Biloxi: an unfortunate step, as the land there is a barren soil, absolutely incapable of culture; the anchorage unsafe, and the coast of difficult access.

The directors sent for publication in the province, a proclamation of theirs, notifying the prices, at which goods were to be obtained in the company's stores at Mobile, Dauphine Island and Pensacola. To these prices an advance of five per cent. was to be added on goods delivered at New Orleans, ten at the Natchez, thirteen at the Yazous, twenty at Natchitoches, and fifty at the Illinois and on the Missouri.

The produce of the country was to be received in the company's warehouses in New Orleans, Biloxi, Ship Island and Mobile at the following rates: Silk, according to quality, from one dollar and fifty cents to two dollars the pound; tobacco of the best kind, five dollars the hundred, rice, four, superfine flour, three, wheat, two dollars; barley and oats, ninety cents the hundred weight; deer skins, from fifteen to twenty-five; dressed, without head or tail, thirty; hides, eight cents the pound.

In the beginning of the year, de la Harpe arrived from Red river. He had established a post at the Cadodaquious, and explored the country around.

Having ascended the Red river, as far as the Natchitoches, with fifty men, in two boats and three pirogues, he found Blondel in command at the fort. Father Manual, a friar of the Spanish mission of the Adayes, had come on a visit. On an island near the fort, were about two hundred individuals of the Natchitoches, Dulcinoes and Yatassee tribes.

Don Martin de Alacorne, governor of the province of Texas, had lately gone to Rio del Norte, after having established several missions, and built a fort on a bay, which he called del Spiritu Santo, near the rivers Guadeloupe and St. Mark; and was expected to return and establish a mission at the Cadodaquious. Laharpe, anxious to pre-occupy the ground, left the fort of Nachitoches and ascended Red river to the Nassonites, who dwelt at the distance of four hundred and fifty miles. The Indians, in these parts, the Cadodaquious and Yatassees, apprised of his approach, had prepared an entertainment, to which they invited him and his officers. Large quantities of smoked beef and fish had been provided. A profound silence prevailed; the Indians deeming it uncivil to address their guests till they are perfectly at rest or begin the conversation; Laharpe waited till his hosts had satisfied their appetites, and then informed them through his interpreter, that the great chief of the French on the Mississippi, of whose mind he was the bearer, apprised of the war the Chickasaws waged against them, had sent him and some other warriors to dwell in their country and protect them against their enemies.

An old Cadodaquiou now rose and observed the time was now come for them to change their mournful mood for scenes of joy; several of his countrymen had been killed and others made prisoners, so that his nation was greatly reduced; but the arrival of the French was about to prevent its utter destruction. He concluded they should return thanks to the great spirit, whose wrath was no doubt appeased, and yield every possible assistance to the French, as his nation well knew that the Naoudishes and other wandering tribes had given them peace since the arrival of some of the French, under Lasalle.

Laharpe, desiring information as to the nearest Spanish settlements, and the neighboring tribes of Indians, was apprised that southerly, at the distance of thirty miles were the Assinais, and one hundred and twenty miles from these the Nadocoes. The Spaniards had lately sent friars and soldiers among these two tribes, whose villages could not be approached by land, except in the lowest waters; as a river was to be crossed, which in the wet season, inundated the country to a large extent. At the distance of one hundred and eighty miles, on the left side of the river, were wandering tribes of Indians, who were at war with the Cadays, in the neighborhood of whom the Spaniards had a mission.

Laharpe purchased the cabin of one of the chiefs, near the river and on the left side of it. The country was flat; but at the distance of one or two miles from the river, were bluffs, and behind these wide prairies. The soil was black, though sandy, and along the stream very suitable to the cultivation of tobacco, indigo, cotton, corn and other grains. The Indians said they sowed corn in April and gathered it in July. The most common trees were the copalm, willow, elm, red and white oak, laurel and plum. The woods abounded in vines, and the prairies were full of strawberries, cranberries and wild purslain.

Laharpe employed his men at first in erecting a large and strong blockhouse, in which he was assisted by the Indians. By repeated observations, he found it in latitude 33. 35. and he reckoned it was distant, in a straight way from the fort of Natchitoches, two hundred and fifty miles.

Don Martin de Alacorne having in the meanwhile returned to the neighborhood, Laharpe dispatched a corporal of his garrison, who spoke the language of several tribes of Indians, with a letter, soliciting Don Martin's friendship and correspondence, and tendering any service in his power; informing him he had it in charge to seek every opportunity of opening a trade with the Spaniards. Laharpe at the same time addressed Father Marsello, the superior of the missionaries in the province of Texas, begging his friendship, and offering a correspondence, advantageous to the mission—observing, the conversion of the Indians ought to engage the attention of all good christians; and as some assistance might be useful, in enabling his reverence successfully to preach the gospel in these parts, and enlist the Indians under the banner of the cross, he suggested the father should write to his friends in Mexico and Bocca de Leon, that they would find at Natchitoches and the Nassonites, any kind of European goods they might have occasion for, on very good terms. He concluded by assuring the holy man he would be allowed a handsome commission on any sale effected through his aid.

By the return of the corporal, Don Martin reciprocated Laharpe's offers of service; but expressed his surprise at the occupation by the French, of a territory, which he observed made a part of the viceroyalty of Mexico.

He requested Laharpe to make it known to his chief that the necessity of using force to remove the detachment might be averted.

The father's reply was of a different cast. He wrote that, as the proposed correspondence was tendered on principles of religion, charity and esteem, he cheerfully accepted it, he would apprise his friends of Laharpe's arrival and views. He added, that, as it did not become the clergy to be concerned in trade, he had to request that the correspondence might be kept secret; especially as he was not on very good terms with Don Martin, who, he intimated, would probably be soon removed.

Laharpe expressed to the latter, he was astonished at the assertion, that the post, just occupied by the French, was within the government of Mexico, as he and his countrymen had always considered the whole country which the Spaniards called the province of Texas, as part of Louisiana, of which Lasalle had taken possession thirty-six years before. He added, he had never understood till now, that the pretensions of Spain had ever been extended to the east of Rio Bravo; all the rivers flowing into the Mississippi being the property of France, with all the country they watered.

There was at the distance of thirty miles to the northwest of the spot occupied by the French, a salt spring, from which they obtained four hundred weight of salt.

A Dulcino Indian, coming from Natchitoches, informed the Nassonites the French were at war with the Spaniards, and the Natchitoches were desirous to be joined by the Nassonites, to assist the French. These Indians replied they would not join in any act of hostility; but they would defend the French if they were attacked.

Moulet and Durivage, two officers of Laharpe's detachment, having gone on a journey of discovery, met, at the distance of one hundred and eighty miles from the Nassonites, on Red river, parts of several wandering tribes, by whom they were well received. These Indians had lately destroyed part of the Cansey nation, who had eleven villages on the head of that river, near which the Spaniards had a settlement and worked mines. In high water, the villages were accessible by the river. Presents were made by the two Frenchmen to these Indians, whom they endeavored to induce to remove to the neighborhood of the Nassonites, to settle in villages and plant corn. They were about two thousand—had no permanent residence; but went out in large parties, erecting huts, in the shape of a dome, and covered with hides.

On the return of these officers, Laharpe, finding his post had nothing to apprehend, made with two others, half a dozen soldiers and a few Indians, an excursion to the northeast. He loaded eleven horses with goods and provisions, and journeyed to the Washitas and Arkansas. He met with a friendly reception from these Indians, and entered into alliance with them. He took possession of their country in the name of his sovereign, and in token of it erected posts with the escutcheon of France. Having disposed of his goods on very advantageous terms, he floated down the Arkansas river to the Mississippi, and reached Biloxi through bayou Manchac and the lakes.

The Chickasaws, excited by the British in South Carolina, began a war against the French colonists. The first act of hostililty was the murder of Sorvidal, an officer whom Bienville had sent among these Indians. This circumstance rendered an increase of population quite welcome. A fleet, commanded by commodore Saugeon, in the month of February, brought five hundred and eighty-two passengers, among whom were a number of females from the hospital-general of Paris.

The settlement of the Illinois began to thrive, many families having come thither from Canada; and Boisbriant, who commanded there, removed its principal establishment to the bank of the Mississippi, twenty-five miles below the Kaskaskia village.

The company having represented to the king that the planters of Louisiana had been enabled by the introduction of a great number of negroes, to clear and cultivate large tracts of land, and that there had been a great migration of his subjects and foreigners, who had been employed in the tillage of the ground; so that the planters found it no longer their interest to employ vagabonds or convicts; as these people were idle and dissolute, and less disposed to labor than to corrupt the poorer white inhabitants, the negroes and Indians, the transportation of vagabonds and convicts to Louisiana was forbidden by an arrest of the king's council, of the ninth of May.

Two line of battle ships came in the latter part of June, from Toulon. They were in great distress; Caffaro, the commodore, and most of their crews had fallen victims to the plague, which some sailors in these ships who had come from Marseilles, had communicated to the others: that city being ravaged by pestilence, brought there by a ship from Seyde, in the Levant. Father Laval, a Jesuit, royal professor of hydrography in the college of Toulon, had by the king's order, taken passage on board of this fleet, with directions to make astronomical observations in Louisiana. The chaplains of the ships having died, the father, considering science an object of minor consideration to a minister of the altar, thought it his duty to bestow all his time in administering spiritual relief to the sick, who for a long time, were very numerous, and he sailed back with the ships.

The settlement of Natchitoches was now in a prosperous situation, though weakened by the migration of some of the settlers who had gone northerly in the hope of enriching themselves by a trade with the Spaniards. This chimerical hope prevented attention to the culture of the land. Bienville now received the king's order to send St. Denys to command there, and Chateaugue, who had gone to France from Havana, came in these ships with the appointment of king's lieutenant in Louisiana, and succeeded St. Denys in command of the fort at Mobile. He had, on his way back, touched at the Havana from whence he brought the French prisoners taken at Pensacola.

One of the company's ships arrived from the coast of Africa, and landed five hundred negroes.

The ill success which had attended every attempt to work the mines that had been discovered in Louisiana, was attributed to the want of skill in those who had been employed, rather than to the poverty of the ore, and the colonial government received orders to engage Don Antonio, a Spaniard, who had been taken at Pensacola, and said he had worked in the mines of Mexico. The hope of obtaining gold from Louisiana could not be easily abandoned in France; the Spaniard was sent up at a great . expense, but did not succeed better than Lochon.

In the meanwhile, Bienville exerted himself to induce his red allies to attack the Chickasaws. He met with considerable difficulty. Part of the

19

Choctaws had been gained by the British: the Alibamons complained that the French allowed them less for their skins than their rivals at Charleston, and sold their goods much dearer. He at last succeeded with the Choctaws, and obtained a promise of neutrality from the Alibamons, and a passage for his men through their country. Pailloux was instructed to secure the aid of the Natchez and Yazous.

The colony received a very large increase of population during the summer and fall. A company ship brought sixty settlers of the grant of St. Catherine, under the order of Beaumanoir, into the country of the Natchez. They were followed by two hundred and fifty others under the orders of Bouteux. Delonne, who had lately been appointed director general, landed at Mobile with a company of infantry, sixty settlers of the grant of Guiche, and one hundred and fifty of that of St. Reine. In another ship, Latour, a brigadier general of engineers and a knight of St. Louis, accompanied by Pauge, led fifty workmen, and Boispinel and Chaville, two officers of the same corps, arrived soon after with two hundred and fifty settlers of the grant of Leblanc and his associates.

The plan of settling the bay of St. Bernard, on the west of the Mississippi, was still a favorite object in France, and Bienville received by these vessels the instructions of the directors of the company, to begin an establishment there immediately, they expressed their apprehension that his delay might defeat their plans, and the bay be occupied by the Spaniards; and, lest their injunction might be overlooked, they had procured the king's special order to Bienville for that purpose. This project was viewed in a different light in Louisiana; the great distance from the other settlements, which were already too spare; the shallowness of water near the coast, which prevented large vessels from approaching, the barrenness of the country the difficulty of protecting and even communicating with it, the small means of defense the colonial government had at command, and the thin population of the province, appeared to forbid the extension of settlements to the west of the Mississippi. None of the colonial officers entertained a different opinion.

The same unanimity did not prevail on a more important question. It was proposed, in a council of war to which the officers of engineers, lately arrived from France, assisted in the month of November, to remove the headquarters to the New Biloxi; a measure which was adopted, notwithstanding the opposition of Bienville and Hubert. These two administrators did not agree as to the place of removal.

Bienville objected to an immediate removal. He thought it would occasion considerable damage to the individuals, who had built at the present place, without any prospect of public or private advantage.

He thought, however, that if a removal was determined upon, New Orleans was the most proper place.

Hubert disapproved also of a removal. His opinion was, that New Orleans would answer only as a place of deposit; that the spot on which the city of Natchez now stands, was the most proper site for the capital of the province, and would ere long become its centre.

He felt so confident, in his hope of being able to induce the directors to adopt his plan, that a few days after, he sailed for France for this purpose; but he died shortly after his landing. He had obtained the grant of an immense tract on St. Catherine's Creek, on which he had made a large plantation with considerable improvements. This circumstance was some evidence, that he considered this part of the province as that which presented the greatest advantage; but his opponents in the council grounded on it a suggestion that his vote was influenced by private interests.

Time has shown that Bienville's view of the subject was the best. The sandy coast of Biloxi, distant from fertile land, difficult of approach for vessels of burden, and without a safe anchorage, offered so many disadvantages, that it is difficult to surmise, on what ground it became the choice of the majority. It presents nothing to the view, but interminable heaps of sand, interspersed with lagoons, and a growth of scattered stunted shrubs. The city of Natchez, after more than a century, has not as yet risen beyond the rank of a smart village. It will in time become the centre of trade, in a circle of a considerable radius; but distant from the sea four hundred miles, and, if time be the measure of distance, situated in those days further from the Balize than Bourdeaux by water, it could have afforded but little protection to the intermediate places between the sea and the settlements at Biloxi or Mobile.

Hubert's views were premature by several centuries. Had the French remained in possession of the whole province of Louisiana, with the extent it then had, no doubt, in the course of time, the spot on which the city of Natchez stands might have become the centre of the population of the colony.

The majority was probably influenced by the commercial agents of the company, who viewed New Biloxi as the spot from which their storekeepers at Biloxi, Pensacola, Ship Island and the old Biloxi might be more conveniently watched.

Bienville complained that these gentlemen thwarted his views and prevented the company from reaping the benefit from his exertions, which they were calculated to produce.

A company ship arrived on the third of January, 1721, with three hundred settlers of the grant of Madame Chaumont, on Pascagoula river, and another landed in the following month eighty girls from the Saltpetriere, a house of correction in Paris, with one hundred other passengers. It seems the late order of council, prohibiting the transportation of vagabonds and convicts, was not considered as extending to females.

In their dispatches to Bienville by these ships, the directors expressed their grief at the division which existed between him and their principal agents in Louisiana, by which the affairs of the company had been brought to such a situation, that it would be preferable that the establishment had now to be begun. The report of the unfortunate condition of their concerns had excited great murmurs in France, and the direction was daily reproached for the immense expenses it had incurred: it was charged with having appointed chiefs too careless of the affairs of the company and too careful of their own. That the regent, who was informed of the discredit in which the stock of the company had fallen, so far from keeping the promise he had made of promoting him to the rank of a brigadier and sending him the broad ribbon of the order of St. Louis, would have proceeded against him with severity, if he had not been informed that the company's agents in the colony had thwarted his views; that the directors flattered themselves, that by sending out new agents, and the new arrangements that were about to be made, the state of things would be changed, and the regent become sensible of his merit; that his royal highness told them, the king's graces were bestowed on effective services only, and as it was suggested that he (Bienville) might now merit them, it was proper to wait till he might prove himself worthy of them.

The directors, while they assured Bienville they would foster the regent's good dispositions towards him, did not conceal their disapprobation of the promotion he had made of some non-commissioned officers. They instructed him for the future to exercise the right of suspension only, and leave to them that of removal and appointment. They recommended to him to correspond with the Marquis de Vaudreuil, governor-general of New France, and to exert himself to induce his Indian allies to declare themselves against the Sioux, whom the Foxes had engaged in their interest.

The fort at Kaskaskias was ordered by the company to be called Fort Chartres; that of Mobile, Fort Conde, and that of Biloxi, Fort St. Louis.

Orders were given to Pauger, to make a survey of the bay of Mobile and the entrance of the Mississippi.

Two hundred German settlers of Law's grant were landed in the month of March at Biloxi, out of twelve hundred who had been recruited. The rest had died before they embarked, or on the passage. They were followed by five hundred negroes from the coast of Africa. This increase of population was rendered less welcome by the great dearth of provisions under which the colony labored.

Bienville dispatched a vessel to St. Domingo for a supply. He employed for this service, Beranger, who had lately arrived from Havana, where he had conveyed the Spanish hostages.

There came among the German new comers a female adventurer. She had been attached to the wardrobe of the wife of the Czarowitz Alexius Petrowitz, the only son of Peter the Great. She imposed on the credulity of many persons, but particularly on that of an officer of the garrison of Mobile, (called by Bossu, the Chevalier d'Aubant, and by the king of Prussia, Maldeck) who having seen the princess at St. Petersburg imagined he recognized her features in those of her former servant, and gave credit to the report which prevailed that she was the duke of Wolfenbuttle's daughter, whom the Czarowitz had married, and who, finding herself treated with great cruelty by her husband, caused it to be circulated that she had died while she fled to a distant seat, driven by the blows he had inflicted on her—that the Czarowitz had given orders for her private burial, and she had travelled incog. into France, and had taken passage at L'Orient in one of the company's ships among the German settlers.

Her story gained credit and the officer married her. After a long residence in Louisiana, she followed him to Paris and the island of Bourbon, where he had a commission of major. Having become a widow in 1754, she returned to Paris with a daughter, and went thence to Brunswick, when her imposture was discovered; charity was bestowed on her, but she was ordered to leave the country. She died in 1771, at Paris, in great poverty.

A similar imposition was practiced for a while with considerable success in the southern British provinces a few years before the declaration of their independence. A female, driven for her misconduct from the service of a maid of honor of princess Matilda, sister to George III., was convicted at the Old Bailey and transported to Maryland. She effected her escape before the expiration of her time, and travelled through Virginia and both the Carolinas, personating the princess and levying contributions on the credulity of planters and merchants; and even some of the king's officers. She was at last arrested in Charleston, prosecuted and whipped.

A company ship had sailed for Louisiana in 1718, with troops and one hundred convicts, and had never been heard of. It was now discovered that, like the fleet of Lasalle, she had missed the Mississippi and had been driven to the west. Her commander had mistaken the island of Cuba for that of St. Domingo, and had been compelled to pass through the old channel to get into the gulf. He made a large bay, in the twenty-ninth degree of latitude, and discovering he had lost his way wandered for several days. His misfortune was increased by a contagious disease breaking out among the convicts. Five of his officers, Bellisle, Allard, Delisle, Legendre and Corlat, thought it less dangerous to land, with provisions for eight days and their arms, than to continue on board. They hoped to meet some Indian who might guide them to the settlements of the French; they were disappointed. All, except Bellisle, fell victims to hunger and fatigue: after burying the last of his companions, he wandered for several weeks on the shore, living on shell fish and roots. At last he fell in with three Indians who stripped him and led him a prisoner to their village, in which he was detained for eighteen months; he suffered much from hunger, fatigue and the cruelty of his captors. At last, one of the latter stole a small tin box, in which Bellisle kept his commission and some other papers. It was purchased by an Indian of the Assinais tribe, and accidentally shown to St. Denys, who prevailed on some of them to go and contract for Bellisle's ransom. He was thus released and found his way to Natchitoches, where after staying a while to recover his strength, he was furnished the means of reaching Biloxi.

Pauger, having completed the survey of the passes of the Mississippi, returned and made his report to Bienville. He found the bar a deposit of mud, about three hundred feet wide, and about twice that in length. It appeared to him it was occasioned by the current of the river and the flux of the sea which, greatly obstructing the current, caused the river to overflow. He took notice that the stream, being very muddy, left on its shores and islands, heaps of timber, covered by annual layers of mud; the smaller timber filling up the interstices. In this manner, islands and new land along the shore were incessantly formed; and after a few years, canes and willows began to rise on the crust formed by several layers. He expressed his opinion, that with little trouble, by giving a proper direction to the floating timber, dykes might be formed along one of the channels, and by sinking old vessels, so as to stop the others, the velocity of the water might be increased in the former, and a very great depth obtained in time; an operation which he said was now forming in some parts of the passes—one of which he had noticed the preceding year, when he found on it but ten or eleven feet of water, and eight months after, from thirteen to fourteen; while a bar had extended to the island of the Balize, which was one hundred and eighteen feet in width, and double that in length with an eminence in the middle, before which ships might ride in eighteen feet of water.

In the spring, a Guineaman landed two hundred and ninety negroes, and reported that another had caught fire at the distance of sixty leagues from the shore; part of the crew had saved themselves in the long boat; the rest perished.

Accounts were received from the Illinois that a party of three hundred Spaniards had marched from Santa Fe to the upper part of the province, while they expected a fleet would attack it on the shore. Seventy of them only had persevered in the attempt, guided by Padouca Indians, who directed them so northerly that they reached the river of the Canseys, near the Missouri, where they fell among Indians, allies of the French, who destroyed them all, except their chief, the swiftness of whose horse secured his safety.

On the fourth of June, two hundred and fifty passengers, chiefly Germans, came in a company ship. Marigny de Mandeville, who had gone to France, where he had obtained the cross of St. Louis and the command of Fort Conde, returned in her, accompanied by d'Arensbourg, a Swedish officer, and three others.

By this vessel the colonists learnt the failure and sudden departure from France of the celebrated Law. This gave room to the apprehension that the settlement of the province might be abandoned or prosecuted with less vigor.

Another Guineaman landed three hundred negroes a few days after.

John Law, of Lauriston, in North Britain, was a celebrated financier, who having gained the confidence of the Duke of Orleans, regent of France, settled at Paris; where, under the auspices of government, he established a bank, with a capital of twelve hundred thousand dollars. Soon after, government became largely interested in it, and it assumed the name of the Royal Bank. The original projector continued at the head of its affairs and, availing himself of the thirst for speculation which its success excited, formed the scheme of a large commercial company to which it was intended to transfer all the privileges, possessions and effects of the foreign trading companies that had been incorporated in France. The royal bank was to be attached to it. The regent gave it letters patent, under the style of the Western Company. From the mighty stream that traverses Louisiana, Law's undertaking was called the Mississippi scheme. The exclusive trade to China and all the East Indies was afterwards granted to the company now called the India Company. Chancellor d'Aguessau opposed the plan with so much earnestness, that the regent took the seals from him and exiled him to his estate.

The stockholders flattered themselves that the vast quantity of land, and the valuable property the company possessed, would enable it to make profits far exceeding those of the most successful adventurers. Accordingly, the directors declared a dividend of two hundred per cent. The delusion was so complete that the stock rose to sixty times its original cost. The notes of the bank took the place of the paper securities government had issued, and so great was the demand for them, that all the metallic medium was paid into the bank.

CHAPTER X.

On the fifteenth of July, Duvergier, who had lately been appointed Director, Ordonnateur, Commandant of the Marine and President of the Council, landed at Pensacola. He brought crosses of St. Louis for Boisbriant, Chateaugue and St. Denys.

The company more intent on extending than improving its possessions in Louisiana, had determined, notwithstanding the unanimous representations of Bienville and all the colonial officers, to have an establishment on the gulf to the west of the Mississippi. For this purpose Bernard de la Harpe came over with Duvergier, having been appointed commandant and inspector of commerce at the bay of St. Bernard. Masilliere, administrator of the grant of the Marquis de Mezieres, Desmarches, Dudemaine and Duplesne, his associates, accompanied him.

The arrival of Duvergier with such ample powers gave much uneasiness to Bienville, who while he remained in command, could not brook to be excluded from the presidency of the council. Chateaugue, who had the rank of a captain in the royal navy, thought himself injured by the command of the navy being given to another, and Delorme imagined his pretensions to the office of ordonnateur had been overlooked.

Three hundred negroes arrived from Africa on the 15th of August.

The occupation of the bay of St. Bernard, notwithstanding the positive orders of which Laharpe was the bearer, was still viewed in Louisiana as a premature operation attended with a considerable and useless expense, requiring a number of men who could not well be spared, and promising, if any, none but very precarious and distant advantages. The difficulty of protecting and supplying so distant a post, the extreme barrenness of the soil to the extent that had been explored, the ferocity of the Indians in the neighborhood, some of whom were said to be anthropophagi, appeared to present insurmountable obstacles while no probable advantage could be contemplated, but the preservation of the possession, which Lasalle had taken of that part of the country, thirty-six years before, in which his life and that of the greatest part of his followers had been sacrificed. Laharpe was now arrived with a commission of which he was impatient to avail himself, and Bienville gave his reluctant assent to the measure.

Beranger was directed to carry the new commandant and thirty men to the bay; fifteen barrels of flour and as many of meat were spared for their use.

The weakness of the detachment and the smallness of the supply (both, in the opinion of Laharpe, inadequate) furnished him irrefragable proof that he was starting on an expedition in which the best wishes of Bienville did not attend him. He weighed anchor on the twenty-sixth of August.

His instructions from the company were to take formal possession of the country, and to set up a post with the arms of France on some conspicuous part of the shore—to build a fort and secure by treaties the amity and good will of as many of the Indian tribes as he could. If he met any Spanish force in the country, he was directed to represent to the commandant that it belonged to the crown of France, by virtue of the possession taken by Lasalle in 1685, and in case he, or any other stranger, insisted on the right of staying, to remove him by force.

The order of the council for the removal of headquarters to Biloxi was now executed, and Bienville, with his staff removed thither, leaving Marigny in command at Fort Conde.

Since the departure of Law from France, the affairs of the company there had fallen into great confusion and disorder, and very little attention was given to the supplies that were needed in Louisiana.   None being procured by agriculture, provisions became extremely scarce.   To provide against the distress of impending famine, such of the troops as could be spared from the service of the posts, were sent, in small detachments, to Pearl river, Pascagoula and among the Indians, to procure their subsistence by fishing and hunting. Their unskilfulness in this mode of seeking sustenance made it necessary to have recourse to impressment.   This measure caused great murmurs among the planters; but the scarcity of provisions was productive of more dreadful consequences among the soldiers.   Twenty-six men, who were in garrison at Fort Toulouse, on the river of the Alibamons, exasperated by hunger and distress, mutinied, and rising against Marchand, their commander, marched off with their arms and baggage, in the expectation of finding their way to the back settlements of Carolina. Villemont, the lieutenant, immediately rode to the village and prevailed on the Indians to go and waylay the deserters; they were overpowered by the savage assailants, but not without great carnage.   Sixteen were killed, and two only escaped.   The other eight being made prisoners were brought to Fort Louis and soon after executed.

In the latter part of September, the colony was, in some measure, relieved by the arrival of a ship from France, with provisions.   She brought accounts that the regent had placed the affairs of the company under the direction of three commissioners.   They were Ferrand, Faget and Machinet.

Laharpe, returned from the bay of St. Bernard on the third of October. He reported he had proceeded three hundred miles westerly from the Mississippi.   On the 27th of August he had entered in a bay in latitude 29.5. which he took for the one he was sent to.   He found, on the bar, at its entrance, eleven feet of water, and having crossed it he sailed westerly; the sounding gave all along from fifteen to twenty feet.   There was a small island at the entrance of the bay.   Bellisle, Laharpe's lieutenant, having gone on shore on the 29th, met a party of Indians, about forty in number, many of whom offered to come on board.   He suffered six of them to enter his boat; others followed in four canoes.   They were entertained on board of the vessel, and among other presents a dog, a cock and a few hens were given them; they seemed greatly pleased with them.

On the next day, Bellisle having again landed with a few soldiers, was met by some of these Indians, who led him to their village.   The French were hospitably received, and made a few presents to their hosts; and the soldiers, with a view of showing them the effects of gunpowder, made a discharge of their pieces.

Bellisle visited the Indians again on the next day.   He told them the intention of the French, in coming to the bay, was to settle and live in friendship with the natives, and afford them protection against their enemies.   They replied they would communicate this to, and consult their countrymen.

On the second of September, the Indians continuing to evince great reserve, the vessel proceeded farther westerly.   Laharpe and Bellisle went several times ashore, attended by a few soldiers, to view the country, without seeing any Indians. Sailing N. W. and N. N. W. for two leagues, they came to an island, at the distance of a musket shot from the main. Here a number of Indians came on board, while many others appeared on the shore on horseback, ranged in battle array. This induced Laharpe to forbear landing. The vessel proceeded to another island near the main, and sailing farther on they found a river flowing through a wide prairie. The river was wide, its water excellent and the current slow.

Sailing along the coast several miles farther, they cast anchor at night before a cluster of cabins. Laharpe and Bellisle going ashore on the next day, were coldly received. The squaws began to yell, striking their sides and screaming horridly. The men asked Laharpe for some goods; he answered all the goods the French had brought were still on board of their vessel and the men in the boat had come with no other intention than to see the country and pay the inhabitants a friendly visit: they were answered one should not come empty handed among strangers. A vehement debate ensued, which induced the French to apprehend that they would be massacred. The party who were for moderate measures, at last prevailed and the French were presented with some dried meat and roots.

Laharpe having repeated his intention of settling on the coast, the Indians expressed their absolute disapprobation of it; urging that they were afraid of the French, notwithstanding he represented to them their opposition would bring down against them the Assinais and other tribes, allies of his nation. They persisted in asserting their fixed determination not to allow him to settle, and their wish that the vessel would depart.

According to the observation Laharpe made, the shore of the bay extended to the south in a series of hills and prairies, interspersed with well timbered land. In the bottom of the bay he saw a river, the mouth of which appeared to be about one hundred yards wide.

On the fifth, a number of Indians came on board unarmed. Laharpe was unable to prevail on them to consent to his making a settlement in their country.

Finding that the number of Indians on the bay was considerable, and that but little dependence could be placed in his soldiers, he united with his lieutenant in the opinion that it would be imprudent to attempt to force himself upon the natives; but he took the ill judged resolution to carry off a few of them by stratagem, in the hope that the manner in which they would be received at Fort St. Louis and the view of the establishment of the French there, might operate on their minds, so as to conquer their obstinacy, and dispose their countrymen to forbear any further opposition to the settlement of the French among them.

Accordingly, he detained twelve of his visitors, as hostages for some of his men who were sent ashore for water, dismissing the other Indians with presents. He learned from his captives that their nation was at war with the Assinais and the Adayes, and that a number of Spaniards had lately passed through their country with large droves of cattle.

The water being brought, the anchor was weighed and the vessel went into deep water. At night the Indians manifested their uneasiness, and wished to be sent ashore, but were told to wait till the morning.

At sunrise Laharpe sent nine of them into the cabin and made a few soldiers stand by with fixed bayonets, to prevent any of them to come out. This precaution excited great alarm among them, and they manifested their apprehension that their destruction was intended. They were told not to fear anything for themselves or their companions—that they would be carried to the chief of the French, in order that he might learn from them the motives of their people in preventing his warriors from settling among them, after receiving the presents he had sent them—that they would be treated kindly and allowed soon to return.

The Indians on deck were now furnished with a canoe to reach the shore. Laharpe made them a few presents, and recommended to them not to allow the Spaniards to settle in their country. Immediately on their leaving the vessel, the guard was removed, the Indians in the cabin allowed to come on deck, and a boat was sent on shore to set up a post on a point of land, with a leaden plate on which the arms of France were engraven.

The Indians on board still imagined they were to be landed; but on the return of the boat, they discovered their error, and endeavored by various means to induce Laharpe to change his determination; sometimes telling him, if he kept in, he would run on the shoals; at other times offering to conduct him to places where good oysters were to be had, or to point out spots in which treasures were hidden.

According to the information of the Indians, and the judgment of Laharpe, the bay he came from was the one Don Martin de Alacorne discovered in 1718, which he placed in twenty-nine degrees, five minutes, and which he called *del Spiritu Santo.*

Bienville highly disapproved the conduct of Laharpe in decoying these Indians, and gave orders to carry them back immediately; but while preparations were making, they escaped and sought their home by land.

No further attempt to settle the bay of St. Bernard appears ever to have been made by the French. Laharpe was greatly mortified at the abandonment of the plan. He thought considerable advantages might have been derived from it, as the situation of the bay afforded safe harbors and a great facility to commerce with the Spaniards, and its navigable rivers invited population. The scarcity of provisions, arms and ammunition in the colony, the smallness of its military force, in relation to the many posts to be protected, were considered by the colonial administration as insuperable obstacles.

On the day after Laharpe's return, Bienville learnt by dispatches from the commissioners, that he was restored in the presidency of the council, and they had resolved that the principal establishment of the colony should be removed to New Orleans. They also directed him to order a survey of the river of the Arkansas, with the view of ascertaining how far it was navigable. It seems the council of the company in France still thought it their interest to extend its possessions in Louisiana, rather than to avail themselves of the advantages the part now occupied presented. They flattered themselves that by pursuing their discoveries to the west, mines of the precious metals might be reached, or a trade with the Spaniards insured. The latter, however, were not inattentive to the views of the French.

St. Denys, who commanded at the fort of Natchitoches, was apprised by a trader from the Adayes, that the Marquis de Gallo, lately appointed governor of the province of Texas, had come among these Indians, with four hundred horsemen, and about fifty thousand dollars worth of goods; he had also a large number of wagons loaded with provisions and effects.

He had begun to burn bricks for a fort which he intended to build immediately. The unpleasant information was received at the same time that the Chickasaws had murdered two Canadians.

In pursuance of the orders of the commissioners, Delorme removed to New Orleans on the first of November.

Laharpe, finding himself unemployed by the determination of the colonial administrators to suspend the execution of the plan of settling the bay of St. Bernard, offered his services to Bienville for the execution of the orders of the commissioners in regard to the river of the Arkansas.

Notwithstanding this measure was positively ordered by the commissioners, the company's agent opposed it strenuously. Bienville however, considered it as one of vital importance. He was anxious to establish a post in that part of the province, to protect the commerce with the Illinois, and facilitate the introduction of cattle from the Spanish provinces.

Laharpe was detached with sixteen men for this service. He was directed after having rested his men, at the mouth of the river, to ascend its main branch as high as he could, to take notice of every island and creek, to look for mines, and in case he discovered any to bring some of the ore. In case of any attempt on the part of the Spaniards to effect a settlement on any of these streams, the same instructions were given him, as when he went to the bay of St. Bernard, to insist on the possession, taken by Lasalle in 1678, when he descended the Mississippi.

In December father Charlevoix reached Louisiana from Canada, by the way of the Illinois. He stopped at the fort of the Yazous, spent the Christmas holidays at the Natchez, and floated down to New Orleans, which he reached on the sixth of January.

He gave out that he had the king's order to seek a northwest passage to China, and to inquire into the state of the southern province; but as he produced no official letter, not much credit was given to his assertion. He was however treated, wherever he went, with considerable attention.

New Orleans, according to his account, consisted at that time of one hundred cabins, placed without much order, a large wooden warehouse, two or three dwelling houses, that would not have adorned a village, and a miserable storehouse, which had been at first occupied as a chapel; a shed being now used for this purpose. Its population did not exceed two hundred persons.

The father stopped at the island of the Balize, which had just been formed. He chaunted a high mass on and blessed it, according to the ritual of his church. He gave it the name of Toulouse island, which it does not appear to have long retained.

The only settlements then begun below the Natchez were those of St. Reine and Madam de Mezieres, a little below Pointe Coupee—that of Diron d'Artaguette, at Baton Rouge—that of Paris near bayou Manchac—that of the Marquis d'Anconis, below Lafourche—that of the Marquis d'Artagnac, at *Cannes Brulees*—that of de Meuse a little below, and a plantation of three brothers of the name of Chauvin, lately come from Canada, at the Tchapitoulas.

Charlevoix reached Fort St. Louis of the Biloxi on the thirty-first of January, and left it on the twenty-fourth of March for Hispaniola.

Duvergier returned to France in the same month.

Loubois, a knight of St. Louis, arrived soon after and took the command of Fort St. Louis, and Latour received the commission of lieutenant-general of the province, much to the mortification of Bienville and Chateaugue.

The Commissioners forwarded for publication a set of rules they had adopted for the management of the company's concerns in Louisiana. They provided that negroes should be sold at six hundred and seventy livres, or one hundred and seventy-six dollars, payable in three annual instalments, in rice or tobacco.

Rice was received at twelve livres or three dollars the barrel, and tobacco at twenty-six livres or six dollars and fifty cents.

Wine was sold at twenty-six livres or six dollars and fifty cents the barrel, and brandy at one hundred and twenty livres or thirty dollars the quarter cask.

A copper coinage had lately been struck for the use of the king's colonies in America, and ordered to be used in the payment of the troops. It was declared a lawful tender in the company stores.

The province for civil and military purposes was now divided into nine districts. Alibamons, Mobile, Biloxi, New Orleans, Natchez, the Yazous, the Illinois and Wabash, Arkansas and Natchitoches. A commandant and judge was directed to be appointed in each.

For religious purposes there were three principal divisions. The first was under the care of the capuchins, and extended from the mouth of the Mississippi to the Illinois. The barefooted carmelites attended to the second, which included the civil districts of Biloxi, Mobile and Alibamons. The Wabash and Illinois formed the last, confided to the Jesuits. Churches and chapels were directed to be built at convenient distances. Before this time in many places large wooden crosses were raised at convenient places, and the people assembled around them, sheltered by trees, to unite in prayer.

The Chickasaws continued their hostilities: they attacked a Canadian pirogue, descending the Mississippi, near Fort Prudhomme and killed two of the men.

In the month of May, Fouquet brought to Biloxi the portion of the late copper coinage for the province.

La Renaudiere, an officer, who had been sent at the head of a brigade of miners by the directors, now led them up the Missouri. Their labor had no other effect than to show how much the company was imposed on and the facility with which the principal agents themselves were induced to employ men without capacity and send them to such a distance and at an enormous expense.

Since the failure of Law and his departure from France, his grant at the Arkansas had been entirely neglected, and the greatest part of the settlers whom he had transported thither from Germany, finding themselves abandoned and disappointed, came down to New Orleans with the hope of obtaining a passage to some port of France, from which they might be enabled to return home. The colonial government being unable or unwilling to grant it, small allotments of land were made to them twenty miles above New Orleans, on both sides of the river, on which they settled in cottage farms. The Chevalier d'Arensbourg, a Swedish officer, lately arrived, was appointed commandant of the new post. This was the beginning of the settlement known as the German coast, or the parishes of St. Charles and St. John the Baptist. These laborious men supplied the troops and the inhabitants of New Orleans with garden stuff. Loading their pirogues with the produce of their week's work, on Saturday evening, they floated down the river and were ready to spread at sunrise on the first market that was held on the banks of the Mississippi, their supplies of vegetables, fowls and butter. Returning, at the close of the market, they reached their homes early in the night, and were ready to resume their work at sunrise; having brought the groceries and other articles needed in the course of the week.

The island which father Charlevoix had lately blessed and to which he had given the name of Toulouse, having been examined under the orders of Bienville, by Pauger, appeared to be a convenient place for the residence of pilots. To afford the entrance of the river some protection, a battery was now raised on it, with barracks, a magazine and chapel, and a small garrison was sent there.

Laharpe returned from his expedition to the river of the Arkansas, on the 20th of May; he had reached the Natchez on the seventeenth of January and found Fort Rosalie a heap of rotten timber; Manneval, who commanded it, had only eighteen soldiers. He staid but one day with him and met, at the mouth of the river of the Yazous, two Canadian pirogues, loaded with 50,000 lb. weight of salt meat. They had killed eighteen bears about the head point of Point Coupee.

Laharpe reached, nine miles up Yazou river, a settlement called Fort St. Peter, commanded by de Grave. There were not more than thirty acres of arable land near the fort; the rest was nothing but stony hills. On digging turf and clay, it was found the water was bad and the place sickly.

A little above the fort were villages of the Coroas, Offogoulas and Oatsees, Their huts were scattered on small hillocks artificially made in the valley. Their whole population did not exceed two hundred and fifty heads. About one hundred miles to the northeast, were the Chouactas, about forty in number, and still higher the Chachoumas, who numbered about one hundred and fifty. In high water, these villages were inaccessible by land. Nine miles higher were the Outaypes, a very small tribe, and fifteen miles farther the Tapouchas, near the Choctaws.

Laharpe left the Yazou river, on the fifteenth day of February, and ascending the Mississippi one hundred and sixty-four miles, came to the lower branch of the river of the Arkansas. He found its current extremely rapid, and stopped a little above its mouth, near that of a stream coming from the northwest from the Osages. The large quantity of rock in its bed prevented its navigation.

The first village was reached on the first of March. It consisted of forty-one cabins and three hundred and twenty persons. Laharpe found here Duboulay, who was there since the month of September; having been sent thither from the fort of the Yazous, to protect these Indians, and the boats from the Illinois, which commonly stopped at this place, to procure provisions.

The Arkansas were not pleased at the arrival of the French among them nor disposed to afford to their leader any information of the topography of their country. They saw with pain his preparations to visit and form alliances with the tribes in the west, and exerted themselves to dissuade him from it; telling him that his party was in great danger of being murdered by the Osages. They refused to accommodate him with a pirogue, although there were upwards of twenty, fastened before the

village, and he found also great difficulty in procuring provisions. He
next proceeded to Law's grant; it lay N. N. W. from the village, on the
right side of the river, at the distance of about seven miles. The buildings
had been erected about a mile from the water. There remained but
forty persons of all ages and sexes; they had a small clearing sown with
wheat.

On the third he sent to the upper village for provisions. The Indians
of it came from the Caenzas a nation who dwelt on the Missouri. This
settlement was insulated, and had a population of about four hundred
persons. Having obtained what he wanted, he sent five of his men forward, directing them to halt on the second day and wait for him. He set
off on the next, with the rest, in all twenty-two men, including Prudhomme
and four others, whom he had taken at the fort of the Yazous.

Proceeding the distance of two hundred and thirty miles, he came to a
remarkable rock on the left bank of the river, mixed with jaspered marble,
forming three steep hillocks, one hundred and sixty-nine feet high. Near
it is a quarry of slate, and at its foot a beautiful cascade and basin. The
water of the river for the first ninety miles is reddish; it afterwards becomes
so clear as to be potable.

The party proceeded seventy miles farther; but the current growing
extremely rapid and disease prevailing among the soldiers, Laharpe
determined to return, much against his inclination; as, according to his
reckoning, he was within three hundred miles of a nation, whom he visited
in 1717, while he was stationed at the Cadodaqueous. He saw red and
white morillos in abundance.

After making a chart of the river, for three hundred and fifty miles from
the first village, he landed and visited several nations on the west side of
the river, and spent some time in exploring the country on the opposite
shore. He then descended the river to Law's grant, where a boat had just
arrived from New Orleans with provisions. They were so needed that
the Germans were making preparations to abandon the settlement.

In floating down the Mississippi, Laharpe was near being surprised by
a party of the Chickasaws.

Peace had in the meantime been made between France and Spain, and
on the thirty-first of May, a Spanish vessel from Vera Cruz landed Don
Alexander Wauchop, a captain of the royal navy of Spain, at the Biloxi.
He was bearer of dispatches to Bienville from the Marquis de Valero,
viceroy of Mexico, enclosing an official copy of the late treaty, which
contained a clause for the restoration of Pensacola, of which Don Alexander was sent to take possession.

Father Charlevoix returned on the fourth of June; the vessel in which
he had sailed for St. Domingo having been wrecked on the Martyr islands,
on the fourteenth of April. He sailed soon after for the place of his
destination.

A large party of the Chickasaws attacked, in the month of July, the
Indians on Yazou river, near Fort St. Peter, robbed them of their
provisions and scalped a sergeant of the garrison and his wife in their
own cabin, within a musket shot of the fort. In apprising Bienville of this
irruption, de Grave, the commandant of Fort St. Peter, added there were
several parties of the hostile Indians hovering in the woods, with a view of
surprising the Coroas, Offogoulas and Yazous. These had sent their
women and children into the fort.

The beginning of August, Bienville removed his headquarters to New Orleans. In the latter part of the month he was visited by a deputation of the Itomapas, a tribe on the western side of the Mississippi, who had stopped in the village of Colapissas, whose chief falling sick during their visit, his countrymen attributed his malady to a spell cast on him by their guests. They followed them to New Orleans, and solicited Bienville's interference, in order to obtain the removal of the spell.

The company, at home, were still less intent to promote agriculture in the parts of Louisiana occupied by the French, than on the discovery of mines of the precious metals, and the extension of trade with the most remote nations of Indians. Yielding to the representations of Boismont, an officer heretofore attached to the garrison of Fort Chartres of the Illinois, who had made several expeditions up the Missouri, and having gone over had been made a knight of St. Louis, they sent him to New Orleans and directed Bienville to furnish him a detachment, pirogues, arms, ammunition and provision, that he might build a fort and begin a settlement on the banks of that river. He landed early in September, bringing to the colonists, as a spiritual relief, three father capuchins and one lay brother.

In their dispatches, the commissioners announced to Bienville that the company expected he should consider himself, not only as the commandant general of its forces in Louisiana, but also, principal director of its concerns, and as responsible for their success—that if they prospered, he should have all the credit of it, but, in case of their miscarriage the loss of the regent's favor.

They inclosed to him a printed copy of a royal proclamation, published on the twenty-first of May, announcing the failure of the bank established by Law. On the following day its notes became absolutely worthless. By its failure an immense number of individuals were ruined, and many rich families reduced to abject poverty. To soothe the general interest, d'Aguesseau was recalled from exile, and the seals were returned to him, About the same time the British nation was gulled, nearly in the same manner, but not to the same extent, by what was called the south sea bubble.

A number of pirogues having been built, Boismont led his detachment to the Missouri.

A most destructive hurricane desolated the province on the eleventh of September. The church, hospital, and thirty houses were levelled to the ground in New Orleans; three vessels that lay before it were driven on shore. The crops above and below were totally destroyed, and many houses of the planters blown down. It prevailed with great violence at the Natchez and Biloxi. Three vessels that were at anchor before the last place, were driven high up on the shore. Famine threatened the colony with its horrors, and the chief dispatched vessels in seach of provisions to Vera Cruz, Havana and St. Domingo.

Hitherto, apprehension in regard to Indian hostility, had been confined to one quarter, and the Chickasaws alone excited the alarm of the French. Dutisne an officer of the garrison of Fort Rosalie, came to New Orleans in the latter part of the month, with distressing accounts from that quarter.

A sergeant having quarrelled with an Indian, an affray ensued. The guard at the fort turned out to quell it. They were attacked by a numerous body of Indians, on whom they at last fired, killing one of them and wounding another. A few days after, Guenot, the director of the grant of St. Catharine, was fired on in the road and wounded; and on the next, the Indians attacked, and attempted to carry away, a cart loaded with provisions, and guarded by a few soldiers. Hiding themselves under high grass, they fired and killed a negro, and wounded another. A party of eighty of them, a few days after, attacked the settlement; but were repulsed with the loss of seven men. They had taken two planters, whose heads they had cut off; they also carried away a considerable number of horses, cattle and hogs.

Two sons of the Natchez were on a visit to Bienville, when Dutisne reached New Orleans. Instead of sending at once a strong force to chastise the offending Indians, presents were made to these chiefs, who promised to go and put a stop to the disorder.

Disease added, in the fall, its horrors to those of impending dearth; but the colonists were in some degree relieved by the appearance of an unexpected crop of rice. The grain scattered by the hurricane had taken root, and promised a comparative abundance.

The directors who had remained at the Biloxi, now joined Delorme at New Orleans.

The scarcity of provisions created such distress, that several of the inhabitants seriously thought of abandoning the colony; and a company of infantry, who had staid behind at the Biloxi being ordered to New Orleans were embarked on board of a schooner; but, as soon as she sailed, the captain and officers forced her master to sail for Charleston—where they landed with their arms and baggage.

Renaud, one of the directors of the company's concerns, had gone to the neighborhood of the Missouri, whither he was industriously engaged in a search after mines. In the belief that several existed on the shores of the Mississippi, Missouri, Marameg and the river of the Illinois, he procured from Boisbriant six grants of land on these streams, each three miles in front on the water, with a depth of eighteen.

The land in Louisiana had appeared very favorable to the culture of indigo; and measures were taken by the company, at the solicitation of the planters to supply them with seed.

Laharpe on his return from Pensacola, where he had been to bring back the troops and effects of the company, on the Spaniards taking possession of the place, reported that Wauchop, who remained there in command, had begun a settlement on the island of St. Rose, where his force was to stay till he was reinforced by a sufficient number to allow a removal to the main: the island being more easily defensible, the post at the bay of St. Joseph had been abandoned.

The Spaniards being badly supplied with provisions, Wauchop made application to the French for flour; intimating that, if he could be accommodated, he would send for it to New Orleans, and probably improve the opportunity of paying his respects to Bienville there, as he was authorized by the viceroy to receive the arms taken at Pensacola; for the restoration of which a clause had been inserted in the late treaty. The council advised Bienville to decline the honor of the intended visit: it being thought imprudent to allow the governor of Pensacola to reconnoitre the passes of the Mississippi, while they were unguarded by any fort, or to become acquainted with the state of the forces of the colony. The flour was accordingly sent to Mobile where Wauchop was requested to send and receive it.

While the Spaniards were thus resuming possession of Pensacola in the east, they were reinforcing their garrisons of the west, in the scattered posts of the province of Texas. St. Denys, in a letter from Natchitoches of the sixteenth of January, informed Bienville the Marquis de Gallo had lately received five hundred soldiers.

On the other hand, accounts were received that the Chickasaws had lately been defeated in a pitched battle by the Choctaws, in which the former had sustained a loss of four hundred men.

The distresses that had followed in France the failure of Law's scheme, were now most heavily felt. Louisiana deeply participated in them, and the French cabinet thought of no better plan of affording relief to the colonists than an alteration of the value of money.

The first attempt was by a rise at the rate of eighty-seven and a half per cent. The dollar of Mexico was the only silver coin in circulation in the province; its value was accordingly raised from four livres, at which it was then received in payment to seven and a half; so that the creditor of a sum of four thousand livres, or one thousand dollars before the edict which bears date the twelth of January, 1723, was compelled to accept in discharge five hundred and thirty dollars and a third.

Matters remained thus during one year. Experience showed the measure adopted was not the right one. As a rise had proved disastrous, it was thought a fall or reduction would have the contrary effect. But, as in the natural body, disease comes on rapidly, and the cure proceeds slowly, it was thought best that the healing of the political should be gradually effected. Accordingly, by an edict of the twenty-sixth of February, in the following year, a reduction of six and two-thirds per cent. was ordered, and the value of the dollar was brought down from seven and a half to seven livres. Thus, the creditor of a sum of four thousand livres before the rise, who had not been tendered after it, five hundred and thirty-three dollars and a third, was now permitted to demand five hundred and sixty-two dollars and eighty-seven cents and a half.

But, this small and tardy relief was paid for by those who had contracted between the publications of the two edicts. He who, on the twenty-fifth of February, had made a note for seven thousand five hundred livres, which could be discharged by the payment of one thousand dollars, was, after the publication of the last edict, compelled to pay an advance of seventy dollars and upwards.

What was intended for, and was called a healing process, was the administration of poison in lieu of a remedy; the doses were not strong, but came in rapid succession. Within sixty days, on the second of May, a new edict proclaimed a further reduction of twenty per cent.; the value of the dollar being lowered to five livres and twelve sous.

Within six months, a farther reduction of twenty per cent. was operated; and the value of the dollar was reduced by an edict of the thirtieth of October, to four livres and a half. Thus, within less than ten months, was the money raised in its value eighty-seven and a half per cent. and gradually reduced to its original rate.

Public and private distresses are curable by the same remedies only:

21

for the former is only the accumulation of the latter. A violent medicine often injures the natural, so do violent measures the political body.

Indolence, improvidence and extravagance, at times, occasion private distress, and this the public. Industry, economy and order alone can relieve the first; and if the latter be curable by the same means only, it is vain to resort to alterations in the value of money, a paper currency, or tender laws—indeed to any such artificial remedies. Loans are palliatives only, and frequently injurious ones. They may, for a moment, mitigate the effect of the disease; but they foment the cause, which should be removed, if a radical cure be intended. If the extravagant, the improvident and the idle be indulged, there can be but little hope of their becoming economical, provident and laborious.

The company, with the view of providing for the spiritual wants of the upper part of the province, in which clergymen were most wanted, entered into arrangements with the order of the Jesuits, by which curates and missionaries were obtained. Persons professing any other religion than the catholic, were not treated with equal charity, and the spirit of intolerance dictated an edict, in the month of March, by which the exercise of any other religion was prohibited in Louisiana, and Jews were directed to be expelled from it, as enemies of the Christian name. A black code for the government of the slaves was given to the colony this year.

Gross infidelities having been committed in the transmission of letters and packets in Louisiana, the king, by an edict of this summer, denounced against persons, intercepting letters and packets in the colony, or opening them and disclosing their contents, a fine of five hundred livres, and the offender, if holding the king's commission was to be cashiered, otherwise put in the pillory.

The colonists considered the preservation of horses and cattle as an object of primary importance; and the superior council had framed regulations for this purpose, as well as for the propagation of these animals. They had proved ineffectual: the interposition of the royal authority had been solicited, and by an edict of the twenty-second of May, the punishment of death was denounced against any person killing or wounding another's horses and cattle. The killing of one's own cow or ewe, or the female young of these animals, was punished by a fine of three hundred livres.

This was a most flagrant instance of the abuse of the punishment of death. It is inflicted for the wounding of an animal; neither does the legislator stop to distinguish between the most deadly stroke and the slightest solution of contiguity.

In no period, in the annals of Louisiana, does the province appear to have engrossed so much legislative attention. Louis the fifteenth had some time in the preceding year, reached his thirteenth, declared himself of age, and assumed the government of his dominions. Happy the country when legislation is never confided to a boy; happier that, in which it is only trusted to representatives chosen by the people, and for a very limited period.

Lachaise and Perrault, lately appointed commissioners to examine and make a report concerning the agents and clerks of the company in Louisiana, reached New Orleans in the fall, with two capuchins. Lachaise was a nephew of father Francois de la Chaise, an eminent jesuit, who, being confessor to Louis the fourteenth, had the firmness to withhold absolution from his royal penitent till he abandoned or married the celebrated madame de Maintenon.

Philip the fifth of Spain gave to the world the rare spectacle of a monarch relinquishing and reassuming a crown within one year. A prey to superstition, melancholy and suspicion, he imitated Charles the first; abdicated the throne in favor of Louis, his eldest son, and retired into a cloister. The new king dying a few months after, from the small pox, the royal monk threw off the cowl, with the same facility as he had the diadem, and leaving in the convent his superstition, suspicions and melancholy, with renovated vigor, successfully directed the destinies of Spain during a second reign.

The superior council now held its sessions in New Orleans, presided over by Lachaise, who had succeeded Duvergier as ordonnateur. Brusle, Perry, Fazende and Fleuriau had lately been called to seats in that tribunal. Fleuriau had succeeded Cartier de la Beaune in the office of attorney general, and Rossart was clerk of that tribunal.

With the view of providing for a speedy determination of small suits, an edict of the month of December, 1725, directed that independently of the monthly sessions of the council, particular ones should be holden, once or twice a week, by two of its members, chosen and removable by it, to try causes in which the value of the matter in dispute did not exceed one hundred livres, or about twenty-two dollars.

The provision lately made for clergymen having proven insufficient for the wants of the colony, and the bishop of Quebec, within whose diocese it was, finding it inconvenient to send the necessary number of curates and missionaries to the upper district, the company entered into a new treaty with the jesuits, on the twentieth of February, 1726.

By this, that of 1724 was annulled. Father Beaubois, the superior of the missionaries, who had come over in that year, was allowed eighteen hundred livres for his services, and a gratification of three thousand livres was divided between his associates for their past services.

The jesuits engaged to keep constantly, at least fourteen priests of their order in the colony, viz: a curate and missionary at Kaskaskias; a missionary in the village of the Brochigomas; a chaplain and missionary at the fort on the Wabash; a missionary at the Arkansas; a chaplain and missionary at fort St. Peter, among the Yazous; another missionary there, whose duty it was to endeavor to penetrate into the country of the Chickasaws, to propagate the Catholic religion, and promote union between these Indians and the French; two missionaries at the Alibamons, one of whom was to preach the gospel to the Choctaws. These locations were not to be altered without the governor's consent.

Father Petit, the superior of the Jesuits in the province, was permitted to reside in New Orleans, but not to perform any ecclesiastical functions there, without the license of the superior of the Capuchins. The company engaged to furnish him with a chapel, vestry room, and a house and lot for his accommodation, that of a missionary, and the temporary use of such priests of his order as might arrive in New Orleans.

The order was to have a grant of land of ten arpents in front on the Mississippi, with the ordinary depth, and negroes, on the same terms as the planters.

The jesuits were to be conveyed to Louisiana at the expense of the company, and a yearly salary of six hundred livres, one hundred and thirty-three dollars and thirty-three cents, was to be paid to each, with an addition of two hundred livres, forty-four dollars and forty-four cents, during each of the first five years; every missionary was to have an outfit of four hundred and fifty livres, or one hundred dollars and a chapel.

Money or goods were furnished at each mission for building a church and presbytery.

Jesuit lay brothers were to receive their passage, and a gratification of one hundred and fifty livres, thirty-three dollars and thirty-three cents, but no salary.

The churches and presbyteries, built at Kaskaskias and the village of the Michigourras, were given to the order.

The treaty received the king's approbation on the seventeenth of August.

Similar arrangements were made with the Capuchins, those with the Carmelites having been annulled.

All the lower part of the province was put under the ecclesiastical care of the Capuchins. Father Bruno, their superior in Louisiana, received the appointment of vicar-general of the bishop of Quebec. A convent was built for them in New Orleans, on the square, immediately below the church. The superior, aided by two monks as his vicars, acted as curate of the parish; a third was chaplain to the military force in New Orleans, and another at the Balize. Curates were stationed at Mobile and Biloxi, the German coast and Natchitoches.

For the purpose of providing for the education of young girls and the care of the hospital, the company entered into an agreement with sisters Marie Francoise Tranchepain St. Augustine and Mary Ann Le Boulanger, St. Angelique, Ursuline nuns of the convent of Rouen, on the thirteenth of September, by which these ladies, assisted by mother Catherine Bruscoli of St. Amand, undertook to pass over to Louisiana with several other nuns of their order. The company engaged to provide for the wants of the hospital, and the subsistence and maintenance of the nuns. The king gave his assent to this arrangement on the eighteenth of August.

During the fall, Perrier, a lieutenant of the king's ships, having been appointed commandant general of Louisiana, reached New Orleans, and shortly after Bienville sailed for France. We have seen that in 1698 he came over at the age of eighteen, with Iberville, his brother; he was then a midshipman; and four years after he succeeded Sauvolle, another brother, in the chief command of the province, which with little interruption he exercised till this period.

George the first, of great Britain, died on the eleventh of June, 1727, in his sixty-seventh year, and was succeeded by George the second, his eldest son.

The Jesuits and Ursuline nuns arrived this summer in a company ship. The fathers were placed on a tract of land immediately above the city, which is now the lowest part of the suburb St. Mary. A house and chapel were erected on it for their use. They improved the front of their land by a plantation of the myrtle wax-shrub. The nuns were for the present lodged in town, in a house on the northern corner of Chartres and Bienville streets, but the company soon after laid the foundation of a very large edifice for a nunnery, in the lowest square on the levee. The ladies removed to it in the latter part of 1730, and occupied it until 1824. It was till the construction of the new convent the largest house in Louisiana. A military hospital was built near it.

A government house was erected immediately below the plantation of the jesuits, and two very long warehouses were built in the two squares below the church, on the levee; one of them was nearly consumed by fire in 1818, the other is now occupied by the United States. This building and the old convent are probably the two oldest edifices in the state.

Barracks were built on each side of the *place d'armes*, the square fronting the cathedral. A house for the sessions of the superior council and a jail, were built on the square immediately above the church.

The land on which the city stands, till protected by a levee, was subject to annual inundations, and a perfect quagmire. The waters of the Mississippi and those of the lakes met, at a high ridge formed by them, midway between the bayou St. John and New Orleans, called the highland of the lepers. To drain the city a wide ditch was dug in Bourbon street, the third from and parallel to the river; each lot was surrounded by a small one, which was in course of time filled up, except the part fronting the street, so that every square instead of every lot, was ditched in. In this way a convenient space was drained.

In the beginning of the winter, a company ship brought a number of poor girls shipped by the company. They had not been taken, as those whom it had transported before, in the houses of correction of Paris. It had supplied each of them with a small box, *cassette*, containing a few articles of clothing. From this circumstance, and to distinguish them from those who had preceded them, they were called the girls *de la cassette*. Till they could be disposed of in marriage, they remained under the care of the nuns.

To the culture of rice and tobacco, that of indigo was now added; the fig tree had been introduced from Provence, and the orange from Hispaniola. A considerable number of negroes had been introduced, and land, which hitherto had been considered as of but little value, began to be regarded as of great relative importance. Much attention had not been paid to securing titles; much less to a compliance with the terms on which they had been granted. This began to create confusion, and confusion litigation: for the purpose of stopping this evil, in its beginning, the king's council published an edict on the tenth of August, 1728.

All orders of the directors of the company in France, issued to those in Louisiana, before the last of December, 1723, not presented to the latter and followed by possession and the required improvement, were annulled.

Landholders were required to exhibit their titles, and to make a declaration of the quantity of land claimed and improved by them, to the senior member of the superior council, within a limited time, under the penalty of a fine of two hundred dollars, and in case of continued neglect, to comply with these requisites, the land was to be resumed and granted to others.

Grants of more than twenty arpents in front, on either side of the Mississippi, below bayou Manshac, were to be reduced to that front, except in cases, in which the whole front had been improved; it was thought necessary to have a denser population above and below the city, for its better protection and security.

Lands, therefore granted, were required to be improved, by one-third of the quantity in front being put in a state to be ploughed and cultivated; but the two chief officers of the colony were authorized, on application, to make exceptions in favor of such landholders who having large herds of cattle, kept their land in pasture.

The depth of every grant was fixed at between twenty and one hundred arpents, according to its situation.

The company, as lords of all the land in the province, were authorized to levy a quit rent of a sou (a cent) on every arpent, cultivated or not, and five livres on every negro, to enable it to build churches, glebes and hospitals.

Grantees were restrained from aliening their land until they had made the requisite improvements.

Hunting and fishing were permitted; provided no damage was done to plantations and enclosures, and no exclusive right thereto was to be granted.

The company were empowered to grant the right of patronage, to persons binding themselves to build and endow churches.

At the departure of Bienville, the colony had made very rapid strides, and reached, in comparison to preceding years, a very high degree of relative prosperity. During the short space of eleven years, since it passed under the care of the company, agriculture had engaged the attention of European capitalists; eighteen hundred negroes had been introduced from Africa, and twenty-five hundred redemptioners brought over; the military force was increased to upwards of eight hundred men. But the moment was approaching when Louisiana was to receive a very severe check, which was to cause her to retrograde, as fast as she had advanced. In the concerns of communities, as in those of individuals, the tide of prosperity does not always flow uninterruptedly; adversity often causes it to ebb, and a change of fortune is often experienced, at the moment a reverse appears less to be dreaded.

CHAPTER XI.

THE Chickasaws instigated, as French writers urge, by the English of Carolina, now meditated the total ruin of Louisiana, and the destruction of every white individual in it. They had carefully concealed their design from the Illinois, the Arkansas and the Tunicas, whose attachment to the French they knew to be unshakeable. All the other tribes had been engaged in the plot. Each was to fall on the settlement of the French designated to it, and the attacks were to be simultaneous. Even the Choctaws, the most numerous nation in the neighborhood and that on whom the French placed the greatest reliance, had been gained though partially only.

Their villages were divided into two distinct settlements. The eastern or the great, and western or the little nation. The former had refused to join in the conspiracy; but they kept it secret, till it would have been too late to have warded off the blow, if it had been struck at the time.

Perrier was informed that these Indians had some misunderstanding with Diron d'Artaguette (the son of the former commissary ordonnateur) successor, in the command of Fort Conde of Marigny de Mandeville, who had died during the preceding year, after having received the appointment of Major General of the troops. He therefore desired the attendance of the head men of every village of both nations, at New Orleans.

In this interview, he succeeded in removing all grounds of complaint. The head men of the western villages left him determined to break the promise they had given to the Chickasaws to fall on the settlement of Mobile, but equally so to deceive him and have the part, that had been cast off to them in the dire tragedy, performed by the Natchez, in the hope of reaping a double advantage from the French, for their assistance; in the pillage made on, and the prisoners taken from the Natchez, whose discomfiture they considered as certain.

Perrier had been sensible, from his arrival in the colony, of the necessity ot strengthening distant posts. The province had indeed many forts; but none of any importance, except that of Mobile. The others were heaps of rotten timber, and hardly one of them was garrisoned by more than twenty men. He had frequently represented his dangerous situation to the company and solicited a reinforcement of two or three hundred men. His fears had been considered as chimerical. It was thought he desired only to increase his command, or sought to embroil the colony in war, in order to display his skill in terminating it.

In the meanwhile, the execution of the plan of the Chickasaws had been abandoned or delayed. Perhaps they had discovered symptoms of defection, in the behavior of the Choctaws. The indiscretion and ill conduct of Chepar, who commanded at Fort Rosalie in the country of the Natchez, induced these Indians to become principals, instead of auxiliaries in the havoc.

This officer, coveting a tract of land in the possession of one of the chiefs, had used menaces to induce him to surrender it, and unable to intimidate the sturdy Indian, had resorted to violence. The nation to whom the commandant's conduct had rendered him obnoxious, took part with its injured member—and revenge was determined on. The suns sat in council to devise means of annoyance, and determined not to confine chastisement to the offender; but having secured the co-operation of all the tribes hostile to the French, to effect the total overthrow of the settlement, murder all white men in it, and reduce the women and children to slavery. Messengers were accordingly sent to all the villages of the Natchez and the tribes in their alliance, to induce them to get themselves ready and come on a given day to begin the slaughter. For this purpose, bundles of an equal number of sticks were prepared and sent to every village with directions to take out a stick every day, after that of the new moon, and the attack was to be on that, on which the last stick was taken out.

This matter was kept a profound secret among the chiefs and the Indians employed by them, and particular care was taken to conceal it from the women. One of the female suns, however, soon discovered that a momentous measure, of which she was not informed, was on foot. Leading one of her sons to a distant and retired spot, in the woods, she upbraided him with his want of confidence in his mother, and artfully drew from him the details of the intended attack. The bundle of sticks for her village had been deposited in the temple, and to the keeper of it, the care had been entrusted of taking out a stick daily. Having from her rank access to the fane at all times, she secretly, and at different moments, detached one or two sticks and then threw them into the sacred fire. Unsatisfied with this, she gave notice of the impending danger to an officer of the garrison, in whom she placed confidence.   But the information was either disbelieved or disregarded.

An accidental circumstance concurred to destroy the intended concert, by hastening the attack without preventing its success.   In the latter part of November, 1729, several boats reached the landing from New Orleans, loaded with a considerable quantity of goods, provisions and ammunition Deceived by the artifice of the female sun, or tempted by the arrival of the boat, the Natchez in the neighborhood determined on a sudden attack, before the day that had been designated.

For this purpose, a number of them equal to that of the French in the fort and on the two grants, went into these places, while another party pretending they were preparing for a great hunting expedition, asked the loan of a few pieces and offered to pay for some powder and shot.   They bartered, in this way, a quantity of corn and fowls.   A supply being thus obtained, the attack was begun at nine o'clock, each Indian among the French falling on his man.   Before noon, upwards of two hundred of the latter were massacred, ninety-two women and one hundred and fifty-five children were made prisoners.

The principal persons who then fell were Chepar, the commandant, Laloire, the principal agent of the company in the post, Kollys father and son, who having purchased Hubert's grant, on St. Catharine Creek, had just arrived to take possession of it, Bailly, Cordere, Desnoyers, Longpre, and father Poisson, the Jesuit, missionary of the Yazous, who was accidentally there.   Two white men only were spared; a carpenter and a tailor—the Indians imagining they might be useful.   No injury was done to any negro.

During the massacre, the great sun with apparent unconcern, smoked his pipe, in the company's warehouse.   His men bringing the heads of the officers, placed that of Chepar near him, and those of the rest around it. Their bodies and those of the other Frenchmen were left, the prey of vermin and buzzards.

The savage foe ripped open the bellies of pregnant women, and killed those who had young children, whose cries importuned them.

As soon as the Great Sun was informed there did not remain a white man alive, except the carpenter and tailor, he ordered the pillage to begin. The warehouse, fort, dwelling houses and the boats were ransacked; the negroes being employed in bringing out the plunder.   It was immediately divided, except the arms and ammunitions which were kept for public use.

As long as the liquor lasted, the nights were spent in gambols and carousing, and the days in barbarous and indecent insults on the mangled bodies of the victims.

Two soldiers who were accidentally in the woods during the tragedy, heard of it on their way back, and set off by land to carry the sad tidings of it to New Orleans.   Perishing with hunger, fatigue and cold, they approached late at night, during a heavy rain, a cabin, from which their ears were saluted with the yells of Indians; they determined on entering it, rather than to remain exposed during the rest of the night to the pelting tempest, and were agreeably surprised to find themselves with a party of Yazous, returning from a friendly visit to the Oumas.

They were supplied with a pirogue, blankets and provisions and requested to assure Perrier the Yazous would ever remain steadfast in their friendship for the French, that they would proceed up the river and warn every white man they should meet of the impending danger.

This humane disposition, however, vanished when on their reaching the Natchez, presents were made them of a part of the spoil. They suffered themselves to be prevailed on to imitate the latter.

Father Soulet, the missionary of the Natchez, was returning from an excursion in the woods, when he was shot near his cabin. His negro attempted to prevent the pillage of his goods; but the Indians immediately dispatched him.

They proceeded, on the next day, to Fort St. Peter, of the Yazous. There were but fourteen men in it under the orders of the Chevalier des Roches. They were massacred with their chief. Two women and five children were carried into slavery.

Some of the Indians had put on the chaplain's clothes and even the sacerdotal vestments. These headed their countrymen back to the village of the Natchez, who soon discovered from the fantastic dress and gestures of the Yazous, that they had imitated their example and destroyed every white man among them.

Father Doutrelau, the missionary of the Arkansas, availing himself of the leisure of the hunting season, to make a trip to New Orleans, was descending the river having left his mission on new year's day. He intended to stop and say mass at father Soulet's, of whose death he was ignorant; but being unable to arrive in time, he had stopped at the mouth of the little river of the Yazous, and begun his arrangements for the celebrating of the holy mysteries. He was dressing his altar when a pirogue full of Indians approached. On being hailed they answered they were Yazous and friends of the French. They came ashore and shook hands with the holy man and his companions. A flock of ducks passing over, the father's fellow travellers fired at them without taking the precaution of reloading their pieces; this imprudence did not escape the attention of the Indians, who placed themselves behind them, as if intending to join in their devotions. The first psalm was hardly finished before a discharge of the pieces of the Indians wounded the father in the arm, and killed one of the men who were waiting on him. The other Frenchmen, seeing their companion dead and the father wounded, imagined he had met the same fate, fled to their pirogue; but, his wound being a flesh one only, he soon rose and running to the river with the sacerdotal vestments on, got on board. The Indians fired again; one of the men had his thigh broke and the father received another small injury.

The pirogue was drifting; the Indians, running along the shore, continued their fire, but without doing any more mischief. The French stopped, as soon as they were out of the reach of a ball, to wash the wounds of their men, and then pushed for the settlement of the Natchez.

On their arrival, seeing the houses burnt or thrown down, they did not suffer themselves to be prevailed on to land, by the invitation of the Indians who hailed them, and soon substituted the fire of their arms to the calls of friendship and hospitality. They determined on avoiding either shore, till they reached New Orleans, and began to apprehend that on their arrival there they would find it necessary to drift to the Balize. On the event of the dire catastrophe, which began at the Yazous, having continued down to the lower settlement on the river, they hoped to find, on board of the shipping, some person escaped from the general massacre.

As they approached bayou Tunica, they rowed close to the opposite shore, but were discovered, and a pirogue left the landing to reconnoitre them.   They pulled faster, but it gained on them: on hearing French spoken on board, joy succeeded to alarm.   Crossing the stream with their countrymen, they soon found themselves in the middle of a small force gathered from Pointe Coupee, Baton Rouge and Manshac.   They were friendly received: surgeons attended their wounds, and all were accommodated with room, in a large and commodious boat that was going to New Orleans for provisions.

As soon as information of the massacre reached the city, Perrier dispatched one of the company ships that were in the colony, to France, for troops and succor.   He sent couriers to the Illinois, by Red river and to Mobile, the Choctaws and the country watered by the Tennessee and Kentucky rivers, on the other side.   Emissaries went also to the Indian tribes in alliance with the French.   Every house in the city, and the plantations near it, was supplied with arms and ammunition out of the company's magazine, and the two remaining ships were directed to proceed as far as bayou Tunica, for the reception and safety of women and children in the last extremity.   The city was surrounded by a wide ditch, and guards were put at each corner.   There were then small forts at the Tchapitoulas, Cannes Brulees, the German Coast, Manshac and Pointe Coupee.

Perrier had collected about three hundred soldiers; having sent for those at Fort St. Louis and Fort Conde.   Three hundred men of the militia had joined this force, and he was preparing to march at their head when it was discovered that the negroes on the plantations evinced symptoms of an intention of joining the Indians against their masters, in the hope of obtaining their liberty, as some had done at the Natchez. There were then nearly two thousand blacks in the colony, a number equal to one-half of the French, but the most of them were in or at a short distance above the city, where their numbers perhaps preponderated over that of the French.   The company had a gang of two hundred and sixty on their plantation, and there were less, but yet very considerable gangs on some of the principal grants.   A few parties of vagrant Indians were hovering around the city, and greatly excited the alarms of its inhabitants.   Perrier, therefore, gave the command of this small army to the chevalier de Loubois, and sent onwards an officer of the name of Mispleix, to procure information of the strength and motions of the enemy.

Lessuer, who had gone to the Choctaws, collected seven hundred warriors of that nation and led them across the country.

Mispleix landed at the Natchez on the twenty-fourth of January, with five men.   The Indians had noticed the approach of this small party; they fired on it and killed three men and made Mispleix and the other two prisoners.

Loubois was advancing; his force had been swelled at bayou Tunica by the militia of Manshac, Baton Rouge and Pointe Coupee and a few Indians. The Natchez, apprised of this by their runners, dispatched some of their chiefs to meet, and offer peace to Loubois.

Their pretensions were high; they required that Broutin, who had before been in command at Fort Rosalie, and the principal chief of the Tunica Indians should be sent as hostages.   They demanded for the ransom of the women and children in their possession, two hundred barrels of powder, two thousand flints, four thousand weight of balls, two hundred knives and as many axes, hoes, shirts, coats, pieces of linen and ginghams, twenty coats laced on every seam, and as many laced hats with plumes, twenty barrels of brandy, and as many of wine. Their intention was to have murdered the men, coming up with these goods.

On the day after the departure of these chiefs, they burnt Mispleix and his two companions.

Lesueur, with his Choctaw force, which on the way had been increased to twelve hundred, arrived on the twenty-eighth, in the evening. Runners, whom he had sent ahead, met him with the information, that the Natchez were not at all aware of his approach, quite out of their guard, and spending their time in dancing and carousing. The intelligence soon spreading in Loubois' camp, he was absolutely unable to retain his Indians, as he was ordered to do, until he was joined by Loubois, with the army from New Orleans.

At daybreak on the twenty-ninth, the Choctaws, in spite of their leader's entreaties, fell on the Natchez, and after a conflict of about three hours, brought away sixty scalps and eighteen prisoners—they liberated the carpenter and tailor, with fifty-one women and children, and one hundred and six negroes. They had only two men killed and eight wounded. After the battle they encamped on St. Catharine's Creek.

The issue of this attack inspired the Natchez with terror. They upbraided the Choctaws for their perfidy and treachery; attesting their solemn promise to join in the conspiracy and afford their aid, in the total destruction of the French.

Loubois came up on the eighth of February. The six hundred men of the regular force and militia, he had taken at New Orleans, had been joined on the way to bayou Tunica by one hundred others, and had found there two hundred French; and three hundred Indians of the Oumas, Chetimachas and Tunicas had joined the army on its march to the Natchez, so that it consisted of upwards of fourteen hundred men mostly white.

The impatience and indocility of the friendly Indians, the now great relative number of the red people, the fatigue of the march, the scarcity of ammunition, which the Indians either wasted or purloined, the strong resistance of the Natchez, who had entrenched themselves and fought like desperadoes, induced Loubois, on the seventh day after the opening of the trenches, to listen to the proposals of the besieged, who threatened, if he persisted, to burn the white women and children still in their possession, and offered to surrender them, if the eleven field pieces he had were withdrawn. There were not in the whole army one man that could manage them, and the only hope entertained of them was, that they might scare the Indians.

On the twenty-fifth, the terms were accepted; and all the prisoners being sent to Loubois' camp, the army moved to the bluff and erected a small fort to keep the Indians in awe, and protect the navigation of the river.

Loubois deemed it necessary, before the departure of the army, to make an example of three of the negroes, who had been the most active and forward in inducing the rest to join the Natchez. They were accordingly delivered to the Choctaws, who burnt them with a cruelty that inspired

the others with the greatest horror for the Indians, and the resort to which
certainly found an apology in the circumstances of the case.

The inhabitants of New Orleans received with open arms, in the bosom
of their families, the widows and children of their friends, who had fallen
under the tomahawk of the Natchez. Benevolence relieved their wants,
and tenderness ministered those succors, which protracted captivity and
sufferings called for. The nuns opened their cloister to the orphans of
their sex; those of the other were divided into the families of the easy and
affluent, and many a matron listened to solicitations to put an early end
to her widowhood.

The Chickasaws had offered an asylum in their nation to the Natchez;
it had been accepted by a number of them. Having thus aided the enemies
of the French, they sought to increase their number, and sent emissaries
to the Illinois to induce them to join in the common cause. These
Indians replied they would assist their white friends on the Mississippi
with all their might, and they sent a deputation to Perrier to assure him
of the dependence he could put in their nation, of their sorrow at the
catastrophe at the Natchez, and their readiness to lose their lives in the
defense of his countrymen.

They returned in the latter part of June to join the Arkansas, in order
to fall on the Yazous and Coroas. A party of the latter, going to the
Chickasaws, were met by one of the Tchaoumas and Choctaws, who
killed eighteen of them, and released some French women and children
they were carrying away. A few days after, a number of Arkansas fell on
a party of Yazous, scalped four men, and took four women, whom they
led into captivity. Returning homewards they met several Canadian
families going to New Orleans; they bewailed with them the disaster of
their countrymen, and particularly the death of father Poisson, who had
been their missionary before he moved to the Yazous; they vowed that, as
long as an Arkansas lived, the Natchez would have an enemy.

While the northernmost tribes remained thus attached to the French,
the smallest ones near the sea, received emissaries from the Chickasaws,
and suffered themselves to be deluded, so far as to admit among themselves
parties of wandering Indians, who much distressed the planters and greatly
alarmed the inhabitants of the city.

The Chouachas, a very small tribe, who originally occupied the margin
of lake Barataria, had removed to that of the Mississippi, a little below the
city, near the English turn, and had proved themselves useful to the
French when they began to occupy the ground on which New Orleans now
stands. They were suspected of being under the influence of the
Chickasaws, and had become obnoxious to the colonists. Their
annihilation was judged indispensable to the tranquillity of the country and
was determined on. The slaves of the neighboring plantations were
incautiously employed in this service, under the idea that the warfare
would sow between them and the Indians, the seeds of such mutual hatred
as would ever prevent a coalition between the red and the black people.
The negroes acquitted themselves with great fury, indiscriminately
massacreing the young and the old, the male and the tenderer sex.

On the tenth of August, the people of New Orleans received the pleasant
intelligence of the arrival at the Balize a few days before, of a company's
ship with troops and succor, under the orders of Perrier de Salvert, a
brother of the commandant general. Much of their joy however was

abated when it became known that there were but three companies of marines on board, each of sixty men.

The company kept in the province six hundred and fifty men of French troops, and two hundred of the Swiss. With this reinforcement, the total barely exceeded one thousand men—a relatively powerful body, if there had been but one settlement to protect; but a very insufficient one, while the establishments were sprinkled over a wide extended territory.

Chagrined at this disappointment, the commandant general made an excursion to Mobile to seek aid among the friendly tribes near Fort Conde.

On his return, he issued a proclamation conjuring every able bodied man, not already under arms, to buckle a knapsack on his back, put a musket on his shoulder and join the army. But little could be expected from this appeal; the whole militia from the Alibamons to the Cadodaquious and from the Balize to the Wabash, not exceeding eight hundred men.

Most of the Natchez Indians, who had not gone over to the Chickasaws, had crossed the Mississippi, and marched through the country of the Washitas to the neighborhood of the Natchitoches, and on Black river.

The departure of the army was delayed by a most distressing event. The negroes who had been employed in destroying the Chouaches, in returning to their labors, began to feel more sensibly the weight of their chain, and the success of the ferocity they had exercised against the Indians gave a hope that liberty might be the result of a similar attempt upon the French. But, their views were discovered, and the arrest and execution of their leaders warded for a while the impending blow.

The Arkansas had promised to come down and join Perrier's force. He now sent a Canadian of the name of Coulangue to meet them, and directed Beaulieu to proceed to Red river and obtain information of the spot to which the enemy had retired, his force and intended movements.

Perrier de Salvert with the vanguard of the army, embarked on the thirteenth of November. It consisted of the three companies of the marines, a few volunteers and Indians; in all about two hundred and fifty. The commandant general set off two days after with the main body, not larger than the van, composed of regulars and volunteers. Benac, who commanded the militia, led the rear, which did not exceed one hundred and fifty. The late alarm rendered it necessary that the forts should continue to be well garrisoned to insure tranquillity and awe the slaves.

The army stopped on the right side of the Mississippi, opposite to Bayou Manshac, where a Colapissa chief led forty warriors. It now consisted of about seven hundred men.

Lesueur was sent forward and ordered to ascend Red river. On his way he received the painful intelligence of the Natchez having surprised Coulange and Beaulieu, killed the former and wounded the latter. Of the twenty-five men who accompanied them, sixteen had been killed or wounded. The Arkansas had come down, according to their promise; but not hearing of the army, grew impatient and returned. He immediately communicated the intelligence to his chief.

Perrier, having ordered the army to proceed to the mouth of Red river, stopped at Bayou Tunica, to join the Indians who had been directed to rendezvous there; one hundred and fifty warriors only met him. He joined the army with these on the fourth of January.

His whole force now consisted of about one thousand men. He ascended Red and Black rivers, and on the twentieth came in sight of one of the enemy's forts, on the banks of the latter. The trenches were immediately opened and the artillery landed on the following day. On the next, the enemy made a sally, wounded an officer, and killed a soldier and a negro. On the twenty-fifth, a white flag was hoisted on the fort and a smaller one displayed on the trenches; soon after an Indian came out with a calumet, suing for peace and offering to surrender every negro in the fort. Perrier told him he would receive the negroes, and if the Indians wished for peace they should send the chiefs to speak with him. The messenger replied the chiefs would not come out; but if Perrier would come forth to the head of the trenches, the chiefs would meet him there. He was directed to go and fetch the negroes, and an answer would be given on his return.

Half an hour after, he brought eighteen negro men and one woman, and said the chiefs would not come out—that peace was wanted, and if the army would return, hostilities would cease. Perrier replied no proposal would be listened to until the chiefs came to speak with him, and if they did not, the attack would be resumed, and quarters given to no one.

The messenger went back and returning soon after, said the warriors insisted on the chiefs not coming out, and except on this head were ready to accede to any proposition. Perrier told him the cannon was ready, and he still insisted on the chiefs coming out—that if they compelled him to fire, he would not stop till the fort was blown to atoms, and no one would be spared.

On the man's return, a Natchez Indian, of the name of St. Come, a son to the head female sun, and as such heir to the sunship, who had always been on a friendly footing with the French, came to Perrier's camp: he told him that now as peace was made, the French army should return, that he grieved much at the conduct of his nation, but everything ought to be forgotten; especially, as the prime mover of all the mischief had fallen in the attack of the Choctaws. Perrier told him he was glad to see him, but he desired to see the great sun also, but would not be played with, and he hoped no Natchez Indian would approach him accept in the company of the latter, as he would order any one to be fired on, who would come with any other proposal.

St. Come took leave, and half an hour after returned with the head sun, and another chief, called the chief of the flour, who was the prime mover of all the mischief; St. Come having sought to screen him.

The Great Sun assured Perrier he had no hand in the massacre of the French, and was very much pleased at the opportunity of treating with him; St. Come exculpated him. The chief of the flour said he was sorry for what had happened. As they were exposed to the rain, which was now increasing, Perrier, pointing to a cabin near them, bid them to take shelter in it; on their doing so, he ordered four men to guard the door, and directed Lesueur and two officers attentively to watch them.

Lesueur, speaking their language, went in, and attempted to get into a conversation with them; but they kept a stubborn silence and lay down to sleep. The other two officers did the same on their rising, Lesueur went to rest towards midnight. About three hours after, he was awakened by a sudden noise, and saw the Great Sun and St. Come, endeavoring to escape from the sentry—the officers and the two other soldiers had gone in pursuit of the chief of the flour, who, having eluded their vigilance, had fled; Lesueur pointing his pistol at the two captives, they refrained from any further attempt to escape.

At daybreak, an Indian came from the fort to visit the Great Sun: being conducted to the cabin, he told him the chief of the flour having reached the fort had called apart ten warriors, and assured them Perrier was determined on burning them all; that for his part he had made up his mind no longer to remain exposed to fall into his hands, and advised them to look for their own safety with him. Accordingly they had followed him, with their women and children, while the rest lost in deliberation the favorable moments, and at daybreak found their flight was no longer possible. The Great Sun observed this chief was an usurper.

Perrier bid his prisoner, towards the evening, to send word to his people to come out with their women and children, and he would spare their lives, and prevent his Indians from hurting them. This was done by the messenger of the morning; but compliance was refused.

In the morning, the Great Sun's wife and some other members of his family visited him. Perrier received them well, because they had afforded protection to the French prisoners. Sixty-five men and about two hundred women came in towards noon.

Word was sent to those in the fort that if they did not leave it, the cannon would be fired and no one spared. The Indians replied the fire might begin, and they did not fear death. They were restrained by the fear of falling into the hands of Perrier's Indians if they went out in small parties, or of being discovered by the French if they went out together.

The cannonade now began: a heavy rain was falling, and it blew very hard. The besieged flattered themselves with the idea the inclemency of the weather would prevent the passes being strictly guarded; they were not deceived. At dusk the cannon was stopped: towards eight at night, an officer reported that the enemy was flying; the cannonade was now resumed, but it was too late—a part of the army went after the foe and brought in upwards of one hundred; Perrier vainly tried to induce his Indians to give the chase; they answered those should do so who had suffered the Natchez to escape. The fort was now entered and no one found in it but a decrepit old man, and a woman who had just lain in

There remaining now no enemy to fight, the prisoners to the number of four hundred and twenty-seven, were secured and embarked. The army set off on the twenty-seventh and reached New Orleans on the fifth of February.

The Great Sun, and the other prisoners, were sent immediately to Hispanolia, where they were sold as slaves.

The war was not, however, at an end, Lesueur had ascertained that the Natchez were not all in the fort Perrier had besieged. They had yet upwards of two hundred warriors, including the Yazous and Coroas, and an equal number of young lads capable of bearing arms. A chief had lately gone to the Chickasaws with forty warriors and many women: another was with seventy warriors, and upward of a hundred women and many children on lake Catahoulou, to the westward of Black river. There were twenty warriors, ten women and six children on the Washita: the strength of the party who had gone towards the Natchitoches was not known.

In the meanwhile, the company finding themselves much disappointed in the hope they had entertained of the profits of their commerce, and the advantages they had imagined would result from their charter; alarmed at the great loss they had sustained at the Natchez, and the great expense necessary to be incurred in the protection and defense of the province, if they retained the possession of it, solicited on the twenty-second of January, 1732, the king's leave to surrender the country and their charter. By an arrest of the council of the following day, and letters patent, which issued thereon, on the tenth of April, the retrocession made by the company of the property, lordship and jurisdiction of the province of Louisiana and its dependencies, together with the country of the Illinois, and the exclusive commerce to those places, was accepted.

The arrest declares the commerce of the retroceded countries free, for the future, to all the king's subjects.

This ended the government of the western company. It lasted during about fourteen years—nearly one-half of the time elapsed since Iberville had laid the foundation of a French colony on the gulf of Mexico.

When the company received its charter, the settlements in the wide extended country ceded to it, were confined to a very narrow space at the Biloxi, Mobile river, Ship and Dauphine islands. Two very small fortifications had been erected on the Mississippi—the one near the sea, the other at the Natchez, and one at the Natchitoches on Red river.

Agriculture had hardly reared its head, though rice was sowed in the swamps. Horticulture supplied the tables of a few with vegetables, and enabled some of the rest to procure a little money by supplying the Spaniards at Pensacola.

Now all the original settlements had considerably extended their limits, a new one had been formed at the Alibamons. On the Mississippi, the foundation of New Orleans was laid: although there was no plantation below it, a considerable one with a gang of upwards of one hundred slaves had been formed opposite the city, and there were many smaller but still considerable ones at Tchapitoulas and Cannes Brulees. A vast number of handsome cottages, lined both sides of the river at the German Coast; grantees of wide tracts had transported a white population, and sent negroes to Manshac, Baton Rouge and Point Coupee, and we have seen a smart settlement had risen at Natchez, the rival of New Orleans. Higher up, small colonies had gone to the Yazous and Arkansas; while others had descended from Canada to the Wabash and the Illinois.

To the culture of rice, that of indigo and tobacco had been added; the forests yielded timber for various uses and exportation: wheat and flour came already down from the Illinois; a smart trade was carried on with the Indians at Natchitoches, Mobile, Alibamons and the Cadadoquious, far beyond the westernmost limits of the present state. Provision had been made for the regular administration of justice; churches and chapels had been built at convenient distances, and without perhaps any exception, every settlement had its clergyman, under the superintendence of a vicar-general of the bishop of Quebec, of whose diocese Louisiana made a part. A convent had been built, the nuns of which attended to the relief of the sick of the garrison, and to the education of the young persons of their sex. The jesuits had a house in New Orleans; a kind of entrepot of their order, from which their priests were located among the neighboring tribes of Indians, or sent, as occasional emissaries, to the most distant; and those men attended to the education of youth.

The monopoly which the company and Crozat had enjoyed and strictly enforced, had checked, and it may be said destroyed, the incipient trade the colony had before the peace of Utrecht; but the produce of the tilled land and the forests, the hides, skins, furs and peltries, which were obtained from the Indians, for goods, which were easily procured in the company's warehouses at the Biloxi, New Orleans, the Natchez and the Illinois, and which were disposed of at an enormous advance, enabled the company to dispose of considerable quantities of merchandise.

The sums, spent by the company in the colony sufficed to furnish the inhabitants with a circulating medium. It had a commandant general, two king's lieutenants, a commissary ordonnateur, six hundred and fifty men of French, and two hundred of Swiss troops in its pay. Besides a number of directors, agents and clerks, it supported upwards of thirty clergymen.

According to the system of all commercial companies, the supreme authority in the province resided in the directors and agents of the corporation; and the military, incessantly controlled by men whose pursuit was wealth, not glory, lost their activity and zeal. A conflict of powers necessarily created dissensions and animosities, fatal to the interest of the company and the province.

It cannot, however, be denied, that while Louisiana was part of the dominions of France, it never prospered but during the fourteen years of the company's privilege.

The white population was raised from seven hundred to upwards of five thousand, and the black from twenty to two thousand.

CHAPTER XII.

SALMON, who on the death of Lachaise, had succeeded him in the office of Commissary Ordonnateur, having been appointed the king's commissioner, received possession of Louisiana in his name, from the company.

The crown had purchased all the property of the corporation in the province. It was not considerable, and the appraised inventory of it, amounted only to two hundred and sixty-three thousand livres; not equal in value to sixty thousand dollars. It consisted of some goods in the warehouses, a plantation opposite the city, which was partly improved as a brick yard, on which were two hundred and sixty negroes, fourteen horses and eight thousand barrels of rice.

The negroes were valued at an average of seven hundred livres or one hundred and sixty-three dollars and a third; the horses at fifty-seven livres or twelve and a half dollars, and the rice three livres or sixty cents and a third, the hundred weight. At these prices, nineteen hundred weight of rice were given for a horse; at the present value of rice, four cents a pound, the animal was worth seventy-six dollars, and the negro nearly one thousand.

The company had contracted a considerable debt with the planters, and obtained on the fourteenth of February, an arrest of the king's council, inhibiting creditors in Louisiana from suing in France. Brusle and Bru, two members of the superior council, were appointed commissioners to receive claims against it, in the province.

In order to facilitate the commerce of the colony, the king, by an ordinance of the fourth of August, dispensed the vessels of his subjects trading thither, with the obligation of transporting redemptioners and muskets, which was imposed on those trading to his other American colonies.

The late change in the government of the province requiring one in the organization of the superior council, this was effected by the king's letter patent of the seventh of May. The members of this tribunal were declared to be the Governor General of New France, of which Louisiana continued to constitute a part, the Governor and the Commissary of Louisiana, the king's lieutenants and the town major of New Orleans, six councillors, an attorney general and clerk.

The members of the council, at this time, were Perrier, Commandant General; Salmon, Commissary Ordonnateur; Loubois and d'Artaguette, the king's two lieutenants; Benac, town major of New Orleans; Fazende, Brusle, Bru, Lafreniere, Prat and Raguet, Councillors; Fleuriau, Attorney General, and Rossart, clerk.

The Natchez Indians continued to wage war with the western parts of the province. The chief of the flour, who had effected his escape from Perrier's camp, on Black river, and who had afterwards left the fort with some warriors, their women and children, had been joined by those whom he had left there, and had not fallen into the hands of the French. After wandering awhile among the Washitas, this party, increased by other individuals of their nation, proceeded to the Nachitoches. St. Denys, who commanded there, having early information of the approach of the Natchez, and finding his garrison weak, dispatched messengers to New Orleans, the Cadodaquious and Assinais, to solicit succor. Accordingly Loubois left New Orleans with sixty men of the garrison; but as he entered Red river, accompanied by one hundred Indians, whom he had taken at the Tunicas, he was met a little below Black river, early in November by Fontaine, who was sent by St. Denys to Perrier. From him Loubois learned the Natchez had attacked the fort, being about two hundred; but they had been repulsed.

The Natchitoches had made a show of resistance; but having but forty warriors, they had been compelled to desist, after having lost four men. The Natchez took possession of their village; St. Denys had been reinforced by his allies, on Red river and the Opelousas. With his garrison, a few Spaniards and these Indians, he sallied out, forced an intrenchment the Natchez had made around their camp, and killed ninety-two of them, among whom were all their chiefs. The rest fled into the woods, and St. Denys' Indians were in pursuit of them when Fontaine left the fort.

With far less means than the commandant general on Black river, St. Denys had effected in much less time a more brilliant and useful exploit. It put an end to the war of the Natchez. The survivors of the nation sought an asylum among the Chickasaws, with whom they became incorporated. These Indians had hitherto pretended to remain neutral; but now excited by a number of English traders, who had settled among them, avowed themselves the open enemies of the French.

There were at the Natchez, on the plantations of the French, a considerable number of negroes; nearly all of whom had joined the murderers of their masters in order to gain their freedom, and had followed their new friends among the Chickasaws. This circumstance, and their consequent emancipation, was known to their former companions who had been recaptured or surrendered, and presented to them the evidence of the possibility of their own release from bondage; they became restless, indocile, and fit subjects to be wrought upon, by persuasion. In the hope of exciting, through them, the other slaves in the colony, to finish the work begun at the Natchez, several of the most artful negroes, among the Chickasaws, were sent to Mobile, New Orleans and along the coast, to sow the seeds of rebellion among the people of their color in those places. These emissaries, being unable to show themselves openly, had no success on the plantations, where the gangs being small, the slaves were fearful. It was in vain urged upon them, the moment was arrived to rid themselves of their masters, and secure their own freedom by removing to the Chickasaws or the English, in Carolina.

On the plantation opposite the city, lately the property of the company, but now of the king, there were upwards of two hundred and fifty hands. Several of these were seduced, and the contagion spread with considerable rapidity up the coast, where, in the vicinity of the city, there were some estates with gangs of from thirty to forty slaves.

Meetings were held without the notice of the French; the blacks improving the opportunity, unsuspectingly furnished them by their owners, to assemble in nightly parties for dancing and recreation.

At last, a night was fixed on, in which, on pretexts like these, the blacks of the upper plantations were to collect on those near the city, at one time, but on various points, and entering it from all sides, they were to destroy all white men, and securing and confining the women and children in the church, expecting to possess themselves of the king's arms and magazine, and thus have the means of resisting the planters when they came down, and carrying on conflagration and slaughter on the coast. They hoped to induce or compel, by a show of strength, the timorous of their color, who had resisted the temptation to swell their number, and with them join parties of the Chickasaws, who they were assured would advance to receive and protect them. Fortunately, the motions of an incautious fellow were noticed by a negro woman, belonging to a Dr. Brasset; she gave such information to her master as led to the discovery of the plot. Four men and a woman, who were the principal agents in it, were detected and seized. The men were broken on the wheel and their heads stuck on posts, at the upper and lower end of the city, the Tchapitoulas and the king's plantation: the woman was hung. This timely severity prevented the mischief.

The king extended further encouragement to the trade of the province, by an arrest of his council of the thirteenth of September, exempting from all duties of exportation, all merchandise shipped by his subjects to Louisiana, and all duties of importation the merchandise of its growth, produce or commerce.

Shortly after, provision was made for its protection and defense, and an arrest of the thirtieth of November ordered a military force to be kept there, consisting of eight hundred men; six hundred and fifty of whom were to be detached from the regiment of Karrer.

The year 1732 is remarkable as the period of the settlement of the last of the British provinces in America, which now constitute the United States.   Charity devised the plan and furnished the means for its execution.   A society, formed in London, selected a large unoccupied tract of land between the rivers Savannah and Alatamaha, a kind of neutral ground, which separated the provinces of South Carolina and Florida, as a spot on which the suffering poor might find an easy and quiet existence.

The abolition of the company's exclusive right to the trade of Louisiana, and the encouragement lately given to its commerce excited the industry of the merchants in several of the seaports of France and her colonies; and several vessels from St. Maloes, Bordeaux, Marseilles and Cape Francois, came to New Orleans in the course of the following year.

The death of Augustus, king of Poland, in 1733, for awhile disturbed the tranquillity of Europe.   Louis XV. supported the claim to the crown of Stanislaus, whose daughter he had married in 1725, and was assisted by Spain, but was opposed by the emperor, who upheld the pretensions of the elector of Saxony.

Bienville was this year re-appointed governor of Louisiana.   He did not, however, reach the province until the following year.   The colonists hailed the return of their former chief, who had devoted the prime of his life to the service of their country.   Perrier, on his arrival, returned to France.

A frigate brought troops to complete the peace establishment of the province, according to the arrest of the king's council of the month of November.

For the double purpose of promoting the king's service, and the extension of agriculture in Louisiana, it was provided by an arrest of the king's council of the month of August, 1734, that there should be annually granted to two soldiers, in each of the companies of French troops serving there, a furlough and a tract of land, subject to a yearly quit rent of a sou for every four acres.   It was stipulated that the grantees should, within three years, clear such a part of the land as the governor should designate, and during that period, their pay and rations were continued to them.

The Swiss soldiers were likewise entitled to such a grant, at the expiration of the time for which they had been enlisted.

We have seen the king kept six hundred and fifty soldiers in the province.   They were divided into thirteen companies of fifty men each, which gave annually twenty-six new farmers.   The Swiss companies gave four in the same period.

In the French troops, the selection was made by the governor, from the soldiers, who conducted themselves the best.   This proved a valuable measure, promoting good order among the men, and extending agriculture. Those, who thus quitted the sword for the plough, became in time the heads of orderly families, and many of their remote descendants are now persons of wealth and respectability.

The French and Spanish arms had this year great success in Italy; Don Carlos, the youngest son of Philip the fifth, who afterwards was Charles the third of Spain, entered the kingdom of Naples, at the head of thirty thousand men, and made himself master of it.

Although large quantities of coin were annually sent over for the pay and maintenance of the troops, and the expenses of the colonial government, the means of remittance which agriculture supplied being comparatively few and small, the merchants hoarded up for exportation all the coin they received. The province found itself drained of its circulating medium, to the great injury to its agriculture and internal trade.

By an edict of the king, which bears date the nineteenth of September, 1735, an emission of card money to the amount of two hundred thousand livres, a little more than forty thousand dollars, was ordered to be struck, and declared receivable in the king's warehouses for ammunition or anything sold there, or in exchange, annually, for drafts on the treasury of the marine in France.

This measure had been solicited by the colonists; cards were accordingly struck of the value of twenty, fifteen, ten and five livres; fifty, twenty-five, twelve and a half, and six and a quarter sous—answering to the emissions of the British provinces of four, three, two and one dollar, halves, quarters and eighths of a dollar.

They bore the king's arms, and were all signed by the comptroller of the marine, at New Orleans. Those of fifty sous and more were also signed by the governor and ordonnateur—the others had the *paraphe* or flourish of these two officers only.

The cards were declared a tender in all payments whatever.

The Natchez and Yazous, who had found refuge among the Chickasaws, now resumed their predatory war on the distant settlements of the colony, and greatly obstructed its communication by the Mississippi to the Illinois, the Wabash and Canada. A number of Chickasaws generally accompanied these marauding parties. As the province could enjoy no tranquillity while such outrages were not suppressed, Bienville sent an officer to the principal village of the Chickasaws to insist on the surrender of the Natchez. He was informed these Indians could not be given up, as they had been received by, and incorporated with the Chickasaw nation. He determined to go and take them, and ordered immediate preparations for an expedition.

For this purpose, he directed the Chevalier d'Artaguette, who was now in command at Fort Chartres of the Illinois, to collect as many French and Indians as he could, and march them down to the country of the Chickasaws, in order to join the troops from New Orleans and Mobile, about the tenth of May.

Leblanc, who was the bearer of these orders to the chevalier, was sent up with five boats laden with provisions and ammunition for Fort Chartres. He successfully resisted the attack of a party of the enemy near the Yazou river. He reached that of the Arkansas, where he landed part of the loading of his boats, which had been too heavily laden. On his reaching Fort Chartres, one of the boats was sent for the provisions left at the Arkansas; but the Indians, who had attacked him on his way up, fell on this boat and killed every man on board, except a lieutenant called Dutisne, who commanded the party, and a half breed of the name of Rosaly.

In the meanwhile, another officer had gone among the Choctaws, for the purpose of inducing some of the chiefs, in the several villages of that nation, to meet Bienville at Fort Conde.

At this meeting the French chief purchased the aid of his red allies, for a quantity of goods, a part of which he brought from New Orleans and now delivered to them. The Choctaw chiefs engaged to collect the warriors of their nation and bring them to the standard of the French; and Bienville returned to New Orleans to hasten the march of the force he had directed to be assembled.

A sufficient number of the militia was left in the forts, and two companies marched with the regulars and some negroes, whom it was not thought imprudent to trust with arms. This force was embarked on the bayou St. John in thirty boats, and as many large pirogues. Bienville reached Fort Conde with it on the tenth of March.

He had before sent a strong detachment, under the order of Lusser, to throw up a small work on the bank of the river, at the distance of two hundred and fifty miles above Fort Conde, and on the same side of the stream, in order to have a safe place of deposit for the provisions, arms and ammunition that had been sent up for the use of the Choctaws. Here some of Lusser's men, instigated by a sergeant of the name of Montfort, formed the design of availing themselves of the facility presented by their great distance from the settlements of the French, to release themselves from subjection, by murdering their officers and seeking refuge among the Chickasaws, whom they were sent to combat, or among the English, in Carolina, through the desert. The plot was luckily discovered, at the moment on which it was to have been executed. The sergeant and five men were arrested, but Lusser postponed their trial till the arrival of his chief.

The army had left Fort Conde on the fourth of April, and reached Tombeckbee on the twentieth; a court martial immediately set on the prisoners, and they were shot. A few days after, the Choctaws, who had been engaged as auxiliaries, joined Bienville, and he delivered to them the balance of the goods he had promised.

Incessant rains and inclement weather prevented the army from leaving Tombeckbee before the fourth of May, and three weeks elapsed before it reached the spot on which it was intended to land. Some time was now spent in erecting a shed for the reception and protection of a part of the provisions and warlike stores, and a few huts for the accommodation of the sick. Here another party of the Choctaws joined the army; the number of these auxiliaries was now twelve hundred.

The nearest village of the Chickasaws was at the distance of twenty-seven miles to the northeast. A sufficient force being left to protect the sick and stores, the army marched in two columns on the twenty-fifth: the Choctaws were on the flanks. A halt was made for the night at the distance of seventeen miles; at daybreak, the troops started in perfect order and silence, and came in sight of the village towards noon: a strong fort had been erected before it. The Choctaws yelling ran forward, in the hope of surprising some of the Chickasaws, but without success.

Bienville, at half past one, formed his army into a regular square; as it approached the fort in this order, he ordered it to halt, and directed the major part of the regulars and militia to form strong detachments and march to the attack. The British flag was flying over the fort, and a few individuals of the nation were perceived in it. Fire had been set to a few cabins near the fort, from which the French might be annoyed; they advanced ten deep, shouting *vive le roi*, but were much distressed by the smoke from the cabins which the wind blew in their faces. The fort now began a galling fire; a lieutenant, a sergeant and two men were killed, and Renaud d'Auterive, an officer of the militia, was severely wounded. The Chickasaws were in a strong fort, surrounded with a thick palissado full of loop holes from which they poured forth an incessant shower of balls; strong and thick planks covered with earth, formed over the palissado, a covering impenetrable to the grenade. The French were unprotected and fell back. They soon advanced again; but the fire from the fort made a great havoc, while they fired in vain against the palissado. At five o'clock, Bienville seeing Noyant, Lusser, Jussau and Girondel, four of his best officers, and many others disabled, and the ammunition of his men nearly exhausted without the hope of success, ordered a retreat, and sent a strong detachment to support it. It was made in good order. The loss was thirty-two killed and sixty-one wounded. The force employed joined the rest without being able to bring away the bodies of their dead.

The evening was employed in throwing up a small entrenchment around the camp. In the morning the French saw the bodies of their countrymen, who fell in the battle, cut into quarters and stuck up on the pickets of the palissado around the fort.

During this day, the Choctaws had several skirmishes with the Chickasaws.

On the twenty-ninth, the army began to retrograde, and encamped within three miles only of the field of battle, and on the next day, within the same distance from their place of landing, which they reached on the third day. Bienville distributing the remainder of his goods among the Choctaws, dismissed them satisfied. Taking in the suite of the army the invalids he had left on the river, he floated down to Fort Conde, where he left a reinforcement in the garrison, and landed the rest of his men on the banks of the bayou St. John, in the latter part of June.

A sergeant of the garrison of the Illinois, who had been made a prisoner by the Chickasaws, succeeded so far in securing the good will of the Indian to whose lot he had fallen, as to obtain his liberty and a sufficiency of provisions to enable him to reach the settlements of the French. He came to New Orleans on the first day of July. Bienville learned from him the unfortunate fate of the Chevalier d'Artaguette.

This officer was the youngest son of the commissary ordonnateur of that name. He had served with distinction during the war of the Natchez, and had been left by Perrier to command the fort which this chief had directed to be built near the site of the present city of Natchez. In compliance with the orders which Leblanc had brought him from Bienville, he had left his command at Fort Chartres, with twelve hundred men, chiefly Indians. Warned by the fate of Lesueur, who having brought a body of Choctaws near the fort of the Natchez, had been unable to contain them, till the arrival of the Chevalier de Loubois; d'Artaguette, by occasionally slacking his march had arrived at the place of rendezvous mentioned in his orders, on the ninth of May; the eve of the very day he was directed to arrive, five days after Bienville had left the small fort at Tombeckbee. He had encamped in sight of the enemy till the twentieth, in anxious expectation of the arrival of Bienville, who did not land until four days after; when his Indians, like the Choctaws at the Natchez, grew impatient and unmanageable, and absolutely insisted on being allowed to fight or to withdraw. Incapable of restraining his turbulent allies, he had accepted the first alternative, and successfully attacked the fort before which he had encamped. He drove the Chickasaws from it and the village it protected. In the pursuit, the valorous youth had driven them to and out of the next fort, and was chasing them to a third, and perhaps their last entrenchment, when he received a wound—then another, which threw him on the ground weltering in his blood. His Indians, on the fall of their leader, retreated in all directions. Forty-eight soldiers, the whole of the garrison of Fort Chartres, which d'Artaguette had been able to bring, and father Senac, its chaplain, stood by, and for awhile defended their prostrated leader. But, what could the deserted few do? They were overpowered, and the Indians led their prisoners to the fort on which, had fate spared d'Artaguette but a few minutes, he would have planted the white banner. His companions washed and dressed his wounds, and his recovery was speedy. For awhile, the Chickasaws treated their captives well: they knew Bienville was advancing with a strong force, and promised themselves great advantages from the possession of the French, and at least a large ransom. But the reports of the arrival and retrograde of the French army were simultaneous, and the foe, elated by success and security, dragged out his unlucky victims to a neighboring field, bound the chevalier and the father to the same stake, and tying his courageous adherents, four by four around their wordly and spiritual leaders, extending protection to the sergeant only, consumed their victims by a slow and often interrupted fire.

Vessels from France, St. Domingo and Martinico frequently came to New Orleans; and early in the next year the king extended a further encouragement to the commerce of the province, by permitting the exportation of any article of its produce to the West India Islands, and the importation of that of these islands, to Louisiana, during ten years. The royal edict is of February, 1737.

The Spaniards at this time began to make great depredations on the commerce of Great Britain in the West India seas. Their guarda costas seized a number of vessels of that nation, which they carried into the ports of the main, the island of Cuba and Hispaniola, for condemnation under the pretense that they were engaged in a contraband trade with the colonies of Spain.

Bienville, on his return from the unsuccessful expedition against the Chickasaws, planned a new one, in which he proposed to reach their country by the Mississippi. He communicated his views to the minister, who submitted them to the chevalier de Beauharnois (the father of the first husband of the Empress Josephine) then Governor General of New France.

Louis XV. was not successful, in the war he had undertaken, to place his father-in-law on the throne of Poland. Tranquillity was momentarily restored to Europe by the peace of 1738, which left the Elector of Saxony in possession of the crown, and Don Carlos, king of Naples. Stanislaus, however, was permitted to retain the title of king, and became Grand Duke of Lorrain and Bar. While the war that had been waged between the emperor and the kings of France and Spain, was thus brought to a close, the latter sovereign began preparations for hostilities against Great Britain, and the garrison of St. Augustine received a very considerable reinforcement, with the view of an attack on the contiguous new British province of Georgia, which Philip V. considered as an encroachment on the dominions of his crown, while George II. sent six hundred men there, under the orders of General Oglethorpe.

As soon as Bienville was informed that the minister approved his plan of an attack on the Chickasaws, with a force, which was to ascend the Mississippi from New Orleans, and come down from Canada and the Illinois, he began his preparations. It is not easy to discover on what ground better success was promised, in this way, than by an approach of the enemy's country up the river Mobile; the greatest fort of the country of the Indians, was to the west of that river—and an army landed on the bank of the Mississippi would have to cross the country of the Choctaws, in its whole width. It is true, the latter were friendly Indians—but though this added much to the security of the forces, it increased equally the trouble, fatigue and expense. By the Mobile, the French landed at once in the centre of the enemy's country.

In the execution of his plans, Bienville ordered a very strong detachment to the river St. Francis, in the present territory of Arkansas, to be immediately employed in building sheds for the reception of the troops, their provisions, arms and ammunition, and a fort for their protection; this spot appearing the most convenient as a place of deposit, and a rendezvous for the forces that might come down from Canada and the Illinois.

In the month of May, of the following year, three of the king's ships, under the command of the chevalier de Kerlerec, landed at New Orleans a few companies of the marines who were commanded by the chevalier de Noailles.

Everything having been previously arranged, the chevalier de Noyant, set off with the vanguard a few days after the arrival of the reinforcements. The main body successively followed in large detachments, and Bienville brought up the rear. The army reached the river St. Francis, on the last of June, and without the loss of much time, crossed the stream to the river Margot, on the opposite side, near the spot on which the present town of Memphis, in the state of Tennessee, stands.

The army was first employed in providing the means of conveyance for the provisions, arms, ammunition and baggage, and in building a fort, which being completed on the fifteenth of August, the day on which the Catholic church celebrates the festival of the Assumption of the Virgin, was called the fort of the Assumption.

Labuissoniere who had succeeded the unfortunate chevalier d'Artaguette in the command of Fort Chartres, arrived a few days after with his garrison, a part of the militia of the Illinois and about two hundred Indians. He was followed the next week by Celeron and St. Laurent, his lieutenants, who commanded a company of Cadets, from Quebec and Montreal, and a number of Canada Indians.

The force from New Orleans consisted of the Louisiana regulars and militia, the companies of marines, lately landed from France, and upwards of sixteen hundred Indians. So that Bienville found himself at the head of upwards of twelve hundred white and double that number of Indian and black troops.

This comparatively very large army, unaccountably spent six months in making preparations for its march. In the meanwhile, the troops lately arrived from France became unhealthy and many died—the climate

25

had an almost equally deleterious influence on those from Canada.   The provisions were now exhausted, and such was the dearth of them, that horses were slaughtered for food.   Early the next year, the regulars and militia of Canada and Louisiana, who had escaped the autumnal disease were prostrated by famine and fatigue, and the chief was compelled to confine his call for service, to his red and black men.   They were his only effectual force.

On the fifteenth of March, Celeron marched the remainder of his Canadian Cadets to whom about a hundred other white soldiers were added.   This small body, with the negroes and Indians, began the march towards the village of the Chickasaws, and Celeron was instructed to promise peace to these Indians if it was asked.

The enemy had been apprised of the arrival of Bienville, with a very large army; and when they perceived the colors of Celeron's company, a few white men and an immense body of Indians, on each flank, they had no doubt that the whole force of Bienville was there.   In the terror which this delusion excited, most of the warriors came out of the fort, and approaching Celeron in an humble posture, begged him to give them peace and vouchsafe to be their intercessor with Bienville; assuring him they would be the inseparable friends of the French; swearing they had been excited to hostilities by the English from Carolina, who had come to their villages; and protesting they had entirely renounced any future connection with them.   They said they had lately made two individuals of that nation prisoners and detained them in the fort; they pressed Celeron to send one of his officers to the fort that he might be satisfied of the truth of what they told him; St. Laurent was accordingly sent.

As he entered, the squaws began to yell and scream loudly, and demanded his head.   On this he was seized and confined in a hut, while the men were deliberating on the demand of the women; at last, the party who deemed it dangerous to grant it, prevailed, and St. Laurent was taken out, and shown the white prisoners.   Pleased at the happy turn the affairs had taken, he promised peace to the Indians in the name of Celeron.   They all followed him to the camp, where the captain ratified his lieutenant's promise.

A deputation of the Chickasaws, joining the French on their retrograde march, Celeron led back his force to the Mississippi, where the calumet was presented, by the Chickasaws, to Bienville.   They renewed to him the protestation of their devotion, to the interests of the French, and presented him the two Englishmen.   The calumet was accepted, and the deputies were permitted to return.

The fort of the Assumption was raised and Labuissonniere and Celeron ascended the river with those of their men, whom disease and famine had spared.   The force from New Orleans stopped at the river St. Francis to dismantle the fort, and then floated down to the city.

Thus ended the Chickasaw war, undertaken by Bienville to compel these Indians to surrender the Natchez, who had found an asylum among the former.   Peace was made on the promise of the Indians of one of the villages of the enemy, to be in future the devoted friends of the French— purchased at the price of many valuable lives, at a vast expense besides, and with great distress and toil.   The French chief acquired no military glory from the war.

While tranquillity appeared thus restored to Louisiana, that of Europe was disturbed, at the death of the Emperor Charles the sixth, on the twentieth of September, 1740, without male issue. According to the pragmatic sanction, by which in 1713 it had been provided, that his eldest daughter should succeed him, Maria Theresa ascended the throne. Louis the fifteenth united with Prussia and Poland, in support of the pretensions of the Duke of Bavaria, to the imperial sceptre, and the dogs of war were let loose.

The chevalier de Beauharnois, Governor-General of New France, was succeeded by the count de la Gallissoniere.

CHAPTER XIII.

THE Marquis de Vaudreuil, a son of the late Governor-General of New France, was in 1741, appointed Governor of Louisiana, and Bienville sailed back to France, much regretted by the colonists. The latter was the youngest son of Lemyone de Bienville, a gentleman of Quebec, who had seven sons in the service of his sovereign. Bienville, the eldest, fell in battle in Canada. Iberville, Serigny, Sauvolle, Chateaugue and St. Helene, have all been mentioned in this work. The youngest, to whom the name of the eldest had been given, came, as we have said, to Louisiana, with Iberville, in 1698. He was then twenty-two years of age, and a midshipman in the royal navy. He remained in the province continually, except during the Administration of Perrier, and was the chief in command, during most of the time. He was called the father of the country, and deserved the appellation.

The commerce of Louisiana, released from the restraints of the exclusive privilege of the company, now began to thrive. Indigo was cultivated to a considerable extent, and with much success, and with rice and tobacco, afforded easy means of remittance to Europe, while lumber found a market in the West India islands. The Chickasaws were less turbulent; a circumstance attributed to the employment which war gave to the people of South Carolina and Georgia.

The increase of trade caused litigation, and it was deemed necessary to create new officers in the superior council. Accordingly, the governor and the commissary ordonnateur were, by the king's letters patent of the month of August, 1742, directed to appoint four assessors, to serve for a period of four years in that tribunal. They were to sit in rank after the councillors; but their votes were received only, in cases in which the record was referred to them to report on, when they were called upon to complete a quroum, or in case of an equality of votes. The choice of the two administrators, for the first time, fell on Delachaise, a son of the late commissary ordonnateur, Delalande d'Aspremont, Amelot and Massy.

The Spaniards this year made an unsuccessful attempt on the province of Georgia.

With a view of having Nova Scotia (which had been restored to Great Britain at the peace of Utrecht) occupied by national subjects, the former French inhabitants had been mostly driven away; three thousand families were brought over, at a great expense defrayed by government, and three regiments were stationed there to protect these people against the French of Canada and the Indians.

George the second having taken arms in support of the claim of Maria Theresa to the throne of her father, and having in person gained the famous battle of Dettingen against the allied forces, war was kindled between France and Great Britain.

Hostilities began in America, by frequent irruptions of the French from Canada into Nova Scotia. A small land and naval force from the island of Cape Breton, afterwards possessed itself of the town of Canceaux, and made its garrison and some of the inhabitants prisoners. A less successful attack was made on Annapolis—the French being driven back by the garrison, which had been reinforced by a strong detachment from Massachusetts. The conquest of Nova Scotia being a favorite object with the people of Canada, Duvivier was sent to France to solicit the minister to send out a sufficient force for this purpose.

Louisiana suffered a great deal from the want of a circulating medium. Card money had caused the disappearance of the gold and silver circulating in the colony before its emission, and its subsequent depreciation had induced the commissary ordonnateur to have recourse to an issue of *ordonances*, a kind of bills of credit, which although not a legal tender, from the want of a metallic currency, soon became an object of commerce. They were followed by treasury notes, which being receivable in the discharge of all claims of the treasury, soon got into circulation. This cumulation of public securities in the market within a short time threw them all into discredit, and gave rise to an *agiotage*, highly injurious to commerce and agriculture.

While Duvivier was gone to France to induce the minister to furnish means for the recapture of Nova Scotia, Governor Shirley, of Massachusetts, had dispatched captain Ryall, an officer of the garrison captured at Canceaux, to represent the danger in which the province of Nova Scotia stood, to the lords of the admiralty, and press them for some naval assistance. The captain was also charged to present a plan, which Governor Shirley had formed, for the surprise and capture of the island of Cape Breton, the possession of which, in the neighborhood of New Foundland, enabled the French to annoy the fisheries and commerce of Great Britain. Although nearly eight millions of dollars had been spent by France on the fortifications of that island, the smallness of the garrison, and the vicinity of the British provinces, induced Shirley to conclude it might be easily taken by surprise : the idea had not originated with him, but had been suggested by Vaughan, a merchant of New Hampshire.

Ryall's mission had no other effect than a direction to the commander of the squadron in the West Indies, to proceed to the north in the spring to afford protection to the commerce and fisheries of the New England provinces, and distress those of the French ; and the governors were instructed to aid him with transports, men and provisions.

In the meanwhile, Vaughan's plan had been submitted to the legislature of the provinces, and those of New Hampshire, Massachusetts and Connecticut, had raised about four thousand men, and the governors of the two first colonies, had taken upon themselves, on this occasion to disregard their instructions, and to give their assent to bills for the emission of paper money.

The colonial forces assembled at Canceaux, towards the middle of April, and were put under the order of Vaughan, and soon after the West India fleet arrived.

A landing on the island was effected a few days after, and while the fleet was cruising off Louisbourg, it fell in with a sixty-four gun ship from France, with five hundred and sixty men, destined for the garrison and an ample supply of provisions and military stores; she was captured, and the land forces soon after compelled the garrison to surrender.

In the meanwhile, the succor that Duvivier had been sent to solicit, had been obtained; seven ships of war, with a considerable land force, sailed from France, in the month of July. They were ordered to stop at Louisbourg, where they were to be joined by a number of volunteers from Canada, for the attack of Nova Scotia. Information reached the fleet, soon after its departure, of the fall of Louisbourg, and of a British fleet cruising in its vicinity; the plan was abandoned and the fleet returned into port.

Great preparations were made by both nations in the following year. The British determined on simultaneous attacks on Canada, from sea and the lakes, and a very considerable force was collected for this purpose. The French equipped a large fleet under the Duke D'Anville for the re-capture of the Island of Cape Breton and Nova Scotia; but like the Spanish armada, this fleet was, if not destroyed, dispersed by the winds and the waves; most of the ships were disabled. The apprehension which its approach excited, induced the British to turn towards the protection of their own territories the forces they had assembled for the reduction of Canada.

Philip the fifth of Spain ended his second reign and his life, in the sixty-third year of his age, on the ninth of July, and was succeeded by his second son, Ferdinand the sixth, having himself been succeeded by, and succeeded, his first.

Louisiana was this year visited by a destructive hurricane, which laid the plantations waste, and totally destroyed the rice crop. This article was used in most families, as a substitute for bread. The consequent distress was greatly increased by the capture of several vessels that had sailed from France, with provisions. The province was, however, relieved by large supplies of flour from the district of the Illinois, amounting it is said, to four thousand sacks. This part of the province was already, at this period, of considerable importance. In a letter to the minister, Vaudreuil wrote, "we receive from the Illinois, flour, corn, bacon, hams, both of bear and hog, corned pork and wild beef, myrtle and beeswax, cotton, tallow, leather, tobacco, lead, copper, buffalo, wool, venison, poultry, bear's grease, oil, skins, fowls and hides. Their boats come down annually, in the latter part of December, and return in February."

War drew off the attention of the people of South Carolina and Georgia; and the Indians, left to themselves, did not annoy the distant settlements of the French, and that in the neighborhood of Fort Chartres was in a very flourishing condition.

The extension of agriculture and commerce drew the attention of the government to the roads in the colony, and regulations were made for their construction and repairs. The office of overseer of the highways was created and given to Olivier Duvezin, who was also appointed the king's surveyor general in the province. His commission bears date the month of October, 1747.

The incapacity of many of the persons who had been appointed, principally in the distant posts, to make inventories of estates of the deceased and similar acts, joined to the impossibility often of finding any person to be appointed, had caused in many instances, the omission of the formalities required by law; great inconvenience had resulted from the necessity imposed on the superior council, of declaring some of these acts absolutely null. On the representations of the colonists, a remedy for this evil was sought, and a declaration of the king's council, of the thirteenth of March, 1748, provided that any inventory or other instrument, made in any of the posts of the province, in which there was no public officer, and even in those in which there was such an officer, as in New Orleans, Mobile and the Illinois, where the legal formalities were omitted, should be valid, provided there was no fraud; and such inventory or other public instrument should, within the year after the publication of the declaration, be presented to the superior council, and on the motion of the attorney-general, recorded, in order to prevent litigation, and promote the peace of families.

New Orleans, Mobile and the Illinois being the only places in the province, where public officers resided, it was directed that elsewhere, inventories and other public acts might in future be made by two notable inhabitants, attended by an equal number of witnesses, and within the year transmitted for registry to the superior council in New Orleans, or the inferior tribunals in Mobile, or the Illinois.

The winter was this year so severe, that all the orange trees were destroyed—a misfortune of which this is the first instance on record.

The peace of Aix la Chapelle, on the eighteenth day of October, settled the dissensions of Europe and put an end to the warfare between Canada and New England. Maria Theresa was recognized as Empress, and Don Carlos, the third son of Philip, retained the crown of the two Sicilies. Louis XV. and George II. agreed that all conquests made during the war should be restored, and the French re-possessed the island of Cape Breton.

The provision made by the treaty of Utrecht for defining the boundary between Canada and Acadia, had not been carried into effect. The cabinet of Versailles urged that by the cession of Acadia, nothing had been yielded, but the peninsula formed by the bay of Fundy, the Atlantic and the gulf of St. Lawrence— that of St. James claimed all the land to the south of the river St. Lawrence. Unfortunately, measures were not taken, at the pacification of Aix la Chapelle, to remove this source of controversy.

On the twenty-fifth of November, the king prolonged for six years, the exemption he had granted to vessels trading to Louisiana, from carrying thither the number of redemptioners and muskets, which were required to be taken to his other American colonies.

Larouvilliere, succededed Salmon as Commissary Ordonnateur, in the latter part of the following year.

Several individuals in England and Virginia had associated themselves under the style of the Ohio company for the purpose of carrying on the Indian trade, and effecting a settlement on the land bordering on that stream. They obtained from the crown a grant of six hundred thousand acres of land on the western side of the Alleghany mountains. Their surveyors and traders soon crossed the ridge, and erected block houses and stores among the Indians. The Marquis de la Jonquiere, who had succeeded the Count de la Gallissoniere in the government of New France, considering the country thus occupied as part of the dominions of his sovereign, complained to governor Colden, of New York, and governor Hamilton, of Pennsylvania, of what he viewed as an encroachment, and assured them that, if this notice was disregarded, he should deem it his indispensable duty to arrest the surveyors and traders, and to seize the goods of the latter.

The French had then a large force at Presquisle on lake Erie, and small detachments on French creek and the Alleghany river, and were making preparations for building a considerable fort, at the confluence of the latter stream and the Monongahela, the spot on which now stands the town of Pittsburg. This fort, with those on lake Ontario, at Niagara, the Illinois, the Chickasaw bluffs, the Yazous, Natchez, Pointe Coupee and New Orleans, was intended to form a connecting line, between the gulfs of St. Lawrence and Mexico.

The quota of troops for the service of the province, on the peace establishment, was fixed by an arrest of the king's council dated the 30th of September, 1750, at eight hundred and fifty men, divided into seventeen companies.

The agriculture of the province was favored by an arrangement with the farmers general of the kingdom, who agreed to purchase all the tobacco raised in Louisiana at thirty livres the hundred, equal to six dollars and two-thirds.

The remonstrances of the Marquis de la Jonquiere to the governors of New York and Pennsylvania having been disregarded, he put his threats into execution by the seizure of the persons and goods of several British traders among the Twigtwees.

The king had favored in 1731, the commerce of his subjects to Louisiana, by exempting all merchandise sent to, or brought from the province, from duty during a period of ten years, and the exemption had in 1741, been extended for a like period. It was by an arrest of the king's council, dated the last of September, farther prolonged during a third period of the same duration : but with regard to foreign merchandise sent there, it was restricted to salt beef, butter, tallow and spices.

Two hundred recruits arrived from France on the seventeenth of April, for the completion of the quota of troops allotted to the province. The king's ships in which they were embarked, touched at the cape, in the island of Hispaniola, where, with a view of trying with what success the sugar cane could be cultivated on the banks of the Mississippi, the Jesuits of that Island were permitted to ship to their brethren in Louisiana a quantity of it. A number of negroes acquainted with the culture and manufacture of sugar, came in the fleet. The canes were planted on the land of the fathers immediately above the city, in the lower part of the spot now known as the suburb St. Mary. Before this time the front of the plantation had been improved in the raising of the myrtle wax shrub ; the rest was sown with indigo.

The myrtle wax shrub is very common in Louisiana, Florida, Georgia, the Carolinas and Virginia, and not rare in the more northern states on the Atlantic. It bears grapes of very diminutive bluish berries, the seeds of which are included in a hard, oblong nucleus, covered by an unctuous and farinaceous substance, easily reducible into wax. In November and December, the berries being perfectly ripe, are boiled in water, and the wax detaches itself and floats on the surface. It is then skimmed off and suffered to cool. It becomes hard and its color a dirty green ; after a second boiling, the color becomes clearer. The candles made of this wax exhale, in burning, a very pleasant odor. Unsuccessful attempts have been made to bleach it. It is apt to crack, and is rendered tenacious, by being mixed with tallow or soft wax.

The ships landed also sixty poor girls, who were brought over at the king's expense. They were the last succor of this kind, which the mother country supplied. They were given in marriage to such soldiers whose good conduct entitled them to a discharge. Land was allotted to each couple with a cow and calf, a cock and five hens, a gun, axe and hoe. During the three first years, rations were allowed them, with a small quantity of powder, shot, and grain for seed.

Macarty, on the twentieth of August, went with a small detachment to take command of Fort Chartres of the Illinois, left vacant by the death of the unfortunate chevalier d'Artaguette. This district had, at this period, six villages; Kaskaskias, Fort Chartres, Caokias, Prairie des rochers, St. Philip and St. Genevieve.

Tranquillity being now restored to the British province, traders from the southernmost, poured in their goods, and erected stores and block houses, in the villages of the Indians, on their back settlements; and those of the French on Mobile and Alibamon rivers began to be distressed by the renewed irruptions of the Chickasaws. In consequence thereof, the Marquis de Vaudreuil marched into the country at the head of a body of seven hundred men of the regular forces and militia, and a large number of Indians. He was not very successful; the enemy had been taught by the British to fortify their villages. Each had a strong block house, surrounded by a wide and deep ditch. The colony was badly supplied with field artillery and soldiers skilled in the management of the pieces. The Marquis lost little time in laying sieges, but wandered through the country, laying the plantations waste. He enlarged the fort of Tombeckbee, left a strong garrison in it, and returned to New Orleans.

The settlements along the Mississippi, above the city and below, as far as the English turn, were now in high cultivation. The Marquis, in a letter to the minister of this year, observed it was almost an impossibility to have plantations near the river, on account of the immense expense attending the levees, necessary to protect the fields from the inundation of sea and land floods. He recommended that the idea of settling the part of the country below the English turn should be abandoned, till the land was raised by the accession of the soil. He observed there had been an increase of three feet in height during the last fifteen years.

A detachment from the troops in Canada had been sent under the orders of Legardeur de St. Pierre, a knight of St. Louis, to erect a fort on the western branch of French creek, which falls into the Ohio. This officer, on the twelfth of December, 1753, received by the hands of major Washington, of Virginia (a man whose name will long attract the admiration of the world and forever that of his country) a letter from governor Dinwiddie, summoning him to withdraw, with the men under his command, from the dominions of the British king. He wrote to the governor, he had been sent to take possession of the country by his superior officer, then in Canada, to whom he would transmit the message, and whose order he would implicitly obey.

In a quarrel between a Choctaw and a Colapissa, the former told the latter, his countrymen were the dogs of the French—meaning their slaves. The Colapissa, having a loaded musket in his hands, discharged its contents at the Choctaw, and fled to New Orleans. The relations of the deceased came to the Marquis de Vaudreuil to demand his surrender; he had in the meanwhile gone to the German coast. The Marquis having vainly tried to appease them, sent orders to Renaud, the commandant of that post, to have the murderer arrested; but he eluded the pursuit. His father went to the Choctaws and offered himself a willing victim: the relations of the deceased persisted in their refusal to accept any compensation in presents. They at last consented to allow the old man to atone by the loss of his own life, for the crime of his son. He stretched himself on the trunk of an old tree and a Choctaw severed his head from the body at the first stroke. This instance of paternal affection was made the subject of a tragedy, by Leblanc de Villeneuve, an officer of the troops lately arrived from France. This performance is the only dramatic work, which the republic of letters owes to Louisiana.

The Marquis de Vaudreuil was this year promoted, and succeeded Duquesne, in the government of New France, and was succeeded, in that of Louisiana by Kerlerec, a captain in the royal navy—and Auberville was on the death of La Rouvilliere, appointed commisary ordonnateur.

On the return of major Washington, the legislature of Virginia directed a regiment to be raised, of which he was appointed Lieutenant-Colonel. He was then in his twenty-second year.

Washington advanced with two companies of his regiment in the middle of April, 1754, and surprised a party of the French, under the orders of Jumonville, a few miles west of a place then called the Great meadows, in the present county of Fayette, in the state of Pennsylvania, and on the first fire this gentleman fell. He was the only man killed, but the whole party surrendered. The rest of the regiment came up soon after. Colonel Fry, its commander, having died on the way, Washington found himself at the head of it, and was soon after reinforced by detachments from New York and South Carolina.

There was then at Fort Chartres of the Illinois, an officer named Villiers, brother of Jumonville, who hearing of his death, solicited from Macarty, who had succeeded La Buissonniere, in the command of Fort Chartres, to be allowed to go and avenge his brother's death, with the few soldiers that could be spared and a large number of Indians. Villiers descended the Mississippi and ascended the Ohio. Washington, having erected a small fort as a place of deposit to which he gave the name of Fort Necessity, the traces of which are still visible near Union, the chief town of the county of Fayette, was marching towards the confluence of the Monongahela and the Alleghany, where the French were building the fort to which they gave the name of Duquesne. He heard of the approach of Villiers, from the Indians, who said that his followers were as numerous as the pigeons in the woods, and was advised by his officers to march back to Fort Necessity, which was at the distance of thirteen miles; he yielded to their suggestion. The party had hardly entered the fort when Villiers approached it, and immediately began a brisk fire, and an engagement now commenced which lasted from ten o'clock till dark, when the assailants offered terms of capitulation, which were rejected; during the night, however, articles were agreed upon. By these Washington having obtained that his men should be allowed to return home with their arms and baggage, surrendered the fort. This was on the now most venerated day in the American calendar, the fourth of July.

26

During the summer, some soldiers of the garrison of Cat Island rose upon and killed Roux, who commanded there. They were exasperated at his avarice and cruelty. He employed them in burning coal, of which he made a traffic, and for trifling delinquencies had exposed several of them, naked and tied to trees in a swamp, during whole nights, to the stings of musquitoes. Joining some English traders in the neighborhood of Mobile, they started in the hope of reaching Georgia, through the Indian country. A party of the Choctaws, then about the fort, was sent after and overtook them. One destroyed himself; the rest were brought to New Orleans, where two were broken on the wheel; the other, belonging to the Swiss regiment of Karrer, was, according to the law of his nation, followed by the officers of the Swiss troops in the service of France, sawed in two parts. He was placed alive in a kind of coffin, to the middle of which two sergeants applied a whip saw. It was not thought prudent to make any allowance for the provocation these men had received. The Indians seldom losing the opportunity of claiming remuneration, the Alibamons made a demand from Kerlerec for the pollution of their land by the self-destruction of a soldier, who had avoided in this manner, the dire fate that awaited him. He accordingly made them a present.

In the latter part of the year, Favrot was sent to the Illinois with four companies of fifty men each, and a large supply of provisions and ammunition.

The Marquis de Vaudreuil, on his arrival at Quebec, had received instructions to occupy and establish forts in the country to the south of the river St. Lawrence.

In the spring, as he was preparing to carry these instructions into effect, the British regular forces in Boston, with two provincial regiments, joined the garrison kept in Nova Scotia; and landing on the main, marched against Beausejour, which was surrendered on the fifth day; and in the summer possession was taken of all the posts of the French in the disputed territory, and every part of Nova Scotia, as claimed by Great Britain, was conquered.

In the cession of Acadia, Louis the fourteenth had stipulated that his subjects there should be allowed to retain their land on swearing allegiance to Queen Anne. They had declined doing so unqualifiedly, and insisted on such a modification of the formula presented to them, as would dispense them from the obligation of turning their arms against their countrymen in the defense of the rights of Great Britain to the country. No oath had been imposed on them. Although this indulgence had been complained of in England, no order had been sent either to require an absolute oath of allegiance or to expel those who had refused to take it: so the Acadians considered themselves as neutrals.

The vicinity of a country, with the inhabitants of which, these people were so intimately connected by the ties of nature, allegiance and national character, who spoke the same language and professed the same religion, prevented them from considering themselves as of a different country, or as subjects of a different crown. They saw in the neighboring Canadians a band of brothers, on whose assistance, in an emergency, they might rely, and considered themselves equally bound to yield theirs in return. They had, on every occasion, enlisted their feelings, their passions and their forces, with these neighbors, and in the late attack against

Beausejour, a considerable number of them were found arrayed against the conquerors, under the banner of France.

Nova Scotia is a rocky, barren country. The winter lasts seven months and is of dreadful severity; it keeps the people in almost as lifeless and torpid state as their vegetables. The summer comes sudenly (for there is no spring) and the heat is greater than is ever felt in England. Perpetual fogs render the country equally unwholesome and unpleasant. It presented so few advantages to new comers that the removal to it of such a number of British subjects, as would give them a preponderance over its former inhabitants, could not soon be effected. The transportation and maintenance of such a body of regular troops, as might keep the latter in awe, was a measure that must necessarily be attended with an expense totally unproportioned to the benefits, which Great Britain could expect from the possession of the country.

It appeared equally dangerous to permit them to depart or stay. For it seemed certain that, if they were left at liberty to choose the place of their removal, they would set down, as nearly as they could, to the country they should leave, that they could be ready to follow any troops the government of Canada might send to retake it.

In this dilemma, it was deemed the safest expedient to remove these people in such a manner as to lessen or destroy, by their division, the danger that might be apprehended from them. They were accordingly, at different periods, shipped off in small numbers to the British provinces to the south of New Jersey. This act of severity, which the circumstances were thought to justify, was not the only one that was exercised against them; their land and goods were taken from them and they were permitted to carry nothing away, but their household furniture and money; of the last article few, very few indeed, had any. It was determined to take from them all means of travelling back; and to deprive them, even of the least hope, as respects this, their fields were laid waste and their dwellings and fences consumed by fire.

Thus beggared, these people were, in small numbers and at different periods, cast on the sandy shores of the southern provinces, among a people of whose language they were ignorant and who knew not theirs, whose manners and education were different from their own, whose religion they abhorred and who were rendered odious to them, as the friends and countrymen of those who had so cruelly treated them, and whom they considered as a less savage foe, than he who wields the tomahawk and the scalping knife.

It is due to the descendants of the British colonists, to say that their sires received with humanity, kindness and hospitality those who so severely smarted under the calamities of war. In every province, the humane example of the legislature of Pennsylvania, was followed, and the colonial treasury was opened to relieve the sufferers; and private charity was not outdone by the public. Yet, but a few accepted the proffered relief and sat down on the land that was offered them.

The others fled westerly from what appeared to them a hostile shore— wandering till they found themselves out of sight of any who spoke the English language. They crossed the mighty spine and wintered among the Indians. The scattered parties, thrown off on the coast of every colony from Pennsylvania to Georgia, united, and trusting themselves to

the western waters sought the land on which the spotless banner waved
and the waves of the Mississippi brought them to New Orleans.

The levee and square of the city presented, on their arrival, a spectacle
not unlike that they offered, about a quarter of a century before on the
landing of the women and children snatched from the hands of the
Natchez.   Like these, the Acadians were greeted with tenderness and
hospitality; every house in the city afforded a shelter to some of these
unfortunate people.   Charity burst open the door of the cloister and the
nuns ministered with profusion and cheerfulness to the wants of the
unprotected of their sex.

Kerlerec and Auberville allotted a tract of land to each family : they
were supplied with farming utensils at the king's expense, and during the
first year the same rations were distributed to them out of the king's
stores, as to the troops.   They settled above the German coast, on both
sides of the Mississippi, and in course of time their plantations connected
the latter settlement with that of Baton Rouge and Pointe Coupee.   It is,
at this day, known by the appellation of the Acadian coast.

In the meanwhile, the British under general Braddock, made on fort
Duquesne an unsuccessful attack, in which the commander lost his life.
Governor Shirley of Massachusetts failed also in an attack against the fort
of the French at Niagara, and in his advance to lake Ontario.   Colonel
Johnson of New York made likewise a vain attempt against Crown point
on lake Champlain.

Although there had been no actual declaration of war between France and
Great Britain, both governments had granted letters of marque, and sent
considerable forces to North America.

The Baron de Dieskau, at the head of a small force marched against
the British post at Oswego, but was overpowered and defeated.

At last, on the seventeenth of May, George the first published his
declaration of war.

This document sets forth that the injurious proceedings of the French
in the West Indies and North America since the peace of Aix la Chapelle,
and their usurpations and encroachments in the Western hemisphere, had
been so frequent and notorious, that they manifested a settled design, and
undeviating resolution of invariably prosecuting the most efficacious
measures for the advancement of their ambitious views, without any
regard for the most solemn engagements and treaties.

The King urges that his frequent and serious representations to the
cabinet of Versailles, on these reiterated acts of violence, and his
endeavors to obtain satisfaction and reparation for the injuries sustained
by his subjects, and to guard against the recurrence of similar causes
of complaint have produced nothing but assurances that everything
should be settled according to existing treaties, and particularly that the
evacuation of the four neutral islands should be effected, as had been
expressly promised to the British Ambassador.   Yet the execution of
this promise and the clause of the treaty on which it was grounded had
been eluded, on the most frivolous pretences, and the illicit practices of
the French governments and its officers had been carried to such a degree
that in April, 1754, they broke out into open hostilities; and in a moment
of profound peace without any previous remonstrance, a body of French
troops openly attacked and captured a British fort on one of the branches
of the Ohio.

Hostilities on the Ohio, as we have seen, had been commenced by the attack of major Washington on the party commanded by Jumonville, in which the latter fell, and the march of Villiers against Fort Necessity was only a matter of retaliation.

It is said in the manifesto, that notwithstanding this act of hostility, which could only be considered as a signal for war, so sincere was the desire of the king to remain at peace, and so sanguine his hope that the French monarch would disown this act of violence and injustice, that he contented himself with sending over to America such forces only as were necessary to the immediate defense of his subjects and their protection against new insults or attacks. But in the meanwhile, a great naval armament was made in France, and a considerable number of troops were sent to Canada; and although the ambassador of France gave the most specious promises of the speedy arrangement of all existing differences, the real design of his court was to gain time, in order that such reinforcements might reach the armies of France in the new world, as would insure superiority, and enable their prince to execute his unjust and ambitious projects. The king complains that the measures which were required from him by the necessity of preventing the landing of the French troops in America, were followed by the departure of the French ambassador, the fortifying of Dunkirk, and the gathering of a considerable number of armed men on the coast of France, threatening his subjects with an invasion.

He declares that in order to avert the impending calamity, and provide for the safety of his kingdom, he was compelled to give orders for the seizure of French vessels. Yet, unwilling to forego the hope, or to throw difficulty in the way, of an amicable adjustment, he had expressly commanded that the cargoes of these vessels should remain in a state of sequestration. But, the actual invasion of the island of Minorca evinced the determination of the French cabinet not to lend its ear to any amicable proposition, but to prosecute the war it had begun, with the utmost violence, and compel him to abandon the system of moderation in which he had so long persisted.

Vast preparations were made under the directions of the Earl of Loudon, who had succeeded General Abercrombie in the chief command of the king's forces in North America. A considerable number of troops were raised in the New England provinces, and in those of New York and Pennsylvania, and lesser bodies were procured in the southern provinces for the campaign of the next year.

In the meanwhile, the Marquis de Montcalm had arrived in Canada and taken the command of the forces of France.

The earl, notwithstanding his great preparations, did not strike any blow—the marquis with far less means was more successful. In the month of August, he made himself master of Fort Oswego: this post, situated at the mouth of Onondago river, commanded a commodious harbor on lake Ontario. It had been erected by Governor Shirley, with a view to the protection of the country of the five nations, the security of the fur trade, the obstruction of the communication between the French establishments, and to open a way for the British forces to Niagara and Fort Frontenac. Montcalm's military means not allowing him to keep it, he ordered the British fort to be raised, and told the Indians his views were not hostile to them—he came into the country for their protection: he wished no strong house to keep them in awe: his nation desired only to live in peace, trade with them and protect them against their enemies, who were those of the French.

The Marquis met with an equal success in the attack of Fort William Henry on lake Champlain, which surrendered in the beginning of August.

This year Auberville died, and was succeeded in the office of commissary ordonnateur of Louisiana by Bobe Descloseaux.

The tide of events turned against France in the following year. The British took the islands of Cape Breton and St. John, and raised Fort Frontenac on lake Ontario, during the summer. In the fall general Forbes marched against Fort Duquesne; the French commander, finding himself unable to defend it, embarked his artillery and ammunition, set fire to the buildings and evacuated it. In the latter part of November, the garrison floated down the Ohio and Mississippi to New Orleans.

In their way, they stopped and built a fort on the right bank of the former stream, not far from the place at which it falls into the latter. It was called Fort Massic, after the officer, who was left to attend to its erection and to command it.

On the arrival of the forces from Fort Duquesne at New Orleans, new buildings were required for the accommodation of the troops, and Kerlerec began the barracks in the lower part of the city.

Although the essay, which the Jesuits had made in 1751, to naturalize the sugar cane in Louisiana, had been successful, the culture of it, on a large scale, was not attempted till this year, when Dubreuil erected a mill for the manufacture of sugar, on his plantation, immediately adjoining the lower part of New Orleans—the spot now covered by the suburb Marigny.

Kerlerec, having been directed to have the part of the province, around lake Barataria and along the sea shore, west of the Mississippi, explored, Marigny de Mandeville, a son of the late commandant of Fort Conde of Mobile, made an accurate map of the southwestern part of the province.

Overtures towards negotiation were made by the cabinet of Versailles, to that of St. James, through the channel of the Dandish ambassador in London.

Rochemore, who had been appointed commissary ordonnateur, arrived early in the following year. Soon after his landing, an unfortunate misunderstanding between him and Kerlerec, disturbed greatly the tranquillity of the colony. It was then the practice of the government to send large quantities of goods for the Indian trade: they were entrusted to the officers sent in command to the distant posts, to whom they furnished the means of considerably increasing their fortunes. The ordonnateur, who had the disposal of these, found in it an opportunity of attaching those officers to his party, which the governor complained, he did not neglect. Each of these chiefs imagined he had grounds of recrimination against the other; a considerable degree of irritation was excited, and a circumstance of no great moment brought matters to a crisis.

Diaz Anna, a Jew from Jamaica, came to New Orleans on a trading voyage. We have seen that by an edict of the month of March, 1724, that of Louis the thirteenth, of the 13th of April, 1615, had been extended to Louisiana. The latter edict declared that Jews as enemies of the christian name, should not be allowed to reside in Louisiana; and if they staid in spite of the edict, their bodies and goods should be confiscated : Rochemore had the vessel of the Israelite and her cargo seized. Kerlerec sent soldiers to drive away the guard put on board the vessel, and had her restored to the Jew. Imagining he had gone too far to stop there, he had Belot, Rochemore's secretary, and Marigny de Mandeville, de Lahoupe, Bossu and some other officers, whom he suspected to have joined the ordonnateur's party, arrested, and a few days after shipped them for France. He entrusted Grandmaison, an officer who having obtained a furlough had taken his passage in the vessel, on board of which these persons were placed, with his dispatches for the minister, containing the reasons which, in his opinion, justified this violent measure.

As the vessel approached the coast of France, she was driven by a storm on that of Spain and entered the port of St. Sebastian. Grandmaison, according to Kerlerec's instructions, went to deposit the dispatches in the hands of the consul of France. Belot and his companions in misfortune accompanied the messenger to the consulate. The dispatches being delivered were placed on a table, from which it is supposed they were purloined by one of the consul's visitors, while he was attending on the others, whose attention had been drawn to some fine engravings on the walls of the apartment.

On their arrival in Paris, Belot and his associates filled the court with their complaints of Kerlerec's arbitrary proceedings. He was universally blamed.

During the summer, the most rapid success attended the British forces in Canada. They possessed themselves of Ticonderoga on the 22d of July, of Crown point, in the beginning of August, of Niagara on the 24th, and of Quebec on the eighteenth of September.

In the following year, they found themselves masters of all Canada, by the reduction of Montreal.

On the eleventh of August, Ferdinand the sixth of Spain died, in the fifty-sixth year of his age, without issue. He was succeeded by Charles the third, his brother, then king of Naples, the third son of Philip the fifth, who wielded the Spanish sceptre.

George the second of Great Britain ended his life, at the advanced age of seventy-seven years, on the twenty-fifth of October; he was succeeded by George the third, his grandson.

On the fall of Canada, a number of the colonists, unwilling to live under their conquerors, sought the warm clime over which the spotless banner still waved; most of them settled in the neighborhood of the Acadians. Others of a more roving disposition crossed the lakes that separate the right bank of the Mississippi from the western prairies and began the settlements of Attakapas, Opelousas and Avoyelles.

The province at this time was inundated by a flood of paper money. The administration, for several years past, had paid in due bills all the supplies they had obtained, and they had been suffered to accumulate to an immense amount. A consequent depression had left them almost without any value. This had been occasioned, in a great degree, by a belief that the officers who had put these securities afloat, had at times, attended more to their own, than to the public interests, and that the French government, on the discovery of this, would not perhaps be found ready to indemnify the holders against the misconduct of its agents. With a view, however, to prepare the way for the redemption of the paper, the colonial treasurer was directed to receive all that might be presented, and to give in its stead, certificates, in order that the extent of the evil, being known the remedy might be applied.

The disastrous situation of the marine of France precluding the hope of recovering any part of her lost territory in America, the Duke of Choiseul, who without the title, exercised the functions of prime minister, made an attempt at negotiation with Great Britain. The conferences began on the twenty-eighth of March, but were closed soon after without success. Disappointed in this quarter, he formed the plan of joining the marine of Spain to that of France, and this was the end of the family compact, which was signed at Paris, on the fifteenth of August.

The avowed object of this arrangement was to give permanence and inviolability to the obligations resulting from the friendship and consanguinity of the sovereigns of France and Spain, and to rear up a solemn monument of the reciprocal interest which was the object of their wishes and insure the continuance of the prosperity of their royal family.

They agree to consider in future any power at war with either of them, as a common enemy; they reciprocally guarantee to each other his respective dominions in every part of the world; but, it is expressly stated that this guarantee is to have no other object than the respective dominions of each crown, as they may exist at the first period of peace with the other powers.

A like guarantee is to be extended to the King of the two Sicilies and the Duke of Parma, on their respective accession to the compact.

Although the mutual guarantee is to be supported with all the forces of the parties, they stipulate that the first succor to be furnished is to consist of a given number of ships, horse and foot.

The wars which the French king may be engaged in, in consequence of his engagements at the treaty of Westphalia, or his alliances with German princes, are exempted from the compact, unless a maritime power takes part in them, or his dominions are attacked.

The stipulated succor is to be considered as the minimum of what the required party is bound to do; and it is the understanding of the parties that on a declaration of war against either, it is to be considered as common to the other. They shall jointly exert all their means: and arrangements will be made, relative to a common plan, and the respective efforts of the parties, according to circumstances.

No proposition of peace from the common enemy shall be listened to, without the joint consent of each party, who in peace and in war, shall consider the interest of the other as his own: all losses and advantages are to be compensated and the two parties are to act as if they formed but one.

The king of Spain stipulates for that of the two Sicilies and engages to procure his accession to the compact.

The *droit d'aubaine* is abolished in favor of the subjects of the parties, and they are to enjoy the advantages and immunities of national subjects.

The powers with whom either party may make a treaty, shall be informed that these advantages and immunities are not to be extended to others.

At the close of the year Rochmore went over to France. His conduct was approved by the minister, and orders were sent to Kerlerec, on the following year, to return and give an account of his : Foucault was sent to succeed Rochmore.

Early the next year, the sovereigns of Great Britain and Spain published formal declarations of war against each other. The success of the British arms, in the West Indies, were as rapid and brilliant as they had been in Canada, in 1759. Martinico, Grenada, St. Lucia and all the other Caribee islands were conquered from France, and the city of Havana from Spain.

On the third of November, a secret treaty was signed at Paris, between the French and Spanish king, by which the former ceded to the latter the part of the province of Louisiana, which lies on the western side of the Mississippi, with the city of New Orleans and the island on which it stands.

The war between Great Britain, France and Spain, was terminated by the treaty of Paris, on the sixteenth of February of the following year.

CHAPTER XIV.

By the treaty of Paris, the king of France renounced his pretensions to Nova Scotia or Acadie, and guaranteed the whole of it, with its dependencies, to the king of Great Britain; to whom he ceded and guaranteed in full right Canada, with all its dependencies, as well as the island of Cape Breton and all the other islands and coasts, in the river and gulf of St. Lawrence.

The limits between the French and British possessions in North America, are fixed irrevocably by a line drawn along the middle of the river Mississippi, from its source to the river Iberville; and from thence by a line in the middle of that stream and lake Maurepas and Pontchartrain to the sea.

The king of France cedes to that of Great Britain the river and port of Mobile, and everything possessed by him on the left side of the river Mississippi, except the town of New Orleans and the island on which it stands.

The navigation of the Mississippi is declared free to the subjects of either sovereign, in its whole breadth and length, from its source to the sea; and it is expressly stipulated that vessels belonging to subjects of either shall not be stopped, visited, or subject to any duty.

The British king promises to allow the inhabitants of Canada, the free exercise of the Roman Catholic religion, and to give the most precise and effective orders that his new Roman Catholic subjects may exercise their religion, according to its rites, in as much as it is permitted by the laws of Great Britain.

Eighteen months are allowed to the inhabitants to sell their property to British subjects, and withdraw wherever they please.

The same rights are granted to the inhabitants of the ceded part of Louisiana.

The king of Spain cedes to that of Great Britain the province of Florida with the fort of St. Augustine and the bay of Pensacola, as well as all the country he possesses on the continent of North America, to the east and southeast of the river Mississippi.

27

We have seen that all the part of Louisiana not ceded to Great Britain, had already been yielded to Spain; so that France did not retain one inch of ground in North America.

The conquered islands were restored to France and Spain.

The island of Grenada and its dependencies were ceded by the king of France to that of Great Britain.\

The islands called neutrals were divided, but not equally; those of St. Vincent, Dominica and Tobago, being yielded to Great Britain, and that of St. Lucia to France.

Clement the thirteenth having expelled the Jesuits from the dominions of the kings of France, Spain and Naples, these monks were now driven from Louisiana, and in the month of July their property, near New Orleans, was taken into the king's hands and sold, under a decree of the superior council. It produced about one hundred and eighty thousand dollars.

On the seventh of October, 1763, the king of Great Britain divided his acquisitions in North America into three distinct governments, those of Quebec, and East and West Florida.

All the coast from the river St. John to Hudson's straits, with the islands of Anticosti and Madeleine, and all other small islands on that coast, were put under the care and inspection of the government of New Foundland.

The islands of St. John, Cape Breton, with the lesser ones adjacent thereto, were annexed to the province of Nova Scotia.

The land between the rivers St. Mary and Altamaha was annexed to the province of Georgia.

The part of the territory acquired from Spain, adjoining Louisiana, was erected into a separate province, called West Florida; it was bounded on the south by the gulf of Mexico, including all islands within six leagues of the sea coast from the river Apalachicola to lake Pontchartrain—on the west by that lake, lake Maurepas and the river Mississippi—on the north, by a line drawn due east from a point in the middle of that river, in the thirty-first degree of northern latitude to the river Apalachicola or Catahouche, and to the east by that river.

In the meanwhile, George Johnston, a captain in the royal navy, appointed governor of the province of West Florida, arrived at Pensacola with major Loftus, who was to command at the Illinois. They were accompanied by a considerable number of highlanders from New York and Charleston. Detachments of these were sent to take possession of Fort Conde, Fort Toulouse, Baton Rouge and the Natchez.

Fort Conde was now called Fort Charlotte, in compliment to the young queen of Great Britain.

Most of the Indians, in alliance with the French, followed the white banner to New Orleans, on its being lowered in the forts of the ceded territory; lands were allotted to them on the western side of the Mississippi.

In the fall, Kerlerec was recalled; and the chief magistracy of the province vested in d'Abadie, under the title of director general. The military force was reduced three hundred men, divided into six companies under the orders of Aubry, as senior captain.

Kerlerec's conduct was highly disapproved of in France; he was confined for some time in the Bastile, and died of grief shortly after his release.

Major Loftus, who commanded the twenty-second regiment, came from Pensacola to New Orleans on his way to the Illinois, early in 1764. He proceeded up the river on the 27th of February, with a detachment of the thirty-fourth, who had been employed in reconnoitring the river Iberville. His whole force consisting of about four hundred men, was embarked in ten batteaux of from sixteen to twenty oars each and two canoes. They reached the heights now called Fort Adams then La roche a Davion, in three weeks.

In the morning of the twentieth of March, the two canoes being a little ahead of the major's batteau and close to the right bank, which was covered with brush, a volley was fired on them and three privates were killed and one wounded in the first canoe and one sergeant and two privates wounded and two privates killed in the second. The boats going back with the stream and there being no possibility of landing on that side, the river having overflowed its banks, the major ordered his small fleet on the opposite shore, and as he approached received a second volley. Both sides of the river appearing strongly guarded by the Indians and the stream narrow, he determined on descending the river and taking post for the present at bayou Manshac. The mount, near which the party was fired on, was afterwards called Loftus' heights.

Having disembarked at bayou Manshac and reconnoitred the ground, major Loftus thought it better to return to New Orleans, where finding a brig ready to sail for Pensacola, he took passage in her; his men floated down in their batteaux, to the Balize, except a captain and twenty men of the twenty-second regiment, whom he ordered to proceed by the lakes to Mobile.

As they were ready to start, d'Abadie received information that sixty Indians of the Colapissa tribe from the western side of lake Ponchartrain were preparing to intercept the batteaux in the rigolets.

The captain represented to the French chief that major Loftus had departed fully suspecting that the French had prevailed on the Indians to prevent his ascent of the river to the Illinois, and an attack of the Indians, who were known to be in the interest of the French, would not fail to increase the suspicion. D'Abadie proposed to send an officer, with a detachment to escort the British. This was declined, and an interpreter, acquainted with the lurking places of the Indians, was sent forward to assure them the British wished to live in peace and friendship with them; and would treat them as brethren. The Captain and his men reached Mobile safely, on the fifth of April.

The Indians, who fired on the British force up the river, were parties of the Tunicas, Oumas, Chetimachas and Yazous.

On the twenty-third of March, the lords commissioners of trade and plantations, in Great Britain, represented to the king that it appeared from observations and surveys made since the province of West Florida was in his possession, that there were considerable settlements on the left bank of the Mississippi, above the thirty-first degree of northern latitude, and recommended that the northern boundary of the province of West Florida should be a line drawn from the mouth of the river of the Yazous, running due west to the river Apalachicola. Accordingly, on the tenth of June, a new commission was issued to governor Johnston, extending thus the limits of his government.

During the summer, a large detachment occupied Fort Rosalie of Natchez.

In the meanwhile, British vessels began to visit the lower banks of the Mississippi—after passing New Orleans, they cast anchor, made fast to a tree above it, opposite the present suburb Lafayette, where the people of the city and neighboring plantations came to trade with them. The spot, at which they stopped on their way up the river, under the pretense of going to bayou Manshac and Baton Rouge, received the appellation of Little Manshac. The wants of the colony induced its chief to overlook and tolerate the illegal traffic—extremely advantageous to the colonists, whose honesty and good faith rendered it equally so to their visitors.

The colonists began now to be distressed by rumors from France of their approaching passage under the yoke of Spain. These fears were realized early in October, when official intelligence of the cession was received by d'Abadie, in a letter of his sovereign, bearing date the first of April preceding.

In this document, the king, after announcing the cession to the director general (copies of the treaty and its acceptance being inclosed) manifests his intention, that, on the receipt of the letter and its inclosures, whether it be delivered him by any Spanish officer, or brought by any French vessel, immediate possession should be delivered to the governor, or any other officer of the Catholic king, of the city of New Orleans and the rest of the ceded territory; It being the object of the cession that the country should in the future belong to the latter sovereign, and be ruled and administered by his governor or chief officer, as being his, in full property and without reserve.

D'Abadie is accordingly instructed, on the arrival of the Spanish officers and troops, after having yielded possession, to withdraw with all the officers, soldiers and other persons in the service of France, who may not be desirous of remaining, and afford them a passage to some of the king's dominions in Europe or the West Indies.

He is directed, immediately after the evacuation, to collect all papers, relative to the finances, and the administration of the province, and to return and give an account of his proceedings; delivering however, to governor or other officer of the Spanish king, such papers, as may especially relate to the affairs of the colony, in regard to the land, the different posts and Indian affairs; taking receipts for his discharge. It is recommended to him to afford such information, relative to the concerns of the colony, as may enable the officers of Spain to administer its affairs to the satisfaction of both nations.

Duplicate inventories are ordered to be made by the director general, and a Spanish commissary, of all the artillery, goods, magazines, hospitals and vessels of the province; so that, after delivery, an appraisement may be made of such articles as may be kept by the Spanish king.

The hope is expressed and the king declares he expects it from the friendship of the monarch of Spain, that, for the advantage and tranquillity of the inhabitants, orders will be given to the governor and other officers, employed in Louisiana, that the regular and secular clergy, acting as curates or missionaries, may be allowed to continue the exercise of their functions and enjoy the rights, privileges and exemptions, granted to them by the royal charters, and that the inferior judges, as well as those of the superior council, may be allowed to continue to administer justice, according to the present laws, forms, and usages of the colony, that the inhabitants may be confirmed in their estates according to the grants of the former governors and commissaries ordonnateurs, and that such grants may be confirmed by the Catholic king, even when they were not so by him. Finally, the king hopes the new sovereign will give to his subjects in Louisiana such marks of his protection and favor, as they have heretofore experienced from the former, of which nothing but the disasters of the war could have prevented them from enjoying the full effect.

The director general is enjoined to cause the royal letter to be transcribed on the minutes of the superior council, that every one in the province may become acquainted with its contents, and recur thereto, in case of need.

This intelligence plunged the inhabitants in great consternation. They bewailed before their estrangement from their kindred and friends in the eastern part of the province; that they were now themselves transferred to a foreign potentate, filled their minds with the utmost sorrow.

The fond hope was however indulged that their united solicitations might avert the impending calamity. Every parish was accordingly invited to send its most notable planters, to a general meeting, in the city of New Orleans in the beginning of the following year.

The council, according to its new organization, on the dismemberment of the province, was composed of d'Abadie, the director general, Foucault, the commissary ordonnateur, Aubry, the commandant of the troops, Delalande, Kernion, Delaunay, Lachaise, Lesassier, Laplace, councillors, Lafreniere, attorney general, and Garic, clerk.

The general meeting was attended by a vast number of the most respectable planters from every part of the province, and almost every person of note in New Orleans. The most prominent characters were Lafreniere, the attorney general, Doucet, a lawyer who had lately come from France, St. Lette, Pin, Villere, the chevalier d'Arensbourg, Jean Milhet, the wealthiest merchant of New Orleans, Joseph Milhet, his brother, St. Maxent, Lachaise, Marquis, Garic, Mazent, Mazange, Poupet, Boisblanc, Grandmaison, Lalande, Lesassier, Braud, the king's printer, Kernion, Carrere and Dersalles.

Lafreniere addressed the meeting in an animated speech, which he concluded by a proposition that the sovereign should be entreated to make such arrangements with his catholic majesty as might prevent Louisiana being severed from the parent stock, and that a person should be immediately sent to France to lay the petition of the inhabitants of the province at the foot of the throne. Without a dissenting vote the proposition was assented to, and with the like unanimity, Jean Milhet was selected for the important mission.

At this period a number of families emigrated to Louisiana from the British provinces, principally from the banks of Roanoke river, in North Carolina, and settled above Baton Rouge; this was the beginning of the settlement which was afterwards called the district of Feliciana.

Till now the post of the Illinois remained in the possession of the French, and St. Ange, the commandant, continued to exercise his authority over it. A proclamation of General Gage, the commander-in-chief of the forces of the king of Great Britain in North America, issued at New York the thirteenth of December, was brought to the post early in the new year by captain Sterling, who was instructed to receive the oath of allegiance and fidelity of the inhabitants to their new sovereign.

By this proclamation they were informed that the taking possession of their country by the king's forces, although delayed had been determined on; and the sovereign had given the most precise and effective orders, that his new Roman Catholic subjects of the Illinois should be allowed the exercise of religious worship, according to the rites of their church in the same manner as the Canadians—that he had agreed that the French inhabitants and others, who had been subjects of the most christian king might retire in full safety and proceed where they pleased; even to New Orleans or other parts of Louisiana, although the Spaniards might take possession of it; that they might sell their estates to the king's subjects and transport themselves and their effects without any other restraint, but that which might result from civil or criminal process. The rights and immunities of British subjects were promised to those who might chose to stay, but they were required to take an oath of allegiance and fidelity.

The commander-in-chief recommended to the people to demean themselves as loyal and faithful subjects, by a prudent conduct to avoid all causes of complaint, and to act in concert with the royal forces on their arrival, so that possession might be taken of every settlement, and good order preserved in the country.

Civil government, being established, under the authority of Great Britain a few months after in the post, St. Ange, the French commandant there, crossed the Mississippi with a number of his countrymen, who were desirous to follow the white flag, and laid the foundation of the town of St. Louis, which with that of St. Genevieve, was the first settlement of the country now known as the state of Missouri.

The province labored under great difficulties on account of a flood of depreciated paper, which, inundating it, annihilated its industry, commerce and agriculture. So sanguine were the inhabitants of their appeal to the throne, that they instructed their emissary, after having accomplished the principal object of his mission, to solicit relief in this respect.

Destrehan, the king's treasurer, and a number of other planters had been induced by the success of Dubreuil, in manufacturing sugar, to erect mills, most of these establishments were below New Orleans and on the same side of the river. Hitherto, the sugar made in Louisiana had been all consumed in the province. This year, a ship was laden for France with this article. It had been so inartificially manufactured, that it leaked out of the hogsheads, and the ship was so lightened by this accident that she was very near upsetting.

Milhet saw, at Paris, Bienville, who having spent the most and best years of his life in Louisiana, and having long presided over its concerns, still felt much interest in its prosperity. He had bewailed its dismemberment, and grieved to see the last remnant of it transferred to Spain; he was then in his eighty-seventh year, having first landed in Louisiana in his twentieth. He attended Milhet to the Duke de Choiseul. This nobleman received the representative of the people of Louisiana with marked civility; but, having been the prime mover of the measures which terminated in the cession, he felt more inclination to thwart, than to promote his views; he artfully prevented Milhet's access to the king, and the mission entirely failed.

The British this year established a post at bayou Manshac, the south-westernmost point of their possessions in North America. A number of traders had opened stores in the neighborhood, from which the planters on the right bank of the Mississippi obtained their supplies, and where they found a sure sale for everything they could raise. A part of the thirty-fourth regiment was sent to garrison the post; but, in the summer, the appearance of the weather, inducing the apprehension it might fall a victim to disease, it was removed beyond Natchez.

While the people of Louisiana were thus distressed by the thought of being severed from the dominions of France, those dissensions prevailed in the British provinces on the Atlantic, which about ten years after, broke asunder the political ties which united them to their mother country. On the twenty-fifth of October, commissioners from the assemblies of Massachusetts, Rhode Island, Connecticut, New York, New Jersey, Pennsylvania, Delaware, Maryland and South Carolina, met in the city of New York. They published a declaration of the rights and grievances of the colonists—asserted their exclusive right to tax themselves, and to the trial by jury, unequivocally expressing the attachment of the colonists to the mother country. They recommended to the several colonies to appoint special agents, with instructions to unite their utmost endeavors, in soliciting a redress of grievances.

The fall was extremely sickly. D'Abadie died, and the supreme command of the province devolved to Aubry, the senior military officer.

The West India seas were at this time greatly infested by pirates; and on the eleventh of March, 1766, the sensibility of the inhabitants of New Orleans was much excited on the arrival of the sloop Fortune, of that port, which on her return picked up, near the island of Cuba, a small boat, in which madam Desnoyers, a lady of St. Domingo, had been committed to the mercy of the waves, with a child, a sucking babe, and a negro woman, by a pirate, who had captured a vessel (in which she was going from the Spanish to the French part of St. Domingo) and had murdered her husband. They had been seven days in the boat when they were taken up. She was received, with great cordiality and after she had spent a few months in New Orleans, the means were furnished her of returning to her friends.

Although Jean Milhet had informed his countrymen of the ill success of his mission, they still flattered themselves with the delusive hope that the cession might be rescinded. Upwards of two years had now elapsed, since the king had directed d'Abadie to surrender the province to any officer who should come to take possession of it for the king of Spain, and that monarch did not appear to have taken any measure to obtain it. These fond hopes vanished, in the summer, by intelligence from Havana, that Don Antonio de Ulloa, the officer appointed by Charles the third to the government of Louisiana, had arrived in that city; from whence, on the tenth of July, he addressed a letter to the superior council of the province, apprising them, that having been honored with the king's command to receive possession of the colony, he would soon be with them for this purpose, and expressing his hope that his mission might afford him a favorable opportunity of rendering them and the other inhabitants any service they might require.

Don Antonio was known in the republic of letters, as an able mathematician, who had accompanied La Condamine, Bourguet and Godin, for the purpose of determining the figure of the earth, under the equator.

He landed at New Orleans, in the fall, with two companies of infantry, under the orders· of Piernas. He was received with dumb respect and declined exhibiting his powers, intimating he wished to delay receiving possession of the country, until such number of the Spanish forces arrived, as would authorize the departure of 'those of France.

In December, the British re-occupied the post at bayou Manshac. A small stockade fort was built by a party of the twenty-first regiment; it was called Fort Bute. The trade, carried on in this neighborhood, at Baton Rouge and Natchez, increased considerably; the French supplied themselves with goods at those places, and British vessels were almost continually anchored, or fastened to the trees, a little above New Orleans. Guinea negroes were now introduced by these vessels, or brought from Pensacola through lake Pontchartrain to bayou Manshac and Baton Rouge. The facility, thus afforded to French planters to supply themselves with slaves, was the origin of the fortunes of many of them.

Ulloa visited the several posts of the province and spent a considerable time in Natchitoches.

According to a census of the inhabitants of the province which was taken this year, it appears it had one thousand eight hundred and ninety-three men fit to bear arms; one thousand and forty-four marriageable women; one thousand three hundred and seventy-five boys, and one thousand two hundred and forty-four girls; in all, five thousand five hundred and fifty-six white individuals. The blacks were nearly as numerous.

This year, the province was visited by a disease, not dissimilar to that now known as the yellow fever. It was severely felt in West Florida, where a number of emigrants had lately arrived. Sixteen families of French protestants, transported at the expense of the British government on the river Escambia, consisting of sixty-four persons, were almost entirely swept away by the deleterious sickness.

Ulloa, in the following year, went to the Balize to await the arrival of a Peruvian lady, the marchioness of Abrado, who landed and whom he married, soon after. He was then in the fifty-first year of his age.

Soon after his return to New Orleans, he received a considerable reinforcement of troops from the Havana, and although again pressed to publish his commission and take formal possession of the country, he persisted in delaying this.

He sent two companies to build a fort on the left bank of the Mississippi, below bayou Manshac, within four hundred yards of Fort Bute; two other companies were sent on the same service, on the opposite side, a little below Natchez, and two others on the left side of Red river, on an eminence between Black river and the Mississippi. A stronger detachment was sent to the Illinois: but its commanding officer was instructed not to interfere with the civil concerns of the inhabitants, who continued under the orders of St. Ange, the British commandant having died.

General Phineas Lyman, contemplating a large establishment on the Ohio, applied to parliament, for an extensive grant of land. He enforced the propriety of the measure by the argument that there could be but little danger of the colonies becoming independent, if confined to agricultural pursuits, and the inhabitants dispersed over the country. "A period," said he, " will no doubt arrive, when North America will no longer acknowledge a dependence on any part of Europe; but it seems to be so remote, as not to be at present an object of rational policy or human prevention, and it will be made still more so, by opening new schemes of agriculture, and widening the space which the colonists must first occupy.

Jean Milhet now returned from France; his protracted absence had kept the hopes of his countrymen alive, and when his presence among them put an end to every expectation from his mission, they became exasperated, and began to manifest their ill disposition towards Ulloa, who, although he continued to decline an official recognition, had gained a powerful influence over Aubry, which was exercised to the injury of some of the colonists.

On the seventeenth and eighteenth of January, 1768, the most intense cold, of which there is any remembrance, was felt in Louisiana. The river was frozen before New Orleans for several yards, on both sides. The orange trees were destroyed throughout the province.

Partial meetings were had in the city and at the German coast. In the latter place, a perfect unanimity prevailed. Father Barnabe, a capuchin missionary, who was curate of that parish, took an active part with the most influential of his flock. At last, the people of the province were invited to a general meeting at New Orleans, to which every parish sent its wealthiest planters. Lafreniere was again the principal speaker, and was supported by Jean Milhet, Joseph Milhet, his brother, and Doucet, a lawyer, lately arrived from France. The proceedings terminated by the subscription of a petition to the superior council to order Ulloa and the principal officers of the Spanish troops away. It was circulated through the province, and received five hundred and fifty respectable signatures. The printing of it was authorized by the ordonnateur, and it was circulated in every parish.

The French, as well as the few Spaniards who had come to the province, blamed the obsequiousness of Aubry towards Ulloa. They believed that the former's instructions might be, occasionally to consult the latter, but they thought that nothing could authorize the subserviency of the French chief to a Spanish officer, who refused to avow the authority with which he was clothed.

Lafreniere having introduced the petition of the inhabitants to the council, this tribunal which was greatly under the influence of Foucault, the ordonnateur, threatened Ulloa with a prosecution as a disturber of the peace of the province. He alleged that Aubry had given him privately possession of the country at the Balize. As none believed that a clandestine act, even if it took place, could authorize any assumption of powers, his declaration was considered as a gross artifice. Aubry, who corroborated Ulloa's assertion, was also disbelieved. He fell into contempt, and Ulloa's opposers were emboldened.

The colonists mistaking their wishes for their belief, indulged the hope that as the taking possession by the officers of Spain was thus protracted, the catholic king must have renounced the acquisition of the province. Others viewed the cessions as a measure feigned for state purposes. Yielding to these delusions they viewed Ulloa with a jealous eye, as a personage who abused the reasons of state, which they supposed to be the

28

cause of his coming among them. Conjectures drawn from the British prints and from conversations with individuals of that nation, who had come to New Orleans on their way to Manshac, Baton Rouge and Natchez, strengthened their belief. The public agitation for awhile subsided, but was at last roused by a rumor that a Spanish armament, destined for Louisiana, had arrived at the Havana.

Frantic and distracted by these alternate impressions of hope and fear some of the popular leaders flattered themselves with the possibility of resistance, and dispatched a messenger to Governor Elliott, who had succeeded Johnston at Pensacola, to ascertain whether the support of the government of West Florida could be obtained. The governor declared himself unwilling to aid his neighbors in an opposition to a king in amity with his own. It was said he transmitted the message he had received to Aubry, who delivered it to Ulloa, and that the latter carried it to Madrid.

Disappointed at this attempt, the leaders pressed the consideration of the petition of the inhabitants, which the council had delayed to act upon. It had been subscribed by five hundred and sixty of the most respectable inhabitants. Lafreniere supported it by an eloquent speech, in which he adverted to the successful opposition of the British American provinces to the stamp act, and drew the attention of the council to the noble conduct of the people of Burgundy in 1526, when summoned by Launoy, the viceroy of Naples, to recognize as their sovereign the emperor Charles the fifth, to whom Francis the second had ceded that province by the treaty of Madrid. The states and courts of justice being convened to deliberate on the emperor's message, unanimously answered that the province was a part of the French monarchy and the king had not the power of alienating it. The nobles resolutely declared that if the king abandoned them they would resort to arms, and the last drop of their blood would be spilt in defense of their country.

At last, on the 29th of October, it was taken up and after some debate the council (notwithstanding the opposition and protest of Aubry) ordered Ulloa to produce his powers from the king of Spain, if he had any, that they might be recorded on its minutes, and published through the province or depart therefrom, within one month. To give weight to the requisition of the council about six hundred of the inhabitants of the city and German coast embodied themselves.

Ulloa took the last of the alternatives proposed to him, and was soon ready to depart; a vessel of the king of Spain that had lately arrived afforded him an opportunity which he improved.

On the evening of one of the first days of November, he went on board of the king's vessel, intending to sail early in the morning. The torch of hymen had been lighted in the house of a wealthy merchant in the city; the dance was protracted till the morning; a number of the planters who had come to the city, had joined the festive banquet. Wine had been sent to others, whose admission the great number of the guests in the house had prevented from attending. At dawn, all parties united, and elated by the nightly orgie, marched to the levee, hallooing and singing. Boats were procured; no apprehension being entertained on board, the vessel was approached, and her cables cut asunder. It does not appear any attempt was made to punish the insult. The vessel was at the moment of departure and floated away.

A few days after, a general meeting of deputies from every parish, was convened at New Orleans, in which it was determined to make a second application, to avert, if possible, the execution of the treaty of cession. This service was confided to St. Lette, a merchant of Natchitoches, and Lesassier, a member of the superior council.

Ulloa proceeded to Havana, where he immediately embarked for Cadiz, and landed after a passage or forty days.

The chevalier Dessales, who sailed with him from New Orleans, saw at Havana, Urissa, the former consul of Spain at Bordeaux, who having been appointed Intendant of Louisiana, was on his way with eight hundred soldiers. He had stopped at Havana, to take in one million of dollars for the king's service in his new acquisition; hearing of Ulloa's ill success, he returned to Europe.

In December the British evacuated and demolished Fort Bute.

The passage of the deputies of the people of Louisiana was not so expeditious as that of Ulloa. They were three months on the water. The complaint of the king of Spain had reached the court, long before their arrival at Paris. Bienville, on whose aid and services they much relied, was now dead, and the Duke of Choiseuil still in power. St. Lette had been a schoolmate of his. The Duke received his former play fellow with open arms, but frowned on the deputy and his colleague. He told them their application was too tardy, as the king of Spain had directed such a force to be sent to New Orleans, as would put down any opposition that could be made. He gave St. Lette a very lucrative office in the East Indies, and Lesassier returned home.

The deputies had been instructed to renew the representation, which Milhet had made in regard to the depreciated paper currency, which inundated the province. They obtained an arrest of the king's council of the twenty-third of March, which is believed to be the last act of the French government concerning Louisiana.

It provided that the bills, emitted by the colonial government, or the receipts for so much of them, as according to a former order had been left with the treasurer, should be reduced to three-fifths of their nominal value.

The holders of these bills or receipts were directed to bring them, before the first of September following, to Marignier, who was authorized to give therefor, (after a deduction of two-fifths) a certificate bearing interest at five per cent.

Provision was made for cases, in which there had been a judicial deposit.

Shortly after the return of Lesassier, the distress, which the accounts he brought excited, was relieved by letters from Bordeaux, intimating that the province was to continue a colony of France.

But on the twenty-third of July, intelligence reached New Orleans of the arrival at the Balize of a Spanish frigate, with twenty-eight transports, having four thousand five hundred soldiers on board, and a large supply of arms and ammunition. This threw the town into great consternation: resistance was spoken of, and messengers were dispatched up the coast.

On the next day, an express, with a message to Aubry, from Don Alexander O'Reilly, the commander of the Spanish forces, landed on the levee.

The inhabitants of the city, on the invitation of Aubry, met him in the church, and he read to them the message. They thus learned that the general was sent by his sovereign to take possession of the colony; but not to distress the inhabitants; that, as soon as he had obtained possession, he would publish the remaining part of the orders of his royal master; but, should any attempt be made to oppose his landing, he was determined not to depart, till he had put his majesty's commands in complete execution.

The inhabitants immediately came to a resolution to choose three gentlemen, to wait in their behalf on the general, and inform him that the people of Louisiana were determined to abandon the colony, and had no other favor to ask from him, but that he would allow them two years, to remove themselves and their effects.

The choice of the meeting fell on Grandmaison, the town major, Lafreniere, the attorney-general, and Mazent, formerly a captain in the colonial troops, now a planter of considerable wealth.

O'Reilly received them with great politeness, and assured them he would cheerfully comply with any reasonable request of the colonists; that he had their interest much at heart, and nothing on his part should be wanting to promote it. He added all past transactions would be buried in oblivion, and all who had offended should be forgiven, and said everything, which he imagined would flatter the minds of the people.

In the meanwhile, the planters of the German, and some of the Acadian coast had taken arms, and a considerable number of them, headed by Villere, marched down to the city.

The deputation reached New Orleans on the first of August, and made public the kind reception O'Reilly had given them, and the fair promises he had made. This considerably quieted the minds of the inhabitants, and many, who had determined on an immediate removal from the province, now resolved to return and gather their crops.

A fortnight had elapsed before the armament reached the city. It cast anchor before it, on the sixteenth; the inhabitants flocked to the levee on the following day, but the landing did not take place till the eighteenth.

At three o'clock, in the afternoon of that day, the Spaniards disembarked, and O'Reilly led his men to the public square, before the church, in the middle of the city, where Aubry, at the head of the troops of France received him; the white banner flying at the top of a high mast, in the middle of the square. It was now slowly lowered, while that of Spain was hoisted, and as they met at half-mast, they were saluted by a *feu-de-joie* from the troops of both nations. The French flag being lowered and the Spanish flying on the top of the mast, O'Reilly, attended by Aubry, and followed by the officers of both nations, who were not under arms, perambulated the square, in token of his being in possession of the colony. His suite then followed him to the church, where a solemn *Te Deum* was chaunted, and the benediction of the host given.

Thus ended, about seventy-one years after the arrival of Iberville, the government of France in Louisiana: and thus was that nation, about one hundred and sixty years after Champlain laid the foundation of Quebec, the oldest town of French origin in North America, left without an inch of ground in that part of the continent.

The exports of the province during the last year of its subjection to France, were as follows:

In Indigo,	. . . . . .	$100,000
" Deer Skins,	. . . . . .	80,000
" Lumber,	. . . . . .	50,000
" Naval Stores,	. . . . . .	12,000
" Rice, Peas and Beans,	. . . .	4,000
" Tallow,	. . . . . .	4,000
		$250,000
An interlope trade with the Spanish colonies, took away goods worth	. . . . .	60,000
The colonial treasury gave bills on government in France, for	. . . .	360,000

So that the province afforded means of remittance for . $670,000

Few merchant vessels came from France; but the island of Hispaniola carried on a brisk trade with New Orleans, and some vessels came from Martinico. King's vessels brought whatever was necessary for the troops, and goods for the Indian trade.

The indigo of Louisiana was greatly inferior to that of Hispaniola; the planters being quite unskillful and inattentive in the manufacture of it; that of sugar had been abandoned, but some planters near New Orleans raised a few canes for the market.

CHAPTER XV.

Don Alexander O'Reilly, a lieutenant-general of the armies of Spain, had, by a commission bearing date Aranjuez, April 16th, 1769, been appointed governor and captain-general of the province of Louisiana, with "special power to establish in this new part of the king's dominions with regard to the military force, police, administration of justice, and finances, such a form of government as might most effectually secure its dependence and subordination, and promote the king's service and the happiness of his subjects."

The intendant of the province was Don Francisco de Loyola.

Don Manuel Joseph de Uristia and Don Felix de Rey, accompanied the captain-general as his assessors or legal advisers in the judicial functions of his office, and his authority was supported by a military force equal to three times the number of persons capable of bearing arms in the colony. We have seen that he took possession of it with as little opposition or difficulty as if he had been a French governor coming to supercede a former one.

He was waited upon by every class of inhabitants with respectful submission. A canopied seat was placed in the largest hall of the house he occupied, where he held a numerous levé, at which the ladies were not unfrequent attendants. An undisturbed tranquillity seemed to prevail. Surprise and afterwards anxiety, were excited by his delay to comply with the promise in his message from the Balize to publish, after he had taken possession of the province the ultimate intentions of his sovereign.

One of the first acts of his administration was an order for a census of the inhabitants of New Orleans. It was executed with great accuracy. It appeared that the aggregate population amounted to three thousand one hundred and ninety persons, of every age, sex and the color. The number of free persons was nineteen hundred and two; thirty-one of whom were black, and sixty-eight of mixed blood. There were twelve hundred and twenty-five slaves, and sixty domesticated Indians. The number of houses was four hundred and sixty-eight: the greatest part of them were in the third and fourth streets from the water, and principally in the latter.

No census was taken in the rest of the province; but from a reference to the preceding and succeeding years, the following statement is believed to be correct:

In the city of New Orleans, as before,	3,190
From the Balize to the city,	570
Bayou St. John and Gentilly,	307
Tchoupitoulas,	4,192
St. Charles,	639
St. John the Baptist,	544
Lafourche,	267
Iberville,	376
Pointe Coupee,	783
Attakapas,	409
Avoyelles,	314
Natchitoches,	811
Rapides,	47
Washita,	110
Arkansas,	88
St. Louis, (Illinois,)	891
	13,538

Towards the last day of August, the people were alarmed by the arrest of Foucault, the commissary-general and ordonnateur, De Noyant and Boisblanc, two members of the superior council; La Freniere, the attorney-general, and Braud, the king's printer. These gentlemen were attending O'Reilly's levé, when he requested them to step into an adjacent apartment, where they found themselves immediately surrounded by a body of grenadiers, with fixed bayonets, the commanding officer of whom informed them they were the king's prisoners. The two first were conveyed to their respective houses, and a guard was left there; the others were imprisoned in the barracks.

It had been determined to make an example of twelve individuals; two from the army, and an equal number from the bar; four planters, and as many merchants. Accordingly, Marquis and De Noyant, officers of the troop; La Freniere, the attorney-general, and Doucet, (lawyers,) Villere, Boisblanc, Mazent and Petit, (planters,) and John Milhet, Joseph Milhet, Caresse and Poupet, (merchants,) had been selected.

Within a few days, Marquis, Doucet, Petit, Mazant, the two Milhets, Caresse and Poupet, were arrested and confined.

Villere, who was on his plantation at the German Coast, had been marked as one of the intended victims; but his absence from the city rendering his arrest less easy, it had been determined to release one of the prisoners on his being secured. He had been apprised of the impending danger, and it had been recommended to him to provide for his safety by seeking the protection of the British flag waving at Manshac. When he was deliberating on the step it became him to take, he received a letter from Aubry, the commandant of the French troops, assuring him he had nothing to apprehend, and advising him to return to the city. Averse to flight, as it would imply a consciousness of guilt, he yielded to Aubry's recommendation and returned to New Orleans; but as he passed the gate, the officer commanding the guard arrested him. He was immediately conveyed on board of a frigate that lay at the levee. On hearing of this, his lady, a granddaughter of La Chaise, the former commissary-general and ordonnateur, hastened to the city. As her boat approached the frigate, it was hailed and ordered away. She made herself known, and solicited admission to her husband, but was answered she could not see him, as the captain was on shore, and had left orders that no communication should be allowed with the prisoner. Villere recognized his wife's voice, and insisted on being permitted to see her. On this being refused, a struggle ensued, in which he fell, pierced by the bayonets of his guards. His bloody shirt thrown into the boat, announced to the lady that she had ceased to be a wife; and a sailor cut the rope that fastened the boat to the frigate.

O'Reilly's assessors heard and recorded the testimony against the prisoners, and called on them for their pleas.

The prosecution was grounded on a statute of Alfonso the eleventh, which is the first law of the seventh title of the first partida, and denounces the punishment of death and confiscation of property against those who excite any insurrection against the king or state, or take up arms under pretense of extending their liberty or rights, and against those who give them any assistance.

Foucault pleaded he had done nothing, except in his character of commissary-general and ordonnateur of the king of France in the province, and to him alone he was accountable for the motives that had directed his official conduct. The plea was sustained; he was not, however, released; and a few days afterwards, he was transported to France.

Braud offered a similar plea, urging he was the king of France's printer of Louisiana. The only accusation against him, was that he had printed the petition of the planters and merchants to the superior council, soliciting that body to require Ulloa to exhibit his powers, or depart. He concluded that he was bound, by his office, to print whatever the ordonnateur sent to his press; and he produced that officer's order to print the petition. His plea was sustained, and he was discharged.

The other prisoners declined also the jurisdiction of the tribunal before which they were arraigned: their plea was overruled. They now denied the facts with which they were charged, contended that if they did take place, they did so while the flag of France was still waving over the province, and the laws of that kingdom retained their empire in it, and thus the facts did not constitute an offense against the laws of Spain; that the people of Louisiana could not bear the yokes of two sovereigns;

that O'Reilly could not command the obedience, nor even the respect of the colonists, until he made known to them his character and powers; and that the Catholic king could not count on their allegiance, till he extended to them his protection.

It had been determined at first, to proceed with the utmost rigor of the law against six of the prisoners; but, on the death of Villere, it was judged sufficient to do so against five only. The jurisprudence of Spain authorizing the infliction of a less severe punishment than that denounced by the statute, when the charge is not proved by two witnesses to the same act, but by one with corroborating circumstances. Accordingly, two witnesses were produced against DeNoyant, La Freniere, Marquis, Joseph Milhet and Caresse. They were convicted; and O'Reilly, by the advice of his assessor, condemned them to be hanged, and pronounced the confiscation of their estates.

The most earnest and pathetic entreaties were employed by persons in every rank of society, to prevail on O'Reilly to remit or suspend the execution of his sentence till the royal clemency could be implored. He was inexorable; and the only indulgence that could be obtained, was, that death should be inflicted by shooting, instead of hanging. With this modification, the sentence was carried into execution on the twenty-eighth of September.

On the morning of that day, the guards, at every gate and post of the city, were doubled, and orders were given not to allow anybody to enter it. All the troops were under arms, and paraded the streets or were placed in battle array along the levee and on the public square. Most of the inhabitants fled into the country. At three o'clock of the afternoon, the victims were led, under a strong guard, to the small square in front of the barracks, tied to stakes, and an explosion of musketry soon announced to the few inhabitants who remained in the city, that their friends were no more.

Posterity, the judge of men in power, will doom this act to public execration. No necessity demanded, no policy justified it. Ulloa's conduct had provoked the measures to which the inhabitants had resorted. During nearly two years, he had haunted the province as a phantom of dubious authority. The efforts of the colonists, to prevent the transfer of their natal soil to a foreign prince, originated in their attachment to their own, and the Catholic king ought to have beheld in their conduct a pledge of their future devotion to himself. They had but lately seen their country severed, and a part of it added to the dominion of Great Britain; they had bewailed their separation from their friends and kindred; and were afterwards to be alienated, without their consent, and subjected to a foreign yoke. If the indiscretion of a few of them needed an apology, the common misfortune afforded it.

A few weeks afterwards, the proceedings against the six remaining prisoners were brought to a close. One witness only deposing against any of them, and circumstances corroborating the testimony, Boisblanc was condemned to imprisonment for life; Doucet, Mazent, John Milhet, Petit and Poupet were condemned to imprisonment for various terms of years. All were transported to Havana, and cast into the dungeons of the Moro Castle.

Conquered countries are generally allowed, at least during a few years, to retain their former laws and usages. Louis the fifteenth, in his letter to d'Abadie, had expressed his hope, and declared he expected it from the friendship of the king of Spain, that, for the advantage and tranquillity of the inhabitants of Louisiana, orders would be given to the governors and other officers sent to the province, that the inferior judges, as well as those of the superior council should be allowed to administer justice according to the laws, forms and usages of the colony. It is oppressive, in the highest degree, to require that a community should instantaneously submit to a total change in the laws that hitherto governed it, and be compelled to regulate its conduct by rules of which it is totally ignorant.

Such was, however, the lot of the people of Louisiana. A proclamation of O'Reilly, on the twenty-first of November, announced to them that the evidence received during the late trials, having furnished full proof of the part the superior council had in the revolt during the two preceding years, and of the influence it had exerted in encouraging the leaders, instead of using its best endeavors to keep the people in the fidelity and subordination they owed to the sovereign, it had become necessary to abolish that tribunal, and to establish, in Louisiana, that form of government and mode of administering justice prescribed by the laws of Spain, which had long maintained the Catholic king's American colonies in perfect tranquillity, content, and subordination.

The premises might be true, but the conclusion was certainly illogical. The indiscreet conduct of a few of the members of the council, the violent measures adopted by some of the inhabitants, could not certainly be attributed to the organization of that tribunal, nor to the laws, customs and usages that had hitherto prevailed in the province. Aubry was about to depart; and were he to stay, the presidency of the council would not belong to him, but to the Spanish chief. Foucault had been transported; La Freniere and De Noyant shot; and Boisblanc was in the dungeons of the Moro Castle. Nothing compelled the new sovereign to retain any of the old members as judges.

The proclamation mentioned, that to the superior council a cabildo would be substituted, and be composed of six perpetual regidors, two ordinary alcades, an attorney-general-syndic, and a clerk; over which the governor would preside in person.

The offices of perpetual regidor and clerk were to be acquired by purchase, and for the first time, at auction. The purchaser had the faculty of transferring his office, by resignation, to a known and capable person, paying one-half of its appraised value on the first, and one-third on every other mutation.

Among the regidors were to be distributed the offices of *Alferez real*, or royal standard-bearer; principal provincial alcade; *Alguazil mayor*, or high sheriff; depositary-general, and receiver of fines.

The ordinary alcades and attorney-general-syndic, were to be chosen on the first day of every year by the cabildo, and were always re-eligible by its unanimous vote, but not by the majority, unless after the expiration of two years. At such elections, the votes were openly given and recorded.

The ordinary alcades were individually judges within the city in civil and criminal cases, where the defendant did not enjoy and claim the privilege of being tried by a military or ecclesiastical judge, *fuero militar*, *fuero ecclesiastico*. They heard and decided in their chambers, summarily, and without any written proceeding, all complaints in which the value of the object in dispute did not exceed twenty dollars. In other cases,

29

proceedings before them were recorded by a notary; and in an apartment set apart for this purpose, and where the value of the object in dispute exceeded ninety thousand maravedis, or three hundred and thirty dollars and eighty-eight cents, an appeal lay from their decision to the cabildo.

This body did not examine itself the judgment appealed from, but chose two regidors, who, with the alcade who had rendered it, reviewed the proceedings; and if he and either of the regidors approved the decision, it was affirmed.

The cabildo sat every Friday, but the governor had the power of convening it at any time. When he did not attend it one of the ordinary alcades presided, and immediately on the adjournment, two regidors went to his house and informed him of what had been done.

The ordinary alcades had the first seats in the cabildo, immediately after the governor; and below them the other members sat, in the following order: The alferez real, principal provincial alcade, alguazil mayor, depositary-general, receiver of fines, attorney-general-syndic and clerk. The office of alferez real was merely honorary, no other function being assigned to the incumbent but the bearing of the royal standard in a few public ceremonies. The principal provincial alcade had cognizance of offenses committed without the city; the alguazil mayor executed personally or by his deputies all processes from the different tribunals. The depositary-general took charge of all moneys and effects placed in the custody of the law. The functions of the receiver-general are pointed out by his official denomination. The attorney-general-syndic was not, as might be suposed from his title, the prosecuting officer of the crown. His duty was to propose to the cabildo such measures as the interest of the people required, and defend their rights.

The regidors received fifty dollars each, annually, from the treasury. The principal provincial alcade, *alguazil mayor*, depositary general, receiver of fines, and ordinary alcades were entitled, as such, to fees of office.

The king had directed a regiment to be raised in the province under the style of the regiment of Louisiana, and had made choice of Don J. Estecheria as its colonel. This officer not having as yet arrived, Unzaga regulated its organization and assumed the provisional command. A number of commissions for officers in this regiment were sent by O'Reilly. They had been filled with the names of such inhabitants as Ulloa had recommended. These commissions were cheerfully accepted; the pay and emoluments in the colonial regiment of Spain being much more considerable than in the French. The ranks of the regiment were soon filled, soldiers in the service of France and in the regiments brought by O'Reilly being permitted to enlist in it.

The supplies which the Spanish government had destined to its military force in Louisiana were unaccountably delayed. The dearth of provisions in New Orleans became excessive, owing to an increase of population, much larger than that of the city before the arrival of the Spaniards. Flour rose to twenty dollars the barrel. A momentary relief was obtained by the arrival of Oliver Pollock in a brig from Baltimore, with a cargo of that article, who offered the load to O'Reilly on his own terms. He declined accepting it thus, and finally purchased it at fifteen dollars the barrel. O'Reilly was so well pleased with the bargain that he told Pollock he should have a free trade to Louisiana as long as he lived, and a report of his conduct on this occasion would be made to the king.

The cabildo held its first session on the first of December, under the presidency of O'Reilly. The regidors' offices had been purchased by Don Francisco Maria Reggio, Don Pedro Francisco Olivier de Vezin, Don Carlos Juan Bautista Fleurian, Don Antonio Bienvenu, Don Jose Ducros, and Don Dyonisio Braud. Don Juan Bautista Garic, who had held the office of clerk of the superior council, had acquired the same office in the cabildo.

Reggio was *alferez real;* de Vezin, principal provincial alcade; Fleurian, *alguazil mayor;* Ducros, depository general; and Bienvenu, receiver of fines.

Don Louis de Unzaga, colonel of the regiment of Havana, one of those who had come with O'Reilly, had the king's commission as governor of the province, but was not authorized to enter upon the duties of that office, until the departure of O'Reilly, or the declaration of his will. Immediately after the installation of the cabildo, he made this declaration, and yielded the chair of that tribunal to Unzaga.

O'Reilly never came to the cabildo afterwards. Unzaga exercised the functions of governor; but the former, as captain-general, continued to make regulations.

He caused a set of instructions, which Don Jose de Uristia and Don Felix de Rey had prepared by his order, to be published. They related to the institution of, and proceedings in, civil and criminal actions, according to the laws of Castille and the Indies, and for the government of judges, officers and parties, till by the introduction of the Spanish language in the province, they might have the means of acquiring a better knowledge of those laws. To them was annexed a compendious abridgment of the criminal laws, and a few directions in regard to last wills and testaments.

From this period, it is believed the laws of Spain became the sole guide of the tribunals in their decisions. As these laws, and those of France, proceed from the same origin, the Roman code, and there is a great similarity in their dispositions in regard to matrimonial rights, testaments and successions, the transition was not perceived before it became complete, and very little inconvenience resulted from it.

The provincial officers of Louisiana were, besides the captain-general, a governor, vested with civil and military powers; an intendant, charged with the administration of the revenue and admiralty matters, the same person acting often in the double capacity of governor and intendant; an auditor of war and assessor of government, whose duty it was to furnish legal advice to the governor, the first in military, the second in civil affairs; an assessor of the intendancy, who rendered a like service to the intendant. Professional characters being very few in Louisiana, the same individual often acted as auditor of war and assessor of the government and intendancy, and he also assisted the cabildo, principal, provincial, and ordinary alcades; a secretary of the government and one of the intendant; a treasurer and a *contador* or comptroller; a storekeeper and a purveyor; a surveyor general; a harbor master; an interpreter of the French and English languages, and an Indian interpreter; three notaries public; a collector and comptroller of the customs; a cashier; *guarda major,* searcher, and notary to the custom house.

Every officer who received a salary of more than three hundred dollars a year was appointed by the crown; others were so by the governor or intendants in their respective departments.

The governor exercised judicial powers in civil and criminal matters throughout the province, as did the intendant in fiscal and admiralty, and the vicar-general in ecclesiastical. These officers were sole judges in their respective courts. The two former were assisted by an auditor or assessor, whose opinion they might, on their own responsibility, disregard.

In every parish, an officer of the army or militia, of no higher grade than a captain, was stationed as civil and military commandant. His duty was to attend to the police of the parish and preserve its peace. He was instructed to examine the passports of all travellers, and suffer no one to settle, within his jurisdiction, without the license of the governor. He had jurisdiction of all civil cases in which the value of the object in dispute did not exceed twenty dollars. In more important cases he received the petition and answer, took down the testimony, and transmitted the whole to the governor, by whom the record was sent to the proper tribunal. He had the power to punish slaves, and arrest and imprison free persons charged with offenses, and was bound to transmit immediate information of the arrest, with a transcript of the evidence, to the governor, by whose order the accused was either discharged or sent to the city. They acted also as notaries public, and made inventories and sales of the estates of the deceased, and attended to the execution of judgments rendered in the city against defendants who resided in the parish.

When the commandant was taken from the army, he continued to receive the pay and emoluments of his rank. When he was not, and had not any pension from the king, an annual sum of one hundred dollars was paid him from the treasury, for stationery and other small expenses. All were entitled to fees in the exercise of judicial and notarial functions.

The Spanish language was ordered to be employed by all public officers in their minutes; but the use of the French was tolerated in the judicial and notarial acts of commandants.

Towards the middle of December, O'Reilly left the city to visit the settlements of the German and Acadian coasts, Iberville and Pointe Coupee.

On the first of January, the cabildo made choice of Lachaise, a grandson of the former commissary-general and ordonnateur, and St. Denis, as ordinary alcades for the year 1770.

Don Cecilio Odoardo arrived with a commission of auditor of war and assessor of the government; and Don Joseph de Uristia and Don Felix de Rey sailed for Havana.

Meetings of the most notable planters were convened, on the arrival of O'Reilly, in each parish, on his way up the river. Although his conduct at New Orleans was ill calculated to attach the people to the sovereign he represented, he was everywhere received with dumb submission; but they did not appear very anxious to improve the opportunity, which his visit was intended to offer, or make him any communication or remonstrance.

A number of French soldiers enlisted in the Spanish service. Many were discharged and received grants of land. Those who did not choose to remain under the authority of the Catholic king, were offered the alternative of a passage to France or Hispaniola. Aubry sailed with those who preferred returning home. The artillery was put on board of a vessel which carried those who were destined for St. Domingo. She was never after heard of.

Bobe Descloseaux, who had acted during a short time, as commissary-general and ordonnateur, on the death of Larouvilliere in 1759, remained in New Orleans by order of the French, and with the consent of the Spanish king, to attend to the redemption of the paper securities, emitted by the former colonial administrations; a very considerable quantity of which was still in circulation.

Peter Chester, on the death of governor Elliott, of West Florida, succeeded him in the latter part of January.

On his return, O'Reilly published on the 8th of February, a number of regulations, in regard to the grants of vacant land.

To every family coming to settle in the province, a tract was to be granted of six or eight arpents in front, on the Mississippi, with a depth of forty; on condition that the grantee should within three years, construct a levee and finish a highway of forty feet at least in width, with parallel ditches towards the levee, and on the opposite side with bridges at regular distances, and enclose and clear the whole front of the grant to the depth of two arpents at least.

The arable land on the points formed by the river, having but little depth, it was provided that grants might be made there of twelve arpents in front, or the land was granted to the owners of the adjacent tracts, in order to secure an uninterrupted continuation of the levee and highway.

In order to secure an early compliance with the conditions of the grants, the grantee was declared incapable of alienating the land until the stipulated improvements were made.

Grants of a square league were authorized in the districts of Attakapas, Opelousas and Natchitoches, where the inhabitants paid more attention to raising cattle than to the culture of the soil. Where the land was less than a league in depth, the grant was of two leagues in front with a depth of half a league. But no grant of forty-two arpents in front and depth was authorized to be made to any person who was not the owner of one hundred head of tame horned cattle, a few horses and sheep and two slaves.

All cattle were required to be branded by the owner before the age of eighteen months; and all older unbranded cattle were declared unclaimable.

Nothing being thought more injurious to the people than strayed cattle, without the destruction of which the tame ones cannot increase, time was given till the first day of June, 1771, to collect the strays; after which period it is declared they may be considered as wild, and killed by any one: none may oppose it, or claim property in such cattle.

All grants are to be made in the king's name by the governor of the province, who is, at the same time, to appoint a surveyor to fix the boundaries both in front and depth, in presence of the ordinary judge of the district, and in that of the two adjoining settlers, who are to be present at the survey, and are to subscribe the process verbal which is to be made. The surveyor is directed to make three copies of it, one of which is to be deposited in the office of the clerk of the cabildo, another in that of the governor, and the third delivered to the grantee.

In a proclamation of the twenty-second of February, the captain-general assigned a revenue to the city of New Orleans. It was to consist of an annual tax of forty dollars on every tavern, billiard table, and coffee house; another of twenty dollars on every boarding house; an imposition of one dollar on every barrel of brandy brought to the city; and a tax of three hundred and seventy dollars, to which the butchers voluntarily submitted, under an express declaration that they thereby meant to authorize no alteration now or thereafter in the price of meat, which they said ought not ever to take place without necessity.

To enable the city to defray the expenses necessary to keep up the levee, an anchorage duty was granted to it, of six dollars upon every vessel of two hundred tons and upwards, and half that sum on smaller ones.

O'Reilly further granted to the city, in the king's name, the ground on both sides of the public square, or place d'armes, from Levee to Chartres and Conti streets, having a front of three hundred and thirty-six feet on the square, and eighty-four feet in depth. The ground was soon afterwards sold on a perpetual yearly rent. Don Andre Almoster became the purchaser of it.

By a special proclamation, the black code, given by Louis the fifteenth to the province, was re-enacted.

With the view of putting an end, in some degree, to the practice of the Indians of dooming prisoners of war to death, with cruel and protracted torments, the colonial government allowed the colonists to purchase and hold them as slaves, and there was a considerable number of them in the possession of planters. O'Reilly, by a special proclamation, declared that the practice of reducing Indians to slavery, was contrary to the wise and pious laws of Spain; but that until the pleasure of the sovereign was manifested, the owners of such slaves might retain them.

With the view of guarding against the introduction of foreigners into the province, all persons were prohibited to receive or entertain any foreigner not provided with a passport from the governor, or to furnish him with any horse, or land or water carriage.

It was also expressly prohibited to purchase anything from persons navigating the Mississippi, or lakes, without a passport: it was, however, permitted to sell fowls and other provisions to boats or vessels, provided the fowls or provisions were delivered on the bank of the river, and payment received in money.

A fine of one hundred dollars, and the confiscation of the articles purchased, was denounced against the delinquent, one-third of the whole being the reward of the informer.

A number of police regulations were made.

No change took place in the ecclesiastical government of the province. Father Dagobert, the superior of the capuchins, was permitted to continue in the exercise of his pastoral functions, as curate of New Orleans, and in the administration of the southern part of the diocese of Quebec, of which the bishop had constituted him vicar-general. The other capuchins were maintained in the curacies of their respective parishes.

The attendance of the Ursuline nuns, in the hospital, according to a bull they had obtained from the pope, was dispensed with; the services of these ladies had become merely nominal, being confined to the daily attendance of two nuns, during the visit of the king's physician. Having noted his prescriptions, they withdrew, contenting themselves with sending from the dispensary, which was kept in the convent, the medicines he had ordered. The Catholic king had directed that two nuns should be maintained at his expense; for each of whom, sixteen dollars were to be paid, monthly, to the convent out of his treasury.

Don Francisco de Loyola died, and was succeeded in the intendancy, *per interim*, by Gayarre, the contador.

By a vessel from Bordeaux, the colonists were informed, in the latter part of the spring, of the fate of their late chiefs. The conduct of Foucault had been disapproved by his sovereign, and he had been lodged in the Bastille, where he was still confined. The vessel, in which Aubry sailed, foundered in the Garonne, near the tower of Cordovan. Every one on board perished, except the captain, doctor, a sergeant, and two sailors. The king evinced his sense of Aubry's services, by pensions to his brother and sister. He had served in Canada and Illinois before he came to Louisiana, and was at Fort Duquesne, when it was attacked by the British under General Forbes,

O'Reilly took passage in the summer, with all the troops he had brought, except twelve hundred men, who were left for the service of the province, leaving behind no favorable impression of the government by whom he was sent. Most of the merchants and mechanics of New Orleans had withdrawn to Cape François, in the island of Hispaniola. Many of the easiest planters (for there were no wealthy ones) had followed them; and the emigration was so great, that O'Reilly, a few days before his departure, determined to check it, by withholding passports from applicants. This measure excited great uneasiness, and a general dissatisfaction pervaded every class of society. The motto on his coat of arms was *Fortitudine et Prudentia*. He does not appear to have attended to the admonition it contained. It is in the combined practice of both these virtues, that those who rule others find their greatest glory; because it best promotes the felicity of the people. The chief, who attends alone to the display of the former, may obtain a momentary glare, but will sooner or later find himself disappointed, and the people will be the victims of his error.

The year of 1770 is remarkable in the annals of North America, by the first effusion of blood, in the dissensions between Great Britain and her colonies, which originated in the passage of the stamp act, soon after the peace of Paris, and terminated in the independence of the latter. The inhabitants of Boston viewed with displeasure two British regiments quartered there. Frequent quarrels had arisen between them and the soldiers. On the fourth of March, an affray took place, near the barracks, which brought out a part of the main guard, between whom and the townsmen blows ensued. The soldiers fired; three of the inhabitants were killed, and five dangerously wounded. The alarm bells were immediately rung, the drums beat to arms, and an immense multitude assembled. Inflamed with rage at the view of the dead bodies, they were with difficulty prevented, by their most influential friends, from rushing on the troops. The officer of the guard and the soldiers who fired were apprehended. He and six of the men were acquitted: two were found guilty of manslaughter.

CHAPTER XVI.

O'REILLY's commission having a particular object, which was now accomplished, Don Antonio Maria Buccarelly, captain-general of the island of Cuba, succeeded him as captain-general of the province of Louisiana.

An appeal lay in certain cases from the tribunals of the province to the captain-general; from him to the royal audience in St. Domingo, in the island of Hispaniola; and from thence to the council of the Indies in Madrid.

Charles the third disapproved of O'Reilly's conduct, and he received, on his landing at Cadiz, an order prohibiting his appearance at court.

The ordinary alcades for the year 1771, were Chabert and Forstall.

The colonists now heard with pleasure that Foucault had been released from his confinement in the Bastille, in which he had remained eighteen months; that the eldest son of Mazent, who was in the Moro Castle, under O'Reilly's sentence of imprisonment, had gone to Madrid, thrown himself at the feet of the king, and solicited his father's pardon, offering, if another victim was indispensable, to take his place. His application was seconded by the court of France, and all those who had been sent from Louisiana to the Moro Castle received a pardon.

Foucault had gone to the island of Bourbon, in the capacity of commissary-general and ordonnateur.

None of the other prisoners, now liberated, returned to Louisiana. Most of them settled in Cape Francois.

The commerce of the province suffered greatly from the restrictive system of Spanish regulations. By a royal schedule, which Ulloa had published in New Orleans, on the sixth of September, 1766, the trade of Louisiana had been confined to six ports of the peninsula. These were Seville, Alicant, Carthagena, Malaga, Barcelona, and Coruna; and no trade was to be carried on in any other than Spanish built vessels, owned and commanded by the king's subjects. Vessels sailing to or from Louisiana, were prohibited from entering any other port in the Spanish dominions in America, except in case of distress, and they were then subjected to strict examination and heavy charges.

By a royal schedule of the twenty-third of March, 1768, however, the commerce of Louisiana had been favored by an exemption from duty, on any foreign or Spanish merchandise, both in the exportation from any of the ports of the peninsula, to which the commerce of the province was permitted, and on the importation into New Orleans; but the exportation of specie or produce was burdened with a duty of four per cent.

Permission had lately been granted for the admission of two vessels from France every year.

The merchants of New Orleans complained of this restrictive system, as very oppressive. They could not advantageously procure, in any of the six ports of the peninsula, named in the schedule of 1766, the merchandise they wanted, nor find there a vent for the produce of the province. The indigo of Louisiana was in no great demand in any port of Spain, where that article might be procured of a much better quality from Guatimala, Caraccas, and other provinces on the main. Furs and peltries were with difficulty sold or preserved in so warm a climate, and timber and lumber could not well bear the expense of transportation to such distant countries. They also complained that the British engrossed all the trade of the Mississippi.

Vessels of that nation were incessantly plying on that stream. Under the pretense of trading to those ports, on the left bank, over which their flag was displayed, they supplied the people in the city and on the plantations, above and below, with goods and slaves. They took in exchange whatever their customers had to spare, and extended to them a most liberal credit, which the good faith of the purchasers amply justified. Besides very large warehouses near the ports at Manshac, Baton Rouge and Natchez, and a number of vessels constantly moored a short distance above New Orleans, opposite to the spot now known as the faubourg La Fayette, the British had two large ones, or floating warehouses, the cabins of which were fitted up with shelves and counters, as a store. These constantly plied along the shore, and at the call of any planter, stopped before his door.

About one hundred and sixty thousand dollars were brought annually from Vera Cruz, since the arrival of O'Reilly, for defraying the expenses of the colonial government: the indigo crops were worth about one hundred and eighty thousand; furs and peltries were exported to the amount of two hundred thousand; one hundred thousand were received for timber, lumber and provisions. All this formed an aggregate of seven hundred thousand dollars to pay for imported goods, which was entirely enjoyed by British traders, except only the cargoes of two French vessels, and about fifteen thousand dollars, the value of boards shipped to Havana for sugar boxes.

Batteaux left New Orleans for Pointe Coupee, Natchitoches, the Arkansas and St. Louis; but most of their cargoes were taken on their way, from the British floating warehouse, or the stores at Manshac, Baton Rouge, or Natchez.

British adventurers found also in Louisiana, the means of forming agricultural establishments, on the left bank of the Mississippi, above Manshac, where land was obtained with much facility. An individual chartered a vessel of about one hundred and fifty tons in Jamaica, for five hundred dollars. He put on board goods and about twenty or thirty slaves, which he obtained on credit. Entering the Mississippi with these he disposed of the goods and three-fourths of the slaves, and received in exchange produce sufficient to pay for the whole and the hire of his vessel. With five or six slaves, he began a plantation, obtaining credit in a store near it, for his farming utensils, and the means of procuring some cattle and his subsistence till he made a crop. After a few years he was a farmer in easy circumstances.

The British owed to this trade with the former subjects of France many, if not all, of their establishments on the left banks of the Mississippi, besides the great advantages they derived from its navigation. A French trader durst not show the flag of his nation, and was compelled to charter a British bottom, and load her with goods; but the British merchant who sold them, and was certain to be paid, realized much greater profits.

Unzaga winked at this infraction of the commercial and revenue laws of Spain, and disregarded the clamors of the merchants of New Orleans,

30

who suspected that the indulgence shown to British traders was not gratuitous.

The ordinary alcades, chosen by the cabildo, for the year 1772, were Amelot and the Chevalier de Villiers.

On the promotion of Buccarelly to the viceroyalty of Mexico, the Marquis de la Torre succeeded him as captain-general of the island of Cuba and the province of Louisiana.

Col. Estacheria arrived and assumed the command of the regiment of Louisiana.

Most of the forces which O'Reilly had left in New Orleans sailed for Havana.

The country was desolated in the summer of this year by a hurricane, of which Roman has preserved the details.   It began on the last day of August and continued until the third of September.   It was not, however, felt in New Orleans, where the weather continued fine, though the wind blew very high from the east.   In lake Ponchartrain and the passes of the Rigolets and Chef Menteur, the water rose to a prodigious height, and the islands in the neighborhood were several feet under water.   The vessels at the Balize were all driven into the marshes, and a Spanish ship foundered and every person on board perished.   Along the coast from lake Borgne to Pensacola, the wind ranged from south southeast and east; but farther west it blew with greatest violence, from north northeast and east. A schooner belonging to the British government, having a detachment of the sixteenth regiment on board, was driven westerly as far as Cat island, under the western part of which she cast anchor; but the water rose so high that she parted her cable and floated over the island.   The wind entirely destroyed the woods for about thirty miles from the sea shore. At Mobile, the effects of it were terrible.   Vessels, boats, and logs were drawn up the streets to a great distance.   The gulleys and hollows as well as the lower grounds of the town were so filled with logs, that the inhabitants easily provided themselves with their winter supply of fuel. The salt spray was carried by the wind four or five miles from the sea shore, and then descended in showers.

For thirty miles up a branch of the Pascagoula, which, from the number of cedar trees on its bank, is called Cedar creek, there was scarcely a tree left standing; the pines were thrown down or broken; and those trees which did not entirely yield to the violence of the wind, were twisted like ropes.

But the most singular effect of this hurricane, was the production of a second growth of leaves and fruit on the mulberry trees.   This hardy tree budded, foliated, blossomed and bore fruit within four weeks after the storm.

With the view of promoting the instruction of the rising generation in the Spanish tongue, a priest was brought over from Spain, at the king's expense, who, with two assistants, taught the elements of that language. Four young women were also sent from Havana, who took the veil in the convent of the Ursuline nuns of New Orleans, and were employed in teaching Spanish to young persons of their sex.   This was the only encouragement given to learning during the whole period of the Spanish government.

The winter was so severe this year that the orange trees perished.

The breach which the stamp act had occasioned between the British

North American provinces and their mother country, was daily widening; and this year, on the suggestion of the province of Massachusetts bay, committees were appointed within the others, for the purpose of correspondence and the organization of a system of resistance to the measures adopted by parliament.

Duplessis and Doriocourt were the ordinary alcades chosen on the first of January, 1773.

It being deemed improper that a Spanish province should continue to form a part of a French bishopric, Louisiana was now separated from that of Quebec, and annexed to that of Cuba, and Don Santiago Joseph de Echevaria, the incumbent of the latter see, appointed Father Dagobert his vicar-general in the province.

Bobe Descloseaux, who had remained in New Orleans to attend to the redemption of the bills of credit emitted by the French government, having previously obtained the consent of his sovereign, now sailed for Cape François. Amelot, an engineer, and Garderat, a major of infantry, took passage in the same ship, with the widow of Carlier, the former comptroller of the marine, her two daughters, and a few other French officers, who had been detained by their private concerns. Neither the ship nor any of the passengers were ever heard of, after she left the Balize.

Time, and Unzaga's mild administration, began to reconcile the colonists to their fate. The resources which they found in a clandestine trade with the British, and the sums brought from Vera Cruz to meet the expenses of government, circulating in the country, had enabled many planters to extend their establishments. But many had employed for this purpose the proceeds of their crops, which justice required to be reserved for the discharge of their debts. To the difficulties which indiscretion had created, were superadded those that were occasioned by the ravages of the late hurricane. The disappointed creditors became clamorous, and some began to attempt coercing payment by legal measures. Over these, the influence of a governor of a Spanish colony was very great. Unzaga exerted his, in allaying the clamors of injured creditors, without distressing honest debtors, by employing coercion against those only who were able, but unwilling to discharge their debts. He gave evidence of his impartiality in this respect, by compelling St. Maxent, a wealthy planter, whose daughter he had married and who sought to avail himself of this circumstance to bid defiance to his creditors. In this manner, he obtained indulgence for those debtors who really required it.

Daniel Boone, with his family and four others, and about forty-five men from Powell's Valley, began this year the first settlement on Kentucky river.

The British East India company having made large shipments of tea to Boston, New York, Philadelphia and Charleston, the people in these cities opposed its landing. In the first, they went much farther. On hearing of the arrival of the company's ships there, it was voted by acclamation, in a numerous meeting of the inhabitants, that the tea should not be landed, nor the duties on it paid; but that it should be sent back in the same vessels in which it had been brought. On the adjournment of the meeting, an immense crowd repaired to the quay, and a number of the most resolute, disguised as Mohawk Indians, boarded the ships; and, in about two hours, broke open three hundred and forty boxes of tea, and discharged the contents into the sea.

The cabildo made choice of Forstall and Chabert, as ordinary alcades for the year 1774; and early in January, Fagot de la Gariniere took his seat in that body, as a perpetual regidor and receiver of fines; having purchased these offices from Bienvenu for fourteen hundred dollars.

On the tenth of May, Louis the fifteenth, the last monarch of France who reigned over Louisiana, died, in the sixty-fifth year of his age, and was succeeded by his grandson, the Duke of Berry, the unfortunate Louis the sixteenth.

By a royal schedule of the fourth of August, the power of granting vacant lands, in the province, was vested in the governor, according to the regulations made by O'Reilly, on the eighth of January, 1770.

The Creeks and Chickasaws this year, sent a number of their chiefs to Charleston, in South Carolina, where they made a cession to the British of several millions of acres of valuable land, in payment of their debts to traders of that nation.

Early in September, delegates from twelve of the British North American provinces met in congress in the city of Philadelphia. They prepared a petition to the king and an address to the people of Great Britain on the subject of their grievances.

The resentment of parliament, on hearing of the destruction of the tea at Boston, was manifested by the occlusion of that port, until reparation should be made to the East India company; and the king declared himself convinced that good order would soon be restored in the town. Another statute was passed annulling the charter of the province of Massachusetts bay, and authorizing the transportation from any of the provinces, for trial in another province or in England, of any person indicted for murder, or any other capital offense. A statute was also passed, for quartering soldiers on the inhabitants. The boundaries of the province of Quebec were extended, so as to include the territory between the lakes, the Ohio and the Mississippi, and its government was vested in a legislative council, to be appointed by the crown. At the request of the Canadians, the French laws were restored to them in civil matters. Two years after, in the declaration of independence, these last measures were urged as grounds of complaint, by the American congress, against George the third, that "he had abolished the free system of English laws in a neighboring province, establishing therein an arbitrary government, and extending its boundaries, so as to render it at once an example and instrument for introducing the same absolute rule in the other colonies."

In the meanwhile, General Gage fortified Bostonack, and had the ammunition and stores in the provincial arsenal at Cambridge, and the powder in the magazine at Charleston, brought to Boston.

Dufossat and Duplessis were the ordinary alcades for the year 1775.

Unzaga was now promoted to the rank of a brigadier-general, and the office of intendant was united to that of governor, in his person.

There were a considerable number of runaway negroes, committing great depredations on the plantations. Unzaga, to remedy or lessen this evil, issued a proclamation offering an amnesty, or free pardon, to such as voluntarily returned to their masters, and absolutely forbidding the latter to punish them. This measure had the intended effect; although the slaves could not absolutely be protected from the resentment of their masters, who might easily have found a pretense for disregarding Unzaga's injunction.

We have seen, in a preceding portion of this work, that general Lyman, of Connecticut, had contemplated, in 1763, an extensive settlement on the Ohio, and had applied to government for a grant of land. This officer had served with distinction during the preceding war. He had been appointed major-general and commander-in-chief of the forces of his native province in 1755; and, in 1762, he was at Havana, in command of all the American troops. On the return of peace, a company had by his exertions been formed, under the style of the Military Adventurers, composed chiefly of officers and soldiers who had lately served in America. Their object was to obtain a considerable extent of territory, on which they might settle, with as large a number of their countrymen as could be induced to join them. General Lyman went to England as the agent of the company, entertaining no doubt of the success of his application. On his arrival, he found that the friends in the ministry, on whom he depended, had been removed, and those who had succeeded them had other persons to provide for, and found it convenient to forget his services and those of his associates. Insurmountable obstacles seemed to embarrass him. At last, after a stay of several years, he obtained grants on the Mississippi and Yazoo rivers, and returned. Many of his former companions had died; several had removed to a distance; many had grown old; and all had passed that period of life, when men are willing to encounter the dangers and hardships attending the settlement of a wilderness, under a different climate, and at the distance of a thousand miles from their homes. After a short stay in Connecticut, he departed, with his eldest son and a few friends, with whom he soon formed a settlement, near Fort Panmure, in the district of Natchez.

Open hostilities broke out, this year, in the contest which terminated by the severance of thirteen British provinces from the mother country. On the 20th of April, the militia of Massachusetts routed a body of regulars at Lexington. In the month of May, the Americans possessed themselves, by surprise, of Ticonderoga; and the fortress of Crown point surrendered to them soon after. On the first of June, congress appointed George Washington commander-in-chief of all the forces of the united colonies; and he proceeded immediately to the vicinity of Boston, where the regular army and the militia of New England kept the royal forces in check, and obtained a decisive advantage on the seventeenth of June, at Breed's Hill.

In the meanwhile, the provincial congresses had organized their militia, and raised a few bodies of regular troops.

Part of the force of New York, and the adjacent provinces, under generals Wooster and Montgomery, marched into Canada, and took possession of Chambly, St. Johns, and Montreal, during the months of October and November. General Arnold, with some troops from Connecticut, crossed the wilderness and formed a junction with Wooster and Montgomery, on the right bank of the river St. Lawrence, opposite to Quebec; and crossing the stream, they made an unsuccessful attack upon the town, in which Montgomery fell, on the thirty-first day of December.

The ordinary alcades, for the year 1776, were d'Ernonville and Livaudais.

Olivier de Vezin took his seat, in the cabildo, as perpetual regidor and principal provincial alcade; Lebarre de la Cestiere, as a perpetual regidor and alguazil mayor; the Chevalier de Clapion, as a perpetual regidor and receiver of fines; and Forstall, as perpetual regidor.

Don Bernardo de Galvez succeeded Estacheria in the command of the regiment of Louisiana.

There were, at this period, a number of merchants from Boston, New York and Philadelphia, in New Orleans: they were all well disposed towards the American cause. Oliver Pollock was the most conspicuous. They had procured a good supply of arms and ammunition for the settlers of the western part of Pennsylvania, which was delivered to colonel Gibson, who came to Pittsburg for it. This had been done with the knowledge of the colonial government, who gave some assistance to the colonel.

Unzaga received the appointment of captain-general of Caraccas. He was much regretted in Louisiana. His mild administration had endeared him to the colonists. He had overlooked the breach of the commercial and fiscal laws of Spain by the British, who had entirely engrossed the commerce of the province. They had introduced a considerable number of slaves, and by the great aid they afforded to planters, had enabled most of them to extend their establishments to a degree hitherto unknown in the province, and others to forms new ones. By the timely exercise of coercion against the dishonest and indolent, he had checked the profligacy of those who misused the facilities which British traders afforded, and compelled them to reduce or surrender establishments which they were unable to sustain. His conduct, in this respect, though not absolutely approved by the king's ministers, did not deprive him of the confidence of his sovereign. His promotion fully proved this. Without this illicit trade Louisiana must have remained an insignificant province.

The British army evacuated Boston on the seventeenth of March, and Washington led his to New York. The united colonies proclaimed their independence on the fourth of July. The royal land and naval forces reached Staten Island, near New York, eight days after. The army landed on Long Island on the twenty-second, and five days after repulsed the Americans at Brooklyn. General Washington abandoned the city of New York in September, leading his force up North river, which he crossed on the thirteenth of November, and had some success in Trenton.

CHAPTER XVII.

BY a royal schedule, of the tenth of July, 1776, Unzaga had been directed to surrender, provisionally, the government and intendancy of Louisiana, on his departure for the province of Caraccas, to Don Bernard de Galvez, colonel of the regiment of Louisiana. This gentleman had powerful friends. His uncle, Don Joseph de Galvez, was president of the council of the Indies; and his father, Don Mathias de Galvez, viceroy of New Spain. He entered on the duties of his office on the first of January, 1777.

The ordinary alcades, for this year, were Forstall and the Chevalier de Villiers.

Don Diego Joseph Navarro succeeded the Marquis de la Torre, as captain-general of the island of Cuba and province of Louisiana.

By a royal schedule of the month of March, the duty of four per cent. on the exportation of colonial produce from Louisiana, was reduced to two.

The commerce of the province was encouraged by the permission given to vessels from the French West India Islands to come in ballast to the Mississippi, and take, at New Orleans or on the plantations, the produce of the country, paying therefor in specie, bills of exchange, or Guinea negroes. The introduction of negroes born, or who had remained some time in the islands, was already considered as dangerous, and had been prohibited. Vessels from Louisiana were also permitted to bring from the islands of Cuba, or Campeachy, produce or European goods. Agriculture was also encouraged by an order to the colonial government to purchase, for the king's account, all the tobacco raised in the colony.

This year, several large canoes came from Fort Pitt to New Orleans, for the purpose of taking the munitions of war which had been collected for the use of the United States, by Oliver Pollock, probably with the aid, but certainly with the knowledge of Galvez. Captain Willing, of Philadelphia, who came in one of these boats, visited the British settlements on the Mississippi, and some of his companions crossed the lakes to Mobile, with the view to induce the inhabitants to raise the striped banner, and join their countrymen in the struggle for freedom. The people of both the Floridas, however, remained steadfast in their attachment to the royal cause. Perhaps those on the Mississippi and in Mobile were deterred by the late tragedy in New Orleans. The thin and sparse population of both the Floridas, their distance from the provinces engaged in the war, and the consequent difficulty of receiving any assistance from them, influenced the conduct of the inhabitants.

The militia of the western part of the state of Virginia made several very successful incursions into the country to the west of the Ohio, and on the banks of the Mississippi. They possessed themselves of Kaskaskia, and some other posts on that stream. By an act of the legislature these were afterwards erected into a county called Illinois. A regiment of infantry and a troop of horse were raised for its protection, and placed under the command of Col. Clark.

The limits of the former province of Carolina to the west, were fixed in the charter of Charles the second on the Pacific ocean. By the treaty between Great Britain and France, the Mississippi was given to North Carolina, as its western limit. By the proclamation of 1763, George the third had forbidden any settlement of white people to the west of the mountains. Nevertheless, a considerable number of emigrants from North Carolina had removed to the banks of the Watauga, one of the branches of the Holston. They had increased to such a degree that in 1776, their claim to representation in the convention that formed the constitution was admitted. This year they were formed into a county which had the Mississippi for its western boundary.

The erection of that county by the state of North Carolina, and that of the county of Illinois by the state of Virginia, are the first instances of measures taken to extend the execution of the laws of the American states to the banks of Mississippi.

Washington was successful in an attack near Princeton, on the twelfth

of January. The British army landed on the banks of Elk river, and
repulsed the Americans at Brandywine on the eleventh of September, and
soon after entered Philadelphia. The Americans were again unsuccessful
at Germantown on the fourth of October; but these misfortunes were in
some degree compensated by their success in the north, and the surrender
of the British army under Burgoyne, at Saratoga, on the twentieth.

The ordinary alcades for the year 1778, were Navarro and Dufossat.

During the month of January, captain Willing made a second visit to
New Orleans. Oliver Pollock now acted openly as the agent of the
Americans with the countenance of Galvez, who now and at subsequent
periods, afforded them an aid of upwards of seventy thousand dollars out
of the royal treasury. By this means the posts occupied by the militia
of Virginia on the Mississippi, and the frontier inhabitants of the state
of Pennsylvania were supplied with arms and ammunition. New hands
were engaged to row up the boats; and Willing with most of the men
who had come down about fifty in number, engaged in a predatory
excursion against the British planters on the Mississippi. They proceeded
to bayou Manshac, where they captured a small vessel which they found
at anchor.   They went in her to Baton Rouge, stopping on their way at
several plantations where they set fire to the houses and carried off the
slaves.

On hearing of their approach the British planters on the left bank of
the Mississippi, crossed the stream with their slaves and most valuable
effects. The inhabitants were so few and so scattered, that they were
unable to make any effectual resistance to the invaders, who proceeded as
far as Natchez, laying waste the plantations, destroying the stock, burning
the houses and taking off such slaves as remained.

Although the government and people of Louisiana were well disposed
towards the United States, this cruel, wanton and unprovoked conduct
towards a helpless community, was viewed with great indignation and
horror, much increased by the circumstance of Willing having been
hospitably received and entertained, the preceding year, in several houses
which he now committed to the flames.

The province now received a considerable accession of population, by
the arrival of a number of families, brought over at the king's expense,
from the Canary islands. A part of them formed a new settlement at the
Terre-aux-Bœufs, below New Orleans, under the order of Marigny de
Mandeville; a part was located on the banks of the river Amite, behind
Baton Rouge, under the order of St. Maxent, and formed the settlement
of Galveztown: the rest formed that of Valenzuela, on bayou Lafourche.

A house was built for each family, and a church in each settlement.
They were supplied with cattle, fowls and farming utensils; rations were
furnished them for a period of four years out of the king's stores, and
considerable pecuniary assistance was also afforded to them.

By a royal schedule of the fourth of May, the indemnity to be paid to
owners of slaves condemned to death, perpetual labor, or transportation,
or killed in the attempt to arrest them, when runaway, was fixed at two
hundred dollars a head; but in the latter case, the indemnity was due
only to those who had previously consented to pay a proportion of the
price of slaves thus killed.

On the twentieth of April, Galvez issued a proclamation, by which,
owing to the distresses of the times, and the difficulty of disposing of the

produce of the province, he permitted its exportation to any of the ports of France; and by another proclamation, on the seventeenth, the permission was extended to any port of the United States.

The king made, on the eighteenth of October, new regulations for the commerce of his American dominions, and particularly for that of Louisiana. Considering it necessary to his service to encourage the trade of that province, and to increase its prosperity, he directed that vessels from New Orleans should no longer be restricted to sail for one of the six ports to which they had been restricted, but might sail to any of the other ports of the peninsula, to which the commerce of the Indies was permitted. The exportation of furs and peltries from Louisiana was at the same time encouraged, by an exemption from duty during a period of ten years; but in the re-exportation from Spain the ordinary duty was to be paid.

Two royal schedules were this year published in Louisiana. By the first, the introduction or reading of a book written by Mercier, entitled *L'An Deux Mille Quatre Cent Quarante*, was prohibited; and the governor was ordered to cause every copy of it found in the province to be seized and destroyed. The other schedule was to the same effect, in regard to Robertson's history of America. Mercier's book had been condemned by the Inquisition, and the king said he had just reason to prohibit Robertson's being read in his American dominions.

There were, at this period, a considerable number of individuals from the United States and West and East Florida and Nova Scotia, in New Orleans. They were all required to take an oath of fidelity to the king of Spain during their residence in his dominions, or depart. It appears the oath was taken by eighty-three individuals.

Colonel Hamilton, who commanded at the British post at Detroit, came this year to Vincennes, on the Wabash, with about six hundred men, chiefly Indians, with a view to an expedition against Kaskaskia, and up the Ohio as far as Fort Pitt, and the back settlements of Virginia. Colonel Clark heard, from a trader, who came down from Vincennes to Kaskaskia, that Hamilton, not intending to take the field until spring, had sent most of his force to block up the Ohio, or to harrass the frontier settlers, keeping at Vincennes sixty soldiers only, with three pieces of cannon and some swivels. The resolution was immediately taken to improve the favorable opportunity for averting the impending danger; and Clark accordingly dispatched a small galley, mounting two four pounders and four swivels, on board of which he put a company of soldiers, with orders to pursue her way up the Wabash, and anchor a few miles below Vincennes, suffering nothing to pass her. He now set off with one hundred and twenty men, the whole force he could command, and marched towards Vincennes. They were five days in crossing the low lands of the Wabash, in the neighborhood of Vincennes, after having spent sixty in crossing the wilderness, wading for several nights up to their breasts in water. Appearing suddenly before the town, they surprised and took it. Hamilton for a while defended the fort, but was at last compelled to surrender.

The prospects of the United States had been much brightened, on the recognition of their independence by France, and the conclusion of a treaty of alliance and commerce with that power, on the sixth of February.

In the summer, the British evacuated Philadelphia, and marched through the state of Jersey to New York. A large detachment of it

31 .

invaded the coasts of the state of Georgia, and took possession of Savannah.

The cabildo made choice of Piernas and Duverger as ordinary alcades, on the first of January, 1779.

Toutant de Beauregard took his seat in that body as a perpetual regidor and principal provincial alcade; and Mazange succeeded Garic as clerk.

Don Juan Dorotheo del Portege succeeded Odoardo in the office of auditor of war and assessor of government.

According to the order made the last year, eighty-seven individuals from the United States, or British provinces, took a temporary oath of fidelity to the Catholic king.

The province, this year, received another accession of population, by the arrival of a number of families brought over, at the king's expense, from Malaga. They were treated as favorably as those who came, in the preceding year, from the Canary islands. It appears, from documents extant, that some heads of families received, besides a grant of land, in cattle, rations, pecuniary and other aid, between three and four thousand dollars. They were sent to form a settlement on bayou Teche, in the district of the Attakapas, under the order of Bouligny. The place was called New Iberia. The industry of the new comers was at first directed to the culture of flax and hemp; but without success.

At the same time, the king sent a spiritual relief to the province, consisting of six capuchin friars; one of whom, at this day, remains in the exercise of his pastoral functions, as curate of the parish of St. Louis, in the city of New Orleans.

The small pox made great havoc in New Orleans and on the plantations, above and below.

Great Britain had considered the recognition of the independence of the United States by France, the treaty of alliance and commerce which she had concluded with them, and the succor which she had afforded them, as equivalent to a declaration of war; and hostilities had actually begun, when Spain offered her mediation, and proposed a general peace for a term of years, with a meeting of the ministers of the belligerent powers at Madrid, to which those of the United States were to be admitted and treated as the representatives of an independent people. Although it was not insisted that the king of Great Britain should formally recognize his former subjects as independent, it was understood that they should be so *de facto*, and absolutely separated from the empire of Great Britain. On the declaration by the cabinet of St. James, that no negotiation would be entered into with the United States, even under the modifications proposed, the Catholic king determined on taking a part in the war, and ordered his embassador at London to deliver a rescript, in which, after reciting several grounds of complaint, he declared his sovereign's determination to use every means in his power to obtain justice. The ambassador left London without taking leave; and letters of marque and reprisals against the ships and subjects of Spain were immediately issued.

On the eighth of May, war was declared by Spain; and on the eighth of July, a royal schedule was issued, authorizing the king's subjects in the Indies to take part in it, the latter document reciting that the king of Great Britain had sought to indemnify himself, for the loss of his American provinces, by the seizure of those of Spain, having, by various artifices, endeavored to raise up new enemies against her, among the

Indian nations in Florida, whom he had induced to conspire against the king's innocent vassals in Louisiana.

With the official account of the rupture, Galvez, who had hitherto exercised the functions of governor *pro tempore,* received the king's commission of governor and intendant. He immediately thought of the attack of the British possessions in the neighborhood, and convened a council of war to deliberate on it. The proposition was rejected, and the council recommended that, until a reinforcement could be obtained from Havana, defensive measures should be alone resorted to.

Impatient of the state of inaction to which the determination of the council condemned him, the chief endeavored to collect a body of men sufficient to justify him in taking on himself the responsibility of acting in opposition to the opinion of his legal advisers. There were a number of men from the United States in and near New Orleans, who offered their services. The militia volunteered theirs. In this manner, with the regular force and many of the people of color, an army of about fourteen hundred men was collected. The fatigue of a forced march and the diseases incident to the climate towards the end of the summer considerably reduced this force before they reached Fort Bute, on bayou Manshac, which was taken by assault on the seventh day of September, within less than sixty days from the date of the royal schedule, authorizing the king's American subjects to take part in the war.

The army marched, without loss of time, to Baton Rouge. Colonel Dickson had there a garrison of little more than four hundred British soldiers and one hundred militia. He was well supplied with arms, ammunition and provisions; but the fort was in ruins, and his men sickly. He was not, however, to be surprised by a *coup de main.* Galvez immediately invested the fort, and began with the erection of batteries, on which he mounted his heavy ordnance. In two hours and a half after the cannonade began, on the twenty-first of September, Dickson proposed a capitulation, which was soon after agreed to. The honors of war were accorded to the garrison, and they were made prisoners. The surrender of fort Panmure, at Natchez, and two small posts, one on Amite river and the other on Thompson creek, were included in the capitulation. Don Carlos de Grandpre was left in command at Baton Rouge, with two officers under him at fort Bute and fort Panmure, and the army marched back to New Orleans.

Julien Poydras, (a gentleman who afterwards became conspicuous by his great wealth and his services in congress, and the territorial and state legislatures) celebrated the achievement of Galvez in a small poem, in the French language, which was printed and circulated at the king's expense.

The elements were not so favorable to Louisiana, as the god of war. A hurricane desolated it in the fall, and the small-pox, the ravages of which were not yet lessened by innoculation or vaccination, made much havoc in the city and its neighborhood.

The arms of the United States were not as successful on the shores of the Atlantic, as those of Spain were on the banks of the Mississippi. During the summer, the Americans made an irruption, under general Howe, into the province of East Florida, and the diseases incident to the climate at that season of the year, proved fatal to a considerable part of the forces. An unsuccessful attempt was also made, during the winter, to dislodge the English from Savannah.

Congress, availing themselves of the rupture between Spain and Great Britain, sent a minister to Madrid to negotiate a treaty. He was particularly instructed to insist on their right to the navigation of the Mississippi, as far as the sea.

The claim was opposed by Spain, and discountenanced by France. The minister of France, at Philadelphia, had urged that his sovereign was anxious to see the independence of the United States acknowledged by Spain, and a treaty of alliance and commerce entered into by these powers; and he had recommended to the consideration of congress several matters which the Catholic king viewed as highly important. These were the rights of Spain to the exclusive navigation of the Mississippi, and to the possession of both the Floridas, and all the territory from the left bank of the stream to the back settlements of the former British provinces, according to the proclamation of 1763. It was contended that no part of the territory, thus claimed, was included within the limits of any of the United States, and the whole of it, with the Floridas, was a possession of the British crown, and consequently a legitimate object against which the Catholic king might direct his arms, with a view to its permanent acquisition. It was suggested that it was expected by the cabinet of Madrid, that congress would prohibit the inhabitants of the southern states from making any attempt towards settling or conquering this portion of territory. The minister concluded that the United States possessing no territory beyond the mountains, except the posts of Kaskaskia and a few others, from which they had momentarily driven the British, would view the navigation of the Mississippi as an unimportant object, in comparison with the recognition of their independence by, and an alliance with Spain. The late declaration of war by Spain, and the hostilities commenced by Galvez, an account of which was received at Philadelphia while congress was deliberating on the communication of the French minister, had, it is believed, considerable influence in the subsequent determination of that body to insist on the claim.

This year a number of French hunters (*coureurs de bois,*) who had strayed to the banks of the Cumberland river, built a few cabins on a spot soon after called the Bluff, and since known as the one on which the town of Nashville stands. It is situated within the limits then claimed by the state of North Carolina, in her constitution, and within the territory afterwards ceded by that state to the United States. The surrounding country was inhabited by Indians only; and the nearest settlement of whites was on the banks of the Watauga, one of the branches of the Tennessee river, at the distance of several hundred miles.

Panis and Duverger were the ordinary alcades for the year 1780.

Galvez' success at Manshac and Baton Rouge was now rewarded by a commission of brigadier-general.

Having received some reinforcement from Havana, he left New Orleans early in January, with a larger force than that which he had led to Baton Rouge during the preceding year. His object was the reduction of Fort Charlotte on the Mobile river. He was overtaken on the gulf by a storm by which one of his armed vessels was stranded. His troops were exposed to great danger and a part of his provisions and ammunition was either totally spoiled or rendered unfit for use for some time. He succeeded at last in landing his army, artillery, military stores, and provisions on the eastern point of Mobile river.

Had general Campbell, who was at Pensacola with a considerable force, sallied out and attacked the invaders their defeat would have been inevitable. Galvez was so conscious of his perilous situation, that he made some preparations for a march by land to New Orleans, leaving his baggage and artillery behind. He, however, determined on proceeding to the fort, and was indebted for his success, to the supineness of the enemy.

On his arrival he erected six batteries, which soon effected a breach in the walls of the fort, the commandant of which capitulated on the fourteenth of March.

General Campbell arrived a few days after, with a force that would have been sufficient to have prevented the capture of the fort, but which, now that it was in the possession of the Spaniards, became useless.

Galvez, on his return to New Orleans, determined on the attack of Pensacola; but the force he could command was insufficient, and he sent an officer to the captain-general to solicit a reinforcement. His messenger returned with the promise of one. Impatient of the delay, he sailed for Havana in order to hasten the intended succor. Having obtained troops, artillery and ammunition, he sailed on the sixteenth of October; but, on the succeeding day, some of his transports foundered in a storm, and the rest were dispersed. He collected and brought them back to Havana, on the sixteenth of November.

In the fall, the British commanding officer at Michilimackinac, with about one hundred and forty men from his garrison, and near fourteen hundred Indians, attacked the Spanish post at St. Louis; but colonel Clark, who was still at Kakaskia, came to its relief. The Indians who came from Michilimackinac, having no idea of fighting any but Spaniards, refused to act against Americans, and complained of having been deceived. Clark released about fifty prisoners that had been made, and the enemy made the best of their way home.

The minister of the United States at Madrid failed in his negotiation, and their independence was not acknowledged by Spain.

The British army was this year successful in South Carolina. Charleston surrendered on the twelfth of May. Tarleton routed, soon after, a party of Americans under Buford, near the southern boundary of North Carolina. Gates was defeated at Camden on the sixteenth of August, and Sumpter, on the Catawba, on the eighteenth. After this, Lord Cornwallis invaded the state of North Carolina.

Don Juan Manuel de Cagigal succeeded, during the year 1781, Navarro, as captain-general of the island of Cuba and the province of Louisiana.

Galvez was promoted to the rank of mariscal de camp. The attention he had to give to military concerns, leaving him no time to be bestowed on the fiscal, Don Martin Nevarro, the contador, was appointed intendant and Don Manuel Serano, assessor of the intendancy. Don Antonio Lopez de Armesto received the appointment of secretary of government, which he held until the cession.

Galvez left Havana for Pensacola on the twenty-eighth of February, with a man of war, two frigates, and several transports, on board of which were fourteen hundred and fifteen soldiers, a competent train of artillery, and abundance of ammunition.   The fleet was commanded by Don Joseph Cabro de Irazabal.

On the ninth of March, he landed his troops, ordnance and military stores, on the island of St. Rosa, and on the next day erected a battery to support the fleet on its passage over the bar.   The attempt to cross it was made on the eleventh; but the commodore's ship having got aground, it was abandoned.   On the next day, Galvez wrote to Irazabal, expressing his uneasiness at the risk which the fleet and convoy must run by remaining long exposed to a storm on a dangerous coast, and requested him to call the captains of the armed vessels on board of his ship and take their opinions as to the best means of getting the fleet and transports over the bar.   This was done, and Irazabal reported that these officers had declared they were unable to form an opinion on the probable success of a second attempt, as they were without a correct chart of the coast.

They complained that the pilots on board of the fleet were incapable of affording any aid; every account which they had given of the soundings having proved erroneous; adding that their ships had nearly all lost their rudders on the eleventh, and expressing their belief that if they had proceeded any farther they should have found prompt and effectual manœuvres impossible.   They observe also that they had all along feared that the artillery of the fort could reach the channel; but they had now the melancholy certainty that it commanded, not only the channel over the bar, but even the island of St. Rosa.   There being in the fort twenty-four pounders, the balls of which would rake, fore and aft, any vessel that should attempt to cross the bar, and the direction of the channel was such that they were obliged to present their sides, poop and prow to the enemy's guns; that the channel was, besides, so narrow that the first ship that got aground would obstruct the passage, and the rapidity of the current preventing any quick manœuvre, the ships would run foul of each other before they could turn, even if that were possible. They came to the conclusion that as the general deemed the crossing of the bar an object of vast importance to the king's service, the commodore should send one or two officers, attended by three or four pilots, to sound the channel as far as Point Siguenza, during the night; a fire being made on that point in order to ascertain the direction in which a vessel might be most easily managed; after which a second trial might be made.

Irazabal expressed his individual opinion that any attempt to attack the British by water would be fruitless, and recommended that the land force should be immediately employed in the reduction of the fort.

Galvez thought he discovered in the commodore and the captains of the armed ships, a reluctance to co-operate with him in any measure, of which they imagined he would exclusively reap the glory in case of success, and that they were disposed to impede rather than to aid his plans.   He replied to Irazabal, that the loss of a ship or two, from which all on board could easily be saved, was not to be put in comparison with that of the whole fleet and the transports, to which they were exposed in case of a storm, and which would entirely prevent the success of their undertaking. After having requested that the captains should again be called together to reconsider their former report, he determined to attempt with the naval means of which he had the immediate command, what he could not obtain from the commodore.

Accordingly, the brig Galvezton, commanded by Rousseau, which had lately arrived with ordnance from New Orleans, cast anchor near the bar; and the captain having sounded the channel as far as Point Siguenza, during the night between the fifteenth and sixteenth, he next morning reported there was water enough in the shallowest part of the channel for the largest ship in the fleet, with her full load.

The captains of the armed ships met on board of the commodore's ship, and having reconsidered their report of the fourteenth, declared they could not do anything but refer the general to it.

Don Joseph de Espeleta had arrived on the sixteenth with the force from Mobile and the militia from the neighborhood, and on the seventeenth, Don Estevan Miro came from New Orleans with the Louisiana forces. They all landed on the western side of Rio Perdido.

Convinced, now, there was no means of inducing Irazabal to make a second attempt to bring the fleet and convoy over the bar, Galvez, from the experience he had on his way to Mobile in the spring, and from Havana in the fall of the preceding year, of the danger he incurred by remaining longer exposed to a storm, directed the brig Galvezton, a schooner just arrived from New Orleans, under the order of Riano, and two gun boats, which constituted all the naval force under his immediate command, to prepare for crossing the bar; in the hope that their success might induce the officers of the royal navy to follow them. Towards noon, Rousseau, with his brig, the schooner, and gun boats, cast anchor near the bar, and at half-past two, Galvez went on board of the brig, directed a pendant to be displayed on her main mast, a salute to be fired, and sail to be set. The fort immediately began a brisk cannonade, principally directed upon the brig, on board of which it was apparent the general was embarked. Neither the brig, schooner, nor gun boats received any injury, except in their sails and rigging; and Galvez landed at the bottom of the bay, on the island of St. Rosa, under a salute, and amid the acclamations of his men.

His success determined Irazabal to send the fleet and convoy over the bar, except his own ship, which, in the meanwhile, had been reladen for her return to Havana. This was effected on the next day. The frigates led the way, and the convoy followed. The fort kept a brisk fire for upwards of an hour, until the hindmost vessel was out of its reach. The shipping received some injury, but no individual was hurt. Galvez had advanced in a boat, and remained in the midst of the convoy until the last vessel anchored.

At four o'clock, he made an effort, with two of his aids, to cross the bar, in order to go and confer with Espeleta and Miro, and devise with them a plan of attack; but the violence of the wind compelled him to desist, and he reached the camp at midnight.

In the morning of the twentieth, he sent one of his aids to general Campbell with a message, in which he informed him that when the British came to Havana in 1762, their commander intimated to the captain-general of the Catholic king, that if any of the king's edifices, ships, or other property were destroyed, the Spaniards would be treated with all the rigor and severity of the laws of war; that the intimation was now made to the general and whoever it might concern, and under the same terms.

At night, the British set fire to a guard house on the beach; and

Galvez sent Riano's schooner, with the launch of the brig Galvezton, which, for awhile, kept up a brisk fire of grape shot on the beach.

A British officer came to the camp, early on the following day, with a message from Campbell, stating that an enemy's threats could only be considered as a stratagem of war, and expressing his hope that, in the defense of Pensacola, he should resort to no measure not justified by the usages of war. He made his acknowledgment for the frank intimation he had received, and gave assurance that his conduct would be regulated by that of the Spanish commander, with regard to certain propositions he had to make, in conjunction with the governor of West Florida.

At noon, an aid of Campbell, accompanied by lieutenant-colonel Dickson, who had been taken the preceding year at Baton Rouge, and liberated on his parol, came in a boat bearing a flag of truce, and delivered to Galvez letters from Campbell and governor Chester.

The first expressed his conviction that humanity required, as much as possible, the exemption of innocent individuals from the disasters necessarily incident to war; and added, that the garrison at Pensacola was unable to resist the force brought against it, without the total destruction of the town, and the consequent ruin of its inhabitants; and he expressed his desire that the town and garrison should be preserved for the victor—a desire, he said, which arose from the hope he entertained that the efforts of the troops he commanded would be crowned with success. He concluded by proposing that the town should be preserved, without receiving any unnecessary injury from either party, during the siege of the redoubt of the marine and Fort George, within which he meant to contend for the preservation of the province for the British crown, under the stipulation that the town of Pensacola should not be used, by either army, for the purpose either of protecting itself or annoying its adversary; but remain the safe asylum of women, children, the aged and infirm. He added, that in case his proposition was rejected, and the Spaniards sought a shelter in Pensacola, it would become his duty to immediately destroy it.

The governor proposed that some Spanish prisoners in his possession should be liberated on their parol, on the assurance of Galvez, that they should not be employed in the military or civil service of the Catholic king, during the war, unless they were sooner exchanged.

Galvez gave orders that his men should be drawn out under arms, in order that the messengers of Campbell and Chester might report what kind and number of troops were under his command. These gentlemen were afterwards dismissed with a verbal message, importing that Galvez was prevented by indisposition from preparing a written answer, and that one would be sent on the next day.

During the night, the British set fire to a few houses near Fort St. George.

In his reply, on the twenty-second, Galvez stated that what he had seen, since the departure of Campbell's aid and lieutenant-colonel Dickson, convinced him that those who sent them had no other object but procrastination, and he was ashamed of his own credulity and their attempt to deceive him; that he would listen to no proposition but that of a surrender; and the conflagration of Pensacola, so long as it was not attributable to any fault of his, would be contemplated with as much indifference as the burning of its incendiaries!

Campbell rejoined, that the haughty style assumed by the Spanish chief, far from its intended effect, would have that of exciting the utmost opposition to the ambitious views of Spain; that the officer commanding at Fort George had done nothing but his duty, in destroying a few houses near it, which afforded protection to the enemy; and that if the invaders sought to avail themselves of Pensacola, by seeking an asylum there, it would be immediately destroyed.

Campbell now retreated into the fort with all the force under his orders, and the Spaniards lost no time in opening a land communication between the bay and the town, and erecting their works on both sides of the British fortifications. They were provided with a good train of artillery.

The attack was not, however, commenced until the beginning of April. From the fleet in front, and the batteries on either side, the British were exposed to a tremendous fire, and their men often driven from their guns. But, they having for a long time anticipated a siege, the fortifications were in excellent repair, and the supply of ammunition and provisions abundant; so that the Spaniards made but little impression. A lower battery, which the British hastily erected, and on which they put heavy cannon, soon enabled them to drive the ships on the opposite side of the bay. Galvez was unable to annoy his enemy by the side batteries, and for a while reduced to comparative inaction. At last, a lucky accident, in the beginning of May, favored his enterprise. The magazine, in one of the advanced redoubts took fire from a shell and blew up. The works were completely destroyed by the explosion, and a free passage opened. Galvez immediately sent Espeleta, with a strong detachment, to occupy the middle ground, in which they were protected by the ruins of the redoubt; and soon after, he sent four field pieces. with which a brisk fire was begun. At this moment a white flag was hoisted in Fort George, and an officer came out to propose a capitulation.

The terms of it were soon agreed on, and it was signed on the ninth of May. The whole province of West Florida was surrendered to Spain, with the garrison, which consisted of upwards of eight hundred men. They were allowed the honors of war, and to retain their baggage and private property, and were transported to their sovereign's dominions, under a stipulation that they should not serve against Spain or her allies, until duly exchanged.

Don Arthur O'Neil, an Irish officer in the service of Spain, was left in command at Pensacola.

CHAPTER XVIII.

AN incident occurred during the siege of Pensacola, which was very near involving some of the British near Natchez in serious difficulties. General Lyman, who, we have seen, had, with some of his adherents in Connecticut, obtained grants of land in the neighborhood of fort Panmure, and formed agricultural establishments in 1775, was now dead, and his followers had seen, with considerable regret, the British force that protected them, driven from the fort, and replaced by Spanish soldiers. During the siege, on the rumor of the approach of a fleet, which had been mistaken for a British one, they considered the success of their sovereign's

32

cause in West Florida so certain, that they determined on giving him an evidence of their loyalty by dislodging the Spaniards from the fort. Having engaged most of the other inhabitants of the district in their plan, and secured the co-operation of a number of the neighboring Indians, they raised, on the twenty-second of April, the British standard in view, but beyond the reach of the guns of the fort. During the night they approached the fort, brought some artillery to bear upon it, but a heavy fire from the guns of the fort soon compelled them to retire.

On the twenty-fourth, the Spaniards fired on, and destroyed a house at small distance, behind which the insurgents had taken shelter: but the latter having procured a field piece, approached and fired on the fort, wounding a corporal, who died on the next day. During the night, the firing was continued with some intervals.

The commandant of the fort sent, on the twenty-eighth, one of his officers to the insurgents, to represent to them the danger to which they exposed themselves, by a rebellion against their lawful sovereign—recommending to them to deliver up their leaders and disperse; and promising that if they did so, the royal clemency should be extended to them. They promised to send an answer the next day. Accordingly, in the morning, a planter came to the fort with a letter from McIntosh, one of the most respectable inhabitants of the district, informing him that what the messenger would say could be relied on. This man on being questioned, said the fort was undermined, and would be blown up the following day. There was a deep valley, at a very short distance from the fort, at which the Spaniards had noticed a considerable number of persons, during the preceding days, a circumstance which gave some credit to the story.

On the twenty-ninth, the men, according to the report of the commandant, being exhausted with fatigue and watching, and the ammunition and provisions nearly consumed, he surrendered the fort, on being permitted to march with his garrison to Baton Rouge.

The evacuation of fort Panmure, by the Spaniards, was soon followed by the report that the rumor that the approach of a British fleet was unfounded, and afterwards by that of Galvez' success at Pensacola.

Those who had taken an active part in this short revolution, among whom were most of the settlers from Connecticut, fearful of meeting the fate of O'Reilly's victims at New Orleans determined on making the best of their way to Savannah in Georgia, now the nearest post occupied by the British—although they had to cross an immense wilderness inhabited by hostile Indians.

The contest between Great Britain, (the subjects of which they were) and the American States, rendering a direct course dangerous, they were obliged to enter North Carolina, descend below the Alatamaha, and cross again the state of Georgia to Savannah, on its northern limit. In the performance of their circuitous journey, they were employed one hundred and thirty-one days.

The caravan was numerous and included women and children, some of the latter at the breast. All were mounted on horseback; but the ruggedness of the ground induced such as were able to walk, to travel most of the way on foot. The country is intersected by numerous, and often broad and deep water courses; steep and lofty mountains obstructed their course; and impervious marshes often required them to make long and tedious circuits. The Choctaws through whose country and along whose border there journey lay to a great extent, having espoused the cause of the Spaniards, were their enemies : and from an Indian foe, no stratagem, no speed, no distance can insure safety. Famine also threatened them in their best circumstances ; often they suffered intensely from thirst ; and disease, at times, compelled those who were well to halt for the recovery of the sick.

They separated into two companies, on reaching the state of Georgia : one was taken by the Americans ; the other crossed the Alatamaha, and journeyed to its mouth where they constructed a raft, on which they crossed with their horses, and finally reached the town of Savannah in the latter part of October.

On the twenty-fourth of August, Louisiana was desolated by a hurricane. This year the Mississippi rose to a greater height than was remembered by the oldest inhabitants. In the Attakapas and Opelousas, the inundation was extreme. The few spots which the water did not reach, were covered with deer.

The affairs of the United States had a very gloomy aspect at the commencement of this year, and a brilliant one towards its conclusion. The new year found the British in possession of the states of Georgia and and South Carolina ; and Lord Cornwallis, who had invaded that of North Carolina, and driven general Green into Virginia, gained a considerable advantage over the latter on his return into North Carolina at the battle of Guilford. The American army was now reduced to a deplorable weakness ; and the remnant of it which still existed, was unpaid, unclothed and often unfed. Under the pressure of these complicated sufferings, a considerable portion of the soldiers had been in open revolt ; and it was not easy to say with confidence, how long the patriotism of the residue would support them under such trying circumstances.

The enemies of America exulted, and her friends desponded. In this inauspicious state of her affairs, congress relaxed, for an instant, the firmness which had uniformly characterized that body, and manifested a disposition to sacrifice remote interests, though of great future magnitude for immediate advantages, and instructed their minister at Madrid to relinquish, should it be absolutely necessary, the claim of the United States to the navigation of the Mississippi, below the thirty-first degree of north latitude and a free port on its banks. The minister, finding himself obliged to comply with the instructions, had the firmness to add, the offer to renounce the claim was made with a view of procuring, at once, the recognition of the independence of the United States, and a treaty of alliance and commerce ; and if these objects were not immediately attained, congress would consider themselves at liberty to insist on their claim thereafter. The cabinet of Madrid did not, however, think proper to negotiate at this period, and the United States afterwards availed themselves of the prudent and spirited conduct of their minister.

Lord Cornwallis had marched from Guilford courthouse to Wilmington, where he staid until the twenty-fifth of April, when he marched to Yorktown, in Virginia. He was afterwards invested by the allied forces of the United States and France, supported by a French fleet commanded by the Count de Grasse, to whom he surrendered on the nineteenth of October.

Galvez' success at Pensacola was rewarded by a commission of lieutenant-general of the king's armies, the cross of a knight pensioner of the royal and distinguished order of Charles the third, and he was appointed captain-general of the provinces of Louisiana and Florida.

Father Cyrillo, of Barcelona, was made a bishop "*in partibus infidelium*," and received the canonical institution of the see of Tricaly, a town in Greece. He was given as coadjutor to Don Santiago Joseph de Estaveria, who still occupied the see of Cuba, and was directed to exercise his episcopal functions in Louisiana.

The Spanish cabinet had directed Galvez to attempt, after the surrender of Pensacola, the capture of the Bahama islands; but a simultaneous attack on the island of Jamaica, by the combined forces of Spain and France, being contemplated, Don Juan Manuel de Cagigal was employed in the former service, and Galvez sailed for Hispaniola, where the combined forces were to assemble, with the view of taking the command of those of Spain.

On the departure of the captain-general, the government of the province was provisionally vested in Don Estevan Miro, colonel of the royal armies.

Cagigal sailed from Havana, in the spring, with three regiments and a large train of artillery; and on the twenty-eighth of May, 1782, the captain-general of the Bahama islands (John Maxwell) signed a capitulation, by which they were surrendered to the arms of the Catholic king.

The war, and the capture of the British forts on the Mississippi, had deprived the planters of Louisiana of the great advantages they derived from the illicit trade carried on by British traders. On the representation of Galvez, considerable privileges were granted to the commerce of the province, on the twenty-second of January, by a schedule which was published in New Orleans in the spring.

In the preamble of this document, the king states that his royal solicitude and wishes have always been to secure to his vassals the utmost felicity, and to enable them to enjoy the advantages of a free trade; that he had never lost sight of so important an object in the regulations he had made for the commerce of his vast dominions in the Indies—firmly persuaded that the protection of trade and industry has a great influence on the wealth and prosperity of a nation. His majesty then adds, that the province of Louisiana has particularly merited his royal attention, since its annexation to his dominions. His paternal love for its inhabitants had induced him to give them repeated proofs that a change of government had not diminished their happiness. But, notwithstanding the favors and exemptions he had been pleased to grant to them, on several occasions, particularly by the regulations of the commerce of the Indies, made on the twenty-eighth day of October, 1778, experience had shown that the advantages he had contemplated were not realized; and the trade in peltries, of that province, with the numerous nations of Indians who surround it, and the articles of exportation to Europe, which the country produces, demanded new regulations. Accordingly, and with the view of rewarding the zeal and fidelity of the colonists, during the late campaigns for the recovery of the territories lately possessed by Great Britain, on the Mississippi and the Gulf of Mexico, the following favors and privileges are granted to the province of Louisiana:

1. Permission is given, during a period of ten years, to be computed from the day on which peace may be proclaimed, to all vessels of the king's subjects in the province of Louisiana, bound to New Orleans or

Pensacola, to sail directly with their cargoes from any of the ports of France, in which a Spanish consul resides, and to return thereto with peltries or the produce of Louisiana or West Florida, (except specie, the exportation of which, in this way, is absolutely forbidden) under the express condition that a detailed invoice of all the merchandise on board, signed by the consul, shall be delivered by him, in a sealed cover, to the captain, to be presented by the latter at the customhouse of the place of destination.

2. In case of urgent necessity in the colony, the existence of which necessity is to be certified by the governor and intendant, permission is given to the colonists to resort to any port in the French West India islands.

3. To encourage the commerce of the province to the ports of the peninsula to which it is allowed, permission is given to export, from New Orleans and Pensacola, any species of merchandise directly imported there from Spain, to be landed in any port within the king's American dominions, to which trade is allowed, paying only the duty with which such merchandise would have been charged on its exportation from the peninsula, according to the regulation of the twelfth of October, 1778; but the exportation of foreign merchandise imported into Louisiana, is forbidden.

4. An exemption from duty is granted, during the same period, on negroes imported into Louisiana or West Florida; and permission is given to procure them in the colonies of neutral or allied powers, in exchange for produce or specie; paying only for such produce and specie, the duties mentioned in the seventh article.

5. In order that the colonists may fully enjoy the favors and privileges now granted, they are permitted during the term of two years, to be computed from the proclamation of peace in New Orleans, to purchase foreign vessels free from duty, and such vessels are to be considered as Spanish bottoms.

6. The exportation of pipe and barrel staves from Louisiana to Spain, is permitted, free from duty.

7. It being just that commerce should contribute to the charges of the the colony, and the expenses it occasions, a duty of six per cent. is laid on all merchandise exported and imported by the king's subjects in the peninsula, Louisiana, and West Florida, according to a moderate assessment.

8. Customhouses are to be established in New Orleans and Pensacola.

The preliminary articles of peace between the United States and Great Britain were signed at Paris, on the thirteenth of November.

Le Breton and Morales were the ordinary alcades for the year 1783, and the following one.

Rodriguez succeeded Mazange in the clerkship of the cabildo.

The king having directed Galvez to select a brigadier-general of his armies, to act as captain-general of the province of Louisiana during Galvez' absence on the intended expedition against Jamaica, he made choice of Don Joseph de Espeleta.

The preliminary articles of peace between Great Britain, France, and Spain, were signed at Paris, on the twentieth of January.

The definitive treaties between Great Britain, the United States, and Spain, were signed at Paris, on the third day of September.

By the first, the king of Great Britain acknowledged the independence of the United States, and recognized, as their southern boundary, a line to be drawn due east from a point in the river Mississippi, in the latitude of thirty-one degrees, north of the equator, to the middle of the river Apalachicola or Cataouche; thence along the middle thereof to its junction with Flint river; thence straight to the head of St. Mary's river; and thence down along the middle of St. Mary's river to the Atlantic ocean.

The description of this line is important, as it became the dividing one between the possessions of Spain and the United States.

By the eighth article, it was expressly provided that the navigation of the Mississippi, from its source to the gulf, should forever remain free and open to the subjects of Great Britain and the citizens of the United States.

By the second, Great Britain warranted the province of West Florida, and ceded that of East Florida to Spain. Eighteen months were given to British subjects, settled in these provinces, from the date of the ratification of the treaty, to sell their property, receive their dues, and transport their persons and effects, without molestation on account of religion, or under any other pretext whatever, excepting that of debt or crime.

The claims of Spain and the United States, under this treaty, were not easy to be reconciled, and soon opened a source of contention, which lasted for a series of years. The Catholic king, under an actual possession, and the guarantee of Great Britain, laid claim to all the territory as far as the mouth of the river Yazoo. We have seen, in a preceding chapter of this work, that immediately after the peace of 1762, on possession being taken by Great Britain, the northern boundary of West Florida was fixed at the thirty-first degree of north latitude; but was afterwards extended to a line drawn due east from the mouth of Yazoo river, in latitude 32. 28. with the view of comprehending, within the limits of the province, some important settlements—Spain contending that the limits being then fixed in the commission of the British governor, had continued the same until the signature of the treaty.

The claim of the United States to the navigation of the Mississippi below their southern boundary was also resisted. The Catholic king, as owner of both banks of the stream, claimed the exclusive ownership of it, and the consequent right of preventing other nations from navigating it.

The United States contended they had the right of going as far as the southern boundary assigned to them by their title—it being a natural one; because the definitive treaties between Great Britain and Spain and them, bearing the same date, that of the preliminary articles ought to be resorted to in order to ascertain the priority of right; and Spain could not urge a warranty stipulated in her preliminary articles against the United States, who had a previous title from her warrantor.

In support of their claim to the navigation of the Mississippi to the gulf, the United States contended that Spain derived every right which she had to the river and its navigation from France, under a treaty posterior to the one by which the latter power had ceded to Great Britain the right of navigating the stream to the gulf; that the United States having succeeded to the rights of Great Britain to the left bank above the bayou Manshac, had equally done so to that of its navigation; which right, moreover, had been expressly ceded by Great Britain in the latter treaty.

The first proposition was not, perhaps, absolutely correct, Great Britain not having ceded her right, but merely a participation in it.

CHAPTER XIX.

THE ordinary alcades on the first of January, 1785, were Forstall and Kernion.

Early in this year, Galvez received a commission of captain-general of the island of Cuba, and of the provinces of Louisiana and East and West Florida, which superseded Espeleta's. In the summer, on the death of his father, he was promoted to the viceroyalty of Mexico, but retained the captain-generalship of Louisiana and the Floridas.

There being a number of persons in the province affected with leprosy, the cabildo erected an hospital for their reception in the rear of the city, on a ridge of high land between it and bayou St. John, which is probably the ridge anciently separating the waters of the Mississippi from those of lake Pontchartrain.

Miro now received and executed a commission of judge of residence of Unzaga.

Residence is a term, which, in the jurisprudence of Spain, is used to designate an inquiry which takes place into the official conduct of any public functionary, whenever by death, removal, or any other cause, he has ceased to execute the duties of his office. The decision of a judge of residence is reviewed on appeal by the council of the Indies. The inquiry is made at the principal place of the district in which the late officer exercised his functions. One would suppose that the fear which the investigation of every act, public or private, of an officer whom any one may accuse, and who is given up, in some measure to every species of reproach and vexation, even from envy and malice, would insure the zealous and upright discharge of his duties; that those who are governed by an officer surrounded by a vigilance which a thousand motives may call into activity, would find in the residence, the most effectual safeguard against his passions, his avarice, and his partiality. And yet, there is no part of the world where abuses of authority are of more frequent occurrence than in the Spanish provinces; and the rapidity with which officers amass large fortunes, is an evidence that there is no obstacle which the love of gain will not surmount, and that the same want of principle which prompts the commission of dishonest acts, will also suggest the means of avoiding their consequences. If any officer thinks of the residence, it is to intimidate those whom he might fear, or to purchase their silence. There is a league between all persons in places subjected to a censure, which has always caused it to degenerate into a mere formality.

An accurate census of the inhabitants of Louisiana and West Florida was taken this year, by order of Galvez, which produced the following results:

Within the city of New Orleans,	4,980
From the Balize to the city,	2,100
At the Terre-aux-Bœufs,	576
On the bayous St. John and Gentilly,	678
Tchoupitoulas,	7,046
Parish of St. Charles,	1,903
CARRIED OVER,	17,283

BROUGHT OVER,	17,283	
St. John the Baptist,	1,300	
St. James	1,332	
Lafourche,	646	
Lafourche, interior,	352	
Iberville,	673	
Pointe Coupée,	1,521	
Opelousas,	1,211	
Attakapas,	1,070	
New Iberia,	125	
Washita .	207	
Rapides,	88	
Avoyelles,	287	
Natchitoches,	756	
Arkansas,	196	
In Lower Louisiana,		27,046
St. Genevieve,	694	
St. Louis,	897	
In Upper Louisiana,		1,591
Manshac,	77	
Galveston	242	
Baton Rouge,	270	
Natchez,	1,550	
Mobile,	746	
Pensacola,	592	
In West Florida		3,477
Grand Total		32,114

Deducting, from the grand total, 3,477 persons, the population of West Florida, and 1,053, the number of those brought, at the king's expense, from the Canary islands and Malaga, there remains a balance of 27,584 souls; which show that the population, at the arrival of O'Reilly, in 1769, was more than doubled in sixteen years by ordinary means.

The number of white persons was 14,217; that of colored free ones, 1,203; that of slaves, 16,594.

A statement was made by the intendant, by order of the captain-general, of the expenses of the province for this year, and is as follows:

ETAT MAJOR.

The governor and captain-general's salary,	$10,000
Assessor of government	2,000
Secretary of government	1,000
First clerk in the secretary's office	600
Town Major	1,200
Aid Major,	740
Adjutant	600
English interpreter,	480
Surveyor-general,	420
Boat's patroon and seamen,	1,380
CARRIED OVER,	$18,420

BROUGHT OVER, ...		$18,420
Officers attached to no particular corps, . . .		
Colonel, with lieutenant-colonel's pay, . . .		1,752
Lieutenant-colonel, ...		1,752
Two lieutenant-colonels with rank, but pay of $372 only, .		744
Four captains, . , ...		1,584
One captain, ...		240
Twelve lieutenants, ...		4,320
Four sub-lieutenants, ...		1,152

ARTILLERY.

A company complete, ...		18,417
A storekeeper		540
An assistant storekeeper, ...		300
A master armorer, ...		220

INFANTRY.

A regiment of infantry, ...		300,838

DRAGOONS.

A company complete, ...		11,230
A house for their barracks, ...		350

CARABINIERS.

An adjutant, ...		330

MILITIA.

An adjutant major, ...		728
A second do.		240
Seven serjeants and four corporals, . . .		1,878
A major commandant of free people of color, . .		240

FORTIFICATIONS.

A director, storekeeper, surveyor of the works, and two servants,		1,620

REVENUE DEPARTMENT.

Intendancy.

An intendant, ...		4,000
Assessor, ...		1,500
Secretary and two clerks, ...		1,100
Office expenses, ...		200
Notary of the marine, ...		500
A boat and crew, ...		1,380

COMPTROLLER'S OFFICE.

A comptroller, (contador)		1,600
Four clerks, ...		1,950
Office expenses, ...		100

TREASURY.

A treasurer, ...		1,200
Two clerks, ...		700
Office rent and expenses, ...		800

CUSTOMHOUSE.

A collector, ...		1,200
Comptroller, ...		1,000

CARRIED OVER, ...	$384,125

33

BROUGHT OVER, ...	$384,125
Cashier, ...	800
Four clerks, ...	1,550
A searcher, ...	700
Guard major, ...	600
Twelve guards, ...	2,400
Boat and crew, ...	1,104

ROYAL HOSPITAL.

A comptroller, $600; commissary, $300, . .	900
Steward, $480; physician, $600, . . .	1,080
Chaplain, $480; first surgeon, $600, . . .	1,080
Assistant surgeon; $360, mate, $192, . .	552
Two minor surgeons; $360, apothecary, $480, . .	840
Apothecary's servant, attendants and cook, . .	964
Provisions and medicines, ...	18,000

SCHOOLS.

A director, ...	700
Two masters, ...	1,050

CHURCH ESTABLISHMENT.

New Orleans, a curate, $480; four assistants, $1,260, .	1,740
Terre-aux-Bœufs, a curate, ...	240
St. Charles, a curate; St. John the Baptist, a curate, .	480
St. James, a curate; Ascension, a curate, . .	480
Iberville, a curate; Pointe Coupée, a curate, . .	480
Attakapas, a curate; Opelousas, a curate, . .	480
Natchitoches, a curate; Natchez, a curate, . .	480
St. Louis, a curate; St. Genevieve, a curate, . .	480
Galvezton, a curate and Sacristan, $540, expenses, $50, .	590
Allowance for wax lights to country parishes, . .	300
Boarding of six nuns, at the king's expense, . .	720
Boarding of twelve orphan girls, . . .	360

CABILDO.

Six regidors, ...	300

POSTS.

Balize—a pilot, $200; two patroons, $240, . .	440
Sixteen seamen, each $72, ...	1,152
Head pilot, ...	360
Allowance for seamen and troops, purchase of boat, etc., .	4,500
Natchez, a garrison and sixty men, . . .	6,000
Adjutant, ...	480

ST. LOUIS.

An adjutant, $510; two storekeepers, $738, . .	1,248
A surgeon, $360; Indian presents, $214, . .	574

CIVIL COMMANDANTS.

Two who do not belong to the army, . . .	200
A keeper of boats in town, ...	180
Extra expenses, ...	10,000

Total expenses in Louisiana, . .	$449,389

BROUGHT OVER, ...		$449,389

MOBILE.

A governor, $2,000; chaplain $360, . . .		2,360
Sacristan, $180; chapel expenses, $50, . . .		230
English interpreter, $180; storekeeper, $600, . .		780
Adjutant, $300; guard, $180, ...		480
Adjutant of artillery, $300; armorer, $360, . .		660
Surgeon, mate, and nurses, ...		1,140
Patroon and hands of city launches, . . .		1,296

DAUPHINE ISLAND.

A pilot and four sailors, ...		696

CATTLE PLANTATION.

A herdsman, an assistant, and a laborer, . .		900
Extra expenses, ...		5,000

PENSACOLA.

A governor, $3000; town-major, $900, . . .		3,900
Adjutant, $720; his aid, $600, ...		1,320
Storekeeper,$ 600; engineer, $1,180, . . .		1,780
Armorer, $360; adjutant of artillery, $420, . .		780
Blacksmith, $350; keeper of the works, $240, . .		800
Military storekeeper and assistants, . . .		1,200
Comptroller, $1,200; two clerks, $780; office expenses, $50,		2,030
Treasurer, $1,200; clerk, $360; office expenses, $50, .		1,610
Hospital director, $780; steward, $360, . . .		1,140
Surgeon, $780; mate, 440; two aids, $600, . .		1,820
Apothecary, $600; an assistant, $300. . . .		900
Four nurses and a cook, ...		1,080
A curate, $440; assistant, $360, ...		800
Sacristan, $180; chapel expenses, $50, . . .		230
Pilot, $330; patroon, $144; twelve sailors, $1,440, .		1,884
A carpenter, cooper and caulker, $360 each, . .		1,080
Extra expenses, ...		12,000
New settlers and Indian affairs, . . .		
A contador, $600; two clerks, $960, . . .		2,560
House rent, $180; office expenses, $50, . . .		230
Storekeeper, $360; commissioner, $360, . .		720
Interpreter, $540; assistant, $300, . . .		840
A surgeon at Terre-aux-Bœufs, ...		360
A commandant, $300; surgeon, $360, Galvezton, .		660
A surgeon, $360; commissary, $180, Valenzuela, .		540
A pensioner, ...		320
An armorer at New Orleans, ...		300
Indian interpreters at Natchez, Natchitoches, and Pointe Coupée		372
Interpreter and armorer at Arkansas, . . .		276
Interpreter and armorer at St. Louis, . . .		340
Commissary and armorer at Mobile, . . .		1,080
A storekeeper and two interpreters at Pensacola . .		1,620
Presents and extra expenses, ...		29,782

		$537,285

Let us contrast these expenses with those of a republican state, that of North Carolina, in the preceding year:

The governor,	$ 2,000
Private secretary,	400
Council of state,	200
Secretary of state,	350
Comptroller,	1,600
His five clerks,	1,100
Stationery,	200
Three judges of the supreme court,	5,200
Attorney-general,	1,320
Three delegates in congress,	6,720
Treasurer,	1,400
Clerks and stationery,	1,400
Ten boards of auditors,	4,800
Commissioners of account,	240
The legislature,	30,000
Public printer,	1,000
	$56,930

The population of North Carolina was, at this period, 377,721 persons; so that her expenses were that year a little more than fifteen cents per head—while those of Louisiana were sixteen dollars and fifty-five cents. Those expenditures, in the first case, were paid by the inhabitants; in the latter, by the sovereign.

An attempt was made to introduce the Inquisition into the province. A clergyman of New Orleans received a commission of commissary of the holy office in Louisiana. Miro had it particularly in charge not to allow the exercise of any inquisitorial functions, within the colony committed to his care. He gave early information of this to the commissary, who thought himself bound to attend to the orders of his spiritual, rather than those of his temporal, superiors: and one night, whilst he was peaceably slumbering, he was disturbed by an officer heading eighteen grenadiers, who lodged him on board of a vessel, which, at break of day, sailed with him to Spain.

According to an arrangement between the courts of France and Spain, the province received this year a very considerable accession of population, by the arrival of a number of Acadian families, who were supported by the French king, and came over to join their friends who had migrated to Louisiana, as we have already mentioned, in 1755. They settled mostly on both sides of the Mississippi river, near Plaquemines; but a number of the families went to increase the settlement on Terre-aux-Bœufs, on the bayou Lafourche, and in the districts of Attakapas and Opelousas.

The period of eighteen months, which had been granted to British settlers to sell their property, collect their debts, and remove their persons and effects from East and West Florida, by the late treaty between Spain and Great Britain, being expired, Miro, with the approbation of Galvez, extended the time, to settlers in West Florida, till the pleasure of the king was known.

The royal schedule of 1782, had revived the trade of New Orleans; and a number of commercial houses from France had established themselves there. The planters, however, regretted the time when British vessels plied on the Mississippi, stopping before every house, furnishing the farmer with whatever he wanted, accepting in payment whatever the latter had to spare, and extending a credit almost unlimited in extent and duration. A number of agents had arrived from Jamaica to collect debts due to merchants of that island, the recovery of which had been impeded during the war. As the trade these creditors had carried on could not now be continued, they pressed for settlement and payment. In some cases legal coercion was resorted to; but Miro with as much prudence as Unzaga on a similar occasion, exerted his influence to procure some respite for those who were really unable to comply with their engagements, and allowed a resort to the last extremity against those only, whose bad faith appeared to require it. Instances are related, in which, unable to obtain a creditor's indulgence for an honest debtor, he satisfied the former out of his own purse.

The cabildo made choice of Orue and Dufossat for ordinary alcades, on the first of January, 1786.

By a royal order, issued at the Pardo on the fifth of April, the king approved the conduct of Miro in the indulgence granted last year to the British subjects at Baton Rouge and Natchez, and declared his will that permission might be granted to such individuals, residing in Louisiana and Florida, to remain where they were on taking an oath of allegiance and fidelity, provided they should not move out of their respective districts without the permission of the governor. Those who neglected to take the oath, were to depart by sea for some of the colonies of North America; and if they were unable to defray the expenses of the voyage, it was to be paid by the king, who was to be reimbursed, as far as possible, by the sale of their property.

The king further ordered that at Natchez and other places, where it might be done conveniently, parishes might be formed and put under the direction of Irish clergymen, in order to bring over the inhabitants and their families to the Catholic faith, by the mildness and persuasion it recommends. For this purpose the king wrote to the bishop of Salamanca, to choose four priests, natives of Ireland, of approved zeal, virtue and learning from among those of his university to be sent to Louisiana at the king's expense.

Miro, on whom the provisional government had devolved on the departure of Galvez, now received a commission of governor, civil and military, of Louisiana and West Florida, and issued his *bando de buen gobierno* on the second of June.

A *bando de buen gobierno*, is a proclamation which the governor of a Spanish colony generally issues on assuming its government to make known the principles by which he intends to direct his conduct, and to introduce necessary alterations into the ordinances of police.

In this document Miro begins by stating that religion being the object of the wise laws of Spain, and a reverend demeanor in church a consequence of it, the bishop having lately published an edict with regard to the respect and devotion with which the faithful are to attend the celebration of the holy mysteries, the proceedings of the vicar-general against delinquents will receive every necessary aid from government. Working on the Sabbath and other holy festivals is prohibited, except in cases of necessity, without the license of the vicar. He forbids the doors of shops or stores being kept open during the hours of divine service, and the dances of slaves on the public square, on those days, before the close of the evening service.

He declares his intention to proceed with severity against all persons living in concubinage. He observes, that the idleness of free negro, mulatto, and quarteroon women, resulting from their dependence for a livelihood on incontinence and libertinage, will not be tolerated. He recommends them to renounce their mode of living, and to betake themselves to honest labor; and declares his determination to have those who neglect his recommendation, sent out of the province—warning them that he will consider their excessive attention to dress, as an evidence of their misconduct.

He complains that the distinction which had been established in the head dress of females of color, is disregarded, and urges that it is useful to enforce it; forbids them to wear thereon any plumes or jewelry, and directs them to wear their hair bound in a handkerchief.

He announces that the laws against gambling and duelling, and against those who carry about their persons, dirks, pistols and other arms, shall be rigorously enforced.

The nightly assemblages of people of color are prohibited.

The inhabitants of the city are forbidden to leave it, either by land or water, without a passport; and those who leave the province are to give security for the payment of their debts.

Persons coming in, by land or water, are to present themselves at the government house.

Those who harbor convicts, or deserters, from the land or naval service, are to be punished.

Any large concourse of people, without the knowledge of government, is inhibited.

None are to walk out at night without urgent necessity, and not then without a light.

No house or apartment to be rented to a slave.

Tavern keepers are to shut their houses at regular hours, and not to sell spirituous liquors to Indians, soldiers or slaves.

Purchases from soldiers, Indians, convicts, or slaves are prohibited.

Regulations are made to prevent forestalling, hogs running at large in the streets, to restrain the keeping too great a number of dogs, and the removal of dead animals.

Measures are taken to guard against conflagrations, for draining the streets, and keeping the landing on the levee unobstructed.

Verbal sales of slaves are forbidden.

Don Pedro Piernas succeeded Miro as colonel of the regiment of Louisiana.

At the close of the war, there had been considerable migrations to the banks of the Ohio and the western part of Virginia. A district had here been formed called Kentucky, the population of which exceeded twelve thousand souls. There was also a large number of settlers in the state of North Carolina, on the western side of the mountains, and many had sat down on the banks of Cumberland river. These found the inconvenience of their situation, from the immense distance of the seat of government, near the shore of the Atlantic. so grievous, that in the preceding year they had made an attempt to erect themselves into a separate government under the style of the state of Franklin.

The people of Kentucky had the same wish, and those of Virginia were not averse to its gratification. They enjoyed no part of the attention of general government. Their communication with the Atlantic was obstructed by an immense wilderness and lofty mountains; and where these obstacles were surmounted, the distance to a sea port was still immense. The climate was favorable to agriculture; and although their land produced much more than they could consume, they could find no market for the surplus. Attempts had been made to seek one on the Mississippi, but their boats had been met and seized by Spanish officers ascending the stream with supplies for St. Louis. A convention of the people met at Danville to deliberate on the propriety of an application to congress, soliciting admission into the Union as an independent state; but the majority of that body concluded that the population of the district was too small and sparse to support the expenses of a separate government. Congress seemed unwilling to take any measure to procure them a free navigation of the Mississippi.

Chabert and Reggio were the ordinary alcades for the year 1787.

The population of the district of Opelousas and Attakapas was heretofore supposed to be so inconsiderable, that it had been thought one commandant was sufficient for both. Don Nicholas Forstall, a regidor, was now appointed commandant of the former, and the Chevalier de Clouet, who before presided over both, was left in charge of the latter. On his departure, Forstall claimed the right, as he was leaving the cabildo on the king's service, to appoint a lieutenant, in proxy, to represent him in it; but that body refused to recognize such a right.

The four Irish priests from the seminary of Salamanca, chosen by the bishop, according to the request of the king, reached New Orleans, and were sent to Baton Rouge, Natchez, and other parts of the territory conquered from Great Britain, during the last war.

Although no treaty had been entered into between the United States and the Catholic king, the latter had sent a minister to the former. This gentleman, Don Diego de Guardoqui, now formed a plan for encouraging migration from the district of Kentucky and the western part of North Carolina, to the right bank of the Mississippi, between the settlements near the river Arkansas and those near the Missouri. George Morgan, of Pennsylvania, who offered himself as the leader of the emigrants, received the grant of a large tract of land, on which he laid the foundation of a city, which he dignified with the name of New Madrid. A company of infantry, under the orders of Pierre Foucher, was sent from New Orleans to build and garrison a fort near the intended site of the city.

At the same time, Don Diego admitted the proposition of the Baron de Steuben, a general officer, who, having served the United States with distinction during the late war, had, together with other officers of rank, and a number of respectable citizens of the United States, solicited an extensive tract of country on the same bank of the Mississippi, for the purpose of establishing a military colony, chiefly composed of such persons as were lately in the army, and were left without employment, on its disbandment. The cabinet of Madrid, however, did not think proper to encourage the formation of a colony, composed of such materials, in the Spanish dominions.

Morgan's plan had but a partial execution.

The foundation was now laid of a commercial intercourse, through the Mississippi, between the United States and New Orleans, which has been continued, with but little interruption, to this day, and has increased to an immense degree; and, to the future extent of which the imagination can hardly contemplate any limit. Hitherto, the boats of the western people, venturing on the Mississippi, were arrested by the first Spanish officer who met them; and confiscation ensued, in every case; all communication between the citizens of the United States and the Spaniards, being strictly prohibited. Now and then, an emigrant, desirous of settling in the district of Natchez, by personal entreaty and the solicitations of his friends, obtained a tract of land, with permission to settle on it with his family, slaves, farming utensils, and furniture. He was not allowed to bring anything to sell without paying an enormous duty. An unexpected incident changed the face of affairs, in this respect.

The idea of a regular trade was first conceived by general Wilkinson, who had served with distinction as an officer in the late war, and whose name is as conspicuous in the annals of the west, as any other. He had connected with it a scheme for the settlement of several thousand American families in that part of the present state of Louisiana, now known as the parishes of East and West Feliciana, and that of Washita, and on White river and other streams of the present territory of Arkansas. For those services to the Spanish government, he expected to obtain the privilege of introducing, yearly, a considerable quantity of tobacco into the Mexican market.

With a view to the execution of his plan, Wilkinson descended the Mississippi, with an adventure of tobacco, flour, butter and bacon. He stopped at Natchez while his boat was floating down the stream to New Orleans, the commandant at the former place having been induced to forbear seizing it, from an apprehension that such a step would be disapproved by Miro, who might be desirous of showing some indulgence to a general officer of a nation with whom his was at peace—especially as the boat and its owner were proceeding to New Orleans, where he could act towards them as he saw fit.

Wilkinson, having stopped at a plantation on the river, the boat reached the city before him. On its approaching the levee, a guard was immediately sent on board, and the revenue officers were about taking measures for its seizure, when a merchant, who was acquainted with Wilkinson and had some influence with Miro, represented to him that the step Navarro was about to take might be attended with unpleasant consequences; that the people of Kentucky were already much exasperated at the conduct of the Spaniards in seizing all the property of those who navigated the Mississippi, and if this system was pursued, they would probably, in spite of congress, take means themselves to open the navigation of the river by force. Hints were, at the same time, thrown out, that the general was a very popular character among those who were capable of inflaming the whole of the western people, and that probably, his sending a boat before him, that it might be seized, was a scheme laid by the government of the United States, that he might on his return, influence the minds of his countrymen; and, having brought them to the point he wished, induce them to choose him for their leader, and, spreading over the country, carry fire and desolation from one part of Louisiana to the other.

On this, Miro expressed his wish to Navarro that the guard might be removed. This was done; and Wilkinson's friend was permitted to take charge of the boat, and sell the cargo, without paying any duty.

On his first interview with Miro, Wilkinson, that he might not derogate from the character his friend had given him, by appearing concerned in so trifling an adventure as a boatload of tobacco, flour, etc., observed that the cargo belonged to several of his fellow citizens in Kentucky who wished to avail themselves of his visit to New Orleans to make a trial of the temper of the colonial government. On his return he could then inform the United States government of the steps taken under his eye; so that in future proper measures might be adopted. He acknowledged with gratitude the attention and respect manifested towards himself, and the favor shown to the merchant who had been permitted to take care of the boat; adding, he did not wish that the intendant should expose himself to the anger of the court, by forbearing to seize the boat and cargo, if such were his instructions, and he had no authority to depart from them when circumstances might require it.

Miro supposed, from this conversation, that Wilkinson's object was to produce a rupture rather than to avoid one. He became more and more alarmed. For two or three years before, particularly since the commissioners of the state of Georgia came to Natchez to claim the country, he had been fearful of an invasion at every rise of the water; and the rumor of a few boats having been seen together on the Ohio was sufficient to excite his apprehensions. At his next interview with Wilkinson, having procured further information of the character, number, and disposition of the western people, and having resolved, in his mind, what measures he could take, consistently with his instructions, he concluded that he could do no better than to hold out a hope to Wilkinson, in order to secure his influence in restraining his countrymen from an invasion of Louisiana, till further instructions could be received from Madrid. The general sailed in September for Philadelphia.

A lucrative trade had begun to be carried on between New Orleans and that city, at which the colonial government appeared to wink. Guardoqui, however, finding that he did not participate in the profits of this new branch of commerce, his friends not obtaining the consignment of the vessels engaged in it, notwithstanding various hints and threats thrown out to the captains and supercargoes, procured a list of the names of the vessels, captains and owners in New Orleans, real or pretended, and forwarded it to Navarro, with a severe reprimand; adding, that he had informed the court of the disregard of the laws in Louisiana. He so worked upon the fears of the intendant, that, apprehensive of losing his place if he did not recur to severe measures, the latter prosecuted, with apparent impartiality and unrelenting rigor, all those against whom information was lodged, seizing vessels on their arrival, confiscating their cargoes, and imprisoning the owners, captains and crews. These were all condemned to the mines for various terms of years.

The spirit of the government and the venality of its officers was, however, apparent. The favorites of those with whom the officers had connexions in business escaped by bringing proofs that were thought sufficient to destroy those sent by Guardoqui, by receiving timely notice of their danger, by orders forwarded to the commandant at the Balize to favor them, by not suffering them to enter, and allowing those who had

34

entered, but not reached New Orleans, to return and put back to sea, with such part of their cargoes as they could not conveniently land on the plantations along the banks of the river—the owners having ordered those vessels to foreign ports, pretended they were lost during their voyage, and they were ignorant of any thing concerning them since they left New Orleans.

It was the practice in Spanish colonies to condemn all contraband traders to the mines; but in such cases the law was rarely carried into execution when there had been no violent resistance or blood shed. The offender was, however, imprisoned, and after a short time, suffered to escape—the jailor reporting him as runaway or dead. Some of the persons who were thus condemned and imprisoned in New Orleans, were soon after liberated. A few were permitted to command other vessels, after having made some change or alteration in their names. One of them who had been imprisoned and returned as dead, by the gaoler, went to Madrid where he obtained the review and reversal of the sentence against him, and came back to New Orleans.

The congress of the United States this year erected the territory to the northwest of the Ohio into a distinct government, at the head of which they placed Arthur St. Clair, an officer of the late revolution, and once their president.

CHAPTER XX.

The ordinary alcades, for the year 1788, were Foucher and Argotte, Pedesclaux now succeeded Rodriguez in the office of clerk of the cabildo, which he held during the remainder of the Spanish government in Louisiana.

On the twenty-first of March, (Good Friday) the chapel of a Spaniard, in Chartres street, New Orleans, took fire about three o'clock in the afternoon; and, the wind being very high at the time, a conflagration ensued, which, in a few hours consumed nine hundred houses, and other property of immense value.

In order to relieve the inhabitants in some degree, from the distress into which this event had plunged them, the colonial government made a large contract for flour, to be purchased within the United States, on which it made great advances in money; and in order to induce contractors to deliver it on the best terms, the privilege was allowed them of introducing an unlimited quantity of merchandise on paying the usual duty. Guardoqui, finding that the information he had given made him enemies in the United States, that the colonial government had seized the opportunity presented by the late conflagration, to release all the individuals imprisoned in consequence of the prosecutions he had instigated during the preceding year, and to restore the property confiscated, (a measure approved by the king, to whom a representation had been made by his officers in Louisiana), and that no benefit could result to him from continuing his interference, desisted from any further attempt to obstruct the commercial intercourse between Philadelphia and New Orleans; and his agents induced by motives of prudence, and perhaps by a share in the profits, did every thing in their power to augment it.

Miro now received and executed a commission of judge of residence of Galvez.

On the eighth of August, Wilkinson's agent in New Orleans procured from the colonial government, permission to send to the city one or more launches loaded with tobacco from Kentucky.

Several individuals from the Wabash, Kentucky and Cumberland rivers, came to Louisiana to ascertain whether their migration to the province would be allowed, and to view the country. They were informed that they would be permitted to introduce their property; such as was for sale, paying a duty of twenty-five per cent; that their slaves, stock, provisions for two years, and farming implements, would be free from duty; that land would be granted and protection afforded them, as long as they demeaned themselves well.

A census, which was taken this year, presents the following results:

Within the city of New Orleans,	5,338	
From the Balize to the city	2,378	
At the Terre-aux-Bœufs,	661	
On the bayous St. John and Gentilly,	772	
Barataria,	40	
Tchoupitoulas	7,589	
Parish of St. Charles,	2,381	
St. John the Baptist,	1,368	
St. James,	1,559	
Lafourche,	1,164	
Lafourche, interior,	1,500	
Iberville,	944	
Pointe Coupée,	2,004	
Opelousas,	1,985	
Attakapas,	2,541	
New Iberia,	190	
Washita,	232	
Rapides,	147	
Avoyelles,	209	
Natchitoches	1,021	
Arkansas,	119	
In Lower Louisiana,		34,142
St. Genevieve,	896	
St. Louis,	1,197	
In Upper Louisiana,		2,093
Manshac,	284	
Galvezton,	268	
Baton Rouge,	682	
Feliciana,	730	
Natchez,	2,679	
Mobile,	1,368	
Pensacola,	265	6,376
Total,		42,611

The increase between the census of 1785, which gave a grand total of 32,114, is 10,497, in three years; which is about thirty-one and a half per cent. This is, perhaps, accounted for, by the accession of population brought by the Acadians since the first census. The increase in Iberville, Manshac, Lafourche, Opelousas and Attakapas, the parts of the province in which these people settled, presents an increase of fifty-one per cent. The number of Acadian emigrants may in this way be reckoned at about 3,500.

The number of white persons was 19,445; that of free persons of color, 1,701; that of slaves, 21,465.

Don Martin Navarro, the intendant, now left the province for Spain; and the two offices of intendant and governor were united in the person of Miro. Navarro's last communication to the king, was a memorial which he had prepared, by order of the minister, on the danger to be apprehended by Spain, in her American colonies, from the emancipation of the late British provinces on the Atlantic. In this document, he dwells much on the ambition of the United States, and their thirst for conquest; whose views he states to be an extension of territory to the shores of the Pacific ocean; and suggests the dismemberment of the western country, by means of pensions and the grant of commercial privileges, as the most proper means, in the power of Spain, to arrest the impending danger. To effect this, was not, in his opinion very difficult. The attempt was therefore strongly recommended, as success would greatly augment the power of Spain, and forever arrest the progress of the United States to the west.

The suggestion was well received at Madrid, and became the ground work of the policy which thereafter actuated the court of Spain.

It would not have been difficult for the king of Spain, at this period, to have found, in Kentucky, citizens of the United States ready to come into his views. The people of that district met this year, in a second convention, and agreed on a petition to congress for the redress of their grievances: the principal of which was, the occlusion of the Mississippi. Under the apprehension that the interference of congress could not be obtained, or might be fruitless, several expedients were talked of, no one of which was generally approved; the people being divided into no less than five parties, all of which had different, if not opposite, views.

The first was for independence of the United States, and the formation of a new republic, unconnected with them, who was to enter into a treaty with Spain.

Another party was willing that the country should become a part of the province of Louisiana, and submit to the admission of the laws of Spain.

A third desired a war with Spain, and the seizure of New Orleans.

A fourth plan was to prevail on congress, by a show of preparation for war, to extort from the cabinet of Madrid, what it persisted in refusing.

The last, as unnatural as the second, was to solicit France to procure a retrocession of Louisiana, and extend her protection to Kentucky.

It was in the western part of the United States, that the inefficacy of the power vested in congress was most complained of. With a view of remedying this evil, a convention of deputies from all the states, except that of Rhode Island. met at Philadelphia; and, on the seventeenth of September, submitted to their fellow-citizens a plan of government for their adoption, calculated to effect a more perfect union, establish justice, insure domestic tranquillity, provide for the common defense, promote the general welfare, and secure the blessings of liberty to them and their posterity.

The choice of the cabildo, for ordinary alcades, for the years 1789 and 1790, fell on Ortega and Almonaster.

Don Andrew Almonaster succeeded Regnio as perpetual regidor and alferez real.

According to the king's order obtained by Forstall, Don Carlos de la Chaise took his seat in the cabildo, as lieutenant in the former.

Charles the third had died on the 14th of December last, in the seventy-second year of his age, and was succeeded by his son, Charles the fourth. Funeral rites were performed, in honor of the departed monarch, on the seventh of May, with as much pomp and solemnity as the smallness of the chapel of the hospital could admit of. This chapel, and that of the nuns, were the only places of worship which the conflagration had spared. On the next day, the new sovereign was proclaimed, under repeated discharges of artillery from the forts and shipping, and the acclamations of the colonists. At night, the city was brilliantly illuminated, and theatrical exhibitions were presented to the people.

Wilkinson visited New Orleans for the second time. Miro informed him he was instructed to permit the migration of settlers from the western country; but he was without information of his sovereign's will as to the grant of land for colonization, on the large scale proposed, or the introduction of tobacco into the viceroyalty of Mexico.

Accordingly, the colonial government granted several tracts of land to such settlers from the western part of the United States as presented themselves. They were favored with an exemption from duty, as to all the property they brought, invested in the produce of their country. Under the denomination of settlers, all those who had an acquaintance with any person of influence in New Orleans, obtained passports, and made shipments, which were admitted free from duty. Pretending to return in order to bring their families, they repeated the speculation several times. Others came with slaves and stock, and returned. A few only remained, and they were those who availed themselves the least of the immunities offered by the Spanish government. They had a few slaves and cattle, and but little of other property. They settled chiefly in the districts of Natchez and Feliciana, where they increased the culture of tobacco, which was the only article of exportation raised in this part of the province. The encouragement thus given to migration and speculation opened a market for the produce of Ohio. Flour was brought down from Pittsburgh; and the farmers, finding a vent for everything they could raise, their land rose in value, and industry was encouraged. Flour was then to be had on the Monongahela, at from eighteen to twenty shillings the barrel, ($2.40 to $2.66.) Its quality was so inferior, that it was used in times of scarcity only, or in making biscuit.

A number of Irish families were desirous of removing to Louisiana or the Floridas, in the hope that the king of Spain would afford them the same aid as had been extended to emigrants from the Canary islands and Malaga a few years before; but on their application, the captain-general was informed from Madrid, that no settlers could be admitted in either of those provinces, whose passage out, or whose maintenance for a limited time, would have to be paid out of the royal treasury; and those foreigners, only, could be received, who of their own free will, should present themselves and swear allegiance to the king. To such, land might be granted, and surveyed gratuitously, in proportion to the number of persons in the family; they were not to be molested on account of their religion, but no other mode of public worship was to be allowed than the Catholic; they were not to be required to bear arms, but in the defense of the province, should an enemy invade it. No other aid or assistance was to be given them, but land, protection and good treatment. They might bring with them property of any kind; but, in case of exporting it, they were to pay a duty of six per cent.

Few or no settlers emigrated from Ireland.

Don Louis de las Casas, a brigadier-general of the royal armies, was appointed captain-general of the Island of Cuba, and of the provinces of East and West Florida.

The bishopric of Cuba, of which the provinces of Louisiana, East and West Florida made a part, was divided. The southern part of the island was erected into the archbishopric of Cuba, and the northern into the bishopric of Havana, of which these provinces now made a part. Don Santiago Joseph de Tres Palacios was the first incumbent of the bishopric.

The people of the several states having adopted the constitution proposed by the late convention, the new government went into operation on the fourth of March of this year, under the auspices of general Washington, the first president of the United States.

The high ground taken by the British government on the attack of the settlements at Nootka Sound, and the vigor with which it armed to support its pretensions, furnished strong ground for the belief that a war would soon be commenced. In the United States, the juncture was considered as a favorable one, for urging their claim to the navigation of the Mississippi; and their charge des affaires at Madrid was instructed not only to press this point with earnestness, but to secure the unmolested use of that river in future, by obtaining a cession of the island on which New Orleans stands, and the Floridas.

The federal government was not yet ready to purchase this cession, for several millions of dollars, as it did afterwards. They expected that in the security of the friendship of the United States, and the security which would be given to the dominions of Spain on the west of the Mississippi, she would find a fair equivalent for the cession; as not only the United States would have no object in crossing the stream, but their real interest would require that Spain should retain the immense possession she claimed to the west.

Carmichael, the charge des affaires of the United States at Madrid, was further directed to draw the attention of the Catholic king's ministers to the peculiar situation of these states, to one-half of which the use of the Mississippi was so necessary, that no effort could prevent them from acquiring it. He was instructed to urge, that their doing so, by acting separately, or in conjunction with Great Britain, was one of those events which human wisdom would in vain attempt to prevent. To the serious consideration of the Spanish government, were submitted the consequences that would result to all the Spanish possessions in America, from hostilities with Great Britain, or the seizure of New Orleans by the United States.

The opinion that in the event of a war between Great Britain and Spain, Louisiana would be invaded from Canada, was not a mere suggestion for aiding the negotiations at Madrid; it was seriously contemplated by the

American government; and the attention of the executive was turned to the measures which would be proper to pursue, should application be made for permission to march a body of troops through the unsettled territory of the United States, into the dominions of Spain, or if such an attempt should be made without permission.

The western people continued loudly and justly to complain of the inattention of congress to the hostile temper of the Indians, to which an unusual degree of importance was given by the apprehension that it was fomented by the intrigues both of Great Britain and Spain. From Canada the northern Indians were understood to be supplied with the means of prosecuting a war, which they had been stimulated to continue; and to the influence of the governor of East Florida, and perhaps to that of Louisiana, had been partly attributed the late failure of a negotiation with the Creeks.

To conciliate the latter Indians, colonel Willet, a distinguished officer of the late revolution, was sent among them. He acquitted himself so well of the duties assigned to him, that the chiefs of that nation, with M'Gillivrey at their head, repaired to New York, where negotiations were immediately begun, and terminated by a treaty of peace on the seventh of August.

On the first information, at St. Augustine, that M'Gillivrey was about to proceed to New York, the intelligence was immediately conveyed to Las Casas, the captain-general at Havana, and the secretary of the government of East Floridas was sent at the same time with a large sum of money as it was said to purchase flour; but his real object was believed to be, to embarrass the negotiations with the Creeks. He was closely watched, and measures were taken to render any attempt he might make abortive.

The overtures the American government made to the Indians on the Wabash and the Miamis, were not so successful. The western frontiers of the middle states were still exposed to the destructive invasion of the savages, and there was reason to believe that the inhabitants could only be released from the terrors of the tomahawk and scalping knife, by the vigorous exertion of military force; and general Hammer was directed by the president of the United States to march against the Indians, bring them, if possible, to an engagement, but in any event to destroy their settlements on the Wabash and Scioto.

With three hundred and fifty regulars and a body of militia of eleven hundred men from the state of Virginia and the district of Kentucky, he received a check early in October; but finally succeeded in reducing to ashes the villages of the enemy on the Scioto, and destroying their winter provisions. He retreated without effecting anything on the Wabash, and the Indians were again successful in a second attack. The supineness of congress, who neglected, notwithstanding the recommendation of the president, to raise a force sufficient to the protection of the western people increased their discontents.

Congress this year accepted a cession made to the United States by North Carolina of all her lands on the western side of the mountain; and a distinct government was established for the people who dwelt to the southwest of the Ohio. It was called the Southwestern Territory, and William Blount was governor of it, until the erection of the state of Tennessee.

Morales and Marigny de Mandeville were chosen ordinary alcades for the year 1791.

Don Nicholas Maria Vidal succeeded Postego, as auditor of war and assessor of government.

Congress now added a new regiment to the military establishment, and authorized the president to raise a body of two thousand men for six months. The president placed this force under major-general St. Clair, governor of the Northwestern Territory, who had served with distinction in the army of the revolution, and had filled the chair of congress.

In the summer and fall, two expeditions were conducted against the villages on the Wabash, in which, with a very small loss, a few of the Indian warriors were killed, some of their old men, women and children made prisoners, and several of their towns with extensive fields were destroyed. The first was led by general Scott in May, and the second by general Wilkinson in September.

The major-general was more unfortunate. His small army consisting of about fourteen hundred effective rank and file, was routed by the Indians on the third of November. His defeat was complete. Six hundred and thirty-one were killed or missing, and two hundred and sixty-seven wounded. Among the killed was the brave and much lamented general Butler. This happened about fifty miles from the Miami villages.

The people of Kentucky complained that congress were too sparing in furnishing means for their protection. They were clamorously calling for admission into the Union as a state. Although Miro favored them with an intercourse with Louisiana, in which they found a vent for their produce, they were dissatisfied with the terms under which they were permitted to enjoy the navigation of the Mississippi.

In the night of the twenty-third of August, a preconcerted insurrection took place throughout the French part of the island of Hispaniola, and an immense portion of its white inhabitants were massacred. Those who were so fortunate as to make their escape, sought a refuge in the islands of Cuba and Jamaica, or the United States, and a few came to Louisiana. Among these, was a company of comedians from Cape François; and the city of New Orleans now enjoyed, for the first time, the advantage of regular dramatic exhibitions. Some of the other refugees, availing themselves of the wants of the province, opened academies for the instruction of youth. Hitherto, the only means of education were confined to a school in which a Spanish priest, aided by two ushers, taught the elements of the Spanish language, and the convent of the Ursuline nuns.

Miro sailed for the peninsula, where he was employed in the army, and obtained the rank of mariscal de camp. He carried with him the good wishes and the regrets of the colonists. Although not a man of superior talents, he governed the province in a manner that accorded with the views of his sovereign and of the colonists. He showed every possible indulgence to a commerce with the United States. Since the conflagration, vessels came freely from Philadelphia, and some other ports of the Union : and the people of Tennessee afterwards manifested their gratitude towards him, by giving his name to one of their judicial districts.

On the fourth of March, the state of Vermont was admitted into the confederacy of the United States, as its fourteenth member.

CHAPTER XXI.

Don Francisco Louis Hector, Baron de Carondelet, colonel of the royal armies, was promoted from the government of San Salvador, in the province of Guatimala, to the rank of governor and intendant of the provinces of Louisiana and West Florida, and entered on the duties of these offices on the first of January, 1792.

The ordinary alcades, for this year, were Marigny de Mandeville and de la Pena.

Don Nicholas Maria Vidal, the auditor of war, received a commission of lieutenant-governor.

The Baron's *bando de buen gobierno* was published on the twenty-second of January. Among the new regulations it introduced, it provided for the division of the city of New Orleans into four wards, in each of which, an alcade *de barrio*, or commissary of police, was to be appointed. In order to procure to government a knowledge of all the inhabitants, and every stranger among them or in the city, it was made the duty of all persons renting houses or apartments, to give the names of their new tenants to the alcade of the district, on the first day of their occupation, or, at farthest, on the succeeding one. The alcades *de barrio* were directed to take charge of fire engines and their implements, and to command the fire and *axe men* companies, in case of conflagration. They were also empowered to preserve the peace, and to take cognizance of small debts.

In one of his first communications to the cabildo, the Baron recommended to them to make provision for lighting the city and employing watchmen. The revenue of the corporation did not amount, at this period, to seven thousand dollars. To meet the charges for the purchase of lamps and oil, and the wages of watchmen, a tax of one dollar and twelve and a half cents was laid on every chimney.

. In a letter to the minister, the Baron, this year, mentioned that the population of New Orleans was under six thousand.

Having received instructions from the king to attend to the humane treatment of slaves in the province, he issued his proclamation on the eleventh of July, establishing the following regulations:

1. That each slave should receive monthly, for his food, one barrel of corn, at least.

2. That every Sunday should be exclusively his own, without his being compelled to work for his master, except in urgent cases, when he must be paid or indemnified.

3. That, on other days, they should not begin to work before daybreak, nor to continue after dark. One-half hour to be allowed at breakfast, and two hours at dinner.

4. Two brown shirts, a woolen coat and pantaloons, and a pair of linen pantaloons, and two handkerchiefs, to be allowed, yearly, to each male slave, and suitable dresses to female.

5. None to be punished with more than thirty lashes, within twenty-four hours.

6. Delinquents to be fined in the sum of one hundred dollars, and in grave cases, the slave may be ordered to be sold to another.

At the solicitation of the cabildo, the Baron issued a proclamation prohibiting the introduction of negroes from the French and British

35

islands, the province being, by such importation, drained of its specie, and apprehension being entertained of an insurrection.

In the month of June, the people of Kentucky were admitted into the Union, as a state.

A settlement of the difficulties relating to Nootka Sound having taken place, without a rupture between Great Britain and Spain, the latter power had expressed a wish for an adjustment of the matters in controversy between it and the United States, by a negotiation to be carried on at Madrid. Carmichael and Short were chosen by the president as commissioners for that purpose. In the meanwhile, the officers of that monarchy persisted in measures calculated to embroil the United States in a war with the southern Indians. By their intrigues, they succeeded in preventing the ratification of the treaty entered into, in 1790, with M'Gillivrey; and the line agreed on as the boundary, was not permitted to be run. The indefinite claim to territory, set up by Spain, was said to constitute a sufficient objection to any line of demarcation, until it was settled; and the previous treaties and relations of Spain with the Creeks were declared to be violated by the acknowledgement of their being under the protection of the United States.

General St. Clair having resigned the command of the western army, it was committed to general Wayne, and the greatest exertions were made to complete its ranks; but so small were the inducements to enter into the service, that the highest grades below the first, were tendered in vain the money. The recruiting service went on so slowly, that no hope was entertained of any decisive expedition this year; and it was thought expedient to negotiate a peace. This attempt proved very unfortunate, at least for those who were engaged in it. Colonel Hardin and major Trueman, having been dispatched severally with propositions of peace, were both murdered by the Indians.

Serano and Daunoy were the ordinary alcades for the years 1793 and 1794.

The king expressed to the Baron his approbation of the prohibition of the importation of slaves from the British and French West India islands, but declared his wish to have their importation from Guinea, by his subjects, encouraged and promoted; and, for this purpose, he issued a royal schedule on the first of January.

After stating that Spain was one of the first nations, the ships of which visited Africa in search of negroes, and his belief that great advantages would result to his subjects if they were to resume that trade, the king declares that every Spaniard may send vessels to the coast of Africa for negroes from any part of his dominions in Europe or the Indies, provided the master and one-half of the crew be Spaniards; and all merchandise purchased for that trade shall be exempted from duty, as well as every foreign vessel expressly purchased for the purpose of being employed therein.

Vessels continued to trade between Philadelphia and New Orleans since the conflagration of 1788. Miro, in the latter years of his administration, and the Baron, from the commencement of his, connived at this violation of the positive instructions of the minister of finance in Europe; but on the representation of the governors of the utility of the measure, it was approved by the king. From this period, a number of merchants in Philadelphia established commercial houses at New Orleans.

All trade is absolutely forbidden in the colonies of Spain, by the letter of the commercial law, to any but natural subjects or naturalized persons residing there. The extreme rigor of this provision had, however, in some degree, defeated it, as the very existence of several colonies depended upon its relaxation, which in New Orleans, began to take place in the latter part of the administration of Miro, after the conflagration, and was continued by the Baron, who extended it in favor of foreign merchants residing in the province, although not naturalized. After this, the officers of the customhouse contented themselves with the simple declaration of an individual, generally the consignee, that he was owner of the vessel. No oath was administered; the production of no document was required. The declaration was even accepted from an individual who did not reside in the province, on his asserting that he meant to do so, or on his producing a license to import goods, No one was thereby deceived, but the customhouse officers were furnished with a pretext for registering a vessel as a Spanish bottom, and thus to preserve an appearance of a compliance with the law. So little attention was paid to this, that at times the governor and intendant certified that a vessel was American property while she appeared on the customhouse books as a Spanish vessel.

Louis the sixteenth died on the scaffold, on the 21st of January, 1793, and the popular party being now predominant in France, the Catholic king declared war against the new republic.

The sympathies and partiality of the people of Louisiana now began to manifest themselves strongly in favor of the French patriots, principally in New Orleans. The situation of the Baron was rendered extremely delicate, by the circumstance of his being a native of France, and obliged by the duties of his station, if not urged by inclination, to restrain excesses against a monarchical government. He prepared, and promoted the subscription of a paper, in which the colonists gave assurances of their loyalty to, and affection for the Catholic king, and bound themselves to support his government in Louisiana. He put a stop to a practice, which had of late been introduced, of entertaining the audience at the theatre with the exhibition of certain martial dances to revolutionary airs. He caused six individuals, who had manifested their approbation of the new French principles, and evinced a desire to see them acted upon in Louisiana, to be arrested and confined in the fort. At the intercession of several respectable inhabitants of New Orleans, he promised to liberate them, but believing afterwards that he had discovered new causes of alarm, which rendered a decisive step necessary, he shipped them for Havana, where they were detained during a twelve-month.

The fortifications, with which the French had surrounded the city being a heap of ruins, he caused new ones to be erected. A fort was built immediately above, and another immediately below the city, upon the river, and a strong redoubt on the back part towards the middle of the city, and one other at each of the angles. They were connected by deep ditches. There was a battery in the middle of each flank of the city, which were also surrounded by strong palisades.

The two batteries built by the French at the English Turn were abandoned, and the fort of St. Philip erected on Plaquemines, with a small one on the opposite bank of the river.

He had the militia trained, and enforced the laws relative to it.

According to a statement which he sent to Madrid this year, it appeared there were between five and six thousand men enrolled, and he was of opinion that the colonial government could, at any time, bring three thousand men, within three weeks, to any given point in the province.

There were four companies, of one hundred men each, between the Balize and the city.

In New Orleans there were five companies of volunteers, one of artillery and two of riflemen; each of one hundred men.

The legion of the Mississippi, consisting of the militia of Baton Rouge, Galvezton, Pointe Coupee, Feliciana, Attakapas and Opelousas, had two companies of grenadiers, ten of fusiliers, and four of dragoons.

At Avoyelles a company of infantry, at Washita one of cavalry; at the Illinois, two of each.

A regiment of the German and Acadian coasts, of one thousand men.

At Mobile, a company of infantry and one of cavalry.

The attention of the colonists was, however, drawn to matters more immediately interesting to them, by the publication of a royal schedule of the month of February, extending great commercial advantages to them.

In the preamble of this document, the king declares his impression of the impossibility of the merchants of New Orleans continuing their expeditions to the ports of France designated in the schedule of the twenty-second of January, 1782, and the consequent necessity of some provision for the exportation of the produce of the provinces of Louisiana, East and West Florida, and for enabling the inhabitants to import the merchandise they stood in need of. With the view of encouraging the national commerce, and that of these provinces, the period of ten years, mentioned in said schedule, is provisionally prolonged, until regulations suitable to these provinces and the general system of commerce in the other colonies of Spanish America may be made.

Permission is given to the inhabitants of these colonies to carry on commerce freely, in Europe and America, with all the nations, with which Spain had treaties of commerce, from the ports of New Orleans, Pensacola, and St. Augustine, to any ports of said nations, (the vessels of which may there be also received) under the condition of stopping, in going and returning, in the port of Concurbion, in Galicia, or that of Alicante, to take a passport.

2. The merchandise, produce and effects, transported, in this foreign commerce, shall be charged with a duty of importation of fifteen per cent. and one of exportation of six; but the exportation of slaves was to continue exempt from duty. The exportation of specie for any purpose whatever, to continue prohibited.

3. The commerce between the peninsula and these provinces is likewise to be free; and the king declares he will view with particular benevolence, those who may in any manner encourage it.

4. Spanish subjects are permitted to trade to the provinces, from any port of the peninsula, to which the commerce of the Indies is permitted, in vessels exclusively Spanish, providing themselves with regular documents.

5. Permission is given to import into the ports of the peninsula, all kinds of foreign goods, wares, and merchandise destined for any of these provinces, although their introduction be prohibited for all other purposes. Likewise tobacco, or any other article of produce of these

provinces, and the importation of which is forbidden to individuals may be brought in, provided it be afterwards exported to a foreign port.

6. Such prohibited produce, the importation of which is only allowed to facilitate returns from these provinces, shall be deposited on landing in the warehouses of the customhouse, from which it shall be drawn only to be carried on board of the vessels in which the importation is to be made.

7. The importation of rice from foreign countries into Spain is prohibited; and the king declares he will likewise prohibit that of any other article of produce, which these provinces may supply, in sufficient quantity for consumption.

8. Goods exported from any of the allowed ports of the peninsula, for the commerce of the provinces, to be exempt from duty and that which may have been paid on their exportation shall be returned.

9. Foreign merchandise coming from any of the allowed ports of the peninsula on its importation in any of these provinces in foreign bottoms, shall pay a duty of three per cent.; but that imported in national vessels shall not pay any.

10. Merchandise or specie, exported from these provinces to any of the allowed ports of the peninsula, shall be free from duty.

11. The exportation to foreign ports of the produce of these provinces, brought to any of the allowed ports of the peninsula, shall be free from duty.

12. The exemptions from duty then granted include that of all local or municipal ones, which, by custom or otherwise, may be claimed.

13. In order to enjoy the exemptions hereby granted, every vessel must be provided with a manifest of her cargo, distinguishing national from foreign goods, certified at the customhouse of the place of her departure, and give bond with security to present it at the place of destination, and bring a certificate of the landing of the goods; and every vessel, on her return, shall be provided with a manifest and certificate that the whole of her cargo is of the produce of the country.

14. Spanish vessels bound from the peninsula to Louisiana or either of the Floridas, which may desire to return with the produce of the country, directly, to any port of Europe, may do so on paying a duty of three per cent. on the produce thus exported.

15. But this advantage is not to be enjoyed by vessels engaged in a direct trade between a foreign port and these provinces.

16. Vessels of the king's subjects, sailing from New Orleans, Pensacola or St. Augustine, are to have a manifest of their cargo, to be presented to his consul, and on their return they are to bring another, subscribed by him, to be presented at the customhouse; and those proceeding directly from Spain to these provinces, are to bring, on their return, besides the manifest of the inward cargo, a certificate of the landing of the outward, in order to have their bonds cancelled.

17. The ports of Bilbao and San Sebastian, which, being in exempt provinces, are reputed foreign, may, as such, trade to these colonies, according to the faculty herein granted, paying the duties imposed thereon; but, in consideration of the importance of enlarging and extending the maritime relations between the mother country and these colonies, vessels from these two ports shall enjoy the favors of exemptions granted to the allowed ports of the peninsula, with the sole difference that the vessels

from Bilbao and San Sebastian shall be bound to touch at San Ander to take a passport, before they proceed on their voyages.

18.   Vessels from the allowed ports, and from Bilbao and San Sebastian, trading to New Orleans, Pensacola, or St. Augustine, are prohibited from entering any other port of the king's dominions in America.

19.   Exportations from New Orleans, Pensacola, or St. Augustine, for any other port of these dominions, are prohibited, except in cases of the most urgent necessity, to be certified by the governor, who will give licenses therefor.   But then nothing can be exported except articles of the produce of the provinces.

20.   The king remits to his subjects all duties heretofore payable on vessels expressly purchased for this trade.

21.   The governor and intendant are directed to make a new tariff, to be submitted to the king.

On the representation of the Baron the office of intendant was separated from that of governor, and Don Francisco de Rendon, who had been employed as secretary of legation from Spain in the United States, having been invested with the former, came to New Orleans in the beginning of the year 1794.

The pope divided the bishopric of Havana; and the provinces of Louisiana, East and West Florida, were erected into a distinct one.   Don Louis de Penalvert, provisor and vicar-general of the bishop of Havana, was called to the new see, and established his cathedral in New Orleans.

Two canons were added to the clergy of the province.

Genet, the minister of the French republic in Philadelphia, had planned two expeditions from the western part of the United States, against the dominions of Spain on the Mississippi and the Gulf of Mexico.   Several citizens of the United States had accepted commissions from him.   Many of these had been seduced by him in Charleston, where he had landed, in Philadelphia, and in the states of North Carolina, Virginia and Maryland. Others (and their number was not small) had yielded their aid to his agents in Kentucky and Tennessee, under the belief that the interests of the western people would be promoted by the success of the enterprise; imagining that the French once in possession of New Orleans, the American government would find it easy to obtain free navigation of the Mississippi.   The idea of a separation of the western people from their brothers on the Atlantic, and an alliance or union with the French of Louisiana, was still fostered by many.   With these views, soldiers were secretly recruited for the enterprise.   Auguste de la Chaise, a creole of Louisiana, (grandson of the former commissary ordonnateur) had been sent to Kentucky to superintend the recruiting service there, and was to be one of the leaders of the expedition against the Spanish territory on the Mississippi.   Another individual, of the name of Clarke, was on a similar errand in the back counties of Georgia, from which state and the neighboring one, another expedition was to be directed against East Florida. The aid of a considerable body of Indians, raised among the Creeks and Cherokees, had been obtained.

The Baron had early information of the danger that threatened the province under his care, from the Spanish minister at Philadelphia, and took early measures to avert it.   He completed the fortifications of New Orleans, and visited most of the parishes to animate the people, and put the militia in a situation of being useful.   His care did not stop here.

He dispatched Thomas Power, an intelligent Englishman, to Kentucky, who, under the pretense of being engaged in collecting materials for a natural history of the western part of the United States, was to prepare the way for the execution of the plan proposed by Navarro, seven years before, by conversing with the most influential individuals, among those who were disposed to promote a separation from the Atlantic states, and an alliance or connection with Spain, and giving them assurances of the cheerful concurrence of the colonial government of Louisiana, and its readiness to supply them with arms, ammunition and money.

This year, *Le Moniteur de la Louisiane,* the only periodical paper published in the province during its subjection to Spain, made its first appearance.

The Baron did not suffer the care he took for the protection of the province to direct his attention from the improvement of the city. On the ninth of May, he gave notice of his intention to dig a canal, which, carrying off the water of the city and its environs into one of the branches of the bayou St. John, would rid New Orleans of the stagnating ponds, which rendered it sickly, and the multitude of mosquitoes, which harrassed the inhabitants.

He mentioned that the expenses of the war allowing no hope of obtaining the assistance of the king for digging a considerable canal of navigation, he had asked from his majesty only the labor of the negro convicts, which, with that of a few hands that might be furnished by able and zealous individuals, might afford a canal for conveying off the water, and in successive years it might be deepened, so as to become a convenient canal, navigable for schooners, facilitating the intercourse between the opposite side of the lakes, Mobile and Pensacola, with New Orleans.

In announcing the king's assent to this proposition, the Baron declared his intention of requesting from the inhabitants of the city, in the month of June following, such a number of negroes as they might spare, to clear the ground through which the canal was to pass, and expressed his belief that, this being done, the convicts might complete the work.

A passage, eight feet in breadth, was to be left on each side, for horses drawing flatboats, and in time, schooners. A wide levee, for foot travelers, was to afford an agreeable promenade, under a double row of trees.

About sixty negroes were sent, and the canal was begun with a depth of six feet only. It turned around the large trees which obstructed its way.

Indigo had hitherto been the principal object of the attention of planters on the banks of the Mississippi; but during several years, its success had sadly disappointed their hopes. At first, the failure of the crops had resulted from the vicissitudes of the seasons; of late, an insect attacked the plant and destroyed its leaves. In the years 1793 and 1794, its ravages were so great that almost every plant perished, and the fields presented nothing to the eye but naked stems.

Since the year 1766, the manufacture of sugar had been entirely abandoned in Louisiana. A few individuals had, however, contrived to plant a few canes in the neighborhood of the city: they found a vent for them in the market. Two Spaniards, Mendez and Solis, had lately made larger plantations. One of them boiled the juice of the cane into syrup, and the other had set up a distillery, in which he made indifferent taffia.

Etienne Boré, a native of the Illinois, who resided about six miles above the city, finding his fortune considerably reduced by the failure of the indigo crops for several successive years, conceived the idea of retrieving his losses by the manufacture of sugar. The attempt was considered by all as a visionary one. His wife, (a daughter of Destrehan, the colonial treasurer under the government of France, who had been one of the first to attempt, and one of the last to abandon, the manufacture of sugar) remembering her father's ill success, warned him of the risk he ran of adding to, instead of repairing his losses, and his relations and friends joined their remonstrances to hers. He, however, persisted; and, having procured a quantity of canes from Mendez and Solis, began to plant.

This year, Don Andre Almonaster, a perpetual regidor and alferez real, completed at his own expense the erection of a cathedral church in New Orleans, having laid the foundation of it in 1792. He had before built and endowed a hospital.

A conflagration reduced a considerable part of the city to ashes, and in the month of August the province was desolated by a hurricane.

The ordinary alcades for the year 1795, were de Lovio and Pontalba. The cabildo made a representation to the king, and prayed that six more offices of regidor might be created; the increase of population rendering, in their opinion, this measure necessary.

They also prayed that the zealous services of the Baron might be rewarded by the appointment of captain-general.

It seems that the progress of the French revolutionary principles was great in the province, and that the hope that Lachaise would succeed in gathering such a force in Kentucky as might enable him, in the language of the day, to "give freedom to the country of his birth," inflamed the minds of many; for, on the first of June, the Baron issued a proclamation for establishing several regulations of police; in the preamble of which he complains of "the success with which evil minded, turbulent, and enthusiastic individuals, who certainly had nothing to lose, had spread false rumors, calculated to give rise to the most complete mistrust between government and the people, whereby the province is threatened with all the disasters to which the French colonies have fallen a prey."

After this the proclamation announces that to restore order and public tranquillity, syndics, chosen among the most notable planters, are to be appointed, residing within about nine miles from each other, to be subordinate to the commandant, to whom they are to give weekly accounts of every important occurrence.

It is made the duty of every one having the knowledge, even by hearsay, of any offense or seditious expressions, tending to excite alarm or disturb public tranquillity to give immediate notice to the syndic, commandant or governor.

Every assemblage, of more than eight persons, to consult on public matters, is absolutely forbidden.

Every individual is bound to denounce to the commandant, any syndic, guilty of an offense in making use of any seditious expressions.

Every traveller found without a passport is immediately to be arrested, carried before the syndic, who is to examine and send him to the commandant.

Every traveller, possessed of any important event, is first to give notice of it to the syndic, who is to take a note of it and register his name, and afterwards, according to circumstances, permit or forbid the communication of the event, giving information of it to the commandant.

Syndics are to direct patrols from time to time.

The vigilance of the executive of the United States was such that Lachaise's efforts proved abortive, and the legislature of South Carolina took measures which ended in the arrest of Genet's agents in the south, and the expedition against East Florida failed.

The Baron thought the strictest vigilance was required in the city, and he availed himself of the circumstance of some nocturnal depredations, to issue a proclamation enforcing a severe police, and directing the shutting of the gates at an early hour.

The canal behind the city was widened to fifteen feet. About one hundred and fifty negroes were sent by the inhabitants of the city and its neighborhood, and all the convict slaves were employed on it. In the month of October, the Baron, by a publication in the Moniteur, brought to view the future grandeur of New Orleans, its increasing commerce, the necessity of opening a communication between the city and the sea, through the lakes, and announced that six days more of the labor of the slaves in the city, and within fifteen miles above and below, would enable the colonial government to complete the canal.

Another publication, on the twenty-third of November, draws the attention of the inhabitants to the facilities they have found in procuring wood through the canal, the marked diminution of mortality during the preceding three months, and asks, as the last assistance which he would require, the labor of the slaves for eight days more.

A number of French royalists had come to New Orleans, and proposed plans for the removal of a number of their countrymen to Louisiana, from the United States, where they had sought an asylum, and the colonial government was induced to make several very extensive grants of land.

The principal was to the Marquis de Maison Rouge, a knight of St. Louis. He offered to bring down thirty families, who were waiting on the banks of the Ohio, and were anxious to form an establishment on those of the Washita, to raise wheat and manufacture it into flour.

The encouragement given by the colonial government was not confined to a grant of land. It covenanted to pay two hundred dollars to every family, composed of at least two white persons, fit for agriculture or the arts necessary in the settlement, as carpenters, blacksmiths, etc. Four hundred dollars to those having four laborers, and the same proportion to those having only an artisan or laborer. They were to be assisted with guides and provisions from New Madrid to Washita. Their baggage and implements of agriculture were to be transported from New Madrid at the king's expense. Each family, consisting of at least two white persons fit for agriculture, was entitled to four hundred acres of land, with a proportionate increase to larger ones. Settlers were permitted to bring white European servants, to be bound to them for six or more years, who, at the expiration of their time, were to receive grants of land in the same proportion.

This agreement was, a few months after, approved by the king.

The Baron, in these plans for colonizing the banks of the Washita, had not lost sight of his favorite one for the separation of the western people from the Union, the idea of which was still entertained by several influential individuals in Kentucky, whom Power had visited, and who had recommended that an officer of rank should be sent by the colonial government, to meet part of them at the mouth of the Ohio. He made choice, for this purpose, of Don Manuel Gayoso de Lemos, who commanded at Natchez, and who set off early in the summer. The ostensible object of this officer's journey was to lead a number of soldiers, who were to erect and garrison a fort at the Chickasaw bluffs. Having set these men at work, Gayoso proceeded to New Madrid, from whence, according to a previous arrangement, he dispatched Power to Red Banks, for the purpose of bringing down Sebastian, Innis, Murray and Nicholas, who had been chosen to hold a conference with the officer to be sent by the Baron at the mouth of the Ohio. Power found Sebastian at the Red Banks, who informed him that some family concerns prevented Innis from leaving home; that, as the courts were now in session, the absence of Nicholas, a lawyer in great practice, would excite suspicion, and that Murray had, for some time past, got into such a state of habitual intoxication, that he was absolutely incapable of attending to any kind of business. He added, he was authorized by Innis and Nicholas, to treat with Gayoso in their names, and accordingly proceeded, in Power's boat, to the Mississippi, where they found Gayoso. He had employed his people in building a small stockade fort, on the right bank of the river, opposite the mouth of the Ohio, with the view of having it believed that this fortification was the object of his journey. He proposed to Sebastian to come down to New Orleans and confer with the Baron. This was agreed to; and, after a short stay, they proceeded down, Gayoso and Sebastian in the former's galley; Power and a Mr. Vander Rogers in a king's barge. They proceeded to Natchez, where they stopped.

Whilst a part of the white population evinced their anxiety to imitate the French in a struggle for freedom, it is not extraordinary that the slaves should have been seduced into an attempt to rise by the reports of the success of the blacks in Hispaniola. An insurrection was planned in the parish of Pointe Coupee, an insulated one, in which the number of slaves was considerable. The conspiracy was formed on the plantation of Julien Poydras, a wealthy planter, who was then absent on a journey to the United States; from thence its progress had been extended to all parts of the parish. The indiscriminate slaughter of every white man was intended. A disagreement as to the day the massacre was to take place, gave rise to a quarrel among the principal leaders, which led to a discovery of the plot. The militia was instantly put under arms; and the Baron on the first information, sent a part of the regular force. The slaves attempted a resistance and twenty-five of them were killed before those that had been selected for trial were arrested and confined. Serano, the assessor of the intendancy, went up to assist Dupart, the civil commandant at the trials. Fifty were found guilty; others were severely flogged. Sixteen of the first were hung in different parts of the parish; the nine remaining were put on board of a galley, which floated down to New Orleans. On her way one of them was landed near the church of each parish along the river, and left hanging on a tree. This timely exercise of severity quieted for awhile the apprehensions of the inhabitants who had been considerably alarmed.

In the meanwhile, Wayne had concluded a treaty of peace with the hostile Indians, on the northwest of the Ohio, on the twentieth of August, and the plenipotentiaries of the United States and Spain had signed a treaty at San Lorenzo, on the twenty-seventh of October.

CHAPTER XXII.

By the Spanish treaty, the southern boundary of the United States, as given by their treaty of peace with Great Britain, was recognized; and their western, as far as related to the boundary of the territory of Spain, was declared to be a line, beginning at a point in the middle of the channel or bed of the Mississippi, on their northern boundary, running along the middle of said channel, to the thirty-first degree of north latitude.

The king agrees that the navigation of the Mississippi, in its whole breadth, from its source to the gulf, shall be free only to his subjects and the colonies of the United States, unless by special convention, he extends the privilege to the subjects of other powers.

The parties promise to maintain, by all the means in their power, peace and harmony among the several nations of Indians inhabiting the country adjacent to the southern boundary of the United States; and the better to attain this object, both parties bind themselves, expressly, to restrain, by force, all hostilities on the part of Indian nations living within their territories, and to make no treaty, except a treaty of peace, with any Indian nation living within the territory of the other.

Provision is made for the protection of vessels, for cases of embargo and seizure for debt or crime, stress of weather, vessels captured by pirates, the estates of the deceased, passports, contraband trade, access to courts of justice, etc.

The principle that free ships make free goods, is recognized.

It is provided that the subjects or colonies of either party shall not make war against those of the other.

Arrangements are made for running the southern boundary line of the United States.

The king promises to permit citizens of the United States, during a period of ten years, from the ratification of the treaty, to deposit their merchandise and effects in the port of New Orleans, and export them free from duty, except a fair charge for the use of stores; and he engages to extend the permission, if it does not, during that period, appear preju-dicial to his interests; and if he does not continue to permit the deposit there, he will assign to them an equivalent establishment on some other spot of the banks of the Mississippi.

Perez and Lachaise were the ordinary alcades for the year 1796.

Early in January, Gayoso, Sebastian, and Power came to New Orleans; and early in the spring the two latter sailed for Philadelphia.

The Count de Santa-Clara succeeded Las Casas as captain-general of the island of Cuba, the provinces of Louisiana and East and West Florida.

The alarm into which the late attempt of the blacks at Pointe Coupee threw the colonists, induced the cabildo, on the 29th of February, to request the Baron to transmit to the king their prayer that the introduction of slaves from any part of the world might be prohibited, and they desired the Baron to issue his proclamation, provisorily, to forbid their import-ation. He complied with their wishes.

Boré's success, in his first attempt to manufacture sugar, was very great, and he sold his crop for twelve thousand dollars. His example induced a number of other planters to plant cane.

By a royal order, given at Aranjuez, on the 20th of June, Don Carlos de Jaen, a licentiate of Havana, was appointed judge of residence of Miro. He did not, however, come over for several years.

Don Francisco de Rendon, having been appointed intendant and corrigidor of the province of Zacatecas, sailed from New Orleans, and the functions of the intendant devolved on Don Juan Benaventura Morales, the contador.

This year the canal behind the city was completed, and a number of schooners went through it to a basin that had been dug near the ramparts. The cabildo, as a mark of their gratitude for the administrator, to whose care this important improvement was due, directed that it should be called "the Canal Carondelet."

The project of inducing French loyalists to migrate to Louisiana, continued to be a favorite one with the Baron; and, with a view of promoting it, very extensive grants of land were made.

The most considerable one was that made to the Baron de Bastrop. It was of twelve square leagues, on the banks of the Washita. The emigrants were intended to be employed in the culture of wheat and the manufacture of flour. The colonial government took upon itself the charge of bringing them down from New Madrid, and of providing for their subsistence during six months. It promised not to molest them on account of their religion; but declared that the Roman Catholic was the only one the rites of which would be allowed to be performed.

Another grant was to James Ceran Delassus de St. Vrain, an officer of the late royal navy of France, who had lost his fortune in the late revolution in his own country, and who, having been compelled to remove to the United States, had rendered himself useful to Spain, in assisting the emissaries of the Baron in defeating the plans of Genet against the king's dominions on the Mississippi and the gulf. This grant was of ten thousand square arpents. The grantee proposed to exert his industry in discovering and working lead mines. The privilege was given him of locating his grant in several mines, salines, millseats, and other places, as might best suit his interests, without any obligation, on his part, of making any settlement thereon, as the execution of his plan would require large disbursements, and could be realized only in places remote from the white population and among the Indians.

Julien Dubuc had made a settlement on the frontiers of the province on land purchased from the Indians in the midst of whom it was effected, and opened and worked several lead mines, which he called "the mines of Spain." The Baron now granted him all the land from the coast above the little river Maquequito to the banks of the Mosquebemanque, forming about six leagues on the west bank of the Mississippi river, by a depth of three leagues.

The Marquis de Maison Rouge having completed his establishment on the Washita, the Baron, on the twentieth of June, appropriated conclusively thirty thousand superficial acres of land for the Marquis' establishment; it being understood that no American settler was to be admitted within the grant.

The expenses of lighting the city of New Orleans and the wages of thirteen watchmen, had originally been provided for by a tax on chimneys.

The destruction of a considerable number of houses by the late conflagration, now rendered this provision insufficient, and the Baron proposed to the cabildo that three hundred toises in depth of the land of the city beyond the fortifications in its rear, should be parcelled out into small tracts, to be leased out for gardens, from which the market could be supplied with vegetables; and he expressed his belief that by the draining of the land, the city would be relieved from the noxious exhalation of such an extent of ground, covered with water during the greatest part of the year. This proposition was not, however, adopted; and a tax was laid on wheat bread and meat. It was thought the tax on bread would fall on the rich only; the poorer class of people using corn and rice; and that a part of both would be borne by travellers and sojourners. The Baron urged the necessity of continuing to light the city, and retaining the watchmen, on the ground of the city being full of French people, the nocturnal assemblages of whom, as well as that of the slaves, it was prudent to prevent.

The king's officers in New Orleans appeared impressed with the idea that the late treaty between Spain and the United States, would never be carried into effect. They thought that, at the time it was entered into, the affairs of Europe rendered the neutrality of the United States of great importance to Spain; and, according to them, the object of Great Britain in her late treaty with those States, was to draw them over to her interests, and render them in some measure dependent on her. They believed that their sovereign had ratified the treaty for the purpose of counteracting the views of Great Britain, and concluded that as that power had failed in her object, Spain on her part, would be no longer interested in fulfilling the stipulations of the treaty.

Accordingly, the Baron had sent Power to Kentucky, in the beginning of the year, to keep alive the hopes of those who still favored the plan of a secession of the western people from the Atlantic states. The messenger delivered the Baron's packets to Wilkinson, at Greenville, in the latter part of May, and was dispatched by him to New Madrid, to take charge of a sum of money (about $10,000) deposited by the Baron in the hands of Don Thomas Portell, the commandant. After overcoming some difficulty, resulting from his having no written order from Wilkinson, the money was delivered to him. He concealed it in barrels of sugar and coffee, and brought it up in safety. On his return to New Orleans, he reported to his employer that whatever might heretofore have been the disposition of the people of Kentucky, they were now perfectly satisfied with the federal government, and their leading men (with very few exceptions) manifested an utter aversion to the hazardous experiments heretofore thought of—especially as their own government had now obtained from them, by the late treaty, the principal object which they expected to attain by a separation from the Union.

The Baron's attention was now momentarily drawn from his favorite plan by the necessity of protecting the province under his care from impending danger. The governor of Canada had assembled a considerable number of troops on the southern border of that province; a circumstance which induced the belief that an expedition was contemplated from thence, through the western territory of the United States, against the dominions of Spain on the Mississippi. The minister of the catholic king at Philadelphia, communicated to the department of state the information he had received on this head, and demanded that, according to a stipulation in the late treaty, the United States should oppose, in the most effectual manner, the intended violation of their territory.

Spain had concluded a treaty of peace with the French republic, and on the 7th of October had declared war against Great Britain. The Catholic king, in the declaration of war, mentions the late treaty between Great Britain and the United States, as one of the motives that had influenced his conduct in this respect.

Serano and Argotte were the ordinary alcades for the years 1797 and 1798.

By a royal order of the fourteenth of May, the royal audience of Santo Domingo was removed to *Puerto del Principe,* a town in the island of Cuba.

The king having acceded to the proposition of the cabildo, in regard to an additional number of regidors, Francisco de Riano, Louis d'Arby d'Anicant, Jayme Jordan, John Leblanc, Gilbert Andry and Francisco Castanedo, took their seats in that body as such.

It had been stipulated, in the late treaty between the United States and Spain, that commissioners of both nations should meet at Natchez, within six months from the ratification. Accordingly, Andrew Ellicot had been appointed commissioner on the part of the United States, and Don Manuel Gayoso de Lemos on that of the Catholic king.

Gayoso, according to the instructions of the Baron, as soon as he heard of Ellicot's approach with a small body of infantry under the orders of Lieut. M'Leary, sent an officer to meet him, with a request that he would not attempt to come to Natchez as yet, but stop at bayou Pierre, as the fort was not ready to be surrendered, and some disorder might result from the approximation of the troops of the two nations.

Ellicot disregarded this message, and reached Natchez with his men in the month of February, and displayed the flag of his country near the fort.

The Baron, wishing to gain time, urged, as his reason for delaying a compliance with the stipulations of treaty, that they were not sufficiently explicit, and doubts had arisen in his mind as to the manner in which the posts were to be delivered. It appeared to him questionable whether they were to be so, with all the forts and edifices standing, as the United States seemed to understand, or evacuated, razed and abandoned, as he conceived, in order that Spain might avoid involving herself into difficulties with the Indian nations, who, by formal treaties, had ceded to her the land at the Chickasaw bluffs, Walnut Hill, and Tombecbee, on the express conditions that she should erect fortifications there, to prevent their country from being invaded. He therefore declared his determination to await the orders of his sovereign, or those of his minister at Philadelphia, retain the posts on the Mississippi, and defend upper Louisiana, until congress, acting upon the representation of the latter, should take measures to restrain any expedition against those Indians, according to the stipulations of the treaty.

For the purpose of receiving possession of the posts to be surrendered, a larger detachment, under the orders of Lieutenant Pope soon followed the former. The instructions of that officer render it probable that the government of the United States apprehended some difficulty from that of Spain. The lieutenant was directed, in the first instance, to proceed to

Fort Massac on the Ohio, and there to await the return of an officer previously sent to New- Madrid for official information in regard to the delivery of the posts; and. on the certainty or probability of such an event, he was to proceed to Natchez, and on his arrival there, to keep up the most perfect discipline among the troops, so as to prevent every kind of disorder, and promote harmony and friendly interchange of good offices with the subjects of the Catholic king, and to treat the Spanish flag with respect.

The commandant at New Madrid, being without instructions, was unable to give any information respecting the views of the colonial government, and lieutenant Pope, concluding that possession would probably be given, descended the Mississippi, and had proceeded as far as New Madrid, where he was met by a messenger from the Baron, warning him to proceed no farther. The lieutenant thought it best, however, to go on. and, at the Walnut Hills, found a letter from Gayoso, requesting him to stop there. He tarried awhile, but on receiving a letter from Ellicot, advising him to come to Natchez, he departed, and joined Ellicot soon after, and immediately increased his force by enlistment, and apprehended several deserters from the army of the United States, who had taken refuge under the protection of the Spanish flag.

The most considerable part of the population of the district of Natchez had removed from the United States, or were descendants of emigrants from the British provinces, after the peace of 1762. They were anxious for a change of government, and appeared to disregard the authority of the officers of Spain. Gayoso issued a proclamation on the twentieth of March, calculated to bring them back to their duty.

The Baron had resolved that his determination, in regard to the delivery of the posts of the United States, should be regulated by the success or failure of a last attempt to detach the western country from the Union, and had accordingly sent Power thither on this errand.

The avowed object of his mission was the delivery of a letter to Wilkinson, who. on the death of Wayne, had succeeded to the command of the American forces, to induce him not to insist on the immediate evacuation of the posts of Spain; the real object of the journey, however, and (concerning which the Baron, in order to avoid all danger of detection, had given only verbal instructions) was to sound the disposition of the western people, whose militia, the Baron had heard, had received orders to be ready to march at the first call. In the event of this proving true, Power was directed to send immediate information of it to the commandant at New Madrid.

He was instructed adroitly to give it out among those with whom he might have an opportunity of conversing in the course of his travels, that the surrender, to the forces of the United States, of the posts occupied by those of Spain, on the Mississippi, was in direct opposition to the interests of the western people, who, as they must one day be separated from the Atlantic states, would find themselves without any communication with the sea, excepting through Louisiana, from whence they might expect powerful succors in artillery, arms, ammunition and money, openly or secretly, as soon as they determined on a secession, which must secure to them independence and prosperity.

The wish was expressed that it might be suggested that, for this reason, Congress was determined on hastening the taking possession of these posts, and the western people would forge fetters for themselves, if they consented to furnish their militia, and other means, which the United States could find among them only.

It was urged that these hints, if diffused through the papers, might make a strong impression on the people, and dispose them to throw off the yoke of the Atlantic states; and if they could be dissuaded from aiding congress, it could not give law to the Spaniards.

Assurances were given that, if one hundred thousand dollars, properly distributed in Kentucky, could induce the people to resist, that sum would be readily furnished. The messenger was authorized to promise this, and an equal sum to procure arms, in case of necessity, with 20 pieces of artillery.

The packet for Wilkinson, securing to the bearer the best opportunity of viewing the army and ascertaining its force, discipline and disposition, he was directed to improve it, and transmit to his employer without delay, the most correct and minute information he could obtain. A doubt was expressed whether a person of Wilkinson's character would prefer the command of the army of the United States, to the glory of being the founder, the liberator, indeed the Washington of the western states. His part was said to be brilliant and easy; all eyes were fixed on him; he possessed the confidence of his fellow-citizens, and principally of the Kentucky volunteers; at the slightest movement, the people would hail him the general of the new republic. His reputation would raise him an army, and France and Spain enable him to pay it.

Pursuing his prophetic strain, the Baron added that, on Wilkinson's taking Fort Massac, he would instantly send him small arms and artillery from New Orleans; and Spain, limiting herself to the posts at Natchez and Walnut Hills, would cede all the left bank of the Mississippi as high as the Ohio, which would form an extensive republic, connected, by its situation and interests, with Spain, who in conjunction with it, would force the Indians to seek its alliance and confound themselves, in time, with its citizens.

The Baron added that the western people were dissatisfied with the tax on whisky, and Spain and France were enraged at the connexion of the United States with Great Britain; the army was weak and devoted to Wilkinson, and the threat of congress authorized him (the Baron) to succor the western people immediately and openly; money would not be wanting; and he was about dispatching a vessel to Vera Cruz for a supply of it, and ammunition; so that nothing was required but an instant of firmness and resolution to render the western people free and happy. But, if they suffered the opportunity to pass unimproved, and the Spaniards were compelled to surrender the posts, Kentucky and Tennessee would forever remain under the oppressive yoke of the Atlantic states.

These instructions concluded with an assurance to Power, that if, by forcibly urging these arguments, he succeeded in bringing over Wilkinson, Lacasagne, Sebastian, Brackenridge, and the other principal men, and if, by dint of promises, which he (the Baron) pledged himself should be faithfully redeemed, and by the general diffusion of these notions among them, the public generally could be engaged to second their efforts, the object of his expedition would be accomplished, and he would acquire imperishable renown, and a claim to the most brilliant rewards; whilst, on the other hand, should he unfortunately fail, his employer would be able to procure him an appointment, which would place him beyond the reach of the envy or hatred of his enemies.

In the meanwhile, other agents were sent among the nations of Indians within the territory of the United States, with speeches calculated to induce them to withdraw from the protection of congress, and take up the hatchet against the citizens of the United States.

The Baron, at the same time, reinforced the garrison of Fort Panmure, and that of the Walnut Hills; a measure which he said was resorted to, as one of precaution against the descent which the British meditated from Canada. The people of the district of Natchez viewed it as a prelude to the arrest of those among them who had manifested a partiality to the government of the United States. Their alarm was such as to drive a few of them to some violent steps. The subsequent commotion in the neighborhood was so great as to induce Gayoso with his family, to seek an asylum in the fort, on the seventh of June.

Four days after, he issued an elaborate proclamation, warning the people of the consequences of their illegal proceedings, requiring them to return to their duty and allegiance to their sovereign, submission to his laws and obedience to his officers; commanding those who had embodied themselves, to disperse and return to their usual and lawful occupations, as the only means of obtaining an amnesty for the past and security for the future.

A general meeting of the people to deliberate on the state of the district, was proposed and was generally approved of, but an apprehension was entertained that Gayoso would break up their assembly, by arresting those who might attend. Lieutenant Pope assured the inhabitants he would protect them at all hazards. He recommended that they should come forward and assert their rights in the most solemn manner, and join the forces of the United States in case the Baron sent more soldiers there from New Orleans. The lieutenant's conduct was countenanced by Ellicot.

The meeting took place on the twentieth of June. They remembered the conduct of O'Reilly in 1769, and felt apprehensive of the consequences of any step they might take; they feared that Gayoso's proclamation might only be intended as a snare, and were anxious to fix the terms of their surrender so as to avoid every ambiguity of expression. At last they assented to Ellicot's proposition for the appointment of a committee of safety, of which lieutenant Pope was a member.

This committee called on Gayoso, and proposed that he should recognize their existence as a body—that none of the people should be injured or prosecuted on account of the part they had taken against government— that they should be exempted from serving in the militia, under the Spanish authorities, except to suppress riots or repress the insults of Indians—that they should be considered as in a state of neutrality, although governed by Spanish laws, and none of them should be sent out of the country under any pretense whatsoever.

Gayoso gave his ready assent to these propositions, and the Baron ratified what he had done, with a single and unimportant exception.

The fall of this year was very sickly in New Orleans, and the city was visited by the yellow fever.

The Baron was now appointed president of the royal audience of the province of Quito, and left Louisiana.

37

This year, the people of the southwestern Territory of the United States were admitted into the Union, as the state of Tennessee, and formed the sixteenth member of the confederacy.

John Adams succeeded general Washington in the presidency of the United States.

CHAPTER XXIII.

Don Manuel Gayoso de Lemos, a brigadier-general of the royal armies, who commanded at Natchez, succeeded the Baron de Carondelet, in the government of the provinces of Louisiana and West Florida, and was succeeded in his former command by Don Carlos de Grandpre. The latter officer, being obnoxious to the people of the district of Natchez, declined going there, and major Minor, a native of New Jersey, who came to Louisiana in the year 1778, and had accepted of a commission in the Catholic king's service, acted as commandant, until the establishment of the government under the authority of the United States.

Power now returned from the western country, and in his report to Gayoso, which bears date on the fifth of December, stated that he met Sebastian at Louisville, and communicated to him the real and ostensible objects of his mission, when, after conferring together, they were of opinion it was indispensable to add four propositions to those the Baron had authorized Power to make. Without the first, neither Sebastian, nor any other person concerned or interested in the important undertaking, would take any step for its success. These propositions were, that:

1. If any person should lose his office, on account of promoting the Baron's views, he should be indemnified by the king of Spain.

2. The northern boundary of the king's dominion should be a line drawn from the mouth of the river Yazoo to the river Tombeckbee; and the northernmost Spanish fort should be six miles below that line.

3. But the king should retain the fort of San Fernando de Barancas (Chickasaw bluffs) with the land around it, ceded to him by the Indians by their treaty with Gayoso.

4. The king should not interfere, directly or indirectly, with the form of government or laws, which the western people should adopt.

Sebastian undertook to communicate the Baron's propositions, with the above amendments, to Innis and Nicholas. To conceal the real object of Power's journey, and avoid the resentment of the people of Louisville, who were enraged at his frequent visits and threatened to tar and feather him, it was agreed that, after having seen Wilkinson at Detroit, he should return by Greenville, Cincinnati, Newport, Georgetown, and Frankfort, to meet Innis and Nicholas, and be informed of the success of their efforts; and that Sebastian, and another person, should accompany him to New Orleans. Notwithstanding he (Sebastian) was of opinion that, for the present, all the means and efforts used to stimulate the western people to secede from the union, would be of no avail, he promised that nothing should be wanting, on his part, to obtain what was so much desired.

Power arrived in the neighborhood of Detroit on the sixteenth of August, and finding that Wilkinson was then at Michilimackinac, he did not enter the fort. The general, immediately after his return, hearing of

Power's arrival, had him arrested and brought to the fort, and thus got the Baron's dispatches. He gave a cold reception to the bearer, and informed him that the governor of the northwestern territory had orders to arrest and send him to Philadelphia, which could be prevented in no other manner than by sending him, under a strong guard, to New Madrid, without delay. He added, the Baron's project was a chimerical one, impossible to be executed, as the western people, having obtained, by the late treaty, all that they wanted, have no need of any connexion or alliance with Spain, nor any motive for a separation from the Atlantic states, even if France and Spain should make them the most advantageous offers— that the ferment which existed four years ago, had now subsided, and the vexations and depredations which the American commerce had suffered from the privateers of France, created an implacable hatred for that nation. He added that the people of Kentucky had proposed to him to raise an army of ten thousand men, to take New Orleans, in case of a rupture with Spain, and the governor of Louisiana had no other measure to pursue, under the present circumstances, than fully to comply with the treaty. He complained that all his plans were overturned, and all his labors for ten years past lost. He added that he had destroyed all his cyphers and burnt his correspondence with the governors of Louisiana, and duty and honor did not permit him to continue it. The Baron, however, need not apprehend his confidence should be abused—that if Spain surrendered the district of Natchez to the United States, they would probably make him governor, and he should not then lack the opportunity of promoting his political projects. He complained that his connection with the colonial government had been divulged—that Don Zenon Trudeau, the commandant at St. Louis, had sent emissaries among the Indian nations within the territory of the United States, inviting them to come and settle within that of Spain, as the Spanish king was at war with the British, and would soon be with the French.

On the sixth, Wilkinson delivered his answer for the Baron, to Power, and immediately compelled the latter to depart for New Madrid, by the way of the Wabash, under a guard commanded by captain Shaumburg. On passing through Vincennes, Power sent an express to Louisville, in order to apprise Sebastian of what happened.

Power concluded his report, by stating that, with regard to the people of Kentucky, Sebastian's opinion differed from Wilkinson's. The former had told him that should war be declared between Spain and the United States, Louisiana would have nothing to fear from the people of Kentucky; and insinuated it would more likely be the circumstance which should stimulate them against the United States. The reporter's own opinion was, that a great proportion of the most influential characters in Kentucky and Tennessee, had been the instigators of the expeditions set on foot, under Lachaise and Clark, against the dominions of Spain, by Genet. The rest were unambitious of conquest from Spain, and desired only to preserve the boundary secured to them by the treaties.

During this winter, general Collet, who had travelled through the states of Kentucky and Tennessee by order of the French government, passed through New Orleans. It was supposed Adet, the French minister at Philadelphia, sent him on an errand similar to that on which Lachaise had been employed by Genet.

Gayoso issued his *bando de buen gobierno*, in the month of January, 1798. It does not contain any important new regulation.

On the following day, he published a set of instructions to commandants, in regard to the grant of land, as follows :

1. They are forbidden to grant land to a new settler, coming from another post, where he has obtained a grant. Such a one must buy land, or obtain a grant from the governor.

2. If a settler be a foreigner, unmarried, and without either slaves, money, or other property, no grant is to be made to him until he shall have remained four years in the post, demeaning himself well in some honest and useful occupation.

3. Mechanics are to be protected, but no land is to be granted to them until they shall have acquired some property, and a residence of three years in the exercise of their trade.

4. No grant of land is to be made to any unmarried emigrant who has neither trade nor property, until after a residence of four years, during which time he must have been employed in the culture of the ground.

5. But if, after a residence of two years, such a person should marry the daughter of an honest farmer, with his consent and be by him recommended, a grant of land may be made to him.

6. Liberty of conscience is not to be extended beyond the first generation : the children of the emigrant must be Catholic ; and emigrants not agreeing to this must not be admitted, but removed, even when they bring property with them. This is to be explained to settlers who do not profess the Catholic religion.

7. In Upper Louisiana, no settler is to be admitted who is not a farmer or a mechanic.

8. It is expressly recommended to commandants to watch that no preacher of any religion but the Catholic comes into the province.

9. To every married emigrant of the above description, two hundred arpents may be granted, with the addition of fifty for every child he brings.

10. If he brings negroes, twenty additional arpents are to be granted him for each : but in no case are more than eight hundred arpents to be granted to an emigrant.

11. No land is to be granted to a trader.

12. Immediately on the arrival of a settler, the oath of allegiance is to be administered to him. If he has a wife, proof is to be demanded of their marriage ; and, if they bring any property, they are to be required to declare what part belongs to either of them ; and they are to be informed that the discovery of any wilful falsehood in this declaration, will incur the forfeiture of the land granted them, and the improvements made thereon.

13. Without proof of a lawful marriage, or of absolute ownership of negroes, no grant is to be made for any wife or negro.

14. The grant is to be forfeited, if a settlement be not made within the year, or one-tenth part of the land put in cultivation within two.

15. No grantee is to be allowed to sell his land until he has produced three crops on a tenth part of it ; but in case of death it may pass to an heir in the province, but not to one without, unless he come and settle it.

16. If the grantee owes debts in the province the proceeds of the first four crops are to be applied to their discharge, in preference to that of

debts due abroad. If, before the third crop be made, it becomes necessary to evict the grantee on account of his bad conduct, the land shall be given to the young man and young woman, residing within one mile of it, whose good conduct may show them to be the best deserving of it; and the decision is to be made by an assembly of notable planters, presided by the commandant.

17. Emigrants are to settle contiguous to old establishments, without leaving any vacant land—that the people may more easily protect each other, in case of any invasion by the Indians; and that the administration of justice, and a compliance with police regulations, may be facilitated.

Early in this year, the dukes of Orleans and Montausier, and the count of Beaujolais, came to New Orleans from the western states. These grandchildren of the duke of Orleans, who was regent of France during the minority of Louis XV. and descendants of Louis XIII. were seen with great interest by the inhabitants. After a stay of a few weeks, they departed for Europe by the way of Havana.

Don Denys de la Ronde and Don Pedro de la Roche took their seats in the cabildo; the former as successor of Almonaster, and the latter as principal provincial alcade.

Captain Guion, an officer of the revolutionary war, came this winter to Natchez, with a strong reinforcement, and took the command of the forces brought by lieutenants M'Nary and Pope. On the 23d of March, the fort at the Walnut Hills, and on the twenty-ninth, Fort Panmure, were evacuated by the troops of Spain, and immediate possession taken by those of the United States. Shortly after, Gayoso gave orders to William Dunbar, (who had succeeded him in the office of commissioner, on the part of Spain, for running the line of demarcation) to make arrangements with Ellicot, in order that the operations might be immediately begun. Major Trueman was the surveyor on the part of the United States, and Power, the Baron's late agent, that on the part of Spain.

Congress on the seventh of April, erected the country bounded on the north by a line drawn due east from the mouth of the river Yazoo to the Catahouche river; on the east by that stream; on the south by the thirty-first degree of north latitude, and on the west by the Mississippi—into a separate government, to be called the Mississippi territory; and a form of government was established therein, similar to that provided for the northwestern territory, by the ordinance of 1787, with the exception of the clause prohibiting slavery.

The state of Georgia laid claim to the land included within the new government, or the greatest part of it; and congress declared that the establishment of the territorial body should not, in any respect, impair the rights to any land west of that state, of any person or persons, either to the jurisdiction or soil of the said territory. The president of the United States was authorized to appoint commissioners to ascertain, conjointly with others appointed on the part of the state, her right to any land west of the river Catahouche, north of the thirty-first degree of north latitude, and south of the land ceded by the state of North Carolina to the United States; and to receive proposals for the relinquishment or cession of the whole or any part of the other territory claimed by the state of Georgia and out of her ordinary jurisdiction.

Winthrop Sergeant was appointed governor of the new territory; and, on his arrival soon after, with the secretary and judges, its government went into operation.

The Northern Indians continuing to manifest pacific dispositions, it was thought proper to transfer the headquarters of the army of the United States to the Mississippi; and, accordingly, Wilkinson came to Natchez with a considerable part of the forces. Here was fixed, at this time, the southernmost post. He removed, with all his men, to the spot called by the French *la Roche a Davion*, and by the English "Loftus' Heights," which was the most southerly tenable point within the United States, and immediately began the fortification which was afterwards called Fort Adams.

By a royal schedule of the twenty-first of October, the intendancy of the provinces of Louisiana and West Florida was put in possession, to the exclusion of all other authority, of the privilege of dividing and granting all kinds of land belonging to the crown—a privilege which, under the royal order of the twenty-fourth of August, 1770, belonged to the civil and military government.

Riano and Fonvergne were the ordinary alcades for the year 1799.

On the 30th of April, Don Joseph Vidal, the commandant of the post of Concordia, opposite to Natchez, entered, by order of Gayoso, into an arrangement with the governor of the Mississippi territory, for the reciprocal surrender of runaway slaves.

Morales, considering that three years had elapsed since the ratification of the treaty between his sovereign and the United States, did not think himself authorized to allow any longer the citizens of the latter a place of deposit in the city of New Orleans; and he issued an order accordingly. A measure which excited great commotion in the provinces and the United States, particularly in Kentucky and Tennessee.

Gayoso and Wilkinson, on the first of March, entered into a provisional convention for the mutual surrender of deserters from the armies of Spain and the United States, seeking an asylum within the limits of their respective adjacent territories.

In the latter part of the month, the running of the line of demarcation was completed, except a small portion of it on the borders of East Florida, which was deferred on account of the hostile appearance of the Indians.

On the seventeenth of July, Morales issued a set of regulations in regard to the grant of land, bottomed on the provisions of the late schedule, as follows:

1. To each newly arrived family, *a chaque famille nouvelle*, who are possessed of the necessary qualifications to be admitted among the number of cultivators of these provinces, and who have obtained the permission of the government to establish themselves on a place which they have chosen, there shall be granted, *for once*, if it is on the bank of the Mississippi, four, six or eight arpents in front on the river, by the ordinary depth of forty arpents; and if it is at any other place, the quantity which they shall be judged capable to cultivate, and which shall be deemed necessary for pasture for their beasts, in proportion and according to the number of which the family is composed; understanding that the concession is never to exceed eight hundred arpents in superfices.

2. To obtain the said concessions, if they are asked for in this city, the permission which has been obtained to establish themselves in the place from the governor, ought to accompany the petition; and if, in any

of the posts, the commandant at the same time will state that the lands asked for are vacant, and belong to the domain, and that the petitioner has obtained permission of the government to establish himself; and referring to the date of the letter or advice they have received.

3. Those who obtain concessions on the bank of the river, ought to make, in the first year of their possession, levees sufficient to prevent the inundation of the waters, and canals sufficient to drain off the water when the river is high; they shall be held, in addition, to make, and keep in good order, a public highway, which ought to be at least thirty feet wide, and have bridges of fifteen feet over the canals or ditches which the road crosses; which regulations ought to be observed, according to the usages of the respective districts, by all persons to whom lands are granted, in whatever part they are obtained.

4. The new settlers who have obtained lands shall be equally obliged to clear and put into cultivation, in the precise time of three years, all the front of their concessions, for the depth of at least two arpents, under the penalty of having the lands granted reunited to the domain, if this condition is not complied with. The commandants and syndics will watch that what is enjoined in this and the preceding article be strictly observed; and occasionally inform the intendant of what they have remarked, well understanding that in case of default they will be responsible to his majesty.

5. If a tract of land, belonging to minors, remain without being cleared, or as much of it as the regulations require; and that the bank, the road, the ditches, and the bridges, are not made, the commandant or syndic of the district will certify from whom the fault has arisen; if it is in the guardian, he will urge him to put it in order; and, if he fails, he shall give an account of it; but, if the fault arises from want of means of the minor to defray the expense, the commandant or syndic shall address a statement of it to the intendancy, to the end that sale of it may be ordered for the benefit of the minor, to whom alone this privilege is allowed; if, in the space of six months, any purchaser presents himself; if not, it shall be granted gratis to any person asking for it, or sold for the benefit of the treasury.

6. During the said term of three years, no person shall sell or dispose of the land which has been granted to him, nor shall he ever after the term, if he has failed to comply with the conditions contained in the preceding article; and to avoid abuses and surprise in this respect, we declare that all sales made without the consent of the intendancy, in writing, shall be null and of no effect; which consent shall not be granted until they have examined, with scrupulous attention, if the conditions have or have not been fulfilled.

7. To avoid for the future, the litigations and confusion of which we have examples every day, we have also judged it very necessary that the notaries of this city, and the commandants of posts, shall not take any acknowledgment of conveyances of land obtained by concession; unless the seller (grantor) presents and delivers to the buyer the title which he has obtained, and in addition, being careful to insert in the deed the metes and bounds, and other descriptions, which result from the title and the *proces verbal* of the survey which ought to accompany it.

8. In case that the small depth which the points, upon which the land on the river is generally formed, prevent the granting of forty arpents,

according to usage, there shall be given a greater quantity in front to compensate it; or, if no other person asks the concession, or to purchase it, it shall be divided equally between the persons nearest to it, who may repair the banks, roads, and bridges, in the manner before prescribed.

9. Although the king renounces the possession of the lands sold, distributed, or conceded in his name, those to whom they are granted or sold ought to be apprised that his majesty reserves the right of taking from the forests known here under the name of cypress woods, all the wood which may be necessary for his use, and more especially which he may want for the navy, in the same manner and with the same liberty that the undertakers have enjoyed to this time; but this, notwithstanding they are not to suppose themselves authorized to take more than is necessary, nor to make use of or split those which are cut down and found unsuitable.

10. In the posts of Opelousas and Attakapas, the greatest quantity of land that can be conceded, shall be one league front by the same quantity in depth; and when forty arpents cannot be obtained in depth, a half league may be granted; and, for a general rule, it is established, that, to obtain, in said posts, a half league in front by the same quantity in depth, the petitioner must be owner of one hundred head of cattle, some horses and sheep, and two slaves, and also in proportion for a larger tract, without the power, however, of exceeding the quantity before mentioned.

11. As much as it is possible, and the local situation will permit, no interval shall be left between concessions; because it is very advantageous that the establishments touch, as much for the inhabitants, who can lend each other mutual support, as for the more easy administration of justice, and the observance of rules of police, indispensable in all places, but more especially in new establishments.

12. If, notwithstanding what is before written, marshy lands, or other causes, shall make it necessary to leave some vacant lands, the commandants and syndics will take care that the inhabitants of the district alone may take wood enough for their use only, well understanding they shall not take more; or, if any individual of any other post, shall attempt to get wood, or cut fire-wood, without having obtained the permission of this intendancy, besides the indemnity which he shall be held to pay the treasury for the damage sustained, he shall be comdemned, for the first time, to the payment of a fine of twenty-five dollars; twice that sum for the second offense; and, for the third offense, shall be put in prison, according as the offense may be more or less aggravated; the said fines shall be divided between the treasury, the judge and the informer.

13. The new settler, to whom land has been granted in one settlement, cannot obtain another concession without having previously proven that he had possessed the first during three years, and fulfilled all the conditions prescribed.

14. The changes occasioned by the current of the river, are often the cause of one part of a concession becoming useless, so that we have examples of proprietors pretending to abandon and re-unite to the domain a part of the most expensive, for keeping up the banks, the roads, the ditches, etc., and willing to reserve only that which is good; and seeing that unless some remedy is provided for this abuse, the greatest mischief must result to the neighbors, we declare that the treasury will not admit of an abandonment or re-union to the domain of any part of the land the

owner wishes to get rid of, unless the abandonment comprehends the whole limits included in the concession or act in virtue of which he owns the land he wishes to abandon.

15. All concessions shall be given in the name of the king, by the general intendant of this province, who shall order the surveyor-general, or one particularly named by him, to make the survey and mark the land by fixing bounds, not only in front, but also in the rear; this (survey) ought to be done in the presence of the commandant or syndic of the district and of two of the neighbors; and these four shall sign the *proces verbal* which shall be drawn up by the surveyor.

16. The said *proces verbal*, with a certified copy of the same shall be sent by the surveyor to the intendant, to the end that, on the original, there be delivered, by the consent of the king's attorney, the necessary title paper; to this will be annexed the certified copy forwarded by the surveyor. The original shall be deposited in the office of the secretary of the treasury, and care shall be taken to make annually a book of all which have been sent, with an alphabetical list, to be the more useful when it is necessary to have recourse to it, and for greater security, to the end that, at all times and against all accidents, the documents which shall be wanted, can be found. The surveyor shall also have another book, numbered, in which the *proces verbal* of the survey he makes shall be recorded; and, as well on the original, which ought to be deposited on record as on the copy intended to be annexed to the title, he shall note the folio of the book in which he has enregistered the figurative plat of survey.

17. In the office of the finances there shall also be a book, numbered, where the titles of concessions shall be recorded; in which, beside the ordinary clauses, mention shall be made of the folio of the book in which they are transcribed. There must also be a note taken in the contadoria (or chamber of accounts) of the army and finances, and that under the penalty of being void. The chamber of accounts shall also have a like book; and, at the time of taking the note, shall cite the folio of the book where it is recorded.

18. Experience proves that a great number of those who have asked for land think themselves the legal owners of it; those who have obtained the first decree, by which the surveyor is ordered to measure it, and to put them in possession; others, after the survey has been made, have neglected to ask the title for the property; and, as like abuses, continuing for a longer time, will augment the confusion and disorder which will necessarily result, we declare that no one of those who have obtained the said decrees, notwithstanding, in virtue of them, the survey has taken place, and that they have been put in possession, can be regarded as owners of land until their real titles are delivered, completed with all the formalities before recited.

19. All those who possess lands in virtue of formal titles given by their excellencies the governors of this province, since the epoch when it came under the power of the Spanish; and those who possessed them in the time when it belonged to France, so far from being interrupted, shall, on the contrary, be protected and maintained in their possessions.

20. Those who, without the title or possession mentioned in the preceding article, are found occupying lands, shall be driven therefrom, as from property belonging to the crown; but, if they have occupied the same more than ten years, a compromise will be admitted to those who

are considered as owners, that is to say, they shall not be deprived of their lands. Always that, after information, and summary procedure, and with the intervention of the procureur of the king, at the board of the treasury, they shall be obliged to pay a just and moderate retribution, calculated according to the extent of the lands, their situation, and other circumstances, and the price of estimation for once paid into the royal treasury. The titles to property will be delivered, on referring to that which has resulted from the proceedings.

21. Those who are found in a situation expressed in the 18th article, if they have not cleared nor done any work upon the land they consider themselves proprietors of, by virtue of the first decree of the government, not being of the number of those who have been admitted in the class of new comers, in being deprived or admitted to compromise, in the manner explained in the preceding article; if they are of that class, they shall observe what is ordered in the article following.

22. In the precise and peremptory term of six months, counting from the day when this regulation shall be published in each post, all those who occupy lands without titles from the governor, and those who, in having obtained a certain number of arpents, have seized a greater quantity, ought to make it known, either to have their titles made out, if there are any, or to be admitted to a compromise, or to declare that the said lands belong to the domain, if they have not been occupied more than ten years; understanding, if it passes the said term, if they are instructed by other ways, they will not obtain either title or compromise.

23. Those who give information of lands occupied, after the expiration of the term fixed in the preceding article, shall have for their reward the one-fourth part of the price for which they are sold, or obtained by way of compromise; and, if desirable, he shall have the preference, either by compromise, at the price of appraisement, and there shall be made a deduction of one-fourth, as informer.

24. As it is impossible, considering all the local circumstances, that all the vacant lands belonging to the domain should be sold by auction, as it is ordained by the law 15th, title 12th, book 4th, of the collection of the laws of these kingdoms, the sale shall be made according as it shall be demanded, with the intervention of the king's attorney for the board of finances, for the price they shall be taxed, to those who wish to purchase; understanding, if the purchasers have not ready money to pay it shall be lawful for them to purchase the said lands at redeemable quit-rent, during which they shall pay the five per cent. yearly.

25. Besides the moderate price which the land ought to be taxed, the purchasers shall be held to pay down the right of *media annata*, or half year's, to be remitted to Spain, which, according to the custom of Havana, founded on law, is reduced to two and a half per cent. on the price of estimation, and made 18 per cent. on the sum, by the said two and a half per cent.; they shall also be obliged to pay down the fees of the surveyor and notary.

26. The sales of land shall be made subject to the same condition, and charges of banks, roads, ditches and bridges, contained in the preceding article. But the purchasers are not subject to lose their lands, if, in the three first years, they do not fulfil the said conditions. Commandants and syndics shall oblige them to put themselves within the rule, begin to

perform the conditions in a reasonable term, and if they do not do it, the said work shall be done at the cost of the purchasers.

27. Care shall be taken to observe in the said sales, that which is recommended in the 11th article, seeing the advantages and utility which result from consolidating the establishments always when it is practicable.

28. The titles to the property of lands which are sold, or granted by way of compromise, shall be issued by the general intendant, who, after the price of estimation is fixed, and of the *media annata* (half year's) rent or quit-rent, the said price of estimation shall have been paid into the treasury, shall put it in writing according to the result of the proceeding which has taken place with the intervention of the king's attorney.

29. The said procedure shall be deposited in the office of the finance, and the title be transcribed in another book, intended for the recording of deeds and grants of land, in the same manner as is ordered by the 17th article, concerning grutuitous concessions. The principal chamber of accounts shall also have a separate book, to take a note of the titles issued for sales and grants under compromise.

30. The fees of the surveyor in every case comprehended in the present regulation, shall be proportionate to the labor and that which it has been customary until this time to pay. Those of the secretary of finances, unless there has been extraordinary labor, and where the new settlers are not poor (for in this case he is not to exact anything of them) shall be five dollars; and this shall include the recording and other formalities prescribed, and those of the appraisers, and of the interpreter. if, on any occasion, there is reason to employ him to translate papers, take declarations or other acts, shall be regulated by the provincial tariff.

31. Indians who possess lands within the limits of the government, shall not, in any manner, be disturbed; on the contrary, they shall be protected and supported; and to this, the commandants, syndics and surveyors, ought to pay the greatest attention, to conduct themselves in consequence.

32. The granting or selling of any lands shall not be proceeded in without formal information having been previously received that they are vacant; and, to avoid injurious mistakes, we premise that, beside the signature of the commandant or syndic of the district, this information ought to be joined by that of the surveyor, and of two of the neighbors, well understanding. If, notwithstanding this necessary precaution, it shall be found that the land has another owner besides the claimant, and that there is sufficient reason to restore it to him, the commandant or syndic, the surveyor, and the neighbors who have signed the information, shall indemnify him for the losses he has suffered.

33. As far as it may be practicable, the inhabitants must endeavor that the petitions presented by them, to ask for lands, be written in the Spanish language; on which ought, also, to be written the advice or information which the commandants are to give. In the posts where this is not practicable, the ancient usage shall be followed.

34. All the lots or seats belonging to the domain, which are found vacant, either in this city, or boroughs, or villages, already established, or which may be established, shall be sold for ready money, with all the formalities prescribed in article the twenty-fourth, and others, which concern the sale of lands.

35. The owners of lots or places, which have been divided, as well as

those in front, as towards the N. E. and S. W. extremities, N. E. and S. W. shall within three months, present to the intendancy the titles which they have obtained; to the end that, in examining the same, if any essential thing is found wanting, it may be supplied, and they assured of their property in a legal way.

36. The same thing must be done before the sub-delegates of Mobile and Pensacola, for those who have obtained grants for lots in these respective establishments; to the end that this intendancy, being instructed thereon, may order what it shall judge most convenient to indemnify the royal treasury, without doing wrong to the owner.

37. In the office of comptroller, contadoria of the army, or chambers of accounts of this province, and other boards under the jurisdiction of this intendancy, an account shall be kept of the amount of sales or grants of lands, to instruct his majesty every year what this branch of the royal revenue produces, according, as it is ordered in the thirteenth article of the ordinance of the king, of the 15th of October, 1754.

38. The commandants, or syndics, in their respective districts, are charged with the collection of the amount of the taxes or rents laid on lands; for this purpose the papers and necessary documents are to be sent to them; and they ought to forward annually, to the general treasury, the sums they have collected, to the end that acquittances, clothed with the usual formalities of law, may be delivered to them.

Gayoso now received and executed a commission of judge of residence of his predecessor. One act of the Baron's administration was deemed reprehensible. He had been deluded, by an excess of zeal for what he conceived to be the public good, to take upon himself the responsibility of condemning to death a slave, who had killed his overseer. The fact was proven, that Vidal, the assessor of government, conceived that the circumstances, which attended it, did not bring the case under any law authorizing a sentence of death and had recommended a milder one. At the solicitation of a number of respectable planters, and of the owner of the slave, Marigny de Mandeville, a knight of St. Louis and colonel of the militia, who represented to the Baron that an example was absolutely necessary, especially so soon after the late insurrection, he disregarded the opinion of his legal adviser and ordered the execution of the slave. It was thought the life of a human being, although a slave, ought not to depend on the opinion of a man, in any case where his sacrifice was not expressly ordered by law. A fine of five hundred dollars was paid by the Baron.

Don Francisco de Bouligny, who had succeeded Piernas in the command of the regiment of Louisiana, died and was succeeded by colonel Howard.

The Marquis de Someruelos, succeeded the Count de Santa Clara, as captain-general of the island of Cuba, and the provinces of Louisiana and East and West Florida. The Marquis retained this office until the cession.

The increase of the commerce of the United States with New Orleans, induced the appointment of a consul there, and the President commissioned Evan Jones as such.

The post of New Madrid was this year annexed to Upper Louisiana.

Gayoso died on the 18th July, in his forty-eighth year. Don Maria Vidal, the lieutenant-governor, now acted as civil governor of the two provinces, and the captain-general, on hearing of Gayoso's death, sent over the Marquis de Casa-Calvo, to act as military governor.

Don Ramon de Lopez y Angullo, a knight pensioner of the royal and distinguished order of Charles III., who had been appointed intendant of the provinces of Louisiana and West Florida, arrived at New Orleans in the latter part of the year.

A report made by Don Carlos Dehault Delassus, commandant-general of Upper Louisiana, presents the following result on the last day of this year:

CENSUS.

St. Louis,	925
Carondelet,	184
St. Charles,	875
St. Fernando,	276
Marais des Liards,	376
Maramec,	115
St. Andrew,	393
St. Genevieve,	949
New Bourbon,	560
Cape Girardeau,	521
New Madrid,	782
Little Meadows,	49
	6,005

The white population was 4,948 souls; the free colored, 197; that of slaves, 883.

During this year there were 34 marriages, 191 births, and 52 deaths.

There were in the different settlements, 7,980 head of horned cattle, and 1,763 horses.

The crops amounted to 88,349 minots of wheat, 84,534 of Indian corn, and 28,627 pounds of tobacco.

The exports to New Orleans, consisted of:

1754 bundles of deerskins, at 40,	$70,160
8 bundles of bearskins, at 32,	256
18 bundles of buffalo robes, at 30,	540
360 quintals of lead, at 6,	2,160
20 quintals of flour, at 3,	60
	$73,176

1340 quintals of lead were exported to the United States, by the Ohio, Cumberland and Tennessee rivers.

One thousand bushels of salt were made yearly.

The United States had been induced, by the conduct of France and Spain, to make warlike preparations; both of those powers having committed spoliations on their trade, and the latter (in violation of her treaty, as the United States considered it) having ceased to allow their citizens a place of deposit in New Orleans. General Washington had accepted the chief command of the armies of his country, but had stipulated that he should not be called on to take the field until his presence became absolutely necessary; and in the meanwhile, the superintendance of the forces had been committed to generals Hamilton and Pinkney. The agency of the former had been extended to all the western army, except that part which might be within the states of Kentucky and

Tennessee; and it was deemed that Wilkinson's presence at his headquarters was indispensable to a full and satisfactory discussion of matters relating to a section of country, with many of the most important transactions of which he had been, in some way or other, concerned. He accordingly descended the Mississippi, and took shipping for New York.

Government had determined on a mode of redress, of which the conception was as bold as its execution was difficult. This was nothing less than the acquisition of New Orleans, which appeared calculated to indemnify the United States for their losses, and appease the fears of the western people. The success of the enterprise depended almost entirely on its being conducted in such a way as not to awake the suspicions of Spain. The differences with France offered a cover for the real design. Twelve regiments were this year added to the army, to serve during the continuance of the differences. Three of these regiments were ordered to the mouth of the Ohio, and to keep their boats in constant readiness. The assent of congress was to be asked at their next meeting.

General Washington died on the fourteenth of December.

The ordinary alcades for the year 1800, were Perez and Poyfarre.

Application having been made to Don Henry Peyroux, the commandant at New Madrid, for the purchase of several very large tracts of land, particularly one of one hundred thousand acres, he consulted Lopez, the new intendant, who refused his assent, being of opinion that it never was the intention of the king to dispose of the vacant lands in quantities so large. He admitted the new regulations were made with a view to the *sale* of lands; but they were to be disposed of in compliance with the previous formalities, and a reference to the abilities and forces of the parties desirous of purchasing; because it would not be just that for a small consideration, one or more speculators should engross a vast extent of land, to the prejudice of others who came to settle, who would consequently find themselves driven to purchase those lands which they might have gratuitously, or at any rate at a low price.

The culture of the cane requiring an additional number of hands, the colonial government, in the beginning of November, at the solicitation of the cabildo, issued a proclamation, suspending, until the pleasure of the king should be known, the existing prohibition of the introduction of African negroes.

On the seventh of May, the northwestern territory of the United States was divided: the western part of it was erected into a distinct government, under a form similar to that established by the ordinance of 1787. It was called the Indian territory.

The marked determination of the people of the United States not to re-elect the president, induced him to abandon the plan he had formed for the seizure of New Orleans.

By the third article of a treaty concluded at St. Ildefonso on the first of October of this year, between the Catholic king and the first consul of the French republic, the former promised and engaged on his part, to cede to the French republic, six months after the full and entire execution of the conditions therein stipulated, in relation to the duke of Parma, the colony and province of Louisiana, with the same extent that it then had in the hands of Spain, and that it had when France possessed it, and such as it should be after the treaties subsequently entered into between Spain and other powers.

Forstall and Caisergues were the ordinary alcades for the years 1801 and 1802.

Don Dominique Bouligny took his seat in the cabildo as a perpetual regidor.

The king having disapproved of the suppression of the right of deposit in New Orleans, allowed to citizens of the United States, right was now restored to them.

The suspension of the prohibition of the introduction of Guinea negroes, met with the king's approbation, and he decreed it to continue until he gave order to the contrary.

On the twenty-first of March, the cession of Louisiana to France was effected. Buonaparte took immediate measures to possess himself of his acquisition. An immense body of troops was destined to this service. A form of government was adopted for the province. Victor was appointed captain-general, Laussat colonial prefet, and Ayme chief justice.

By a royal schedule of the tenth of May, the king gave his assent to the proposition of the Baron de Carondelet, that three hundred toises of the commons behind the city and near the fortifications, which in their then situation produced nothing, being covered with water during one-half of the year, should be divided into lots of seventy toises in front, and one hundred and forty in depth, and let out for a moderate rent to such inhabitants of the city as might wish to occupy them as gardens, and the money thus raised applied to the lighting of the city, so that in the course of a few years the whole ground could by tillage be raised above the level of the water, and the occupier of these lots draining them by trenches into the canal Carondelet, would put an end to the putrid fevers occasioned by the stagnation of water in ponds near the city, which was the cause of much mortality.

Thomas Jefferson succeeded John Adams in the presidency of the United States, on the fourth of March.

The differences that had prevailed between the United States and the French republic, were terminated by a treaty entered into at Paris, and ratified on the first day of June.

CHAPTER XXIV.

Don Juan Manuel de Salcedo, a brigadier-general of the royal armies, arrived towards the middle of June, with a commission of governor of the provinces of Louisiana and West Florida, and the Marquis de Casa-Calvo sailed for Havana.

Daniel Clark, a citizen of the United States, residing in New Orleans, was appointed consul of these states in said city.

Lopez sailed for Spain, and the duties of his office were provisionally performed by Morales, the contador.

The Mississippi territory was separated from the United States, by lands belonging to Indians, through which travelling was often difficult; a remedy was now applied to this evil.

On the twenty-fourth of October, a treaty was concluded on the Chickasaw Bluffs, between the United States and the Chickasaw nation of Indians, by which the latter permitted the former to lay out, open, and make a convenient wagon road through the Indian land, between the settlements of the Miro district, in the state of Tennessee, and those of Natchez in the Mississippi territory; and it was provided that the necessary ferries over the water courses crossed by the road, should be deemed the property of the Indians.

On the seventeenth day of December, another treaty was concluded at Fort Adams, on the Mississippi, between the United States and the Choctaw nation of Indians, by which the latter gave their consent that a convenient and durable wagon road might be explored, marked, opened, and made through their land, to commence at the northwestern extremity of the Mississippi territory, and extend to the land of the Chickasaws. The Choctaws agreed that the old boundary line, heretofore established by the officers of the king of Great Britain and the Choctaw nation, which runs in a parallel direction with the Mississippi river eastward, should be retraced and plainly marked, and be held ever after as the boundary between the settlements of the Mississippi territory and the Choctaw nation. The Choctaws relinquished to the United States all their rights to the land between this line and the Mississippi, bounded on the south by the thirty-first degree of north latitude, and on the north by the river Yazoo, where the line shall strike the stream. The United States engaged that all persons who might settle beyond this line, should be removed within it, on the side towards the Mississippi, together with their slaves, household furniture, tools, stock, and materials, and their cabins or houses demolished.

On the twenty-fifth of March, 1802, a definite treaty of peace, between Spain, France and Great Britain was signed at Amiens.

Don Carlos de Jaen came over with and executed a commission of judge of residence of Miro.

By a royal schedule of the eleventh of June, the contribution to be paid on legacies, devises, and successions *ab intestato*, in favor of relatives and relations of deceased persons or strangers, was reduced to and fixed at four per cent. That on legacies or devises to a husband or wife, at one-half of one per cent. This charge, however, was not to extend to estates of less than two thousand dollars, nor to bequests for the benefit of the soul of the deceased.

The Baron de Bastrop having ceded to Moorhouse, a citizen of the United States, a part of the grant he had obtained from the Baron de Carondelet, in 1769, on the Washita, the king disapproved of this arrangement, and by a royal schedule of the eighteenth of July, forbade the grant of any land in Louisiana to a citizen of the United States.

Serano, the assessor of the intendancy, died on the first of December. Morales, in consequence of this event, and of the absence of a legal character to supply his place, closed the tribunal of affairs and causes relating to grants and compositions of royal lands, the ordinance for the intendants of New Spain, providing that for conducting the affairs of that tribunal and sustaining its acts, there should be the concurrence of such a character.

During the last quarter of this year, citizens of the United States were not allowed the right of a deposit, in or near New Orleans, and the importation of goods in American bottoms was not permitted.

Lopez having lost the office of intendant by the cession of Louisiana to France, was appointed consul-general of Spain at New Orleans, and embarked on board of a vessel for that city, but died on the passage.

On the twenty-ninth of November, the people of the E. division of the N. W. territory of the United States, became a state under the name of the state of Ohio, being the seventeenth.

Forstall and Lanusse were the ordinary alcades during the year 1803.

Towards the latter part of January, Morales issued a proclamation, allowing the importation of flour and provisions from the United States on payment of a duty of six per cent. subject to exportation in Spanish bottoms only.

On the first of March, the king disapproved of the order of Morales, prohibiting the introduction and deposit of goods, wares and merchandise from the United States, in the port of New Orleans: and ordered that the United States should continue to enjoy their right of deposit in New Orleans, without prejudice of his to substitute some other spot on the banks of the Mississippi.

By an act of congress of the ninth of February, provision was made for granting licenses at the customhouse at Fort Adams, to vessels owned by citizens of the United States, lying on the Mississippi, below the thirty-first degree of northern latitude.

General Victor had been appointed, by the first consul, commissioner for receiving possession of the province of Louisiana, and his arrival being daily expected, the cabildo, on the twenty-third of March, 1803, caused the supply of meat for the French troops accompanying him, to be put at auction to the lowest bidder, with the exclusive right of supplying the inhabitants of the city. The contractor was required to keep constantly a stock of at least one thousand head of cattle in or near the city of New Orleans.

A vessel arriving from Havre-de-Grace, on the following day, brought the baggage of Laussat, the colonial prefect, who was preceding the captain-general, with a special mission, for the purpose of providing whatever might be necessary on the arrival of the troops, and making arrangements for the establishment of the government of the republic.

By this vessel the people of Louisiana were informed of the form of government provided for the province by its new master.

Its principal officers were a captain-general, a colonial prefect, and a commissary of justice.

The captain-general was commander-in-chief of the land and naval forces, and had the care of the exterior and the interior defense of the colony. He provisorily filled the vacancies in military offices, according to the order of advancement, as far as the grade of chief of division or squadron, and proposed to the minister proper persons to fill higher grades. He delivered passports, regulated the bearing of arms, and corresponded with the governors of other colonies, whether belonging to allies, neutrals, or enemies. With the colonial prefect, he regulated the works to be done on the fortifications, and the new roads to be opened; and finally exercised all powers formally granted to governors-general. He was forbidden to interfere with the attributions of the colonial prefect or commissary of justice; but was authorized to require from either of them information on any matter relative to the service. Power was given him to suspend provisorily the execution of laws, in whole or in part, on his

39

responsibility, after having consulted the colonial prefect, or the commissary of justice, according to the nature of the case.

Copies of every deliberation were to be sent yearly to the minister.

Vacant lands were to be granted by the captain-general and colonial prefect; but in case of disagreement the opinion of the former was to prevail.

Vacancies in the departments of the colonial prefect and commissary of justice, were to be filled by the captain-general on their nomination; but no appointment was final until confirmed by the first consul.

In case of the absence of the captain-general, he was to be represented by the colonial prefect, or by the highest military officer.

The colonial prefect's powers extended to the administration of the finances, the general accountability and destination of all officers of administration. He was exclusively charged with the police of the colony, including all that related to taxes, receipts and expenditures, the customhouse, the pay of the troops, the public stores, agriculture, navigation, commerce, the census, the suppression of contraband trade, the police of slaves, highways, levees, public instruction and worship, the press, and generally all the powers formerly exercised by intendants, commissaries-general, and ordonnateurs. In the assessment of taxes he was to consult three merchants and three planters. In case of absence, he was to be represented by the officer of administration next in rank.

The commissary of justice had the superintendence of all courts of justice and their ministerial officers; he was to have an eye to the regular administration of justice, the safety and salubrity of gaols, as well as the conduct of officers and clerks. He might preside and vote in any court of justice. He was to require monthly statements from the president and clerk of each court, of every case tried, and communicate it to the captain-general. He was authorized to make rules for the administration of justice, and, with the consent of the captain-general, order them to be observed. Agents of government were not suable for any matter relating to their officers, nor any citizen in the public service arrested without his *fiat*, and he was to give an account of his proceedings in this respect to the minister. He was to prepare a civil and criminal code, and submit it to the captain-general and colonial prefect for their examination, and transmit it, with the proces verbal of their deliberations thereon, to the minister. He had the police of vagrants.

In the latter part of the month, notice reached New Orleans, of the arrival, at the Balize, of a French national brig, having on board Laussat, the colonial prefect. Salcedo immediately dispatched a captain and a lieutenant of infantry in the government barge, and Morales, an officer of administration, in that of the customhouse, to meet and congratulate the representative of the French republic. Laussat came up in the government barge, landed at the levee on the twenty-sixth, and was immediately conducted to the government house, where Salcedo and Morales, surrounded by the staff of the garrison and army, the officers of the militia, and the head of the clergy, were assembled for his reception.

In this interview Laussat announced the fixed determination of the French government to promote the prosperity of the colony, to cause order to prevail in it, to maintain its laws, to respect the treaties with Indian nations, and protect the exercise of public worship without any change therein. He added that the captain-general and troops, who had left

Holland, as he believed, in the latter end of January, would probably arrive here towards the middle of April.

A few days afterwards, he issued a proclamation in the name of the French republic.

This document begins by stating that the separation of Louisiana from France marked in the annals of the latter one of the most shameful eras under a weak and corrupt government, after an ignominious war and dishonorable peace. With this unnatural abandonment by the mother country, the love, loyalty and heroic courage of the people of Louisiana formed a noble contrast, with which every heart in France was now moved, and would long preserve the remembrance of. The French still remembered that a portion of the inhabitants of Louisiana were their descendants, with the same blood running in their veins. As soon as France, by a prodigious succession of triumphs, in the late revolution, had recovered her own freedom and glory, she turned her eyes towards Louisiana, the retrocession of which signalized her first peace. But the period was not yet arrived—it was necessary that a man, who is a stranger to nothing that is national, great, magnanimous or just; who, to the most distinguished talent for conquering, adds the rare one of obtaining for his conquests the happiest results, and by the ascendancy of his character, at once strikes terror to his enemies, and inspires his allies with confidence—whose expansive mind discovered at once the true interests of his country, and was bent on restoring to France her pristine grandeur and her lost possessions—should accomplish this important work.

This man, said the prefect, presides over the destinies of France and Louisiana, to insure their felicity. In the latter nothing more was necessary than to improve the bounties of which nature had been so prodigal towards her.

He observed it was the intention of government to do this—to live in peace and amity with the neighboring Indians, and protect the commerce of the colony; encourage its agriculture, people its deserts, promote labor and industry, respect property, opinions, and habits, protect public worship, preserve the empire of the laws, amend them slowly and with the light of experience only, maintain a regular police, introduce permanent order and economy in every branch of administration, tighten the bonds which a common origin and a similarity of manners had already established between the colony and the mother country, was the honorable object of the mission of the captain-general, colonial prefect, and commissary of justice, sent by the first consul.

After a short eulogy of the two high magistrates with whom he was associated, and of the officers who had hitherto governed the colony under the authority of Spain, whom he said the former would endeavor to imitate, he concluded with an assurance that the devotion of the people of Louisiana to the French republic, their gratitude to those by whom they were reunited to it, and the spectacle of their prosperity, were the rewards which he aspired to and should endeavor to deserve by a zeal which would know no limits but the fulfilment of its duties.

In an address, which was presented to him a few days afterwards, subscribed by a considerable number of the most respectable planters and merchants, assurance was given him that France had done justice to the sentiments of the people of Louisiana, in giving them credit for the attachment they had preserved for her. Thirty-four years of foreign domination had not extinguished or even diminished in their hearts the sacred love of their country; and their joy on returning under her banner, could only be equalled by the grief which they had felt on seeing it lowered in the midst of them. They were happy in having lived long enough to witness the reunion of the colony to France—an event which they had never ceased to desire, and which now gratified their utmost wishes.

They added that in an age so fruitful in astonishing events, greater, more important and memorable had occurred, but none in its history could present a more affecting and interesting spectacle than that of victorious and triumphant France holding out a protecting hand to children heretofore cast out from her bosom, by a weak and vacillating government, and calling them to a share in the fruits of a glorious peace, terminating in the most brilliant manner a bloody and terrible revolution.

They observed that the prefect had signalized the return of the French government, by bearing an authentic testimony of its beneficent views. His proclamation had filled the people with gratitude for its parental care, and they had already felt the happiness of their union with the French Republic. The happy selection of some of her most virtuous citizens to govern them, and her choicest troops to protect them, were sure pledges of their future happiness and prosperity. They offered in return their love and obedience, and swore to endeavor to prove themselves worthy of the title of French citizens.

The answer concludes by expressing the belief that France would attach less value to the assurance the people of Louisiana gave of their loyalty and fidelity, if they did not, at the same time, manifest some regret at the dissolution of their allegiance to a sovereign who had heaped on them his choicest favors, during the time they had lived under him. They protested that their hearts entertained no such guilty indifference; their grief, on separating from him, was mingled with joy on recovering their country; and they would prove themselves worthy members of the French republic, in preserving during their lives the remembrance of his paternal care.

The Marquis de Casa-Calvo, who had acted as military governor after the death of Gayoso, arrived from the Havana on the tenth of April, having been joined to Salcedo in a commission for the delivery of possession of the province to the commissioners of France. On the eighteenth of May, Salcedo and he issued a proclamation, announcing the intention of their sovereign to surrender the province to the French republic, and that his majesty, retaining the same affection as ever for the inhabitants of the province, and desiring to continue to them the same protection which he had hitherto extended to them, had determined:

1.   That the cession of the colony and island of New Orleans should be on the same terms as that of his Most Christian to his Catholic majesty; and consequently, the limits on both sides of the river St. Louis, or Mississippi, should continue as they remained by the fifth article of the definitive treaty of peace concluded at Paris on the tenth of December, 1763; and accordingly, the settlements from the bayou Manshac, as far as the line which separated the dominions of Spain and those of the United States, should remain a part of the monarchy of Spain and be annexed to the province of West Florida.

2. Every individual, employed in any branch of the king's service, and wishing to remain under his government, might proceed to Havana or any other part of his dominions, unless he preferred entering into the service of the French republic, which he might do : but if any just reason prevented his immediate departure, he might urge it in proper time.

3. The king's generosity induced him to continue to widows and others their respective provisions, and he would make known, in due time, in what manner he wished they should avail themselves of this favor.

4. He declared his expectation, from the sincere friendship and alliance which existed between him and the French republic, that orders would be given to the governors and other officers employed by France in Louisiana, that the clergy and religious institutions should be permitted to remain in the discharge of their offices, within their respective curacies and missions, and enjoy their former emoluments, privileges and exemptions ; that the tribunals established for the administration of justice, and ordinary judges, should be allowed to continue to administer it according to the former laws and usages of the province ; the inhabitants maintained in the peaceable possession of their property, and all grants made to them by the former governors confirmed, even when not finally ratified by the king ; and finally, that the French government should continue to the people of Louisiana the favor and protection they had enjoyed under Spain.

Everything seemed now ready, and the arrival of Victor, the commissioner of France for receiving possession, was hourly expected ; every one had his tri-colored cockade ready to be stuck in his hat as soon as the Spanish flag was lowered and the French hoisted, when a vessel from Bordeaux brought accounts of the sale of the province by Bonaparte to the United States.

By a treaty concluded at Paris on the thirtieth of April, the first consul had ceded, in the name of the republic, to the United States, forever and in full sovereignty, the province of Louisiana, with all its rights and appurtenances in full, and in the same manner as they had been acquired by the republic from the Catholic king.

2. In the cession are included the islands adjacent to Louisiana, all public lots and squares, vacant lands, and all public buildings, fortifications, barracks, and other edifices, which are not private property. The archives, papers and documents, relative to the domains and sovereignty of the province, are to be left in the possession of the commissioners of the United States, and copies given afterwards in due form to magistrates and principal officers, of such papers, and documents as may be necessary to them.

3. It is provided that the inhabitants of the ceded territory shall be incorporated into the union of the United States, and admitted as soon as possible, according to the principles of the federal constitution, to the enjoyment of all the advantages and immunities of citizens of the United States ; and in the meantime be unrestrained and protected in the free enjoyment of their liberty, property and the religion which they possess.

4. The government of France is to send a commissioner to Louisiana, to the end that he may do all acts necessary to receive possession of the country and its dependencies, from the officers of Spain, in the name of the French republic, and deliver it over to the commissioners or agents of the United States.

5. Immediately after the ratification of the treaty, by the president of the United States, in case that of the first consul shall have been obtained the commissioner of the French republic shall surrender all military posts in New Orleans, and in the rest of the ceded territory, to the commissioners of the United States, and the troops of France are to be withdrawn.

6. The United States promise to execute all treaties entered into by Spain with the Indians.

7. French vessels coming directly from France or her colonies, loaded only with the produce or manufactures of France or her colonies; and those of Spain, coming directly from the peninsula or her colonies, loaded only with the produce or manufactures of Spain or her colonies, are to be admitted, during twelve years, into the ports of the ceded territory, in the same manner as vessels of the United States coming directly from France, Spain, or any of their colonies, without paying any higher duty on tonnage or merchandise than citizens of the United States. During these twelve years no other nation shall enjoy the same advantages.

8. Afterwards and forever, French vessels are to be treated upon the footing of the most favored nations in these ports.

By two separate conventions of the same date, the United States engaged to pay sixty millions of francs to France, and discharge certain claims of their citizens on that power. A stock of eleven millions, two hundred and fifty thousand dollars, was created, bearing interest at six per cent. payable in London, Amsterdam, or Paris; the principal to be reimbursed at their treasury in annual instalments of not less than three millions, the first of which was to be paid fifteen years after the exchange of the ratifications. The French government promised, if disposed to sell the stock to do so to the United States, on the best terms. The value of the dollar of the United States was fixed at five livres eight sous.

The Catholic king made a solemn protest, on being informed of the sale of Louisiana by the first consul; and his minister at Washington city sent to the department of state a representation on the defects which in the opinion of the cabinet of Madrid, impaired the alienation; detailing the motives which had induced his sovereign to protest against it—the principal of which was, that France had promised never to alienate the ceded territory. After this representation, an opinion prevailed, both in Europe and America, that the king had given or would give, orders to prevent the delivery of the province to the French. The minister of the United States at Madrid, was therefore, instructed to ascertain whether there was any ground for the rumor.

In the month of June, the Spanish nuns in the convent of the Ursulines, unwilling to live under the government of the French republic, sailed for Havana, where the government gave them a house, and they established a convent of their order.

Congress, on the last day of October, authorized the President of the United States to take possession of the ceded territory; and in order to maintain therein the authority of the United States, to employ such a part of the navy and army of the union, and of the militia of the neighboring states and territory, as he might deem necessary. In the meanwhile, all the military, civil and judicial powers exercised by the existing government, were to be vested in such person or persons, and to be exercised in such a manner, as the President of the United States should direct, for the maintenance and protection of the inhabitants of Louisiana, in their liberty, property, and the religion which they professed.

The President of the United States appointed, accordingly, governor Claiborne, of the Mississippi territory, and general Wilkinson, commissioners for receiving possession of the ceded territory from the commissioner of France; and he gave to the former a commission, authorizing him provisorily to exercise, within the ceded territory, all the powers with which the Spanish governor-general and intendant were clothed, except that of granting lands.

In the meanwhile, the first consul had, on the sixth of June, appointed Laussat commissioner on the part of France, to receive possession of the province from those of Spain, and deliver it to those of the United States.

On Wednesday, the thirtieth of November, the Spanish colors were displayed from a lofty flag staff, in the centre of the public square. At noon, the Spanish regiment of Louisiana was drawn out, with a company of Mexican dragoons on the right, and the militia of the city on the left. The commissioners of Spain proceeded to the city hall, where the commissioner of France came soon after. He produced to them an order from the king of Spain for the delivery of the province, and the powers of the first consul to receive it; whereupon Salcedo immediately handed him the keys of New Orleans, and the Marquis de Casa-Calvo declared that such of his majesty's subjects in Louisiana as made it their election to live under the authority of the French republic, were absolved from their oath of fidelity and allegiance to the crown of Spain. A record was made of these proceedings, and the three commissioners walked to the main balcony, when the Spanish flag was saluted by a discharge of artillery on its descent, and that of the French republic greeted in the same manner, on its ascent.

Thus ended the government of Spain in Louisiana, after the lapse of thirty-four years and a few months.

In a proclamation which Laussat issued immediately afterwards, he informed the inhabitants that the mission which brought him among them, and on which he had built many fond hopes, and entertained many honorable expectations for their welfare and happiness, was changed; and that of which he was now charged, though less gratifying to him, was equally flattering, as it afforded him the consolation that it was more advantageous to them. The flag of the republic now displayed, and the sound of her cannon, announced the return of French domination; but it was for an instant only, as he was on the eve of delivering possession of the colony to the commissioners of the United States.

He observed that the commencement of a war under the most sanguinary auspices, carrying terror into all parts of the world, had induced the French government to turn its views towards Louisiana; considerations of prudence and humanity, connected with vast and permanent objects, worthy of the genius who balanced the grand destinies of nations, having given a new direction to the benevolent intentions of France towards the colony, it was ceded to the United States, and its inhabitants became the surest pledge of the increasing friendship between the two republics.

He drew their attention to that part of the treaty of cession, by which their incorporation into the union was secured; and congratulated them on becoming part of a nation already numerous and powerful—a people renowned for their industry, patriotism and enlightened understanding.

He remarked that, however pure and benevolent the intentions of the mother country might be, the people of a distant colony were ever exposed to the cupidity and malversations of those who were sent to govern them. Distance affording the means of concealment, operated as a temptation, and often corrupted the most virtuous—while the nature of the government under which they were about to pass, rendered rulers dependent on the will of the people, and connected their political existence with public suffrage.

He reminded them that the period was not distant when they would adopt a form of government for themselves, adapted to the maxims of the federal constitution, and suited to their manners, usages and localities. They would feel and appreciate as a singular attribute of a free constitution, the invaluable advantage of an upright, impartial and incorruptible administration of justice, in which the public and invariable forms of proceeding would combine with the moral and national character of judges and jurors, to ensure to the citizens security for person and property.

Monopoly, he added, more or less exclusive, is peculiar to, and invariably attendant on, colonial government; but from the United States the people of Louisiana ought to expect, at the same time, protection from such abuses, by the faculty of exporting, free from duty, every article of their produce. The ports of the Mississippi ought to be expected to become vast places of deposit, as this Nile of America, flowing not through parched deserts, but across fertile plains, would be navigated by vessels of all nations.

He expressed a hope that, among different flags, the people of Louisiana, would ever view that of France with complacency; as, in securing to his countrymen certain advantages during a limited time, in their intercourse with the ceded country, the first consul had a view to the renewal, strengthening, and perpetuating the ancient bonds between the French of Europe and those of Louisiana—so that Louisianians and Frenchmen would never hereafter meet in any part of the world, without mutually feeling a tender emotion, and exchanging the affectionate appellation of brothers—alike expressive of their lasting friendship and dependence on reciprocal kind offices.

On the same day, the colonial prefect issued a number of other proclamations in regard to the government of the province; the principal of which was for the substitution of a municipality to the cabildo. A mayor, two adjoints, and ten members, constituting the new body. The mayoralty was given to Boré: Destrehan and Sauvé were associated with him. The members were Livaudais, Petit Cavelier, Villere, Jones, Fortier, Donaldson, Faurie, Allard, Tureaud, and Watkins. Derbigny was secretary, and Labatut treasurer.

By a special proclamation, the black code, given by Louis the fifteenth to the province, excepting such parts of it as were inconsistent with the constitution and laws of the United States, was declared to be in force.

The citizens of the United States in New Orleans, about one hundred and twenty in number, formed themselves into a company of infantry, under Daniel Clark, the consul, and offered their services to the colonial prefect for the preservation of order and tranquillity; and, at his request, performed regular duty until the commissioners of the United States received possession of the province.

From the disposition manifested a few years before, by the colonial government, to retain possession of the posts above the thirty-first degree, and the protest of the Catholic king, apprehensions were entertained by the government of the United States that difficulties might arise. The president ordered a part of the militia of the states of Ohio, Kentucky, and Tennessee, to be held in readiness to march at a moment's warning. The military force in the west had been assembled at Fort Adams, and five hundred men of the militia of Tennessee came as far as Natchez, under the orders of colonel Dogherty.

Claiborne had given orders to the volunteer company of horse of the Mississippi territory, to prepare to accompany him, on the tenth of December.

Wilkinson who, since his return from the Atlantic states, had been employed as a commissioner in the treaties, lately entered into with the Choctaws, Chickasaws, and Creeks, was, at the time of his appointment as joint commissioner with Claiborne, engaged in running the line between the lands of the western states and those of the latter Indians. He reached New Orleans on the day after Laussat had received possession, and did not hear of his appointment till then. Crossing the lake, he met his colleague at Fort Adams. On the seventeenth of December, the two commissioners, the troops of the United States, and the Mississippi volunteers camped within two miles of New Orleans. On the following day Claiborne and Wilkinson paid a visit to Laussat, who came to their camp on the next, accompanied by the municipality, and a number of militia officers.

On Monday, the twentieth, the tri-colored flag was displayed at the top of the staff in the middle of the public square, at sunrise. At eleven, the militia paraded near it, and precisely at noon, the commissioners of the United States, at the head of their forces, entered the city. The American troops occupied the side of the square opposed to that on which the militia stood. The colonial prefect, attended by his secretary and a number of his countrymen, left his house under a discharge of cannon, and proceeded to the city hall, where the municipality and a large concourse of the most respectable inhabitants attended.

The commissioners of the United States now came, and the prefect gave them formal possession of the province by the delivery of the keys of the city. He then declared such of the inhabitants as chose to pass under the government of the United States, absolved and released from their allegiance to the French republic.

Claiborne now rose, and offered to the people of Louisiana his congratulations on the event which placed them beyond the reach of chance. He assured them the United States received them as brothers, and would hasten to extend to them a participation in the invaluable rights forming the basis of their unexampled prosperity, and in the meanwhile, the people would be protected in the enjoyment of their liberty, property, and religion—their commerce favored, and their agriculture encouraged. He recommended to them to promote political information in the province, and guide the rising generation in the paths of republican economy and virtue.

40

The tri-colored made room for the striped banner, under repeated peals of artillery and musketry.

A group of citizens of the United States, who stood on a corner of the square, waved their hats, in token of respect for their country's flag, and a few of them greeted it with their voices. No emotion was manifested by any other part of the crowd. The colonists did not appear conscious that they were reaching the *Latium sedes ubi fata quietas ostendunt.*

CHAPTER XXV.

When the French enjoyed the undisturbed possession of Louisiana, its extent in their opinion, had scarcely any bounds to the northwest; and its limits were ill defined anywhere, except on the sea coast. As its sovereign claimed all the neighboring country which was totally without inhabitants, or occupied by savage enemies, a demarcation of its limits was impossible, even if it had been desirable. During the Spanish government, a dispute with Great Britain, respecting Nootka Sound and her discoveries in that quarter, was terminated by a recognition of her right to New Albion, the boundary of which to the south being agreed on became the northern one of California, which, prolonged eastwardly to a certain point, was to mark the extent of New Albion in that direction. Where New Albion ended, Louisiana was said to begin.

On the bayou *des Lauriers* (Laurel creek) six miles S. W. by S. from the town of Natchitoches, on Red river, and fifteen miles from the Adayes, where the road to Nacogdoches crosses the bayou, the French had placed leaden plates on a tree on each side of the road, with an inscription expressing that the spot was the boundary between the French and Spanish dominions, without indicating the continuation of the line on either side. Similar plates were also fixed at Yatassees, a village of the Nadoca Indians, fifty leagues N. W. of Natchitoches.

The boundary line, from bayou *des Lauriers* to the sea, was never run, and each party claimed much more than the other was willing to allow. The Spaniards contended that the line was to be run due south, in which case it would strike the sea near the river Carcassou.

The eastern boundary of Louisiana, as far as the thirty-first degree, and the northern on the eastern side of the Mississippi, which separated the territories of Spain and the United States, were fixed by a treaty—the first in the middle of the stream, and the latter at the thirty-first degree of northern latitude. But the province of Louisiana did not extend far beyond the Mississippi below Iberville, and was separated from West Florida by a line drawn through the middle of that stream, and lakes Maurepas and Pontchartrain, to the sea.

Before the peace of 1763, the French recognized no other boundary of Louisiana, to the north, than the southern line of Canada.

To the east, the *rio Perdido* was recognized as affording the beginning of the boundary line, but the direction in which it ran, from the mouth or source of the stream, never engaged the attention of France or Spain.

The province of Louisiana and that of West Florida, were laid off into the following divisions: Pensacola, Mobile, the land between the Balize and New Orleans, the city, and the land on both sides of lake Pontchartrain, the first and second German coasts, Cabahanosse, La Fourche, Venezuela, Iberville, Galveztown, Baton Rouge, Pointe Coupee, Atakapas Opelousas, Avoyelles, Rapides, Natchitoches, Arkansas and the Illinois, in each of which there was a commandant.

In the Illinois, there was a commandant-general at St. Louis, to whom were subordinate those of New Madrid, St. Genevieve, New Bourbon, St. Charles and St. Andrew.

Baton Rouge had been made a government, in favor of Don Carlos de Grandpre, who had been appointed governor of Natchez, on Gayoso being promoted to that of the two provinces. The districts of Manshac, Thompson Creek and the Feliciana, Bayou-Sara, made part of it.

Chapitoula and Terre-aux-Bœufs had once separate commandants, but of late, they made part of the district of the city.

All the lands, on both sides of the Mississippi, from fifty miles below the city to Baton Rouge, had been granted, to the depth of forty arpents, or one mile and a half, which is the depth of all original grants. Some had double, and others treble grants, that is to say, a depth of eighty or one hundred and twenty arpents. A few grants extended as far as the sea, or lake behind them. In the other parts of the country, the people being generally settled on the banks of a river or creek, had a front of from six to forty arpents, and the grant generally expressed a depth of forty arpents.

The ungranted lands on the island of Orleans, and on the opposite bank of the river, were supposed to be unfit for cultivation; but a considerable portion might be drained. There are, in this part of the country, valuable cypress swamps belonging to the public.

It was supposed that all the land free from inundation, from the Balize to Manshac, as far back as the swamps, were fit for the cultivation of the cane. Above Manshac, it was supposed the cane would be affected by the cold, and its produce uncertain. The culture of the cane was not attended to elsewhere.

The buildings, fortifications and fixed property of the public, were chiefly in New Orleans. They consisted of:

Two very extensive brick stores, one being one hundred and sixty, the other one hundred and twenty feet in length; each about thirty feet in width, one story high, with a large loft, and covered with shingles.

A government house, outhouses and gardens, on a lot of about two hundred and twenty feet in front, with a depth of three hundred and thirty-six.

A military hospital.

A powder magazine, on the opposite bank of the Mississippi.

An ill-constructed customhouse of wood, almost in ruins.

Extensive barracks, calculated to accommodate nearly fifteen hundred men.

Five ill-constructed redoubts, with a covered way, pallisade, and ditch.

A large lot, adjoining the king's stores, used as a park of artillery, in which were a few sheds.

A town house, market house, assembly room and prison.

A cathedral and presbytery, to which a square of ground, well built on, was attached.

A charity hospital, with a few houses, yielding to it a revenue of about fifteen hundred dollars a year.

No authentic census of the inhabitants of the province, since that of 1788, is extant; but one made for the department of state, by the consul of the United States at New Orleans, from the best documents he could procure, in 1803, presents the following result:

In the city of New Orleans,	8,056
From the Balize to the city,	2,388
At Terre-aux-Bœufs,	661
Bayou St. John and Gentilly,	489
Barataria,	101
Tchoupitoulas,	7,444
Parish of St. Charles,	2,421
Parish of St. John the Baptist,	1,950
Parish of St. James,	2,200
Lafourche,	1,094
Lafourche, Interior,	2,064
Valenzuela,	1,057
Iberville,	1,300
Galveztown,	247
Baton Rouge,	1,513
Pointe Coupee,	2,150
Attakapas,	1,447
Opelousas,	2,454
Washita,	361
Avoyelles,	432
Rapides,	753
Natchitoches,	1,631
Arkansas,	368
Illinois, St. Louis, etc.,	6,028
Mobile,	810
Pensacola,	404
Total,	**49,473**

On the left bank of the Mississippi, about seventy-five miles above New Orleans, were the remains of the Oumas, (Red men) not exceeding sixty persons. There were no other Indians settled on this side of the river, in Louisiana or West Florida; although wandering parties of the Choctaws and Creeks were often rambling over the country.

On the right side of the Mississippi, above the settlement of Pointe Coupee, were the remains of the Tunica nation, not exceeding fifty or sixty persons.

On the left side of bayou Plaquemine, about twelve miles from the Mississippi, were two villages of the Chilimackas, consisting of about twenty cabins; each village had about sixty persons.

In the lower part of bayou Teche, at the distance of thirty-six miles from the sea, was another village of the Chetimachas, in which were about one hundred persons.

The nation of the Attakapas (Man-eaters) was nearly extinct. They had a village on bayou Vermillion, in which were about one hundred and twenty persons. Wandering families were scattered through the district, and a number of females were domiciliated among the planters.

The Choctaws, Biloxis, and Pascagoulas, had villages on bayou Crocodile and bayou Bœuf, in the parish of Rapides.

The Alibamons had a village of about one hundred persons, on the bayou Courtableau in the district of Opelousas.

Several small villages of the Cunhates were dispersed on the banks of the Meritao and Carcasu rivers. There were in them about three hundred and fifty of these Indians.

At the Avoyelles, there was a village of the Choctaws, or red men, at the distance of about sixty miles from the Mississippi, and another on the lake of the Avoyelles. These two villages had not more than one hundred persons.

At the Rapides, twenty miles higher up, was a village of the Chactas, which had about one hundred persons; and six miles farther, was a village of the Biloxis of the same size.

At the river *aux Cannes* was another village of the same nation, of about fifty persons.

The males of all these villages were frequently employed as boatmen.

About two hundred and fifty miles from the town of Natchitoches, on Red river, was the nation of the Cadodaquious, called, by abbreviation, Cados. They could raise five hundred warriors.

Four or five hundred families of the Choctaws were dispersed in the district of Washita, and the whole nation would have moved to the west side of the Mississippi, had they not been prevented by the Spaniards, and the Indians in their alliance there, who had suffered much from the aggressions of the Choctaws.

Between Red river and that of the Arkansas, were a few Indian families, the remains of tribes almost extinct. The nation that gave its name to the last river, was reduced to about two hundred and fifty warriors. They had three large villages on the river; the first was at the distance of forty miles from the Mississippi; the others at the distance of nine and eighteen miles from the stream.

On the river St. Francis, and on the right bank of the Mississippi, near New Madrid and Cape Girardeau, were wandering families, who had emigrated from the Delaware, Shawanees, Miamis, Cherokees, and Chickasaws—in all about five hundred families. They were at times troublesome to the boats descending the Mississippi, plundering them, and even committing murders. They had been attracted to this part of the country several years before the cession, when the views of the government of Louisiana were hostile to the United States.

The scarcity of game to the east of the Mississippi, had lately induced a number of Cherokees, Chickasaws, and Choctaws, to frequent the country to the west, where game was still abundant. Some of them had contracted marriages with Arkansas women, and many others were inclined to incorporate themselves in that nation. Their number was unknown, but supposed to be considerable.

On the river *des Moines*, which falls into the Mississippi from the west, were the Ayoas, a nation that formerly dwelt on the Missouri. They had two hundred warriors. Its number had lately been much reduced by the small-pox.

Higher up, and about nine hundred miles above St. Louis, on the banks of the Mississippi, were the Sacs and Renards, who together had about five hundred warriors.   They traded with St. Louis and Michilimackinac, who had always been peaceable and friendly.

The nations on the Missouri were cruel, treacherous and insolent.

The officers of the province were:

A governor, invested with civil and military authority.

An intendant, charged with the revenue, granting of land, and admiralty matters.

An auditor of war.

An assessor of the intendancy.

(The same individual often acted in both these capacities.)

A secretary of the government, and one of the intendant.

A treasurer and a comptroller.

A surveyor-general.

A storekeeper.

A purveyor, who made purchases for the king.

Three notaries, who acted as auctioneers, and whose offices were the repositories for law proceedings and deeds.

An interpreter of the French and English languages, and one for the Indians.

A harbor master.

A marine officer.

A physician to the military hospital—surgeon, and apothecary.

Another to the charity hospital—surgeon and apothecary.

A collector, treasurer, guarda mayor, notary, two head clerks, and about twenty inferior officers, in the customhouse.

Besides these, there was a cabildo in New Orleans, composed of two ordinary alcades, twelve regidors, an attorney-general, syndic and clerk; four alcades *de barrio*, and a number of syndics, or officers of police.

In the country, there was a commandant in each parish, who had a number of syndics under him.

In a communication to the department of state, in 1803, the consul of the United States at New Orleans, says: "the auditors of war, and assessors of government and intendancy, have always been corrupt; and to them only may be attributed the mal-administration of justice, as the governor and other judges, who are unacquainted with law, seldom dare to act contrary to the opinions they give.   Hence, when the auditor, or assessor was bribed, suitors had to complain of delays and infamous decisions.   All the officers plunder when the opportunity offers; they are all venal.   A bargain can be made with the governor, intendant, judge, or collector, down to the constable; and if ever an officer be displeased at an offer of money, it is not at the offer or offerer, but because imperious circumstances compel him to refuse; and the offerer acquires a degree of favor which encourages him to make a second offer, when a better opportunity is presented."

The duties at the customhouse, in the year preceding the cession, amounted to $117,515.

The imposts paid in Louisiana, were:

1.   A duty of six per cent. on the transfer of shipping. It was exacted on the sum the parties declared, which seldom exceeded one-half the real, as no oath was required.

2.   A duty on legacies or inheritances of collateral relatives, when

exceeding the value of two thousand dollars, and of four per cent. when the legatee or heir was not a relation of the deceased.

3. A tax on all civil employments, the salary of which exceeded three hundred dollars a year, called *media annata*, amounting to one-half of the first year's salary, payable, in some cases, in two yearly instalments, and in others in four. The first incumbent of a newly created office was exempt from this tax.

4. Seven dollars, deducted from twenty, paid for pilotage by every vessel entering or leaving the Mississippi : but the treasury provided boats, and paid the wages of pilots and sailors employed at the Balize. The remainder of the twenty dollars was distributed as follows : four dollars to the head pilot, four to the pilot who boarded the vessel, and five to the crew of the boat who brought him.

5. A tax of forty dollars on licenses to sell spirituous liquors.

6. A tax on saleable offices, as those of regidors, clerk of the cabildo, and notaries.

Exclusive of paper money, emissions of which were made in the early part of the Spanish government, there existed, at all times, a debt due by the government, for expenses incurred, for supplies furnished to the troops, and the king's stores and salaries of officers and workmen, for which *liberanzas*, or certificates, were regularly issued, of which there was afloat, at the cession, a sum of from four hundred and fifty to five hundred thousand dollars. They bore no interest, and were commonly to be bought at a discount of from 25 to 50 per cent. At the change or government, the discount was thirty. This depreciation was not the result of a want of confidence, or any apprehension that the certificates would not be paid, but from the value of money and the scarcity of it in the market.

With the view of removing from circulation a part of those *liberanzas* which inundated the market, the intendant, on the fifteenth of July, 1802, announced that he would furnish bills, or *cartas de paga*, on the treasury of the army, or that of the marine, at Havana, and receive one-half of the amount in *liberanzas* issued in New Orleans, and the other in cash ; under the condition that, in regard to the *cartas de paga* on the treasurer of the army, should there not be, at their presentation, funds appropriated to the province of Louisiana, the holder should wait until the arrival of such funds. By this measure, a considerable part of the *liberanzas* were withdrawn from circulation.

The church of Louisiana was under the direction of a bishop and two canons, New Orleans having been erected into a bishopric in 1792, the first incumbent of which, Don Luis de Penalvert, was promoted in 1801 to the archbishopric of Guatimala. A successor had been appointed to him, but he never came to the province. The reverend Thomas Haslett, one of the canons, died a short time before the cession, and had not been replaced.

The province, for ecclesiastical purposes, was divided into twenty-one parishes ; four of which were without a church, and as many more without a priest, so that the whole clergy did not consist of more than nineteen individuals. There was a chaplain to the convent, one to the troops, and one in each of the hospitals ; and the curate of New Orleans had three assistants.

The bishop had a salary of four thousand dollars, charged on some bishoprics in Mexico and Havana. The canons received a salary of six hundred dollars; and those of the curates and chaplains were from three hundred and sixty to seven hundred and twenty dollars, paid out of the treasury. They besides received fees for masses, marriages, and burials.

The king, besides, paid a salary of one hundred and eighty dollars a year to each of the sacristans of most of the parishes, and a sum of one hundred dollars a year to the cathedral, and twenty-four dollars to each parish, for bread, wine, and wax lights.

The cathedral church owned a square in the city, the rent of the houses of which, and the hire of the pews, with the sum paid by the king, constituted its revenue. The other churches derived one from the hire of pews.

Besides the cathedral, there were two chapels in New Orleans, in which divine service wes regularly performed—that of the convent, and that of the charity hospital.

There were but eleven nuns in the convent. They attended to the education of young persons of their sex; receiving pay from the wealthy, and educating a few poor girls gratuitously.

The catholic religion was the only one of which the rites were allowed to be publicly performed. None were compelled to attend its service. In public, respect was expected for the ceremonies of that church; but every one was permitted, at home, to worship his maker as he deemed proper.

RECEIPTS AND EXPENDITURES OF THE PROVINCE,
DURING THE YEAR 1802.

RECEIPTS.
Common Branches.

Balance of last year, ...	$ 51,932 27
Invalids, ...	5,959 13
Sale of effects from the artillery store, . .	630 38
Dues received from ships entering the Balize, . .	3,240 50
Payments to the treasury of debts due it, . .	16,024 75
Sale of effects from the king's store, . . .	2,005 62
Sums received from the customhouse, . .	130,724 88
Rent of the tenements belonging to the king, . .	336 00
Rations, deducted from the soldier's pay, . .	31,998 75
Hospital fees, likewise deducted, . . .	5,177 88
Loans to the treasury, ...	14,106 00
Sale of waste lands, ...	188 50
Duty of *media annata* on said lands, . .	5 50
Cash received from Vera Cruz, ...	402,258 00
Returns for supplies to the navy, . . .	20,000 00
Cash received for drafts on other treasuries, . .	49,512 88
Returns of overcharge to the treasury, . .	3 75

Private Funds.

Balance of the year before, ...	30,880 51
Balance of accounts, ...	217 63
Media annata of officers, . . .	1,226 26
Donation, ...	121 00

Funds not the King's Property.

Balance of the year before, ...	$ 53,775 62
Monte Pio of surgeons, ...	167 00
Monte Pio of military officers, ...	1,619 25
Deposits, ...	19,364 50
Monte Pio of officers of civil employments, . .	341 13
Monte Pio of offices, ...	1,209 76
	$843,043 37

EXPENDITURES.

Common Branches.

Expenses of people condemned to public works, .	6,971 63
Ordinary expenses of the city, ...	3,614 50
Expenses of fortifications, ...	4,210 25
Returns of loans made to the treasury, . .	42,015 63
Buildings, ...	6,152 88
Extraordinary expenses, ...	6,679 50
Maintenance of prisoners of war, . . .	824 37
Maintenance of poor, confined for their rations, .	519 75
Supplies to the navy, ...	8,844 88
Supplies to other treasuries, ...	10,316 13
Pay to the people employed in the galleys, . .	21,922 62
Expenses for the chapel service, ...	526 25
Hospital expenses, ...	27,716 02
Indian expenses, ...	25,418 26
Salaries of officers and people employed in the different offices of the revenue, ...	46,307 00
Expenses of the general store, etc., . . .	108,620 75
Expenses for the galleys, ...	4,004 38
Return of duties, ...	1,542 63
Allowances for table to officers, ...	5,367 88
Rations, ...	1,446 63
Civil and military salaries, ...	9,293 26
General expenses of revenue department, . .	19,523 00
Remittances to other treasuries, ...	74,000 00
Salaries to Indians, ...	4,851 00
Salaries to invalids, ...	540 50
Pay of the regular troops, ...	186,387 14
Allowances to professional corps, . . .	158 26
Pay of the militia, ...	12,704 13
Office expenses, ...	1,138 50
Department of artillery and workmen, . .	5,241 37
Half pay to officers retired, ...	300 00
Employed in the customhouse, . . .	7,386 26
Pensions, ...	2,328 00
House rent, ...	1,068 00
Salaries of persons employed in forming settlements, .	1,320 00
Salaries of officers and sergeants in half pay, .	2,902 00
Salaries of French emigrant officers, . . .	744 00
Premiums to soldiers for services, . . .	4,811 26

41

Conveyances of dispatches, ... $ 230 37
Purchase of naval stores for Vera Cruz,   .   .   9,453 63
Passage money of soldiers and criminals,   .   .   166 00
Expenses of demarcation of limits, .   .   .   7,540 00
Returns of sundries from the treasury, .   .   .   2,400 00
Secret expenses, ...   2,000 00
Secret expenses, military, ...   25 00
Sums charged to the treasurer, not received,   .   4,184 01

Private Funds.

Balance of accounts, ...   49 75
Expenses of justice, ...   10 00

Funds not King's Property.

Deposits, ...   6,682 76
Monte Pio of officers, ...   399 89
Monte Pio of military, ...   4,553 88
Monte Pio of offices, ...   957 39
Balance in the treasury, ...   136,674 13
                                                             _____
                                                             $843,048 38

The foregoing statement shows that the expenses actually paid in cash
in all the year 1802, including those of the *ramos agenos*, etc., or funds not
royal property, amounted to seven hundred and six thousand three
hundred and seventy-four dollars and fourteen cents, to which if we add
the salaries and pay due to many officers of the revenue department, and
crew of the squadron of galleys, the extraordinary expenses caused by the
different expeditions, particularly those which are renewed to the post of
Apalaches, for its defense against the attacks of the adventurer, Bowles,
and his party among the Creeks; the amount of bills drawn on the royal
chests by the king's storekeeper of Illinois, New Madrid, Baton Rouge,
Plaquemines, Apalaches, Mobile, and other posts, which not being yet
present are unpaid, it will appear that the quota (or *situado*) of this
province, reduced to five hundred and thirty-seven thousand, eight
hundred and sixty-nine dollars and fifty-six cents, is exceeded, by extraordinary expenses, upwards of three hundred thousand dollars, notwithstanding there are 820 men wanting to complete the regiment on the war
footing, and independent of the sums received for duties at the customhouse, and many considerable savings in the establishment, which have
taken place since it was formed in 1785, and the causes of said expenses,
and considerable debt incurred by this treasury, are those mentioned in
the foregoing statement.

It is likewise remarked that the royal chests owe 255,518 dollars to the
fund of deposits, 48,372 dollars and 31 cents to that of tobacco, 60,000
dollars to the fixed regiment and other corps, 12,000 dollars to the public
deposit, 1000 dollars to the pious fund of the cabins of female orphans,
and 337,760 dollars and 37 cents in certificates of credit, which, for want
of cash, have been issued in payment to the public, without comprehending what may be owing in Pensacola, as this office has no knowledge
of its means and resources.

New Orleans, 23d March, 1803.

                         (Signed)   GIBERTO LEONARD.
[Translation.]   MANUEL ALMIREZ.

This fund of deposit is cash deposited for a particular purpose, such as the fortifications of Pensacola, etc., to which it has not been applied.

The *ramos particulares*, or private funds are those of individuals under the royal protection, for the payment of pensions, etc., to officers' widows, etc.

The *ramos agenos* are funds which do not belong to the king, but are destined for the purposes mentioned, being generally discounts from salaries, to pay invalids, etc.

The deposits constituting a part of this fund, proceed from property in dispute to which the king has a claim, and the amount is deposited until the claim is decided.

The sum due to the fund of tobacco, is a balance which remained of that particular fund, after the purchases for the king's account were completed.

That due to the public deposit is the amount of certain property for which suits are depending between individuals.

That the regiment of Louisiana is taken from the military chest of that regiment, which has considerable funds of its own in cash.

The amount of certificates is the sum then due to the public, for supplies, salaries, and wages, which have not been paid for want of cash.

SALARIES AND EXPENSES,

Not comprehended in the Provincial Regulation.

ANNUAL.

Governor, late of Natchez, now Baton Rouge,	$ 2,500
Secretary to governor,	840
A colonel of artillery,	2,000
Two captains of said companies,	1,680
One lieutenant of said companies,	528
Two engineers,	2,000
Allowances for table expenses (when employed, $25 per month,) cannot be specified,.	
Officers of the army, additional, who have been put on pay viz., 2 captains, 1 lieutenant, and 3 sub-lieutenants,	3,096
Officers added to the etat-major de place: 5 captains, 2 lieutenants, and 1 on half pay,'	2,476
Augmentation of pay to the public interpreter,	264
An interventor or comptroller of public stores,	800
Two officers for revision of accounts,	1,140
One officer added to the secretary's office of the intendancy,	360
Auditor of war,	2,000
Storekeeper, interpreter, and baker of New Madrid; interpreter and baker of Illinois,	1,200
An additional clerk to the public stores,	360
Storekeeper at Baton Rouge,	360
Storekeeper, surgeon, interpreter, and baker, at Apalaches,	1,300
Commandants of the posts of St. John the Baptist, of the German parish, Opelousas, New Bourbon, Cape Bourbon, Cape Girardeau, St. Andrew, and St. Fernando of Illinois,	600
A French engineer,	1,200

An emigrant captain of the same nation,   .   . $ 744
Expenses of artillery department, ...   10,000
Provincial hospitals in various places,   .   .   .   5,000
Indian presents and expenses, in addition to the sum men-
    tioned in the provincial regulation,   .   .   .   30,000
Allowances to couriers yearly, ...   1,000
Supply of provisions, medicines, etc., to the garrison of
    Pensacola, ...   20,000
Secret expenses of government—cannot be precisely fixed,
Pay of 9 dragoons, at $25 per month and rations, on condi-
    tion of finding their own horses, at Pensacola,   3,500
Four corporals of militia, employed in various posts of the
    province under the orders of the commandants, at $10
    per month, ...   480
Pay of the harbor master, ...   2,000
Assistant to the harbor master,   .   .   .   360
Salary of the two canons, ...   1,200
An assistant to the curate, ...   720
A ranger of the forest at Concordia, opposite Natchez,   240
One ranger in Ouachita, ...   240
Fifteen sergeants on half pay, ...   2,025
Pensions to four officers of the royal hacienda, who have
    retired, ...   1,550
Seven sacristans appointed since the establishment of the
    regulation for St. Bernard, Baton Rouge, New Feliciana,
    or Thompson's creek, Rapides, Natchitoches, Arkansas,
    and New Madrid, at $15 per month each,   .   .   1,260
House rent in various places, viz:
Commandant at Baton Rouge, ...   360
Curate of Baton Rouge, ...   180
Curate of Feliciana, ...   180
Commandant of Natchitoches, ...   300
Commandant of Concord, ...   240
Commandant of New Madrid, ...   240
Six seamen at the Balize, at $6 per month and rations,   .   837
Four seamen for the boat of the revenue officer employed
    there, ...   480
Two seamen at Mobile, to look after the king's launch at $10
    each, per month, and rations, ...
Allowance to the commandant of the encampment at Espe-
    ranza, opposite the Chickasaw Bluffs,   .   .   72
Storekeeper, surgeon, apothecary, and assistant to the hos-
    pital at Plaquemines, ...   984
                                    ————————
                                  $109,271

EXTRAORDINARY.

Brigade of *presidarios*, or people condemned to the public
    works; their maintenance, clothing, etc.,   .   .   25,000
Pay of the officers and people employed in the galleys and
    gun-boats, etc., ...   60,000
Rations for officers and repairs of vessels,   .   .   40,000

Expenses of fortifications and repairs, in the capital and
    other posts, ... $ 20,000
Transportation of troops and presidarios, . . 1,000
Maintenance of criminals, ... 1,500
Expenses of running the line of demarcation with the U. S.
    from the beginning of 1797, not brought into account
    until the whole was completed; exceeding, . 150,000
Premiums to soldiers of good character, who have served
    beyond a certain period, ... 4,500

                                                     $302,000

Grand total, annual and extraordinary expenses, . $411,271

Expenses which, for want of cash, were paid in Certificates, in the year 1802.

Salaries of the revenue department, . . $ 5,735 38
General expenses of revenue department, . . 3,665 37
General expenses of the king's store, for supplies, . 28,990 87
General expenses of extraordinaries, . . . 713 50
General expenses for chapel service, . . 197 88
General expenses of the military hospital, . . 1,132 37
General expenses of criminals condemned to public
    works, ... 42 62
General expenses for the city guards, . . . 684 74
House rent, ... 1,365 00
Maintenance of persons confined, . . . 280 12
Purchase of stores for Vera Cruz, . . . 1,194 37
Passage of troops discharged, ... 28 00
Pay of soldiers, ... 15 00
Pay of militia, ... 3,166 62
Pay of half pay officers and servants, . , 45 00
Department of artillery and workmen, . . . 1,088 37
Pay of the crew of the galleys, . . . 44,444 56
Repairs of the galleys, ... 960 94
Repairs of fortifications, etc., . , . 3,319 31
Allowance for table expenses to officers on service, . 1,197 00
Salaries to the Indian department, . . 2,021 75
General expenses of the Indian department, . . 15,983 31
Rations to officers on service, . . . 80 00

                                                     $116,352 37

Annual Revenues of the City of New Orleans.

Hire of the stalls in the beef market, . . . $ 2,350
Tax of seven-eighths of a dollar on every carcass of beef
    exposed to sale, calculated at 3,325
Hire of the green and fish markets, etc., . . 1,383
Tax of one quarter of a dollar on every carcass of veal,
    mutton, or pork, exposed to sale, (supposed) . . 1,200

Tax of half a dollar per barrel on flour, baked in the city,
for which the bakers do not render a just account, $ 2,800

Tax of $40 on taverns, $20 on lodging houses, and $40 on
billiard tables, estimated at   .   .   .   3,500

Tax of $3 on all ships for anchorage, destined for the
repairs of the levee of the city; this tax not being paid
by the American shipping, ...   500

Tax of $2 per pipe on taffia imported,   .   .   .   800

Ground rents on the great square, ...   132

Rent of the old market house, now turned into a gaming
house and ball-room, ...   1,800

Ground rents, arising from the sale of the square opposite
the hospital, ...   693

Movable shops and stalls, ...   360

Tax of a dollar on all vessels entering the bayou St. John,   470

$19,278

MEM.—Some of the above items are casual, and depend on the hiring of stalls, and greater or less consumption of the city.

Expenses of the City.

A commission of five per cent. to the treasurer for all sums
he may receive.   .   .   .   .   .   .

To the six regidors or members of the cabildo or town council
first created, ... $ 350

The notary who serves as clerk to the council,   .   .   200

To the two porters of the council, who are likewise employed
by the treasurer in collecting the hire of the stalls,
etc., at $35 per month, ...   420

To the sergeant employed to look after the city carters, who
are obliged to bring weekly two loads of earth for
repairing the streets which are unpaid: at $12 per
month, ...   144

To the corporal who looks after the persons condemned to
the public works; at $12 per month,   .   .   .   144

To the city cryer, $12 per month, ...   144

To the executioner, $15 per month, ...   180

For lighting the lamps of the city, about 1800 gallons of oil
annually, ...

Repairing lamps, ladders, candlewick,   .   .   .   400

To 14 watchmen, who serve likewise as lamplighters,   .   2,580

To the guard appointed to attend at the Bayou bridge,   .   62

Repairs of the Bayou bridge, (casual)   .   .   .

Repairs of the city levee, or dyke, now in a dangerous state,
being partly carried away this spring by the under-
mining of the river, and which will be very expensive
to repair, ...

Repairs of the streets, gutters and city drains, uncertain,   .

There are besides the above, many casual and extraordinary expenses, which cannot be particularly enumerated.

IMPORTS AT NEW ORLEANS, IN 1802.

Fans assorted, dozens,	468
Fan for cleaning rice,	1
Steel, lbs.,	34,834
Olive oil in bottles, doz.,	1,648
Olive oil, common, in flasks, doz.,	420
Olive oil in jars,	50
Oil, essentials, phials, doz.,	6
Oil, linseed, galls.,	1,132
Oil, fish, galls.,	3,931
Oil, turpentine, lbs.,	215
Olives, in flasks, doz.,	236
Brandy of Provence, galls.,	1,960
Brandy of Bordeaux, galls.,	5,178
Brandy, bottled, doz.,	194
Brandy of peaches, galls.,	30
Taffia, hhds.,	67
Whiskey, galls.,	300
Scented waters, bottles,	485
Hungary and other waters, bottles,	103
Capers, in flasks, doz.,	264
Copperas, lbs.,	800
Carpets, wool,	6
Cotton, lbs.,	39,808
Red lead, lbs.,	1,120
Almonds, in shell, lbs.,	3,917
Almonds, shelled, lbs.,	400
Starch, lbs.,	130
Tar, (brought in vessels originally bound to other ports) bbls.,	325
Bitters, bottles,	288
Broadcloths, ells,	600
Anchovies, bottles,	283
Eels, salted, flasks,	30
Anniseed, in baskets,	662
Telescopes,	26
Indigo, lbs.,	1,597
Ploughs,	4
Herrings and Pilchards, lbs.,	21,400
Press of mahogany,	1
Harness with brass mountings,	6
Glass bottles, cases,	3
Filberts, lbs.,	500
Quicksilver, lbs.,	24,210
Sugar, white, lbs.,	704
Sugar, brown, lbs.,	23,992
Sulphur, lbs.,	4,650
Codfish, dried, quintals,	348
Baftas, pieces of 10 ells,	507
Scales, pairs,	2
Balls for muskets,	300

Buckets, doz.,	159
Varnish, common, galls.,	5,889
Varnish, fine, bottles,	24
Dresses for womeń, in piéces	110
Cambricks, in 6 ell pieces,	132
Trunks, empty,	40
Baize, ells,	4,250
Beaufort, unbleached, ells,	1,488
Calf skins, doz.,	123
Bath coatings, ells,	4,290
Book-cases, mahogany,	2
Bidets,	48
Screens, (paper)	10
Biscuit, quintals,	153
Blondes, silk, etc., ells,.	901
Purses, silk, doz.,	50
Fire engines,	2
Puffs, swansdown, doz.,	21
Boots, pairs,	98
Bootlegs, pairs,	425
Half-boots, pairs,	269
Half-bootlegs, pairs,	617
Empty bottles,	100,140
Bramantes or Flanders, ells,	14,451
Butter, bbls.,	38
Britanias, pieces,	15,472
Brin of all breadths, ells,	30,144
Buffets, mahogany,	6
Busts of plaster,	74
Cables, lbs.,	59,487
Cacao, lbs.,	1,024
Coffee, lbs.,	189,910
Coffee pots of iron, tinned,	42
Callimancoes, ells,	9,049
Copper kettles for sugar boilers,	4
Chaises,	2
Chairs,	15
Breeches patterns, cotton web,	110
Breeches and pantaloons made,	1,482
Bedsteads, mahogany,	1
Sheets, linen, doz.,	46
Sheets, check and ticking, doz.,	925
Canapees or sofas,	21
Canvass, ells,	4,350
Cinnamon, lbs.,	200
Cotton bagging, ells,	38
Hemp, lbs.,	65,822
Quills for writing,	57,000
Carabines,	10
Sea coal, hhds.,	100
Cotton cards, pairs,	1,524
Verdigris, lbs.,	21

Pork, salted, bbls.,	2,537
Beef, salted, bbls.,	237
Bacon, lbs.,	68,556
Venison, smoked, lbs.,	100
Carts and drays,	3
Carts with their harness,	6
Feathers, cartons,	24
Flowers, artificial, cartons,	60
Check jackets,	10
Caps, leather, doz.,	29
German rolls, ells,	10,125
Casimirs, ells,	919
Onions, quintals,	127
Sieves, wire, etc., doz..	887
Lace, ells,	4,069
Sashes for women,	82
Wax, manufactured, lbs.,	1 550
Beer, hhds.,	92
Beer, bottled, doz.,	807
Shoe blacking balls, lbs.,	200
Waiscoats of various materials,	875
Jackets of various materials, doz.,	191
Vermillion, lbs.,	530
Girt webb, ells,	485
Ribbons, silk, pieces,	9,443
Ribbons, velvet, pieces,	677
Ribbons for the hair, 60 ell pieces,	329
Tape, dozen pieces,	3,176
Binding, worsted, pieces,	2,430
Satin ribbon, pieces,	204
Cotton tape, gross of pieces,	3
Prunes, lbs.,	6,308
Nails, assorted, lbs.,	133,738
Cloves, lbs.,	280
Copper, manufactured, lbs.,	400
Copper in sheets, lbs.,	180
Head dresses for women,	58
Iron chests,	3
Glue, lbs.,	205
Counterpanes, quilted,	330
Oznaburg, white, ells,	6,371
Oznaburg, brown, ells,	53,945
Sweetmeats, dried, lbs.,	417
Sweetmeats in syrup, lbs.,	87
Coral, boxes,	26
Neck handkerchiefs, boxes,	23
Fishing lines,	5,444
Leather dressed, dozen skins,	17
Cider, galls.,	1,050
Cider, bottled, doz.,	374
Saddles,	208
Windsor chairs, doz.,	179

Riding chairs,	1
Mahogany arm chairs,	8
Seersuckers, pieces of 12 ells,	24
Hats, doz.,	1,357
Sole leather, lbs.,	500
Cork soles, pieces,	50
Suspenders, elastic, pairs,	162
Kentucky tobacco, lbs.,	241,846
Kentucky twist, lbs.,	948
Rapee snuff, bottles,	363
Corks,	778,000
Corks for demijohns,	8,000
Tea, lbs.,	5,567
Ticken, ells,	14,241
Tiles,	27,000
Whiting, casks,	67
Ink, bottles,	349
Inkstands, doz.,	50
Toilette glasses,	12
Molasses casks, broke up,	130
Turpentine, lbs.,	1,786
Velvets, cotton,	1,182
Glass for doors and windows,	2,980
Watch glasses,	504
White wine vinegar, galls.,	5,145
Red wine vinegar, galls.,	105
Composition vinegar, bottles,	75
Catalonian wine, galls.,	6,972
Andalusian wine, galls.,	3,171
Andalusian wine, bottled, doz.,	40
Corsican wine, pipes,	5
Claret, hhds.,	3,575
Claret, bottled, doz.,	4,062
White wine, Bordeaux, casks,	144
White wine, Bordeaux, bottled, doz.,	1,371
Provence wine, hhds.,	234
Provence wine, bottled, doz.,	334
Canary wine, galls.,	1,620
Madeira wine, galls.,	150
Madeira wine, bottled, doz.,	20
Frontignac, galls.,	271
Champagne, galls.,	35
Alicant, galls.,	16
Violins,	36
Soap, lbs.,	156,752
Soap balls, lbs.,	146
Cordage, lbs.,	323,645
Cages,	40
Syringes,	1,119
Syringes, small,	97
Shoes, men's and women's, of every description, pairs,	9,758

EXPORTS FOR 1802.

Garlic, ropes,	500
Cotton, clean, lbs.,	2,161,498
Tar, barrels,	1,846
Anchors,	1
Indigo, (produce of former years, long in store)	336,199
Rice, quintals,	46
Masts,	127
White sugar, lbs.,	100
Brown sugar, lbs.,	2,493,274
Pitch, bbls.,	258
Cables,	1
Cane, reed,	9,000
Beef, bbls.,	217
Pork, bbls.,	636
Tables of common wood,	18
Black lead, lbs.,	118
Corn mills,	122
Fire dogs gilt, pairs,	40
Mustard, doz. bottles,	132
Muslins, different kinds, ells,	15,793
Muslinets, different kinds, ells,	3,236
Petticoats made,	12
Nanquinets, ells,	3,158
Cards, grosses of packs,	375
Walnut plank, feet,	1,000
Nutmegs, lbs.,	71
Hand organs,	4
Guayac wood, quintals,	280
Cloths, ells,	14,950
Strouds, 16 ell pieces,	673
Handkerchiefs, all descriptions, doz.,	9,583
Potatoes, quintals,	410
Letter paper, reams,	516
Common writing paper, reams,	6,144
Paper hangings, pieces,	6,342
Wrapping paper, reams,	1,360
Writing desks. mahogany,	2
Parasols,	3,462
Raisins, lbs.,	34,617
Chocolate, lbs.,	1,880
Pickled turkeys and geese, bbls.,	3
Satin cloaks,	12
Pewter, quintals,	20
Wigs for men and women,	111
Pears, bbls.,	86
Shot, lbs.,	10,059
Flints,	349,000
Grindstones,	1,116
Mill stones, pr.	140
Whetstones, doz.,	8
Dripstones,	38

Beaver, lbs.,	36
Fox and raccoon,	22
Otter, lbs.,	272
Bearskins,	26
Deerskins in hair, lbs.,	93
Deerskins shaved, lbs.,	1,900
Pepper, lbs.,	2,070
Paints, common, lbs.,	10,563
Paints, fine, lbs.,	230
Pipes, clay, gross,	577
Pistols, pairs.	31
Slates,	165,000
Slates for schools, doz.,	6
Coined money, marks,	184
Platillas, white, pieces,	2,670
Platillas, brown, pieces,	244
Lead in sheets, lbs.,	3,800
Powder. lbs.,	6,420
Hair powder, lbs.,	10,090
Pomatum, pots and sticks, doz.,	262
Cheese, lbs.,	38,579
Hardware, packages,	416
Gold watches,	10
Clocks for staircases,	1
Clocks for chimney pieces,	12
Rosin, quintals,	40
Ploughshares,	30
Rum, gallons,	13,798
Russia sheetings, pieces,	1,970
Sheets ready made, pairs,	3
Salt, bbls.,	4,727
Bologna sausages, lbs.,	100
Salmon, lbs.,	2,880
Sardines, lbs.,	3,180
Serges, woolen, ells,	736
Frying pans,	2,985
Tallow, lbs.,	610
Tallow, manufactured, lbs.,	26,065
Secretaries, mahogany,	2
Sewing silk, lbs.	278
Silk of other descriptions, lbs.,	1,000
Garden seeds, lbs.,	100
Boot stockings, doz.,	18
Bacon, lbs.,	8,068
Wax, lbs.,	120
Peas and beans, bbls.,	123
Nails, lbs.,	200
Sugar, boxes,	2,050
Beef, hides,	2,409
Calf skins,	144
Staves,	24,000
Flour, bbls.,	5,575

Hams, lbs., ...	2,998
Wool, lbs., ...	462
Earthenware, crates, ...	2
Hogs' lard, ...	11,889
Molasses, casks, ...	312
Logwood, tons, ...	433
Beaver skins, lbs., ...	179
Otter skins, ...	6
Raccoon and fox skins, lbs., ...	138
Deer, in hair, lbs., ...	103,897
Deer, shaved, lbs., ...	121,608
Bearskins, ...	982
Buffalo robes, ...	32
Pimento, lbs., ...	7,281
Lead, in pigs, lbs., ...	167,192
Ash oars, ...	200
Snuff, bottles, ...	54
Tobacco, Kentucky, lbs., ...	87,622
Tobacco, in carrots, lbs., ...	7,768
Boards, of 10 to 12 feet, ...	690
Shingles, ...	30,000
Vanilla, per M. pods, ...	92

The annual produce of the province was supposed to consist of:
    3,000 lbs. of indigo, rapidly declining.
    20,000 bales of cotton of 300 lbs. each.
    5,000 hhds. of sugar of 1000 lbs. each.
    5,000 casks of molasses, of 50 gallons each.
There were but few domestic manufactures. The Acadians wrought some cotton into quilts and homespun, and in the more remote parts of the province, the poorer kind of people spun and wove wool mixed with cotton, into coarse cloth. There was a machine for spinning cotton in the parish of Iberville, and another in Opelousas; but neither was much employed. In New Orleans, there was a considerable manufacture of cordage, and a few small ones of hair powder, vermicelli and shot. There were near the city, about a dozen of distilleries, in which about four thousand casks of taffia, of fifty gallons each, were made, and a sugar refinery which produced about 200,000 lbs. of loaf sugar.

In the year 1802, two hundred and fifty-six vessels of all kinds entered the Mississippi: eighteen of which were public armed vessels: the others, merchantmen, as follows:

	American.	Spanish.	French.
Ships,	48	14	0
Brigs,	63	17	1
Polacres,	0	4	0
Schooners,	50	61	0
Sloops,	9	1	0
	170	97	1

Of the American vessels, twenty-three ships, twenty-five brigs, nineteen schooners and five sloops came in ballast.

Five Spanish ships and seven schooners came also in ballast.

The tonnage of the merchantmen, that entered the Mississippi, was twenty-three thousand seven hundred and twenty-five registered tons.

In the same year, there sailed from the Mississippi:

158 American vessels, . . .	21,383 Tons.
104 Spanish vessels, ...	9,753 Tons.
3 French vessels, . . .	105 Tons.

Total,	265	31,241

The tonnage of the vessels that went in ballast, not that of public armed ones, is not included. The latter took off masts, yards, spars and naval stores.

There was a considerable coasting trade from Pensacola, Mobile and the rivers and creeks falling into lakes Pontchartrain and Maurepas and the neighboring coast. From it, principally, New Orleans was supplied with ship timber, lime, charcoal and naval stores; cattle was also brought from these places. Schooners and sloops of from eight to fifty tons, some of them but half decked, were employed in that trade. Reckoning their repeated trips, five hundred of them entered the bayou St. John in 1802, with thirteen galleys and four boats.

There was also some coasting trade between New Orleans and the districts of Attakapas and Opelousas by the Balize.

Estimate of the produce shipped from New Orleans, in the year 1802, including that of the settlements on the Mississippi, Ohio, etc.:

	TONS.
Flour, 50,000 barrels, ...	5,000
Salt beef and pork, 3,000 barrels, . . .	500
Tobacco, 2,000 hogsheads, ...	1,400
Cotton, 34,000 bales, ...	17,000
Sugar, 4,000 hogsheads, ...	3,000
Molasses, 800 hogsheads, ...	500
Peltries, ...	450
Naval stores, ...	500
Lumber, chiefly sugar boxes, ...	5,000
	33,350
Potash, Indian corn, meal, lead, cherry and walnut planks, hemp, masts, spars, hams, butter, lard, peas, beans, biscuit, ginseng, garlic, cordage, hides, staves, tobacco, in carrots.	6,650
	40,000

CHAPTER XXVI.

THE first act of Claiborne, on his entering on the functions of governor-general and intendant of the province of Louisiana, was a proclamation of the twentieth December, 1803, by which he declared that the government heretofore exercised over the province, as well under the authority of Spain as under that of the French republic, had ceased, and that of the United States was established over it; that the inhabitants would be incorporated in the Union, and admitted, as soon as possible, according to the principles of the federal constitution, to the enjoyment of all the rights, advantages and immunities of citizens of the United States, and in the meantime maintained and protected in the free enjoyment of their liberty, property and religion, that the laws and municipal regulations in force, at the cessation of the late government, still remained in vigor. He made known the powers, with which he was invested, that the officers charged with the execution of the laws (except those whose powers were vested in himself, or in the person charged with the collection of the revenue) were continued in the exercise of their respective functions. He exhorted the people to be faithful and true in their allegiance to the United States, and obedient to the laws, under the assurance, that their rights would be under the guardianship of the United States, and their persons and property protected against force or violence, from without and within.

Trist, the collector of the United States, at Fort Adams, had been appointed superintendent of the revenue in the province.

By the substitution of a municipal body to the cabildo, Laussat had abolished the offices of principal, provisional and ordinary alcades; so that there remained in New Orleans, no tribunal or officer, vested with judicial powers, but Claiborne and the alcades *de barrio*: to remedy this evil, he established, on the thirtieth of December, a court of pleas, composed of seven justices. Its civil jurisdiction was limited to cases, which did not exceed in value three thousand dollars, with an appeal to the governor, in cases where it exceeded five hundred. Its criminal jurisdiction extended to all cases, in which the punishment did not exceed a fine of two hundred dollars and imprisonment during sixty days.

The justices had individually summary jurisdiction of debts, under the sum of one hundred dollars; but from all their judgments an appeal lay to the court of pleas.

Early in the new year, the Marquis de Casa Irujo, Spanish minister at Washington City, gave assurance to the department of state that his sovereign had given no order whatever for opposing the delivery of Louisiana to the French, and that the report current in the United States, and elsewhere, of the existence of such an order, was wholly without foundation; since there was no connection whatever between the pretended opposition and the representation made last year, by the Spanish minister to the government of the United States, on the defects which impaired the sale of Louisiana, by France, to these states, in which he had manifested the just motives of the Spanish government, in protesting against that alienation. The Marquis added, that he was commanded to make it known, that his majesty had since thought it proper to renounce his protest, notwithstanding the solid grounds on which it was founded; affording, in this way, a new proof of his benevolence and friendship for the United States.

The President ratified a convention between the United States and Spain on the 11th of August, 1802, which he had laid before the Senate, during the last session, and which had not been definitively acted on, when that body adjourned.

By an act of congress, of the twenty-sixth of March, the province of

Louisiana was divided.   That part of it, south of the Mississippi territory, and an east and west line, beginning on the river Mississippi, on the thirty-third degree of northern latitude, was erected into a distinct government, denominated the territory of Orleans: and the other was annexed, under the name of the district of Louisiana, to the Indiana territory.

The executive powers of government, in the territory, were vested in a governor, appointed for three years, unless sooner removed, by the president of the United States.   He was commander-in-chief of the militia, and had power to grant pardon for offenses against the territory, and reprieve, as to those against the United States, till the pleasure of the president was known; he had the appointment of all civil and military officers, except those for whom other provisions were made by the act.

A secretary of the territory was to be appointed, for four years, unless sooner removed, by the president.   His duty was, under the direction of the governor, to record and preserve all the papers and proceedings of the executive, and the acts of the legislature, and transmit authentic copies of the whole, every six months, to the president.   In case of the vacancy of the office of governor, his duties devolved on the secretary.

The legislative power was vested in the governor, and a legislative council, composed of thirteen freeholders of the territory, having resided one year therein, and holding no other appointment under the territory or the United States.   The territorial legislature was restricted from passing laws, repugnant to the constitution of the United States, laying any restraint, burden or disability, on account of religious opinion, profession or worship, preventing any one from maintaining his own, or burdening him with that of others: for the primary disposal of the soil, or taxing the lands of the United States.   The governor was charged with the publication of the laws and the transmission of copies of them to the president, for the information of congress; on whose disapprobation they were to be void.   The governor had power to convene and prorogue the council.

He was to procure and transmit to the president, information of the customs, habits and dispositions of the people.

The judicial powers were vested in a superior court, and such inferior court and justices of the peace, as the legislature might establish; the judges and justices of the peace holding their offices during four years. The superior court consisted of three judges, one of whom constituted a court.   It had jurisdiction of all criminal cases, and exclusively of capital ones, and original and appellate jurisdiction of all civil cases of the value of one hundred dollars and upwards: its sessions were monthly.   In capital cases, the trial was to be by jury: in all others, civil or criminal, either party might require it to be so.

Provision was made for the writ of *habeas corpus*, admission to bail in cases not capital and against cruel or unusual punishments.

The judges, district attorney, marshal, and general officers of the militia, were to be appointed by the president, with the advice and consent of the senate,

The compensation of the governor was fixed at five thousand dollars, that of the secretary and judges, at two thousand each, and that of the members of the legislative council at four dollars a day.

The importation of slaves from foreign countries was forbidden, and that of those brought from the United States was allowed only to citizens, *bona fide* owners, removing to the territory.

All grants for land within the ceded territories, the title whereof was at the date of the treaty of San Ildefonso, in the crown, government or nation of Spain, and every act and proceeding subsequent thereto, towards the obtaining any grant, title or claim to such lands, were declared to be null and void. There was a proviso, excepting the titles of actual settlers, acquired before the twentieth of December, 1803. The obvious intention of this clause was to act on all grants made by Spain, after her retrocession to France, and without deciding on the extent of that retrocession, to put the titles thus acquired under the control of the American government.

The President of the United States was authorized to appoint registers and recorders of land titles, who were to receive and record titles acquired under the Spanish and French governments, and commissioners who should receive all claims to lands, and hear and determine, in a summary way, all matters respecting such claims. Their proceedings were to be reported to the secretary of the treasury, and laid before congress for their final decision.

By two subsequent acts, congress made provision for extending the collection and navigation laws of the union to the territory.

Every vessel possessed of, or sailing under, a Spanish or French register and belonging wholly, on the twentieth of December last, to a citizen of the United States, then residing within the ceded territory, or to any person being, on the thirtieth of April preceding, a resident thereof, and continuing to reside therein, and of which the master was such a citizen or resident, was declared capable of being enrolled, registered or licensed, according to law, and afterwards to be denominated and deemed a vessel of the United States, Such inhabitants were, however, required before they availed themselves of these provisions, to take an oath of allegiance to the United States, and to abjure their former one to the king of Spain or the French republic.

The inhabitants, thus taking the oath, were entitled to all the benefits and advantages of holding vessels of the United States, as resident citizens.

The ceded territory and all the navigable waters, rivers, creeks, bays, and inlets, within the United States, emptying themselves into the gulf of Mexico, east of the river Mississippi, were annexed to the former Mississippi district.

The city of New Orleans was made a port of entry and delivery, and the town of Bayou St. John a port of delivery.

The district of Natchez was established, of which the city of that name was the sole port of entry and delivery.

Foreign vessels were permitted to unload in the port of New Orleans only, and the same restraint was imposed on vessels of the United States coming from France or any of her colonies.

Vessels from the cape of Good Hope, or any place beyond it, were admitted to an entry, in the port of New Orleans, only.

The President of the United States was authorized, whenever he should deem it expedient, to erect the shores, waters and inlets, of the bay of Mobile, and the other rivers, bays and creeks emptying themselves into the gulf of Mexico, east of the river Mobile and west of the river Pasca-

43

goula, into a separate district, and designate within it a port of entry and delivery. The territory was erected into a judicial district of the United States, and a district court, with circuit court powers, was established therein.

It having been represented to the President of the United States, that many persons, formerly engaged in the military service of the United States, and having deserted from it, had become inhabitants of the ceded territory, chiefly in that part of it immediately below the line of demarcation, on the left bank of the Mississippi, where they had establishments of property and families, and were in such habits of industry and good conduct as gave reasons to believe they had become orderly and useful members of society, he granted to every such deserter, as an inhabitant of the ceded territory, on the twentieth of December, 1803, a free and full pardon for his desertion, and a relinquishment of the term during which he was bound to serve.

In the latter part of that month, Laussat sailed to the island of Martinico. He concluded his last communication to the minister from New Orleans, with the following observations: "The Americans have given fifteen millions of dollars for Louisiana; they would have given sixty rather than not possess it. They will receive one million of dollars for duties, at the customhouse in New Orleans, during the present year, a sum exceeding the interest of their money, without taking into consideration the value of the very great quantity of vacant lands. As to the twelve years, during which our vessels are to be received on the footing of national ones, they present but an illusive prospect, considering the war and the impossibility of our being able to enter into competition with their merchantmen. Besides, all will in a short time turn to the advantage of English manufactures, by the great means, this place will exclusively enjoy, from its situation, to supply the Spanish colonies, as far as the equator. In a few years, the country, as far as the *Rio Bravo*, will be in a state of cultivation. New Orleans will then have a population of from thirty to fifty thousand souls; and the new territory will produce sugar enough for the supply of North America and a part of Europe; let us not dissimulate; in a few years the existing prejudices will be worn off, the inhabitants will gradually become Americans, by the introduction of native Americans and Englishmen; a system already begun. Many of the present inhabitants will leave the country in disgust; those who have large fortunes will retire to the mother country; a great proportion will remove into the Spanish settlements; and the remaining few will be lost amidst the new comers. Should no fortunate amelioration of political events intervene, what a magnificent *Nouvelle France* have we lost. The creoles and French established here unite in favor of France, and cannot be persuaded that the convention for the cession of Louisiana is anything but a political trick: they think that it will return under the dominion of France."

Wilkinson sailed to New York, about the same time, leaving the command of the few companies of the regular troops in the district to Major Porter; a company had been detached to Natchitoches, under Captain Turner; there was a smaller command at Pointe Coupee; the rest were at New Orleans and Fort Adams.

The people of Louisiana, especially in New Orleans, were greatly dissatisfied at the new order of things. They complained that the person whom Congress had sent to preside over them, was an utter stranger to their laws, manners and language, and had no personal interest in the prosperity of the country—that he was incessantly surrounded by new comers from the United States, to whom he gave a decided preference over the creoles and European French, in the distribution of offices—that in the new court of pleas, most of the judges of which were ignorant of the laws and language of the country, proceedings were carried on in the English language, which Claiborne had lately attempted to introduce in the proceedings of the municipal body, and the suitors were in an equally disadvantageous situation, in the court of the last resort, in which he sat, as sole judge, not attended, as the Spanish governors were, by a legal adviser; that the errors into which he could not help falling, were without redress. They urged that, under the former government, an appeal lay from the governor's decision to the captain-general of the island of Cuba, from thence to the Royal Audience in that island, and in many cases from them to the council of the Indies at Madrid.

To these, a new cause of complaint was superadded by the late act of Congress, establishing the new form of government. The people murmured at the division of the province, which put off, to an almost indefinite period, their admission into the Union, as an independent state. They saw with displeasure that their rights continued, in the new supreme court, at the discretion of one individual, and that the introduction of slaves, from foreign countries, was absolutely prohibited, and that from the United States allowed only to new comers.

Considerable distress was felt from the great scarcity of a circulating medium. Silver was no longer brought from Vera Cruz by government, and the Spaniards were not very anxious to redeem a large quantity of *liberanzas*, or certificates, which they had left afloat in the province, and which were greatly depreciated. Claiborne sought a remedy for this evil in the establishment of the Louisiana Bank, the extension of the capital of which, was allowed to two millions of dollars; but the people being absolutely unacquainted with institutions of this kind, and having suffered a great deal by the depreciation of paper securities, heretofore emitted in the province, were tardy in according their confidence to the bank.

The former militia was completely disorganized. Most of the individuals, who had lately arrived from the United States, had enrolled themselves in independent companies of volunteers, rangers, riflemen, artillery and cavalry, which Claiborne had formed and patronized. These military associations, in which very few of the natives entered, gave a more marked character to the new government, and more distinctly drew the line between the two populations.

The exploring of the region between the Pacific Ocean and the Mississippi was an object, in which the then President of the United States, had felt an early and lively interest. While he was at the court of France, about twenty years before, he had employed a countryman of his, Ledyard, the famous traveller, to proceed to Kamschatka, take passage in some of the Russian ships, bound to Nootka Sound, and, landing in the middle states of the Union, to seek his way to them by land. Passports had been obtained from the Empress of Russia, and Ledyard took his winter quarters, within twenty miles from Kamschatka. In the spring, he was about to proceed, when he was arrested by an officer, sent after him by the Empress, whose disposition had changed.　He was shut up in a close carriage, and driven with great rapidity and without interruption, till he was left on the frontiers of Poland to follow the route his inclination pointed out.　He took that of Egypt, with the view of reaching the sources of the Nile, and died at Cairo, on the 15th of November, 1788.

In the year 1792, Jefferson proposed to the American Philosophical Society, a subscription for attaining the same object, in the opposite direction; funds were raised and the services of Michaux, a botanist, sent by the French government to the United States, were engaged.　This man left Philadelphia, with a single companion, to avoid existing suspicion among the Indians; but he had scarcely reached Kentucky, when he was overtaken by an order of the French Minister at Philadelphia, to desist from his undertaking and pursue his botanical inquiries in the western states.

In 1803, the act of congress for establishing trading houses with the Indians, being about to expire, some modifications of it were recommended by a confidential message of the President, on the 8th of January, with an extension of its views to the tribes on the Missouri.　In order to pave the way for that purpose, the message proposed to send an exploring party to trace that stream to its source across the highlands, and seek a water communication to the Pacific Ocean.　Congress entered into the views of the President, and an appropriation was accordingly made.

The command of the expedition was given to Merriwether Lewis, a captain of the army of the United States, who had for some time acted as private secretary to the President and, who being desired to select the officer next in command, made choice of William Clark, a brother of colonel Clark, who, we have seen, distinguished himself as a partisan officer, on the banks of the Mississippi and the Wabash, during the revolutionary war.　Fourteen soldiers, some young men from Kentucky, two French boatmen, a hunter, and a negro man belonging to captain Lewis, with the two commanders, composed the party.

Passports were obtained from the Spanish, French and British ministers at Washington City.

The expedition did not reach St. Louis until December; and Delassus, the commandant-general there, having no official direction, refused, notwithstanding the passport of the minister of the Catholic king, to permit an armed force to cross his dominions, in that part of America. The party, therefore, wintered on the left side of the Mississippi, and did not set off till the fourteenth of May, possession of upper Louisiana having then been taken by the United States.

In the meantime, the dissatisfaction of the inhabitants of New Orleans, rose to such a degree, that a determination was taken, by a few individuals, to induce their countrymen to solicit relief from congress at its next session.　For this purpose a meeting of the most influential merchants in the city, and planters in the neighborhood was called for the first of June, when it was almost unanimously determined to make application to congress for the repeal of so much of their late act, as related to the division of the ceded territory and the restrictions on the importation of slaves, and to require the immediate admission of Louisiana into the Union.　Jones, Livingston, Pitot and Petit were appointed a committee, charged with preparing and submitting to the next meeting the draft of a memorial to congress.

They made their report to a much more numerous meeting towards the beginning of July, by whom it was approved, and who made choice, from among themselves, of a committee of twelve, who were charged with circulating copies of the memorial in the parishes, and procuring the signatures of the most notable inhabitants, and to collect voluntary contributions for defraying the expenses of a deputation to be sent to Washington City with the memorial. They were further instructed to lay before a future meeting the names of six individuals, out of whom there were to be chosen the deputation.

At this last meeting, on the eighteenth, Derbigny, Destrehan and Sauvé were chosen, and they set out in the fall.

We have seen, in a preceding chapter of this work, that on Great Britain having obtained possession of the left bank of the Mississippi, in the former century, there had been a great migration thither, from her colonies. It had since increased at various periods, and the Spanish government, in Louisiana, had favored it. Few French and Spanish families had come to settle in a neighborhood in which the English language alone was spoken. An annexation to the United States was as much desired by the inhabitants of Thompson's Creek, Bayou Sara and Baton Rouge, as a continuation of the government of the French republic, below Manshac, or on the right bank of the Mississippi. The people, immediately below the line of demarcation, were disappointed at the omission of the commissioners of the United States to insist on receiving possession of the country, as far as *Rio Perdido*. The late acts of congress, for extending the collection and navigation laws of the United States, having made provision for the establishment of a port of entry and delivery at Mobile, and ports of delivery in its vicinity, had satisfied them that the federal government considered the country they inhabited, as part of the territory it had lately acquired. A considerable number of them assembled and determined on an attempt to drive the Spanish garrison from the fort at Baton Rouge. The standard of revolt was raised, and a number of men armed themselves and rode through the country, in various directions, to induce others to join them. Their efforts were not at first absolutely unsuccessful, and about two hundred men were collected; but some misunderstanding having taken place among the principal leaders, the project miscarried, and the latter crossed the line, to seek a refuge in the Mississippi territory.

The government lately provided for the territory of Orleans, went into operation on the first of October.

Claiborne had been appointed governor, and Brown, secretary.

Bellechasse, Boré, Cantrelle, Clark, Debuys, Dow, Jones, Kenner, Mongan, Poydras, Roman, Watkins, and Wikoff, had been selected as members of the legislative council.

Duponceau, Kirby and Prevost, were appointed judges of the superior court.

Hall was the district judge of the United States; Mahlon Dickenson, district attorney, and Le Breton d'Orgeney, marshal.

Prevost opened the first territorial court, alone, on the ninth of November, Duponceau having declined his appointment, Kirby having died.

Boré, Bellechasse, Jones and Clark, having taken an active part in the meetings of the inhabitants, deemed it inconsistent to give their aid to a form of government, against which they had remonstrated, and declined accepting their seats. An ineffectual attempt to procure a *quorum* was made in the latter part of November; many of the other members refusing, or being tardy in giving, their attendance; so that the formation of the legislative council must have been protracted to a very distant period, had not Claiborne availed himself of an accidental circumstance. The christian names of the persons selected by the president not being known at the department of state, blank commissions had been transmitted to Claiborne. He filled those for the four gentlemen who had declined, with the names of Dorciere, Flood, Mather and Pollock, and a mere quorum was obtained on the fourth of December.

The territory was divided into twelve counties, in each of which an inferior court was established, composed of one judge. Acts were passed, to regulate the practice of the superior and inferior or county courts. Suits were to be instituted by a petition, in the form of a bill in chancery. The definition of crimes and mode of prosecution in criminal cases, according to the common law of England, were adopted. Provision was made for the inspection of flour, pork and beef. Charters of incorporation were given to the city of New Orleans, and to library, navigation and insurance companies. An university was established, which was charged with locating schools in each county; but as no appropriation was made, nor funds provided for these seminaries, the views of the legislature were not successfully carried into execution, and the plan, in a few years, absolutely failed.

The council adjourned in February, after having appointed a committee to prepare a civil and a criminal code, with the assistance of two professional men, for whose remuneration five thousand dollars were appropriated.

The bank of the United States, having procured an amendment to their charter, to authorize them to establish offices of discount and deposit in the territories, established one in New Orleans.

This winter, William Dunbar and Doctor Hunter, with a party, employed by the United States, explored the country, traversed by the river Washita, as high up as the hot springs, in the vicinity of that stream.

Another party, by a Mr. Freeman, ascended Red river, to a considerable distance above Natchitoches; but, being met by a detachment of Spanish troops, were compelled to retrograde.

Previous to the acquisition of Louisiana, the ministers of the United States had been instructed to endeavor to obtain the Floridas from Spain. After that acquisition, this object was still pursued, and the friendly aid of the French government towards this attainment was requested. On the suggestion of Talleyrand, that the time was unfavorable, the design was suspended. The government of the United States, however, soon resumed its purpose; the settlement of the boundaries of Louisiana was blended with the purchase of Florida, and the adjustment of heavy claims made by the United States, for American property, condemned in the ports of Spain, during the war which terminated by the treaty of Amiens.

On his way to Madrid, Monroe, who was empowered in conjunction with Pinckney, the American minister at the court of his Catholic majesty, to conduct the negotiation, passed through Paris, and addressed a letter to the minister of external relations, in which he declared the object of his mission, and his views respecting the boundaries of Louisiana. In his answer to this letter, dated the twenty-first of December, 1804, Talleyrand declared in distinct terms, that the treaty of San Ildefonso, Spain retroceded to France no part of the territory east of Iberville, which had been held and known as West Florida, and that, in all the negotiations between the two powers, Spain had constantly refused to cede any part of the two Floridas, even from the Mississippi to the Mobile. He added, that he was authorized by his imperial majesty to say, that in the beginning of the year 1802, Bournonville had been charged to open a negotiation, for the acquisition of the Floridas; but this project had not been followed by a treaty. Soon after Monroe's arrival at his place of destination, the negotiation commenced at Aranjuez. Every word in that article of the treaty of San Ildefonso, which retroceded Louisiana to France, was scanned by the ministers on both sides, with all the critical acumen which talents and zeal could bring into their service. Every argument drawn from collateral circumstances, connected with the subject, which could be supposed to elucidate it, was exhausted. No advance towards an arrangement was made, and the negotiation was terminated, leaving each party firm in its original opinion and purpose; each persevered in maintaining the construction with which he had commenced.

Don Dio Premiro, Bishop of Montelrey, in the province of New Leon, whose diocese included, besides that province, those of San Andero, Coaguilla, and Texas, being on a pastoral visit to Nacogdoches, came to the town of Natchitoches, where he spent a week. He was treated with great respect by the inhabitants.

The deputation from the territory of Orleans was not successful in their application to congress; that body passed a law, on the second of March, authorizing the President of the United States to establish within that territory a government similar to that of the Mississippi territory, in conformity with the ordinance of the old congress, in 1787, except so far as relates to the descent and distribution of the estates of persons dying intestate and the prohibition of slavery. Provision was made for the admission of the inhabitants into the Union, on the same footing as other states, as soon as the population of the territory amounted to sixty thousand souls.

The bill became an act, in the shape in which it was introduced, notwithstanding the strenuous efforts of the deputation for the introduction of three amendments, to which they attached great importance. The first was, that the governor should be chosen by the President of the United States, out of two individuals, selected by the people; the second, that an equity jurisdiction should be given to the superior court: the last, a clause allowing the inhabitants permission to purchase slaves in the United States,

An act was also passed for the confirmation of inchoate titles to land, and for grants to occupants of tracts, cultivated before the 20th of December, 1803, with the permission of the local authorities.

The legislative council held its sessions in New Orleans, on the twentieth of June. Annual sessions of the superior court were directed to be holden in each county, except Concordia and Washita. Provision was made for the relief of insolvent debtors, and the improvement of the inland navigation.   A court of probates was established.   The council adjourned early in July.

Towards the middle of the following month, lieutenant Pike, set out from St. Louis, on an exploring party to the sources of the Mississippi, in a large keel boat. He had with him a sergeant, two corporals and seventeen privates.

Burr, the late Vice President of the United States, this year made an excursion in the western states.

The expedition, under the orders of captain Lewis, reached the extreme navigable point on the Missouri, on the seventeenth of August, in latitude 43. 20. at the distance, according to his computation, of two thousand five hundred and seventy-five miles from the Mississippi. On the twenty-sixth they began their march, and reached Flat river, a stream flowing into the Columbia river, at the distance of three hundred and forty miles from the spot on which they had landed on the Missouri.   The gap of the Rocky Mountains, which they crossed, was at the distance of sixty-eight miles from the Missouri.   Their route was for one hundred and forty miles, over high mountains, nearly half of which were covered with snow, eight or ten feet deep; in the latter part of the way, the route was very fine.

At the distance of four hundred and sixty-two miles from the place where they embarked, the tide became sensible, and one hundred and seventy-eight miles farther, they reached the ocean, on the seventh of November, in latitude 46. 15. and longitude 124. 57. from Greenock, and at the distance according to their computation, of three thousand five hundred and fifty-four miles from the Mississippi.

The width of Columbia river was, at its mouth, one hundred and fifty yards; its utmost five hundred, and its least eighteen.

The officers of Spain had protracted their stay, in New Orleans, for several months, beyond the time limited by the treaty, until the American government, distrustful of such an unreasonable delay, had actually forced their departure; the Marquis de Casa-Calvo, did not depart till the summer, when he made an excursion through the provinces of Spain, in the neighborhood of the United States, as far as Chihuahua.   After their departure, the Spanish troops which had remained in New Orleans, left it for Pensacola.

By a pope's bull of the first of September, the spiritual administration of the diocese of Louisiana, was committed to bishop Carrol of Baltimore.

The few Spaniards, that remained in the territory and many of the creoles, were unwilling to believe the country was really lost to its former master, and the opinion was cherished among them, that the United States held Louisiana, in trust, during the war.   On the east and the west, the Spaniards were still in great relative force.   Many parties were hovering on the frontiers, provoking vexatious contests about limits, occasionally violating, with armed force, and even with outrage, the unequivocal and undisturbed territories of the Union.

In the night of the twenty-third of September, a party of armed men from Baton Rouge came to Pinckneyville, in the Mississippi territory, and forcibly seized three brothers of the name of Kemper, who, having taken an active part in the insurrection at Bayou Sara, in the preceding year, had sought refuge beyond the line of demarcation. The party returned with their prisoners, as far as Bayou Tunica, where, after much ill treatment, they were put on board of a boat for Baton Rouge. As they came to a part of the river where it makes a large bend, they were discovered by a negro man, who crossing a narrow neck, reached Pointe Coupee, where he gave information to lieutenant Wilson of the artillery, who without loss of time manned a boat, and soon after met the one, in which the Kempers were; he made himself master of and brought her to Pointe Coupee, where they were liberated, and their captors lodged in prison.

On the Mobile, the American trade was incessantly harrassed with searches and obstructions, and at times, subjected to heavy exactions.

From Nacogdoches, the American settlements, near the Sabine and on Red River, were occasionally menaced and disturbed. From the Sabine to New Orleans, the country was absolutely open to an invader. There was but one place of strength, besides New Orleans: Baton Rouge in a settlement, still occupied by the Spaniards, although within the territory claimed by the United States.

By a treaty concluded at Tellico, on the seventh of October, the Cherokee Indians agreed that, as the mail of the United States was ordered to be carried from Knoxville to New Orleans through the Cherokee, Choctaw and Creek countries, the citizens of the United States should have, as far as it goes through their country, the free and unmolested use of a road leading from Tellico to Tombigbee.

By a convention between the United States and the Creeks, at Washington City, on the fourteenth of November, these Indians agreed that the United States should forever thereafter have a right to a horse path through the Creek country, from the Ocmulgee to the Mobile river, and their citizens should, at all times, have a right to pass peaceably on said path. The Indians promised to have boats kept at the several creeks for the transportation of travellers, their horses and baggage, and houses of entertainment, at suitable places along said path, for the entertainment of travellers.

CHAPTER XXVII.

THE new form of government, provided by the late act of congress for the territory of Orleans, differed principally from the former, in the election of the house of representatives immediately, and a legislative council mediately, by the people.

The governor, secretary and judges of the superior courts were to be appointed by the President of the United States, with the advice and consent of the senate; the first of these officers for three, and the second for four years, unless sooner removed by the President of the United States, The judges held their offices during good behavior.

The legislative council was composed of five, and the house of representatives of twenty-five members.

The members of the legislative council were chosen by the President, with the advice and consent of the senate, out of ten individuals, selected by the house of representatives of the territory. Their period of service was five years, unless sooner removed by the President of the United States. The only qualification required from them was a freehold estate, in five hundred acres of land.

The members of the house of representatives were elected for two years. Citizenship of one of the United States for three years, and a residence in the territory, or three years residence in the territory, were required from the elected, and, in either case, a fee simple estate in two hundred acres of land. The qualifications of the electors, were citizenship of the United States, and a residence in the territory, or two years residence in the territory.

The salaries of the officers above mentioned were the same as under the preceding form of government.

All other officers were to be appointed by the governor.

The act of congress had a bill of rights.

The people of Louisiana complained, that in this form, as in the preceding, their lives and property were, in some degree, at the disposal of a single individual, from whose decision there was no appeal; the law declaring any one of the judges of the superior court a *quorum*.

Claiborne had been appointed governor, Graham, secretary, and Prevost, Sprig and Mathews, judges of the superior court.

The house of representatives met on the fourth of November, for the purpose of nominating to the President of the United States ten individuals, out of whom he was to choose a legislative council. Their choice fell on Bellechasse, Bouligny, the chevalier d'Ennemours, Derbigny, Destrehan, Gurley, Jones, Macarty, Sauvé, and Villere.

The bishop of Baltimore made choice on the twenty-ninth of December, of Olivier, the chaplain of the nunnery in New Orleans, for his vicar-general in the territory.

The marquis de Casa-Calvo reached Natchitoches, on his return from the neighboring Spanish provinces, on the first day of the new year. He was visited by major Porter, who commanded the small garrison at that post, and by his officers; but he was not permitted to enter the fort. He tarried but three days and proceeded to Pensacola, by the way of Baton Rouge.

A short time afterwards, a small detachment from the garrison of Nacogdoches came to establish a new post, at the Adayes, on the road from Nacogdoches to Natchitoches, within fourteen miles from the latter place; and accounts were received, that don Antonio Cordero, governor of the province of Texas, had marched from San Antonio, with a body of six hundred regulars, some militia, a few Indians and a considerable number of horses, mules and cattle. He had stopped on the banks of the river Trinity, where he had been joined by don Simon Herrera, the commandant of Montelrey, in the province of New Leon, who had been sent with a reinforcement by don Nemesio Salcedo, the captain-general of the internal provinces.

Porter received on the twenty-fourth of January, orders from the department of war, to require from the commanding officer at Nacogdoches, assurance that there should be no further inroads, nor acts of violence committed by the forces of Spain, on the eastern side of the river Sabine, and in case the assurance was refused or disregarded, to be on the alert for the protection of the citizens of the United States, pursuing their lawful concerns, westward of the Mississippi. He was instructed to send patrols through the country, eastward of the Sabine, which was considered as part of the territory of the United States, especially when armed men, not under the authority of the United States, attempted to cross that stream; to repel invasion by pursuing and arresting invaders; avoiding, however, the spilling of blood, when this could be done without it. He was directed to deliver any Spanish subject, thus arrested, to the commanding officer, at Nacogdoches, if he would give assurances to have them punished, but otherwise, to deal with them as Claiborne would advise. It was recommended to him in patrolling the country around the settlement of Bayou Pierre, which was within the territory of the United States, but of which no possession had yet been taken, not to disturb the inhabitants, unless an aggression made it necessary to take possession of the settlement and send the garrison to Nacogdoches. In case the commandant of the latter post gave the assurance required from him, any peaceable intercourse between it and the settlement on Bayou Pierre was not to be objected to; but if the assurance was refused, all intercourse between the two places was to be prohibited.

Porter, accordingly, sent lieutenant Piatt, with a corresponding message to Nacogdoches. Don Sebastian Rodriguez, to whom it was delivered, answered that no encroachment had been intended, nor any violence offered, by any part of his garrison, except so far as was necessary to prevent a contraband trade and the exportation of horses. He added, duty forbade him to give the assurance required, and he had ordered his parties to patrol as far as *Arrojo Hondo*.

On Piatt's return, Porter sent captain Turner, with sixty men, to remove the Spanish force from the post they had lately occupied at the Adayes, near Natchitoches. This was effected without difficulty on the fifth of February, and Turner went to patrol the country as far as the Sabine.

In the meanwhile, Don Sebastian had sent an officer of his garrison to the settlement of Bayou Pierre, to remind the inhabitants of the allegiance they owed to the Catholic king, and the obligation they were under to join his standard, whenever called upon by any of his officers. He gave them assurances, that Red river would soon be the boundary between the territory of Spain and that of the United States.

Cordero had sent a large reinforcement to Nacogdoches; Porter had not two hundred men, under his orders, on Red river. In a letter to the secretary of war, of the fifteenth of February, he stated the great disaffection of the people around him; nineteen of whom, out of twenty, preferred the government of Spain to that of the United States. He attributed this disposition to the intrigues of the marquis de Casa-Calvo, who had assured the inhabitants, on his way, that the period was not very distant when his sovereign would resume possession of the country.

The first territorial legislature, under the new form of government met in New Orleans, on the twenty-fifth of January; the members of the legislative council, appointed by the President of the United States, were Bellechasse, Destrehan, Macarty, Sauvé and Jones.

The session lasted for upwards of five months. Among the most important acts, is a black code, or statute regulating the police of slaves. Provision was made for establishing schools in the several counties, for regulating the rights and duties of masters, apprentices and indented servants, and for the improvement of the navigation of the canal of Lafourche and the Bayou Plaquemines.

The attempt of the former legislative council to procure a civil and criminal code for the territory, having failed, two professional gentlemen were employed to prepare a civil code, and directed to take the former laws of the country as the basis of their work.

The assemblage of several bodies of Spanish troops, on the eastern boundary of the province of Texas, rendering the reinforcement of the military posts, in the lower part of the Mississippi necessary, orders had been transmitted from the department of war, as early as the fourth of March, to Wilkinson, who was then at St. Louis, to make the necessary arrangements for the removal of all the troops in his neighborhood, (except one company) to Fort Adams; and four days after he was directed to order colonel Cushing, with three companies and four field pieces, to proceed to Natchitoches, without stopping at Fort Adams, and to send the rest of the forces down the river, under the orders of lieutenant-colonel Kingsbury. On the sixth of May, Wilkinson received orders to repair to the territory of Orleans, or its vicinity, take the command of the regular forces in that quarter, and of such volunteer bodies and militia as might turn out for the defense of the country, and, by all means in his power, to repel any invasion of the territory of the United States.

The secretary of war recommended, that the earliest opportunities should be taken to give to the governors of the provinces of Texas and West Florida, a clear view of the principles on which the government of the United States was acting, viz: that, while negotiations were pending, the military posts of neither party should be advanced; that whatever opinion might be entertained with regard to the boundaries of Louisiana, no military measures should be pursued on either side; and it might be depended upon, that none would be resorted to, on the part of the United States, unless the officers of the Catholic king should attempt a change in the existing order of things: that the actual quiet possession by the United States of the country, east of the Sabine, should be insisted upon, (with the trifling exception of the settlement of Bayou Pierre): and any attempt on the part of Spain to occupy any new post east of the Sabine, would be viewed by the United States, as an invasion of their territorial rights, and resisted as such.

Measures were, at the same time, taken by the department of war for erecting fortifications, at New Orleans and near it. Nine gunboats were sent to the Mississippi, and a considerable number of recruits were sent down the Ohio, and by sea, to fill the companies in that quarter.

Cushing reached Natchitoches on the first of June.

The attention of government was not, however, engrossed by these military preparations. Lieutenant Pike was sent, towards the middle of July, up the Missouri, with lieutenant Wilkinson, a son of the general, a surgeon, a sergeant, two corporals, sixteen privates and an interpreter. The object of this expedition was to escort several chiefs of the Osage and Pawnee nations, who, with a number of women and children, were returning from a visit to the President of the United States, with their presents and baggage. These Indians, fifty-one in number, had been redeemed from captivity among the Potomatomies, and were to be restored to their friends at the Osage towns.

Although the escorting of these Indians was the first object to which Pike's attention was directed, it was not the principal one: it was next to be turned to the accomplishment of a permanent peace between the Osages and Kanses: a third object was his effecting an interview with the Yanetons, Tetans and Comanches, in order to establish a good understanding among these tribes.

It being an object of much interest with the President of the United States to ascertain the direction, extension and navigation of the Arkansas and Red rivers, Pike was instructed to go to the head of these streams, and to detach a party, with a few Indians, to descend the first stream, to take the courses and distances, observe the soil, tribes, etc., and note the creeks or bayous falling into the river; this party was, on reaching the Mississippi, to make the best of its way to Fort Adams and wait for further orders.

Pike was next to proceed with the rest of the party to the head of Red river, making particular remarks on the geographical structure, natural history and population of the country: he was furnished with instruments to ascertain the variation of the magnetic needle and the latitude of every remarkable point; to observe the eclipses of Jupiter's satellites, and the periods of immersions and emersions, in order that, afterwards, by a resort to particular tables, the longitude of the places of observation might be ascertained. He was directed to descend Red river to Natchitoches.

On the rise of the legislature, Claiborne had ordered parts of the militia of the counties of Opelousas and Rapides, to Natchitoches. On his arrival at the latter place, towards the end of August, he found that the Spanish force, on the eastern boundary of the province of Texas, was divided into two main bodies: Cordero was at Nacogdoches, with the one; the other was encamped on the western bank of the Sabine, under Herrera. He was informed that an armed Spanish party had lately gone to the Caddo village, within the territory of the United States, in which that flag was displayed, and had cut down its staff, menacing the peace and tranquillity of these Indians, in case they persisted in acknowledging any dependence on the government of the United States, or in keeping up an intercourse with their citizens: that three of the latter, Shaw, Irwin and Brewster, had been apprehended by a Spanish patrol, within twelve miles of Natchitoches, and forcibly carried to Nacogdoches; and that several slaves, the property of citizens of the United States, had escaped from the service of their masters to the latter place, where they had found an asylum.

On the twenty-sixth, he dispatched Hopkins, the adjutant-general of the territory of Orleans, to Herrera, to make representations to that officer, of the insults offered to the government of the United States last winter, by a Spanish patrol, who had compelled the exploring party under Freeman, who was ascending Red river, to retrograde, and, also, in relation to the recent outrages. Herrera informed Claiborne that he had transmitted his communication to Salcedo, the captain-general; that the exploring party had ascended Red river far above the limits of the United States, and the officer who commanded the patrol that met him, had discharged his duty in insisting on the party's descending the river, till they reached the boundary line; that the Caddo village was within the acknowledged territory of Spain, and these Indians had been notified that if they chose to live under the protection of the United States, they should remove to some part of the territory of their new friends, and, if they chose to continue to dwell in their village, they should take down the flag of the United States; that having chosen the last alternative, and being more tardy in lowering the flag than appeared reasonable, it had been done by the Spaniards; that Shaw and his companions were found twice, on different days, observing the position and movements of the troops under Herrera, and did not agree in the motives assigned by them for encroaching on the king's dominions, and finally avowed their intention of settling in the province; whereupon they had been sent under an escort to San Antonio; finally, that the detention of a number of slaves from Louisiana, at Nacogdoches, was a matter now under the consideration of the captain-general.

Wilkinson reached Natchez on the sixth of September. At this place, he made arrangements with the executor of the Mississippi territory, for holding its militia in readiness. He sent an order to New Orleans for stationing four galleys on lake Pontchartain and the rigolets, and for reinforcing the detachment at Pointe Coupee to seventy-five men; a number which he deemed sufficient, with some militia, to take Grandpre, and his garrison, at Baton Rouge, on this first order; and he instructed the commanding officer on the Tombigbee to prepare with his garrison, and two hundred militia, to invest Mobile, while another body of militia should be sent to make a feint on Pensacola, in order to prevent succor being sent from thence to Mobile.

Claiborne had been desirous of making an immediate attack on Herrera's camp; but the force he could command was insufficient, and the officer who commanded the garrison, had orders to avoid a resort to offensive measures till the arrival of the general. The two chiefs met at Alexandria; Claiborne returned to New Orleans, in order to take measures for holding the militia of the territory in readiness, and Wilkinson proceeded to Natchitoches.

On the twenty-fourth, he, dispatching Cushing to Nacogdoches with a communication to Cordero, couched in the style recommended by the secretary of war, and demanded the immediate removal of the Spanish troops to the west of the Sabine. Cordero replied he would transmit the communication to the captain-general, without whose orders he could not act. On this, Wilkinson informed him the troops of the United States would march to the Sabine—that the sole object of this movement was to settle the boundary, claimed by his government, and that it was without any hostile intention against the troops of Spain, or her territory; this march being rendered essential by some of Herrera's late movements, and the position newly taken by some of the troops, immediately under Cordero's orders, close on the western bank of the Sabine, within sixty miles from Natchitoches.

In the meanwhile, the President of the United States had received information, that designs were in agitation in the western states, unlawful and unfriendly to the peace of the union; and that the prime mover of them was Burr, the late Vice President of the United States. The grounds of that information being inconclusive, the object uncertain, and the fidelity of the western states known to be firm, no immediate step was taken. A rumor was gaining ground, that a numerous and powerful association, extending from New York, through the western states, to the gulf of Mexico had been formed—that eight or ten thousand men were to rendezvous in New Orleans, at no distant period. and from thence, with the co-operation of a naval force, follow Burr to Vera Cruz—that agents from Mexico had come to Philadelphia, during the summer, and had given assurances that the landing of the expedition would be followed by such an immediate and general insurrection, as would ensure the subversion of the existing government, and silence all opposition within a very few weeks—that a part of the association would descend the Alleghany river, and the first general rendezvous would be at the rapids of the Ohio towards the twentieth of October, and from thence the aggregate force was to proceed, in light boats, with the utmost velocity, to New Orleans, under an expectation of being joined on the route by men raised in the state of Tennessee, and other quarters.

It was said that the maritime co-operation relied on, was from a British squadron in the West Indies; that active and influential characters had been engaged in making preparations for six or eight months past, which were in such a state of readiness, that it was expected the van would reach New Orleans in December, when it was expected the necessary organization and equipment would be completed with such promptitude, that the expedition would leave the Mississippi towards the first of February; it was also added, that the revolt of the slaves, along the river was depended upon as an auxiliary measure, and that the seizure of the money in the vaults of the banks in New Orleans, was relied on to supply the funds necessary to carry on the enterprise.

Giving full credit to these reports, Wilkinson determined on making the best arrangement he could with the Spaniards, in order that he might descend to New Orleans, with the greatest part of his force. Accordingly, on the twenty-ninth of October, being on his march to the Sabine, he sent Burling, one of his aids-de-camp, to Cordero, with a written message, proposing that, without yielding a pretension, ceding a right, or interfering with discussions which belonged to their superiors, the state of things, at the delivery and possession of the province to the United States, should be restored by the withdrawal of the troops, of both governments, from the advanced posts they occupied, to those of Nacogdoches and Natchitoches, respectively. He proposed that Cordero's accession to this proposal should be conclusive, and promised to begin his retrograde march on the day the Spanish camp, on the right bank of the Sabine, should be broken up, under a stipulation that the troops of the United States should not cross *Arrojo Hondo*, as long as those of Spain should not cross the Sabine, or until further orders were given by their respective governments.

Cordero assured Burling that Wilkinson's proposition entirely met his views; but he added, his hands were tied by the captain-general's orders, whom he was bound to consult. Burling had been furnished with a copy of the message to Cordero, which he had on his way left with Herrera, who on his return informed him, that the officer next in command would, on the next day, visit Wilkinson, and everything should be arranged. It appears that Herrera was less punctilious than Cordero; for on the following day, the officer brought to Wilkinson, Herrera's assent to his proposition.

On the fifth of November, Wilkinson, having received information that the Spanish camp on the Sabine, would be broken up on that day, began his march towards Natchitoches. Immediately on his arrival there, he directed Porter to proceed to New Orleans, with the utmost expedition, and to repair, mount and equip for service every piece of ordnance in the city, to employ all hands in preparing shells, grape, canister and musket cartridges with buck shot, to have every field piece ready, with hose, harness and drag ropes, and to mount six or eight battering cannons on fort St. Charles and Fort St. Louis, below and above the city, and along its front, flanks and rear.

In the meanwhile, the President of the United States began to perceive the object of the conspiracy; but his information was so blended and involved in mystery, that nothing certain could be sought out for pursuit. In this state of uncertainty he thought it best to order to the field of action, a person in whose integrity, reliance and confidence could be placed, with instructions to investigate the plot' going on, to enter into conferences (for which he was furnished with sufficient credentials) with the civil and military officers of the western states, and with their aid to call on the spot, whatever should become necessary to discover the designs of the conspirators, arrest their means, bring their persons to punishment, and call out the force of the country to suppress any enter-prise in which they were found to be engaged. His choice fell on Graham, the secretary of the territory of Orleans.

It being known, at this time, that many boats were in preparation, stores and provisions collected, and an unusual number of suspicious characters in motion on the Ohio and its tributary streams, orders were given to the governors of the Mississippi and Orleans territories, and to the commander of the land and naval forces there, to be on their guard against surprise, and in constant readiness to resist any enterprise that might be attempted: and on the eighth of November, instructions had been sent to Wilkinson to hasten an accommodation with the Spanish commander on the Sabine, and fall back with his principal force on the hither bank of the Mississippi; a measure, which we have seen, he had already anticipated.

The report was, that Burr had in contemplation three distinct objects, which might be carried on jointly or separately, and either first, as circumstances might require. One of these was the separation from the union of the portion of country west of the Alleghany mountains—another an attack on Mexico—the last was provided as merely ostensible: it was the settlement of a vast tract of land, heretofore granted to the Baron de Bastrop, on the banks of the Washita river. This was to serve as the pretext of all the preparations of Burr, an allurement for such as really wished for a settlement on that stream, and a cover under which to retreat on the event of a final discomfiture.

Such was the state of information at Washington City, in the latter part of November, when specific measures were openly adopted by government. On the twenty-seventh, the President of the United States issued a proclamation, announcing the existence of a conspiracy, and warning such citizens as might have been led, without due knowledge or consideration, to participate therein, to withdraw and desist therefrom, and calling on all officers, civil and military, to be vigilant and active in suppressing it.

Orders were sent to every important point on the Ohio and Mississippi, from Pittsburg to the Balize, for the employment of such part of the civil authority, as might enable them to seize all boats and stores, provided for the enterprise and arrest all persons concerned. A short time before these orders were received in the state of Ohio, Graham, the President's confidential agent, had been diligently employed in tracing the conspiracy and had acquired sufficient information to apply for the immediate exer-tion of the authority of that state to crush the combination. Governor

Tiffin and the legislature, with zeal and energy, effected the seizure of all the boats, provisions and other things provided, within their reach.

Thus, was the first blow given, materially disabling the enterprise in the onset.

In Kentucky, a premature attempt to bring Burr to justice, without sufficient evidence to convict him, had procured a momentary impression in his favor; which gave him the opportunity of hastening his equipments. The arrival of the President's proclamation and orders and the application of Graham, at last awakened the authorities of the state to the truth, and produced the energy and promptitude of which the neighboring state had given the example. Under an order of the legislature, the militia was instantly ordered to different important points, and measures were taken for effecting whatever could be done; but a small number of men, in a few boats, had, in the meanwhile, passed the falls of the Ohio, to rendezvous at the mouth of Cumberland river, with others coming down that stream.

Porter had left Natchitoches for New Orleans, with all the artificers and a company of one hundred men, and had been followed by Cushing with the rest of the forces, leaving only one company behind. Wilkinson, on his way to New Orleans, stopped at Natchez, and made application to the executive of the Mississippi territory, for a detachment of five hundred men of its militia, to proceed to New Orleans, but declining to communicate his motives in making this requisition, was refused. From this place, on the fifteenth of November, he dispatched Burling, one of his aids, to Mexico, for the ostensible purpose of apprising the viceroy of the danger, with which his sovereign's dominions were menaced; but, as the general mentions in his memoirs, "on grounds of public duty and professional enterprise to attempt to penetrate the veil which concealed the topographical route to the city of Mexico, and the military defences which intervened, feeling that the equivocal relation of the two countries justified the *ruse*."

Wilkinson reached New Orleans, towards the end of November, and in his first communication to the President of the United States, after his arrival, mentioned, that among his countrymen, he had discovered characters, who had hitherto been distinguished for integrity and patriotism, men of talents, honored by the confidence of government and distinguished by marks of its regard, who, if not connected with the flagitious plan by active co-operation, approved it, and withheld timely and important information.

Accounts of the requisition made for a detachment of the neighboring territory, and of the refusal of its executive, were soon received in New Orleans, and excited much surprise. The inhabitants wondered that, after the amicable adjustment of all difficulties with the Spaniards, the territory of Orleans, with a reasonable force of regular troops, and an efficient militia well armed and disciplined, should require any aid from the Mississippi territory. As yet, Burr's plans were but partially spoken of and disbelieved; the people had heard of an apprehended insurrection in some of the western states; but the merchants who had frequent accounts from above, understood that things were perfectly tranquil there. Surprise was further excited at the appearance of an uncommon number of men at work on the old fortifications, and on the hearing of a contract for a sufficient number of pickets to enclose the whole city. This and

45

other contracts, entered into since the arrival of Wilkinson, instead of being offered, as was usual, to any who would engage in them on the lowest terms, were entered into secretly and as if intended to be kept from the public eye.

On the seventh of December, Wilkinson dispatched lieutenant Swann, of the army, to Jamaica, with a letter to the officer commanding the naval force on that station, informing him of Burr's plans, and that a report was afloat that the aid of a British naval armament had been either promised or applied for, and warning him and all British military and naval officers, that their interference or any co-operation on their part, would be considered as highly injurious to the United States, and affecting the present amicable relations between the two nations. The communication concluded with the expression of a hope that the British government would refrain from any interference or co-operation, and prevent any individual from affording aid ; and the assurance that the writer would, with all the force under his command, resist any effort of a foreign power to favor Burr's projects.

On the ninth of December, a meeting of the merchants and some of the principal inhabitants was called at the government house, where Claiborne and Wilkinson attended to apprise them of the danger to which the country was exposed. The first said that the object of the preparations of the latter was to defend New Orleans, against a numerous and powerful party, headed by one of the first characters in the union. Wilkinson spoke of the co-operation of the British navy with Burr, and the ultimate destination of the expedition for Mexico, after they had plundered the banks, seized on the shipping, and helped themselves with everything, which an army of seven thousand men might want.

It was then proposed to the meeting, that the shipping in the river should be detained and the crews discharged, that they might be employed on board of the vessels of the United States. This was immediately agreed to, and a subscription was opened for extra bounty and clothing for such sailors, as would enter the public service, and within a short space of time a considerable sum was raised.

In a letter to the President of the United States, Wilkinson stated he had offered to Hall, the district judge of the United States, and Mathews, one of the territorial judges, on the twelfth and thirteenth, all the testimony he possessed against Burr and Bollman, to the end that the former might be proclaimed for apprehension throughout the United States, and the latter committed to close confinement to secure his testimony, and prevent his correspondence and machinations in aid of Burr's plans. The first proposition was rejected, as " it would be too late, as Burr might be on his way;" the second was rejected, as Bollman's offense was bailable and a writ of habeas corpus would set him at large ; that after some reflections judge Hall said : " I believe it will be the best for the general to exercise his discretion ;" Mathews did not say anything, and as they left Wilkinson, he told them he hoped they would not hang him for what he would do, and they both answered in the negative.

On Sunday, the fourteenth, Dr. Erick Bollman, was arrested by order of Wilkinson and hurried to a secret place of confinement, and on the evening of the following day application was made on his behalf, for a writ of habeas corpus, to Sprigg, one of the territorial judges, who declined acting till he could consult Mathews, who could not then be found.   On the sixteenth, the writ was obtained from the superior court; but Bollman was, in the meanwhile, put on board of a vessel and sent down the river.   On the same day, application was made to Workman, the judge of the county of Orleans, for a writ of habeas corpus, in favor of Ogden and Swartwout, who had been arrested a few days before, by order of Wilkinson, at Fort Adams, and were on board of a bomb ketch of the United States, lying before the city.   Workman immediately granted the writ, and called on Claiborne to inquire whether he had assented to Wilkinson's proceedings; Claiborne replied he had consented to the arrest of Bollman, and his mind was not made up as to the propriety of that of Ogden and Swartwout.   Workman then expatiated on the illegality and evil tendency of such measures, beseeching Claiborne not to permit them, but to use his own authority, as the constitutional guardian of his fellow-citizens, to protect them; but he was answered that the executive had no authority to liberate those persons, and it was for the judiciary to do it, if they thought fit.   Workman added, that he had heard that Wilkinson intended to ship off his prisoners, and if this was permitted, writs of habeas corpus would prove nugatory.

From the alarm and terror prevalent in the city, the deputy sheriff could procure no boat to take him on board of the ketch, on the day the writ issued.   This circumstance was made known early on the next morning to Workman, who, thereupon, directed the deputy sheriff to procure a boat by the offer of a considerable sum of money, for the payment of which he undertook the county would be responsible.   The writ was served soon afterwards, and returned at five in the evening by commodore Shaw and the commanding officer of the ketch, lieutenant Jones; Swartwout had been taken from the ketch before the service of the writ.   Ogden was produced and discharged, as his detention was justified on the order of Wilkinson only.

On the eighteenth of December, Wilkinson returned the writ of habeas corpus into the superior court, stating that, as commander-in-chief of the army of the United States, he took on himself all responsibility for the arrest of Erick Bollman, charged with misprison of treason against the government of the United States, and he had adopted measures for his safe delivery to the government of the United States: that it was after several conversations with the governor and one of the judges of the territory, that he had hazarded this step for the national safety, menaced to its basis by a lawless band of traitors, associated under Aaron Burr, whose accomplices were extended from New York to New Orleans; that no man held in higher reverence the civil authorities of his country, and it was to maintain and perpetuate the holy attributes of the constitution, against the uplifted arm of violence, that he had interposed the force of arms in a moment of the utmost peril, to seize upon Bollman, as he should upon all others, *without regard to standing or station*, against whom any proof might arise of a participation in the lawless combination.

This return was, afterwards, amended by an averment that, at the time of the service of the writ, Bollman was not in the possession or power of the person to whom it was addressed.

On the following day Ogden was arrested a second time by the commanding officer of a troop of cavalry of the militia of the territory, in the service of the United States, by whom Alexander was also taken in custody; on the application of Livingston, Workman issued writs of habeas corpus for both prisoners.

Instead of a return, Wilkinson sent a written message to Workman, begging him to accept his return to the superior court, as applicable to the two traitors, who were the subjects of his writs. On this, Livingston procured from the court, a rule that Wilkinson make a further and more explicit return to the writs, or show cause why an attachment should not issue against him.

Workman now called again on Claiborne, and repeated his observations and recommended, that Wilkinson should be opposed by force of arms. He stated, that the violent measures of that officer had produced great discontent, alarm and agitation in the public mind; and, unless such proceeding were effectually opposed, all confidence in government would be at an end. He urged Claiborne to revoke the order, by which he had placed the Orleans volunteers under Wilkinson's command, and to call out and arm the rest of the militia force, as soon as possible. He stated it as his opinion, that the army would not oppose the civil power, when constitutionally brought forth, or that, if they did, the governor might soon have men enough to render the opposition ineffectual. He added, that, from the laudable conduct of commodore Shaw and lieutenant Jones, respecting Ogden, he not only did not apprehend any resistance to the civil authority from the navy, but thought they might be relied on. Similar representations were made to Claiborne by Hall and Mathews; but they were unavailing.

On the twenty-sixth, Wilkinson made a second return to the writ of habeas corpus, stating that the body of neither of the prisoners was in his possession or control. On this, Livingston moved for process of attachment.

Workman now made an official communication to Claiborne. He began by observing that the late extraordinary events, which had taken place within the territory, had led to a circumstance, which authorized the renewal, in a formal manner, of the request he had so frequently urged in conversation, that the executive would make use of the constitutional force placed under his command, to maintain the laws, and protect his fellow citizens against the unexampled tyranny exercised over them.

He added, it was notorious that the commander-in-chief of the military forces had, by his own authority, arrested several citizens for civil offenses, and had avowed on record, that he had adopted measures to send them out of the territory, openly declaring his determination to usurp the functions of the judiciary, by making himself the only judge of the guilt of the persons he suspected, and asserting in the same manner, and as yet without contradiction, that his measures were taken after several consultations with the governor.

He proceeded to state, that writs of habeas corpus had been issued from the court of county of New Orleans: on one of them, Ogden had been brought up and discharged, but he had been, however, again arrested, by order of the general, together with an officer of the court, who had aided professionally in procuring his release. The general had, in his return to a subsequent writ, issued on his behalf, referred the court to a return made by him to a former writ of the superior court, and in the further return which he had been ordered to make, he had declared that neither of the prisoners was in his power, possession or custody; but he had not averred what was requisite, in order to exempt him from the penalty of a contempt of court, that these persons were not in his power, possession or custody, at the time when the writs were served, and, in consequence of the deficiency, the court had been moved for an attachment.

The judge remarked, that although a common case would not require the step he was taking, yet, he deemed it his duty, before any decisive measure was pursued against a man, who had all the regular force, and in pursuance of the governor's public orders, a great part of that of the territory at his disposal, to ask whether the executive had the ability to enforce the decrees of the court of the county, and if he had, whether he would deem it expedient to do it, in the present instance, or whether the allegation by which he supported these violent measures, was well founded?

Not only the conduct and power of Wilkinson, said the judge, but various other circumstances, peculiar to our present situation, the alarm excited in the public mind, the description and character of a large part of the population of the country, might render it dangerous, in the highest degree, to adopt the measure usual in ordinary cases, of calling to the aid of the sheriff, the *posse comitatus*, unless it were done with the assurance of being supported by the governor in an efficient manner.

The letter concluded by requesting a precise and speedy answer to the preceding inquiries, and an assurance that, if certain of the governor's support, the judge should forthwith punish, as the law directs the contempt offered to his court; on the other hand, should the governor not think it practicable or proper to afford his aid, the court and its officers would no longer remain exposed to the contempt or insults of a man, whom they were unable to punish or resist.

The legislature met on the twelfth of January. Two days after, general Adair arrived in the city, from Tennessee, and reported he had left Burr at Nashville, on the twenty-second of December, with two flatboats, destined for New Orleans. In the afternoon of the day of Adair's arrival, the hotel at which he had stopped was invested by one hundred and twenty men, under lieutenant-colonel Kingsbury, accompanied by one of Wilkinson's aids. Adair was dragged from the dining table and conducted to headquarters, where he was put in confinement. They beat to arms through the streets, the battalion of the volunteers of Orleans, and a part of the regular troops, paraded through the city, and Workman, Kerr and Bradford were arrested and confined. Wilkinson ordered the latter to be released, and the two former were liberated on the following day, on a writ of habeas corpus, issued by the district judge of the United States. Adair was secreted until an opportunity offered to ship him away.

Accounts arrived a few days after, that Burr was at Bayou Pierre, a little above the city of Natchez, with fourteen boats. He had been joined, at the mouth of Cumberland river, by a dozen boats, that had descended the Ohio; there were from eighty to one hundred men with him, and he had about forty stands of arms.

Claiborne made an ineffectual attempt to induce the legislature to pass an act for the suspension of the writ of habeas corpus. The draft of a memorial to be presented to congress by the territorial legislature, was introduced in its lower house; the object of it was to place the conduct of Wilkinson in its true light before the national council. After an animated debate, which lasted during several days, the memorial was rejected by a majority of seven out of twenty-one members.

On the twenty-eighth, advices were received from Natchez, that on the fifteenth, Claiborne, colonel of the militia of the Mississippi territory, had marched at the head of a large detachment towards the part of the river at which Burr had stopped; that Burr had written to the secretary of the territory, who exercised the functions of governor, that he was ready to surrender himself to the civil authority; that the secretary had met him, and they had rode together to Natchez, where Burr gave bond for his appearance before the territorial court at its next term. He, however, left the territory, and the governor issued a proclamation, offering a reward of two thousand dollars for his apprehension.

In the latter part of that month, Burling, who had been sent by Wilkinson to Mexico, had returned. The viceroy had not been the dupe of Wilkinson's *ruse*, and gave a very cold reception to his messenger, who was strictly watched, and permitted to stay but a short time in the country.

Lieutenant Swann, who had been sent to Jamaica, came back about the same time. Admiral Drake observed to Wilkinson, that from the style and manner in which the communication he had received was written, he was at a loss how to answer it; but he begged him to be assured that British ships of war would never be employed in any improper service, and that he should ever be ready most cheerfully to obey the orders of his sovereign. Sir Eyre Coote trusted and sincerely believed that the representation made to Wilkinson was totally groundless, as his letter contained the only intelligence received on the subject.

Workman resigned his office, finding that Claiborne paid no attention to his communications.

Towards the middle of March, Burr was arrested near Fort Stoddart, and placed under a strong guard, by whom he was conveyed to Richmond, in Virginia, where he was admitted to bail.

Lieutenant Wilkinson, who had accompanied Pike up the Missouri, now reached New Orleans. In his report, dated the sixth of April, he stated that the Osage Indians had been left in their village, about the fifteenth of August; after which, Pike's party traced the Osage river to its source, and reached the towns of the Pawnees, on the twenty-fifth of September. These Indians had lately been visited by a body of armed Spaniards, from Santa Fe. The flag of Spain was waving over their council room. Pike induced them to substitute that of the United States for it. Proceeding thence, westward, the party came to the Arkansas river, on the fifteenth of October. After a short halt, the lieutenant was detached, with five men, down the stream, to explore the country, and float down to the Mississippi. Pike and the rest of the party, set out for the source of Red river.

The legislature adjourned towards the end of April, after having passed several very important acts. The country courts were abolished; a court was established in each parish, the judge of which was ex-officio judge of probates, and acted as clerk, sheriff and notary. It having been found, that annual sessions of the superior court, out of New Orleans, were inconvenient, semi-annual ones were directed to be holden at Lafourche, Pointe Coupee, Alexandria, Opelousas and Attakapas. The number of members of the house of representatives was fixed at twenty-five: six of these were to represent the county of Orleans; the counties of German Coast, Acadie, Lafourche, Iberville, Pointe Coupee, Rapides, Opelousas and Attakapas, were to send two members each; and one was to come from each of those of Concordia, Washita and Natchitoches. The territory was divided into nineteen parishes.

Wilkinson sailed to Virginia, towards the middle of May, for the purpose of attending Burr's trial, in Richmond.

On the first of July, Pike reached Natchitoches, We have seen that he had sent a small detachment from his party down the Arkansas river in October. From thence he had travelled westwardly, and rambled throughout the Rocky mountains, till the beginning of the new year, when he reached a branch of the Rio del Norte, which he mistook for one of those of Red river. He was overtaken by two Spanish officers and one hundred men, sent by don Joachim Allencaster, who commanded at Santa Fe. The officers, at the head of the Spanish party, were sent to escort Pike and his party to that city, from whence, he was informed they would be conducted, by the most direct route to the navigable waters of Red river which they would descend to Natchitoches. Although dubious of the sincerity of this invitation, and believing he was in a situation to defend himself, as long as his provisions lasted, or till an opportunity offered of escaping by night; yet, mindful of the pacific disposition of the government of the United States, and of his instructions in case he reconnoitered a party of Spanish troops, he determined on complying with don Joachim's request.

On his arrival at Santa Fe, he was informed that don Nemesio de Salcedo, the captain-general of the interior provinces had given orders that he should be sent with his men to the city of Chihuahua, in the province of Biscay, the residence of the captain-general. He, accordingly, left Santa Fe, on the second day after his arrival, and reached Chihauhua on the twentieth of April.

Here, he was compelled to open his trunk, in presence of don Nemesio and an Irishman, in the service of Spain. All his official papers, his correspondence with Wilkinson, his diary, the notes he had taken on the geology, topography and climate of the country, and the Indian tribes he had visited, were seized and detained. He was supplied with money, guides and an escort, and set off for Natchitoches, three days after his arrival at Chihauhua.

In a letter, which Salcedo gave him for Wilkinson, he observed that the latter could not be ignorant of the repeated representations made by the Spanish minister at Philadelphia, and by the marquis de Casa-Calvo, while he was in Louisiana, warning the government of the United States, from extending its expeditions into territories unequivocally belonging to the Catholic king. He added that the papers taken from Pike, afforded evident and incontestible proof of his being guilty of a direct violation of the territorial rights of the crown of Spain, which would have justified his detention, and that of every individual accompanying him, as prisoners; but a desire to give the utmost latitude to the system of harmony and good understanding, subsisting between the two governments, and a hope that such measures would be taken by the officers of the United States, as would prevent any ill consequences resulting from the moderation of those of Spain, had induced him to detain, in the archives of the captainship-general, all the papers Pike had presented, and permit him and his party to return home.

CHAPTER XXVIII.

A MOTION being made on the twenty-fifth of December, 1807, in the house of representatives of the United States, that the President be requested to institute an inquiry into the conduct of Wilkinson, who was suspected of being a pensioner of Spain, he, on the second of January, made application for a court of inquiry, and one was accordingly ordered to assemble.

A short time after, Clark, the delegate of the territory of Orleans, delivered to the house, under the sanction of his oath, a statement of several transactions, which had come to his knowledge, within the preceding twenty years, strongly implicating Wilkinson's conduct, as a pensioner of Spain and an accomplice of Burr.

The second territorial legislature began its second session, on the eighth of January. The professional gentlemen, who had been appointed in 1805, to prepare a civil and criminal code, Moreau Lislet and Brown, reported " a digest of the civil laws now in force in the territory of Orleans, with alterations and amendments adapted to the present form of government." Although the Napoleon code was promulgated in 1804, no copy of it had as yet reached New Orleans: and the gentlemen availed themselves of the project of that work, the arrangement of which they adopted, and *mutatis mutandis*, literally transcribed a considerable portion of it. Their conduct was certainly praiseworthy; for, although the project is necessarily much more imperfect than the code, it was far superior to anything, that any two individuals could have produced, early enough, to answer the expectation of those who employed them. Their labor would have been much more beneficial to the people, than it has proved, if the legislature to whom it was submitted, had given it their sanction as a system, intended to stand by itself, and be construed by its own context, by repealing all former laws on matters acted upon in this digest.

Anterior laws were repealed, so far only, as they were contrary to, or irreconcilable with any of the provisions of the new. This would have been the case, if it had not been expressed.

In practice, the work was used, as an incomplete digest of existing statutes, which still retained their empire; and their exceptions and modifications were held to affect several clauses by which former principles were absolutely stated. Thus, the people found a decoy, in what was held out as a beacon.

The Fuero Viejo, Fuero Juezgo, Partidas, Recopilationes, Leyes de las Indias, Autos Accordados and Royal schedules remained parts of the written law of the territory, when not repealed expressly or by a necessary implication.

Of these musty laws the copies were extremely rare; a complete collection of them was in the hands of no one, and of very many of them, not a single copy existed in the province.

To explain them, Spanish commentators were consulted and the *corpus juris civilis* and its own commentators were resorted to; and to eke out any deficiency, the lawyers who came from France or Hispaniola read Pothier, d'Aguesseau, Dumoulin, etc.

Courts of justice were furnished with interpreters, of the French, Spanish and English languages; these translated the evidence and the charge of the court, when necessary, but not the arguments of the counsel. The case was often opened in the English language, and then the jurymen, who did not understand the counsel, were indulged with leave to withdraw from the box into the gallery. The defense, being in French, they were recalled and the indulgence shown to them was enjoyed by their companions, who were strangers to that language. All went together into the jury room; each contending the argument he had listened to was conclusive, and they finally agreed on a verdict, in the best manner they could.

Among the most useful acts that were passed, at this session, was one for the establishment of a school in each parish.

The court of inquiry on Wilkinson's conduct did not terminate its investigation, till the month of June; its report was in favor of the general, and was approved of by the President of the United States.

In the fall, the foreign relations of the union assumed an aspect which produced a general impression that a rupture with Great Britain was neither improbable nor distant, and the executive received information that the disposable force at Halifax, was held in readiness to serve in the West Indies, or take possession of New Orleans, (should the forces of the United States move northerly) and keep that city as an equivalent for what might be lost in Canada.

Accordingly, on the second of November, the secretary of war directed Wilkinson to take measures, without delay, for assembling at New Orleans and its vicinity, as large a portion of the regular troops as circumstances would allow. The third, fifth and seventh regiments, with a battalion, composed of four companies of the sixth and the companies of light dragoons, light artillery and riflemen, raised in the states south of New Jersey, were destined to the service, and the general was instructed to make arrangements for reaching New Orleans in order to take the command of the forces in that department, as soon as possible, and to make such a disposition of them as would most effectually enable him to defend the country against an invading foe. He was authorized, in case of necessity, to call on the executives of the territories of Orleans and Mississippi, for such parts of their militia as might be wanted.

He embarked at Baltimore on the twenty-fourth of January, 1809, and touched at Annapolis, Norfolk and Charleston to accelerate the motions of the troops in those places, and sailed to Havana, on a special mission to the captain-general of the island of Cuba.

On the ninth of February, congress passed an act authorizing the President of the United States to cause the canal Carondelet to be extended to the Mississippi and deepened throughout, so as to admit of an early and safe passage to gunboats from the river to the lake, and if, on a survey, he should be convinced that this was practicable and would conduce to the defense of New Orleans, and an appropriation of twenty-five thousand dollars was made therefor.

On the fourth of March, James Madison succeeded Jefferson in the presidency of the United States.

Wilkinson, on his return from Havana, stopped at Pensacola, and reached New Orleans on the nineteenth of April.

The force which he found in that city was a little less than two thousand men, and one third of it was on the sick list. He spent some time in reconnoitring the country around, in search of a spot from which the troops might readily be brought into action, in case of an attack, and in which they might, in the meanwhile, enjoy as much health and comfort as the climate would allow; his choice fell on an elevated piece of ground on the left bank of the Mississippi, about eight miles below the city, near the point at which the road leading to the settlements of Terre-aux-Bœufs leaves that which runs along the river.

Between the nineteenth of May and the eighteenth of July of this year, thirty-four vessels from the island of Cuba, with 5,797 individuals, of whom 1,828 were white, 1,978 free blacks or colored perons, and 1,991 slaves. These people had sought a refuge in that island, on the insurrection of the blacks in Hispaniola.

A large detachment was sent to Terre-aux-Bœufs to make the necessary preparations and the rest of the troops gradually followed; on the thirteenth, seven hundred non-commissioned officers and privates had assembled.

They had hardly been three weeks encamped, when the most peremptory order from the department of war, of the twenty-fourth of October, was received by Wilkinson, directing him immediately to embark his whole force, leaving only sufficient garrisons of old troops at New Orleans and Fort St. Philip, and proceed to the high grounds on the rear of Fort Adams and Natchez, and by an equal division of his men form an encampment at each place.

A difficulty in procuring boats, and other circumstances, did not allow the troops to begin ascending the river, before the fifteenth of September; their progress lasted forty-seven days; during which, out of nine hundred and thirty-five men, who embarked, six hundred and thirty-eight were sick, and two hundred and forty died.

Although the report of the court of inquiry, in the preceding year, had been favorable to Wilkinson, the general impression, that he had received large sums of money from the Spanish government in Louisiana to favor its views in detaching the western people from the Atlantic states, was not absolutely effaced. Clark had published a statement of different transactions, in which Wilkinson had been concerned, during the preceding years, and had annexed to it copies of a number of authentic documents, from which he concluded the proof was irresistible, that the general had been a pensioner of Spain and an accomplice of Burr, whom he had betrayed, when he found his plans could not succeed. Clark's publication excited suspicion in many and caused conviction in some. The disasters, attending the forces sent to the Mississippi, were attributed by Wilkinson's enemies to his misconduct and the clamor against him became so general, that it was thought proper to call him to the seat of government. Wade Hampton, who was sent to supersede him, assumed the command of the troops on the nineteenth of December.

The total number of non-commissioned officers and privates, during the last ten months of this year, never exceeded nineteen hundred and fifty-three. Out of it, seven hundred and sixty-four died and one hundred and sixty-six deserted. So that the total loss was nine hundred and thirty, almost one half of the whole. The greatest sickness was in the month of August, when five hundred and sixty-three men were on the sick list.

The third territorial legislature held its first session on the ninth of February, and adjourned late in March, without having passed any very important public act. By one of its resolutions, however, twenty thousand dollars were appropriated to the establishment of a college.

Early in May, Claiborne having obtained leave of absence, left the territory on a visit to the eastern states—and the executive functions devolved on the secretary, Thomas B. Robertson.

In the summer, a number of citizens of the United States, who had removed to the neighborhood of Bayou Sara, joined by others from the Mississippi territory, took up arms, embodied themselves and marched to the fort of Baton Rouge. Delassus, who commanded it, having but a handful of men, was unable to prevent their taking it. The people of the district sent delegates to a convention, that met at St. Francisville, declared their independence and framed a constitution. Fulwar Skipwith was appointed governor of the new state.

By a census taken this year, by the marshal of the United States, under an act of congress, it appears that the population of the territory was as follows:

City and suburbs of New Orleans,	17,242	24,552
Precinct of New Orleans,	7,310	
Plaquemines,		1,549
St. Bernard,		1,020
St. Charles,		3,291
St. John Baptist,		2,990
St. James,		3,955
Ascension,		2,219
Assumption,		2,472
Lafourche,		1,995
Iberville,		2,679
Baton Rouge,		1,463
Pointe Coupee,		4,539
Concordia,		2,895
Ouachita,		1,077
Rapides,		2,200
Catahoula,		1,164
Avoyelles,		1,209
Natchitoches,		2,870
Opelousas,		5,048
Attakapas,		7,369
		76,556

On receiving information that the garrison of the fort at Baton Rouge had been driven out, the President of the United States issued a proclamation, on the 16th of October, setting forth that the territory south of the 31st degree of northern latitude, east on the Mississippi, as far as *Rio Perdido*, of which possession had not yet been delivered to the United States, had ever been considered and claimed by them as part of the country they had acquired by the treaty of the 30th April, 1803, and their acquiescence in its temporary continuation under the authorities of Spain, was not the result of any distrust of their title, as had been particularly evinced by the general tenor of their laws, but was occasioned by their conciliatory views, a confidence in the justice of their cause, and the result of candid discussion and amicable negotiations with a friendly power; that a satisfactory adjustment of existing differences, too long delayed, without the fault of the United States, had been for some time, entirely suspended, by events over which they had no control; and a crisis was now arrived, subversive of the order of things under the authority of Spain, whereby a failure of on the part of the United States, to take the country into their possession, might lead to events ultimately contravening the views of both parties; while in the meantime the security and tranquillity of their adjoining territories were endangered, and new facilities given to the violation of their revenue and commercial laws, and of those for the prohibition of the importation of slaves; the failure might farther be considered as a dereliction of their title, and an insensibility to the importance of the stake.

It was urged, that the acts of congress, although comtemplating a present possession by a foreign prince, had also had in view an eventual one by the United States, and had accordingly been so framed, as in that case to extend their operations thereto.

The President concluded by announcing that under these weighty and urgent considerations, he had deemed it right and requisite, that possession should be immediately taken of the said territory, in the name and behalf of the United States. The governor of the territory of New Orleans was accordingly directed to carry the views of the United States into complete execution, and to exercise over that part of the territory the authority and functions, legally appertaining to his office; the people were charged to pay due regard to him in his official character, to be obedient to the laws, to cherish harmony and demean themselves as peaceful citizens, under assurance of protection in the enjoyment of liberty, property and the religion they profess.

Claiborne, on his return from the United States, stopped at Natchez, where governor Holmes furnished him with a detachment of the militia of the Mississippi territory, which was joined by a volunteer troop of horse, from the neighborhood. They marched to St. Francisville, the first town below the line of demarcation, where, on the 7th of December, without any opposition, he hoisted the flag of the United States, in token of his having taken possession of the country, in their name and behalf, the inhabitants cheerfully submitting to his authority. He announced this event by a proclamation, and by subsequent ones established, in this new part of the territory of Orleans, the parishes of Feliciana, East Baton Rouge, St. Helena, St. Tammany, Biloxi and Pascagoula.

No attempt was made to occupy the town of Mobile, nor any part of the country around it, and the Spanish garrison of Fort Charlotte was left undisturbed; Claiborne having been especially instructed not to take possession, by force, of any post in which the Spaniards had a garrison, however small it might be,

We have seen that in the latter part of the preceding year, Wilkinson had been ordered to the seat of government: he reached it towards the middle of April. There were then two committees of the house of representatives, charged with enquiries on matters that concerned him, viz: the cause of the great mortality among the troops on the Mississippi, during the preceding year; his public life, conduct and character: and while the attention of the house was thus arrested on the general, the executive deemed it proper to suspend any proceeding in regard to him. Congress adjourned, without either of the committees making a report.

Soon after the meeting of congress, in the winter, the first committee made a report, which did not implicate Wilkinson's conduct; the other, without an expression of their opinion, submitted to the house the whole evidence before them: without acting on it, the house directed it to be laid before the President of the United States.

Claiborne came to New Orleans early in January, to meet the third territorial legislature, at its second session; but an uncontrollable event induced him to prorogue it till the fourth Monday of that month.

The slaves of a plantation, in the parish of St. John the Baptist, on the left bank of the Mississippi, about thirty-six miles above New Orleans, revolted and were immediately joined by those of several neighboring plantations. They marched along the river, towards the city, divided into companies, each under an officer, with beat of drums and flags displayed, compelling the blacks they met to fall in their rear; and before they could be checked, set fire to the houses of four or five plantations. Their exact number was never ascertained, but asserted to be about five hundred. The militia of the parish and those above and below, were soon under arms; major Milton came down from Baton Rouge, with the regular force under his orders, and general Hampton, who was then in the city, headed those in Fort St. Charles and the barracks. The blacks were soon surrounded and routed; sixty-six of them were either killed during the action, or hung on the spot, immediately after. Sixteen were sent to the city for trial, and a number fled to the swamps, where they could not be pursued: several of these had been dangerously wounded, and the corpses of others were afterwards discovered. The blacks sent to New Orleans, were convicted and executed. Their heads were placed on high poles, above and below the city, and along the river as far as the plantation on which the revolt began, and on those on which they had committed devastation. To insure tranquillity and quiet alarm, a part of the regular forces and the militia remained on duty, in the neighborhood, during a considerable time.

The general assembly made provision for the representation of the inhabitants of the new part of the territory in the legislature. They erected two new judicial districts, viz: those of Feliciana and Catahoula; the town of Vidalia, in the parish of Concordia, opposite to the city of Natchez, was established; a charter of incorporation was granted to a number of individuals, who had formed themselves into companies, for establishing two banks, the Planter's bank and the bank of Orleans; these institutions appeared to be called for by the expiration of the charter of the bank of the United States. The first had a capital of six hundred thousand dollars, and the duration of its charter was fifteen years; the capital of the other was five hundred thousand dollars, and its charter had the same duration.

An act was passed, granting to Livingston and Fulton, the sole and exclusive right and privilege to build, construct, make use, employ and navigate boats, vessels and water crafts, urged or propelled through the water by fire or steam, in all the creeks, rivers, bays and waters whatsoever, within the jurisdiction of the territory, during eighteen years from the first of January, 1812.

Before the adjournment of the legislature, official information was received, that congress had, on the eleventh of February, passed an act, to enable the people of the territory to form a constitution and state government, and the admission of such state in the union.

Congress had not, as yet, determined that the part of the ceded territory, of which possession had been taken a few months, should be part of the new state, and its inhabitants were not authorized to appoint members of the convention, for framing the constitution.

The qualifications of the electors were citizenship of the United States, one year's residence in the territory and having paid a territorial, county, district or parish tax; persons having, in other respects, the legal qualifications for voting for representatives of the general assembly of the territory, were also authorized to vote.

The act was silent as to any qualifications, with regard to the members of the convention; their number was not to exceed sixty; the third Monday of September was named for their election, and they were directed to meet on the first Monday in November. The members who were to compose it were to be apportioned among the counties, districts and parishes by the legislature.

The election was to be held at the same place and conducted in the same manner, as that for members of the house of representatives.

The convention was to assemble in the city of New Orleans.

That body was first to determine, by the majority of the whole number elected, whether it be expedient or not, at that time, to form a constitution or state government, for the people of the territory, and if it was determined to be expedient, was to declare, in the same manner, in behalf of the people, that it adopted the constitution of the United States.

Congress required that the constitution to be formed, should be republican; consistent with the constitution of the United States; contain the fundamental principles of civil and religious liberty; secure to the citizens the right of trial by jury in criminal cases, and that of the writ of *habeas corpus*, conformably to the provisions of the constitution of the United States; and that after the admission of the new state into the union, the laws which suit a state may pass and be promulgated, and its records of every description, be preserved, and its legislative and judicial written proceedings be conducted in the language in which the laws, the legislative and judicial written proceedings were then published and conducted.

The convention was further required to provide, by an ordinance irrevocable, without the consent of the United States, that the people of the territory do agree and declare that they do forever disclaim all right or title to the waste or unappropriated lands, lying within the territory, and that the same shall be and remain at the sole and absolute disposition of the United States; and, moreover, that each and every tract of land sold by congress, shall remain exempt from any tax laid by the order, or under the authority of the state, county, township, parish, or any other purpose whatever, for the term of four years from the respective days of the sale thereof: further, that the lands of citizens of the United States, residing without the state, shall never be taxed higher than the lands belonging to persons residing therein; and no tax shall ever be imposed on lands belonging to the United States.

Congress agreed that five per cent. on the net proceeds of the sales of the public lands of the United States, should be applied to laying out and constructing public roads and levees, in the state, as the legislature may direct.

The act finally provided that if the constitution or form of government to be made, was not disapproved by congress, at their next session after they received it, the new state should be admitted into the union, upon the same footing with the original states.

The legislature apportioned the number of members of the convention among the parishes, and made provision for the expenses attending it, and adjourned in the latter part of April.

In the summer, a court martial was ordered for the trial of Wilkinson, to meet at Frederickstown, and, on the 11th of July, he was furnished with a copy of the charges against him.   He was accused of having corruptly combined with the government of Spain, in Louisiana, for the separation of the western people from the Atlantic states; of having corruptly received large sums of money from Spain; of having connived at the designs of Burr; of having been an accomplice in them; of waste of public money; and finally, of disobedience to orders.

In the month of November, the convention assembled at New Orleans. The constitution of the United States was adopted; a constitution was formed, and received the signatures of all the members of the convention on the 22d of January.

The preamble of this document, describes the limits of the new state, and declares the erection of the territory into a state, by the name of Louisiana.

The powers of government are divided into three distinct branches, each of which is confided to a separate body of magistracy, the legislative, executive and judiciary; and it is declared that no person or number of persons, of any of the magistracies, shall exercise any power confided to any of the others.

The legislative powers are vested in a general assembly, composed of a senate and house of representatives.

The election is to take place on the first Monday of July, in every other year.

The qualifications of electors are the same, in regard to the senate and house of representatives.

Every free white male citizen of the United States, having attained the age of twenty-one years, and resided one year in the country, and having within the last six months paid a state tax, or being a purchaser of lands of the United States, is entitled to a vote.

Free white male citizens of the United States, having attained the age of twenty-one years, resided in the state during the two preceding years, and during the last in the county or district, and holding landed property therein to the value of five hundred dollars, are eligible as members of the house of representatives.

The number of representatives is to be ascertained and regulated by the number of qualified electors; a census thereof is to be taken in every fourth year.

The state is divided into fourteen senatorial districts, which are forever to remain indivisible, and each of which elects a senator.

Each senator must be a citizen of the United States, have attained the age of thirty years, and have double the time of residence, and value of property, required of a member of the house of representatives.

Senators are elected for six years, one-third of them going out every second year.

In either house, a majority of its members constitutes a quorum, but a less number may adjourn and compel attendance.

Each is judge of the qualifications and elections of its own members; appoints its officers; determines the rules of its proceedings; may punish and, with the concurrence of two-thirds, expel a member, but not a second time for the same offence; keeps and publishes a weekly journal of its proceedings; and enters, thereon, the yeas and nays, at the desire of two members.

Neither, during the session, can without the consent of the other, adjourn for more than three days, nor to any place, than that in which they respectively sit.

The members of each house receive a compensation for their services, from the treasury. Except in cases of treason, felony and breach of the peace, they are privileged from arrest, while sitting in, going to, or returning from the house, and for any speech therein, cannot be questioned elsewhere. They are, during the period of their service and the following year, ineligible to any office created, or the emoluments of which were increased during the period for which they were elected, unless the office be filled by the suffrages of the people.

Clergymen, priests or teachers of any religious persuasion and collectors of public taxes, not duly discharged, are ineligible as members of the general assembly.

Every bill is to be read three times, in each of the houses.

Bills for raising a revenue originate in the house of representatives; but the senate may propose amendments.

The executive power is vested in the governor.

He must be, at least, thirty-five years of age, have resided six years in the state, immediately before the election, and hold in his own right, a landed estate of the value of five thousand dollars, according to the tax list.

Members of congress, persons holding any office under the United States, and ministers of any religious society, are ineligible as governor.

Every fourth year the electors of members of the legislature vote for a governor, at the time and place at which they vote for the legislature: and, on the second day after the meeting of that body, the members of both houses meet in the house of representatives, choose a governor out of the two individuals having received the greatest number of votes from the people: but, if more than two have such a number, the members vote for them in the same manner: but if more than one individual have an equal number of votes, next to the one who had the highest, they vote for one of the former, to be voted for with the latter.

In this, as in all other elections, the votes are taken by ballot.

The governor is commander-in-chief of the army and navy, and the militia, except when the latter is in the service of the United States; but does not act personally in the field, unless so advised by the legislature. He nominates and appoints, with the advice and consent of the senate, judges, sheriffs and all other officers, created by the constitution, whose appointment it does not vest in other persons; he fills, provisionally, all vacancies happening during the recess of the legislature; he has power to remit fines and forfeitures; except in cases of impeachment, he grants reprieves, and, with the approbation of the senate, pardons; in case of treason, he grants reprieves till the meeting of the general assembly, who alone may pardon.

He may require information, in writing, from any officer in the executive department, on any matter relating to their respective offices.

He gives, from time to time, to the general assembly, information respecting the situation of the state, and recommends measures to their consideration, and takes care that the laws be executed.

On extraordinary occasions, he convenes the general assembly, at the seat of government, or elsewhere in cases of danger. If the houses disagree, at the time of their adjournment, he adjourns them to any day within four months.

He visits the several counties, at least, once in every two years.

Every bill, after having passed both houses, is sent to the governor, who signs it, if he approves of it; otherwise he returns it to the house from whence it came, with his objections, where, after they are entered on the journal, the bill is reconsidered, and if two-thirds of the members elected, vote for it, it is sent, with the objections, to the other house, and becomes a law, if voted for there, by two-thirds of the members elected.

Resolutions, to which both houses made assent, are sent to the governor in the same manner as bills.

If the governor does not return a bill or resolution within ten days after receiving it, his approbation is presumed, unless the house, in which it originated, prevents its return by an adjournment.

A secretary of state is appointed for the same period as the governor; he attests the latter's official acts, and is the keeper of the archives.

The governor's compensation cannot be increased or diminished during the incumbent's period of service.

The judicial power is vested in a supreme and inferior courts. The first is composed of not less than three nor more than five judges. It sits at New Orleans during the months of January, February, March, April, May, June, July, November and December, for the eastern district; and at Opelousas during the rest of the year, for the western. The legislature may change the place of sitting, in the western circuit, every fifth year. Its jurisdiction is appellate only, and extends to civil cases, in which the value of the matter in dispute exceeds three hundred dollars.

Inferior courts are established by law.

The judges are conservators of the peace throughout the state; they hold their offices during their good behavior. They are removable on impeachment, and, for any reasonable cause, not sufficient for impeachment, they may be removed by the governor, on the address of three-fourths of each house of the general assembly.

The power of impeachment is vested in the house of representatives alone. The senate is the sole judge, and conviction cannot take place without the concurrence of two-thirds of the senators present.

The governor and all civil officers are liable to impeachment for any misdemeanor in office. The judgment extends only to removal and disqualification, but is subject to prosecution in other courts.

In case of the governor's impeachment, death, resignation or removal, his functions devolve on the president of the senate.

Provision was made for the freedom of the press; the writ of *habeas corpus;* the trial by jury, and the due administration of justice in criminal

47

cases; admission to bail, and the exclusion of cruel and unusual punishment.

The clauses recommended by congress were inserted.

A mode for revising the constitution was provided.

Arrangements were made, in a schedule, for the march of the state government, at the expiration of the territorial, by continuing the officers of the former, until superseded by law.

Those who prepared the first form of a constitution, submitted to the convention, took the constitution of Kentucky for a model; they made several alterations, and others were introduced by the convention.

One of the principal was a provision for the salary of the judges of the supreme court, which was fixed at five thousand dollars; another was the obligation imposed on the judges of all courts, as often as it may be possible, in every definitive judgment, to refer to the particular law, in virtue of which, the judgment is rendered, and, in all cases, to adduce the reasons on which it is founded.

CHAPTER XXIX.

On the tenth of January, 1812, the inhabitants of New Orleans witnessed the approach of the first vessel, propelled by steam, which floated on the Mississippi, the New Orleans, from Pittsburg. The captain stated, he had been but two hundred and fifty-nine hours, actually, on the way.

We have seen that soon after the cession, the Pope had placed the ecclesiastical concerns of the success of Louisiana, under the care of bishop Carrol, of Baltimore; he now confided them to the abbe Dubourg, a French clergyman, who had resided for several years in Baltimore, and who came to New Orleans with the appointment of Apostolic Administrator.

The President of the United States approved, on the 14th of February, 1812, the sentence pronounced by the court martial, on the 23d of December preceding, acquitting Wilkinson of all the charges exhibited against him.

Early in the month of April, congress passed an act for the admission of the territory of Orleans, as a state, into the Union; but the act was not to be in force till the 30th of the month, the ninth anniversary of the treaty of cession. It was declared to be a condition of the admission of the new member, that the river Mississippi, and the navigable waters leading into it, and into the gulf of Mexico, should be common highways, and forever free, as well to the inhabitants of that state as to those of the other states and territories of the United States, without any tax, duty, impost or toll therefor, imposed by the state, and that this condition and all others, stated in the act of the preceding session, for enabling the inhabitants of the territory to form a constitution, etc., should be considered as the fundamental terms and conditions of the admission of the state into the union.

A few days after, another act was passed, for extending the limits of the state, by annexing thereto, the country south of the Mississippi territory, and east of the Mississippi river and the lakes, as far as Pearl river.

The legislature was required, in case it assented to this accession of territory, to make provision, at its next session, for the representation of the inhabitants, in the legislature, according to the principles of the constitution, and for securing to them equal rights with those enjoyed by the people of the other parts of the state; the law passed for this purpose being liable to revision, modification and amendments by congress, and, also, in the mode, provided for amendments to the constitution, but not liable to change and amendment by the legislature of the state.

On the 12th of the same month, Wilkinson was directed, by the secretary of war, to return to New Orleans and resume his command.

Authentic copies of the late acts of congress having reached New Orleans in the beginning of June, Poydras, the president of the late convention, in compliance with a provision of the schedule, annexed to the constitution, issued his proclamation for the election of a governor and members to the legislature.

General Wilkinson reached New Orleans on the 8th of June.

Congress declared war against Great Britain on the 18th.

The senate and house of representatives, according to the constitution, assembled on the 27th, and on the following day proceeded to the election of a governor; Claiborne and Villere, the son of the gentleman who, we have seen, fell under the bayonets of a Spanish guard, in 1769, were the individuals who had received the highest number of votes from the people; the former, who had a larger number than the latter, was chosen.

The first act of the legislature, was that by which the proposed extent of territory was assented to; and the next was that providing for the representation of the new citizens of the state, in its legislature, and the extension to them of all the rights enjoyed by the inhabitants of the other parts of the state. They were allowed three senators and six members of the house of representatives.

It was thought best to postpone the establishment of the judiciary department, till the new members of the legislature could be elected and take their seats; and after attending to such matters as required immediate attention, the legislature adjourned early in September, to the 23d of November.

On the nineteenth of August, the county suffered a great deal from a hurricane, the ravages of which exceeded those hitherto known by any of the inhabitants. Several buildings were blown down in New Orleans, particularly a very large and elegant market house.

At their second session, a supreme, district and parish courts were organized; the first was to be composed of three judges, and Hall, Mathews and Derbigny were, accordingly, appointed. The state was divided into seven districts, in which a court was to be holden, in each parish, except the first, by a district judge, who had the same jurisdiction as the late territorial superior court. In the first district the court was to be holden in New Orleans only.

The parish courts were continued on the same footing, except that of New Orleans, to which the jurisdiction of a district court was given.

The arms of the United States were unsuccessful on the northern frontier, during the year 1812; general Hall surrendered his army to the enemy, who possessed themselves of the whole Michigan territory. General Van Ranselaer was more fortunate, at the battle of Queenstown, where he drove off the assailants, with a considerable loss, particularly that of their leader, general Brock.

The navy acquired much eclat: the British frigates Guerriere, Macedonian and Java, were taken by captains Hull, Decatur and Bainbridge; the sloop of war Alert, by captain Porter, and the brigs of war Detroit and Caledonia, by lieutenant Jones.

The United States lost the brigs Nautilus and Vixen and the sloop of war, the Wasp.

On the 12th of February, 1813, congress authorized the President of the United States, to occupy and hold that part of West Florida, lying west of the river Perdido, not then in the possession of the United States. Orders for this purpose were sent to Wilkinson, who immediately took measures with commodore Shaw, and the necessary equipments being made, the forces employed in this service reached the vicinity of Fort Charlotte, in the night between the 7th and 8th of April, having on their way dispossessed a Spanish guard, on Dauphin island, and intercepted a Spanish transport, having on board detachments of artillery, with provisions and munitions of war, Don Gayetano Perez, who commanded in Fort Charlotte, received the first information of Wilkinson's approach from his drums. The place was strong and well supplied with artillery, but the garrison consisted of one hundred and fifty effective men only, and was destitute of provisions, as the troops depended upon the town for daily subsistence. Don Gayetano capitulated on the thirteenth. The garrison was sent to Pensacola, but the artillery of the fort was retained, to be accounted for by the United States; with part of it, Wilkinson established a small fortification on Mobile point, which commanded the entrance of the bay; he left colonel Constant in command at Fort Charlotte, and returned to New Orleans, which he left a few days after, being ordered to join the army on the frontiers of Canada.

General Flournoy, of Georgia, was sent to command the forces on the Mississippi.

The British had sent emissaries from Canada, among the southern Indians, with a view to induce them to take up the hatchet against the frontier inhabitants of Georgia and the Mississippi territory. Those men were successful among the Creeks, who, on the 20th of June, manifested their hostile temper by the massacre of several individuals of their own tribes, who were friendly to the United States. This event was not, however, followed by any positive act of hostility against the United States, till the 13th of September, when they committed a sudden, unprovoked, and daring outrage against them.

Major Beasley had been sent to command a small garrison, which it had been deemed proper to put in Fort Mimms, in the Tensau settlement of the Mississippi territory; a Creek Indian came and informed him, in an apparently friendly manner, that he was to be attacked within two days; having made his communication, he departed and was hardly out of sight when twenty or thirty of his countrymen came in view, and forcibly entered the fort. In the attempt to shut the gate, Beasley was killed; the garrison revenged his death by that of all the assailants. This first party was, however, soon followed by a body of about eight hundred: the garrison was overpowered, the fort taken and every man, woman and child in it slaughtered, with the exception of four privates, who, though severely wounded, effected their escape and reached Fort Stoddard.

This misfortune was considerably heightened by the circumstance of a number of the settlers near the fort having sent their families there for protection: the number of white persons who thus perished amounted to three hundred and fifty. The garrison made a most obstinate defense; two hundred and fifty Indians were killed and the number of the wounded could not be known.

This event broke up the settlement: its inhabitants sought the protection of the white people, at Mobile and Forts Stoddard and St. Stevens.

A forty-fourth regiment of infantry had been ordered to be raised, and exclusively employed in the state of Louisiana and West Florida. Colonel G. T. Ross, to whom the command of it had been given, entered on the recruiting service early in the month of October.

On the first account of the disaster at Fort Mimms, very large parties of the militia of the states of Tennessee and Georgia, volunteered their services, and took the field under generals Jackson and Floyd, to avenge their countrymen. The first blow was struck on the third of November, at the Tallusatche towns, where one hundred and eighty-six warriors were killed, and eighty-four women and children made prisoners: the militia had five men killed and forty-one wounded. A week after, Jackson, with about two thousand Tennessee volunteers, fell on the Indians at Talledoga and defeated them, killing three hundred warriors: he had only six men killed and eighty wounded.

On the eighteenth, a division of the Tennessee volunteer militia, under general White, destroyed the towns of Little Oakfulkee, Genalga and Hillsbee; in an action in which he had not a man killed or wounded, and he killed sixty Indians and made two hundred and fifty-six prisoners.

General Floyd, with nine hundred and sixty men, of the Georgia militia, and three hundred and fifty friendly Indians, attacked fifteen hundred hostile Creeks, at Antossee and Tallassee. He burnt upwards of four hundred houses, and killed two hundred warriors, including the kings of the two towns. His loss was seven killed and fifty-four wounded.

Congress, on the seventeenth of December, laid a general embargo.

In the latter part of that month, Flournoy, by order of the United States, made a requisition of one thousand men of the militia of the state, to be employed in the service of the United States, during six months, unless sooner discharged. Claiborne complied with the requisition immediately.

The arms of the United States were more successful on the northern frontier during this year, than in the preceding, yet but little advantage was obtained. The enemy made considerable havoc on the Chesapeake, in the towns of Hampton, Havre de Grace, Georgetown and Frederickton.

The navy acquired much glory: the British ships Detroit and Queen Charlotte, brig Hunter, schooners Lady Prevost and Chippewa, and sloop Little Belt, were taken by commodore Perry. The brigs Peacock and Boxer by captain Lawrence and lieutenant Brown, the schooners Dominica and Highflyer by a privateer, and captain Rodgers. The United States lost the frigate Chesapeake, and schooners Viper, Asp, Julia and Growler, and brig Argus.

The legislature began its third session on the third of January, 1814, but did not pass any very important act.

General Claiborne, at the head of a detachment of the Mississippi territory, on the twenty-third of January, burned the town of Etchenachaca, (holy ground) and routed the Indians. Two days after, general Floyd was attacked, on his encampment, forty-eight miles west of Catahouchee, but the enemy retreated after a severe conflict. The loss of the general was twenty-two killed and twenty-seven wounded.

A decisive blow was at last struck on the twenty-seventh of March, when general Jackson attacked the enemy's entrenchments, and, after an action of five hours, completely defeated them, killing seven hundred and fifty warriors, and taking two hundred and fifty women and children. His loss was twenty-five killed, and one hundred and five wounded.

Congress, on the fourteenth of April, repealed the embargo and new importation laws.

In the course of that month the banks in New Orleans ceased to pay specie for their notes.

Lieutenant-colonel Pearson, with two hundred and fifty of the North Carolina militia, and seventy friendly Indians, having scoured the banks of the Alabama, made six hundred and twenty-two men, women and children prisoners.

Official accounts were received at Washington City, of the fall of Bonaparte; the restoration of Louis XVIII., and the consequent general pacification in Europe. These events leaving to Great Britain a large disposable force, and offering her the means of giving to the war in America a character of new and increased activity and extent; although the government of the United States did not know that such would be its application, nor what particular point or points would become objects of attack, the President deemed it advisable to strengthen the line of the Atlantic and the gulf of Mexico. His directions were accordingly communicated by the secretary of war to Claiborne, to organize and hold in readiness a corps of one thousand militia infantry, the quota of Louisiana, also a requisition made on the executive of the several states for ninety-three thousand five hundred men. Claiborne lost no time in carrying the views of the general government into execution.

The Creek Indians having sued for peace, power was given to Jackson to conclude it. This was done at Fort Jackson, on the ninth of August.

This treaty strongly marks the temper of the United States' agent. It begins by stating that an unprovoked, inhuman and sanguinary war, waged by the hostile Creek Indians, against the United States, has been repelled, prosecuted and determined successfully on the part of the latter, in conformity with the principles of national justice and honorable warfare, and consideration is due to the rectitude of the proceeding, dictated by instructions relating to the re-establishment of peace; that prior to the conquest of that part of the Creek nation, hostile to the United States, numberless aggravations had been committed against the peace, the property and the lives of the citizens of the United States and those of the Creek nation in amity with them, at the mouth of Duck river, Fort Mimms and elsewhere, contrary to national faith, and an existing treaty; that the United States, previously to the perpetration of such outrages, endeavored to secure future amity and concord between the Creek nation and their citizens, in conformity with the stipulations of former treaties, fulfilled with punctuality, and good faith, their engagements to the Creek nation, and more than two-thirds of the whole number of chiefs and warriors, disregarding the genuine spirit of existing treaties, suffered themselves to be instigated to violations of their national honor, the respect due to the part of the nation faithful to the United States and the principles of humanity, by impostors, denominating themselves prophets, and by the duplicity and misrepresentations of foreign emissaries, whose governments are at war, open or understood, with the United States— wherefore:

The United States demand an equivalent for all expenses, incurred in prosecuting the war to its termination, by a cession of all the territory belonging to the Creek nation, within certain limits, expressed in the treaty.

The United States guaranty to the Creek nation the integrity of the rest of their territory.

They demand that the Creek nation abandon all communication and cease to hold any intercourse with any British or Spanish post, garrison or town, and that they shall not admit among them any agent or trader, who shall not have authority, to hold commercial or other intercourse with them, from the United States.

The United States demand an acknowledgment of the rights of establishing military posts and trading houses, and to open roads within the territory, guaranteed to the Creek nation, and a right to the free navigation of all its waters.

The United States demand the immediate surrender of all the persons and property of their citizens and their friendly Indians, and promise to restore the prisoners they made in the nation, and the property of any of its members.

The United States demand the capture and surrender of all the prophets and instigators of the war, whether foreigners or natives, who have not submitted to the arms of the United States, or become parties to the treaty, if ever they shall be found within the territory, guaranteed by the United States to the nation by the treaty.

The Creek nation being reduced to extreme want and not having, at present, the means of subsistence, the United States, from motives of humanity, will continue to furnish gratuitously, the necessaries of life, until crops of corn be considered competent to yield the nation a supply, and will establish trading houses among them to enable the nation, by industry and economy, to purchase clothing.

The Creek nation acceding to these demands, it is declared, that a permanent peace shall ensue, from the date of the treaty forever, between the Creek nation and the United States, and the Creek nation and the Cherokee, Chickasaw and Choctaw nations.

Early in the month of August, the British brig Orpheus, brought several officers of that nation to the bay of Apalachicola, with several pieces of artillery. There object was to enter into arrangements with the chiefs of the Creek nation of Indians for obtaining a number of their warriors to join the British force, which was soon expected, and intended for the attack of the fortification which Wilkinson, after he had taken Fort Charlotte, had established at Mobile point, and the possession of which was considered an an object of great importance towards the execution of ulterior operations, which were meditated against Louisiana. These officers easily succeeded in rallying a number of Indians around the British standard. Individuals from almost all the tribes who dwelt to the eastward of the Choctaws, joined the Creeks; they were supplied with arms and drilled.

Soon after, colonel Nichols arrived at Pensacola. He had sailed from Bermudas with a few companies of infantry, and touched at the Havana, in expectation of obtaining from the captain-general of the island of Cuba, a few gunboats and small vessels, with permission to land his men and some artillery at Pensacola. He obtained no aid: but it is imagined the captain-general did not seriously object to his effecting a landing at Pensacola, as he did so without any effort made by the Spanish officers there, to maintain the neutrality of the place. He was soon joined by the officers of his nation, who had preceded him in West Florida, accompanied by a very considerable number of Indians. He established his headquarters in the town, from which he issued, on the twenty-ninth of August, his proclamation to the people of Louisiana.

He announced, that on them the first call was then made to assist in the liberation of their natal soil, from a faithless and weak government. To Spaniards, Frenchmen, Italians and Englishmen, whether residents or sojourners in Louisiana, application was made for assistance. The colonel said he had brought a fine train of artillery and everything requisite, was heading a large body of Indians, commanded by British officers, and was seconded by numerous British and Spanish fleets. His object was to put an end to the usurpation of the United States, and restore the country to its lawful owners.

He gave assurances that the inhabitants had no need to be alarmed at his approach, as the good faith and disinterestedness, which Britons had manifested in Europe, would distinguish them in America. The people would be relieved from taxes imposed on them to support an unnatural war: their property, their laws, their religion, the peace and tranquillity of their country, would be guaranteed by men, who suffered no infringement of their own.

The Indians, he added, had pledged themselves in the most solemn manner, to refrain from offering the slightest injury to any but the enemies of their Spanish or British fathers. A French, Spanish or British flag, hoisted over any house, would be a sure protection, and no Indian would dare to cross the threshold of such a dwelling.

Addressing himself to the people of Kentucky, he observed, they had too long borne with grievous impositions; the whole brunt of the war had fallen on their brave sons. He advised them to be imposed on no longer, but either to revenge themselves under the standard of their forefathers, or observe the strictest neutrality: assuring them, that, if they complied with his offers, whatever provisions they might send down would be paid in dollars, and the safety of the persons accompanying them, as well as the free navigation of the Mississippi would be guaranteed to them.

He called to their view, and he trusted to their abhorrence, the conduct of those factions which had hurried them into a civil, unjust and unnatural war, at a time when Great Britain was straining every nerve in the defense of her own and the liberties of the world; when the bravest of her sons were fighting and bleeding in so sacred a cause; when she was spending millions of her treasure, in endeavoring to put down one of the most formidable and dangerous tyrants that ever disgraced the form of man; when groaning Europe was almost in her last gasp; when Britain alone showed an undaunted front; when her assassins endeavored to stab her; from the war, she had turned on them, renovated from the bloody, but successful struggle; Europe was now happy and free, and she now hastened justly to avenge the insult. He besought them to show they were not collectively unjust, and leave the contemptible few to shift for themselves; to let the slaves of the tyrants send an embassy to the island of Elba, to implore his aid, and let every honest American spurn them with united contempt.

He asked, whether the Kentuckians, after the experience of twenty-one years, could longer support those brawlers for liberty, who called it freedom, when themselves were free. He advised them not to be duped any longer and accept of his offers, assuring them what he had promised he guaranteed to them on the *sound honor* of a *British officer.*

In an order of the day for the first colonial battalion of the royal corps of marines, colonel Nichols informed them they were called upon to perform a duty of the utmost danger, and to begin a long and tedious march through wildernesses and swamps, and their enemy, being enured to the climate, had a great advantage over them; but he conjured them to remember the twenty-one years of 'glory and toil of their country, and to resolve to follow the example of their noble companions, who had fought and shed their blood in her service; to be equally faithful and trust in their moral discipline, and the least and most perfidious of their enemies would not long maintain himself before them.

He added, that a cause, so sacred as that which had led them to draw their swords in Europe, would make them unsheath them in America, and use them with equal credit and advantage. In Europe their arms had not been employed for the good of their country only, but for that of those who groaned in the chains of oppression, and in America they were to have the same discretion, and the people they were now to aid and assist, groaned under robberies and murders, committed on them by the Americans.

He said, the noble Spanish nation had grieved to see her territories insulted, having been robbed and despoiled of a portion of them, while overwhelmed with distress and held down by chains a tyrant had loaded her with, while gloriously struggling for the greatest of all possible blessings, true liberty; the treacherous Americans, who call themselves free, had attacked her, like assassins, while she was fallen; but the day of retribution was fast approaching; these atrocities would excite horror in the hearts of British soldiers, and would stimulate them to avenge the oppressed.

He recommended to his men to exhibit to the Indians the most exact discipline, and be a pattern to those children of nature; to teach and instruct them, with the utmost patience, and correct them when they deserve it; to respect their affections and antipathies and never give them a just cause of offense.

He concluded by reminding them, that sobriety above all things, should be their greatest care; a single instance of drunkenness might be their ruin, and he declared, in the most solemn manner, that no consideration whatever should ever induce him to forgive a drunkard.

Emissaries were sent, with copies of this proclamation over the country, between Mobile river and the Mississippi.

On the capture of the island of Guadaloupe, by the British, most of the privateers, commissioned by the colonial government, unable to find a

48

shelter in the West India islands, resorted to lake Barataria, to the west of the city of New Orleans, for supplies of water and provisions, recruiting the health of their crews and disposing of their prizes, which they were unable to do elsewhere. At the expiration of the period, during which their commissions, from the governor of Guadaloupe, authorized them to cruise, these people went to Carthagena, where they procured commissions, authorizing the capture of Spanish vessels; the neutrality of the United States, preventing vessels thus captured from being brought to their ports, they were brought to Barataria. Under that denomination was included all the coast on the gulf of Mexico, between the western mouth of the Mississippi and that of the river or bayou Lafourche. Near the sea between those streams, are the small, large and larger lakes of Barataria, communicating with one another by bayous, the numerous branches of which interlock each other. A secure harbor afforded a shelter to the vessels of those people, who had established near it a small village, in which they met individuals from the settlements of Attakapas and Lafourche, and the right bank of the Mississippi, and even New Orleans, who, having but few competitors, purchased merchandise on advantageous terms, and obtained good prices for the provisions they brought. Besides privateersmen, the village was resorted to by interlope and negro traders from foreign ports; and it was reported, that some of the Barataria people were addicted to piratical pursuits. The violation of the laws of neutrality, the fiscal regulations and those against the importation of slaves, by the men of Barataria, though persisted in for a number of years, had not, till very lately, attracted the notice of the general or state government. Commodore Patterson had just received orders, from the secretary of the navy, to disperse those marauders, the schooner Carolina had been ordered to New Orleans, for that purpose, and colonel Ross, of the forty-fourth regiment, had been directed to co-operate in this measure. These officers were now making preparations for this purpose.

On the thirty-first of August, colonel Nichols, addressed a letter to Lafitte, the most influential individual at Barataria, informing him of his arrival at Pensacola, for the purpose of annoying the only enemy Great Britain had in the world, and called on him and his brave followers to enter into the service of Great Britain, in which he should have the rank of a captain, and lands would be allowed to them all, according to their respective ranks, on a peace taking place.

An officer of the marine corps was dispatched with this letter, and the commander of the king's ships at Pensacola wrote also to Lafitte, referring him to captain Lockyer, of the Sophia, who was sent to convey Nichols' emissary. On the third day of September, these letters were delivered to a brother of Lafitte, who was absent. He amused his visitors and encouraged them to hope he would come into their views, but asked the delay of a fortnight before he made his final determination known. He instantly sent to a merchant in New Orleans, the letter he had received and Nichols' proclamation, with directions to communicate them to Claiborne, and deliver him a letter, in which Lafitte offered his services, and those of his people, to defend the part of the state he occupied, or be otherwise employed against the enemy, asking only that a stop might be put to the proscription of his brother, himself and their adherents, by an act of oblivion. He concluded, with the assurance that, if his request was not granted, he would forthwith leave the state, to avoid the imputation of having co-operated in an invasion of Barataria.

Claiborne called together the principal officers of the army, militia and navy, and laid before them Lafitte's letter, and the papers he had received; they recommended that he should not have any intercourse, or enter into correspondence with any of those people. Major-general Villere and Claiborne were the only persons, at this meeting, who disapproved of the recommendation.

At the expiration of the delay, captain Lockyer came to the place indicated, to receive Lafitte's final answer, but being met by no one, he returned.

Early in this month, the quota of the militia in the state, which had been ordered to be held in readiness, in consequence of a requisition of Jackson, who had succeeded Flournoy, in command of the seventh military district, was directed by Claiborne to rendezvous in New Orleans, to be organized and taken into the service of the United States.

Fort Boyer, the fortification which Wilkinson, after the Spanish garrison was driven out of Fort Charlotte, at Mobile, had erected, on a point of land which commands the entrance of Mobile bay, was found a great obstacle to the operations of the British in Louisiana, and an effort was made, in the middle of September, to take possession of it.

Commodore Perry, with a flotilla of four vessels of war, in which he had brought Nichols and his troops to Pensacola, took on board thirteen hundred men, six hundred of whom were Indians; his ships had ninety-two pieces of heavy artillery. Major Lawrence, who commanded the fort, had a garrison of one hundred and thirty men and twenty pieces of cannon. Perry landed a part of his soldiers, who erected a battery, the guns of which and those of the ships, began at once a tremendous fire: but the fort was so gallantly defended and his own ship was so injured that he was obliged to set fire to her: the other three were so absolutely disabled, that the commodore took the men he had landed, on board, and sailed away, having had one hundred and sixty-two men killed and as many wounded.

On the eighteenth of September, the expedition that had been prepared, in New Orleans, by commodore Patterson and colonel Ross, reached the settlement of Barataria men; those people had abandoned it, as soon as they perceived the vessels, leaving a quantity of goods, that were saved; the houses were all destroyed.

On the return of the British flotilla, which had been repulsed before Fort Boyer, the British were permitted to garrison the forts at Pensacola. Jackson, who was then at Mobile, determined on taking possession of that town, in order to deprive the enemy of a place of shelter and refuge. He accordingly assembled at Fort Montgomery, on the Alabama river, a body of about four thousand men, composed of regulars and militia from the state of Tennessee and Mississippi territory, and, soon after, led them towards Pensacola, and halted within two miles of the town, on the sixth of November.

Major Peire, an aid of Jackson, was now dispatched with a communication to the Spanish governor, announcing to him, that the army of the United States did not approach with any hostile views to Spain, and had no object but to deprive the British, with whom they were at war, of a place of refuge, in which they prepared the means of annoying the inhabitants of the adjoining territory of the United States.   He therefore required, that the governor should admit a garrison out of the army of the United States in Fort St. Michael and that of the Barrancas, till a sufficient Spanish force, to enable the colonial government of Pensacola, to support the neutrality of the Catholic king's territory, should arrive. The major was fired on, although he approached alone, and bore a conspicuous white flag; he reconnoitred the fort and distinctly saw it occupied by British troops; the Spanish flag was displayed over it; but information was received that, on the preceding day, both the Spanish and British flags had been simultaneously hoisted.

Jackson, on the return of Peire, sent a letter to the governor, by a prisoner, demanding an explanation. A Spanish officer soon after arrived with a letter from the governor, containing assurances of his having had no participation in the transaction complained of, and that if the communication was renewed the messenger would be received with due respect. Peire went in accordingly, at midnight, and on Jackson's proposition being rejected, declared that recourse would be had to arms.

Accordingly on his return, on the seventh, three thousand men were marched in three columns, along the beach, in order to avoid the fire of Fort St. Michael; but when in sight of the town, the artillery proving too heavy for the sand, the middle column was ordered to charge, and as soon as the head of it appeared in the principal street, a Spanish battery of two pieces of cannon, was opened on it: it was immediately carried at the point of the bayonet, with the loss of eleven men killed or wounded; the Spaniards had one man killed and six wounded.

The governor now made his appearance, with a white flag in his hand and being met by some officers, at the head of the troops, declared his intention to accept the proposition made to him.   Jackson, on being informed of this, hastened to the house of the intendant, who assured him the town, arsenals, forts and munitions of war would be surrendered. On this, Jackson ordered hostilities to cease, and his troops to march out of town.

Notwithstanding the strong assurances of the governor and intendant, the forts were not surrendered. Jackson was making preparations to storm Fort St. Michael, when the officer commanding it, lowered his flag and yielded the fortress, before a single blow was struck.

The troops were marching towards Fort St. Charles, of the Barrancas, when the British blew it up, and retreated to their shipping, with some of their Indians. Those of the latter, who did not go on board, fled across the country; the others were landed on the Apalachicola, and, immediately after, the vessel sailed away.

The American army, shortly after, returned to Mobile.

CHAPTER XXX.

THE second state legislature had began its first session on the tenth of November, 1814. The following extract from Claiborne's speech shows how little foundation there was in the rumor, that circulated, of the disaffection of the inhabitants of Louisiana: "In the patriotic ardor, which pervades the state, I behold a pledge of its fidelity and devotion to the

American union. This ardor, this American spirit, has been tested by the facility with which the late requisition, for an auxiliary force of militia infantry, has been carried into effect, by the laudable zeal with which the volunteer cavalry and riflemen have pressed forward in their country's cause. In meeting the requisition, I am satisfied with the conduct of every officer, whose duty it was to co-operate; and I have noticed, with pleasure, the promptitude with which most of the regiments furnished their contingent. But, for the valuable services of the cavalry and riflemen, we are particularly indebted to the distinguished patriotism of the citizens of Feliciana and Attakapas. You cannot, gentlemen, too highly appreciate the patriotic, the martial spirit which at present exists."

General Jackson reached New Orleans on the second of December, and, on the next day, descended the river to view Fort St. Charles, at Plaquemines, and other works which were projecting on the opposite bank. A committee of the legislature waited on him, with the copy of a resolution of that body, testifying to the great and important services lately rendered by him and the gallant army under his command, entitled them to the thanks and gratitude of the general assembly.

Accounts were now received from Pensacola, that a very large naval force of the enemy was off that port, and it was generally understood New Orleans was the object of the attack; eighty vessels were in sight, and more than double that number were momentarily looked for. There were vessels of all descriptions and a large body of troops. Admiral Cochrane commanded the fleet, and his ship the Tonnant, was off the port.

Lieutenant Jones, who commanded on lake Borgne, a flotilla consisting of five gunboats and a schooner, was ordered to reconnoitre and ascertain the disposition and force of the enemy, and in case they should attempt, through this route, to effect a disembarkation, to retire to the Rigolets, the principal pass between lakes Borgne and Pontchartrain, and there, with his flotilla, make an obstinate resistance and contend to the last. He remained off Ship Island till the twelfth, when the enemy's force being much increased, he retired to a position near the Malheureux island, from whence, on his being attacked, he had a better opportunity of making his retreat to the Rigolets, where alone he was instructed to make opposition. This pass and that of Chef Menteur, unite at the entrance of the lakes, and form a narrow channel, on reaching which the gunboats would be enabled to present as formidable an opposition, as could be made to all the force that could be brought against them, and put at defiance any effort that could be made against the city through that route.

On the thirteenth, Jones perceived the enemy's barges approaching him, and immediately weighed his anchors, with the design of reaching the Rigolets: but found this absolutely impracticable. A strong wind having blown for some days to the east, from the lake to the gulf, had so reduced the depth of water, that the best and deepest channels were insufficient to float his little squadron; the oars were resorted to, but in vain. Everything that could be spared was thrown overboard; but this was also ineffectual. At last, a sudden tide brought a momentary relief, lifted the boat from the shoals, and Jones directed his course to the Rigolets, and came to an anchor at one o'clock on the next morning, in the west passage of the Malheureux island, and at daybreak saw the pursuit had been abandoned.

There was, at the bay of St. Louis, some public stores, which he had sent the schooner Sea Horse, to bring off. The British barges made two vain attempts to capture this vessel. Her commander deeming it impossible to execute Jones' orders, destroyed the stores: and seeing the enemy returning in great force, blew up the schooner and retreated by land.

On the morning of the fourteenth, the enemy's barges were seen approaching the gunboats; a retreat became impossible, the wind was entirely lulled, a perfect calm prevailed, and a strong current setting to the gulf, rendered every effort, to reach the Rigolets unavailing, the resolution was taken to fight as long as there remained the hope of the least success. The line was formed, with springs on the cables. Forty-three barges, mounting as many cannon, with twelve hundred fine men, were advancing in an extended line, and came soon in reach; at half after eleven o'clock they commenced to fire, and the action immediately became general. Owing to a strong current setting out to the east, two of the boats were unable to keep their anchorage, and floated about one hundred yards in advance of the line. The enemy advanced in three divisions; the centre one bore down on the centre boat, commanded by the senior officer, and twice attempting to board, was twice repulsed, with an immense destruction of officers and men and the loss of two boats, which were sunk. Jones being too severely wounded to maintain the deck, the command devolved on Parker, who no less valiantly defended his flag, till his wounds compelled him to retreat, and the boat was soon after carried; another boat, though gallantly defended, was soon after taken and the guns of both turned on the others, which were compelled to surrender. The loss on board of the gunboats was ten men killed and thirty-five wounded; that of the British not less than three hundred. The Americans had five boats, one hundred and eighty-two men, and twenty-three guns. The force of the assailants has already been stated.

The loss of the gunboats has left the enemy complete master of the lakes to the east of the island on which the city of New Orleans stands, and gave him the facility of reaching it by any of the waters running easterly to any of these lakes.

The crisis appeared really alarming. The force in New Orleans consisted only of seven hundred men of the seventh and forty-fourth regiments of the United States, and one thousand state militia, besides one hundred and fifty sailors and marines. Three thousand men of the militia of Tennessee, under general Carrol, and a body of twelve hundred and fifty riflemen of the same state, under general Coffee, were looked for; and it was reported, a body of twenty-five hundred men from Kentucky, under general Thomas, were on their march; and it was deemed, that after leaving a sufficient part of the militia of the state in the different parishes to keep the slaves in awe, three thousand men might be brought to the defense of the city—making, with some aid from the Mississippi territory, a general total of about twelve thousand: but the enemy was much nearer to the city than three-fourths of this force.

Although the population of New Orleans was composed of individuals of different nations, it was as patriotic as that of any city in the union. The creoles were sincerely attached to liberty and the general goverment; they had given a strong evidence of this, on their admission into the union, by the election of the governor, judges, and almost every other officer sent to them by the President of the United States. The Spaniards were very small in number, and a few of them might have been elated to see the flag of their nation raised in the country, but they had no sympathetic feeling for the British; the individuals of that nation who were not naturalized had retired into the interior. There were a few from almost every other European nation, but nothing was apprehended from them.

Claiborne was sincerely attached to the government of his country, and the legislature was prepared to call forth and place at Jackson's disposal all the resources of the state.

The disappointment of some, who had unsuccessfully struggled for ascendency, had united them in opposition to Claiborne's measures. There were a few citizens of the United States of considerable talents and influence among them, many of whom had seats in the legislature; and hitherto when no immediate danger seemed to threaten, had thrown some difficulty in the way of Claiborne on his attempt to bring a part of the militia into the service of the United States. The governor, who in 1806, had joined Wilkinson in the cry of spies and traitors, was disposed to consider his opponents as of that character.

Hall, the district judge of the United States, had become obnoxious to a few individuals; he had been from the beginning very strict in enforcing the laws of congress, and persons brought before him for breaches of the revenue, embargo or non-importation laws, had conceived the idea that he was extremely severe. Among the papers of Lafitte, which had been lately taken at Barataria, had been found letters of several merchants, who had hitherto sustained a good character, affording evidence of their being accomplices of that man, and prosecutions had been instituted against some of them. The stern impartiality of the judge had induced a belief they had much to apprehend; the counsel, whom they had employed, were generally the opponents of Claiborne.

The want of an able military chief was sensibly felt, and notwithstanding any division of sentiment on any other subject, the inclination was universal to support Jackson, and he had been hailed on his arrival by all. There were some, indeed, who conceived that the crisis demanded a general of some experience in ordinary warfare; that one whose military career had begun with the current year, and who had never met with any but an Indian force, was ill calculated to meet the warlike enemy who threatened; but all were willing to make a virtue of necessity, and to take their wishes for their opinions, and manifested an unbounded confidence in him. All united in demonstrations of respect and reliance, and every one was ready to give him his support. His immediate and incessant attention to the defense of the country, the care he took to visit every vulnerable point, his unremitted vigilance and the strict discipline enforced, soon convinced all that he was the man the occasion demanded.

Unfortunately he had been surrounded, from the moment of his arrival, by persons from the ranks of the opposition to Claiborne, Hall and the state government, and it was soon discovered that he had become impressed with the idea, that a great part of the population of Louisiana was disaffected and the city full of traitors and spies. It appears such were his sentiments as early as the eighth of September; for in a letter of Claiborne, which he since published, the governor joins in the opinion and writes to him, " I think with you that our country is full of spies and traitors." The governor was not unwilling to increase his own merit, by magnifying the obstacles he had to surmount: he therefore stated in his correspondence with Jackson every opposition he met with, and did not fail to represent every one, who did not think as he did, as inimical to the country. Those who immediately surrounded Jackson on his arrival, with a view to enhance his reliance on them, availed themselves of every opportunity to increase his sense of danger.

Time, which is the true test of the soundness of opinions, has shown that the people of Louisiana deserved well of their country during the invasion, and that not one shadow of treason or disaffection appeared in them.

An instance of what is called the machinations of foreigners, has been recorded. Colonel Coliel, a Spanish officer of the garrison of Pensacola, had an only daughter married to Lacroix, a wealthy planter, and was on a visit at his farm, a few miles below the city: in writing thence to one of his friends in Pensacola, he stated the weakness of the force the British would have to encounter in Louisiana, and expressed his belief of their success. This letter was intercepted and sent to Claiborne, who submitted it to the attorney-general. The latter thought there was no room for his interference, but gave it as his opinion, that in time of war, when an invasion was apprehended, the governor might send away any foreigner whom he suspected of any concert with the enemy. On this, the colonel was ordered away, and obeyed. The communication between New Orleans and Pensacola was opened; there was no British force in the latter place, and the information conveyed was such as might have been had from any traveller. The colonel acted perhaps indiscreetly, but it is far from being clear he had any hostile view.

Jackson had Claiborne's assurance that the latter would receive and obey his orders, and support all his measures for the common defense.

The legislature was in session, since the beginning of the preceding month. We have seen that Claiborne, at the opening of the session, had offered them his congratulations on the alacrity with which the call of the United States for a body of militia had been met, which, with the detail of the proceedings of that body, is the best refutation of the charges which have been urged against them. It will show, that in attachment to the Union, in zeal for the defense of the country, in liberality in furnishing the means of it, and in ministering to the wants of their brave fellow-citizens who came down to assist them in repelling the foe, the general assembly of Louisiana does not suffer by a comparison of its conduct with that of any legislative body in the United States. The assertion, that any member of it entertained the silly opinion, that a capitulation, if any became necessary, was to be brought about or effected by the agency of the houses, any more than by that of a court of justice, or the city council of New Orleans, is absolutely groundless.

As early as the twenty-second of November, Louaillier, one of the members of the house of representatives for the county of Opelousas, whose name will be frequently mentioned in the sequel of the work, in a report, which he made as chairman of the committee of ways and means, had drawn the attention of the legislature to the necessity of their making suitable provision for the defense of the country. "Who," it is said in this document, "has not admired the patriotic ardor which was displayed in the execution of the works deemed, by the principal cities of the union and our sister states, necessary for the protection of such as could be assailed by the enemy? The magistrates, the citizens, the officers of the general government, manifested the utmost zeal to obtain the desired object—their safety and the ignominious retreat of the enemy were the glorious result of their efforts. How does it happen that such a noble example has not been followed in this part of the union? Are we so situated as to have no dangers to dread? Is our population of such a description as to secure our tranquillity? Shall we always confine ourselves to addresses and proclamations? Are we always to witness the several departments entrusted with our defense, languishing in a state of inactivity hardly to be excused, even in the most peaceable times? No other evidence of patriotism is to be found than a disposition to avoid every expense, every fatigue—nothing as yet has been performed; it is the duty of the legislature to give the necessary impulse, but it is only by adopting a course entirely opposite to that which hitherto has been pursued, that we can hope for success—if the legislature adds its own indolence to that which generally prevails, we can easily foresee that ere long, a capitulation, similar to that obtained by the city of Alexandria, will be the consequence of a conduct so highly culpable.

"A considerable force is now assembled under the orders of general Jackson, which will speedily receive large reinforcements from the militia of the western states, but it is nevertheless true that the principal avenues to our capital are not in a situation to insure its preservation; and that unless we are determined to provide for its safety ourselves, unless we act with a promptness and energy equal to the torpor which seems to have invaded the principal branches of our government, that force will only be employed in retaking this territory, which must fall an easy prey to the first efforts of an invading foe; the legislature has been convened for the purpose of raising a fund adequate to the expenses necessary to ward off the dangers by which we are threatened—this is the object which must be accomplished—little does it matter whether this or that expenditure ought to be supplied by the general or by the state government, let us not hesitate in making such as safety may require; when this shall have been secured, then our claims to a reimbursement will be listened to."

On the same day, Roffignac, the chairman of the committee of defense, presented a plan, which was directed to be communicated to Claiborne, for the information of Jackson.

Commodore Patterson having, on the seventh of December, suggested a plan of defense against any attempt of the enemy to ascend the Mississippi, the legislature, after having ordered it to be laid before Jackson, directed the committee of defense to ascertain what number of men, and the quantity of ordnance and other arms, the commanding officers of the land and naval forces would require, that it might be known what was to be supplied by the state.

On the thirteenth, the sum of seventeen thousand dollars, the remaining part of twenty thousand, which Claiborne had borrowed during the recess of the legislature, for the defense of the country, on account of the state, was directed to be applied, under the orders of Jackson, in procuring materials and workmen for the completion of such batteries and other fortifications as he had directed, and a further sum of eleven thousand dollars was appropriated to the same object.

Claiborne was at the same time requested to recommend it to the planters of the parish of Orleans and the neighboring ones, to place immediately as many of their working hands as they could spare at the disposal of Jackson, to be employed on these fortifications—a requisition which was complied with so generally, that more hands were sent than could be employed.

At the suggestion of Patterson and Jackson, Claiborne proposed to the legislature, on the following day, the suspension of the writ of *habeas corpus,* in order to enable the commodore immediately to press hands for the service of the United States and the general, in case the enemy landed, to apprehend and secure disaffected persons.

Great doubts were entertained by the legislature, whether any person arrested by the commanding officers of the land and naval forces of the United States could be relieved on writs of *habeas corpus,* issued by a state court or judge, and they knew from the firmness and inflexibility which Hall, the district judge of the United States, had manifested in 1806, that he would not consider himself relieved from the obligation of affording relief to the meanest individual, in whose favor a writ of *habeas corpus* was applied for, till congress itself decreed a suspension of it. Wilkinson had disregarded the writs of territorial judges, but had not dared to disobey those of Hall, who he knew would not suffer it to be done with impunity.

Coming from every part of the state, the representatives had witnessed the universal alacrity with which Jackson's requisitions for a quota of the militia of the state had been complied with; they knew their constituents could be depended on; they knew that Jackson, Claiborne, and many of the military, were incessantly talking of sedition, disaffection and treason; but better acquainted with the people of Louisiana than those who were vociferating against it, they were conscious that no state was more free from sedition, disaffection and treason, than their own; they thought the state should not outlaw her citizens when they were rushing to repel the enemy. They dreaded the return of those days, when Wilkinson filled New Orleans with terror and dismay, arresting and transporting whom he pleased. They recollected that in 1806 Jefferson had made application to congress for a suspension of the writ of *habeas corpus,* but that the recommendation of the President was not deemed sufficient to induce the legislature of the union to suspend it: that of Claiborne, as far as it concerned Jackson, was not therefore acted on. The members had determined not to adjourn during the invasion, and thought they would suspend the writ, when they deemed the times required it, but not till then.

Louaillier, in his report as chairman of the committee to whom was referred the consideration of suspending the writ, in order to enable Patterson to impress seamen, considered the measure as inexpedient. The committee thought the country would be ill defended by men *forced* into her service; that it was better to induce sailors, by the offer of ample bounties, to repair on board of the ships of the United States, than forcibly to drag them on board. A sum of six thousand dollars was therefore placed at the disposal of the commodore, to be expended in bounties; and to remove the opportunity of seamen being tempted to decline entering the service of the United States, by the hope of employment on board of merchant vessels, an embargo law was passed.

On the requisition of Jackson, Claiborne issued a proclamation for calling out the militia of the state *en masse* into the service of the United

States. His call was obeyed everywhere with promptness and alacrity: they were ordered to hold themselves in readiness to march at a moment's warning.

On the sixteenth of December, Claiborne sent a message to the legislature, stating that the time was certainly inauspicious for that cool and mature deliberation necessary to the formation of good laws; that the enemy menaced the capital, and how soon he would effect his landing was uncertain; every hand should be raised to repel him, and every moment occupied in arranging and completing means of defense: he therefore suggested the expediency of the houses adjourning for twenty or twenty-five days.

The house of representatives concurred with the report of their committee, who considered an adjournment at the present crisis as inexpedient. They thought that it might be highly dangerous; accidents might happen, unforeseen cases might occur, in which the interference of the legislature might be necessary. Should this happen after the adjournment, and the state be thereby endangered, the members should incur the just reproaches of their constituents. Should the houses adjourn for the proposed period, few members would have time to leave the city, and if they did, their mileages would exceed their expenses, if they continued their sitting. The committe therefore recommended, that the members stay at their post, ready, on any emergency, to contribute, as far as in them lay, to the defense of the country.

The suspension of the writ of *habeas corpus*, and adjournment of the houses, were measures which Jackson anxiously desired. There was a great inclination in the members of both houses to gratify him, in every instance in which they could do it with safety; in these two only, they were of opinion it would be unsafe to adopt his views.

He now issued a general order, putting the city of New Orleans and its environs under strict martial law, and directed that

1. Every individual entering the city, should report himself to the adjutant-general's office, and on failure, be arrested and held for examination.

2. None should be permitted to leave the city or bayou St. John, without a passport from the general or some of his staff.

3. No vessel, boat or craft, should leave the city or bayou St. John, without such a passport, or that of the commodore.

4. The lamps of the city to be extinguished at nine o'clock, after which, every person found in the streets or out of his usual place of residence, without a pass or the countersign, to be apprehended as a spy and held for examination.

The proclamation of martial law was understood in Louisiana, as it is believed to be in other states, a solemn warning that the martial law of the United States would be strictly enforced. Martial law was known to be that system of legitimate rules by which the martial affairs of the nation are regulated. It was not imagined that the President of the United States himself, as commander-in-chief of the forces of the union, could add aught to or change these legitimate rules; that he could make *martial law*, any more than *fiscal, commercial*, or *criminal* law.

The collection of the rules by which the conduct of the citizens of a nation in time of peace towards all belligerent nations is regulated, are called the laws of neutrality.

When Washington found that the sympathies of his fellow-citizens with the French nation, might tempt some of them to violate the laws of neutrality, to the injury of the British nation, with which his was at peace, he issued a proclamation, reminding them of their obligations and warning them of the consequences those should expose themselves to, who would violate the laws of neutrality. This was not an useless ceremony. It no doubt had the effect of preventing breaches of those laws. In 1806, when a spirit of enterprise seemed likely to delude some of the citizens of the United States into measures that might involve this country in a war with Spain, Jefferson, actuated by the same motives of Washington, issued a proclamation of the laws of neutrality. It was not considered that a proclamation of martial law could add anything to that law, any more than the proclamation of the laws of neutrality by Washington and Jefferson, add to these laws. To enact and to proclaim, or impose a law, were thought distinct acts, the first the province of the legislature, the other the exclusive right of the executive power.

That necessity *justifies* whatever it commands, was admitted as a principle to which every law must bend. That whatever measure became *necessary* to the defense of the country, might be legitimately enforced, was admitted, and we have seen that the attorney-general had given out as his opinion to Claiborne, that the governor of a place, in time of war, might send out of the country a person attempting anything which might afford aid to the enemy. This principle was known to result from *martial* law, which justifies whatever circumstances require for the defense of the country or to annoy the foe. It was known to be independent of the *proclamation* of martial law, which was thought to add nothing to the authority of the officer who made it—to render anything whatever lawful or unlawful, that was otherwise before.

Such were the ideas entertained by the general government of martial law. "In the United States," said the secretary of war (Dallas) in a communication to Jackson, of the first of July, 1815, "there exists no authority to declare or impose martial law, beyond the positive sanction of the act of congress. To maintain the discipline and insure the safety of his camp, an American commander possesses indeed highly important powers: but all these are compatible with the rights of the citizen, and the independence of the judicial authority."

A number of individuals who had heretofore joined, or been concerned with privateers lately resorting to Barataria, were deterred from entering into the service of the United States, by the apprehension of prosecutions. With the view of quieting their fears, the legislature, on the seventeenth, entered into resolutions requesting Jackson to endeavor to procure an amnesty in favor of such of them as should enlist themselves to serve during the war, and earnestly recommended it to the President of the United States, to grant them a full pardon. The governor was at the same time desired to endeavor to prevail on the attorney of the United States, with the leave of the court, to enter *nolle prosequis* on all prosecutions against such persons then under confinement, on the above condition. This measure was adopted, because it was represented to the houses that Jackson was anxious for it. A number of members had strong objections to it, deeming it improper to accept the services of persons of this description. Claiborne having issued a proclamation, to make the intention of the legislature in this respect known, a considerable number of these people came in and were enrolled.

The crisis obliging every one to take up arms, to quit their homes and abandon their private affairs, in a manner that exposed many to great inconvenience, the legislature passed an act forbidding the protest of any bill or note till the expiration of four months, and forbade during the same period the institution or any suit.

On the nineteenth, general Carrol, with a brigade of the militia of the state of Tennessee, consisting of twenty-five hundred men, arrived, and on the following day he was joined by general Coffee and twelve hundred riflemen from the same state.

The legislature, on the motion of Louaillier, appointed a committee, at whose disposal they placed a sum of two thousand dollars, for the relief of the militia of the state, seafaring men and persons of color, in the service of the United States. The committee were instructed to invite their fellow-citizens to make donations of woollen clothes, blankets, and such other articles, as, in case of an attack, might be useful to the sick.

At this period the forces at New Orleans amounted to between six and seven thousand men. Every individual exempted from militia duty, on account of age, had joined one of the companies of veterans, which had been formed for the preservation of order. Every class of society was animated with the most ardent zeal; the young, the old, women, children, all breathed defiance to the enemy, firmly disposed to oppose to the utmost the threatened invasion. There were in the city a very great number of French subjects, who from their national character could not have been compelled to perform military duty; these men, however, with hardly any exception, volunteered their services. The chevalier de Tousac, the consul of France, who had distinguished himself and had lost an arm in the service of the United States, during the revolutionary war, lamenting that the neutrality of his nation did not allow him to lead his countrymen in New Orleans to the field, encouraged them to flock to Jackson's standard. The people were preparing for battle as cheerfully as if for a party of pleasure; the streets resounded with martial airs; the several corps of militia were constantly exercising, from morning to night; every bosom glowed with the feelings of national honor; everything showed nothing was to be apprehended from disaffection, disloyalty or treason.

On the twenty-first, major Villere, by order of major-general Villere, his father, sent a detachment of the third regiment of the militia, consisting of eight men and a sergeant, attended by two mulattoes and a negro, to a village of Spanish fishermen, on the left bank of bayou Bienvenu, at the distance of a mile and a half from its mouth on lake Borgne. The village in which from thirty to forty fishermen dwelt, was found deserted by them, with the exception of a sick man. The sergeant sent out a few of his men in a boat, to ascertain whether there was any of the enemy's shipping near; on the next day, at daybreak, another party was sent out for the same purpose, and other parties were frequently out during the day, without discovering any vessel or craft approaching. Towards evening, three men arrived from Chef Menteur, having traversed the lake without seeing any enemy.

A little after midnight, the sentinel below the village gave the alarm; by the last gleams of the setting moon, five barges full of men, with some artillery, were discovered ascending the bayou. The sergeant judging, from the smallness of his party, it would be imprudent to fire, ordered them to conceal themselves behind one of the cabins. They were however, discovered and taken, except a man, who attempting to escape through the prairies, lost his way, and reached Chef Menteur, after a ramble of three days.

The first division of the British army, composed of about three thousand men, under general Kean, proceeded up the bayou and the canal of Villere's plantation; they surrounded the house, in which was a company of militia, whom they made prisoners, and surprised major Villere, who, notwithstanding several pistols fired at him, effected his escape, and running to some distance below, crossed the river and reached the city.

Jackson received the first intelligence of the enemy's landing at two o'clock, and in half an hour a detachment of artillery, with two field pieces and a body of marines, were sent in advance. Generals Carrol and Coffee, who were encamped with the force of Tennessee four miles above the city, soon reached it, and at four o'clock the Tennessee riflemen, Mississippi dragoons and Orleans riflemen took their stations two miles below the city. The battalion of men of color, the forty-fourth regiment, and a battalion of the city militia, soon followed; and commodore Patterson, on board of the United States schooner Carolina, floated down towards the enemy.

Claiborne, with two regiments of the state militia, and a company of horse, took a position in the rear of the city, on the Gentilly road, to oppose any force that might come from Chef Menteur.

A negro was apprehended on the levee, a few miles from the city, with a number of copies of a proclamation by Admiral Cochrane and general Keane, inviting the Louisianians to remain quiet in their houses, and assuring them, that their property would be protected, the invaders being at war with the Americans only. As the army proceeded, several copies of this proclamation were seen stuck up along the road.

At seven o'clock, the Carolina came to anchor on the bank of Villere's batture, opposite to the centre of the enemy's encampment, within musket shot. Such was their security that taking this vessel for a common craft plying on the river, a number of them came to the levee to examine her more closely. She now began so dreadful a fire, that one hundred of them were killed before the consternation which her salute created subsided. An unsuccessful attempt was made to annoy her with a fire of musketry: Congreve rockets were resorted to with as little success, and in less than half an hour, the schooner drove the enemy from his camp.

At this moment colonel Piatt drove in one of the enemy's outposts from the main road, opposite to Lacoste's plantation.

In the meanwhile the seventh regiment advanced by heads of companies to the distance of one hundred and fifty yards, where it formed in battalion before the enemy, with whom it instantly engaged, with a very brisk and close fire. The forty-fourth now came up, and forming on the left of the seventh, commenced firing. Two pieces of artillery were put in battery on the road, and the marines drawn up on the right, on the bank of the river. The engagement now became general on both sides. The front of the British line greatly outflanking our line on the left, and the enemy seeing he could not make our troops give way, caused some of his to file off on the old levee, by a gate three hundred yards from the river, with the intent to turn our right flank. The forty-fourth had already been obliged to oblique on the left, in order to avoid being flanked, when two battalions of the state militia and a few Indians advanced. The enemy's column silently approached in the dark to turn the troops of the line, fell suddenly almost within pistol shot of the extremity of one of the battalions of militia, and instantly commenced a brisk fire, One of these battalions forming the centre, advanced in a close column and displayed under the enemy's fire, which was then kept up by his whole front. Already had the enemy been forced to give way, and our troops continued to advance, keeping up a brisk fire, when he began to retreat, favored by darkness now increased by a fog and by the smoke, which a light breeze blew in the faces of our men.

In the meantime, Coffee's division had advanced, in order to fall on the enemy's rear, followed by a company of riflemen of the state militia: this company, after having penetrated into the very camp of the enemy and made several prisoners, pushed forward to the right, following the movements of Coffee, but unfortunately part of them, through a mistake occasioned by the darkness, fell among a corps of one hundred and fifty British, who were moving on rapidly towards the camp, mistaking them for part of Coffee's division, and were made prisoners. Coffee soon took a position in front of the old levee, where he continued a destructive fire.

At half-past nine, the enemy fell back to his camp, where all the troops passed the night under arms and without fire.

Jackson, finding that darkness rendered it useless to continue the pursuit, led back his troops to his former position.

At about half after eleven, a firing of musketry was heard in the direction of Jumonville's plantation, that contiguous to and below Villere's.

A detachment of three hundred and fifty men, of the state drafted militia, had been stationed at the English Turn, under general Morgan. On the first intelligence of the landing of the enemy, these men insisted on being instantly led to oppose him. Morgan, being without orders from Jackson, on this head declined gratifying them. But when the fire from the Carolina, and the subsequent discharges of artillery and musketry on shore announced that the conflict was commenced, the entreaties of the officers and men of this detachment became so pressing that Morgan could no longer resist them. He had reached, at the head of them, the spot at which the road that leads to Terre-aux-Bœufs leaves that which runs along the levee, during the hottest part of the action, and continued to advance, preceded by two pickets, the one on the high road, the other in the fields, near the woods. The former, as it approached the bridge of Jumonville's plantation, exchanged a fire with some of the enemy's troops, who instantly fell back behind the canal. Darkness preventing Morgan to ascertain the force of the enemy near him, or the relative situation of the two armies, he took a position in a neighboring field, to avoid an ambush. In a council, to which he called all his officers, it was deemed inexpedient to remain, and the detachment moved back a little before daylight.

The enemy, who had received a reinforcement during the action, had a force of very near five thousand men: that which opposed him was not much above two thousand. His loss exceeded four hundred: Jackson had twenty-four men killed, one hundred and fifteen wounded, and seventy-five made prisoners.

During the night, whilst anxiety kept the mind of the inhabitants of New Orleans, who had remained in the city, in painful suspense on their impending fate, an unfortunate occurrence excited much alarm among them. A report was spread that Jackson, before his departure, had taken measures and given positive orders for blowing up the magazine and setting fire to various parts of the city, in case the British succeeded in forcing his ranks. His conduct, in this respect, was considered by some, as an evidence of his deeming his defeat a probable event. The old inhabitants, who had great confidence in the natural obstacles which the situation of the capital presents to an invading foe, and which they thought insurmountable if proper attention was bestowed, concluded that it had been neglected: they lamented that the protection of the city had been confided to an utter stranger to the topography of its environs, and while frequent explosions of musketry and artillery reminded them that their sons were facing warlike soldiers, they grieved that an officer, who, in the beginning of the year had hardly ever met any but an Indian enemy, and whose inexperience appeared demonstrated by the rash step attributed to him. The truth or falsity of the report was sought to be ascertained by an application to the officer left in command at the city, who declined to admit or deny that the steps had been taken, or the order given.

A circumstance tended to present the conflagration of New Orleans as a more distressing event than that of Moscow. The burning of the houses of several planters, above the city, in 1811, was remembered, and apprehension had been entertained that British emissaries would be ready, a short time before the main attack, to induce the slaves towards Baton Rouge or Donaldsonville, to begin the conflagration of their owners' houses, and march towards the city, spreading terror, dismay, fire and slaughter; and a dread prevailed that Jackson's firing of the city would be taken by them for the signal at which they were to begin the havoc—even in case the apprehensions from British emissaries were groundless. The idea of thus finding themselves, with their wives, children and old men, driven by the flames of their houses towards a black enemy, bringing down devastation, harrowed up the minds of the inhabitants.

Persons, however, who hourly came up from the field of battle, brought from time to time, such information as gradually dispelled these alarms, and in the morning a present sense of safety inspired quite different sensations, and the accounts which were received of Jackson's cold, intrepid and soldierlike behavior, excited universal confidence.

CHAPTER XXXI.

At four o'clock, on the morning of the twenty-fourth, Jackson ordered his small army to encamp on the left bank of Rodriguez's canal, about two miles below the field of battle, leaving the Mississippi mounted riflemen and Feliciana dragoons near it, to watch the motions of the enemy. The canal was deepened and widened, and a strong wall formed in front of it, with the earth which had been originally thrown out. The levee was broken, about one hundred yards below, and a broad stream of water passed rapidly over the plain, to the depth of about thirty inches, which prevented the approach of troops on foot.

Embrasures were formed in the wall, and two pieces of artillery placed so as to rake the road which runs along the levee.

Morgan was now directed to send a strong detachment from the English Turn, who advanced as near as they could towards the enemy's camp and destroyed the levee, so as to let in the water of the Mississippi, whereby the British army was completely insulated, and the march above and below obstructed.

On the twenty-sixth, Jackson, fearing for the situation of Morgan, who, as the British occupied the intermediate space, was entirely detached from his camp, ordered him to abandon his position, carry off such of the cannon as he conveniently could, and throw the remainder into the river, from whence they might be recovered when the water subsided; to cross the stream, and take and fortify a position opposite to the American lines.

The height of the Mississippi and the discharge of water through the openings made in the levee, had given an increased depth to the canal through which the enemy had come; this enabled them to advance their boats much nearer to their encampment, and to bring up a new supply of artillery, bombs and ammunition.

Early on the twenty-seventh, a battery was discovered on the bank of the Mississippi, which had been erected during the previous night, from which a fire was now opened on the Carolina, which was lying near the opposite shore. The repeated discharges of bombs and red hot shot from this battery were spiritedly answered, but without effect, there being on board but one long twelve-pounder that could reach. A red hot shot was lodged under her cables, from which it could not be removed, and soon set her in a blaze. Another discharge extended the ravages of the devouring element, and flames began to burst from numberless places. Orders were now given to abandon her; one of the crew was killed and six wounded; the rest reached the shore in safety, and soon after the fire reached the magazine and the vessel was blown up.

The battery's fire was now directed against the sloop of war Louisiana, which lay at some distance higher up, the preservation of which was the more important, as she was the only public vessel remaining on the river. She was accordingly towed up, out of the reach of the enemy's guns.

In the afternoon the British moved forward, and obliged Jackson's advanced guard to fall back, and during the night they began to erect several batteries on the river.

By break of day, the enemy displayed in several columns and drove in the advanced guards. He now advanced, preceded by several pieces of artillery, part of which played on the Louisiana, and the rest on Jackson's line.

The Louisiana now opened a tremendous and well directed fire on the assailants, which was at first briskly answered, but her guns and those of the line soon silenced the enemy's, broke his columns and forced him to disperse and fall back into the fields, where he took a position, beyond the reach of the Louisiana and Jackson's artillery. His loss was estimated at from two to three hundred men; seven were killed and ten wounded

50

on the American line, and one man slightly wounded, by the bursting of a shell on board of the Louisiana.

The legislature had ceased to sit, on the first intelligence of the arrival of part of the British army on Villere's plantation. Several of the members held commissions in the militia, and had joined their respective corps; the younger had volunteered their services, and the aged joined the several companies of veterans, which had been organized for the maintenance of order in the city and its suburbs. Several were attending a military committee, and others, appointed by the legislature to superintend the supply of the wants of indigent families, whose heads were on the line, and to provide succor for those who daily reached the city to assist in its defense. The apprehension from the black population which had been excited by the rumor of Jackson's intention to fire the city, had induced a few respectable individuals from the country, who possessed influence in their respective parishes, and whose age and habits disqualified them from active military service, to visit those neighborhoods, in order to contribute by their presence, to the general maintenance of order. The city council were active in providing means for the support of the needy, and Girod, the mayor, was incessantly engaged in collecting arms and in driving stragglers to the field. Never was an army more abundantly supplied with provisions—the calls of Jackson for negroes to work on his line, for tools and munition, were instantly attended to.

Every day, towards noon, three or four of the members of each house, who served among the veterans or on the committees, attended in their respective halls to effect an adjournment, in order that, if any circumstance rendered the aid of the legislature necessary, it might be instantly afforded. On going for this purpose to the government house, Skipwith, the speaker of the senate, and two of its members, found a sentinel on the staircase, who, presenting his bayonet, forbade them to enter the senate chamber. They quietly retired and proceeded to the hall of the sessions of the city council, where an adjournment took place. The members of the other house, who attended for the same purpose, were likewise prevented from entering its hall, and acted like those of the senate.

An unsuccessful attempt, notwithstanding great exertions were used, was made on the thirtieth to obtain a quorum, and the next day it failed in both houses. The crisis had so scattered the members, that those who assembled found themselves obliged to send the sergeant-at-arms and other messengers to require the attendance of the absent members. With great difficulty, a quorum was obtained in each house, late in the evening, and a joint committee was appointed, to wait on Jackson and inquire into the reasons that had occasioned the violent measures resorted to against the legislature.

This committee, having performed this service, received from the general a written statement, in the following words:

CAMP AT M'CARTY'S, 4 MILES BELOW NEW ORLEANS.

Headquarters, December 31, 1814.

The Major-General commanding has the honor to acknowledge the receipt of the joint resolution of both houses of the honorable the legislature of the state of Louisiana, now in session, dated the 30th inst. and communicated to him by a joint committee of both houses, to which the general gives the following answer:

That just after the engagement between the British and American armies had commenced on the 28th inst., when the enemy was advancing, and it was every instant expected they would storm our lines; as the general was riding rapidly from right to left of his line—he was accosted by Mr. Duncan, one of his volunteer aids, who had just returned from New Orleans; observing him to be apparently agitated, the general stopped, supposing him the bearer of some information of the enemy's movements, asked what was the matter. He replied that he was the bearer of a message from governor Claiborne, that the assembly were about to give up the country to the enemy. Being asked if he had any letter from the governor, he answered in the negative. He was then interrogated as to the person from whom he received the intelligence; he said it was from a militia colonel; the general inquired where the colonel was, that he ought to be apprehended, and if the information was not true, he ought to be shot, but that the general did not believe it. To this Mr. Duncan replied, that the colonel had returned to New Orleans, and had requested him, Mr. Duncan, to deliver the above message.

The general was in the act of pushing forward the line, when Mr. Duncan called after him and said, "the governor expects orders what to do." The general replied that he did not believe the intelligence; but to desire the governor to make strict inquiry into the subject; and if true to blow them up. The general pursued his way, and Mr. Duncan returned to the city. After the action, Mr. Duncan returned, and on the general's stating to him the impropriety of delivering such a message publicly in the presence of the troops, as well as the improbability of the fact, he excused himself by the great importance of the intelligence, and then, for the first time, the general heard the name of colonel Declouet, as Mr. Duncan's author.

The above statement, the general gives as a substantial one, of the matter referred to in the resolutions of the senate and house of representatives; and to this he adds, that he gave no order to the governor to interfere with the legislature, except as above stated.

ANDREW JACKSON,
Maj. Gen. Commanding.

This statement clearly shows, that Jackson did not believe that the general assembly had the least thought of offering terms to the enemy—and that the violence exercised against them was the effect of a real or pretended misunderstanding of what he had said.

Duncan, on his examination before a committee of the houses, stated that soon after the beginning of the attack, he met colonel Declouet, who was hastening from the city, apparently in great perturbation, who requested him to inform the general of the existence of a plot, among several members of the legislature, to surrender the country to the enemy, and that he had heard, that Jackson was carrying on a Russian war, and it was better to capitulate and save the city: that he had been invited to join in the plot. Duncan added, that Declouet did not say he was sent by Claiborne, and that as far as he recollected, Jackson's order was to tell Claiborne to inquire into the matter, and in case they (the legislature) made any such attempt, to blow them up; and afterwards, he (Duncan) meeting one of Claiborne's aids, directed him to inform the governor, the general wished him to prevent the legislature from assembling.

Declouet stated, that on the night between the twenty-seventh and twenty-eighth, he slept at his brother's, below the city, and noticed the consternation of several of the inhabitants, and conversed with several members of the legislature, who apprehended direful consequences from the war. Hence, he feared a proposition would be made by the legislature to capitulate, which would occasion a disastrous division in the country. In the morning, he set off with the view of communicating his apprehensions to Jackson, but as he did not reach the line till after the beginning of the attack, he requested Duncan to make his communication to the general. He added, no member of the legislature had manifested to him an intention of doing anything positive. The step he took, was grounded on the apprehensions he entertained—apprehensions which he never would have had, if he had been acquainted with the good intentions and beneficent views of the legislature.

Jackson's biographers have seized on this event, a most erroneous account of which they have given, to blazon his character, to the injury of the state of Louisiana.

Eaton, who cannot be supposed to have wanted the best means of information, assures his readers that Jackson was apprehensive of a design in the general assembly to propose a capitulation to the enemy, and intended to have had them confined in the government house. By placing the statement of Jackson side by side with Eaton's, the reader will be conscious of the gross error under which Eaton must have labored.

"Jackson's object," says Eaton, "was not to restrain the legislature in the discharge of their official duties; for although he thought, that such a moment when the sound of the cannon was constantly pealing in their ears, was inauspicious to wholesome legislation, and that it would have better comported with the state of the times for them to abandon their civil duties and appear in the field, yet it was a matter indelicate to be proposed; and it was hence preferred that they should adopt whatever course might be suggested by their own notions of propriety. This sentiment would have been still adhered to; but when, through the communication of Mr. Duncan, they were represented as entertaining opinions and schemes, adverse to the general interest and safety of the country, the necessity of a new and different course of conduct was at once obvious. But he did not order governor Claiborne to interfere with, or prevent them from proceeding with their duties; on the contrary, he was instructed, so soon as anything hostile to the general cause should be ascertained, to place a guard at the door, and keep the members to their post and to their duty. My object in this, remarked the general, was that then they would be able to proceed with their business without producing the slightest injury; whatever schemes they might entertain would have remained with themselves, without the power of circulating them to the prejudice of any other interest than their own. I had intended to have had them well treated and kindly dealt by; and thus abstracted from everything passing without doors, a better opportunity would have been afforded them to enact good and wholesome laws; but governor Claiborne mistook my order, and instead of shutting them indoors, contrary to my wishes and expectation, turned them out."

The other writers, who have preserved details of the events of these days, have all fallen into great mistakes, and Jackson himself appears to have been egregiously deceived. One of his letters to the postmaster-general, of the 22d of March, 1824, which found its way into the public prints, contains the following paragraph:

"When I left the city, and marched against the enemy on the night of the 23d of December, 1814, I was obliged to leave one of my aids in command, having no other confidential officer that could be spared from command. A few days after, Mr. Skipwith, in person, applied to my aid to be informed what would be my conduct, if driven from my lines of defense and compelled to retreat through New Orleans—whether I would leave the supplies for the enemy or destroy them? As reported by my aid to me, he wanted this information for the assembly, that in case my intention was to destroy them, they might make terms with the enemy. Obtaining no satisfaction from my aid, a committee of three waited on me for satisfaction on this subject. To them I replied, 'If I thought the hair of my head knew my thoughts, I would cut it off or burn it'—to return to their honorable body, and to say to them from me, that if I was to be so unfortunate as to be driven from the lines I then occupied, and compelled to retreat through New Orleans, they would have a warm session of it."

These charges were noticed by Skipwith, in a letter to Jackson of the thirteenth of May, 1827, which appeared in the Richmond Enquirer, in the following manner:

"It was on one of the nights, about the time alluded to by major Butler, that, returning from patrol duty from the grand round of the city, in passing and seeing lights in the house of Mrs. F——, an old and much respected acquaintance of mine, and a great admirer of yours, I called in to pay her my respects, and found with her another very interesting lady, Mrs. E——, who in the course of her conversation mentioned a report, as circulated in the city, and I think she said, by some Kentuckians just from your lines of defense, that, if forced, you would destroy, rather than see the city fall into the hands of the enemy. A day or two after, at the request of the military council of the city guards, of which I was a member, I waited on major Butler concerning a citizen under arrest, and not directly, nor indirectly, charged with anything concerning that report; and being asked by him, 'If there was anything new in the city,' I remember replying, that such was the report 'among women.' Conscious, general, of having through life treated the names and characters of married ladies with the most scrupulous caution and respect, I cannot believe that I mentioned the names of the two ladies, between whom I heard the report: and never having, at any time attached to it, myself, either belief or importance, I could not have made it a subject of serious communication to the senate, to the military council, or to any member, individually, of them. I am willing, therefore, to rest the truth of my assertions, in repelling this most slanderous and bolstered charge of yours, and consequently its utter falsehood, as far as it criminates my conduct and views, on the testimony not only of the remaining individuals, who composed the senate and the military council, but on the testimony of any two, or three remaining individuals in society, who were eye witnesses of my conduct at the invasion of New Orleans, and whose oaths would be respected by a well composed jury of their vicinity.

"I may well, then, sir, pronounce this last charge of yours to be false, utterly false! as applying to me individually, or to the senate over which

I presided, or to the military council of which I was a member, or, that the most distant hint, or wish, was ever expressed in any of their deliberations, or in private, by any one of their members, with my knowledge or within my hearing, " to make terms with the enemy." And more false, if possible, is it still, that ' the legislature should, with my consent or connivance, depute a committee to wait on you on that subject,' or on any other, during the invasion, in which I had any agency, that was not founded, in my humble estimation at least, on principles of patriotism and honor. I may, therefore, hope to find indulgence in every honest breast, for having expressed in some degree, the profound contempt which this charge so justly merits, and which it is impossible for me with life, to cease to feel."

Thibodaux, then a member of the senate, who afterwards exercised, as president of that body, the functions of chief magistrate of the state, on the resignation of governor Robertson, expressed his indignation on the subject, in a letter to Skipwith, on the 10th of September, 1827.

"The notorious," said he, "ungenerous and unmerited accusation, which has been cast upon the whole legislature of Louisiana, and particularly upon the senate, by general Jackson, in his published letter to the postmaster-general, in order to defeat your pretensions as a candidate in opposition with his favorite, Mr. Crogan, is, in my humble opinion, such as ought to be taken up and repelled with the indignation it really deserves. This charge was not laid upon you alone, but it embraces the whole senate. Could you not, sir, as being then the president of that honorable body, could you not, with propriety, call upon the members who were sitting with you, and prevail upon them to join in clearing, through the same medium that was made use of, those shameful stains with which that body has been stigmatized? And would it not be but fair, if this infamous calumny was recoiled towards its source and against its very author? A supine silence appears to operate on the part of the members of the general assembly, as a conviction of the truth of the accusation : and this opinion, as you may know yourself, is circulating in the public, by the exertions of the general's friends.

" I beg leave to be excused for attempting to suggest the right course you have to follow ; these are the dictates of a heart indignantly offended at the rash attack of the general,*and although it does not fall upon me directly, (for you will recollect I was on active military service,) it rebounds upon me very heavily, and wounds me to the very heart's core."

The journal of neither of the houses makes any mention of the motion for, nor of the appointment of, the committee of which Jackson speaks. The members of the house of representatives have universally expressed their indignation at the unfounded charge, and their astonishment at the egregious imposition, under which Jackson must have been, when he made it.

Major-General Villere, of the state militia, reached the camp on the twenty-ninth, with six hundred men of the militia of his division, and was directed by Jackson to take the command of a second line, which was now formed between the first and the city.

On new year's day, a thick fog concealed the movements of the enemy, till towards eight o'cclock. He now opened a brisk fire from three batteries he had just completed. The left, on the road, had two twelve-pounders ; the centre eight eighteen and twenty-four-pounders, and some carronades; the right, close to the woods, mounted eight pieces of cannon and carronades of different calibres. A flash of congreve rockets accompanied the balls, and for a quarter of an hour the fire was kept up with unexampled celerity, and answered in so brisk, steady and well directed a manner, that it now slackened in a perceptible degree. The cannonade was, however, kept up on both sides, but with varied intervals, for an hour, during which seven of the enemy's guns were dismounted, and when the fire ceased, the greater part of his artillery was unfit for service. At one o'clock he abandoned his battery near the woods; the centre one and that near the road continued to throw a few balls and rockets till three, when they were silenced.

Soon after, major-general Thomas, of the second division of state militia, arrived with five hundred men, who encamped behind the main line on Dupre's plantation, and three days after, a detachment of the militia of the state of Kentucky, amounting to two thousand two hundred and fifty men, under major-general Thomas and brigadier-general Adair, arrived and encamped below the city, on Prevost's plantation. Afterwards, a part of this force, under general Adair, advanced and took a position, a little in the rear of Jackson's line.

The deplorable condition of a great part of the militia of the states of Kentucky and Tennessee, who were in want of warm clothing, and from the nature of the service, occasionally exposed in the open air, the winter being extremely severe, excited the sensibility of the legislature of Louisiana, and on the motion of Louaillier, an appropriation was made of six thousand dollars. This sum was placed in the hands of a committee, of which the mover was an efficient member. An equal sum was added, by subscription in the city; the planters of the German Coast sent thirty-six hundred dollars, and those of Attakapas transmitted five hundred. By these means, with other aid, a sum of sixteen thousand dollars was obtained, as an addition to that appropriated by the legislature, and the whole was expended in the purchase of blankets and woollen cloths, which were distributed among the ladies of New Orleans, to be made into wearing apparel: and within one week twelve hundred blanket coats, two hundred and twenty-five waistcoasts, eleven hundred and twenty-seven pairs of pantaloons, and eight hundred shirts, were completed and distributed. Specific donations of several boxes of hats and shoes, and a considerable number of mattresses, were made by merchants and shop-keepers.

A number of debtors, who had taken the benefit of the acts establishing the prison bounds, were anxious to join in the defense of the city, but were apprehensive of exposing their sureties. On this being represented to the legislature, an act was passed, extending the prison bounds, until the first of May following, so as to include Jackson's line.

From deserters, desultory accounts were received, of a considerable reinforcement having arrived, under the orders of lieutenant-general Packenham and major-general Lambert; it was reported, that the British army now consisted of fourteen thousand men. Jackson had information that for several days, the communication between the army and fleet had been unusually active, and that a general attack was preparing—that the enemy was deepening Villere's canal and extending it, in order to bring his boats to the Mississippi.

Early on the morning of the eighth, signals, to produce concert in the enemy's movements, were noticed. A rocket ascended on the left, near the swamp, and soon after, another on the right, near the river; and a few minutes after, the charge was began with such rapidity that our soldiers at the outposts, with difficulty fled in.

The enemy's batteries, which had been demolished on new year's day, had been repaired during the night, and furnished with several pieces of heavy artillery. These now opened, and showers of balls and bombs were poured on our line, and the air was lighted with congreve rockets. The two divisions under generals Keane and Gibbs were led by Packenham : both pressed forward, the one against the centre, the other against the redoubt on the levee. A thick fog enabled them to approach within a short distance, before they were discovered. They advanced, with a firm, quick and steady pace, in solid columns, with a front of sixty or seventy deep. On perceiving them, Jackson, who had been for some time waiting their appearance, gave a signal, on which our men, who were in readiness, gave three cheers, and instantly the whole line was lighted with the blaze of their fire. A burst of artillery and small arms, pouring with destructive aim upon the British, mowed their front and arrested their advance. In the musketry, there was not a moment of intermission, as one party discharged their pieces, another succeeded : alternately loading and firing, no pause could be perceived—it was one continued volley. Notwithstanding the severity of the fire, some British soldiers pressed forward, and succeeded in gaining the ditch in front of the line. At this moment, Packenham fell, in front of his men, mortally wounded, and soon after, Gibbs and Keane were borne from the field, dangerously wounded. Lambert, who was advancing, at a small distance in the rear with the reserve, met the columns precipitately retreating and in great confusion. His efforts to rally them were unavailing—they reached a ditch, at the distance of four hundred yards from our line, where, finding a momentary safety, they were rallied and halted.

They shortly after returned to the charge; but Jackson's batteries had not ceased their fire—their constant discharge of grape and cannister, and volleys of musketry, cut down the enemy's columns as fast as they could be formed; they now abandoned the contest and the field in disorder, leaving it entirely covered with the dead and the wounded.

A strong detachment which formed the left of Keane's command, was sent under colonel Rennie, against our redoubt, on the right. This work was in an unfinished state. Rennie, urging forward with stern bravery reached the ditch. His advance was greatly annoyed by Patterson's battery, on the right bank, and the cannon mounted on the redoubt; but he passed the ditch, and leaping, sword in hand, on the wall, called to his men to follow him, when the fatal aim of a rifleman brought him down. Pressed by the impetuosity of superior numbers, who were mounting the wall and entering at the embrasures, the men in the redoubt had retired to the rear of the line, when the city riflemen, cool and self-possessed, opened on the assailants, and at every discharge brought the object to the ground. The followers of Rennie abandoned the attempt, in which he had fallen; they retired, galled by such part of the guns in the line as could be brought upon them; they sought a shelter behind the levee, but the fire of Patterson's battery, on the right bank of the river, severely annoyed them on their retreat.

The efforts of the enemy to carry Jackson's line of defense, were seconded by an attack, which was intended to have been simultaneous, on the opposite bank. Col. Thornton, before daybreak, had crossed the Mississippi with eight hundred men: but he hardly effected his landing, when the day broke, and he hastened forward against Morgan's entrenchment.

Jackson had foreseen an attack on that side of the river, and during the previous night, he had sent two hundred of the militia of the state to asssist in opposing it. This detachment had advanced a mile down the river, and Arnaud, who commanded it, supposing that the general was mistaken, or deeming that the spirits of his men would be resuscitated by repose had directed them to lie down and sleep. Hearing the rattling noise made by the British, who were approaching, Arnaud aroused his sleeping companions, and before they could be formed, the foe was so near that they became confused, and moved off in the direction in which they had come. A body of Kentuckians, who had reached Morgan's camp at five in the morning had been sent on to support Arnaud: they had proceeded about three-fourths of a mile when they met his men hastily retreating up the road.

These two detachments ran along together, and formed behind a saw-mill race, skirted with a quantity of plank and scantling, which afforded them a tolerable shelter. The enemy now appeared; his approach was resisted, and a warm and spirited opposition made for awhile. A momentary check was given him. He retired, returned and again received a heavy fire. One of Morgan's aids now arrived, and ordered a retreat. Confusion ensued—order could not be restored, and the whole precipitately fled to Morgan's entrenchment, when they were instantly formed, and ordered to extend themselves in line to the swamp, to prevent the entrenchment being turned.

Thornton halted, at the distance of about seven hundred yards, and soon after advanced to the attack, in two divisions, against the extreme right and centre of the line, now defended by about five hundred men. A well directed discharge of the artillery, which had been mounted on the works, caused his right division to oblique and unite with the left, and press forward to the point occupied by the Kentucky troops. These men finding themselves thus exposed, and not having yet recovered from the disorder of their hasty retreat, now gave way, and soon after abandoned their position. The Louisiana militia gave a few fires and followed the example. The officers succeeded in obtaining a momentary halt; but a burst of congreve rockets happening to set fire to a field of sugar cane and to other combustible materials, their fears were again excited—they hastily moved away, and could not be rallied, till, at the distance of two miles they reached a small race and were formed and placed in an attitude of defense.

The loss of the British in the main attack, on the left bank, is supposed to have been between twenty-five hundred and three-thousand killed—the number of wounded was much greater. The loss of the Americans in killed and wounded was but thirteen.

General Lambert, on whom the command of the British army devolved on the fall of Packenham, Gibbs and Keane, now solicited permission to send an unarmed detachment to bury the dead and bring off the wounded, lying near Jackson's line. This was allowed, and a suspension of hostilities agreed on for twenty-four hours.

A considerable naval force of the enemy had been destined to co-operate in the late attack by ascending the Mississippi. They succeeded in passing the Balize, and made prisoners of a small detachment that had been stationed there, but were unable to pass Fort St. Phillip, at Plaquemines.

The squadron, which consisted of two bomb vessels, a brig, schooner and sloop, approached the fort, on the ninth, at ten o'clock in the morning, within striking distance, and soon after commenced to discharge an immense quantity of bombs and balls against the fort. A severe and well directed fire from its water battery compelled the shipping to retreat to the distance of two miles, where they could reach the fort with the shells from their largest mortars, while they stood beyond the reach of its artillery. The bombardment, with various intervals, was continued till the seventeenth, when a heavy mortar having been mounted and turned against them, they retreated on the morning of the eighteenth.

At midnight, between the eighteenth and nineteenth, the enemy precipitately abandoned his encampment on the left bank of the Mississippi, to return to his shipping, leaving under medical attendance, eighteen wounded, including two officers, fourteen pieces of artillery and a considerable quantity of shot. Such was the situation of the ground they abandoned, and that through which they retreated, protected by swamps, canals, redoubts and intrenchments, that Jackson could not, without encountering a risk, which policy neither required or authorized, annoy him much on his retreat. He took eight prisoners only.

One of the medical men, left to take care of the wounded, handed to Jackson a letter from Lambert, imploring protection for the men thus remaining behind, and announcing that he had relinquished, "for the present, all further operations against New Orleans."

"Whether," says Jackson's communication to the Secretary of War, of the nineteenth, "it be the purpose of the enemy to abandon the expedition altogether, or to renew his efforts at some other point, I shall not pretend to decide with positiveness. In my own mind, there is but little doubt that his last exertions have been made in this quarter; at any rate for the present season, and by the next, if he shall choose to revisit us, I hope we shall be fully prepared for him. In this belief, I am strengthened by the prodigious loss he sustained, on the position he had just quitted and by the failure of his fleet to pass Fort St. Phillip. His loss since the debarkation of his troops, as stated by all the prisoners and deserters, and as confirmed by many additional circumstances, exceeds, in the whole, four thousand men.

Jackson now determined to withdraw his troops from the position they had occupied and place them near the city, whence they might easily be advanced whenever it might be necessary. The seventh regiment of infantry was left to protect the point he was leaving, and further in advance on Villere's canal, where the enemy landed, he posted a detachment of Louisiana and Kentucky militia.

Having made these arrangements, he brought the rest of his army to the city, on the twentieth.

On the twenty-third, a solemn service of thanksgiving was performed in the Cathedral—exactly one month after the first landing of the enemy at Villere's plantation.

If the vigilance, the activity, and the intrepidity of the general had been conspicuous during the whole period of the invasion, his prudence, moderation and self-denial, on the departure of the enemy, deserves no less commendation and admiration. An opportunity was then presented to him of acquiring laurels by a pursuit, which few, elated as he must have been by success, could have resisted. But, he nobly reflected that those who fled from him were mercenaries—those who surrounded his standard, his fellow-citizens, almost universally fathers of families :—sound policy, to use his own expressions, neither required or authorized him to expose the lives of his companions in arms, in a useless conflict. He thought the lives of ten British soldiers would not requite the loss of one of his men. He had not saved New Orleans to sacrifice its inhabitants. With tears of gratitude they greeted him on his return, in the strains which Arisoto addresses to his patron :

> Fu il víncer sempre mai laudábil cosa,
> Vincasi e per fortuna o per ingegno :
> Gli e ver, che la vittoria sanguinosa
> Spesso far suole il capitán men degno ;
> E quella eternamente e gloriosa,
> E dei divini onori arriva al segno,
> Quando, servando i suoi senz'alcúu danno,
> Si fa che gl'inimici in rotta vanno.
>
> La vostra, signór mio, fu degna loda,
> Quando al leone, in mar tanto feroce,
> Ch' avéa occupata l'una e l'altra prodo,
> Del Po, da Francolín sin alla foce,
> Faceste si, che ancór che ruggír l'oda,
> S' io vedro voi, non temeró la voce.
> Come vincer si de' ne dimostrate ;
> Ch' uccideste i nemici, e noi saivaste.

ORLANDO FURIOSO, XIV.

Thus paraphrased :

> Great honor every victor must obtain,
> Let fortune give success or conduct gain :
> Yet oft a battle, won with blood, will yield
> Less praise to him who boasts the conquered field.
> But ever glorious is that chieftain's name—
> And pure and sacred is his martial fame,
> Who, while the forces of his foes o'erthrown
> Proclaim his might, from loss preserves his own.
> Such was the war by thee, brave Jackson, wag'd,
> When Britain on the waves had fiercely rag'd—
> Had seiz'd each shore that to the Gulph descends,
> And to our Lakes from Pensacola bends :
> Tho' yet afar, her lion's roar seem'd near,
> But present thou, what beast could harbor fear.
> Nobly thou taught's us victory to gain—
> By thee our friends were sav'd, our foes were slain.

CHAPTER XXXII.

THE legislature made an appropriation of two thousand dollars for the benefit of the Charity Hospital, the resources of which had been diminished by the liberal succor it had yielded to the sick of the states of Kentucky and Tennessee. Provision was also made for the immediate relief of the wounded and the families of those who had been killed.

Danger had now evidently subsided. The levy en masse of the militia had been arriving in regiments and companies. "Everything," says Latour, "was in readiness to repel the enemy on whatever point he might make an attack. All the damaged arms had been repaired, and a barge had arrived from Pittsburg, with muskets, cannon and balls. Louisiana had been defended and saved with means much inferior to those of the enemy, and towards the end of January she was in a condition to defy double the number that had at first attacked her. Time had shown how groundless were the apprehensions which were pretended to be entertained from the disaffection of the people, and had evinced the wisdom of the legislature in rejecting the propositions which had been made to suspend the writ of *habeas corpus*. They adjourned on the sixth of February.

On the twelfth, the British possessed themselves of Fort Boyer, at the entrance of Mobile Bay.

By a communication of the following day, from admiral Cochrane, Jackson was informed that the admiral had just received a bulletin from Jamaica, (a copy of which was inclosed) proclaiming that a treaty of peace had been signed by the respective plenipotentiaries of Great Britain and the United States, at Ghent, on the twenty-fourth of December. The dispatch did not arrive till the twenty-first, by the way of the Balize, but the intelligence had been brought to the city on the preceding day by one of Jackson's aids, who had returned from the British fleet with a flag of truce.

In announcing this event, by an address to the army and the people of Louisiana, the general forewarned them from being thrown into security by hopes that might be delusive; observing it was by holding out such, that an artful and insidious foe too often seeks to accomplish objects, the utmost exertion of his strength will not enable him to effect. He added that to place them off their guard, and attack them by surprise, was the natural expedient of one, who, having experienced the superiority of their arms, hoped to overcome them by stratagem.

On the twenty-second, the gladsome tidings were confirmed, and a gazette of Charleston was received, announcing the ratification of the treaty by the Prince Regent.

We have seen that on the first account of the arrival of part of the British army on Villere's plantation, the French subjects who resided in New Orleans and its environs, animated by Tousard, their consul, had flocked round Jackson's standard, "determined to leave it with the necessity that called them to it, and not till then." As long as the foe remained in the state, they patiently submitted to toil, privation and danger, with exemplary fortitude and patience; they had left their families in penury and distress, but the liberality of the city council had ministered to their wants; that body had distributed among the needy inhabitants thirty-four thousand rations of bread, and thirteen thousand of meat. But, whether the means of the corporation were exhausted, or the absence of danger rendered its officers less attentive, these supplies did not flow as abundantly as at first, and, pressed by the anxiety of coming to the help of their families, and no longer elated by the hope of gaining laurels, being useful to the country they lived in, or excited by their antipathy to the invaders, they grew tired of a service which they now thought perfectly useless. A few solicited their discharge from the officers under whom they were immediately placed; Jackson was consulted, and insisted on their being retained. On this, a number of them demanded from Tousard certificates of their national character, which they presented to the general, by whom they were countersigned, and the bearers permitted to return home. The example was followed by so many, that Jackson was induced to believe that Tousard too easily gratified the applicants with certificates, and considering his compliance with his duty, as evidence of his adhesion to the enemy, ordered him out of the city.

Yielding to the advice of many around him, who were constantly filling his ears with their clamors about the disloyalty, disaffection and treason of the people of Louisiana, and particularly the state officers and the people of French origin, Jackson, on the last day of February, issued a general order, commanding all French subjects, possessed of a certificate of their national character, subscribed by the consul of France, and countersigned by the commanding-general, to retire into the interior, to a distance above Baton Rouge; a measure, which was stated to have been rendered indispensable by the frequent applications for discharges. The names were directed to be taken of all persons of this description remaining in the city after the expiration of three days.

Time has shown this to have been a most unfortunate step, and those by whose suggestions it was taken, soon found themselves unable to avert from the general the consequences to which it exposed him. The people against whom it was directed were loyal; many of them had bled, all had toiled and suffered in the defense of the state. Need, in many instances, improvidence in several, had induced the families of these people to part with the furniture of their houses to supply those immediate wants which the absence of the head of the family occasioned. No exception, no distinction was made. The sympathetic feeling of every class of inhabitants were enlisted in favor of these men; they lacked the means of sustaining themselves on the way, and must have been compelled, on their arrival at Baton Rouge, then a very insignificant village, to throw themselves on the charity of the inhabitants. Another consideration rendered the departure of these men, an evil to be dreaded. The apprehension of the return of the enemy was represented, as having had much weight with Jackson in issuing his order. Their past conduct was a sure pledge, that, in case of need, their services would again be re-offered; there were among them a number of experienced artillerymen; a description of soldiers, which was not easily to be found among the brave who had come down from Kentucky, or Tennessee, or even in the army of the United States. These considerations induced several respectable citizens to wait on Jackson, for the purpose of endeavoring to induce him to reconsider a determination, which was viewed as productive of flagrant injustice and injury to those against whom it was directed, without any possible advantage, and probably very detrimental, to those for whose benefit it was intended.

Eaton has informed his readers that "Promptitude and decision constitutes one of the leading traits of Jackson's character." Those who called on the general, were soon convinced, that hasty determinations are seldom patiently re-examined, or willingly changed; they found him inexorable. The recommendation was therefore given to the French exiles, to forbear the manifestation of any positive resistance, but to remain quietly at home, in the hope, that official accounts from the seat of government, changing the state of affairs, should soon enable Jackson to withdraw his late orders, without admitting they were too precipitately issued. They were assured that the laws of the country would protect them, and punish, even in a successful general, a violation of the rights of, or a wanton injury to, the meanest individual, citizen or alien. They were referred to the case of Wilkinson, against whom an independent jury of the Mississippi territory had given a verdict in favor of Adair, who had been illegally arrested and transported during the winter of 1806.

The mail now brought northern gazettes, announcing the arrival of the treaty at Washington, on the 14th. The hope, that had been entertained, that Jackson would now allow those unfortunate people to stay with their families, was disappointed; a circumstance which induced several of their countrymen, who had become citizens of the United States, to imagine, that antipathy to the French population influenced the general's determination. It has justly been allowed, that those who are ignorant of each other's language, often lack the liberality of giving the best construction to each others acts; and the inhabitants of New Orleans had often complained, that the government of the United States had not had the indulgence, which the king of Spain had always extended to them, of sending superior officers to preside over them, who spoke their language. Jackson had uniformly kept aloof from the French part of the population, and did not appear to treat the officers of the state government, with the attention which was believed to be due them: and those who were considered, as his most confidential friends, were believed to be in opposition to the officers of the state.

Louallier, the member of the house of representatives for the county of Opelousas, a native of France, had been an efficient member of the legislature, and had been remarked for his constant and steady efforts, in bringing forth the energies of the state for its defense, and in providing and distributing assistance for its needy defenders. He had been hitherto extremely useful in the regulation of the finances—we have seen he was one of those, who thought the legislature should remain in session, while danger hovered over the state. He had thought it better to open the treasury, and induce sailors to go on board of public vessels, by ample bounties, than to empower the commodore to send out press gangs—he thought that the state should not outlaw its defenders, by suspending the *habeas corpus*—he did not believe in the cry of Jackson and Claiborne, of disaffection, sedition and treason. He thought every citizen owed to the state the exertion of his utmost faculties, during the pending crisis; he accordingly enrolled himself in one of the companies of veterans, patroled the city during the night, and sat, during the day, in a military council, and a committee of succors. Of the latter, he had been the most efficient member. In distributing relief to the indigent, he had frequently visited in person the mansions of those, who had abandoned their families, buckled a knapsack on their backs, placed a musket on their shoulders, and followed Jackson; and he had witnessed the distresses of their families. He had given credit to the admiral's communication; being unable or unwilling to believe, that officer entertained so unfavorable an opinion of those who opposed him, as to conceive the idea, that they could be imposed upon, by so flimsy a means, as a forged newspaper. He had approved the caution of Jackson; but the confirmation of the signature of the treaty, in a Charleston gazette, had sanctioned the belief that the admiral's information was correct. The frequent and uncontradicted repetition of the intelligence in letters and newspapers, placed it beyond all doubt. When he heard, that the treaty was before the senate, he entertained very little doubt of its instant ratification.

A report, which now was afloat, that those who surrounded Jackson were laboring to induce him to arrest some individuals, alluded to in the general orders of the 28th of February, roused his indignation, to which (perhaps more honestly than prudently) he gave vent in a publication, of which the following is a translation, in the *Courier de la Louisiane* of the 3d of March:

COMMUNICATION.

" Mr. Editor:—To remain silent on the last general orders, directing all the Frenchmen, who now reside in New Orleans, to leave it within three days, and to keep at a distance of 120 miles from it, would be an act of cowardice, which ought not to be expected from a citizen of a free country; and when every one laments such an abuse of authority, the press ought to denounce it to the people."

" In order to encourage a communication between both countries, the 7th and 8th articles of the treaty of cession secure, to the French who shall come to Louisiana, certain commercial advantages, which they are to enjoy, during a term of twelve years, which are not yet expired. At the expiration of that time, they shall be treated in the same manner as the most favored nation. A peace which nothing is likely to disturb, uniting both nations, the French have until this moment been treated in the United States with that regard which a great people deserves and requires, even in its reverses, and with that good will, which so eminently distinguishes the American Government in its relations with foreign nations. In such circumstances, what can be the motives which have induced the commander-in-chief of the 7th district to issue general orders of so vexatious a nature ? When the foreigners of every nation—when the Spaniards, and even the English, are permitted to remain unmolested among us, shall the French alone be condemned to ostracism; because they rendered too great services? Had they remained idle spectators of the last events, could their sentiments towards us be doubted, then we might merely be surprised at the course now followed with regard to them. But now, are we to restrain our indignation, when we remember that these very Frenchmen, who are now exiled, have so powerfully contributed to the preservation of Louisiana? Without speaking of the corps who so eminently distinguished themselves, and in which we see a number of Frenchmen rank either as officers or privates; how can we forget, that they were French artillerists, who directed and served a part of those pieces of cannon, which so greatly annoyed the British forces? Can any flatter himself that such important' services could have so soon been forgotten? No, they are engraved in everlasting characters on the hearts of all the inhabitants of Louisiana, and they shall form a brilliant part in the history of their country; and when those brave men ask no other reward, but being permitted peaceably to enjoy among us the rights secured to them by treaties and the laws of America, far from sharing in the sentiments which have dictated the general order, we avail ourselves of this opportunity to give them a public testimony of our gratitude.

"Far from us be the idea, that there is a single Frenchman so pusillan-imous as to forsake his country merely to please the military commander of this district, and in order to avoid the proscription to which he has chosen to condemn them; we may, therefore, expect to see them repair to the consul of their nation, there to renew the act which binds them to their country—but supposing that, yielding to a sentiment of fear, they should consent to cease to be French citizens, would they, by such an abjuration, become American citizens? No, certainly they would not; the man who would be powerful enough to denationalize them, would not be powerful enough to give them a country. It is better, therefore, for a man to remain a faithful Frenchman, than to suffer himself to be scared even by the *martial law*, a law useless, when the presence of the foe and honor call us to arms, but which becomes degrading, when their shameful flight suffers us to enjoy a glorious rest, which fear and terror ought not to disturb.

"But could it be possible, that the constitution and laws of our country should have left it in the power of the several commanders of military districts, to dissolve all at once, the ties of friendship, which unite America to the nations of Europe? Would it be possible, that peace or war could depend upon their caprice, and the friendship or enmity they might entertain for any nation? We do not hesitate in declaring, that nothing of the kind exists. The President alone has, by law, the right to adopt against *alien enemies* such measures as a state of war may render necessary, and for that purpose he must issue a proclamation; but this is a power he cannot delegate. It is by virtue of that law, and a proclamation, that the subjects of Great Britain were removed from our seaports and seashores. We do not know any law, authorizing general Jackson to apply to *alien friends* a measure which the President of the United States, himself, has only the right to adopt against *alien enemies*.

"Our laws protect strangers, who come to settle or reside among us. To the sovereign alone belongs the right of depriving them of that protection; and all those who know how to appreciate the title of an American citizen, and who are acquainted with their prerogatives, will easily understand, that, by the sovereign, I do, by no means, intend to designate a Major-General, or any other military commander, to whom I willingly grant the power of issuing general orders like the one in question, but to whom I deny that of having them executed.

"If the last general order has no object but to inspire us with a salutary fear; if it is only destined to be read; if it is not to be followed by any act of violence; if it is only to be obeyed by those who may choose to leave the city, in order to enjoy the pure air of the country, we shall forget that extraordinary order; but should anything else happen, we are of opinion that the tribunals will, sooner or later, do justice to the victims of that illegal order.

"Every alien friend, who shall continue to respect the laws which rule our country, shall continue to be entitled to their protection. Could that general order be applied to us, we should calmly wait until we were forced by violence to execute it, well convinced of the firmness of the magistrates, who are the organs of the laws in this part of the union, and the guardians of public order.

"Let us conclude by saying, that it is high time the laws should resume their empire; that the citizens of this state should return to the full enjoyment of their rights; that in acknowledging, that we are indebted to general Jackson for the preservation of our city, and the defeat of the British, we do not feel much inclined, through gratitude, to sacrifice any of our privileges, and less than any other, that of expressing our opinion about the acts of his administration; that it is time the citizens accused of any crime should be rendered to their natural judges, and cease to be dealt with before special or military tribunals, a kind of institution held in abhorrence even in absolute governments; and that having done enough for glory, the moment of moderation has arrived; and finally, that the acts of authority which the invasion of our country, and our safety may have rendered necessary, are, since the evacuation of it by the enemy, no longer compatible with our dignity and our oath of making the constitution respected."

Man bears nothing with more impatience, than the exposure of his errors, and the contempt of his authority. Those who had provoked Jackson's violent measure against the French subjects, availed themselves of the paroxysms of the ire which the publication excited; they threw fuel into the fire, and blew it into a flame. They persuaded him Louallier had been guilty of an offense, punishable with death, and he should have him tried by court martial, as a spy, Yielding to this suggestion, and preparatory to such a trial, he ordered the publication of the second section of the rules and articles of war, which denounces the punishment of death against spies, and directed Louallier to be arrested and confined. Eaton is mistaken when he asserts that the section had been published *before.* The adjutant's letter to Leclerc, the printer of the *Ami des Lois,* requesting him to publish it, bears date of the *fourth* of March, the day *after* Louallier's publication made its appearance. The section was followed by a notice that "the city of New Orleans and its environs, being under martial law, and several encampments and fortifications within its limits, it was deemed necessary to give publicity to the section, *for the information of all concerned.*"

Great, indeed, must have been Jackson's excitement, when he suffered himself to be persuaded, that Louallier could successfully be prosecuted as a spy. Eaton informs us Louallier was prosecuted as one *owing allegiance to the United States.* The very circumstance of his owing that allegiance, prevented his being liable to a prosecution as a spy. He was a citizen of the United States: his being a member of the legislature was evidence of this. If he, therefore, committed any act, which would constitute an alien a *spy,* he was guilty of high treason, and ought to have been delivered to the legitimate magistrate, to be prosecuted as a traitor.

The second section of the act of congress, for establishing rules and articles of war, is in the following words:

"Sec. 2. *In time of war,* all persons, *not citizens of, or owing allegiance to the United States,* who shall be found, lurking as spies, in or about the

52

fortifications or encampments of the armies of the United States, or any of them, shall suffer death, according to the laws and usages of nations, by sentence of a general court martial."

It is certain the article applies only to aliens; persons who are *not* citizens of the United States, *nor* owing temporal allegiance to them. A spy gives *aid* to the enemy : and he, who owing allegiance (perpetual or temporal) to the United States, adheres to their enemies ; *giving* them *aid* or comfort, is not a spy, but a traitor.

This distinction has been recognized by the department of war of the United States. In the beginning of the last war, a natural born citizen of the United States, who before the declaration of war had removed his domicil into Canada, was found lurking about as a spy, near a fortification of the United States, arrested, tried and convicted by a general court martial, and condemned to death, as a spy. The President disapproved of the sentence, on the ground that as the culprit was a citizen of the United States, and owed allegiance to them, he could not be a spy; he was accordingly, by order of the secretary of war, surrendered to the legitimate magistrate, to be dealt with according to law.

Louallier was arrested on Sunday, the fifth day of March, at noon, near the Exchange Coffeehouse. He immediately desired Morel, a gentleman of the bar, who was near him, to adopt legal means for his relief.

Application was made to one of the members of the supreme court, Martin, who was being prevented by the imperfection of his sight to be otherwise useful, had enrolled himself in one of the companies of veterans, organized for the maintenance of order in the city. That court had determined in the preceding year, in the case of a British subject, arrested by the marshal for the purpose of being sent into the interior, that its jurisdiction being appellate *only*, it could not issue the writ of *habeas corpus*. Morel was, therefore, informed that the judge did not conceive he could interfere; especially, as it was alleged the prisoner was arrested and confined for trial, before a court martial, under the authority of the United States.

Morel, having consulted other gentlemen of the profession, applied to Hall, the district judge of the United States, for a writ of *prohibition*, to stay proceedings against his client, in the court martial. Hall expressed a doubt of his authority to order such a writ at chambers, and said he would take some time to deliberate. Morel withdrew, but soon after returned with a petition for a writ of *habeas corpus*, on which the judge gave his *fiat*, after having received Morel's promise, that he would inform the general of his application for the writ, and the order made for issuing it.

On receiving Morel's communication, the ebullition of Jackson's anger was such that reason appeared to have lost its control. Those who had suggested the harsh measures against the French citizens, and the still more harsh one against Louallier, imagined the moment was come when their enmity towards Hall might be gratified. We have seen that a number of individuals, who had hitherto sustained a fair character, were now known as accomplices of the Barataria pirates. Prosecutions had been commenced against some of them, and Hall manifested that stern severity of character, which appals guilt. The counsel of these men had conceived the idea that he did not view their efforts to screen their clients, with the liberality and indulgence they deserved. The opportunity now offered of humbling this worthy magistrate, was not suffered to remain unimproved; and Jackson was assured that Hall, like Louallier, was guilty of an offense punishable with death.

The general's attention was drawn to the seventh section of the rules and articles of war, which denounces the last punishment against persons aiding or abetting mutiny; and he was pressed to prosecute the judge before a court martial. As a preparatory step, with that promptitude of decision, which Eaton says is a leading trait in his character, he signed an instrument at once, the warrant for the arrest, and the *mittimus* for the imprisonment of Hall. He wrote to colonel Arbuckle, who commanded at the barracks, that having received proof that Dominic A. Hall had been *aiding, abetting, and exciting mutiny* in his camp, he desired that a detachment might be ordered forwith, to arrest and *confine* him, and that a report might be made as soon as he was arrested. "You will," as it is said in the conclusion of this paper, "be vigilant; as the agents of our enemy are more numerous than we expected. You will be guarded against escapes."

The prosecution of the judge was intended to be grounded on the seventh section of the articles of war, which is in these words: "Any *officer or soldier*, who shall begin, cause, excite or join in, any mutiny or sedition, in any troop or company, in the service of the United States, or in any post, detachment or guard, shall suffer death, or any other punishment, as by a court martial shall be inflicted."

Hall was not an officer, in the sense of the act of congress—he was not a soldier, in the ordinary meaning of that word; but, according to the jurisprudence of headquarters, the proclamation of martial law had transformed every inhabitant of New Orleans into a soldier, and rendered him punishable under the articles of war.

The judge was accordingly arrested in his own house, at nine o'clock, and confined in the same apartment with Louallier, in the barracks.

As soon as this was reported at headquarters, major Chotard was dispatched to demand from Claiborne, the clerk of the district court of the United States, the surrender of Louallier's petition, on the back of which Hall had written the order for issuing the writ of *habeas corpus*. It has been seen that there was not any officer of the state government, nor of the United States, out of the army, who imagined that a proclamation of martial law gave the general any right, nor imposed on others any obligation, which did not exist before. The clerk accordingly answered that there was a rule of court, which forbade him to part with any original paper lodged in his office; and he was ignorant of any right, in the commander of the army, to interfere with the records of the court. He, however, was after much solicitation, prevailed on to take the document in his pocket, and accompany Chotard to headquarters.

In the meanwhile, an express from the department of war had arrived, with the intelligence that the President of the United States had ratified the treaty, and an exchange of the ratifications had taken place at Washington, on the 17th of February, the preceding month. By an accident, which was not accounted for, a packet had been put into the hands of the messenger, instead of the one containing the official information of the exchange of the ratifications. But the man was bearer of an open order of the Postmaster, to all his deputies on the road, to expedite him with the utmost celerity, as he carried *information of the*

recent peace.   He declared he had handed an official notice of this event
to the governor of the state of Tennessee.

On the arrival of the clerk at headquarters, Jackson asked him whether
it was his intention to issue the writ; he replied it was his bounden duty
to do so, and he most assuredly would.   He was threatened with an arrest,
but persisted in his asseveration that he would obey the judge's order.
He had handed Louallier's petition to Jackson, and, before he retired,
demanded the return of it; this was peremptorily refused, and the paper
was withheld.   It appears the date of the *fifth* of March had been originally on this document, and that being Sunday, Hall had changed it to
that of the following day, the *sixth*.   The idea had been cherished, that
this alteration might support an additional article, in the charges against
Hall.   It is not extraordinary, that those who imagined that, as Louallier
might be tried for a *libel*, in a court martial, Hall might for *forgery*.   Thus
one inconsistency almost universally leads to another.

Duplessis, the marshal of the United States, had volunteered his services
as an aid to Jackson; a little after midnight he visited headquarters.   The
imprisonment of Hall, and the accounts from Washington, had brought a
great concourse of people near the general; who, elated by the success of
the evening, met the marshal at the door, and announced to him, *he had
shopped the judge.*   Perceiving that Duplessis did not show his exultation,
he inquired whether he would serve Hall's writ.   The marshal replied, he
had ever done his duty, which obliged him to execute all writs directed
to him by the court, whose ministerial officer he was, and, looking sternly
at the person who addressed him, added, he would execute the court's writ,
on any man.   A copy of the proclamation of martial law, that lay on the
table, was pointed to him, and Jackson said, he *also* would do his duty.

A large concourse of people had been drawn to the Exchange Coffeehouse, during the night, by the passing events, which were not there, as
at headquarters, a subject of exultation and gratulation.   The circumstances
were not unlike those of the year 1806, which Livingston describes as " so
new in the history of our country, that they will not easily gain belief, at
a distance, and can scarcely be realized by those who beheld them.   A
dictatorial power, assumed by the commander of the American army—the
military arrest of citizens, charged with a civil offense—the violation of
the sanctuary of justice.   An attempt to overawe by denunciations, those
who dared, professionally, to assert the authority of the laws—the
unblushing avowal of the employment of military force, to punish a civil
offense, and the hardy menace of persevering in the same course, were
circumstances that must command attention, and excite the corresponding
sentiments of grief, indignation and contempt."

There were some who recommended, that application should be made
to Claiborne, to put himself at the head of the militia of the state, and
to Duplessis, to call out the *posse comitatus* of the district, to support the
authority of the judiciary; but the sentiment of those prevailed, who
harangued the people in the strains of Livingston's address to his fellow-
citizens, about eight years before.   " We must suffer the evils to which we
are exposed.   Let us, however, do it with fortitude, and never be tempted
to any act, which may enlist us, on the side of those, who trample on our
constitution, sport with our liberties, and violate our laws.   Let us
remember, that the day of retribution will arrive, and is not far distant,
when a strict account will be taken, as well of the wanton abuses, as of

the shameful dereliction which permits them.   But, let us strive by our zeal in the support of our country, by our submission to lawful authority, by our opposition to every foreign or domestic foe, that there is no pretext for the dictatorial power that is assumed over us."

" I have said that we *must suffer*.   Never were two words more applicable to our situation: it is one the most dreadful to an independent mind, of any that can be imagined—subject to the uncontrolled will of a single man, to whom the hearsay tales of slander are proofs; and who, on his own evidence, arraigns, condemns and punishes, the accused; dooms him to imprisonment, by whom the tribunals are insulted.   What state of things can be worse?   No caution can protect! no consciousness of innocence secure.   The evidence is taken in private; malicious, cowardly informers, skulk around the proconsul's office.   Their tales give food to pre-existing enmity, and avenge their own quarrels by secret denunciations of guilt.   The objects of official suspicion are confined."

Repose having restored calmness to Jackson's mind, and the intelligence of peace depriving his measures of the only ground on which they could be justified—necessity—he acted on the suggestions of his own reflections, and considering the British as no longer the enemies of his country, he determined on an attempt to anticipate, as much as him lay, the blessings of returning peace.   With this object in view, one of his first acts on the *sixth*, was a communication to Lambert, which Latour has preserved.   It is in the following words:

" I have just received intelligence from Washington, which leaves little doubt, in my mind, that the treaty, signed at Ghent, between the United States and Great Britain, has been ratified by the president of the senate of the United States.   But, by some unaccountable accident, a dispatch, on another subject, has been substituted for the one intended to give me official notice of this event.   The one I have received is accompanied by an order from the postmaster general, desiring his deputies to forward the express, carrying intelligence of the recent peace.   Of this order I enclose a copy.   From other circumstances, to which I give credit, I learn that the same express brought official notice of the ratification of the treaty, to the governor of Tennessee.   I have deemed it my duty, to communicate the exact state of these circumstances, without loss of time, that you might determine whether they would not justify you, in agreeing to a cessation of hostilities, to anticipate the happy return of peace between our two nations, which the first direct intelligence must bring to us, in an official form."

Jackson now paused to deliberate whether these circumstances did not require him, by a cessation of all measures of violence, to allow his fellow-citizens in New Orleans, to anticipate this happy return of peace, the account of which the first direct intelligence was to bring to him, in an official form—the untoward arrival of an orderly sergeant, with a message from Arbuckle, to whom the custody of Hall had been committed, prevented Jackson coming to that conclusion which his unprejudiced judgment would have suggested.   The prisoner had requested that a magistrate might be permitted to have access to him, to receive an affidavit which he wished to make, in order to resort to legal measures for his release.   Arbuckle desired to know the general's pleasure on this application.   Naturally impatient of anything like control or restraint, the idea of a superior power to be employed against his decisions, threw

Jackson into emotions of rage. Before they had sufficiently subsided to allow him to act on the message, some of his ordinary advisers came in, to recommend the arrest of Hollander, a merchant of some note. What was the offense of this man has never been known; but Jackson's temper of mind was favorable to the views of his visitors. He ordered the arrest of the merchant and forbade the access of the magistrate to Hall; the idea of allowing his fellow-citizens to anticipate the happy return of peace, was abandoned, and measures were directed to be taken for the trial of Louallier.

Seven distinct charges were exhibited against the prisoner:

1. Mutiny. The specification on this head was that he did write, and cause to be published, the piece in the *Courier de la Louisiane*, of the 3d of March, 1815.

2. Exciting mutiny. The specification was the same as the preceding.

3. General misconduct. The specification was as before.

4. Being a spy. The specification was that the prisoner was found lurking about the fortifications and encampment of the United States, in New Orleans, being much disaffected, and writing, and causing to be published, as before.

5. Illegal and improper conduct, and disobedience to orders.

Specification 1st. Violating the fifty-sixth article of the rules and articles of war, viz: "Whoever shall relieve the enemy with money, victuals, or ammunition, or shall knowingly harbor or protect an enemy, shall suffer death, or such other punishment as shall be ordered by the sentence of a court martial." This specification concluded with an averment that the prisoner did write and cause to be published, etc., as before.

Specification 2d. Violating the 57th article, viz: "Whosoever shall be convicted of corresponding with, or giving intelligence to the enemy, either directly or indirectly, shall suffer death, or such other punishment as shall be ordered by the sentence of the court martial." The averment on this specification was the same as the preceding.

6. Writing a wilful and corrupt libel.

7. Unsoldierlike conduct, and contrary to the proclamation of martial law. The specification was that the prisoner did write, and cause to be published, the piece, etc.

The supreme court of the state being in session, application was made to it for a writ of *habeas corpus* in favor of Hollander. The two judges present, Derbigny and Martin, severally declared they should not think themselves justified in rejecting the application, on account of any proclamation of martial law, if they were convinced they had authority to issue the writ; and expressed their readiness to hear an argument, if any gentleman of the bar had a doubt of the former decision of the tribunal, in the case of Laverty, the British subject arrested by the marshal during the preceding summer. This man claimed the citizenship of the United States, and wished to test his pretension by a writ of *habeas corpus;* but the court declined interfering, being of opinion, theirs was an *appellate* jurisdiction *only confined* to *civil* cases, and they could not inquire into the legality of an arrest, on *criminal* or *political* grounds. They permitted the case to be argued; but, before the argument was concluded information was received that Hollander had been discharged by Jackson.

Dick, the attorney of the United States, made application to Lewis, one of the district judges of the state, who was serving as a subaltern officer, in the Orleans rifle company, and whose conduct during the invasion had received Jackson's particular commendation. Believing that his duty as a military man, did not diminish his obligation, as a judge, to protect his fellow-citizens from illegal arrest, Lewis, without hesitation, on the first call of Dick, laid down his rifle, and allowed the writ.

Information of this having been carried to headquarters, Jackson immediately ordered the arrest of Lewis and Dick.

Arbuckle, to whom Lewis' writ, in favor of Hall, was directed, refused to surrender his prisoner, on the ground he was committed by Jackson, under the authority of the United States.

The orders for the arrest of Lewis and Dick were countermanded.

The court martial for the trial of Louallier, of which major-general Gaines was president, met on the 7th.

The prisoner's counsel confined his defense to a plea, to the jurisdiction of court; contending that he was, as a member of the legislature, exempt from militia service; that the rules and articles of war, were expressly established for the government of the *army* of the United States, and extended to the militia of the state; when in the service of the United States; that their client was neither of the *army or militia*, although, during the invasion, he had performed military duty in one of the volunteer companies, embodied for the maintenance of order in the city; that the *proclamation* of martial law, *made* no one a soldier, who was not so before; that it vested no right in the general, nor imposed on any one, any obligation, which did not exist before.

The irritation of the public mind manifested itself, in the evening, by the destruction of a transparent painting, in honor of Jackson, which the proprietor of the Exchange Coffeehouse displayed in the largest hall.

A general order on the 8th, announced that, although the commanding general had not yet received official information, that the state of war had ceased, by the ratification of the treaty, he had persuasive evidence of the fact, and credited it, at the risk of being misled by his wishes, and under this impression, his first duty was to discharge from actual service, the body of the militia of the state, which had taken the field, under the order for the levy en masse.

The French subjects had remained perfectly quiet at home, regardless of the order of the 28th of February. Louallier's publication had opened the eyes of the community, whose sympathy was enlisted in favor of these defenders of the country, and under the present excitement of the public mind, the execution of a sentence of exile against them, would have been dangerous. The governor, who, in Wilkinson's time, had been charged with a co-operation in his illegal measures, or at least with a dereliction of duty, appeared now disposed to act, in such a manner, as to give room for a similar imputation; and Eaton tells us, " he had been heard to declare, in words of mysterious import, that serious difficulties would be shortly witnessed in New Orleans." It was deemed most prudent, at headquarters, to make a virtue of necessity. With a view of enabling Jackson to do so, with a good grace, an address was procured from the officers and men of the principal volunteer corps of the militia of the city, soliciting the suspension of the order of the 28th of February, and pledging themselves for the future good conduct of the French subjects. On receiving this address, a general order was issued, stating that, time having been given to the people, to consider whether they would avail themselves of their degrading exemption, at a distance from the camp, or enrol themselves among them who defended the state; and the delay being expired, the order would have been strictly enforced, had it not been for the application and guarantee of the officers and men of the volunteer companies. The execution of the order was therefore suspended, till the general's pleasure was further signified.

There is a manifest inconsistency between these two orders. Had the latter been penned by a friend of Jackson's, the order of the 28th of February would have been rescinded, on the reason assigned in the first, viz: the *persuasive evidence*, which had reached headquarters, that the state of war had ceased. There would have been much more dignity, in this admission than in the boast that the subjects of a friendly nation, entitled by treaty to peculiar privileges in Louisiana, could be exiled from New Orleans and compelled to march to the distance of one hundred and twenty miles, in time of peace, on the mere *signification* of any man's *pleasure*.

A number of officers had compelled the proprietor of the Exchange Coffeehouse, to exhibit a new transparent painting, and to illuminate the hall in a more than usual manner. They attended in the evening, and stood near the painting, with the apparent intention of indicating a determination, to resist the attempt of taking down the painting. It was reported a number of soldiers were in the neighborhood, ready to march to the coffeehouse, at the first call. This was not calculated to allay the excitement of the public mind. The prostration of the legitimate government; the imprisonment of the district judge of the United States, the only magistrate, whose interference could be successfully invoked, on an illegal arrest, under color of the authority of the United States, the ascendancy assumed by the military, appeared to have dissolved all the bands of social order in New Orleans.

It is not easy to say, to what extremity matters would have been carried if the good sense of the most influential characters in the city, had not induced them to interfere. They represented, to those who were disposed to run all hazards, that a few days, perhaps a few hours, would bring the official account of the exchange of the ratifications of the treaty; that Jackson's day of reckoning would then arrive; that Hall, with the authority (though now without the power) of checking the encroachments of the military, possessed the authority, and would soon have the power to punish the violators of the law—presenting the idea without using the eloquent language of Workman, in 1807: "the law is not dead, but sleepeth; the constitution is eclipsed indeed, but the dark bodies of hideous and ill-omened form, which have intercepted its light, and deprived us of its genial influence, will soon pass away, and we shall again behold the glorious luminary, shining forth in all its original splendor."

On the 9th, the court martial sustained Louallier's plea to their jurisdiction, as to all the charges except the fourth; that of being a spy—manifesting, that all judicial institutions possess, in the United States, an essential purity and energy. They thought the rules and articles of war, were expressly established by the congress, for the government of the army, and were not binding on any individual out of it; that neither the President, or any commander, can, by a proclamation of martial law, vest in himself right, or impose on others any obligation that did not exist before; nor render anything lawful or unlawful, that was otherwise before.

They acquitted Louallier of the fourth charge. There was no evidence before them, that he was found lurking about any fortification or encampment of the army of the United States; none of his disaffection; and his conduct, in the legislature, had evinced that, in zeal and patriotism, he did not yield even to Jackson. If he had published a libel, it was the duty of the attorney-general of the state to indict him, and the province of the grand jury to present him, if that officer neglected his duty. He was placed before them as a person owing allegiance to, they knew he was a citizen of the United States, and that government had in the beginning of the war, declared that a spy must essentially be an alien.

Jackson was greatly disappointed at the conclusion to which the court martial had arrived; he, however, did not release either of his prisoners, and on the tenth issued the following general order:

"The commanding general disapproves of the sentence of the court martial, of which major-general Gaines is president, on the several charges and specifications exhibited against Mr. Louallier; and is induced by the novelty and inportance of the matters, submitted to the decision of that court, to assign the reasons of this disapproval.

" The charges against the prisoner were mutiny, exciting mutiny, general misconduct, for being a spy, illegal and improper conduct, and disobedience of orders, writing a wilful and corrupt libel against the commanding general, unsoldierly conduct, and conduct in violation of a general order; all of which charges are, on the face of them, proper to be inquired into by a court martial. The defendant pleaded to the jurisdiction of the court, and founded his exceptions on matters of fact, which exceptions, as to all the charges and specifications but one, the court sustained, without inquiring into the truth of the facts (which not otherwise could have appeared to them), upon which those exceptions were bottomed.

"The commanding general is not disposed, however, to rest his objections upon any informality in the mode of proceeding adopted by the court, but presuming that the court really believed the truth of the facts set forth in the exceptions, deems it his duty to meet the doubts as he supposes them to have existed. The character of the prisoner (a citizen not enrolled in any corps, and a member of the state legislature, though that legislature was not in session) probably, in the opinion of the court, placed him without their reach, upon the several charges on which they declined acting.

" The enemy having invaded the country, and threatening an attack on New Orleans, many considerations, growing out of this emergency, and connected with the defense of the city, rendered the adoption of the most energetic and decisive measures necessary. Martial law, as the most comprehensive and effectual, was therefore proclaimed by the commanding general—a state of things which made it the duty of every inhabitant, indiscriminately, to contribute to the defense of his country—a duty, in the opinion of the commanding general, more positive and more urgent than any resulting from the common and usual transactions of private, or even public life. The occasion that calls it forth, involves at once, the very existence of the government, and the liberty, property and lives of the citizens.

53

"Martial law being established, applies, as the commanding general believes, to all persons who remain within the sphere of its operation; and claims exclusive jurisdiction of all offenses, which aim at the disorganization and ruin of the army over which it extends. To a certain extent, it is believed to make every man a *soldier*, to defend the spot where chance or choice has placed him, and to make him *liable* for any misconduct calculated to weaken its defense.

"If martial law, when necessity shall have justified a resort to it, does not operate to this extent, it is not easy to perceive the reason or the utility of it. If a man, who shall, from choice, remain within the limits of its operation, and whose house is without these limits, and there labor by means in his power to stir up sedition and mutiny among the soldiery, inspire them with distrust towards the commanding officer, and communicate to the enemy intelligence of the disaffection and discontent, which he himself has created, he may safely avail himself of what he may please to call his constitutional rights and continue his dangerous machinations with impunity; the commanding general believes he cannot easily conceive, how a man thus influenced and thus acting, might render the enemy more important services, and do his country more injury, than he possibly could, by entering the ranks of the enemy, and aiding him in open battle. Why is martial law ever declared? Is it to make the enlisted or drafted soldier subject to it? He was subject to it before. It is, that the whole resources of a country, or of that district over which it is proclaimed, may be successfully applied for its preservation. Every man, therefore, within the limits to which it extends, is subject to its influence. If it has not this operation, it is surely a perfect nullity. Apply this view of the subject to the case before the court—and how is it? After the adjournment of the legislature, of which the defendant claims to be a member, he remained within the camp of the American army, and within the limits, which are declared to be embraced by martial law. How does he there deport himself? Instead of contributing to the defense of his country; instead of seeking to promote that unanimity, which a love of country, and the important trust which had been reposed in him, might have led us to expect, we behold him endeavoring to stir up discord, sedition, mutiny—laboring to disorganize and destroy an army which had so lately defended his country, and might so soon again be necessary for its defense. Not only inviting the enemy to renew his attempt, but contributing his utmost to enable him to succeed, if he should obey the invitation. Is there no power to restrain the efforts, or to punish the wickedness of such a man? If he aids and comforts the enemy, by communicating to him information of the mutinous and seditious spirit, of the distraction and confusion which he himself has created—why this is treason, and he cannot be punished by a court martial. If he excites mutiny, disobedience to orders, and rebellion among the soldiery, he is not attached to the army, and cannot be restrained! Why, is he not attached to the army? Why, at such a moment, when he remains within it, is he not subject to its rules and regulations? If the enemy comes, may he fold his arms and walk unconcernedly along the lines, or remain inactive in his room? Can he not be called upon for his exertions? May he not only refuse to render any assistance himself, but without fear or reproach, do all in his power to render ineffectual the exertions of others; of that army which, in the most threatening crisis, is fighting for the liberty and safety of that country, whose liberty and safety he professes to have so much at heart? May he, at such a moment, proclaim to the enemy, that we are dissatisfied with our general, tired of the war, determined no longer to bear the restrictions which it imposes; in a word, disaffected and disunited, and ready to yield to him on his first approach. May this man, a foreigner, retaining the predilections for the country which gave him birth, and boasting of those predilections; may such a man, under such circumstances, excite sedition and mutiny, division and disorganization in our army; and when he is called before the court martial to answer for his crimes, say—gentlemen, you have no right to take cognizance of the offences of which I am charged? Decide with the accused, no army can be safe, no general can command; disaffection and disobedience, anarchy and confusion must take place of order and subordination, defeat and shame, of victory and triumph. But the commanding general is persuaded, that this is a state of things which the government of no country can or does tolerate. The constitution of the United States secures to the citizen the most valuable privileges; yet, the same constitution contemplates the necessity of suspending the exercise of the same, in order to secure the continuance of all. If it authorizes the suspension of the writ of *habeas corpus* in certain cases; it, thereby, implicitly admits the operation of martial law, when in the event of rebellion or invasion public safety may require it. To whom does the declaration of this law belong? To the guardian of the public safety; to him who is to conduct the operations against the enemy, whose vigilance is to descry danger, and whose arms are to repel it? He is the only authority present to witness and determine the emergency which makes such a resort necessary and possessed of the means to make suitable provisions for it. For the correctness of his conduct, under the circumstances which influenced him, he stands responsible to his government."

The court martial consoled themselves by the reflection, that their sentence, though disapproved by Jackson, was in perfect conformity with decisions of the President of the United States, and of the supreme court of the state of New York, in similar cases.

In August, 1812, Elijah Clark was condemned to be hung as a spy, at Buffalo, in the state of New York, by sentence of a court martial. "It appeared that he was born in the state of New Jersey, and that he continued to reside in the United States, as a citizen thereof, until within about eight months, when he removed to Canada, and there married; that his wife and property are yet in Canada, and within the dominion and allegiance of the king of the united kingdom of Great Britain and Ireland. For these reasons, the court was of opinion, that (although the said Elijah Clark was a native born citizen of the United States, and was yet holden under the allegiance, which, as such citizen, he owed to the United States) he was nevertheless liable to be tried and convicted, as a spy in the United States, for his acts of a spy, committed during the continuance of such temporary allegiance to the king of the united kingdom of Great Britain and Ireland, with whom the United States were at war."

General Hull suspended the execution till the pleasure of the President of the United States was known.

On the second of October, the secretary of war wrote to the general, that Clark, "being considered a citizen of the United States, and not liable to be tried by a court martial as a spy, the President directed that unless he should be arraigned by the civil court for treason, or a minor crime, under the laws of the state of New York, he must be discharged."

One Smith, a naturalized citizen of the United States, and a Scotchman by birth, was arrested during the last war, and imprisoned in the barracks at Sackett's Harbor, on the charge, among others, of his being a spy. On the restoration of peace, he brought his action of false imprisonment against the commanding officer of the garrison. The case was brought before the supreme court, where it was argued, on the part of the defendant, that, on the principle of natural or perpetual allegiance, he remained a British subject, he was a spy, and could be treated as such; and at all events, the officer who detained him was justifiable in doing so, until by due investigation in a court martial, it could be ascertained whether he was a citizen or an alien. For the plaintiff, it was insisted that a naturalized citizen enjoys all the rights and privileges of a native born, who is entitled, in every possible case, to protection from military power. The authority of Sir Matthew Hale was quoted, that even in England, martial law is no law, but something indulged as a law; and the opinion of Lord Loughborough was relied on, that martial law, even as described by Sir Matthew Hale, does not exist at all. The court said, "the defendant's conduct does not appear harsh or offensive; but it is the principle invoked that renders the result so important. None of the offenses, charged against the plaintiff, were cognizable before a court martial, except that which relates to his being a spy: and, if he was an American citizen, he could not be chargeable with such an offense. He might be amenable to the civil authority for treason; but could not be prosecuted, under *martial law*, as a spy." One of the judges dissented, on the ground that the officer was justifiable in detaining the plaintiff, till it was ascertained whether he was a citizen; but the judge expressly admitted, that if he was a citizen, he was not liable to be tried as a spy.

It is evident, that by the expression, *martial law*, in the last part of the opinion of the court, reference is made to the second section of the act of congress, for establishing rules and articles of war, for the government of the armies of the United States, in which the punishment of death is denounced against spies.

The independent stand, taken by the court martial, had left no glimpse of hope, at headquarters, that the prosecution of Hall, on the charge of mutiny, on which he had been imprisoned, could be attempted with any prospect of success—the futility of any further proceedings against Louallier was evident—Jackson, therefore, put an end to Hall's imprisonment on Saturday, the 11th of March. The word *imprisonment* is used, because Eaton assures his readers, that "*Judge Hall was not imprisoned; it was merely an arrest.*" Hall had been taken from his bedchamber, on the preceding Sunday, at 9 o'clock in the evening, by a detachment of about one hundred men, dragged through the streets, and confined in the same apartment with Louallier, in the barracks. Three days after it had been officially announced to the inhabitants of New Orleans, that Jackson was in possession of persuasive evidence, that a state of peace existed, and the militia had been discharged, the door of Hall's prison was thrown open, but not for his release. He was put under a guard, who led him several miles beyond the limits of the city, where they left him, with a prohibition to return, "till the ratification of the treaty was *regularly* announced, or the British shall have left the southern coast."

This last, and useless display of usurped power, astonished the inhabitants. They thought, that, if the general feared the return of the British, the safety of New Orleans would be better insured, by his recall of the militia, than by the banishment of the legitimate magistrate. It was the last expansion of light, and momentary effulgence, that precedes the extinguishment of a taper.

At the dawn of light, on Monday, the 13th, an express reached headquarters, with the dispatch which had accidentally been misplaced, in the office of the secretary of war, three weeks before. The cannon soon announced the arrival of this important document, and Louallier was indebted for his liberation, to the precaution, which Eaton says, the President of the United States had taken to direct Jackson to issue a proclamation for the pardon of all military offenses.

CHAPTER XXXIII.

HALL's return to the city was greeted by the acclamations of the inhabitants. He was the first judge of the United States they had received, and they had admired in him the distinguishing characteristics of an American magistrate—a pure heart, clean hands, and a mind susceptible of no fear, but that of God. His firmness had, eight years before, arrested Wilkinson in his despotic measures. He was now looked upon to show, that if he had been unable to stop Jackson's arbitrary steps, he would prevent him from exulting in the impunity of his trespass.

Dick was anxious to lose no time, in calling the attention of the district court of the United States, to the violent proceedings, during the week that had followed the arrival of the first messenger of peace; but Hall insisted on a few days being exclusively given to the manifestation of the joyous feelings, which the termination of the war excited. He did not yield to Dick's wishes till the 21st. The affidavits of the clerk of the district court, of the marshal of the United States, of the attorney of Louallier and of the commander at the barracks, were then laid before the court.

The case they presented, was this—that Jackson, desirous to punish the author of a publication, which he called a false and corrupt libel, upwards of six weeks after the departure of the British, had yielded to the advice of those who recommended that the publisher should be prosecuted, before a court martial, as a spy, and had him arrested. The prisoner sought legal advice, and was informed, that in case of conviction, sentence of death would inevitably be passed on him—and that the court martial by whom he was to be tried, was without jurisdiction. He implored the interference of the tribunal, especially charged with preventing a military court from stepping out of the bounds of its legitimate jurisdiction. The judge took the proper step, to have the complaint legally inquired into. With the view of obstructing the course of justice, and depriving his victim of the protection he had sought, Jackson had the judge arrested and imprisoned, till the trial was over. The clerk of the court was compelled to bring a record of the court, to headquarters, where it was taken and withheld from him.   He and the marshal were threatened. Some of these transactions happened after accounts of the cessation of the state of war was received.   The proceedings did not appear to have the least semblance of necessity, or even utility.

On the motion of the attorney of the United States, a rule to show cause, why process of attachment should not issue against Jackson, was granted.

On the return day, Reid, one of the general's aids, accompanied him to the court house, and presented to the court a paper, sworn to by Jackson, as his answer to the rule.

In the preamble of this document, a solemn protest was made against the unconstitutionality and illegality of the prosecution—the authority of the attorney of the United States to institute it, was denied, as well as that of any court of the United States, to punish for a contempt.   It averred that no criminal prosecution could be carried on, in any of these courts, except upon a presentment or indictment, or for an offense not created by a statute—it insisted on a trial by jury; it urged that the contempt had not been committed in presence of the court, that the writ of *habeas corpus* was not returnable into court; and that the authority of the judge, who issued it, was confined to the case of a prisoner under, or by color of the authority of the United States.

In the conclusion, the proclamation of martial law was justified, on the report which the general had received of the disaffection and seditious disposition of the French part of the population of Louisiana, and various extracts were given from letters of the governor, on the difficulties he had to encounter, the opposition he met with from the legislature, and the little dependence there was for success, except on a regular force, to be sent by the United States. The interference with the records in the clerk's office, was justified on the belief the defendant entertained, that it was within his authority.   The proclamation of martial law was held to have made the publisher of the libel a soldier, and his offense cognizable by a court martial; and the imprisonment of the judge was said to have been a measure of necessity.

The attorney of the United States, opposed the reading of this paper. He said that, in no case, the defendant was permitted to make evidence for himself, and justify himself, by swearing he was innocent; although, on a process of attachment, the defendant's answers to interrogatories, put by the officer who conducted the prosecution, were conclusive evidence.

In the present stage of the cause, the inquiry was confined to the sufficiency of the facts sworn to—whether they did not constitute an offense, and one which did support a prosecution, by process of attachment. When the hearing would be on the merits, the defendant might avail himself of his answers to interrogatories to show that the facts, in the affidavits, on which the rule was obtained, were not true.   The judge took time to deliberate.

On the next day, he said   "The court has taken time to consider the propriety of admitting the answer, offered yesterday.   It was proper to do so; because it is the first proceeding, of any importance, instituted in a matter like the present, since the establishment of the court; and because, by the constitution of the court, it is composed of one judge only; and it so happens, that one of the charges of contempt, is his imprisonment, and the consequent obstruction of the course of justice. This is no reason why the proceedings should not have been instituted, and be persevered in; but it is a good one for much deliberation. No personal consideration ought, for a moment, to allow the abandonment of the defense of the laws, the support of the dignity of the tribunal, and of the rights of the citizen.

"I have considered the case, and I think I see a clear course.

"On a rule to show cause, the party called on may take all *legal* grounds, to show that the attachment ought not to issue. He may take exceptions to the *mode* of proceedings, and prove, from the affidavits on which the rule was obtained, that the facts do not amount to a contempt.

"If the court be convinced that the attachment may legally issue, it goes to bring the party into court—the interrogatories are propounded—he may object to any of them, as improper, or deny the facts charged, and purge himself of the contempt, on oath. His single testimony counteracts all other that may have been adduced.

"I will hear any of the exceptions taken in the answer, or any question of law that may be urged."

Reid now expatiated on the unconstitutionality and illegality of a mode of proceeding, which deprived the defendant of the benefit of a trial by a jury, and on the protestations, and exceptions in the preamble of Jackson's answer. He dwelt on the necessity there was for the proclamation of martial law, and attempted the justification of the facts, stated in the affidavit, which were the basis of the prosecutions, by martial law.

The attorney of the United States stated his conviction, that it was now too late to speak of the unconstitutionality of the process of attachment—a construction and interpretation of the constitution, contemporaneous with that instrument, and coeval with the present government, had received the sanction of the judiciary, and the house of representatives:—that no jury was called in, because the facts, if contested, were to be settled by the oath of the defendant, in his answers to interrogatories propounded to him, in behalf of the United States; it being the duty of their attorney, to draw forth, by these interrogatories, as by cross-examination, in the audition of witnesses, the facts, which the defendant had an interest to conceal. After his conscience was thus probed, the evidence resulting from his answers, counteracted all the testimony adduced against him.

The attorney urged, that he was willing to admit that the arrest of Louallier was not made under any authority derived from the United States, but it was his duty to say, it took place, under color of such an authority; and in either case, it was the duty of the magistracy of the United States, to inquire into the legality of the arrest. He added, that with regard to such writs, which the judges were authorized to issue, at their chambers, it had never been doubted, that obedience to them was to be enforced, and contempt of them punished, in the same manner as if the writ had been issued by the clerk.

He added that, when the case should be before the court on the merits, the defendant would have every benefit that could be derived from martial law.

The rule was made absolute.

Jackson's advisers now found he could not be defended on the merits, with the slightest hope of success, as the attorney of the United States would probably draw from him by interrogations, the admission, that both Louallier and the judge were kept in prison, long after persuasive evidence had been received at headquarters, of the cessation of the state of war. They therefore recommended to him not to answer the interrogatories, which would authorize the insinuation that he had been condemned unheard.

It appears that some of his party, at this period, entertained the hope that Hall could be intimidated, and prevented from proceeding further. A report was accordingly circulated that a mob would assemble in and about the courthouse—that the pirates of Barataria, to whom the judge had rendered himself obnoxious before the war, by his zeal and strictness, in the prosecution that had been instituted against several of their ringleaders, would improve this opportunity of humbling him. Accordingly, groups of them took their stands, in different parts of the hall, and gave a shout when Jackson entered. It is due to him to state, that, it did not appear that he had the least intimation that a disturbance was intended, and his influence was honestly exercised to prevent disorder.

On his being called, he addressed a few words to the court, expressive of his intention not to avail himself of the faculty he had to answer interrogatories; a determination, which he said was grounded on the court's refusal to allow his answer to the rule being read.

The court informed him, every indulgence had been extended to him, which the law authorized.

The attorney of the United States now rose, and said that his task was much simplified by the course the defendant had taken. The defendant stood charged with having obstructed the course of justice and prevented the interference of the court, in order that an illegal prosecution, for a capital offense, might be carried on, before a military tribunal, against a citizen absolutely unconnected with the army or militia. His protestations and exceptions had already been disposed of. The greatest part of the paper, which he had produced on his first coming into court, was filled with extracts of letters, and arguments, by which his issuing a proclamation of martial law, was intended to be justified. No one had ever seen any degree of guilt in this act. It was very proper, in the beginning of an invasion, for the commander of the army raised to oppose it, to warn, by a solemn appeal, his men and all his fellow-citizens around him, that circumstances required the exertion of the faculties of all, to repel the enemy; and that the martial law of the United States, *i. e.*, the system of rules established by the acts of congress and the laws and usages of nations, with regard to martial matters, would be strictly enforced.

The words of Judge Bay, of the supreme court of South Carolina, in *Lamb's* case, were quoted: "If by martial law is to be understood that dreadful system, the *law of arms*, which in former times was exercised by the King of England and his lieutenants, when *his word was the law*, and his *will the power*, by which it was *exercised*, I have no hesitation in saying that such a monster could not exist in this land of liberty and freedom. The political atmosphere of America would destroy it in embryo. It was against such a tyrannical monster that we triumphed in our revolutionary conflict. Our fathers sealed the conquest by their blood, and their posterity will never permit it to tarnish our soil by its unhallowed feet, or harrow up the feelings of our gallant sons, by its ghastly appearance. All our civil institutions forbid it; and the manly hearts of our countrymen are steeled against it. But, if by this military code are to be understood the rules and regulations for the government of our men in arms, when marshalled in defense of our country's rights and honor, then I am bound to say, there is nothing unconstitutional in such a system."

The attorney of the United States candidly admitted, that, although the acts of the defendant could not by any means, be justified by his proclamation; they could certainly be so, by necessity, which justifies any act it commands—and the defendant was entitled to every benefit under the plea of necessity; and on the part of the United States, success in the prosecution was neither expected nor wished, if that necessity could be shown.

To show that no necessity existed to authorize the acts of violence complained of, the attorney stated, that the defendant had admitted that "most of the acts mentioned in the rule took place, after the enemy had retired, from the place he had at first assumed—after they had met with a signal defeat—and, after an unofficial account had been received of the signature of the treaty." This had been verified by the affidavit of the defendant, that the material facts contained in his answer he believed to be true—but the general had not sworn that his answer contained the whole truth, and the counsel by whom the document was prepared, had carefully suppressed some most material circumstances. The charges, which were the basis of the illegal proceedings, which it was the bounden duty of the court to arrest, were exhibited, after several confirmations of the account of the signature of the treaty were received —after the ratification of that treaty by the Prince Regent had been announced—after it was known that the treaty had arrived at Washington, and the senate had advised its ratification—after the President had ratified it, and the mutual exchange of the ratifications. It was admitted that the official annunciation of all these circumstances had not been received by the defendant, but to use his own words, in an official document, he had *persuasive evidence* of these facts, and he credited them. The untoward accident, which had prevented his receiving the dispatch of the secretary of war containing the official intelligence, was known to him. He even confessed the state of war no longer existed—that his duty forbad him to persist in measures, which the return of peace rendered unnecessary and illegal. Under this impression, he proposed a suspension of hostilities to Lambert—he discharged the militia of the state, and consented that the French subjects, residing in New Orleans, should no longer be required to return to his camp.

In the conclusion of his argument, Dick observed, that credulity itself could not admit the proposition, that persuasive evidence that the war had ceased, and belief that necessity required that violent measures should be persisted in to prevent the exercise of the judicial power of the legitimate tribunal, could exist at the same time, in the defendant's mind.

The general made a last effort to avert the judgment of the court against him, by an asseveration, he had imprisoned Dominick A. Hall, and *not the judge :* his attention was drawn to the affidavit of the marshal, in which he swore Jackson told him " I have *shopped the judge.*"

The court, desirous of manifesting moderation, in the punishment of the defendant for the want of it, said that, in consideration of the services the general had rendered to his country, imprisonment should make no part of the sentence, and condemned him to pay a fine of one thousand dollars and costs, only.

A check was immediately filled by Duncan, signed by Jackson, and handed to the marshal, who accepted it in discharge of the fine and costs.

On Jackson's coming out of the courthouse, his friends procured a hack, in which he entered, and they dragged it to the Exchange Coffeehouse, where he made a speech, in the conclusion of which he observed that, " during the invasion, he had exerted every faculty in support of the constitution and laws—on that day, he had been called on to submit to their operation, under circumstances, which many persons might have deemed sufficient to justify resistance.   Considering obedience to the laws, even when we think them unjustly applied, as the first duty of a citizen, he did not hesitate to comply with the sentence they had heard pronounced ;" and he entreated the people, to remember the example he had given them, of respectful submission to the administration of justice.

A few days after he published in the *Ami des Lois*, the answer he had offered to the district court, preceded by an exordium, in which he complained that the court had refused to hear it. He added, that the judge " had indulged himself, on his route to Bayou Sara, in manifesting apprehensions as to the fate of the country, equally disgraceful to himself, and injurious to the interest and safety of the state," and concluded: " should judge Hall deny this statement, the general is prepared to prove it, fully and satisfactorily.

The gauntlet did not long remain on the ground, and the following piece appeared in the *Louisiana Courier:*

" It is stated in the introductory remarks of general Jackson, that ' on the judge's route to Bayou Sara, he manifested apprehensions as to the safety of the country, disgraceful to himself, and injurious to the state.' Judge Hall knows full well, how easy it is for one, with the influence and patronage of general Jackson, to procure certificates and affidavits. He knows that men, usurping authority, have their delators and spies; and that, in the sunshine of imperial or dictatorial power, swarms of miserable creatures are easily generated, from the surrounding corruption, and rapidly changed into the shape of buzzing informers. Notwithstanding which, judge Hall declares, that on his route to Bayou Sara, he uttered no sentiment disgraceful to himself, or injurious to the state. He calls upon general Jackson, to furnish that full and satisfactory evidence of his assertion, which he says he is enabled to do."

The pledge was never redeemed. The general's silence showed, that those, on whose reports he had ventured to charge Hall, could not enable him to administer proof of what they had advanced. The accusation appeared as destitute of foundation, as the charge brought against the legislature, of having entertained the idea of proposing a capitulation. Never was a virtuous community, more gratuitously charged with disaffection, sedition and treason, than the population of Louisiana. Time has shown, that, in patriotism, zeal and courage, it did not yield to that of any state in the confederacy. Before danger was impending, they canvassed every measure that was proposed to them ; they investigated every claim on their services. But, as soon as it was necessary to act, they did so, promptly and effectually. All the resources of the state, were put at the disposal of Jackson—every branch of government, with all its might seconded him—the people submitted to every privation, every duty, which circumstances imposed.

It is true, the general assembly did not join Jackson in the belief, that the suspension of the writ of *habeas corpus*, was a proper measure. They knew, better than he, the population of their country—they did not err, when they concluded it could be trusted. They remembered the time of Wilkinson, and experience that his violent measures and those of Jackson, after danger had ceased to exist, were absolutely ill timed—productive of disorder and confusion, and unattended by any advantage; and the people, as soon as danger was over, manifested their determination not to submit to oppression or unnecessary hardships. The French subjects had shown, they were not afraid of the enemy; they showed they did not fear the general. Nothing but the certainty, that the day of retribution was at hand, and that the insult, offered to the court of the United States, was about to be avenged, prevented those serious difficulties, which Claiborne, as Eaton informs us, believed would soon be witnessed in New Orleans.

The national council rendered to Louisiana, that justice, which she ought to have received at the headquarters of the seventh military district.

Congress passed a resolution, expressive of the high sense they entertained, of the patriotism, zeal, fidelity and courage, with which the people of Louisiana had promptly and unanimously stepped forward, under circumstances of imminent danger, from a powerful invading enemy, in defense of all the *individual,* social and *political* rights *held dear to man.* A like sense was also expressed of the generosity, benevolence and humanity displayed by the inhabitants of New Orleans, in voluntarily affording the best accommodations in their power, and giving their best attentions, to the wounded, not only of the army of the United States, but also to the wounded prisoners of a vanquished foe.

In receiving this testimonial of the approbation of the legislature of the Union, well might the people of Louisiana exclaim, *laus laudari a te.* It was calculated to induce them to disregard, as it effectually counteracted the assertions and insinuations of Jackson's advisers and panegyrists.

If, on the arrival of O'Reilly, at New Orleans, in 1769, he had attended to the maxim, in the motto of his coat of arms, *Fortitudine et prudentia,* the lives of five individuals, in whose attachment to their former sovereign, he should have seen a pledge of their future devotion to his own, would have been spared. If Jackson had been as *prudent* after the invasion, as he had been *brave* during its continuance, he would have spared to himself and others, very disagreeable consequences. May his conduct during one period, be a pattern, and, during the other, a warning to future commanders!

It is the duty of history to record the virtues and errors of conspicuous individuals. In free governments, dangerous precedents are to be dreaded from good and popular characters only. Men of a different cast can never obtain sufficient sanction for their measures, to make their acts an example for others. Hence, the necessity of exposing the false grounds of the actions of the former, and pointing out the evil consequences to which they lead.

The history of every age, and every country, shows that, the higher man is placed in authority, the greater the necessity of his bridling his passions, lest others should believe anger and resentment have prompted measures, which should have had no other motive but public utility—and that a temper, which can bear no contradiction, and a will spurning all control, are the characteristics of a man in power.   It teaches us how important it is, he should not select for his advisers, men who have enlisted themselves in the ranks of those who oppose the measures of government—men having private interests to subserve, private enmities to gratify, and private injuries to avenge—that he should abstain from acting personally, in cases, which present great latitude for the improper indulgence of his feelings; and leave to dispassionate tribunals, the punishment of those who have wounded his pride, by setting his authority at defiance: refraining to become the prosecutor and arbiter of his own grievances, and to place himself in situation, in which, reason having but little control, he may do great injustice: and suspicion always, and censure often, attach to his determination.

May the citizens of these states ever find in the annals of their country, reasons to cherish and venerate, that branch of government, without the protection of which it is in vain that the invader is repelled—the benign influence of which, man feels before he enters the portals of life—which guards the rights of the unborn child—throws its broad shield over helpless infancy—the solicitude of which, watches over man's interests, whenever disease or absence, prevents his attention to them—to which the woodsman confidently commits his humble roof and its inmates, in the morning, when shouldering his axe, he whistles his way to the forest, assured it will guard them from injury, and secure to him the produce of his labor—from which the poor and the rich are sure of equal justice—which neither the *ardor civium, prava jubentium,* nor the *vultus instantis tyranni,* will prevent from coming to the relief of the oppressed—which secures the enjoyment of every domestic, social and political right, and does not abandon man after he has passed the gates of death—leaving him in the grave, the consoling hope that the judiciary power of his country, will cause him to hover a while, like a beneficent shade over the family he reared—directing the disposition of the funds his care accumulated for their support, and thus, by a sort of magic, allow him to *continue to have a will,* after he has *ceased to have an existence.*

ANNALS OF LOUISIANA.

FROM THE CLOSE OF MARTIN'S HISTORY,
A. D. 1815.

TO THE COMMENCEMENT OF THE CIVIL WAR,
A. D. 1861.

"*   *   *   *the abstracts and brief chronicles of the time.*"

1816. An era of commercial and agricultural activity, resulting in general prosperity, ensued upon the close of the war. Specially to be noted was a marked increase in the area of sugar production, the amount of capital invested in this industry, at the time, being estimated at forty million dollars. Many planters from other Southern States, who had come hither with their slaves, engaged in the cultivation of the cane. The commerce of New Orleans speedily developed and extended; the "town, the number of her warehouses rapidly increasing, her port crowded with ships and steamboats, and her building lots rising to an enormous value. The old town was no longer large enough,   *   *   and its extension became necessary." [Bunner.]

The long term of service of the State's first governor closed with this year. Claiborne, who had occupied the executive chair, territorial and State, for thirteen years, was succeeded in December by General James Villeré, a citizen standing high, deservedly, in the opinion of all classes. The election was by the General Assembly, and so continued to be for years.

1817. In January, ex-Governor Claiborne was elected United States Senator, but did not live to wear his senatorial honors long, as he died in November following. Henry Johnson, who was subsequently governor, was his successor in the senate.

Judging from the number of penal laws enacted, these were wild as well as "flush" times in the more thickly settled portions of the State. Without concerning ourselves with the several "black codes" enacted in this and succeeding years—having for us, now-a-days, but a curious interest—we may note a few points in other directions.

Insolvent debtors were not liable to imprisonment if they surrendered their property to their creditors, but if the debtor were guilty of fraud, he was thereby ineligible to any office of honor or profit in the State.

Simple theft was punishable with hard labor.

Death was the punishment decreed to any robber arrested with arms on his person, and to any one killing another in a duel.

And, any one seeking to corrupt a judge; or, who should obstruct a public highway, or keep a house of ill-fame, or become accessory after the fact to any of these offenses, might be punished with fine and imprisonment, at the discretion of the court.

A branch of the Bank of the United States was established in New Orleans this year.

1818. If prosperity continued to increase, there was still a dark and darkening side to the picture. Wild times were these in Louisiana, owing in great measure to the large element of lawless character in the immigration, which at this period caused—according to Governor Villeré—so prodigious an increase in the population. The governor made the matter the subject of a special message, in March of this year, calling the legislature's attention to "the disorders and crimes of which, during nearly all last month, this city has been the theatre;" and strongly intimating, if not nakedly asserting, that this lawless element was composed in the main "of those men who, lately, under the false pretext of serving the cause of the Spanish patriots, scoured the Gulf of Mexico, making its waves groan under the direful weight of their vessels fraught with depredations, * * * and of foreigners, whom the calamities, the revolutions, and the peace of Europe compel or induce to emigrate."

Within the month an act was passed and approved, establishing the "Criminal Court of the City of New Orleans."

The "Louisiana State Bank," the first established since Louisiana had become a State, was incorporated this year, capital two million dollars. The State took stock to the amount of five hundred thousand dollars, and received a bonus of one hundred thousand. There were to be five branches at interior points.

In this year was also organized the "First Presbyterian Church, and Congregation of the City and Parish of New Orleans." Not a few of the names among the forty odd incorporators have become prominently associated with the city's annals.

"The Medical Society of New Orleans" organized.

Frank's Island, near the Northeast Pass, mouth of the Mississippi, was ceded to the United States for the site of a lighthouse.

New Orleans was extended by pushing the upper boundary to the lower limits of the Miss Macarty Plantation. The annexed portion was made the eighth ward.

The law relating to "vagabonds and suspicious persons," arriving in the State from foreign countries, was made still more stringent, while at the same time very humane and provident legislation was enacted for "the relief and protection of persons brought into this State as redemptioners," immigrants under contract to service, or labor, for the payment of their passage money.

Further stringent enactments were added to the Penal Code this year. The crime of murder in the second degree was expunged from the criminal law, and that of manslaughter substituted.

Richard Claiborne, its inventor, was granted the exclusive right, for fourteen years, of navigating or propelling boats on the waters of the State by means of the "hinge, or duck-foot paddle."

1819. "The city is now in the enjoyment of the most perfect security," says Gov. Villeré in his annual message, 6th of January. The Criminal Court has fully realized the ends for which it was instituted: "violators of the laws, malefactors of every description, had suffered or were undergoing, the punishment due to their crimes"; and while society could thus congratulate itself on the supremacy of law, all the pursuits of industry continued to flourish. Somewhat of financial embarrassment there was, owing to a spirit of hazardous commercial speculation. But these were features common throughout the country at the time. Prosperity, broad, substantial and growing, still marked undeniably the progress of Louisiana. Indeed, these were halcyon days for the State, according even to executive testimony. [See Gayarré, Vol. IV., p. 636]. In addition to the expanding and development of her rich and varied resources, and growing trade and commerce, to disorders and violence had succeeded (as above noted) the reign of law, while even "party spirit," says his excellency, "had almost entirely disappeared, and hardly did any remembrance remain of those dangerous distinctions which had been created by idle prejudice between citizens of foreign birth."

In the legislation of this year, we note: all regular lodges constituted by the Grand Lodge of the State declared bodies corporate.

The Medical Society of New Orleans authorized to raise the sum of $15,000, by lottery, for the purchase of a library, philosophical apparatus, etc.

Such parts of the *Partidas* as were held to have the force of law in the State, were ordered to be translated and published.

The Louisiana Bank authorized to liquidate its affairs within two years, from March 12, 1820.

An annual appropriation of $600 was voted each parish (except Orleans) for the support of public schools, and $3,000, annually, to the College of New Orleans. The Regents of the latter were empowered to raise, by lottery, the sum of $25,000, in aid of the institution.

Stabbing or shooting, with intent to commit murder, by persons lying in wait, or in the perpetration of arson, rape or burglary, was made punishable with death.

The Board of Health was abolished, and the governor authorized to make proclamation of quarantine, prescribe regulations thereof, etc.

The "Louisiana State Insurance Company," capital five hundred thousand dollars, incorporated.

Benj. N. B. Latrobe and associates, who had a contract with the city, were made a body corporate, under the name and style of the "New Orleans Water Company"—to continue only during the existence of its contract.

The most important work projected this year, which may be classed under the head of internal improvements, was that designed by the "Orleans Company," of which Bernard Marigny, P. Delaronde, and L. B. Macarty, were leading spirits. It was proposed to dig a "basin which shall be situated on the spot of the Marigny's Canal, and shall communicate with the river Mississippi, by dams or any other means, deemed the best for that purpose." * * For the site of the basin ground was to be purchased of Marigny, "on the spot of" his canal; but at what point the proposed canal from this basin was to strike the river, is not stated in their charter. Conjecture derives but little aid from the bare statements that " a solid and sufficient bridge " was to be erected where the canal and river met, so that traffic along the highway by the levee should not be interrupted. A " bridge was also to span the canal " in front of Moreau street, and another one in front of Greatmen street. Of course, tolls were to be imposed ; and the corporation was to have perpetual succession. But their projects

> " melted into air, into thin air,"
> leaving " not a rack behind."

The city had its usual yellow fever intliction during the summer of this year ; and referring to this annual scourge, Mr. Gayarré makes a *naive* declaration in behalf of the population of the *ancien regime*. After saying that a great portion of her inhabitants had become reconciled to its ravages, from the frequency of its returns, he adds :   " There were even some who felt friendly to the scourge, as, in their opinion, it checked that tide of immigration which, otherwise, would have speedily rolled its waves over the old population, and swept away all those landmarks in legislation, customs, language and social habits to which they were fondly attached.

" A flattering unction " from a grim source, surely !

1820. These were still days of pleasantness and peace, of increasing commerce and richly renumerative husbandry. The financial system of the country having emerged from its embarrassments, the sinews of general industry and trade were again in full and active play. Gov. Villeré, in his January message, says the population of the State had trebled. The inhabitants now numbered 153,407, of whom 53,041 were engaged in agriculture, 6,251 in commerce, 6,041 in manufactures. The number of slaves amounted to 69,060. Bunner, who is our authority for these figures, says the population had more than doubled in ten years.

Under the law for the organization of the militia, passed this year, the Louisiana Legion was projected.

Alexander Milne and others were empowered to open a turnpike road from Lake Pontchartrain to the Mississippi, the first section to run in as direct a line as practicable from the margin of the lake to the Gentilly Road, and the second section thence by the most practicable route to the river. The franchises to continue twenty-five years.

The late war of invasion had impressed the public mind with the necessity of enlarged and improved military and maritime defense. Gov. Villeré was instructed by the legislature to correspond with the President of the United States on the subject, and to urge the expediency of completing the fortifications already commenced in this quarter of the Union. His Excellency was also requested to correspond with the President on the subject of running off and making the western and northern boundary line of the State, " to-wit: the line beginning on the Sabine river, at the thirty-second degree of north latitude, thence running north to the northernmost part of the thirty-third degree of latitude, thence along the same parallel of latitude to the Mississippi river."

Up to this period, the General Assembly met annually on the first Monday of January. At this year's session the time of assembling was changed to the third Monday of November of each year, commencing with the present, and the day for the convening of both Houses in joint session for the choosing of Electors of President and Vice President of the United

States, from the first Monday of November [year of Presidental election] to the first Monday following the meeting of the General Assembly. The expense and trouble of a special assembling for the choosing of Electors were thus obviated. On the second day of the regular session, the General Assembly proceeds to the election of governor. The election of a chief magistrate, federal or State, was not in those days submitted directly to the people. Salutary conservative checks upon universal suffrage prevailed unquestioned. As yet, the demagogue's *vox populi vox Dei*, was but a far off murmur.

Trials by jury were granted to the parish courts of St. Helena and Washington, this year.

Clergymen were exempted from jury duty and working on public roads.

It was enacted that no petition for divorce be received by the legislature unless a separation of bed and board be previously obtained, and that no one obtaining a divorce be allowed to marry again till the expiration of a year.

The town of Franklin made the seat of justice, St. Mary parish.

The governor authorized to receive plans and estimates for the erection of a penitentiary.

Sickness would appear to have prevailed to a considerable extent, at this period, among those engaged in the commerce of the river, the chief sufferers being the unacclimatized from the west. It was proposed to establish hospitals for the relief of such persons, one to be situated at Baton Rouge, one at Covington, and one at some point on Red river, and to the carrying out of the design, the governor was instructed to enter into correspondence with the Executives of the Western States and Territories, inviting their co-operation in the establishing and support of such institutions.

Monroe, Ouachita parish, incorporated.

Persons duly qualified, could be admitted to practice by the Medical Board of the Eastern District. Hitherto, the strange ceremony of an examination before the Mayor and two aldermen of the City of New Orleans, was required by law of the State.

Parish judges empowered to celebrate marriages.

The Physico-Medical Society, of New Orleans, incorporated. Object— the discussion of subjects relating to medicine and natural philosophy. Among the founders was Dr. W. N. Mercer.

One W. H. Robertson obtained at this time the exclusive privilege of supplying New Orleans with live fish. They were brought to market in " smacks, smackers and carrs," and the monopolist was bound to have never less than sixty tons of such craft in the business.

A separate retreat for the insane was ordered erected in connection with the new buildings for the Charity Hospital.

The law empowering the Mayor and City Council of New Orleans to fix the wages for day laborers, repealed.

P. Derbigny and associates establish a steam ferry between New Orleans and the opposite bank.

From this time forward, all proceedings in Courts of Probate, and the records thereof, were to be kept in the English language.

A New Orleans recorder, was required to possess real estate in the city to the amount of $3,000.

Property qualifications were also required of the Mayor and aldermen.

Thomas B. Robertson was elected successor of Governor Villeré, at the November session of the legislature. He had been for several years a representative in Congress. The new executive, in his first message, congratulated the State upon its condition and prospects, but complained of the General Government's failure to open up the public domain to settlement, as had been done in "other frontier States of the Union." Another question, much agitated at the time, was coast defense. This, as well as the admission of Missouri, and the slavery agitation, in connection therewith, were also dwelt upon in the inaugural.

1821. The commerce of New Orleans, continuing to grow. it became necessary to define clearly the limits of the port. It was declared to extend along the left bank, or city front, from the lower limit of Bourg Declouet, to the lower limit of Rousseau's plantation, and on the right bank, from the upper limit of John McDonogh's plantation, to the lower limit of the Duverjé plantation.

About this time, also, further evidence of the aspiring character of the city were shown in prohibiting the reconstruction of wooden buildings within certain limits.

In connection, it is of interest to note that the city government was empowered to sell its landed property, [*i. e.,* land within its corporate limits] on the terms of perpetual ground rent. Redemption of the rent, by payment of the capital, was expressly prohibited.

Law-breakers, and evil-doers generally, in city and suburbs, having been made to feel that society would protect itself by strict and swift enforcement of its laws, the business of the Criminal Court no longer required the services of three judges. The number was reduced to one; and this tribunal was made the Criminal Court of the First District.

A "Code of Public Health" was enacted this year. It provided for a Board of Health, and defined at much length the duties of such body as to quarantine, hospitals, indigent sick, [particularly strangers,] and the sanitary condition of the metropolis and suburbs generally. The enactment is lengthy and elaborate, divided into five chapters, embracing fifty-eight articles. Nominees of the governor and five aldermen, constituted the Board. No salary.

Subsequently, the City Council was empowered to have the indigent sick, found in boarding-houses, or aboard any water craft, conveyed to the Charity Hospital.

The law of libel was materially amended.

Hitherto, the ruling was, "the greater the truth, the greater the libel." It was now enacted, that in any civil suit for slander, etc., the defendant might plead the truth of defamatory words or publication.

Further efforts to extend and improve the public school system were made this year. The parish schools were withdrawn from the superintendance of the police juries, and placed in control of five trustees in each parish, to be appointed annually by said juries, and the annual appropriation for each parish was raised from six to eight hundred dollars. In addition to this sum, the police juries might, in their discretion, levy a tax on land and slaves to the amount of one thousand dollars, for public school purposes. Parishes in which there was no public school building and which had received no appropriation for such object, were entitled each to eight hundred dollars from the State, for the erection of public schoolhouses. An additional sum of one thousand dollars was voted to the University of Orleans, making the annual appropriation five thousand dollars. The Regents of the University were replaced by a Board of Administrators, appointed by the governor. Here is a provision worth resurrecting: "the trustees shall admit in the school, or schools, of their respective parishes, eight day scholars, taken from those families who are indigent, which day scholars shall be apportioned in the different schools by the said trustees, and shall receive instruction gratis, and be, moreover, furnished with classical books, quills and paper, at the cost of said school or schools." It is evident the general assembly had no "Committee on Style," nor as yet entertained the idea of "Public *Free* Schools." Then, too, this quaint phraseology of "classical books," taken in such questionable connection is worth noting, while "quills" seem the echo of sound from out the remote past.

A census of the electors of the State, to be taken by the assessors of each parish, was ordered taken this year.

How to deal with gambling has always been a vexed problem with the authorities of New Orleans. Licensing and total suppression have each in turn been tried, but with results in either case equally disheartening to the moralist. The legislatures of those years resorted to both repressive and tolerant enactments, but still, gambling, like the "problem of the existence of evil," continued to mock solution. The law of 1811, which forbade gambling throughout the State, under severe penalties, was so far amended in 1814, as to permit the licensing of gaming houses in New Orleans and with the inevitable results. So rank and widespread became the demoralization, notwithstanding municipal regulations, that the prohibitory statute, with all its pains and penalties, was re-enacted this year for the benefit of the city. Municipal control, regulations, inspection, not merely failed to repress the evil, " but on the contrary," says the preamble of the act, " have encouraged this most alarming vice under the sanction of law."

The first Methodist Episcopal Church, and the Mechanic Society, of New Orleans, were organized and incorporated. Several old familiar names figure in the list of incorporators of both bodies.

Opelousas, St. Landry Parish, incorporated, and Franklin made the seat of justice for Washington Parish.

The penal code of this period dealt vigorously with certain crimes and misdemeanors. Wanton or malicious killing of a horse, mule, cow, etc., or even of a dog, was punishable by a fine within the amount of two hundred dollars, or by imprisonment, not to exceed six months, with damages to the amount of the value of the animal and costs of court. Mere cruelty to such animals was punished proportionately.

Embezzling, or any other unlawful diverting of the funds of a bank by the president, or other officer of such institution, was punishable by imprisonment at hard labor for a term of one to seven years.

Provision was made at this session of the General Assembly for a codification "of criminal laws in both the French and English language? "

1822. The State continued on her prosperous career, blessed also with "domestic tranquillity," wherever throughout her borders there was organized society. The lawless element had been put down, and, as we have seen in the reorganization of the Criminal Court of New Orleans, stern justice could reduce her forces and enjoy a comparative degree of repose. The distribution of the public lands within the State, and her maritime defense, were the main public questions.

As to the public lands, it was complained that the Federal government had not done as liberally by Louisiana as by the Western States; and in regard to maritime defense, the governor in his annual message declared his inability "to perceive the wisdom of that policy which had sent our naval force to Africa, whilst our own coasts, particularly those of the Gulf of Mexico, had been permitted for years to exhibit scenes of blood and rapine, unequaled in atrocity in the annals of the world."

The "great national road" from Nashville, Tenn., to Madisonville, La., undertaken by the general government, was, so far as it extended within her territory, the object of much care on the part of the State. This highway ran through St. Tammany and Washington parishes, and was required to be kept in repair by the inhabitants living within five miles of each side of the road. *

Meantime, the senators and representatives in congress were formally invited by the legislature to urge upon the general government the practicability and expediency of a new and shorter mail route between New Orleans and Washington City than was then traversed. The committee of the legislature to whom the subject was referred, sketched a route by which it was thought the time between the two cities could be reduced to twelve days! How marvellous is our progress in annihilating time and space! Do we appreciate?

A revision of the civil code was ordered, together with a complete system of commercial laws. Edward Livingston's report on a code of criminal law was accepted by the legislature, and the great jurisconsult was authorized to proceed with the plan of codification outlined in his report.

The authorized translation of the *Partidas*, or rather of such portions as had the force of law in the State, appeared this year.

By act of the General Assembly, the State was divided into three congressional districts. The first comprised "the counties of Orleans, German Coast, Acadie, and Lafourche; the second, the counties of Iberville, Pointe Coupee, and Feliciana; the counties of Attakapas, Opelousas, Rapides, Natchitoches, Ouachita, and Concordia," composed the third congressional district.

Members of the legislature acting as Presidential electors were prohibited from receiving any compensation.

The Eighth Judicial District, composed of the Parishes of Washington, St. Helena, and St. Tammany, established.

Appropriations to the amount of $7,000 were made for the improvement of navigation in the Pearl and Red rivers. And in connection, it should be noted, that charters were all but annually granted to companies or individuals for the improvement of the interior water-courses.

New Orleans was authorized by legislative act to create a public fund or stock to the amount of $300,000.

The sum to be raised was to be expended exclusively in "paving and watering the city."

* Bunner erroneously supposes—so asserts, indeed—that this great national road was constructed in part, at least, by the State. She simply provided for keeping it in repair within her borders.

The " Louisiana Bank " was further allowed to March, 1823, to complete its liquidation.

An appropriation of $1000 was made for the purchase and distribution of genuine vaccine matter throughout the State.

By act of the legislature, a residence of one year on the part of a bankrupt was no longer required to entitle him to the benefit of the insolvent laws of the State.

The volunteer companies of New Orleans were formed into one corps, under the title of the Louisiana Legion, and made the first brigade of the State militia. It was composed of infantry, cavalry, artillery and riflemen, and admitted to be one of the finest bodies of volunteer soldiery of the country.

It is noteworthy that fines incurred by the militia were collectible by the Sheriff of each parish. Militiaing in those days seems to have been something more than mere playing at soldier.

The apportionment of this year gave to the House of Representatives forty-six members. The " county of Orleans " elected nine, and the county of Feliciana, ten.

The parish of Terrebonne created out of the county of Lafourche.

A large number of the leading ladies of New Orleans—American and French—united in establishing the "Female Charity Society," [chartered] for the purpose of relieving the sick and destitute of the city.

The raising of money by a lottery was a popular expedient in those days. The legislature was no niggard in granting the privilege to its own constituents, but required lottery agencies from other States to pay an annual license tax of $50,000.

A lottery was authorized to raise funds for the improvement of Bayou Lafourche; and the First Presbyterian Church of New Orleans had recourse to the same expedient to relieve itself of a debt of $30,000.

This year, the parish of Orleans was incorporated. In the language of the legislative act: "That the free white inhabitants of the parish of St. Louis, of Orleans, be, and are hereby formed and constituted a body, civil and politic, styled, 'The inhabitants of the parish of Orleans.' "

1823. This year is memorable for the extraordinary cold weather which set in about the middle of February.

To unusually warm weather, there succeeded on February 16, a frost of such severity, that, " the river at New Orleans, was partially frozen over, and people skated on the marshes." * * " Several watermen perished with cold in their boats, also negroes in their cabins, and animals were found dead in the woods." All the orange trees are said to have perished.

The disposal of the government lands was again a prominent topic in Gov. Robertson's message.

It being understood that the garrison of regulars at Baton Rouge were to be removed from the State, the General Assembly requested the congressional delegation "to be unceasingly urgent with the Executive of the United States, in remonstrating and protesting against " the measure. The governor, too, in official correspondence with the President, pressed the need for the presence of troops within the State. The great importance of the coast defense was likewise urged both by the legislature and governor.

The old problem of the gambling evil came again before the legislature, and once more there was a change of front.   Six gaming houses were allowed to be licensed in New Orleans and suburbs, on payment, each, of a State tax of $5,000.   The Charity Hospital and College of New Orleans were to be the beneficiaries.

The parish of Lafayette formed from the county of Attakapas.

"The New Orleans Steam Ferry Company" was relieved of the obligation of using steam, and were permitted instead to employ horse-power.   Tedious, and rather hazardous navigation, and which, now-a-days, would attract an immense throng of spectators.

The town of Donaldson [laid off by Wm. Donaldson] was incorporated.

The charter of the Bank of Orleans, which would expire in 1826, was extended to 1847, the bank paying the State a bonus of $25,000.

Commissions for the survey of rivers and bayous, for established or projected roads and canals, were appointed by the legislature.

1824.   Perhaps the most noticeable event of this year, was the creation of the Bank of Louisiana, with a capital of $4,000,000, the State being shareholder to the extent of one-half.   Agriculture, commerce and trade generally, yielded rich returns, and further stimulated a questionable spirit of commercial adventure.   Capital was in demand, and the Bank of Louisiana was ready to discount.

Sound, conservative financiering could not sanction the creation of such an institution, at least under the circumstances of the day; much less decree its chartered existence to the year 1870.

The continued failure of the general government to pursue the same policy with regard to the public lands of Louisiana, as it had done and was now doing in other States, was once more brought to the attention of the legislature, by the governor in his annual message.

The Revised Civil Code, and the new Code of Practice, in connection therewith, were promulgated this year.   An act of the legislature appropriates compensation to "three jurisconsults," for their services in preparing these Codes, and the Criminal Code.   But history recognizes Edward Livingston's as the master mind in this work of codification.

"Louisiana," says Bunner, " is also indebted for her Penal Code to the learning and persevering industry of this gentleman.   After having nearly completed this arduous work, it was destroyed by fire, but the next day he was seen again at his labors, and by untiring application he completed his task in an incredibly short space of time."   The legislature extended the time to January, 1826.*

The Alexandria Library Society incorporated.

County of Feliciana formed into the parishes of East and West Feliciana.

About the usual number of lotteries were sanctioned this year.

The Hibernian Society, of New Orleans, incorporated—its revenues to

---

*Bunner makes the impression that the "Penal (or Criminal) Code," projected by Livingston, was finally adopted.   Neither the Commercial Code nor the Criminal were ever enacted.   The latter encountered increasing opposition, and with its adjunct, the Code of Criminal Procedure and Prison Discipline, it was laid to rest.   Notable among the means of defeat were Judge Seth Lewis' masterly expositions, vindicating the prevailing common law system, and showing the evils of change.   The first argument, sixty-five pages, was published in 1825; and the second, one hundred and forty-two pages, on a renewal of the codifying attempt, in 1831.

be applied exclusively to charitable purposes. Among the incorporators were G. W. White, N. J. Dick, T. Mellon, H. K. Gordon, J. Dumoulin, etc.

A Free Library Society was formed in New Orleans, under the auspices of Ex-Governor Robertson, J. A. Maybin, Alfred Hennen, Beverly Chew, Theo. Clapp, etc., " for the purpose of extending knowledge and promoting virtue among the inhabitants of that city." As it was understood that the philanthropic Judah Touro would provide a suitable building, in the act of incorporation, the name of it was changed to the " Touro Free Library of New Orleans."

Vermillionville, Lafayette parish, laid off by Jean Mouton, Sr.

Governor Robertson did not remain in office to the close of his term. Having been tendered, by President Monroe, the position of Judge of the U. S. District Court, for the District of Louisiana, he resigned a few weeks before its expiration; and President Thibodaux, of the senate, became acting governor. Henry Johnson, the new governor, was inaugurated in December. He had been United States Senator for a number of years. "In his inaugural address," says Gayarré, " he recommended to the heterogeneous population of Louisiana, the observance of a spirit of concord and good will, which could hardly be supposed to prevail, without interruption, among the discordant elements which composed it."

1825. The illustrious Lafayette honored New Orleans with a visit early in this year, to the delight, as was apparent, of all classes of its " heterogeneous population." He landed on the battle-field of Chalmette, and, as witnesses testify, was conducted in triumph to the city. The State voted the handsome sum of $15,000, to give to its distinguished guest such a reception as would "be worthy of the patriotic warrior whom the American people delight to honor."

A law was enacted prohibiting aliens from holding any office, civil or military, within the State.

The bridging of Red river at Alexandria authorized.

The " City Court of New Orleans " organized, composed of one presiding and four associate judges. It absorbed the offices of Justices of Peace, but in the act creating the court, the Mayor, Recorder and Aldermen, were authorized to exercise such functions.

The opening of a public road from Vidalia to Harrisonburgh ordered.

The " College of Louisiana," a State institution, to be established at Jackson, East Feliciana, was authorized by acts approved February 18, this year. It was to be supported by the public school funds of East and West Feliciana, and by the annual appropriation of $5,000, heretofore voted the College of Orleans. The latter was left to depend upon a certain proportion of the tax derived from the gambling houses of New Orleans.

A company was incorporated for the opening of a turnpike road, " beginning at Canal street, in the City of New Orleans, below the line of Rampart street, and proceeding in a direct line, as near as practicable, across the head waters of the Bayou St. John, until it strikes the Mississippi, above the city." The franchises were to be held through fifty years from the opening of the road. John Hagan, Richard Clague, David Urquhart and Stephen Henderson, were among the incorporators.

The act of 1821, with its elaborate Code of Public Health, was repealed this year, and the rights and duties of a Board of Health conferred upon the City Council of New Orleans. Quarantine and gambling appeared to be insoluble problems with the General Assembly.

The Louisiana State Bank authorized to discontinue its branches, excepting that at St. Martinsville.

A memorial to Congress was adopted by the legislature, urging the construction of a canal direct from Lake Pontchartain to the Mississippi river.

The "Mississippi Marine and Fire Insurance Company," capital $300,000, established in New Orleans. Bank of Louisiana was authorized to hold stock to the amount of $50,000.

A law of this year declared every individual convicted of bribery, perjury, forgery or other high crimes, ineligible to office of trust and profit, and incapable of exercising the rights of suffrage.

Parish of Jefferson formed from parish of Orleans.

The General Assembly, by resolution, requested of the general government the cession of a lot of ground in New Orleans, within the area bounded by Common, Canal, Tchoupitoulas and Magazine streets, as the site of a banking house and exchange for the Bank of Louisiana, on condition that a portion of the building be appropriated to the Post Office.

President Monroe's term of office, now nearing its close, the same body adopted joint resolutions, expressing in earnest language Louisiana's warm appreciation of his official and personal character, as well as grateful recollection of his services in securing the State to the Union.

By act approved February of this year, the seat of government was to be transferred from New Orleans to Donaldsonville, from and after the first of December, 1825.

1826. The slavery agitation was a growing and irritant issue. Governor Johnson devotes a portion of his January message to this subject, in laying before the legislature officially communicated declarations of this character.

Disorders and depredations on the frontier, along the Sabine, owing in part to "our proximity to the province of Texas, and the peculiar situation of that country," were also dwelt upon, and earnestly pressed upon the attention of legislators.

The legislature politely non-concurred in the Ohio resolution regarding emancipation of slaves; but concurred in the amendment to the constitution of the United States, proposed by Georgia, respecting the importation of slaves. The amendment provided: "That no part of the constitution of the United States ought to be construed, or shall be construed, to authorize the importation, or ingress, of any person of color into any one of the United States, contrary to the laws of such State."

At the same session, an act was passed prohibiting, after the first day of June, of this year, the bringing of any slave into the State merely for the purpose of sale. Immigrants and *bona fide* citizens might introduce slaves for their own service, but could not sell or exchange them within two years after their introduction. According to the apportionment of this year, under the fourth constitutional census, the House of Representatives consisted of — members .The county of Orleans was entitled to ten representatives, of which the parish and city of Orleans had seven, and the parishes of Plaquemines, St. Bernard and Jefferson, one each. The county of the German Coast, comprising the parishes of St. Charles and St. John Baptist, had two; and the county of Feliciana, embracing the parishes of East and West Feliciana, East Baton Rouge, Washington, St. Helena and St. Tammany, sent ten members, thus ranking with the county of Orleans in the matter of representation.

The closing of Bayou Manchac was authorized, and a Board of Internal Improvements created, consisting of five unsalaried members—elected annually—with the governor as ex-officio president.

Gentlemen of the long robe, or rather the unworthy among them, were the objects of decidedly minatory attention on the part of the legislature this session. It was enacted that an attorney neglecting or refusing—without any legal ground—to pay to his client money collected on the latter's account, should, upon conviction, have his license cancelled, and his name stricken from the roll; and that no lawyer be entitled to relief under the insolvent debtor laws for any sum collected in the capacity aforesaid.

The New Orleans Steam Tow-Boat, and the Balize Steamboat Companies, were organized. The latter was also a tow-boat enterprise, running on the Mississippi.

The board of trustees of the College of Louisiana, at Jackson, were invested with police authority over the town in the interest of the scholastic discipline and good morals.

Two primary schools and one central were established in New Orleans, and the College of Orleans discontinued. The State support of the latter was now voted to the schools; and an unlimited issue of gambling licenses by the State Treasurer was decreed in order to raise a fund for the support [in part] of the Charity Hospital, Orphan Asylums, the College of Louisiana and these newly founded city schools. The latter were under the management of a Board of Regents, who organized the plan of education and system of administration, or delegated the necessary authority to a director elected by them. Reading, writing and arithmetic, with the elements of French and English grammar, were taught in the primary schools. The Central was entrusted to Professors of French, English and Latin languages, mathematics, literature, etc.

It was provided that at least fifty children of the poorer classes should be admitted " in each of those schools " free of charge, but would not be received if under seven or over fourteen years of age.

Another source of revenue for the schools was the tax on the two theatres of the city, which amounted to $3,000—fifteen hundred dollars for each license. Mr. Caldwell, the pioneer of theatrical entertainments in the American quarter, was the proprietor of the theatre in fauxbourg St. Mary—as this quarter was then officially known—the building being the recently demolished Armory Hall. The other was the old Orleans Theatre, then under the management of Mr. Davis. In the imposition of the license tax, the law-makers solemnly declare that the object is not alone an increase of the school fund, but " at the same time to encourage two public establishments, alike useful and ornamental, in this city."

Few Louisianians need to be told what coco or nut grass is. Many and many a broad field have our planters been forced to abandon to the indestructible pest. One Francisco Mow represented to the legislature that he " had discovered an effectual means of destroying the plant known by the name of grass nut," [coco Amer.] and asked that an act be passed authorizing him to charge certain sums for the use of his method of destruction. The legislature appointed a commission to report upon the alleged "effectual means," as well as Mow's claims as the discoverer. Two years were allowed the commissioners within which to report. Whether they reported or not, we are unable to say, but *bon gré, mal gré* Mow, coco flourishes.

Even before this early period, mechanical invention had done much to advance the interests of the cotton producer. Whitney had given him the gin, but a good press was as yet a desideratum. L. A. Verniville was the inventor of the " Lafayette Cotton Press," of those days, which would seem to have possessed some good points, for the legislature protected him in its exclusive manufacture and sales for the period of ten years.

An urgent and very important move in the effort to preserve valuable archives of the State was undertaken this year, under official auspices. A great number of ancient titles to land, running from the year 1702 to the year 1771, and other documents affecting the rights of property in Louisiana, were " kept barely in files in the office of Philip Pedesclaux, notary for New Orleans, exposed to decay," and much in need of intelligent arrangement and classification. Felix Percy was authorized, by act of the legislature, to undertake the needed measures. The documents were to be arranged chronologically and alphabetically, numbered and placed on a general index, and then put away in cedar boxes.

The Parish Judge of East Baton Rouge was required to do the same by any similar documents that might be found in his office.

The remuneration of this labor was at the munificent rate of one cent for each page arranged, numbered and put in the index.

1827. Louisiana was becoming restive under the continued indifference of the general government to her oft repeated demand for an impartial adjustment of the public lands question. She asked simply that the government make such disposition of them in this State as had been had in the older States. Until such disposal of the government lands was had, Louisiana could make but slow advances in the development of those rich and varied resources with which nature had so bounteously endowed her. The grievance was once again brought to the legislature's attention by the governor. A memorial was adopted and forwarded to the Louisiana representatives and senators for presentation in both houses of Congress.

An act, in which members could be equally unanimous—and infinitely more pleasing in its character—was the grateful and gracefully expressed tribute to the memory of President Jefferson. The official record is before us, but we adopt Mr. Gayarré's clear and concise statement :

The legislature, being officially informed by the governor of the death of Thomas Jefferson, and of his having left to his family no other inheritance than that of his illustrious name, voted the sum of ten thousand dollars to his heirs, which was delicately tendered as "a tribute of gratitude" from the State, to the representatives of the man by whom " she had been acquired to the union," and to whom she was indebted for the " blessings of civil and political liberty."

A significant amelioration in the Penal Code was made at this session ; white persons were no more to be sentenced to the pillory. The act refers only to the pillory ; nor is there, in the enactments of this session, any mention made of the whipping post. Maintaining [or supposing] the abolition of both punishments at the same time, Bunner, writing more than forty years back, observes : " It had, indeed, been a matter of wonder, that in such a state of society, where part of the population was free and part in a state of slavery, a punishment of this kind, common to both, should ever have been in force." This is pertinent, perhaps. But, Louisiana corrected the vicious anomaly over half a century ago, while the whipping-post and pillory abide to this day in some parts of the country, where, if slavery no longer prevails, caste asserts itself, *ex necessitate rei.*

Facile dissolution of the marriage tie was regarded with but little favor by society, however complaisant may have been the action of the General Assembly in some instances. But, even with this admission, legislation on this question, had, on the whole, been conservative; the total number of divorces granted from the session of the first State legislature to the present, not being quite two score ; not, indeed, three for each year. Yet, at this session, divorces were made more difficult of attainment. It was enacted that divorce should not be allowed, except for infidelity in either husband or wife, ill-treatment, condemnation to ignominious punishment, or desertion for a period of five years. In case of divorce for adultery, the guilty party could not marry his [or her] partner in guilt, under penalty of being prosecuted for bigamy. Alimony was allowed the wife obtaining a divorce. District Courts throughout the State, and the Parish Courts of New Orleans, were invested with exclusive original jurisdiction in divorce cases, parties being allowed right of appeal.

The Civil Code abolished certain impediments to marriage, on account of affinity, which existed under the Spanish law. To remove all doubt and prevent litigation, the legislature declared valid all marriages between brothers-in-law and sisters-in-law, contracted previous to the promulgation of the Code.

Slaves, under thirty years, might be emancipated in certain cases.

The " New Orleans Steam Ferry," between the city and opposite bank, organized.

The Grand Lodge was authorized to raise by lottery the sum of $35,000, for the erection of a Masonic hall in New Orleans.

A lottery was also permitted for internal improvements in lower portion [left bank] of Iberville parish.

The legislature invited the hero of New Orleans to participate in the celebration of the Eighth of January, the ensuing year.

A survey and map of Red river raft, ordered by the general government, and just completed, copies were presented to the State by the officers engaged thereon, Captain Burch and Lieutenant Lee.

Cotton and raw sugar, of home production, were exempted from auction duties when so disposed of.

The Barataria and Lafourche Canal Company, formed for the purpose of building a canal from the Mississippi to Bayou Lafourche.

Ten weighers of cotton and two of hay, for New Orleans, authorized to be appointed by the governor. A Registrar of Conveyances was also appointed.

The public school system was further amended. The annual appropriation for each parish [Orleans excepted] was at the rate of two dollars and five-eighths for every voter, no parish to receive a greater sum than $1,350, nor less than $800. Parish administrators were to be appointed by the several police juries, school ward trustees by the administrators,

and duly qualified teachers by the latter, after examination. Pay of the
teacher was made dependent upon voucher of the trustees, that he had
complied with the conditions imposed for the management of his school;
among these, that he had not refused admittance to the prescribed
number of indigent children. Any one declining—unless duly excused
—to serve as administrator, was liable to a fine of from twenty-five to
fifty dollars. But administrators and treasurers of their boards were
exempt from jury duty, and from militia duty in time of peace.

The old expedient of a lottery is again resorted to. The College of
Louisiana was allowed to raise $40,000, for buildings, library, etc., and
the Regents of the New Orleans schools a like sum for the erection of a
central and primary schoolhouses. The number of pupils to be received
gratis in each of these city schools was limited to one hundred. These
are the more important points in the laws of this year.

Some important legislation passed this year respecting the State's
interests in the Bank of Louisiana. Our limits forbid more than a
reference. See Act and Resolution, approved March 4, 1827.

The boldest—and most questionable—financing scheme yet devised
was legislated into existence at this session. As it was remarked—the
merchants had their banks, and the planters thought they ought to have
one also. So a charter was obtained incorporating, "The President,
Directors & Co. of the Consolidated Association of the Planters of
Louisiana," capital $2,000,000, [eventually $2,500,000] and exempt from
all taxes. The Association was authorized to deal in all kinds of movable
and immovable property, take mortgages, discount, etc., to the extent of
double its capital, while this itself was based on stock secured by
mortgage on real estate to the extent of each holder's subscription. A
loan of two million dollars was permitted on the issue of bonds, and the
borrowers and lenders of the Association, with sincere reciprocal felici-
tations, went swimmingly down a "bright and shining river" to ——.
Well, let us not anticipate. Such alluring, but delusive, banking wrought
the ruin of not a few fine estates; and the end is not yet. A grim spectre
of the "Association" now haunts our courts and legislative halls.

The pay of the recorder of New Orleans was raised to $1000 this year,
being double that previously paid.

New Orleans at this time consisted, as to municipal divisions, of eight
wards. "The first, beginning at the levee, where it is intersected by the
piece of ground reserved for the prolongation of the Canal Carondelet,
thence running along the intended canal until it intersects the lower line
of the commons of the city; thence along the lower limits of said
commons until it shall intersect the middle of St. Louis street, thence up
the middle of St. Louis street to the levee; thence along the levee to the
place of beginning." So much for the local antiquarian reader. The
eighth ward was circumscribed [in part] by the upper boundary of the
city, which was advanced in 1818 to the lower limits of the Macarty
Plantation. The land thus annexed was constituted the eighth. The
first and sixth wards elected two aldermen each, the others but one each.

The now well known malady, *dengue,* or as it was written in those
days, *denguet,* made its appearance. It was understood to have been
introduced in New Orleans by refugees from Mexico, at the period of her
revolt.

1828. The most interesting event of this year was the visit of General Jackson, in compliance with the request of the legislature, to be present at the celebration of the anniversary of the victory of January 8, 1815. Liberal provision had been made for his reception and entertainment, and both were such as must have deeply stirred the heart of the old soldier, while they were no less worthy of the fervid and generous people whom he had signally served.

Free persons of color from the North and from abroad were not desirable accessions to the population. The wisdom of excluding such being evident, the legislature passed a bill "more effectually to prohibit free negroes and persons of color from entering into this State," but Gov. Johnson vetoed it on the ground of its being opposed to certain provisions of the federal constitution. The presence of free persons of color among the crews of foreign commercial marine in Southern ports had been and continued to be a troublous question in State and federal, and federal international relations.

In his last annual message the governor again brings up the question of the public lands; and the legislature, by unanimous resolve, declared the policy of the government to have "retarded and repressed" the progress of the State. Her senators and representatives were urged to press upon the general government the justice and necessity of an early adjustment.

They were also requested again to bring before the government the scheme of a canal from Lake Pontchartrain to the Mississippi.

Administrators of parish schools were now required to make reports to the grand juries.

The prohibition upon the introduction of slaves for sale was removed.

A decision of the Supreme Court still recognizing the old doctrine, and the new Civil Code not having expressly abrogated it, the legislature declared widows, and unmarried women of age, competent to bind themselves as sureties and endorsers—just as men might enjoy the same seldom envied privilege.

Pensions granted by the State to persons wounded in her defense were made payable five years longer.

A digest of the laws of the State was authorized, and Moreau Lislet commissioned to undertake the same.

The capital of the Planters' Consolidated Association was increased to two million five hundred thousand dollars, the guarantee subscriptions to three millions, and the faith of the State pledged for the payment of the borrowed capital as well as the interest thereon. Duration of the charter was extended to 1843. In return, the State received [nominally] stock to the amount of one million dollars, but could, at no time, be allowed a credit exceeding $250,000, and upon this interest had to be paid. And planters and speculators went on rearing *chateaux en Espagne.*

Among other enactments, arson was made punishable with death, and attempted arson with imprisonment from ten to fifteen years. Pickpockets were incarcerated for terms running from two months to two years, as well as made liable to a fine of five hundred dollars.

A Real Estate Association, with a capital of $300,000, was formed in New Orleans, for the erection of buildings and making other improvements. There were likewise organized, the Mariner's Church Society, Law Society,

Society of Israelites, the Company of Architects, and the New Orleans Jockey Club.

With the close of the year, Pierre Dérbigny succeeded Governor Johnson in office. We quote from Gayarré:

"Governor Dérbigny had previously occupied conspicuous positions in the State, such as Judge of the Supreme Court, and he had also been Secretary of State. His administration was short, for he was killed on the 7th of October, 1829, by being thrown out of his carriage. The constitution devolved the office on the President of the Senate until a governor should be elected by the people and duly qualified. A. Beauvais and J. Dupré, successfully officiated in that capacity, from the governor's death until the 31st of January, 1831, when A. B. Roman was sworn into office."

1829. A census of the voters was ordered.

Land! Land! the acquisition of, and title to, seem to have been among the most absorbing questions of the day. While the State, through her legislature, executive and congressional delegation, was insisting upon an equitable disposal of the public lands within her limits, the governor himself was in correspondence with the authorities of Cuba, "in order to obtain the delivery of the titles and other papers relative to lands and other property in Louisiana, which may be deposited in the Havana."

District Courts were empowered to emancipate minors above the age of nineteen, upon certain prescribed conditions.

The great legist, Edward Livingston, was elected United States Senator.

It is noteworthy, that even in this early period in the political career of the United States, Louisiana had pointed out the vice in our scheme of a federal executive, and proposed the only remedy suggested even to this day. The General Assembly adopted a resolution—inviting concurrence of the other States—that the constitution be so amended as to make the term of the President and Vice President six years, and that the President be ineligible afterwards.

Also deserving of attention is the legislation regarding the introduction of slaves. Its main aim was the exclusion of slaves of a worthless or vicious character, brought hither for sale or hire, from the other Southern States. It was made unlawful to introduce a slave child of ten years, or under, separate from its mother; and any one selling such child [separate from its mother] was liable to a fine of one to two thousand dollars, with imprisonment from six months to one year, and forfeiture of the slave so sold.

As to the slave marts and the public sale of slaves, the City Council of New Orleans was required to make such regulations as were meet and proper, being expressly enjoined from permitting the exposition of slaves in the public and most frequented quarters. Copies of the act were transmitted, by resolution of the General Assembly, to the governors of Mississippi and Alabama, and publication made in the newspapers of Maryland, Virginia, Kentucky, Tennessee and Missouri.

A law was enacted providing for a complete levee system throughout the State, and the maintenance of the same. It is elaborate in its provisions, amounting to no fewer than fifty-six sections. In connection, mention may be made of the resolutions of the legislature calling upon the general government to undertake the improvement of the Louisiana reach of the Mississippi, its tributaries, outlets and passes, and the bayou St. John, with the suggestion that General Bernard be detailed to make a sketch of a general system of improvements.

Covington made the seat of justice of St. Tammany parish.

Malicious destruction of the public works of a corporation, carrying of concealed weapons, infliction of a wound, with intent to kill, or the procuring of the escape of a criminal condemned for a capital crime, were punishable with imprisonment at hard labor of from one to ten years.

Owners were required to make oath that the lists of their taxable property given to the assessors were "full and true." The attorney-general and district attorneys were charged with enforcing the requirement, and bringing it to the attention of the grand juries. Here is a lesson of the past for these days of fraudulent assessments.

The New Orleans Gas Light Company was incorporated—charter to run twenty-five years.

1830. Donaldsonville was now the seat of government, and the second session of the tenth legislature was "begun and held" on Monday, January 4. Among its first acts—if not the first—was the incorporation of our now venerable Pontchartrain Railroad Company. The enterprise was, we believe, the fifth of the kind in the United States. The list of incorporators included names then, or subsequently, prominent in the city's progress—Ex-Gov. Claiborne, Saml. J. Peters, Edmund Forstall, George Eustis, John L. Lewis, and others. All, save one, are but memories. General Lewis still moves among us, a fine type of the old-time Louisiana gentleman—his

> "* * Age as a lusty winter,
> Frosty, but kindly."

About this period, says Bunner, several persons were detected travelling about the country and endeavoring to excite the blacks to insurrection; and the populace would have punished them very summarily had they been permitted. The legislature, thereupon, passed a law, making it death for any one to excite the slaves against the whites, either by writings, sermons, speeches made at the bar or in the theatre, or to bring into the State any pamphlets having that tendency and for that object. Teaching slaves to read was also forbidden.

Any slave, selling liquor without permission of his master, was punished by whipping, and any white man buying liquor of a slave was liable to a fine.

Provision was made for running the line marking the boundary between Louisiana and the Territory of Arkansas, agreeable to Act of Congress, approved May 19, 1828.

An act of the legislature provided that a governor should be voted for in the general election of July, and that one of the persons so voted for, be afterwards chosen as governor, for the constitutional term of four years.

The great rafts, which forbid navigation of the Atchafalaya up to this time, were now being brought to the attention of the general government.

Two thousand dollars were appropriated for opening bayou des Glaises to navigation.

The agent engaged to distribute vaccine matter throughout the State, was voted an annual compensation of five hundred dollars.

Another step towards the abolition of imprisonment for debt; an insolvent debtor might, after serving his term of imprisonment, take the benefit of the insolvent laws as to a fine and costs, for which he had been sentenced and committed, until they were paid.

The famous Louisiana Legion was voted twenty-five hundred dollars from the State Treasury, to provide uniforms, etc., for such members as could but ill-afford the expense.

Stringent laws were enacted, excluding free persons of color from the State, requiring even the departure, within sixty days, of free negroes and mulattoes, who had arrived since the year 1825. Those who had settled in the State between the years 1812 and 1825 were required to register their names with the parish judges, and such free persons of color amenable to this law as were property owners, were allowed one year for the disposal of their estates.

Every provision of the law makes it evident that it was a time for vigilance. Fine and imprisonment were decreed for any white person— for any free person of color, severe measures of incarceration and fine, with banishment to follow—who by writing, printing or speaking, disturb the public peace or security " in relation to the slaves of the people of this State, or [tend] to diminish that respect which is commanded to the free people of color for the whites,   *   *   *   or to destroy that line of distinction which the law has established between the several classes of this community." All which was a necessity of the situation. The dominant race in a mixed community is now and then forced to assert, with more or less emphasis, its supremacy. Especially is a sharp lesson salutary for the aspiring mongrel.

A company was formed in New Orleans for the refining of sugar, under the W. A. Archbald patent rights; also were incorporated the first German Protestant Church, the " Mississippi Fire Company," and the "Volunteer Fire Engine Company, No. 1," same city.

Franklin, St. Mary parish, and Thibodauxville, Lafourche Interior, declared incorporated towns.

Louisiana was not in accord with other Southern States on the tariff of 1828. Declining to concur in the resolutions of Mississippi, the legislature declared it did not perceive the unconstitutionality or impolicy of the measure, or that the State had suffered any injury therefrom. In this great tariff issue Louisiana ranged herself on the side of Vermont. *Tempora mutantur, etc.*

The severity of the winter, which set in early in December, and lasted through February, destroyed the orange trees.

The population of Louisiana now amounted to 215,275, having increased two-fifths in the last ten years.

1831. New Orleans was again made the seat of government. The first session of the tenth legislature was begun in Donaldsonville on Monday, January 3, was adjourned, and resumed in the city on the 8th of January. On the 31st, A. B. Roman was inaugurated as governor. The new executive had much experience in public affairs, having been Speaker of the House of Representatives, and previously a District Judge.

The law of 1829, respecting the introduction of slaves, was relieved of some of its restrictive features. The prohibition, however, was made absolute as to slaves from Alabama, Mississippi, Florida and Arkansas.

The edict of last year, with regard to free persons of color and residence, was also deprived of its harshest feature. Expulsion was reserved only for the worthless element.

Maunsel White, Joseph Lallande, Persifer Smith and others, this year organized the Orleans Fire Company.

Natural fathers, or mothers, were empowered to legitimate their natural children, *provided* the parents could have lawfully contracted marriage, and that there did not exist on the legitimating parent side, "ascendants or legitimate descendants." The act revived law seventh, title fifteenth, of the fourth *Partidas*, repealed in the Civil Code.

Monroe, Ouachita parish, ceased to be an incorporated town.

Pierre Abadie was another discoverer of "an efficient method of destroying the plant known by the name of nut grass, [coco Amer.]"

He, too, sought the intervention of the legislature for the protection of his property rights in his "discovery," and as in the case of Miro, had his legislative commission to examine and report. So far as reports may be looked for, both these discoveries would appear to have fallen stillborn. It may be, though, that pigeon-holing was not unknown even in this early period.

Gambling houses were prohibited outside of New Orleans.

Six hundred copies of Mr. Gayarré's "Historical Essay on Louisiana," were purchased by the State for distribution to the several parishes, under the supervision and in the discretion of their respective Boards of School Administrators.

An annual appropriation of five thousand dollars each, for four years, was voted to Franklin College, St. Landry parish, Jefferson College, St. James, and College of Louisiana, East Feliciana. Other State support of the latter was not affected by this appropriation.

The sum of twenty thousand dollars was allowed for the arming and equipping of the volunteer military.

Charters were granted to the New Orleans Canal and Banking Company, capital, four million dollars; the City Bank, capital, two millions; the College of Jefferson, the West Feliciana Railroad Company, and the New Orleans Hotel Company.

Mr. Livingston having resigned, Geo. A. Waggaman was elected United States Senator.

A tremendous storm setting in from the east, afterward shifting to the south, and continuing from the 16th to the 17th of August, drove back the waters of the Gulf into the lakes and bayous, so as to flood New Orleans and the whole country bordering the sea. The water, indeed, was so high that many vessels were driven on to the levee. The damage to the town exceeded a hundred thousand dollars, and the loss of the planters was still more severe. [Bunner.]

The condition of the passes of the Mississippi was now a subject of grave consideration. The legislature affirmed that the difficulties in the way of entrance were daily increasing, and demanded the immediate interposition of the general government for their removal.

1832. The subject was again brought up in the legislature this year, and the plan of Mr. Buisson for the Fort St. Philip Ship Canal, was warmly approved. He submitted a chart of the mouths of the river with the adjacent coast, and proposed to dig a canal, six miles and a half long, commencing a few miles below the fort, and entering the sea about four miles south of Breton Island. Government undertook the work a few years later, but the scheme "was found to be impracticable, as it [the canal] filled with fresh accumulations of sand nearly as fast as it was dug out, and was accordingly abandoned."

In connection with the scheme just noticed should be chronicled the "Lake Borgne Navigation Company," as it was corporately styled. Commissioners were appointed to procure surveys, plans and estimates for a canal six feet deep, from Bayou Mazart, which debouches from [or embouches into] Lake Borgne, to some part of New Orleans, or its suburbs. As soon as these preliminary steps had been satisfactorily taken, the commissioners—who were really the soul and body of the movement—were to commence the work. There were to be buying of lands, with or without consent of owners; much digging and bridging and basining, buoys and beacons at the bar, and a lighthouse at the entrance to Bayou Mazart. And, it all went out in darkness.

Another large banking establishment, with, of course, the credit of the State pledged for its borrowed millions! "The Union Bank of Louisiana," capital eight million dollars. The State gave its bonds, and the subscribers to the bank stock gave mortgages on real estate, improved or unimproved, and slaves. How recklessly they borrowed and endorsed in those years.

Other incorporated enterprises this year were the Amite Navigation Company, Levee Steam Cotton Press, and the Western Marine and Fire Insurance Company.

Jackson, East Feliciana, and Covington, St. Tammany, were incorporated.

Office of State Civil Engineer created.

The old Charity Hospital was purchased from the city for a statehouse. It was situated in the square bounded by Canal, Phillipa, Common and Carondelet streets.

Extensive powers were given the municipal council for the laying out of new streets, improvements of public places, etc., in New Orleans, its suburbs and banlieues.

Parishes of Carroll and Livingston established.

Fifty thousand dollars were appropriated for the erection of a penitentiary at Baton Rouge.

More legislative dealing in gambling. Any one could now open a gambling hell in New Orleans, who could pay the annual tax of seven thousand five hundred dollars. This revenue and the tax on the two theatres, [now raised to four thousand dollars each] were devoted to asylums, Charity Hospital and schools of New Orleans.

This year the Asiatic cholera, after extending its ravages over Asia and a part of Europe, made its appearance in Canada, whither it was supposed to have been brought by an English vessel. Passing through the States to the north and west, says Bunner, it at length reached Louisiana; and in New Orleans alone, not less than five thousand persons fell victims. The yellow fever was raging at the time. Many unfortunates were supposed to have been buried alive; while others, thus suffering under quite different illnesses, were treated for cholera, and killed by the violence of the remedies. The blacks had been spared by the yellow fever, but the cholera almost exterminated them. There were plantations in the environs of New Orleans which lost from seventy to eighty slaves in two or three days. And, adds our chronicler, the disease appeared again the following year, but with greatly diminished violence.

1833. A census of the voters was taken, and a State Agricultural Society established. The latter was another of those speculative, financing concerns, in which Louisiana has been so fecund.

Nor was the year without its usual fungus growth of banks. Now came into being the Citizens Bank, with a capital of twelve million dollars, the Commercial, which was to expend $100,000 annually in the construction of water works, and the Mechanics and Traders, with a capital of two million dollars. The acts incorporating these banking institutions are among the most suggestive readings that have ever fallen in the way of this writer. The performances have sadly fallen short of the hope inspiring programmes.

J. H. Caldwell obtained an "exclusive privilege [25 years] for introducing and vending gas lights in New Orleans and its faubourgs, and particularly the faubourgs of St. Mary and Marigny."

The College of Jefferson was voted twenty thousand dollars, annual instalments of five thousand.

Old St. Patrick's and the first Congregational Church were incorporated, also the Orleans Cotton Press, the Lyceum, the New Orleans Steam Ferry Co., Bayou Bœuf and Red River Navigation Co., the Louisiana Sugar Refining Co., the Louisiana Steam Tow-boat Co., and the New Orleans Commercial Library.

Lafayette, now the favorite Garden District of New Orleans, was raised to the dignity and responsibilities of a town.

A Board of Public Works was created, with a fund for improvement of navigable waters and highways.

The Secretary of State had shouldered upon him the office of Superintendent of Public Schools, with an allowance for "only reasonable expenses," and provision was made for a State Library.

Charters was granted to the New Orleans and Carrollton Railroad, the Clinton and Port Hudson, for two in Rapides parish, and the governor was instructed to take one hundred shares in the West Feliciana. But this year lotteries were abolished.

This is one of the most interesting years in our annals, and a few more words are needed to complete the annalist's sketch.

The exports of New Orleans were estimated at this time to be about thirty-seven million dollars, twenty millions of which were the produce of Louisiana alone. Sugar was a large element in the productive industry of the State, and the continued prosperity of this industry depended in no small measure upon the tariff policy of the general government. In regard to this subject, we quote the following: "The first blow to the agricultural industry of Louisiana was from the new tariff, providing for a gradual reduction of duties on foreign goods to 20 per cent., taking off every two years one-tenth of all there was above that, as fixed by the former tariff. The minimum was to be reached on the first of July, 1842. The effect of this change would be to diminish the price of foreign sugars, and, consequently, that of the domestic article. The first few years but little alteration took place, and the sugar trade was in a highly flourishing condition. On the strength of the tariff of 1816, fixing the duty on imported sugars at three cents, the culture had been greatly extended, and the crop had increased since 1828 from fifteen thousand to forty-five thousand hogsheads. At that time there were more than three hundred sugar plantations, with a capital of thirty-four million dollars, twenty-one thousand men, twelve thousand head of working cattle, and steam engines equal to sixteen hundred and fifty horse power, being employed in this branch of industry; and from this time to 1830, nearly four hundred new establishments were formed, with a capital of six millions, making the whole number of sugar plantations no less than seven hundred, with a capital of forty millions. Louisiana already furnished half the sugar consumed in the country, and bade fair to supply the rest. The sugar planters were at this time looked upon as the most prosperous class in society. They had two banks, which liberally supplied them with funds; and a third, called the Citizens' Bank, with a capital of twelve million dollars, was now started. The plan of this institution was to advance to any planter, on a mortgage of his lands, slaves and cattle, one-half of their estimated value in specie, at six per cent. for twenty years, he being obliged to pay back each year one-twentieth of the sum lent.

The abundance of paper money gave rise also to other speculating companies, and among them four new railroad companies. In short, there were chartered this year corporate institutions with an aggregate capital amounting to the enormous sum of eighteen million nine hundred and eighty-four thousand dollars. Never had the legislative assembly been so extravagantly liberal. In this stock-jobbing system, real estate was inflated to an exorbitant nominal value. During the past year a banking corporation had paid half a million dollars for a piece of land which might have been bought for fifty or sixty thousand but a short time before. Towns were laid out in the environs of New Orleans; and the purchasers of lots no sooner began to realize large profits by their sale, than they rose to twice, ten times, nay, a hundred times their actual value.
*   *   *   *   *   *   *

Money difficulties came on apace at this time, and 15, 18, and 24 per cent. was demanded on good paper. Bankruptcies * * began to take place, * * and to remedy, or rather increase the evil, there was a loud call for more banks. * * [Bunner.]

1834. After the reckless chartering of the late years, it is somewhat reassuring to know that the aggregate capital of the institutions incorporated this year amounted to but one million six hundred and twenty thousand dollars. Among these institutions were the following:

The Company of Architects of the 8th District of New Orleans; a building association for the district named, among whose directors were Pierre Soulé and Th. Pilie; the Pontchartrain Steamboat Company, a leading spirit of which was Wm. Bagley; the Commercial Insurance Company; the Atlantic Marine & Fire Insurance Company; the St. Bernard Railroad Company, which was to construct a road from the Mississippi to some point on Bayou Terre-Aux-Bœufs in St. Bernard Parish; the Planters' Sugar Refining Company, an association of sugar planters of the parishes of St. James, Ascension, Assumption, and Lafourche Interior, for the purpose set forth in corporate title; and the New Orleans Improvement Company, whose efforts were restricted to the section bounded by Levee, Canal, Rampart and Esplanade streets.

The port limits of the city were again extended to the lower line of the parish of Jefferson, and three miles down the left bank, "from the centre of the square of the city."

A Chamber of Commerce was organized, and the "Presbyterian Church and Congregation for the city and parish of New Orleans" incorporated; among the incorporators being Saml. H. Harper, Chas. Gardiner, Alfred Hennen, J. S. Walton, and J. A. Maybin.

Audubon received from his native State the paltry recognition of the purchase of one copy of his great work, "The Birds of America."

Jurisdiction over the island of Petites Coquilles, opposite western branch of Pearl river; over Gordon's Island, near South Pass of the Mississippi; and over Wagner's Island, Southwest Pass, was ceded to the United States, as sites for the erection and maintenance of lighthouses; and over Grand-Terre for the erection of a fort. In the act ceding jurisdiction over these sites, Louisiana asserts her sovereignty and right of eminent domain by the usual proviso of reversion, execution of State process, etc. If no better than a county, or at best a province, how could she thus vaunt herself? and the "national government" accepted without protest!

The most important legislation of the year was the "Act relative to Steamboats." Explosions, collisions and sinkings had been so frequent, and had resulted in such appalling loss of life and great destruction of property, that public opinion demanded legislative interference in the running and general management of river steam craft, provided inspection as to condition, etc. The Louisiana law required all captains and owners of steamboats to have their boilers examined by an engineer appointed by the State, under penalty of fine and imprisonment, besides being responsible for all losses or damage to the goods aboard, and in case of the loss of life, to the punishment provided for manslaughter. The engineer was punishable for giving a false certificate; the amount and storage of gunpowder as freight had prominent attention, and rules were prescribed to be observed by boats when passing each other on rivers and streams. Copies of the law, in French and English, were required to be posted in conspicuous places on board every boat. It is on record that from 1816 to 1838, two hundred and thirty steamboats were lost, of which one hundred and thirty-seven were destroyed by explosions, occasioning a loss of nearly seventeen hundred lives. In the explosion of the Ben Sherrod, one hundred and thirty persons were blown up; and in that of the Monmouth, three hundred. Both occurred on the Mississippi in 1837.

This year, says our chronicler, Bunner, was marked by a horrible discovery. One of those interpositions of Providence, which often brings to light crimes perpetrated in darkness, disclosed the dreadful atrocities committed by a woman who had hitherto been admitted to the first society of New Orleans. Her name was Lalaurie. The house taking fire, while efforts were making to extinguish it, a rumor was spread that some slaves were confined in an outhouse which was locked up. Mr. Canonge, judge of the Criminal Court, applied to her for the key, which she refused. He, with some other gentlemen broke into the building, and discovered in different parts of it, seven slaves chained in various ways, and all bearing marks of the most horrible treatment. One of them declared that he had been confined for five months, with no other sustenance than a handful of meal a day.

* * * As soon as she found that her barbarity was on the

58

point of being discovered, she contrived to make her escape, and, strange to tell, by the aid of some of her own slaves, who conveyed her to a carriage, while the crowd was occupied at the other end of the house.

Had she remained, her life probably would have been taken, for the fury of the people knew no bounds; they broke into the house, destroyed every article of furniture, and would have even torn down the house itself had they not been restrained by the authorities.   *   *   Further evidences of her cruelty were discovered the next day, when more than one body was dug up in the yard.   The guilty woman reached a northern port in safety, and embarked for France under an assumed name, the husband and youngest child had joined her, and some suspicion being excited among the passengers, they questioned the child, and ascertained who she was. No one spoke to her during the rest of the voyage. Arriving in France, she was soon discovered and universally shunned; on one occasion being driven out of the theatre.   If she is still living, speculates the chronicler, she has probably been obliged to seek a deeper retirement to conceal her guilt.

1835.   E. D. White, who had served several years in Congress, succeeded Governor Roman.   The new executive, in his inaugural, touched upon the tariff compromise measures, so far as they affected the State's agricultural interest, and the still unsettled land question.

The twelfth legislature proved itself equal to the seemingly required standard of prodigality, in the chartering of banks, etc., and pledging the credit of the State.   Among the earliest of its measures was the incorporating of the New Orleans and Nashville Railroad Company, whose proposed enterprise is yet to be accomplished.   The city had also charters for two Insurance Companies, the Medical Society, the Firemen's Charitable Association, the Louisiana Cotton Seed Oil Factory, for the building of the Exchange, and for a grand speculating concern, called "The New Orleans Draining Company"—with a capital of one million dollars—which was to drain, clear and open out for settlement all the swamps between the city, its suburbs and Old Ponchartrain; the State and municipality both to be shareholders.

The legislature likewise generously voted to make the State a stockholder in the Barataria & Lafourche Canal Company, to the extent of five hundred shares, and commendably granted appropriations for improving several rivers.

Springfield, Livingston parish, was made the seat of justice, and Washington, St. Landry, incorporated.

The banks chartered were: the New Orleans Gaslight and Banking Company, capital $6,000,000; Exchange Bank, capital $2,000,000; Carrollton Railroad Bank, capital $3,000,000, and the Atchafalaya Railroad, capital $2,000,000.

While the banker was thus being made a "chartered libertine," gambling of the non-respectable kind was receiving its *coup de grace.*   A law was enacted at this same session imposing a fine of from five to ten thousand dollars, with imprisonment for not less than one nor more than five years, upon the keepers of gambling hells.   Still the fraternity throve; they only hid their heads.

1836.   So far as their external relations were concerned, Louisianians were moved mainly by the struggles of the Texans for independence.

Their sympathies were so ardent as to call from the governor a proclamation of neutrality. Next in interest, was the war against the Seminoles in Florida. The general government having made its requisition on the State for troops, "her quota," says Mr. Gayarré, "was furnished with great alacrity in ten days." Seventy-five thousand dollars was appropriated by the State for the equipment, etc., of its military contingent.

At its session this year the general assembly chartered the Merchants Bank, capital one million dollars; conferred banking privileges on the New Orleans Improvement Company, capital two millions; the same upon the Pontchartrain Railroad Company, and allowing an addition of one million to its capital, and pledged the credit of the State in favor of the Citizens' Bank, "an overgrown institution, * * which paid its cashier ten thousand dollars a year, and attempted to negotiate a loan of twelve million dollars in Europe, in which it failed for want of security," and the St. Charles Hotel Company, born of the Exchange and Banking Company.

Six railroad companies were incorporated, viz: the Springfield & Liberty, the Livingston, Lake Providence & Red River, Baton Rouge & Clinton, Iberville, and the Orleans & Plaquemine, the latter to construct a road through the prairie between the city and the English Turn.

Mr. Caldwell got a charter for his "St. Charles Theatre, Arcade & Arcade Bath Company;" Mr. T. J. Davis his for the "Orleans Theatre Company," and the New Orleans Floating Dry Dock Company was launched.

Cheneyville, Rapides parish, and Vermillionville, Lafayette parish, incorporated.

Robert Carter Nicholas, was chosen United States Senator.

By act of the legislature New Orleans was "divided into three separate sections, each with distinct municipal powers," the Mayor exercising the same powers in each municipality, and ruling as chief magistrate of the whole city.

The aggregate capital of the institutions chartered by this twelfth general assembly, amounted to $39,345,000. "The mania of speculation had now seized on all minds and turned all heads, and the effervescence of the people of Paris, excited by the Mississippi lands in the time of Law, had never been more violent. * * * A state of affairs now existed in Louisiana of the most extraordinary character. An enormous value was placed upon lands covered with water; towns were laid out in the midst of cypress swamps; prairies were set on fire, and speculators were ready to snatch at every islet. Some few, shrewder than the rest, or favored by fortune, succeeded in amassing riches, but a far greater number were irretrievably ruined." To make the existing state of things in the end still worse, the banks were profuse in their discounts, and did not scruple to issue paper to five times the amount of the available capital."

1837. At length, continues our authority, on the 13th of May, the disaster which had been so long preparing for Louisiana, fell upon her. Fourteen of the banks of New Orleans suspended specie payments. In this emergency, and to afford the community a temporary and partial relief, the three municipalities each issued bills from the value of one shilling to four dollars, and in a short time companies and even individuals claimed the same privilege, so that the State was inundated with rag money. Another cause of the existing distress was the new tariff, which had depreciated the value of American sugar in proportion as the duty had been reduced on the foreign article. At a former period the culture of cotton had been abandoned for that of sugar. The contrary was now the case; cane was destroyed and cotton planted in its place. One hundred and sixty-six sugar plantations were given up; and cotton alone was destined to restore prosperity to Louisiana. The crop of this article in 1834 had been 150,000 bales—equivalent to sixty-two million pounds—and this year it increased to 225,000 bales, or ninety-four million pounds. The large profits that had been realized increased the rashness of speculators, and their eagerness to purchase raised the price to 18 and 20 cents. These prices were wholly unwarranted by the state of the markets in Europe, and the losses were immense. Numerous bankruptcies followed, some for great amounts. Lands could no longer be sold; plans of towns were of no value but to be gazed on as pictures, and the fortunes based on them fell even more suddenly than they had risen. Usurers were now the only class that prospered, and they reaped a rich harvest from the calamities of others.

Still associations went on forming for this or that more or less legitimate venture, and were duly incorporated by the legislature. Among these were the New Orleans & Texas Navigation, and Mexican Gulf Railway Companies; the Madison & Covington, Natchitoches & Sabine, Vidalia, Harrisonburg & Alexandria, and the Louisiana and Mississippi railroad projects; and the Lake Borgne Navigation Company, which proposed to dig a canal from a point in the lower portion of New Orleans to Bayou Bienvenu.

A loan to the amount of five hundred thousand dollars in State bonds was made to the New Orleans & Nashville Railroad, and its nominal stock increased by three million dollars.

The State accepted her allotted portion under the act of Congress making distribution of the surplus revenue of the general government.

Resolutions approving the views of the governor, as set forth in his message, respecting abolition societies, concurring in the declarations of Kentucky and South Carolina on the same crusading organizations, and recommending a convention, were adopted by the general assembly; and Hon. Alex. Mouton was chosen United States Senator, vice Hon. Alex. Porter, resigned.

1838. The great financial crash could not be retrieved in a day. Property of all kind was more or less depreciated in value, and industry was all but paralyzed. Doctors of finance, or financial quacks, were on hand with their nostrums, and many were looking for an extra session of the legislature, expecting relief from that quarter. There was no extra session.

A bill passed the senate, at the regular session of the general assembly, appointing a commission to examine into and report upon the conditions of the banks, imposing certain restrictions upon the privileges of these institutions, but allowing them to issue post-notes payable in 1840. But the house and senate were not in accord, and the measure fell through. It embodied the suggestions of Mr. Albert Hoa.

Subsequently, the banks determined upon the issue of post-notes, the expedient to be confined to the period of suspension of specie payments.

The Red River, Baton Rouge & Clinton, and the Mexican Gulf Railroad Companies, were recipients of State aid, in bonds to the amount of $275,000, and the " Bath Railroad Company," a charter. " Bath " is now but a little known name of some indefinite spot on the shore of Lake Ponchartrain, parish of Jefferson.

Caldwell, Caddo and Madison parishes were erected, and Port Hudson, Springfield and Thibodeaux, incorporated.

Preliminary steps toward the education of the deaf and dumb—which culminated in the State asylum—were authorized at this session.

The agitation of the slavery question was spreading and growing. The lower house of Congress was becoming the scene of unseemly debate. Eastern and Western members vituperatively inveighed; Southern members vainly appealed to the guarantees of the federal constitution, or parliamentary rules, or, when some negrophilist's speech exceeded all license, left the house. The general assembly of Louisiana, at the present session, declared in emphatic language, its approval of the course pursued by the Southern members of Congress, "in manifesting their determination, manfully and with energy, to resist by all constitutional means, any attempt which may be made to abolish slavery in any portion of the Union by the action of Congress."

1839. The banks had resumed specie payments, and the general assembly, recognizing that the suspension was "the result of a general derangement of the monetary system of the country," [as the act expressed it,] reinstated them in their chartered rights, privileges, etc. The general assembly also passed resolutions in endorsement of the United States Bank, declaring that a national bank, properly constituted, an important auxiliary in carrying into effect the power of Congress to create and regulate a currency of equal value, credit and use, wherever it may circulate, and to facilitate the fiscal operations of the government.

The Citizens' Bank was required to establish seven branches, with an aggregate capital of $3,000,000, and State bonds to the amouut of $1,400,000, were emitted to the three municipalities of New Orleans.

" To promote direct intercourse between New Orleans and Europe," the State took two hundred thousand dollars of the capital stock of the " Steam Trans-Atlantic Company of Louisiana," and to " expedite the construction of Clinton and Port Hudson Railroad," issued bonds to the amount of five hundred thousand dollars. The Attakapas Canal [through Lake Verret] Company received twenty-five thousand dollars of State funds.

Union parish was created, and the towns of Iberia and Shreveport incorporated. The Milne Asylums for Orphans, the Roman Catholic Church of St. Vincent de Paul, and the Methodist Episcopal Church in New Orleans, were incorporated. Among the trustees of the latter were Ed. McGhee and T. K. Price.

The number of justices of the Supreme Court was raised to five, the Commercial Court of New Orleans created, and a law against betting on elections enacted. The latter forbade any person to stake or hazard upon elections, popular or in legislature, under penalty of a fine equal to the amount hazarded.

The office of auditor on auction sales in New Orleans was created.

Emissaries of New England's intermeddling philanthrophy had become objects of legislative attention, and an act was passed respecting the carrying away of slaves, making the captain or owner of any vessel, on board which a slave should be found, without the consent of his owner, responsible to the latter for any loss he might sustain, also liable to a fine of five hundred dollars for every such slave.

On the 12th of February, the New Orleans Exchange, a splendid edifice, was destroyed by fire. The loss is set down by one authority at the very high figure of six hundred thousand dollars.

February 4, A. B. Roman succeeded Governor White, being a second time elected governor. In his inaugural he referred in emphatic language to the anti-slavery agitation, and the invasion of the State by a body of armed men from the Republic of Texas.

The State was now divided into thirty-eight parishes and ten judicial districts.

1840. The fourteenth legislature signalized itself at the second session by abolishing imprisonment for debt. It also made appropriations for the improvement of several bayous, the cutting of a channel through the falls at Alexandria, and for the removal of Red River raft; created the parishes of Union and Calcasieu; incorporated the town of Mandeville, and the old Jefferson & Lake Ponchartrain Railroad, and gave registrars of mortgages to Natchitoches and Jefferson parishes.

The year is memorable for an extraordinary rise of the Mississippi. "Never had the river worn so terrific an aspect since 1782, when the Attakapas and Opelousas were partly covered by its waters. It was now swollen to within a few inches of the highest levees, and in several places flowed over them, and inundated the country. The crevasses were numerous, and some of them of great width. The lands of Lafourche and Concordia were completely under water. The Red River, driven back by the increased volume of the Mississippi, inundated its fine cotton lands. But at last the flood subsided, and compensated by the rich deposit it left for the mischief it had done. New fertility was given to the soil, and never was the crop more abundant." [Bunner.]

The number of sugar plantations at this time amounted to 525, employing 40,000 laborers, and a mechanical power equal to ten thousand horse. The population of the State amounted to 350,000; at the time of its cession, the number of inhabitants of the Territory was but 60,000. Her progress was as undoubted, as were her resources for great and enduring prosperity. But the banks, unable to stem the tide of general financial embarrassment, again suspended specie payments.

1841. Their condition was, however, daily growing better, and their reputation for solvency widening. Their notes were but little below par, and circulated extensively through the Southwest.

The State was their debtor at this period to the amount of $850,000, "and it was generally believed at the time," says Gayarré, "on the authority of persons who had made the calculation, that the members of the legislature, in their private capacity, owed to these institutions about one million dollars." Such relations render sound, not to say honest banking, impossible. Little wonder legislators pledged the credit of the State so wantonly.

The Clinton & Port Hudson Railroad was ordered forfeited to the State, the company being unable to meet the interest on the bonds

[$389,000] authorized by the legislature to expedite the construction of the road.

The work of opening the mouth of the Atchafalaya at the Mississippi, and that of Grand River at its junction with Bayou Plaquemines, was undertaken by the Board of Public Works; the cutting off of points on Red River, by the removal of which its navigation might be improved, was ordered, and appropriations continued for the cleaning out of several navigable bayous.

Lotteries were *again* "generally abolished."

The long unheeded claim of the State to her share of the public lands within her domain had been at length acceded to. But many thousand acres of the grant were of little or no value.

A bill was passed at this session [first of the fifteenth legislature] submitting to popular vote the question of calling a convention to amend the constitution.

1842. The closing session of this legislature was marked by earnest work; the chief matter for consideration being what we may term the financial situation. Some remedial measures were urgently demanded. Banking privileges had been so inconsiderately accorded and so recklessly used, there had been so much borrowing, discounting, and of speculative venture based on unlimited credit, that only the law-making power could interpose with the needed corrective and restrictive legislation. A law was enacted prohibiting banks from further violation of their charters, providing for the liquidation of such as were insolvent, and creating a "Board of Currency" to see that they rigidly complied with their charters and by-laws. Two were paying specie; during the year seven of them went by the board, leaving nine in sound financial condition, with a reserve of $4,565,925 against the comparatively trivial circulation of $1,261,514. But so severe had been the lesson, that even with this strength the banks would not venture to afford the usual aid to even legitimate commercial and industrial enterprise.

A law was also passed retrenching the expenses of the State government. Its expenditures had for years been extravagant and in excess of revenue. A direct tax upon real estate in the several parishes, as well as other levies in the way of taxation, made, to increase the resources of the government.

According to the apportionment of this year, the house of representatives consisted of fifty-nine members, the parish of Orleans sending ten.

A much more efficient organization of the militia—in detail, and as a whole—was ordered this year.

In the general financial scheme of retrenchment and reform, the public school system also received attention. The parishes [Orleans excepted] were now to provide each a school fund of from two hundred to four hundred dollars, receiving from the State double the amount it raised; Orleans received $7,500, the parish being required to tax itself for the balance necessary to meet the authorized expenditure; the sums of ten thousand dollars to the Louisiana College, five thousand to the College of Franklin, annually to each, and ten thousand a year to the College of Jefferson, were voted. The cutting of a channel through the falls at Alexandria was abandoned, and State appropriations for several other purposes were withdrawn.

The legislature was in a penitent mood. Asylums, however, and the Charity Hospital, were not neglected : to do so would not be like Louisiana in any period of her history. That truly philanthropic body, the Howard Association of New Orleans, organized this year, and the First Presbyterian Church of the City of Lafayette—now Fourth District of New Orleans.

The Civil Code was so amended that it was no longer required a minister of religion should be a resident of the parish when he performed the marriage ceremony.

A disastrous fire having occurred in Baton Rouge, the legislature voted the sum of two thousand dollars for the relief of the destitute sufferers : also incorporated the towns of Bayou Sara, Farmerville and St. Charles, of Grand Coteau.

Further legislation was had respecting the immigration of free persons of color into the State, and resolutions were adopted as to the action of New York in her inter-State obligations under the fugitive slave law.

1843. Governor Roman was succeeded by Alexander Mouton in January. The new executive was an experienced politician, having been United States Senator for several years, and previously speaker of the general assembly. His outgivings show him to be a Democrat of pronounced Jeffersonian type. This he evidenced in his inaugural, wherein he also dwelt upon the old question of the public lands, and spoke with unreserve of the lamentable condition of the finances of the State. Her liabilities—loans and faith pledged—amounted to some millions, while the ordinary expenses of the government exceeded the income by about one hundred thousand dollars. The old banking system was at fault, and it was necessary to render its revival impossible. Acts were passed to facilitate the liquidation of insolvent banks—a special enactment for the property banks—and the insolvent laws were revived.

Under the new congressional apportionment, the State was entitled to four members in the lower house, and accordingly there was a re-districting of the State.

Louisianians were not growing unmindful of the great services rendered them by "Old Hickory." Resolutions were adopted by the legislature this year, pledging the State to refund to General Jackson, the fine (with interest) imposed upon him by Judge Hall, of the United States District Court at New Orleans, in the event congress should fail to do so.

Five new parishes were created, viz : Bossier, DeSoto, Franklin, Sabine, and Tensas. Marksville and St. Martinsville incorporated.

A court of errors and appeals in criminal cases was organized.

The opening of a road around the raft in Red River was authorized. The Metropolis had, besides other attention from the legislature, incorporation of the Medico-Chirurgical Society; the Medical College of Louisiana; Medical College of Orleans; the French Society, and the Association of Veterans.

A Glass Manufacturing Company, parish of Jefferson, received a charter; and in this year the New Orleans & Carrollton Railroad was allowed to use locomotives in the running of cars to and from the corner of Baronne and Poydras streets.

1844. The project of a State Convention to revise the constitution having been carried, an election for members was held in July, and on

August 5th, those chosen convened at Jackson, East Feliciana. Subsequently the convention adjourned to New Orleans.

Hon. Henry Johnson was elected United States Senator.

A movement towards the erection in New Orleans of a " National Monument of 1814–15," was inaugurated by the legislature.

The office of State Librarian was created; also the parishes of Morehouse and Vermillion; and the Agricultural & Mechanics' Association; St. Charles Hotel Company; and the Odd Fellows' Grand Lodge incorporated.

An act was passed providing for the liquidation of the debts proper of the State, but the Bank of Louisiana and others, declining to go into the arrangement, nothing came of the effort till the succeeding session. Governor Mouton was able, however, to congratulate the legislature upon the reviving prosperity of the State and a greatly improved financial condition.

1845. The new constitution which was adopted in convention, May 14, was ratified by the popular vote. It did away with many of the conservative features of the existing regime, while it imposed wise and marked restrictions upon the legislative power to confer charters, and absolutely prohibited the State from partnership in any bank or other corporations. No monopoly was to be created, nor divorces granted by the legislature, and lotteries were forbidden. Suffrage was extended, the term of judicial office reduced; a public school system ordained, with a State University at New Orleans; the office of lieutenant-governor created, and a new apportionment made. Under it, the general assembly consisted of 91 representatives and 32 senators; the parish of Orleans having twenty members of the house and four of the senate. An election was to follow for a new general assembly, governor, etc.

Next in interest was the final disposal of the relations between the State and the banks. Under the act for the adjustment and liquidation of the debts proper of the State, [which was revived at this session, with amendments acceptable to the banks] there was an adjustment of mutual obligations, a renunciation by the State of all interference in bank management; and she was relieved of about three million dollars of debt. Louisiana was steadily emerging from her financial embarrassments. The banks, too, were extinguishing their bonded debts; the city of New Orleans had retired her depreciated " promises to pay; " public credit was restored; a sound currency in circulation, and the State treasury in a most prosperous condition, thanks to the wonderful resources of the State, the commercial advantages of the metropolis, the recuperative powers of the people, and the able, eminently prudent, watchful and courageous administration of Governor Mouton.

Can it be believed that Louisiana was opposed to the annexation of Texas? We learn from Mr. Gayarré, that it was with difficulty a resolution favoring such measure went through the General Assembly, even "with a proviso tacked to it, which was not free from objections." The veteran historian was himself the chief champion in the house, of this declaration of the undoubted wishes of Louisianians.

The law against the introduction of free persons of color, drew remonstrances from some of the eastern States as well as from Great Britain. It was a measure common to the southern States—certainly to the seaboard

States—was enacted in the interest of domestic tranquillity, and held to be clearly within the scope of the legislative powers, to say nothing of their inalienable sovereignty. Foreign powers might, so far as the enforcement of the law affected their maritime interests, enter diplomatic protest with the general government, but the Southern States rightly rejected interference from any quarter. Massachusetts, in her anti-slavery zealotry, sent an agent to Louisiana to enquire as to the reported imprisonment of such of these free persons of color as were citizens of that commonwealth, with the view of making up a case which might ultimately be brought before the United States Supreme Court. Hubbard's [agent's name] presence in New Orleans, evoked a deep but suppressed feeling of resentment; there was no violence shown him nor even insult, and his stay was short. He, himself, has left on record the hopeless and irritating character of his mission, and the intense excitement his arrival created, in the same connection bearing handsome testimony to "the courteous, bland and humane manner in which" these facts had been conveyed to him.

The legislature passed suitable resolutions upon this attempted inter-position of Massachusetts in the police regulations of Louisiana.

This year a Board of Commissioners for the better organization of the public schools was created; and the appropriation to those in New Orleans doubled; the City of Carrollton was incorporated, likewise the Polytechnic School, [now no more]; the "College of Louisiana," which had received many thousands from the State treasury, ordered sold; an appropriation for the encouragement of silk culture in the State; the First Baptist Church, of New Orleans, incorporated; the parish of Jackson created, and the charter of the Mexican Gulf Railway Company renewed.

1846. At the election in January, held under the new constitution, Hon. Isaac Johnson was elected governor, and Trasimon Landry, lieutenant-governor.

The new general assembly convened on the 9th February, and the inauguration took place on the 12th.

For months the relations between Mexico and the United States had been severely strained, and the attitude of their respective military forces on the Rio Grande was threateningly hostile. Early in the year hostilities broke out, and General Taylor, who held the American lines, was in imminent danger of being crushed by a greatly superior Mexican force. News of his critical position reaching New Orleans, the enthusiasm of patriotic men fired all classes. The legislature voted $100,000 for raising, equipping, and transporting four regiments of volunteers to the army of General Taylor. "In an incredible short space of time," says Governor Johnson, "several thousand brave and devoted men were forwarded to the seat of war, where they happily arrived in time to enable General Taylor more confidently to assume an offensive attitude against the enemy, and to crown the brilliant victories of the 8th and 9th, [of May] already achieved, with the conquest of Matamoras."

The legislature passed resolutions tendering the thanks of the State to General Taylor and his army, for the additional lustre they had shed upon American arms during the short but brilliant campaign, and voted a sword to the General himself.

General Gaines, too, was voted resolutions of thanks, but in language that would make the typical sophomore burst with envy.

Jurisdiction over the sites of Forts Jackson, St. Philip, Wood and Pike, the sites of Battery Bienvenu and Tower Dupré, and the site for a fortification at or near Proctor's Landing, on Lake Borgne, was granted or ceded to the United States for military purposes, June 1st.

The State was divided into seventeen judicial districts; and the Court of Errors and Appeals in Criminal matters, abolished, its jurisdiction being transferred to the Supreme Court.

The new constitution having decreed that the seat of government should be moved from New Orleans, Baton Rouge was selected by the legislature as the new capital. But no change was to take place till after September, 1849.

The general assembly, at this session, fixed the salaries of the executive and other State officers, as follows: Governor, $6,000; Secretary of State, $2,000; Treasurer, $4,000; Auditor, $3,000. The new constitution fixed the pay of the Chief Justice of the Supreme Court at $6,000, and each of the three Associate Justices at $5,000.

Unionville and Donaldsonville were merged and incorporated as the town of Donaldsonville, Lafayette was made the seat of justice of Jefferson parish, and a stretch of territory, reaching from that city to Bloomingdale, in same parish, and fronting the river, was incorporated as the Borough of Freeport.

The seat of justice of Plaquemine parish, was fixed at Point-a-la-Hache, and the town of Plaquemine, Iberville, incorporated.

1847. The war with Mexico continuing, another regiment of volunteers was raised, and presented by the State with a stand of colors costing three hundred dollars.

Liberal appropriations had been made through several years, for the improvement of interior navigation, but the results were neither commensurate with the expenditure nor encouraging. Money was, however, still voted for this purpose, as well as for the closing of the crevasses at New Carthage and Grand Levee; the erection of a breakwater opposite Bayou Lafourche, the Raccourci Cut-off, etc., and work continued under the superintendence of the State engineer.

One hundred and fifty thousand dollars was appropriated for the erection of the new State House at Baton Rouge; $37,000 for the completion of the Penitentiary Cotton Factory, and the purchase of new machinery for the same. The penitentiary was now leased out, whereby the State was relieved of the annual expenditure of several thousand dollars required for its support.

A State University, with the title of University of Louisiana, to be located in New Orleans, and to be composed of four faculties, viz: law, medicine, natural science and letters, with an academical department, was called into existence this year. The Medical College of Louisiana was merged in it, and an appropriation of $25,000 made for the erection of the central of that group of white, oblong buildings, fronting on Common street, between Baronne and Dryades [then Phillippa] streets, and known as the University buildings. The site was a donation from the State. After many and chequered years, the University of Louisiana, seems now, [1882] to have awakened to a new and vigorous life.

Hitherto, judicial advertisements were published in English and French, in compliance with the laws. But the American population was becoming larger year by year, opening extensive areas, creating and giving names to new parishes, and irresistibly asserting itself. In recognition of the situation—as the phrase now is—the legislature declared the publication in French not necessary, in twenty [specified] parishes, mostly northern, in which the American population was largely in the ascendant.

This year also witnessed the establishment of the State Insane Asylum at Jackson, East Feliciana.

A census of the population of the State, with varied statistical returns, was made.

Bankrupt banks and shattered corporations, that never ought to have been created, were still liquidating. To facilitate their disappearance, the State appointed a liquidator for each of the following, viz : Exchange and Banking Company, Atchafalya Railroad and Banking Company, Merchants' Bank, Bank of Orleans, Clinton & Port Hudson Railroad Company, Mexican Gulf Railway Company, and the Nashville Railroad Company. There were in liquidation besides, the New Orleans Company of Architects, and the New Orleans Improvement and Banking Company, which latter was to drain the swamp regions between the city and Lake Pontchartrain, and make it blossom like the rose. They built the St. Louis hotel, exchange and ball room, and some stores, in a single structure, which, under corrupt, carpet-bag rule, was bought for a State House.

There was created at this time, a Treasury Department in the State Government, a union of the offices of auditor and State treasurer, with these officials as heads of the Department. Those curious in the matter, are referred to Act 18, second session ; approved January 26th, 1847.

Another Act of the same session, provided for the disposal of the " Improvement lands " granted by Congress.

Disposal of the public school lands was a more difficult matter. These grants of the general government were too often located on irreclaimable sea marsh, and other lands of no value, and the laws of congress imposed such restrictions on their sale, as made the donation all but barren. An ordinance of the new constitution required the establishment of a system of free public schools, to be supported mainly by the proceeds from the sale of these school lands ; and a memorial to congress was adopted by the legislature, praying that other than sea marsh, etc., be appropriated, and for such amendments in the act as were evidently necessary to make the system of free public schools something more than a mere scheme. At this session, also, an Act was passed in accordance with the requirements of the constitution in this matter of public education, and a school fund created, based upon the proceeds of the sale of public lands. Additional legislation was, however, required before any practical results could be had.

The parish of Orleans was extended to Felicity road, which was then within the City of Lafayette, parish of Jefferson, and three municipalities of New Orleans, were authorized to fund their debts in thirty-year bonds, bearing seven per cent. interest.

Houses of refuge, for vagrants and juvenile delinquents, were established in the city.

Mansfield, De Soto parish, was incorporated.

Resolutions of respect, for the memory of Ex-Governor White, were adopted by the legislature.

The storming and capture of Monterey also elicited from that body eulogistic "resolutions of thanks," to General Taylor and the Louisiana officers and soldiers engaged in that brilliant achievement. General Worth was voted a sword, in recognition of his services in the same engagement. General Scott received a similar testimonial for his capture of Vera Cruz and victory of Cerro Gordo, and General Taylor a gold medal, in recognition of his victory of Buena Vista.

Hon. Pierre Soulé was elected United States Senator.

1848–9. The general assembly consisted at this time of thirty-three senators and ninety-seven representatives, on an apportionment of 375 electors for each representative. In his message to the legislature at the opening of the session, Governor Johnson took decided ground against the adoption of the "Wilmot proviso"—a virtual declaration of exclusion of the South from all territory acquired from Mexico—which had been introduced in the Federal House of Representatives by Mr. Wilmot, of Pennsylvania.

Internal improvements were pushed with much vigor.

We spoke above of how little had been accomplished, in proportion to the expenditures, in the way of internal improvements. Much reformation had been had in this direction. But the abuses must have been great when the governor could sarcastically observe [January message] that the State engineer's "report would announce the startling and unprecedented fact that he had performed all the duties imposed on him by the last legislature."

A "road and levee fund" and an "internal improvement fund" were created, and large sums voted for public works. Thirty-five thousand dollars in the erection of buildings, purchase of apparatus, books, etc., for the University of Louisiana. A Bureau of Statistics was created in connection with the office of Secretary of State, and measures taken for the classification and preservation of the archives of the State. The records, surveys, etc., of Francis Gonsoulin, made under the Spanish domination, were ordered purchased. We may note in connection herewith that a large quantity of printed State documents—including even the decisions of the Supreme Court—were this year bestowed upon the Louisiana Historical Society. The volumes were deposited with the society "for reference and preservation," says the act authorizing the donation. But this society is long since defunct.

An act of the legislature placed absentees and non-residents on the same footing with residents, in relation to the law of prescription.

The law was so amended that married persons might reciprocally claim divorce, when their marital relations were such as rendered their living together insupportable.

Bienville parish was created, and the towns of Houma, Vienna and Providence incorporated.

General Persifer F. Smith was voted a sword by the legislature, and Pope Pius IX., who had signalized his assumption of the tiara with the declaration of a decidedly liberal policy and the inauguration of many reforms, was warmly eulogized in resolutions adopted by the same body.

Hiram Powers, the sculptor, received a commission for a full length statue of Washington.   This—one of the finest of Powers' efforts—stood for years in the Capitol at Baton Rouge, till all-appropriating General Butler arrested it as the counterfeit presentment of a rebel, and as rebel property confiscated and shipped it North.

An extra session* of the legislature, was begun December 4th, in compliance with the proclamation of the governor. The main object of the session was to complete and set in action the system of free public schools, though considerable other legislation of interest was also enacted.

The sum of five hundred and fifty thousand dollars was appropriated for the organization and support of schools. Liberal sums were voted from the improvement fund, among others, $10,000 for the completion of the Barataria & Lafourche Canal. the State undertaking the work, and securing itself by a lien on the property of the company.

A revision of the Statutes and Codes was ordered, and twelve thousand dollars voted for the purpose.

Mr Caldwell was granted the exclusive privilege of lighting the City of Lafayette with gas, for the term of twenty years.

A measure looking towards the establishment of a " State Seminary of Learning," was also adopted by the legislature.

1850–2. The legislature convened in the new State House at Baton Rouge—now the capital—on the 21st January. On the 28th, Hon. Joseph Walker, who had been elected successor of Gov. Johnson, was inaugurated. The session was a busy one, no fewer than 355 acts and resolutions being the outcome. Among those most deserving of note was the grant of the right of way through lands belonging to the State, to the New Orleans & Jackson Railroad Company.

The Mechanics' & Traders' Bank and the City Bank were authorized to go into liquidation.

Very liberal appropriations were made for the opening up of new roads, the construction of levees, and the improvement of interior navigation; twenty thousand dollars being granted for the completion of the Barataria & Lafourche Canal.

The towns of Abbeville, Bayou Sara, Homer, Minden, Shreveport, Trinity and Vernon were incorporated. The latter was also made the seat of justice of Jackson parish. This year Jefferson City, too, came into corporate existence.

The limits of the parish of Orleans was extended "to that portion of Felicity road,   *   *   falling within the northern and middle lines thereof, extending parallel from Levee street to the rear of the city." A new charter was adopted for the city of New Orleans, under which the three municipalities were re-united. An act providing for the liquidation of their debts was also passed, and a Board of Health created. The New Orleans Navigation Company's charter was declared forfeited and the governor authorized to lease out the Bayou St. John and Canal Carondelet. The Mechanics' Society of New Orleans received from the State a grant of the lot upon which was erected the Mechanics' Institute. Some two million acres of the swamp and overflowed lands within her limits

* Under the new constitution the sessions were triennial.

had been granted to the State by Congress, on condition of their reclamation, etc. The grant, with its conditions, was accepted.

Gen. Philemon Thomas, a soldier of the revolution and of the war of 1814-15, the leader in the capture of Baton Rouge from the Spaniards in 1810, and who had served for many years in the legislature and Congress, having passed away, appropriate resolutions were adopted by the legislature.

The constitution of 1845 did not give unqualified satisfaction. What form of government does ? It was not Democratic enough—not up with the spirit of "progressive Democracy." There was at this period much bosh in the air about the infallibillity and omnipotence of the ballot. Divine right of monarchy had given place to divine right of manhood suffrage, and in keeping therewith, every functionary was to owe his office to popular vote. This radicalism which had its birth in the Eastern and Western States, invaded the slave-holding, conservative South, and Louisiana, by popular vote, called another convention to revise her constitution in accordance with the "spirit of the age." This body met at the capital early in July; gave to the people as radical a charter of the organic law as could well be carried out at the time. All offices were made elective—the judiciary even becoming the foot-ball of popular caprice, and sessions of the legislature again made annual.

In the matter of State aid to enterprises, more or less legitimate, incorporating of banks, etc., the State was once more free "to foster and promote" progress backwards.

A re-districting for congressional representation was made. The parish of Orleans [left bank] constituted the first, the other parishes making up the three remaining districts.

The Bureau of Statistics was abolished, and may be it was out of the saving thereof, that $138,000 was given for school expenses. The City of Lafayette—now Fourth District—was annexed to New Orleans, and the Lafayette & Lake Pontchartrain Railroad Company given the right of way through streets and public squares. New Orleans took her municipalities together again and constituted herself one city.

A pension of $6 per month, to be paid semi-annually, in advance, was granted the veterans (or widows) of 1813–15. Any person making a cut-off, from the Mississippi river, without authority of law, was made liable to a fine of from one hundred to one thousand dollars, with imprisonment not less than one week, nor more than one year.

The towns of Alexandria, Bastrop, Clinton, Farmerville, Madisonville, Mansfield, Port Hudson, Sparta, Trenton, Trinity and Vernon were incorporated.

Another chimerical project of connecting the Mississippi with Lake Borgne, by way of Bayou Bienvenu, was authorized by the legislature. A State institute for the deaf, dumb and blind was founded by the State, this year, at Baton Rouge.

Chairs constructed from the platform of a battery in the Castle of San Jua de Ulloa, harbor of Vera Cruz, were presented by Gen. Persifer F. Smith for the presiding officers of the legislature. The thanks of this body are on record, but what has become of the chairs ? Ten thousand dollars were appropriated towards the erection of the equestrian statue of Jackson, in Jackson Square; five hundred dollars for a block for the Washington monument, and measures taken for securing a site whereon to erect the monument in commemoration of the victory of January 8th, 1815.

1853. Paul O. Hebert, who had been chosen governor, in the election held under the new constitution, was inaugurated early in January. W. W. Farmer was elected lieutenant-governor.

The year is memorable in our annals, from the prevalence of the most appalling epidemic of yellow fever that had ever ravaged Louisiana. It raged during summer and autumn, extended in various directions into the interior, and subsided only after its victims could be counted by the thousands. "Notwithstanding the heavy blow," says Mr. Gayarré, "she [the State] was otherwise prosperous, and energetically engaged in the construction of railroads, and in carrying on the works of internal improvement."

The State at this time was divided into four congressional and eighteen judicial districts.

A general system of free banking received the sanction of the legislature, but the issue or circulation of any note less than the denomination of five dollars was prohibited.

There was had a reorganization of the public school system, and ample provision was made for its support; the reclamation of the swamp and overflowed lands granted by congress was begun; the New Orleans, Jackson and Great Northern, the New Orleans, Opelousas and Great Western, the Vicksburg, Shreveport and Texas, and the New Orleans and Baton Rouge Railroad Companies, were incorporated, with State aid for the three first.

Parishes and municipalities were forbidden to contract any debt without at the same time making provision to meet the principal and interest, and the homestead law was repealed. The State Seminary of Learning, at Alexandria, was this year practically projected.

The suffix *Interior* was henceforward to be discarded, and the parish to be designated simply Lafourche. The town of Mount Lebanon, Bienville parish, and that noble charity, St. Anna's Asylum, New Orleans, were incorporated.

These were the days of filibustering expeditions, and New Orleans was the headquarters and *point d'appui* of the filibusters. Cuba was, in the language of our late war correspondents, the objective point. It was hoped, with the aid of the disaffected on the island, to start an uprising that would blaze into successful revolution, culminating not only in the overthrow of Spanish rule, but in the annexation of Cuba to the United States. The tragic ending of the Lopez expedition, and others equally disastrous, must still be fresh in the memory of the American people.

The news of the fate of Lopez, young Crittenden and others, reaching New Orleans, riotous demonstrations took place at the Spanish Consulate. President Fillmore had, in accordance with international obligations, issued his proclamation denouncing these filibustering expeditions. It was as ineffective as the mythical Papal bull against the comet.

1854. This was another yellow fever year, but the epidemic did not rage with the virulence that marked the scourge of 1853.

The apportionment of this year gave to the general assembly thirty-two senators and eighty representatives; the latter on a representative number of seven thousand.

The opinion was prevalent that Spain intended abolishing slavery in Cuba. The South, at least, was apprehensive of such a measure, and Louisiana but gave expression to the views of her sister slave-holding States, in the resolution adopted by her general assembly. It was claimed that the consummation of the policy of abolition in Cuba, would have a most pernicious effect on the institutions and interests of the United States, and that the situation called for energetic action on the part of the Federal Government.

The notable Ostend Conference, in which figured three United States Ministers to the European courts, Messrs. Soulé, Buchanan and Mason, was the response of the Federal Government to the demand of the South for "the most decisive and energetic measures."

Up to this date no practical system of free public schools had been established. Acts, original and mandatory, had passed the general assembly year after year, but they sketched no broad and practical scheme, nor could any amount of legislation evoke the genius of organization. This year was created the "Free School Accumulating Fund."

The City of New Orleans was empowered, by legislative act, to take stock of the New Orleans, Opelousas & Great Western, New Orleans & Jackson, and the Pontchartrain Railroad Companies, in the aggregate amount of five million dollars.

Besides the sum of $50,000, for the reclamation of the swamp and overflowed lands, appropriations on an unusually liberal scale were made for internal improvements of various character, and fifteen thousand dollars placed to the credit of the pension fund for the veterans of 1814–15.

It was decreed that in the parish of Orleans, death sentences should be carried out within the precincts of the parish prison, in presence of the sheriff and at least four witnesses, residents therein, who should duly attest, under oath, the fact of the execution to the court which rendered the sentence.

A revision of the Statutes of a general character was authorized.

A "local option law," passed the legislature this year. It is doubtful whether such an enactment could be procured in this, the year of grace, 1882.

That "blessing in disguise" for the real estate owners of New Orleans, the drainage tax, was now for the first time imposed. All the swamp lands within the corporate limits were to be drained, and—still are to be.

"Man never is, but always to be, blest."

The employees in the United States Mint at New Orleans were exempted from jury duty. Abbeville was made the seat of justice of Vermillion parish, and the Grand Conclave of the S. W. M. was incorporated.

John Mitchell, the sterling Irish patriot and brilliant writer, was invited by the legislature to visit the seat of government.

1855. Mr. Gayarré notes this year as being marked by the demolition of the "Know-Nothing" Party in Louisiana. As a sop to "nativeism," no doubt, the act prohibiting aliens from holding office of honor or profit was re-enacted, and a very proper enactment it was.

The legislature was prodigal in its appropriations this year, voting the sum of $50,000 to establish quarantine; $30,000 to the State Seminary of Learning; $13,000 for the completion of the University buildings in New

Orleans; $10,000 to Centenary College; $15,000 for merely setting up in the capitol Powers' statue of Washington, and upwards of $20,000 for improving the grounds around the State House. Another act, establishing a system of free banking, was passed, a requisition of births and deaths made obligatory, and the State Insane Asylum established.

New Orleans was empowered to establish public schools; there was another re-organization of the State system of free public education, and once more the permanent fund was established. Cemeteries were exempted from taxation, seizure for debt, and declared non-susceptible of being mortgaged. Judges of the District Courts were authorized to celebrate marriages, married women enabled to contract debts, a Recorder of Mortgages and Registrar of Conveyances for the parish of Orleans appointed; Arcadia and Ringgold, Bienville parish; Monroe, Claiborne parish; Winfield, Winn parish; the Southern Pacific Railroad; the Louisiana College, St. James parish, and that noble benefaction, the Town Alms-House, were incorporated. Let us also make note, that this year witnessed the incorporation of the New Orleans Savings' Institution, which a few years ago made so disastrous a wreck.

1856. Governor Hebert, in his January message to the legislature, deplores, and in nervous terms condemns, the mockeries of the freedom of the ballot. In the same paper—in which was his final message—he testifies to the solid and advancing prosperity of the State, and takes a decidedly advanced Southern position on the anti-slavery agitation.

Hon. Robert C. Wickliffe, who succeeded Governor Hebert in the executive office, gave expression, in his inaugural, to sentiments even more strongly pro-southern on this issue, and though not wishing to speak highly of the Union, did not shrink from calculating the value of the bond to the South.

There is but little deserving of note in the legislation of this year. Registration of voters in the parish of Orleans was provided, and assessment and collection of taxes authorized for public improvements in Algiers, which was then coming prominently into notice. The usual liberal appropriations were made, including $50,000 for the State Seminary of Learning at Alexandria. Bellevue, Bossier parish, Floyd, Carroll parish, and Natchitoches, were incorporated. Charters were granted the Louisiana Central Stem of the Pacific, and the Vicksburg, Shreveport & Texas Railroads; and a site for the Marine Hospital, in New Orleans, ceded to the general government. The Kane Arctic Expedition was the object of generous recognition in joint resolutions of the general assembly.

This year is made sadly memorable in our annals by that appalling calamity, the Last Island storm. This island is the last of a chain extending westward from the mouth of the Mississippi—hence the name. It is some twenty-five miles long by three-fourths to one mile in width, and distant about five to six miles from the nearest shore. It was the summer resort of planters and their families from the Lafourche and Attakapas regions; and on Saturday, August 9, 1856—the eve of the frightful visitation—there were gathered thereon some three hundred souls. On the night of that day, a strong N. E. wind set in, and continued to grow in violence up to 10 A. M., Sunday, when it swelled into a terrific hurricane, accompanied with rain that beat like hail. Every building was prostrated, and everything afloat wrecked. But the worst was yet to come. About 4 P. M.—the storm still raging—the waters of the Gulf and bay met, rose, and rolled their whelming waves over the whole island, sweeping over one hundred human beings into eternity, and leaving but a waste of waters, where, but yesterday, was the pleasant and healthful retreat of happy summer idlers. Those who were not swallowed up in the rush of the devouring waves, found refuge aboard a wrecked steamboat, or escaped by clinging to floating spars, timbers of the demolished houses, etc.; many were carried into the neighboring marshes, and some found precarious refuge in trees. When news of this dire catastrophe reached the mainland, measures looking to the rescue of the survivors were promptly set afoot. Some days, however, elapsed before the several places of refuge of many of the unfortunates were discovered, and, in the meantime, not a few perished from exhaustion or exposure. The number who were finally rescued bore but a small proportion to the number of victims. The latter were estimated to have amounted to nearly two hundred. They yielded up the spirit in lone and scarce accessible spots, whither the surging waves had carried them, or with loosened grasp of spar—or other straw of hope—sunk into the remorseless deep; many were buried beneath the whirling sand and debris of the island, but, by far, the greater were suddenly entombed in the Gulf.

1857. Governor Wickliffe, in his January message, bears this strong official testimony: "It is a well known fact that at the two last general elections, many of the streets and approaches to the polls were completely in the hands of organized ruffians, who committed acts of violence on multitudes of naturalized fellow-citizens who dared to venture to exercise the right of suffrage. Thus, nearly one-third of the registered voters of New Orleans have been deterred from exercising their highest and most sacred prerogatives." Such an election he denounced as an open fraud on the popular will, and called upon the legislature to adopt the needed repressive measures.

No less a sum than one hundred and thirty thousand dollars was taken from the State treasury this year for the penitentiary. It would be an interesting calculation to ascertain how many hundreds of thousands of dollars this institution has cost the taxpayers of Louisiana. And, apropos, let it be noted down, that only $50,000 were given this year to charitable institutions.

There were incorporated, the American Hook and Ladder Company, No. 2; Mechanics' & Dealers' Exchange; Phœnix Fire Company, No. 8; St. Mary's Orphan Boys' Asylum: the Carondelet Canal & Navigation Company; and the Washington Monument Association, all of New Orleans. The latter body died, and gave no sign.

The Towns of Campte, Natchitoches, and Winnsborough, Franklin parish, received incorporation.

1858. For this year, political antagonism, for a few days, threatened New Orleans with fearful disaster.

On the night of the fourth of June, an armed body of men, about five hundred, claiming to act under the orders of a *Vigilant Committee,* took possession of the courthouse and State arsenal at Jackson Square, fortified themselves by barricading the streets, and were the next day joined by about one thousand more men, under the same authority, and also armed for deadly strife.

The Native American, or Know-Nothing Party, took possession of

Lafayette Square, planted cannon there, and arming themselves, prepared for the expected conflict.

Wiser counsels, however, prevailed, and the city election was held on the seventh of the same month, and was concluded in the most quiet and orderly manner, not even the slightest disturbance occurring, Gerard Stith, the Native American candidate, being elected mayor. Colonel G. T. Beauregard being the candidate of the Vigilant Committee party.

The "financial crisis" of 1857 [common to the United States] had been completely tided over by the opening of the year 1858. But the State treasury was not in a healthy condition, the expenditures for some years past exceeding the revenues. And yet the old extravagant rate of appropriation went on for expenses of general assembly, internal improvements, education, etc., while the returns were, indeed, beggarly. Many of the beneficiaries of the public funds had no legitimate claim upon State support. Here, for instance, we find Mount Lebanon University getting $10,000; the New Orleans School of Medicine a like sum; and State bonds to the amount of $40,000 were issued to the Baton Rouge, Gross Tete & Opelousas Railroad. Let us not omit to note, however, that $1500 was appropriated for the instruction of the deaf and dumb of the State Asylum in the art of printing.

Within this period were incorporated the towns of Shiloh and Spearsville, Union parish; Ville Platte, St. Landry; Breaux Bridge, St. Martin; Vernon, Jackson, Waterproof, Tensas, Creola, [name subsequently changed to Montgomery] Winn; and that pleasant suburb of New Orleans—the City of Carrollton.

The breed of dogs in Louisiana in those days must have been of far more worth than that of which she can now boast, for an act of the legislature declared them personal property.

1859. "Quaint and curious" reading, in the light of these after-years, is the act of the legislature of 1859, permitting "free persons of African descent to choose their own masters and become slaves for life."

Judah P. Benjamin was elected United States Senator the same year.

The apportionment of 1859 gave to the general assembly thirty-two senators and ninety-eight representatives—the latter "at a representative number of six thousand nine hundred and twenty."

1860. This year, which opened on a prosperous and contented commonwealth, closed in gloom and apprehension. The returns of agricultural industry were unusually large; money was abundant; city and country alike basked in the smiles of good fortune; and the metropolis was blessed with a summer of exceptional healthiness, and with exemption from the yellow fever.

The presidential canvass of that year was heated, notably so in Louisiana, where fear, and dread of the future, were beginning to take possession of the public mind. But this high-toned, gallant and chivalrous people, conscious of being a republic, and able to govern themselves, canvassed with dignity; voted with entire freedom and order; and the voice of the commonwealth met no dissent or murmur. Breckinridge received 22,681 votes; Bell, 20,204; and Douglas, 7,625. The electoral vote was cast for the first.

The vote of the country at large is thus given: Lincoln, 1,857,610; Douglas, 1,365,976; Breckinridge, 847,953; Bell, 500,631.

It could but be seen that the dividing and conquering of the conservative strength of the country, must, as it did, result from the split in the Charleston convention; but, in spite of that, Louisiana, as we shall see, not only exhibited high republican character in the election, but she afterwards proceeded with due deliberation and dignity, in accordance with her political nature, to exercise (perhaps with impolicy) that self-defense which the Creator, in making her a society of people, had charged her with.

At the election referred to, the choice for a governor to succeed Robert C. Wickliffe, fell upon Thomas Overton Moore, a wealthy planter of Rapides parish, with conservative views, and some legislative experience. He called an extra session of the legislature, which met December 10th, and within a few days, passed an act for an election on January 7, 1861, for delegates to a State convention. It also appropriated $500,000 for the arming and equipping of volunteers; the purchase of military stores, etc. A military commission was also provided for and appointed.

On the 12th, Hon. Wirt Adams, commissioner for Mississippi, addressed the legislature in joint session, announcing the course of action determined on by his State, and urging the co-operation of Louisiana.

Meanwhile, the long continued anxiety and fear of the masses, together with gloomy "thought for the morrow," resulting from anti-slavery agitations and aggressions, were giving rise to a popular conviction that the "domestic tranquillity" and "the blessings of liberty" the federal system was devised to secure, could not be enjoyed in the Union. The public mind became much excited, especially in New Orleans, where, on the 21st of December, an immense popular meeting was held; one hundred guns were fired; the pelican flag was unfurled; and various other enthusiastic demonstrations were made, upon the news of the secession of South Carolina.

1861. The result of the election of January 7th, to the State Convention, showed 20,448 for the professedly "southern rights" candidates against 17,296 for opponents favoring various policies, the leading one of them being a co-operation of the Southern States within the Union. This was futile then, because South Carolina and other States had already seceded, which seemed to make it necessary for all the South to do likewise, and stand or fall together!

The Convention met at the capital January 23, and with little delay, organized itself by the election of the venerable and universally respected Ex-Governor Alexander Mouton as president.

On the fourth day, or January 26th, an ordinance of secession was adopted, by a vote of 113 yeas against 17 nays, the president voting with the majority. Upon the proposition to submit the ordinance to the popular vote, the yeas were 45, nays 84. One hundred and twenty-one delegates signed the Ordinance of Secession, only seven refusing.

When the vote was declared, the president said: " In virtue of the vote just announced, I now declare the connection between the State of Louisiana and the Federal Union dissolved, and that she is a free, sovereign and independent power." *

Immediately after the adoption of this Ordinance, the following resolution passed unanimously: *Resolved*, That we, the people of the State

* The Ordinance of Secession and the names of the signers will be found in the Appendix.

of Louisiana, recognize the right of the free navigation of the Mississippi river and its tributaries by all friendly. States bordering thereon. And we also recognize the right of egress and ingress of the mouth of the Mississippi by all friendly States and Powers, and we do hereby declare our willingness to enter into any stipulations to guarantee the exercise of said rights.

On the same day the Convention adjourned, to re-assemble in New Orleans, January 29th.

The legislature met in regular session, January 21st. The Governor, in his message, gave a succinct history of the decisive measures which he deemed the situation called upon him to adopt. " Respecting the manifest will of the people," " and convinced, moreover, that prompt action was the more necessary in order to prevent a collision between the federal troops and the people," he had taken possession of the military posts and munitions of war within the State, " without opposition or difficulty."

In order that the deliberations of the Convention should not be over-awed by the presence of a federal garrison, the barracks and arsenal at Baton Rouge were the first occupied. These were quietly surrendered to the State troops, January 11, the federal forces—far too feeble for resistance —departing on the 13th. About the same time, Forts Jackson, St. Philip, Pike and other posts,were occupied. A resolution, approving the Governor's course, was adopted by the legislature ; and later, acts were passed trans-ferring the State forces and munitions of war to the Confederate Government.

The Convention re-assembled January 29th, in New Orleans, and the following day elected delegates to the Convention called to meet in Montgomery, for the formation of a Southern Confederacy. March 22d, it ratified the Constitution adopted by that body.

Louisiana, at this period, was enjoying remarkable prosperity. Her banks were among the soundest in the Union, and her finances were in a most satisfactory condition, there being a surplus in the State Treasury. Her chief city exhibited a great increase of commercial activity, attracting capital, mercantile enterprise, and desirable immigrants from other sections, and from foreign parts. Her population notably increased, the census of 1860 showing 666,431.

Moreover, her character was high, her credit good, and her faith untar-nished. She had a fair proportion of religious and educational institutions. Her lawyers, doctors, preachers and great men were at least up to the average, while the charitable institutions of her principal city were, in number, character and beneficence, unequalled. The Charity Hospital, the Howard Association and the Free Market, to say nothing of many others, would have added glory even to the greatest of cities. Nay, more, she had, for two generations, shown full competency for self-government, not only at home, but by sending a *quota* to the federal agency that would have done credit to any of her sisters.

This annalist here gladly concludes his task, because the annals of war and reconstruction, and the changes wrought thereby, have no attractions for his pen. If " history is philosophy teaching by example," it can be properly written only by him who can do it with judicial temper and fairness.

APPENDIX.

TREATY AND CONVENTIONS BETWEEN THE UNITED STATES AND THE FRENCH REPUBLIC.

Treaty between the French Republic and the United States, concerning the Cession of Louisiana, signed at Paris the 30th of April, 1803.

The President of the United States of America, and the first consul of the French republic, in the name of the French people, desiring to remove all source of misunderstanding relative to objects of discussion, mentioned in the second and fifth articles of the convention of the 8th Vendemiaire, an 9, (30th of September, 1800) relative to the rights claimed by the United States, in virtue of the treaty concluded at Madrid, the 27th of October, 1795, between his Catholic Majesty and the said United States, and willing to strengthen the union and friendship which at the time of the said convention was happily re-established between the two nations, have respectively named their plenipotentiaries, to-wit: the President of the United States of America, by and with the advice and consent of the senate of the said States, Robert R. Livingston, minister plenipotentiary of the United States, and James Monroe, minister plenipotentiary and envoy extraordinary of the said States, near the government of the French republic; and the first consul, in the name of the French people, the French citizen, Barbé Marbois, minister of the public treasury, who, after having respectively exchanged their full powers, have agreed to the following articles:

ARTICLE 1. *Whereas,* by the article the third of the treaty concluded at St. Ildephonso, the 9th Vendemiaire, an 9, (1st October 1800) between the first consul of the French republic and His Catholic Majesty, it was agreed as follows: "His Catholic Majesty promises and engages, on his part, to retrocede to the French republic, six months after the full and entire execution of the conditions and stipulations herein relative to his Royal Highness the Duke of Parma, the colony or province of Louisiana, with the same extent that it now has in the hands of Spain, and that it had when France possessed it; and such as it should be after the treaties subsequently entered into between Spain and other States." And, whereas, in pursuance of the treaty, and particularly of the third article, the French republic has an incontestable title to the domain, and to the possession of the said territory. The first consul of the French republic, desiring to give to the United States a strong proof of his friendship, doth hereby cede to the said United States, in the name of the French republic, forever and in full sovereignty, the said territory, with all its rights and appurtenances, as fully and in the same manner as they had been acquired by the French republic, in virtue of the above-mentioned treaty concluded with His Catholic Majesty.

Art. 2. In the cession made by the preceding article are included the adjacent islands belonging to Louisiana, all public lots and squares, vacant lands, and all public buildings, fortifications, barracks, and other edifices, which are not private property. The archives, papers, and documents, relative to the domain and sovereignty of Louisiana and its dependencies, will be left in the possession of the commissaries of the United States, and copies will be afterwards given in due form to the magistrates and municipal officers of such of the said papers and documents as may be necessary to them.

Art. 3. The inhabitants of the ceded territory shall be incorporated in the Union of the United States, and admitted as soon as possible, according to the principles of the federal constitution, to the enjoyment of all the rights, advantages, and immunities of citizens of the United States; and in the meantime they shall be maintained and protected in the free enjoyment of their liberty, property, and the religion which they profess.

Art. 4. There shall be sent by the government of France a commissary to Louisiana, to the end that he do every act necessary, as well to receive from the officers of His Catholic Majesty, the said country and its dependencies, in the name of the French republic, if it has not been already done, as to transmit it in the name of the French republic to the commissary or agent of the United States.

Art. 5. Immediately after the ratification of the present treaty by the President of the United States, and in case that of the first consul shall have been previously obtained, the commissary of the French republic shall remit all the military posts of New Orleans, and other parts of the ceded territory, to the commissary or commissaries named by the President to take possession; the troops, whether of France or Spain, who may be there, shall cease to occupy any military post from the time of taking possession, and shall be embarked as soon as possible, in the course of three months after the ratification of this treaty.

Art. 6. The United States promise to execute such treaties and articles as may have been agreed between Spain and the tribes and nations of Indians, until, by mutual consent of the United States and the said tribes or nations, other suitable articles shall have been agreed upon.

Art. 7. As it is reciprocally advantageous to the commerce of France and the United States to encourage the communication of both nations for a limited time in the country ceded by the present treaty, until general arrangements relative to the commerce of both nations may be agreed on, it has been agreed between the contracting parties, that the French ships coming directly from France or any of her colonies, loaded only with the produce or manufactures of France or her said colonies; and the ships of Spain, coming directly from Spain or any of her colonies, loaded only with the produce or manufactures of Spain or her colonies, shall be admitted, during the space of twelve years, in the ports of New Orleans, and in all other legal ports of entry within the ceded territory, in the same manner as the ships of the United States coming directly from France or Spain, or any of their colonies, without being subject to any other or greater duty on merchandise, or other or greater tonnage than those paid by the citizens of the United States.

During the space of time above mentioned, no other nation shall have a right to the same privileges in the ports of the ceded territory; the twelve years shall commence three months after the exchange of ratifications, if it shall take place in France, or three months after it shall have been notified at Paris to the French government, if it shall take place in the United States; it is, however, well understood, that the object of the above article is to favor the manufactures, commerce, freight and navigation of France and of Spain, so far as relates to the importations that the French and Spanish shall make into the said ports of the United States, without in any sort affecting the regulations that the United States may make concerning the exportation of the produce and merchandise of the United States, or any right they may have to make any such regulations.

ART. 8. In future, and forever after the expiration of the twelve years, the ships of France shall be treated upon the footing of the most favored nations in the ports above mentioned.

ART. 9. The particular convention, signed this day by the respective ministers, having for its object to provide for the payment of debts due to the citizens of the United States by the French republic, prior to the 30th of September, 1800, (8th Vendemiaire, an 9) is approved, and to have its execution in the same manner as if it had been inserted in the present treaty, and it shall be ratified in the same form, and in the same time, so that the one shall not be ratified distinct from the other.

Another particular convention, signed at the same date as the present treaty, relative to the definitive rule between the contracting parties, is in the like manner approved, and will be ratified in the same form, and in the same time, and jointly.

ART. 10. The present treaty shall be ratified in good and due form, and the ratifications shall be exchanged in the space of six months after the date of the signature by the ministers plenipotentiary, or sooner, if possible.

In faith whereof, the respective plenipotentiaries have signed these articles in the French and English languages; declaring, nevertheless, that the present treaty was originally agreed to in the French language; and have thereunto put their seals.

Done at Paris, the tenth day of Floreal, in the eleventh year of the French republic, and the 30th of April, 1803.

ROBERT R. LIVINGSTON,
JAMES MONROE,
BARBE MARBOIS.

CONVENTION BETWEEN THE UNITED STATES OF AMERICA AND THE FRENCH REPUBLIC, OF THE SAME DATE WITH THE PRECEDING TREATY.

The President of the United States of America, and the first consul of the French republic, in the name of the French people, in consequence of the treaty of cession of Louisiana, which has been signed this day, wishing to regulate, definitively, everything which has relation to the said cession, have authorized to this effect the plenipotentiaries, that is to say: the President of the United States has, by and with the advice and consent of the senate of the said States, nominated for their plenipotentiaries, Robert R. Livingston, minister plenipotentiary of the United States, and James Monroe, minister plenipotentiary and envoy extraordinary of the said United States, near the government of the French republic; and the first consul of the French republic, in the name of the French people, has named as plenipotentiary of the said republic, the French citizen, Barbé Marbois, who, in virtue of their full powers, which have been exchanged this day, have agreed to the following articles:

ARTICLE 1. The government of the United States engages to pay to the French government, in the manner specified in the following articles, the sum of sixty millions of francs, independent of the sum which shall be fixed by another convention for the payment of debts due by France to citizens of the United States.

ART. 2. For the payment of the sum of sixty millions of francs, mentioned in the preceding article, the United States shall create a stock of eleven millions two hundred and fifty thousand dollars, bearing an interest of six per cent. per annum, payable half yearly in London, Amsterdam, or Paris, amounting by the half year to three hundred and thirty-seven thousand five hundred dollars, according to the proportions which shall be determined by the French government, to be paid at either place; the principal of the said stock to be reimbursed at the treasury of the United States, in annual payment of not less than three millions of dollars each; of which the first payment shall commence fifteen years after the date of the exchange of ratifications; this stock shall be transferred to the government of France, or to such person or persons as shall be authorized to receive it, in three months at most after the exchange of the ratifications of this treaty, and after Louisiana shall be taken possession of in the name of the government of the United States.

It is farther agreed, that if the French government should be desirous of disposing of the said stock to receive the capital in Europe, at shorter terms, that its measures for that purpose shall be taken so as to favor, in the greatest degree possible, the credit of the United States, and to raise to the highest price the said stock.

ART. 3. It is agreed that the dollar of the United States, specified in the present convention, shall be fixed at five francs $\frac{3333}{10000}$, or five livres eight sous tournois. The present convention shall be ratified in good and due form, and the ratifications shall be exchanged in the space of six months, to date from this day, or sooner if possible.

In faith of which, the respective plenipotentiaries have signed the above articles both in the French and English languages; declaring nevertheless, that the present treaty has been originally agreed on and written in the French language; to which they have hereunto affixed their seals.

Done at Paris, the tenth of Floreal, eleventh year of the French republic, (30th April, 1803.)

[L. s.]	ROBERT. R. LIVINGSTON,
[L. s.]	JAMES MONROE,
[L. s.]	BARBE MARBOIS.

CONVENTION BETWEEN THE UNITED STATES OF AMERICA AND THE FRENCH REPUBLIC, ALSO OF THE SAME DATE WITH THE LOUISIANA TREATY.

The President of the United States of America, and the first consul of the French republic, in the name of the French people, having by a treaty of this date terminated all difficulties relative to Louisiana, and established on a solid foundation the friendship which unites the two nations, and being desirous, in compliance with the second and fifth articles of the convention of the 8th Vendemiaire, ninth year of the French republic, (30th September, 1800) to secure the payment of the sum due by France to the citizens of the United States, have respectively nominated as plenipotentiaries, that is to say : the President of the United States of America, by, and with the advice and consent of the senate, Robert R. Livingston, minister plenipotentiary, and James Monroe, minister plenipotentiary and envoy extraordinary of the said States, near the government of the French republic, and the first consul, in the name of the French people, the French citizen Barbé Marbois, minister of the public treasury; who, after having exchanged their full powers, have agreed to the following articles :

ARTICLE 1.   The debts due by France to the citizens of the United States, contracted before the 8th Vendemiaire, ninth year of the French republic, (30th September, 1800) shall be paid according to the following regulations, with interest at six per cent., to commence from the period when the accounts and vouchers were presented to the French government.

ART. 2.   The debts provided for by the preceding article are those whose result is comprised in the conjectural note annexed to the present convention, and which, with the interest, cannot exceed the sum of twenty millions of francs.   The claims comprised in the said note, which fall within the exceptions of the following articles, shall not be admitted to the benefit of this provision.

ART. 3.   The principal and interest of the said debts shall be discharged by the United States, by orders drawn by their minister plenipotentiary, on their treasury; these orders shall be payable sixty days after the exchange of the ratifications of the treaty and the conventions signed this day, and after possession shall be given of Louisiana by the commissioners of France to those of the United States.

ART. 4.   It is expressly agreed, that the preceding articles shall comprehend no debts but such as are due to citizens of the United States, who have been and are yet creditors of France, for supplies, embargoes, and for prizes made at sea, in which the appeal has been properly lodged within the time mentioned in the said convention of the 8th Vendemiaire, ninth year, (30th September, 1800.)

ART. 5.   The preceding articles shall apply only : 1st, to captures of which the council of prizes shall have ordered restitution; it being well understood that the claimant cannot have recourse to the United States otherwise than he might have had to the government of the French republic, and only in case of the insufficiency of the captors; 2d, the debts mentioned in the said fifth article of the convention, contracted before the 8th Vendemiaire, an 9, (30th September, 1800) the payment of which has been heretofore claimed of the actual government of France, and for which the creditors have a right to the protection of the United States; the said fifth article does not comprehend prizes whose condemnation has been or shall be confirmed; it is the express intention of the contracting parties not to extend the benefit of the present convention to reclamations of American citizens, who shall have established houses of commerce in France, England, or other countries than the United States, in partnership with foreigners, and who by that reason and the nature of their commerce, ought to be regarded as domiciliated in the places where such houses exist.   All agreements and bargains concerning merchandise, which shall not be the property of American citizens, are equally excepted from the benefit of the said convention, saving, however, to such persons their claims in like manner as if this treaty had not been made.

ART. 6. And that the different questions which may arise under the preceding article may be fairly investigated, the ministers plenipotentiary of the United States shall name three persons, who shall act from the present and provisionally, and who shall have full power to examine, without removing the documents, all the accounts of the different claims already liquidated by the bureau established for this purpose by the French republic; and to ascertain whether they belong to the classes designated by the present convention and the principles established in it, or if they are not in one of its exceptions, and on their certificate, declaring that the debt is due to an American citizen or his representative, and that it existed before the 8th Vendemiaire, ninth year, (30th September, '1800) the creditor shall be entitled to an order on the treasury of the United States in the manner prescribed by the third article.

ART. 7. The same agents shall likewise have power, without removing the documents, to examine the claims which are prepared for verification, and to certify those which ought to be admitted by uniting the necessary qualifications, and not being comprised in the exceptions contained in the present convention.

ART. 8. The same agents shall likewise examine the claims which are not prepared for liquidation, and certify in writing those which in their judgments ought to be admitted to liquidation.

ART. 9. In proportion as the debts mentioned in these articles shall be admitted, they shall be discharged with interest at six per cent. by the treasury of the United States.

ART. 10. And that no debt which shall not have the qualifications above mentioned, and that no unjust or exorbitant demand may be admitted, the commercial agent of the United States at Paris, or such other agent as the minister plenipotentiary of the United States shall think proper to nominate, shall assist at the operations of the bureau, and co-operate in the examination of the claims; and if this agent shall be of opinion that any debt is not completely proved, or if he shall judge that it is not comprised in the principles of the fifth article above mentioned; and if, notwithstanding his opinion, the bureau established by the French government should think that it ought to be liquidated, he shall transmit his observations to the board established by the United States, who, without removing the documents, shall make a complete examination of the debt and vouchers which support it, and report the result to the minister of the United States. The minister of the United States shall transmit his observations, in all such cases, to the minister of the treasury of the French republic, on whose report the French government shall decide definitively in every case.

The rejection of any claim shall have no other effect than to exempt the United States from the payment of it, the French government reserving to itself the right to decide definitively on such claim so far as it concerns itself.

ART. 11. Every necessary decision shall be made in the course of a year, to commence from the exchange of ratifications, and no reclamation shall be admitted afterwards.

ART. 12. In case of claims for debts contracted by the government of France with citizens of the United States, since the 8th Vendemiaire, ninth year, (30th September, 1800) not being comprised in this convention, they may be pursued, and the payment demanded in the same manner as if it had not been made.

ART. 13. The present convention shall be ratified in good and due form, and the ratifications shall be exchanged in six months from the date of the signature of the ministers plenipotentiary, or sooner, if possible.

In faith of which, the respective ministers plenipotentiary have signed the above articles, both in the French and English languages, declaring, nevertheless, that the present treaty has been originally agreed on and written in the French language; to which they have hereunto affixed their seals.

Done at Paris, the tenth day of Floreal, eleventh year of the French republic, (30th April, 1803.)

[L. S.]	ROBERT R. LIVINGSTON,
[L. S.]	JAMES MONROE,
[L. S.]	BARBE MARBOIS.

"ORDINANCE OF SECESSION."

THE STATE OF LOUISIANA.

An Ordinance to dissolve the Union between the State of Louisiana and other States united with her, under the compact entitled :

"THE CONSTITUTION OF THE UNITED STATES OF AMERICA."

We, the people of the State of Louisiana, in Convention assembled, do declare and ordain, and it is hereby declared and ordained, that the Ordinance passed by us in Convention on the 22d day of November, in the year, Eighteen Hundred and Eleven, whereby the Constitution of the United States of America, and the amendments of the said Constitution, were adopted; and all laws and ordinances by which the State of Louisiana became a member of the Federal Union, be and the same are hereby repealed and abrogated; and that the Union now subsisting between Louisiana and other States, under the name of "The United States of America," is hereby dissolved.

We do further declare and ordain, That the State of Louisiana hereby resumes all rights and powers heretofore delegated to the Government of the United States of America; that her citizens are absolved from all allegiance to said government; and that she is in full possession and exercise of all those rights of sovereignty which appertains to a free and independent State.

We do further declare and ordain, That all rights acquired and vested under the Constitution of the United States, or any acts of Congress, or treaty, or under any law of this State, and not incompatible with this Ordinance, shall remain in force and have the same effect as if this Ordinance had not been passed.

The Legislature met at Baton Rouge on the 21st of January, 1861, and on the 18th of February, the following Joint Resolution was signed by the Governor:

1st. *Be it resolved by the Senate and House of Representatives of the State of Louisiana, in General Assembly convened,* That the right of a sovereign State to secede or withdraw from the Government of the Federal Union and resume her original sovereignty when in her judgment such act becomes necessary, is not prohibited by the Federal Constitution, but is reserved thereby to the several States, or people thereof, to be exercised, each for itself, without molestation.

2d. *Be it further resolved, etc.,* That any attempt to coerce or force a sovereign State to remain within the Federal Union, come from what quarter and under whatever pretense it may, will be viewed by the people of Louisiana, as well on her own account as of her sister Southern States, as a hostile invasion, and resisted to the utmost extent.

C. H. MORRISON,
Speaker of the House of Representatives.

B. W. PEARCE,
President pro tem. of the Senate.

Approved, February 18th, 1861.

THOS. O. MOORE,
Governor of the State of Louisiana.

A true copy:
PLINY D. HARDY,
Secretary of State.

A Joint Resolution was also passed approving the action of the Governor in taking possession of the Forts and Arsenals within the limits of the State.

An act was passed authorizing the Governor to transfer and cause to be mustered into the service of the Provisional Government of the Confederate States of America, the regular military force of this State, organized under an ordinance of the Convention of the people of Louisiana, passed on the 5th of February, 1861.

Two hundred and seventy-three acts in all were passed, but few of which were of general interest or worthy of mention here.

CONVENTION OF 1861.

On the 23d day of January, 1861, in pursuance of an Act of the Legislature, passed at its Special Session of 1860, the Convention of the people of the State of Louisiana, met at Baton Rouge; one hundred and twenty-eight of the one hundred and thirty delegates answering roll call at the opening Session.

List of Delegates.

Adams, W. R . . . . Orleans.
Anderson, W. D . . . . Tensas.
Avegno, B . . . . Orleans.
Barbin, Ad . . . . Avoyelles.
Barrow, W. R . . . . . West Feliciana.
Bermudez, E . . . . Orleans.
Bienvenu, C . . . . St. Bernard,
Plaquemines, Orleans, Right Bank, and Jefferson.
Bonford, P. R . . . . Orleans.
Bonner, A . . . . Franklin.
Briscoe, C. C . . . . Madison.
Burton, W . . . . St. Landry.
Bush, L . . . . Lafourche, St. Charles.
Butler, E. G. W . . . . Iberville.
Caldwell, T. J . . . . Bossier.
Cannon, F . . . . Avoyelles.
Carr, W. C . . . . Union.
Clark, George . . . . Orleans.
Cook, T. A . . . . St. Landry.
Connelly, G. F . . . . Terrebonne.
Conner, L. P . . . . Concordia, Tensas and Madison.
Conner, S. S . . . . St. Tammany.
Cottman, T . . . . Ascension.
Davidson, W. A . . . . Livingston.
Davison, E. C . . . . Sabine.
Declouet, A . . . . St. Martin, Vermillion.
DeBlanc, A . . . . St. Martin,
Dorsey, S. W . . . . Tensas.
Duffel, E . . . . Ascension.
Dupre, L. J . . . . St. Landry, Calcasieu and Lafayette.
Elam, J. B . . . . DeSoto.
Elgee, J. K . . . . Rapides.
Estlin, W. R . . . . Orleans.
Fusilier, G. L . . . . St. Mary.
Fuqua, J. O . . . . East Feliciana, East and West Baton Rouge.
Gladden, A. H . . . . Orleans.
Gardere, F . . . . Plaquemines, St. Bernard and Orleans, Right Bank.
Garrett, J . . . . Ouachita.
Gaudet, J. K . . . . St. James.
Graves, Y. W . . . . DeSoto.
Gray, A. M . . . . . Avoyelles, Pointe Coupée and West Feliciana.

Gill, W. E . . . . Calcasieu.
Girard, M. E . . . . Lafayette.
Griffin, S. H . . . . Union.
Hernandez, J . . . . Orleans.
Herron, A. S . . . East Baton Rouge, East Feliciana and West Baton Rouge.
Hough, W. H . . . . Caldwell, Catahoula and Winn.
Hodge, B. L . . . . Caddo, Natchitoches, Sabine and DeSoto.
Hodges, R . . . . . Bienville, Bossier.
Hollingsworth, S . . St. John Baptist.
Johnston, F . . . . Iberville.
Kennedy, T. H . . . . Orleans.
Kidd, W. M . . . . . . Jackson, Union.
Labutut, F . . . . Orleans.
Lawrence, E . . . . Plaquemines.
Lagroue, C. T . . . . Jefferson.
LeBlanc, C. O . . . . Orleans.
LeBourgeois, L. S . . . . . . St. James.
Lewis, F . . . . Bienville.
Lewis, J. L . . . . Claiborne.
Lewis, G. W . . Orleans, Right Bank.
Manning, T. C . . . . Rapides.
Marshall, H . . . . . . DeSoto, Caddo, Sabine and Natchitoches.
Marrero, A . . . . St. Bernard.
Marks, L. D . . . . Caddo.
Marks, I. N . . . . Orleans.
Martin, N. C . . . . Assumption, Ascension and Terrebonne.
Martin, J. H . . . . Carroll.
Magee, N . . . . Washington.
Melançon, O. E . . . . . . Assumption.
Meredith, C. C . . . . Caldwell.
Miles, W. R . . . . Orleans.
Michel, J. J . . . . Orleans.
Miller, J. E . . . . Concordia.
Moore, J . . . . St. Martin.
Mouton, A . . . . Lafayette, St. Landry and Calcasieu.
McCloskey, J . . . . Orleans.
McCollam, A . . . . Terrebonne.
McFarland, H . . . . Bossier.
McNeely, S. W . . . . . Pointe Coupée.
Norton, M. O. H . . . . Orleans.
Olivier, J. G . . . . St. Mary.
O'Brien, D . . . . Vermillion.
Patterson, W . . . . . . East Feliciana.

LIST OF DELEGATES.—*Continued.*

Perkins, J. S. . . . . Lafourche.
Perkins, J., Jr . . . . Madison,
 Tensas and Concordia.
Perkins, W. M . . . . Orleans.
Peck, W. R . . . . Madison.
Pemberton, J . . . . Orleans.
Pierson, A. H . . . . Natchitoches.
Pierson, D . . . . Winn.
Pike, W. S . . . . . East Baton Rouge.
Polk, H. M . . . Morehouse, Ouachita.
Pope, N. W . . . . West Baton Rouge.
Provosty, A . . . . Point Coupée.
Pugh, W . . . . Assumption.
Richardson, H . . . . Washington,
 St. Helena, Livingston and St.
 Tammany.
Roman, A. B . . . . St. James,
 St. John Baptist.
Roselius, C . . . . Jefferson.
Rozier, J. Ad . . . . Orleans.
Slawson, J. B . . . . Orleans.
Smart, W. W . . . . Rapides.
Swayze, E. L . . . . St. Landry.
Semmes, T. J . . . . Orleans.
Stewart, C. D . . . . . . Point Coupée.
Scott, T. W . . . . East Feliciana.
 Avoyelles and West Feliciana.

Sparrow, E . . . . Carroll.
Sompayrac, J . . . . Natchitoches.
Scott, N. G. . . . . Claiborne.
Stocker, W. T . . . . Orleans.
Smith, W. M. M . . . . St. Mary.
Tappan, B. S . . . . Orleans.
Talbot, A . . . . Iberville.
Taliaferro, J. G . . . . Catahoula.
Taylor, R . . . . St. Charles.
Taylor, J. A . . . . St. Landry.
Texada, L . . . . Rapides.
Thomasson, J. S . . . . Claiborne.
Todd, R. B . . . . Morehouse.
Towles, J. T . . . . . . West Feliciana.
Tucker, C. J . . . . Lafourche.
Valentine, M . . . . Carroll, Franklin.
Verret, A . . . . Terrebonne,
 Ascension and Assumption.
Warren, W. B . . . . Jackson.
Walker, A . . . . Orleans.
Williams, I. A . . East Baton Rouge.
Williams, J. A . . . . St. Helena.
Williamson, G . . . . Caddo.
Wilkinson, J. B., Jr . . Plaquemines.
Wiltz, P. S . . . . Orleans.
York, Z . . . . Concordia.

Of the above, Manning, of Rapides, and Gladden, of Orleans, were the only delegates absent at the opening of the Convention. Alexander Mouton, of Lafayette, was elected President on the first ballot. J. T. Wheat, of Orleans, was elected Secretary.

Roster of Louisiana Troops in the Confederate Service.

No.	Command	Arm of Service.	Commander.	Date of Rank.	Remarks.
1st	Regiment	Cavalry..	Col. John S Scott......	May 4, 1861.	
1st	"	Artillery.	Col. C. A. Fuller.......	Aug. 14, 1861.	
1st	{ C. C. Reg't }	Infantry.	Col. M. J. Smith........	May 31, 1862	
1st	Enlisted Men.	" ...	{ Col. Jas. Strawbridge....	Feb. 16, 1863.	
			{ Col. Dan'l W. Adams...	....	Promoted Brigadier-General.
1st	Regiment	" ...	{ Col. W. R. Shivers......	June 16, 1862.	
			{ Col. A. R. Harrison......		
2d	"	" ...	{ Col. J. M. Williams......	June 6, 1862.	
			{ Col. W. M. Levy.......	....	
3d	"	"	Col. J. B. Gilmore.......	Nov. 5, 1862.	
4th	"	" ...	{ Col. A. C. Hunter.. ...	Mch. 29, 1863.	
			{ Col. R. J Barrow.......		
5th	"	"	{ Col. Henry Forno.......	July 31, 1862.	
			{ Col. T. G. Hunt........	....	
6th	"	"	{ Col. Wm. Monaghan....	Nov. 7, 1862.	
			{ Col. I. G. Seymour......	....	
7th	"	" ...	{ Col. Davidson B. Penn...	July 20, 1862.	
			{ Col. Harry T. Hays.....	....	Promoted Major-General.
8th	"	"	Col. H. B. Kelly.........	June 10, 1861.	
9th	"	" ...	Col. Leroy A. Stafford. .	Apr. 24, 1862.	Promoted Brigadier-General.
10th	"	" ...	{ Col. Eugene Waggaman.	Oct. 1, 1862	
			{ Col. M. Marigny........	....	
11th	"	" ...	Col. S. F. Marks.........	Aug. 9, 1861.	
12th	"	" ...	Col. Thos. M. Scott......	Aug. 9, 1861.	Promoted Brigadier-General.
13th	"	" ...	Col. R. L. Gibson........	Sept. 16, 1861.	Promoted Brigadier-General.
14th	"	" ...	{ Col. Z. York...........	Aug. 15, 1862.	Promoted Brigadier-General.
			{ Col. R. W. Jones		
15th	"	"	Col. Edmund Pendleton.	Oct. 14, 1862.	
16th	"	" ...	{ Col. Dan'l Gober........	May 8. 1862.	
			{ Col. P. Pond.....	....	
17th	"	" ...	{ Col. Robt. Richardson ...	May 23, 1862.	
			{ Col. S. S. Heard........		
18th	"	" ...	{ Col L. L. Armant......,	Sept. 26, 1862.	
			{ Col. A. Mouton..........	....	Promoted Brigadier-General.
19th	"	" ...	{ Col. W. P. Winans......	July 17, 1862	
			{ Col. B. L. Hodge........		
20th	"	" ...	{ Col. Leon Von Zincken ..	July 7, 1862.	
			{ Col. Aug. Reichard	....	
21st	"	" ...	{ Col. Isaac W. Patton	May 15, 1862.	
			{ Col. M. L. Smith...	....	
			{ Col. Edward Higgins		
22d	"	" ...	{ Col. Charles H. Herrick.	May 26, 1862	
			{ Col. Paul E. Theard......	....	
23d	"	" ...	....	....	
24th	"	" ...			
25th	"	" ...	Col. J. C. Lewis..........	Dec. 31, 1862.	
26th	"	" ...	{ Col. Winchester Hall ...	Nov. 25, 1862.	
			{ Col. Alex'r Declouet.....	....	Delegate to Provisional Congress at Montgomery.
27th	"	"	Col. Leon D. Marks.......	Apr. 19, 1862.	
28th	"	"	Col. Henry Gray.........	May 1, 1862.	
29th	"	"	Col. Allen Thomas.......	May 3, 1862.	Promoted Brigadier-General.
30th	"	"	Col. G. A. Breaux........	....	
31st	"	" ...	Col. Chas. H. Morrison..	June 16, 1862.	.
32d	"	"	Col. J. C. Denis..........		
2d	"	Cavalry..	Col. W. G. Vincent......	Sept. 1, 1862.	
1st	Battalion.	Artillery.	Lt Col J B. Walton......	....	
1st	"	Infantry.	Lt. Col. Rightor	....	
1st	"	Zouaves..	Lt. Col. Coppens.........	....	
2d	"	Infantry.	Major Wheat..............	....	
3d	"	"	....	....	Afterwards changed to 15th regim't
4th	"	" ...	Lt. Col. J. McEnery.....	....	
5th	"	" ...	Lt. Col. Kennedy........	....	
6th	"	" ...	Lt. Col. C. H. Morrison..	....	

INDEX

COMPILED BY STUART O. LANDRY

The index is for Martin's History proper beginning with Chapter 1 (Pg. 31) and ending with Chapter XXXIII (Pg. 412). It does not include Martin's Preliminary Chapter, "A Topographical View of the State of Louisiana"; the Introduction; the biographical sketch by Judge W. W. Howe; and the "Annals of Louisiana from 1815 to 1861" appended to Martin's History.

INDEX

INDEX

Bonapart, Napoleon—287, 293, 358
Boone, Daniel—219
Bore, Etienne (Mayor)—263, 267, 296, 325
Bossu—191
Boston—Treaty of, 66; 90, 94, 111, 186; Massacre, 215; Tea Party, 219; 220
Bouligny—226
Boulikny, Don Dominique—287
Bouligny, Don Francisco de—284, 330
Bourdon—Atty. Gen. of New France, 64
Bourgeois—94
Bourgoing, Vicar—Gen. in La. —110
Bourguet—200
Bouteux—138
Bowles—306
Bradford—341
Braddock, Gen.—188
Braud—Printer, 193, 206, 207
Braud—Don Dyonisio—211
Brandywine—224
Brasset, Dr.—171
Breckenridge—282
Brebeuf, Father Jean de—54
Breda, Treaty of—66
Brewster—333
British—Traders in Lower La., 117; Dissensions of colonies, 199; Vessels in Miss. River, 196, 200, 217; Planters in La., 224; Army retires (Bat. of N. O.), 386
Brocard, Duplessis—61
Broutin—162
Brown—Sec. of Orleans Ter., 325, 344
Bru—169, 170
Brule—57
Bruno, Father—156
Bruscoli, Mother Catherine—156
Brusle—155, 169, 170
Buccarelly, Don Antonio Maria—216
Budget of La.—240
Buford—229
Burgoygne—224
Burling—335, 337, 342
Burr, Aaron—To Western States, 328; Designs against U. S., 334-344; 346; 351
Butler, Gen.—256
Butler, Maj.—at Battle of N. O., 381

C

Cabahanosse—299
Cabildo—Instituted, 209-212; 220, 222, 226, 237, 239, 245, 247, 250, 253, 257, 264, 268-270, 277, 286, 296, 302, 319
Cabot—31, 38
Caday Indians—135
Caddo Indians—127, 134, 150, 168, 170, 301, 333
Cadillac, Lamotte—117, 121
Caen, Edmund de—54
Caen, Emery de—58
Caen, William—54
Caenza Indians—150
Cagigal, Don Juan Menuel de—Caffaro, Commodore—137 229, 236
Caisergues (Alcalde)—287

California—298
Callieres—Gov. of Montreal, 90, 95; Of Canada, 105, 106
Cambray, Peace of—32, 33
Campbell, Gen.—Defends Pensacola, 229-233
Canada—Name, 34; 36; 37; 38; Education, 61; Earthquake, epidemic, 62; Conquered, 191; to Great Britain, 193; Invaded, 221; 269; 356
Canary Island Settlers—129, 224, 253
Canaveral—41
Canceaux—180
Cannes Brulees—127, 147, 162, 168
Cannibalism—among French, 40; Attakapas Indians, 300
Cantrelle—325
Caouis—121
Cape Breton Island—56, 180, 190
Cape Cod—46, 53
Cape Girardeau—301
Capital to Mobile—104
Cappa Indians—77
Capuchins—148, 151, 154, 156, 156, 214, 226
Carcasu River—301
Caresse—206, 208
Carigan Salieres Reg.—64
Carlos, Don—182
Carmelites—148, 156
Carlier, Widow—219
Caron, Father Joseph le—52, 54
Carolina (Carolana)—39, 41, 55, 58 105, 117, 118, 171, 174, 178, 223
Carolina Schooner—At N. O., 374; blows up, 377
Carondelet, Don Francisco Louis Hector, Baron de—Arrives in La., 257-264; Widens canal, 265; his regime, 266-273; 274, 275, 277, 284, 287
Carondelet Canal—263, 265, 268, 287, 345
Carrere—197
Carroll, Bishop—328, 354
Carroll, Gen.—at Battle of N. O., 366, 373, 374
Carthagena—362
Cartier—33, 34, 37, 46
Casa Calvo, Marquis de—284, 287, 292, 328, 330, 331, 343
Casa Irujo, Marquis de—319
Casket Girls—157
Castenado, Francisco—270
Cat Island—96, 186, 218
Catahoula—349
Catahoulou Lake—167
Catahoushe River—277
Catawba Indians—118
Catholics only—154
Cattle Branded—213
Causey Indians—136
Cavelier, Petit—296
Celeron, Lieut.—177, 178
Censorship of books—225
Cenis Indians—86
Census—Canada, 89, 95; Upper La., 285; New Orleans (1766), 200; (1769), 206; (1785), 239; 300; 347
Cestiere, Lebarre de la (Regidor)—222
Chabert (Alcalde)—216, 220, 247

Chachoumas Indians—149
Chaise, Father de la—68
Chaise, Auguste de la—262
Chaise, Don Carlos de la—253
Chaise, Francois de la—154, 155, 179
Chambly—at Acadie, 65, 68
Canada, 46, 48; Founds Quebec, 49, 50; Discovers Lake Champlain, 51; in Canada, 52-57; Gov. of Canada, 58; death, 59; 204
Champmeslin, Count de—131, 132
Chandeleurs Islands—96
Charles I (England)—54, 57, 58, 60
Charles I (Spain)—31, 33, 34
Charles II (England)—61, 64, 65, 68, 75, 76, 81, 223
Charles II (Spain)—65, 103, 172
Charles III—191, 199, 216, 253
Charles IV—253
Charles V—179
Charles VIII (France)—31
Charles IX (France)—39, 42, 43
Charleston (S. C.)—attacked by French frigate, 106; 118, 152, 220, 262
Charleston—Newspaper repotrs end of War of 1812, 388
Charlevoix, Father—61, 147, 149, 150
Charter—of Crozat, 114; of Western Co., 124
Chartres St. (N. O.)—250
Chaville (Officer)—138
Chateague—107, 112, 127, 130, 132, 137, 143
Chateaumorent, Naval Capt.—96
Chatte, Commander de la—46
Chauvin, Capt.—in Canada, 46
Chaumont, Madame—grant, 127, 139
Chauvin Bros.—147
Chef Menteur—218, 365, 373, 374
Cheney (of S. C.)—110
Chepar, Commandant—159, 160
Cherokee Indians—35, 106, 109, 118, 119, 262, 301, 329, 359
Chesapeake Bay—48
Chester, Gov.—232
Chester, Peter—213
Chetimaches Fork—100
Chetimaches Indians—97, 110, 163, 195, 300
Chickasaw Indians—35, 76, 77, 79, 99, 104, 105, 107-111, 117, 134, 136, 137, 147, 148, 150, 151, 153, 158, 159, 164, 165, 167, 170, 171, 173-179, 184, 220, 287, 297, 301, 359
Chickasaw Bluffs—287
Chilimacka Indians—300
Chihauhua—343
Chinonoa Indians—85
Choctaw Indians—36, 104, 107-112, 117-119, 138, 149, 153, 158, 159, 162-164, 166, 173-175, 177, 184-186, 234, 288, 297, 300, 301, 329, 359, 360
Choiseuil, Duke de—192, 198, 203
Chotard, Maj.—395
Chouacha Indians—119, 164, 165
Chouactas Indians—149
Church in La.—303

INDEX

INDEX

INDEX

INDEX

INDEX

INDEX

INDEX

INDEX